Basic Legal Instruments for the Liberalisation of Trade

The interpretation and application of the rules of international and regional trade is becoming an increasingly specialised field. This study provides an in-depth analysis of the core legal concepts characterising the two most prominent and successful efforts in the regulation of international trade to date. Adopting a comparative method, it analyses the basic legal instruments employed by the EU and the WTO for the purpose of liberalising trade in goods among their respective Members. To this end, this study offers a fresh look at the principles underlying the basic rules of international trade law, including the prohibition of border measures, the principle of non-discrimination on grounds of nationality, and the principle of reasonableness.

VOLUME 1 in the series Studies in International Trade Law

Studies in International Trade Law
Titles in this series:

Basic Legal Instruments for the Liberalisation of Trade by *Federico Ortino*
Appellate Decisions in the WTO by *Rob Howse*

Basic Legal Instruments for the Liberalisation of Trade

A Comparative Analysis of EC and WTO Law

Federico Ortino

·H A R T·
PUBLISHING

OXFORD AND PORTLAND OREGON
2004

Published in North America (US and Canada) by
Hart Publishing
c/o International Specialized Book Services
5804 NE Hassalo Street
Portland, Oregon
97213-3644
USA

Hart Publishing is a specialist legal publisher based in Oxford, England.
To order further copies of this book or to request a list of other
publications please write to:

Hart Publishing, Salters Boatyard, Folly Bridge, Abingdon Rd, Oxford,
OX1 4LB Telephone: +44 (0)1865 245533 Fax: +44 (0) 1865 794882
email: mail@hartpub.co.uk
WEBSITE: http//:www.hartpub.co.uk

British Library Cataloguing in Publication Data
Data Available

ISBN 1-84113-425-2 (hardback)

Typeset by Olympus Infotech Pvt. Ltd., India, in Palatino 10/12 pt.
Printed and bound in Great Britain by
Biddles Ltd, _www.biddles.co.uk_

In memoria di Chiara Ciappi
il cui amore e coraggio
rimarranno sempre vivi

Acknowledgements

This book is based on the thesis that I submitted for the degree of Doctor of Laws of the European University Institute, Florence. I sincerely thank my supervisor, Professor Claus-Dieter Ehlermann, for dedicating time, patience and inspiration to my work. He has been, inside and outside his supervising role, a guiding light. I would also like to thank the other members of my jury: Professors Piet Eeckhout (King's College London), Paolo Mengozzi (Court of First Instance, Luxembourg) and Ernst-Ulrich Petersmann (European University Institute). They all have at different times provided much needed support and encouragement.

I am moreover greatly indebted to Lorand Bartels, Gráinne de Búrca, Gabrielle Marceau, Joanne Scott, Francis Snyder, Gaëtan Verhoosel, and Joseph Weiler, all of whom have, in several important ways, contributed to the making of this book. None of the above friends and colleagues, of course, bears responsibility for the views expressed in this work. Particular thanks go to everybody in the Legal Affairs Division of the WTO who in the fall of 2000 have warmly welcomed me as a stagiaire and showed me the ropes of that game.

I would also like to thank Professor Allen Mendelsohn at Georgetown University Law Center and Professor Nicolò Trocker at the Department of Comparative Law of the University of Florence whose support and guidance have been indispensable since the early stages of my academic career. My gratitude goes to Richard Hart and his team in Oxford for making the publication of this work a smooth 'walk in the park'.

I am grateful to my parents for their continuous and unconditional support over the years; to my friends, in particular Philip and Costanza, who have accompanied me throughout this journey; and last, but not least, to my wife, Maria, for making everything worthwhile.

Federico Ortino
Florence/Geneva, September 2003

Table of Contents

Table of Cases

EUROPEAN COURT OF JUSTICE DECISIONS

GATT PANEL REPORTS

WTO PANEL AND APPELLATE BODY REPORTS

Introduction

Defining the Boundaries of the Research

$\int$ $\mathbf{T}$RADE OF GOODS and services has been a constant feature of human history, and has played a fundamental role in economic, social, technological and cultural development. Based on economic theories developed in the eighteenth and nineteenth centuries suggesting that States should, in the interest of the world's aggregate gains, pursue *liberal* trade policies, exchanging goods and services according to their comparative advantage, the second half of the twentieth century witnessed an intensification of efforts to impose restraints on national governments' capabilities to adopt *protectionist* policies restricting international trade. The resulting liberalisation of international trade has occurred at bilateral, regional and multilateral levels. The two most prominent and successful of these efforts are without doubt the European Union (EU)—formerly the European Economic Community (EEC)—and the World Trade Organisation (WTO), established in 1995, which builds on the former General Agreement on Tariff and Trade (GATT) of 1947.

The object of this study is a comparative analysis of the basic legal instruments employed by the EU and the WTO for the purpose of liberalising trade in goods among their respective Members. Accordingly, rather than focusing on the interrelationships between the two systems of law (eg the direct effect of WTO law in the EC legal order), this study analyses the interpretation and application of the basic rules (such as the prohibition of border measures, the principle of non-discrimination on grounds of nationality and the principle of reasonableness) which both systems employ in order to guarantee that their respective Members do not implement protectionist policies restricting trade among themselves.

In this introductory chapter the boundaries of the research will be defined. First of all, a justification for such a comparative analysis will be put forward, together with its underlying methodology. Subsequently, the several types of national rules that can represent obstacles to the free movement of goods across national borders, as well as the different modalities that can be employed to address such obstacles will be examined. Lastly, the actual analytical framework for carrying out the proposed comparison will be outlined.

1. THE EC AND THE WTO: JUSTIFICATION FOR A COMPARISON

It is undeniable that a comparison between two legal and political realities as far apart as the European Union and the World Trade Organisation might be a "superfluous" endeavour. Although the immediate political[1] and macro-economic objectives[2] of both constructs were almost identical, the ultimate goals of the EEC went well beyond those of the GATT even at the time of its conception. The 23 Contracting Parties of the GATT were simply pursuing the "substantial reduction of tariffs and other barriers to trade and [...] the elimination of discriminatory treatment in international commerce". By contrast, the original six Member States of the EEC were "determined to lay the foundations of an ever closer union among the peoples of Europe"[3] by, first of all, "establishing a common market and progressively approximating the economic policies of Member States".[4] In other words, while the GATT aimed exclusively at "trade liberalisation", the EEC embarked on a process of deeper economic as well as political "integration."[5]

---

[1] International economic co-operation is essential in preserving peace and stability among nations. One of the basic premises of those who sought international regulation of international trade was that "self-interest economic policies on the international scene contribute to misunderstanding, instability, and war in international relations generally." J Jackson, *World Trade and the Law of GATT* (1969) at 9–10. See the Preamble to the Treaty of Rome, which states as follows: "intending to confirm the solidarity which binds Europe and the overseas countries and desiring to ensure the development of their prosperity, in accordance with the principles of the Charter of the United Nations, Resolved by thus pooling their resources to preserve and strengthen peace and liberty, and calling upon the other peoples of Europe who share their ideal to join in their efforts."

[2] In the preamble to GATT, the Contracting Parties recognised that "their relations in the field of trade and economic endeavour should be conducted with a view to raising standards of living, ensuring full employment and a large and steadily growing volume of real income and effective demand, developing the full use of the resources of the world and expanding the production and exchange of goods". Similarly, Art 2 of the Treaty of Rome determined that the task of the Community was "to promote throughout the Community a harmonious development of economic activities, a continuous and balanced expansion, an increased stability, an accelerated raising of the standard of living and closer relations between the States belonging to it."

[3] Preamble, Treaty of Rome.

[4] Art 2, Treaty of Rome.

[5] In this context, the distinction between "liberalisation" and "integration" depends thus on the different long-term objectives characterising the GATT and EC experiences respectively. Cf A von Bogdandy, "Legal Equality, Legal Certainty and Subsidiarity in Transnational Economic Law, in A von Bogdandy, P Mavroidis and Y Mény (eds), *European Integration and International Co-ordination—Studies in Transnational Economic Law in Honour of Claus-Dieter Ehlermann* (The Hague/London/New York, Kluwer Law International, 2002) at 33–34:

However, neither the lack of a "political" project in GATT nor the limited scope of any long-term "economic" objective—mainly due to the specific nature of the General Agreement and the premature death of the more wide-ranging International Trade Organisation (ITO)—should undermine the relevance of comparing the laws of the European Community and the new World Trade Organisation.[6]

Aside from its preambular statement of "political" intent, the heart of the European Community—not only its Economic Community—has been the establishment of an "economic" space in the form of a "common market".[7] The bulk of the activities entrusted to the new regional entity refers principally to this task, which is carried out by means of "the elimination, as between Member States, of customs duties and of quantitative restrictions on the import and export of goods, and of all other measures having equivalent effect", "the abolition, as between Member States, of obstacles to freedom of movement for persons, services and capital", "the institution of a system ensuring that competition in the common market is not distorted" and "the approximation of the laws of Member States to the extent required for the proper functioning of the common market".[8]

By contrast, the WTO does not formally pursue the establishment of a "global market". However, the new features added by the Uruguay Round—for example, the inclusion of services, intellectual property and investment-related issues, as well as the more biting disciplines regulating technical and sanitary standards—have almost entirely bridged the gap that existed between the EC and the GATT with regard to the "core subject-matter" covered by these two frameworks for regulation of transnational trade. This was indeed a change in focus of WTO law. Like its regional counterpart, the WTO is no longer limited to the reduction—at the border—of trade barriers and the elimination—within the borders—of discriminatory treatment, but deals increasingly with national regulation that is "unnecessarily" or "unreasonably" trade restrictive.[9]

"The free trade obligations in the EC Treaty and similar provisions in EU agreements with third States have been developed into individual economic rights because of the function they serve in the gradual establishment and maintenance of a market as goals of the treaties. [...]WTO law [does not] provide for a global market as a normative aim. To put it in another way, from a public law perspective there is legally no global market, but only a number of domestic markets, and WTO law can be best understood as an instrument to co-ordinate the interdependence between them."

[6] JHH Weiler, "Cain and Abel—Convergence and Divergence in International Trade Law", in JHH Weiler (ed), *The EU, the WTO and the NAFTA: Towards a Common Law of International Trade?* (Oxford, OUP, 2000) at 1.
[7] Cf R Dehousse, "Rediscovering Functionalism", *Jean Monnet Working Papers* (Harvard Law School, N 7, 2000) at 9.
[8] Art 3 lett. (a), (c), (f) and (h) of the Treaty of Rome.
[9] F Roessler, "Increasing Market Access under Regulatory Heterogeneity: The Strategies of the World Trade Organization", in OECD, *Regulatory Reform and International Market Openness* (1996) at 117: "The GATT has now been supplemented by agreements annexed to

As occurred in the EEC in the 1970s and 1980s, this change has increased the tension between what is still the principal aim of the multilateral trade regime, which is the liberalisation of international trade, and the need to foster other non-economic values or policies.[10] This tension is to some extent recognised in the preamble to the 1994 Marrakesh Agreement Establishing the WTO, in which the Members, after having faithfully repeated the original GATT macro-economic objectives, emphasise the need to allow "for the optimal use of the world's resources in accordance with the objective of sustainable development, seeking both to protect and preserve the environment and to enhance the means for doing so in a manner consistent with their respective needs and concerns at different levels of economic development".

Moreover, the establishment within the WTO of a newly improved, compulsory dispute settlement system centred on a permanent court of appeal (the Appellate Body) has rightly been said to represent "the most important systemic outcome of the Uruguay Round".[11] Thus, the shift from the diplomatic-based dispute settlement procedures characterising the old GATT to the new quasi-judicial system of the WTO (what has been termed the "juridification" of the WTO dispute settlement system and of the WTO as a whole) has meant that both procedurally and substantively the WTO legal system has indeed adopted many of the features of its European counterpart. Since most of the pro-liberalisation rules employed in both EC and WTO law are general in nature, the existence and, more importantly, the *modus operandi* of the dispute settlement system, play a crucial role in the actual interpretation, application and development of such rules.

the Agreement establishing the World Trade Organization [...] that go beyond the mere prohibition of discrimination and establish requirements for domestic regulations, that is, regulations equally applicable to domestic and foreign goods, services and service suppliers. The distinction between foreign trade policies, in respect of which governments accept to be bound, and domestic economic policies, which they may conduct autonomously, is no longer being made." As the analysis will show, even the apparently innocuous non-discrimination principle may represent a very pungent tool for the liberalisation of trade, at least if taken to its extremes. Cf T Cottier, "A Theory of Direct Effect in Global Law", in A von Bogdandy, P Mavroidis and Y Mény (eds), *European Integration and International Co-ordination—Studies in Transnational Economic Law in Honour of Claus-Dieter Ehlermann* (The Hague/London/New York, Kluwer Law International, 2002) at 100; MP Maduro, "The Constitution of the Global Market", in F Snyder (ed), *Regional and Global Regulation of International Trade* (Oxford, Hart Publishing, 2002) at 55. See below chs 2 and 3 on the National Treatment principle and related bibliography.

[10] JHH Weiler, "Epilogue: Towards a Common Law of International Trade", in JHH Weiler (ed), *The EU, the WTO and the NAFTA: Towards a Common Law of International Trade?* (Oxford, OUP, 2000) at 202: "[...] it is almost amusing to see how the WTO must suddenly grapple with the consequences of a *Dassonville*-style approach with all the difficulties that result from the inevitable encroachment on national sovereignty, policy choices, legitimacy of governance, and accountable decision making."
[11] JHH Weiler, "The Rule of Lawyers and the Ethos of Diplomats: Reflections on the Internal and External Legitimacy of WTO Dispute Settlement", *Jean Monnet Working Paper* (Harvard-NYU School of Law, 2000) at 1.

Accordingly, while the experience of the EC cannot "provide a ready-made template for global regulation and liberalisation",[12] it can certainly be the subject, together with its multilateral counterpart, of a comparative study on the legal tools employed for the liberalisation of trade in goods.

This conviction may be said to be based on the basic methodological principle, which has been used in recent legal comparative analysis, ie the principle of "functionality".[13] From this basic principle stem all the other rules which guide the comparatist in determining such matters as the choice of laws to compare, the scope of the undertaking, and the creation of a system of comparative law. As noted by Zweigert and Kötz, "incomparables cannot usefully be compared, and in law the only things which are comparable are those which fulfil the same function."[14] With the change of focus in the tasks of the WTO compared to GATT, the "function" of WTO law has come to equate the basic function of EC law as characterised by the *Dassonville* jurisprudence of the European Court of Justice (ECJ), that is to tackle all national rules which are capable of hindering trade.[15]

However, I prefer to consider the present comparative study as premised more simply on the belief that the comparative method is principally a means for the attainment of knowledge. Since the social scientist does not enjoy the benefit of the laboratory conditions that are available to the natural scientist, the comparative method becomes the only available means of dealing with the issues characterising political, legal and economic analysis.[16] In other words, the comparative analysis of legal systems or of legal norms employed in different legal systems provides the tools that are indispensable for the comprehension of those same systems and norms as well as possibly for the construction of the "science" of (international) economic law.

---

[12] J Rollo and L Winters, "Domestic Regulation and Trade: Subsidiarity and Governance Challenges for the WTO", mimeo, at 13.

[13] Cf K Zweigert and H Kötz, *Introduction to Comparative Law* (Oxford, OUP 1998) at 34 (in the field of private law); G de Vergottini, *Diritto Costituzionale Comparato* (Padova, CEDAM, 1999) at 74–75 (in the field of constitutional law).

[14] K Zweigert and H Kötz, *Introduction to Comparative Law* (Oxford, OUP 1998) at 34: "The proposition rests on what every comparatist learns, namely that the legal system of every society faces essentially the same problems, and solves these problems by quite different means though very often with similar results."

[15] I use the word "tackle" because of its imprecise and neutral meaning. Cf J Pelkmans, "Removing Regulatory Access Barriers: The Case of 'Deep' Integration", OECD Paper (Feb 1996) at 2; Communication from the Commission concerning the consequences of the Judgment given by the Court of Justice on 20 Feb 1979 in Case 120/78 (*"Cassis de Dijon"*) [OJ 1980, No C256/2].

[16] M Cappelletti, M Seccombe, J Weiler (eds), *Integration Through Law—Europe and the American Federal Experience, Vol 1: Methods, Tools and Institutions, Book 1: A Political, Legal and Economic Overview* (Berlin/New York, Walter de Gruyter, 1986) at 5. For an example of this broader function of the comparative method *see* J Hazard, *The Soviet System of Government* (Chicago/London, University of Chicago Press, 1968).

This second more pragmatic and relaxed methodological approach appears to be at the basis of the increasing number of comparative studies recently focussing on EC and WTO law.[17] For example, Professor Weiler justifies his comparative analysis of the law of the market in the EU and the WTO on the basis that (a) one cannot simply read critically the jurisprudence of the European Court of Justice on the free movement of goods without a firm grasp of the law of the GATT/WTO, and vice versa, and (b) there is enough convergence between the substantial and procedural features of the two regimes

[17] Cf in *general* CD Ehlermann, "Some Personal Experiences as Member of the Appellate Body of the WTO" (EUI, Policy Paper No 9, 2002); G de Búrca and J Scott (eds), *The EU and the WTO: Legal and Constitutional Aspects* (Oxford, Hart Publishing, 2001); JHH Weiler (ed) *The EU, the WTO and the NAFTA: Towards a Common Law of International Trade?* (Oxford, OUP, 2000); P Eeckhout, "After *Keck and Mithouard*: Free Movement of Goods in the EC, Market Access, and Non-Discrimination", in T Cottier and P Mavroidis (eds), *Regulatory Barriers and the Principle of Non-Discrimination in World Trade Law* (Ann Arbor, Michigan University Press, 2000); N Emiliou and D O'Keefe (eds) *The European Union and World Trade Law: After the GATT Uruguay Round* (London, John Wiley and Sons, 1996); G Verhoosel, *National Treatment and WTO Dispute Settlement—Adjudicating the Boundaries of Regulatory Autonomy* (Oxford, Hart Publishing, 2002); J Scott, "GATT and Community Law: rethinking the 'regulatory gap'" in J Shaw and G More (eds) *New Legal Dynamics of European Union* (New York, Clarendon Press, 1995); T Oppermann and J Cascante, "Dispute Settlement in the EC: Lessons for the GATT/WTO Dispute Settlement System?" in EU Petersmann (ed) *International Trade Law and the GATT/WTO Dispute Settlement System* (London, Kluwer Law International, 1997); M Hilf, F Jacobs and EU Petersmann (eds), *The European Community and GATT* (Deventer-Boston, Kluwer, 1986). In particular with regard to *environmental protection*, N Notaro, *Judicial Approaches to Trade and Environment: The EC and the WTO, alias The Comparative Disadvantage of Dolphins and Turtles* (London, Cameron May International Law Publishers, 2003); J Wiers, *Trade and Environment in the EC and the WTO: a Legal Analysis* (Groningen, Europa Law Publishing, 2002); EU Petersmann, *International and European Trade and Environmental Law after the Uruguay Round* (London/The Hague/Boston, Kluwer Law International, 1995); D French, "The Changing Nature of 'Environmental Protection': Recent Developments Regarding Trade and the Environment in the European Union and the World Trade Organization", XLVII *Netherlands International Law Review* (2000) 1; J Wiers, "Regional and Global Approaches to Trade and Environment: the EC and the WTO", 25 *Legal Issues of European Integration* (1998) 93; S Walker, *Environmental Protection Versus Trade Liberalisation: Finding the Balance—An examination of the Legality of Environmental Regulation under International Trade Law Regimes* (Bruxelles, Faculté Saint-Louis, 1993); D Vogel, "The WTO, International Trade and Environmental Protection: European and American Perspective", *EUI Working Paper* (34, 2002); E Neumayer, "Greening the WTO Agreements—Can the Treaty Establishing the European Community be of Guidance", 35 *Journal of World Trade* (2001) 145; R Steinberg, "Trade-Environment Negotiations in the EU, NAFTA, and WTO: Regional Trajectories of Rule Development", 91 *American Journal of International Law* (1997) 231; D Esty and D Geradin, "Market Access, Competitiveness, and Harmonisation: Environmental Protection in Regional Trade Agreements", 21 *Harvard Environmental Law Review* (1997) 265; B Condon, "Reconciling Trade and Environment: A Legal Analysis of European and North American Approaches", 8 *Cardozo Journal of International and Comparative Law* (2000) 1. With regard to the *taxation* field, PJ Kuyper, "Booze and Fast Cars: Tax Discrimination Under GATT and the EC", 23 *Legal Issues of European Integration* (1996) 129. In the field of *trade in services*, CD Ehlermann and G Campogrande, "Rules on Services in the EEC: A Model for Negotiating World-Wide Rules?" in EU Petersmann and M Hilf (eds) *The New GATT Round of Multilateral Trade Negotiations—Legal and Economic Problems* (Deventer-Boston, Kluwer Law and Taxation Publishers, 1991); L Radicati Di Brozolo, "Un primo confronto tra la liberalizzazione delle telecomunicazioni nel sistema del WTO e della Comunità Europea" in SIDI

to justify a redefinition of the field—international economic law as a single field comprising its various siblings and families and sharing a common doctrinal core—as close, perhaps, as the Common Law doctrines in the Old British Commonwealth.[18]

While perhaps not sharing in full Weiler's findings with regard to the existence of *a* common doctrinal core in international trade law, I strongly believe in the correctness of his methodological approach. It is only through comparative analysis that one is capable of fully understanding the features, as well as appreciating the peculiarities, of each individual legal system or norm under consideration. Thus, the principal aim of the present analysis is to shed some light on the two sovranational systems at issue and the norms they employ in order to liberalise trade.

2.   BARRIERS TO INTERNATIONAL TRADE

Following a pragmatic approach in describing the rules for the liberalisation of trade in the EC and WTO law, it seems appropriate at this stage to describe the types of "barriers" to international trade which both legal systems aim to reduce or eliminate.

In summary, trade barriers can be categorised in four main ways: according to their nature, location, effect and origin.[19]

A.   Tariff v Non-tariff Measures

A first criterion is based on the distinction between a tariff and a non-tariff trade barrier. While a tariff, also known as an import or custom duty, is basically a tax imposed at the border on imported goods, a non-tariff barrier refers to any law, regulation, policy, or practice of a government, other than an import duty, that has a restrictive effect on trade.[20]

(Società Italiana di Diritto Internazionale), *Diritto ed organizzazione del commercio internazionale dopo la creazione della Organizzazione Mondiale del Commercio*, Il Convegno, Milano 5–7 giugno 1997 (Editoriale Scientifica, 1998); P Eeckhout, "Constitutional Concepts for Free Trade in Services", in G de Búrca and J Scott (eds), *The EU and the WTO: Legal and Constitutional Aspects* (Oxford, Hart Publishing, 2001).

[18] JHH Weiler, "Cain and Abel—Convergence and Divergence in International Trade Law", in JHH Weiler (ed), *The EU, the WTO and the NAFTA: Towards a Common Law of International Trade?* (Oxford, OUP, 2000) respectively at 3 and 4.
[19] These criteria are not the only ones according to which trade barriers stemming from national regulations may be categorised. Cf B Jansen and M Lugard, "Some Considerations on Trade Barriers Erected for Non-Economic Reasons and WTO Obligations", 1 *JIEL* (1999) at 530.
[20] Kelly, "Non Tariff Barriers", in B Balassa (ed), *Studies in Trade Liberalization: Problems and Prospects for the Industrial Countries* (Baltimore, Johns Hopkins Press, 1967) at 266.

This distinction, which has lost today some of its value, can be explained by taking into consideration the evolution of the international economic system.

In 1947, at the time the GATT was drafted, governments used four main instruments to restrict imports: tariffs, quotas, subsidies and state trading enterprises. Among these four, the most prominent was the tariff.[21] By the end of the 1960s, following the remarkable success of the Kennedy Round of negotiations under the GATT in reducing tariffs, negotiators increasingly began to focus on measures other than tariffs as sources of distortion to international trade.[22] As one writer put it then, "the lowering of tariffs has, in effect, been like draining a swamp. The lower water level has revealed all the snags and stumps of non-tariff barriers that still have to be cleared away...".[23]

The tariff/non-tariff dichotomy has today lost its value both because tariffs have been drastically reduced during GATT Rounds over the last 50 years, and because the negatively defined category of non-tariff barriers, which has since taken centre stage, comprises a broad and diversified number of barriers.[24] A similar development, though at an accelerated pace, also characterises the experience of EC integration.

B.   Border v Domestic Measures

A more modern and meaningful criterion for classifying trade barriers is based on the "location" of the measure (or barrier) itself. Accordingly, one may distinguish between border measures and domestic (or internal) measures. Within the first category, next to "tariffs", one also finds "quantitative restrictions", which, for example, specify the quantity of a particular good or the total value of service transactions or assets that a country will allow to be "imported" during a specified time period,[25]

---

[21] J Jackson, W Davey and A Sykes, *Legal Problems of International Economic Relations: Cases, Materials and Text* (St Paul, Minnesota, West Publishing, 1995) at 373. Cf P Picone and G Sacerdoti, *Diritto internazionale dell'economia: Raccolta sistematica dei principali atti normativi internazionali ed interni con testi introduttivi e note* (Milano, Angeli, 1989).

[22] R Baldwin, *Nontariff Distortions of International Trade* (Washington DC, The Brookings Institution, 1970) at 1.

[23] BA Jones, *New York Times*, 10 July 1968, cited in R Baldwin, *Nontariff Distortions of International Trade, ibid.*, at 2.

[24] In his 1970 study, Baldwin analysed non-tariff trade distortions in 12 groupings including: quotas and restrictive state-trading policies, export subsides and taxes, discriminatory government and private procurement policies, selective indirect taxes and selective domestic subsidies and aids, restrictive customs procedures, antidumping regulations, restrictive administrative and technical regulations, restrictive business practices, control over foreign investment, etc. *Ibid.*, at 11–12. J Rollo and L Winters, "Domestic Regulation and Trade: Subsidiarity and Governance Challenges for the WTO, at 7–8, mimeo.

[25] It should be noted that a quantitative restriction can also take the form of an absolute ban on the importation of a specific good or service (a so-called zero-quota).

as well as "customs procedures and regulations" for classifying and valuing commodities as a basis for levying import duties.[26] The second category, "domestic measures", comprises all other taxes and charges (fiscal measures) as well as laws, regulations and requirements (non-fiscal regulations) that adversely affect international trade.[27]

The central characteristic of this second dichotomy lies in a fundamental difference between "border" and "domestic" measures. As a consequence of their "geographical location" (applied "at the border" or "internally"), these measures have a different scope of application. While domestic measures potentially apply to all goods or services, whether or not they have entered the stream of international commerce, border measures apply exclusively to imported or exported goods or services.[28] Border measures can also be described as "pure trading rules", since their main function is to regulate trade between States.[29] From this, it follows that border measures have a strong protectionist feature, since they cannot but afford better treatment to domestic products (which by definition are not subject to them).

This is certainly true for tariffs. However, it is possible that a quantitative restriction may apply to both imported and domestic goods or services. Such a measure could be characterised not as a border measure but as a domestic measure. Imagine, for example, that a State decides to set a limit on the number of cars, whether imported or produced domestically, to be sold in its territory, or that it decides to grant licenses to only ten (foreign and domestic) construction companies. In both cases, the quantitative restriction applies not just to the *importation* of the good or service, but to the specific *good* or *service* (or *service provider*) itself. Accordingly, while a "border" quantitative restriction has an *inherently* strong protectionist feature, a "domestic" quantitative restriction does not (this latter measure may however have de facto protectionist effects depending on the circumstances).

The relevance of the dichotomy of border and domestic measures differs depending on whether one is referring to measures restricting trade

---

[26] So-called "rules of origin", which determine the "exact" origin or nationality of a product, are functionally similar to valuation and classification rules. Cf E Vermulst, P Waer and J Bourgeois (eds), *Rules of Origin in International Trade: a Comparative Study* (Ann Arbor, University of Michigan Press, 1994).

[27] Antidumping duties and countervailing duties are also considered border measures. Antidumping duties are charges imposed on imports when it is alleged that those imports are under priced compared to their domestic market price or their real cost of production. Countervailing duties are charges imposed on imports to counteract the subsidisation of exports or outputs by a foreign government. These trade restrictive measures, however, will not be considered in the present analysis.

[28] Border measures are also said to apply to the "import and export" of goods or services.

[29] As will be explained later, domestic measures can, and actually do, regulate trade as such, but this is evident only in certain specific circumstances (for example when the domestic measure "formally" discriminates against foreign goods or services).

in goods or trade in services. While "trade in goods" is a relatively simple concept, involving in its most general terms the physical movement of a product from the place of production to the place of consumption,[30] the concept of "trade in services" is more complex.[31] Services may be traded in different ways, or "modalities", depending on the element of the service transaction (the "service" itself, the service "provider" or the service "recipient") which "moves" from one State to another.[32] The concept of border measures is in general difficult to apply to trade in *services*. This is for the simple reason that, unlike trade in goods, services do not "pass the frontier" and are therefore difficult to regulate at that point.[33] In particular, with regard to the "cross-border provision of services" mode of trade in services, the customs authorities will not be able to detect the service as it crosses the frontier, since the service is by definition an intangible product and can be supplied through a simple telephone call, a fax, or an email. With regard to the other modes of supply, while customs agents might still not be able to see the service, they will at least be able to observe service suppliers or recipients as they pass the frontier. However, the value or volume of any service transactions that occur cannot be known or even anticipated until after they have actually been produced or consumed.[34]

---

[30] Cf B Hoekman and M Kostecki, *The Political Economy of the World Trading System—The WTO and Beyond* (Oxford, OUP, 2001).

[31] P Eeckhout, "Constitutional Concepts for Free Trade in Services", in G de Búrca and J Scott (eds), *The EU and the WTO: Legal and Constitutional Aspects* (Oxford, Hart Publishing, 2001) at 220. Cf P Nicolaides, "Economic Aspects of Services: Implications for a GATT Agreement", 23 *JWT* (1989) at 126–27, where the author lists three important characteristics of services: (a) services are processes, (b) transactions in services may require personal contact between the provider and the consumer, and (c) some services may have to be regulated.

[32] P Eeckhout, *The European Internal Market and International Trade: A Legal Analysis* (Oxford, Clarendon Press, 1994) at 10; R Snape, "Principles in Trade in Services" in P Messerlin and K Sauvant (eds), *The Uruguay Round. Services in the World Economy* (Washington, DC, World Bank, 1990) at 5–7. The case where the "service" itself moves without the provider or the recipient having to travel to another country is referred to in WTO terms as "cross-border provision of service" *stricto sensu* (for example, an architect who sends his designs abroad via internet is providing his services across the border). When the recipient of the service or the "consumer" moves to the country where the service provider is established is "consumption abroad", or "movement of consumer" (for example, a consumer who travels to a different country to undergo medical surgery is the beneficiary of a service provided to him within the territory of another country). When the "business" itself moves to the country where the service is to be provided, it is "commercial presence" (a bank established in Country A sets up a branch in Country B). Cf Art I GATS. With regard to EC law, see notions of "temporary provision of service" pursuant to Art 49 (ex 59) and of "permanent establishment" pursuant to Art 43 (ex 52).

[33] B Hoekman and C Primo Braga, "Protection and Trade in Services: A Survey", World Bank paper, (March 1997) at 5. See also, P Eeckhout, *The European Internal Market and International Trade: A Legal Analysis* (Oxford, Clarendon Press, 1994) at 11; A Mattoo, "National Treatment in the GATS: Corner-Stone or Pandora's Box?", *JWT* (1997) at 113.

[34] B Hoekman and C Primo Braga, "Protection and Trade in Services: A Survey", *World Bank Paper* (March 1997) at 5.

Accordingly, while tariffs, together with classification and valuation procedures and regulations, constitute perhaps the first and more evident barrier to the international movement of products, they are practically non-existent with regard to trade in services.[35] Quantitative restrictions, on the other hand, play a role in regulating and restricting trade in both goods and services, in the latter case at least with regard to those service sectors where cross-border provision is not technically or economically feasible.[36] However, the intangible nature of many services implies that quantitative restrictions on trade in services cannot be imposed on the "importation" of the service itself. In fact, as Hoekman and Primo Braga have explained, the intangible and nonstorable nature of many services implies that quantitative restrictions may only be applied to providers of services rather than to services per se.[37] Thus, quantitative restrictions in trade in services might be characterised both as border and domestic barriers. While the former can only take the form of immigration policies[38] and have by definition a protectionist character, the latter comprise a wider range of measures that are not inherently protectionist in character.[39]

When one moves from border to domestic measures, the regulation of trade in goods and trade in services is more similar.

As with the definition of "non-tariff barriers", the concept of "domestic measures" is usually defined negatively, in opposition to border measures. Accordingly, every trade restrictive measure that is not imposed at the border on the importation (or export) of goods or services is considered to be a "domestic" barrier to trade. Within this category one may distinguish between fiscal measures (such as direct and indirect taxes or other internal charges) and non-fiscal internal regulations that take

---

[35] J Trachtman, "Trade in Financial Services under GATS, NAFTA and the EC: A Regulatory Jurisdiction Analysis", 34 *Columbia Journal of Transnational Law* (1995) 37 at 45. An exception to this general conclusion relates to services that are incorporated in goods (such as films, television programmes and computer software) or goods that are necessary inputs into the production of services (such as computers and telecommunications). Cf B Hoekman and C Primo Braga, "Protection and Trade in Service: A Survey", above n 34, at 7–8.

[36] In theory, though probably not in practice, it would be possible to impose quotas on the number of designs an architect can send abroad via the internet.

[37] B Hoekman and C Primo Braga, "Protection and Trade in Service: A Survey", above n 34, at 5.

[38] Eeckhout has rightly pointed out that a fundamental implication of the fact that trade in services can involve the international movement of the actors in the service transaction, is that "one has to draw a line between international movement of people as such—in other words migration, which is a very sensitive issue—and service transactions involving people moving across borders. Often, it is not so easy to draw this line." P Eeckhout, *The European Internal Market and International Trade: A Legal Analysis* (Oxford, Clarendon Press, 1994) at 10.

[39] B Hoekman, "Market Access Through Multilateral Agreement: From Goods to Services", 15 *The World Economy* (Nov 1992) at 721.

the form, for example, of technical, health and safety standards, or licensing and authorisation requirements.[40]

It is common knowledge that both goods and services (as well as their transactions) are today extensively regulated by governments, usually in the pursuit of a wide-range of public policy goals (for example, the protection of consumers, public health, development objectives, or the protection of standards in regard to specific sectors).[41] As already explained in the previous paragraph, a fundamental characteristic of this type of regulation is its "domestic" nature. In other words, the rules governing goods and services are not aimed at regulating international trade in any specific or direct way, as is the case with border measures. However, although they often pursue legitimate policy objectives, such measures have the potential to affect negatively the competitiveness of foreign products or services (or services suppliers) vis-à-vis domestic products or services. It has been noted, for example, that domestic regulation may treat foreign product manufacturers and service providers unfavourably compared to domestic manufacturers and providers simply because the latter have grown accustomed to local regulations, have structured their affairs optimally in light of local regulations, or have had their business structures considered in the formulation of local regulations.[42] The mere cumulative application of both host and home state regulation may also constitute a cause for tilting the competitiveness scale in favour of domestic goods or services (what is usually referred to as the "dual-burden" or "regulatory overlap" phenomenon).[43] Accordingly, the fundamentally "domestic" nature of regulations of this sort should not be taken to exclude their potential "extraterritorial" effect. With regard to trade in goods, this extraterritorial effect is potentially inherent in any measure regulating the many aspects of the life of a product, from the manner in which a product is manufactured or produced (process standards), its characteristics (product standards) and the way in which it is sold in the marketplace (marketing standards).[44]

---

[40] Subsidies and state aids should also be considered as falling within this category. Like antidumping and countervailing duties they are usually subject to specific disciplines and will thus not be considered in the present analysis.

[41] See P Eeckhout, *The European Internal Market and International Trade: A Legal Analysis* (Oxford, Clarendon Press, 1994) at 11; P Mengozzi, "I servizi nell'Organizzazione Mondiale del Commercio" in SIDI (Società Italiana di Diritto Internazionale), *Diritto ed organizzazione del commercio internazionale dopo la creazione della Organizzazione Mondiale del Commercio*, Il Convegno, Milano 5–7 giugno 1997 (Editoriale Scientifica, 1998).

[42] J Trachtman, "Trade in Financial Services under GATS, NAFTA and the EC: a Regulatory Jurisdiction Analysis", 34 *Columbia Journal of Transnational Law* (1995) 37 at 46.

[43] See below in particular the sections dealing with the ECJ judgments in *Cassis de Dijon* and *Keck* in Part II.

[44] This is particularly true for national disciplines regulating trade in services. For example, because of their generally more personalised character, most barriers to international trade in services are found in regulations of the service-producing persons and companies, rather

In any event, it should be clear that domestic or internal measures constitute the largest category of restrictions of international trade. Furthermore, with regard to service transactions in particular, they constitute the only barrier, with the exception of immigration policies. Accordingly, while any attempt to liberalise trade in services will be faced right from the start with trade-restrictive domestic regulation, the liberalisation of trade in goods ideally follows a gradual progression, beginning with border measures and then with domestic measures.[45]

C.   Market Access v Market Regulation Barriers

A further criterion used to categorise barriers to international trade is based on the "intensity" of the restrictive effect of these barriers. Measures barring or restricting entry to a specific market fall within the category of "market access barriers" (for example, a ban on the importation of apples or a nationality requirement for the provision of legal services). On the other hand, measures that increase the cost of trade by simply regulating the market fall within the category of "market regulation barriers" (for example, a requirement that apples be sold within 15 days from their harvest or a requirement that lawyers take additional legal courses every year).

Scholars have employed a variety of terms to describe these two types of barriers: some distinguish between "market entry restrictions" and "cost-increasing barriers",[46] others (in particular with regard to trade in services) between "pre-entry" and "post-entry barriers."[47] At first sight, there would seem to be a certain similarity between this dichotomy and

than on the service itself, raising even more clearly the issue of the extraterritorial effect of domestic regulation (at least with regard to those services that do not involve the movement of the service provider). Should a company established in State A providing insurance services to customers residing in State B by means of the internet be subjected to the requirements and regulations of State B? A similar regulatory interest could in theory exist in the case of those same customers travelling to State A to receive there the specific service. Cf P Eeckhout, "Constitutional Concepts for Free Trade in Services" in G de Búrca and J Scott (eds), *The EU and the WTO: Legal and Constitutional Aspects* (Oxford, Hart, 2001) at 223 *et seq*. On the extraterritorial issue in WTO law, see L Bartels, "Article XX of GATT and the Problem of Extraterritorial Jurisdiction: The Case of Trade Measures for the Protection of Human Rights", 36 *JWT* (2002) 353.

[45] This explains in part why the GATS has adopted a less biting approach with regard to internal measures restricting trade in services compared to the GATT. For example, the National Treatment obligation in Art XVII GATS only applies in the sectors and at the conditions specified in each Member's schedule.

[46] P Robson, *The Economics of International Integration* (1998) at 93.

[47] J Trachtman, "Trade in Financial Services under GATS, NAFTA and the EC: a Regulatory Jurisdiction Analysis", 34 *Columbia Journal of Transnational Law* (1995) 37 at 64, "It is worth distinguishing between national treatment regarding entry or establishment, on the one hand, and national treatment regarding post-entry operations, on the other hand. National treatment

the distinction between "border" and "domestic" measures. However, there is a fundamental difference between the two sets of criteria. While the dichotomy between border and domestic measures is principally based on the "location" of the trade restrictive measure (and focuses on whether the measure is inherently discriminatory), the distinction between "market access" and "market regulation" barriers is based only on the restrictive "effect" of the measure. Accordingly, a tariff, which is the classical type of border measure, will not necessarily constitute a "barrier" to market access if it sufficiently low. On the other hand, an across-the-board prohibition on the sale of red meat, a solely domestic measure, would therefore be considered to be a market access barrier.

As is usually the case with generalisations, it is sometimes hard to determine whether a measure should be considered a barrier to market access or a simple market regulation. The two examples given above with regard to trade in apples are fairly easy to distinguish; how about a measure which requires that apples be sold within two days of harvesting? Is not this measure, for all purposes, equivalent to a ban on the importation of apples? What if it were three days, or four days? When does a market regulation become a market access barrier?

There does not seem to be any easy way of determining which measures restrict market entry or simply regulate the market, except by investigating the intensity of the restrictive effect of the measures on a case-by-case basis. In this regard, the difficulties encountered by the ECJ in its attempt to envision a criterion for distinguishing between measures that restrict market access and those that do not (the so-called *Keck* jurisprudence), may just represent a confirmation of the problematic nature of this distinction.[48]

With regard to trade in services, this determination may even be more complex, as there are several ways of providing a specific service and, correspondingly, an equal number of means of restricting the provision of these services. For example, imagine that the laws of State A require that only nationals of State A may own banking institutions, thereby preventing the establishment in that State of foreign banks. At the same time, State A does not ban the cross-border supply of banking services, thus allowing foreign banks to provide their services through this particular

---

regarding entry or establishment is related to market access, although failure to provide national treatment regarding operations may also be viewed as a barrier to market access." Cf A Mattoo, National Treatment in the GATS: Corner-Stone or Pandora's Box?, 31 *JWT* (1997) 113 at 114, "measures affecting entry of the supplier into the market and those affecting post-establishment activity".

[48] For a recent attempt in distinguishing the various categories of legal tests articulated by the Court of Justice for determining market access see C Barnard and S Deakin, "Market Access and Regulatory Competition" in C Barnard and J Scott (eds), *The Law of the Single European Market: Unpacking the Premises* (Oxford, Hart Publishing, 2002) at 204 *et seq*. On the *Keck* jurisprudence see below ch 3 on the prohibition of de facto discrimination in EC Law.

mode of supply. Could it be argued that the above mentioned "nationality" requirement restricts access to the banking market of State A or that, having regard to the option of cross-border supply of banking services, foreign banks still have access to that market?

In light of all of these problems, it might be argued that, at least for legal purposes, there is not much sense in employing two general categories distinguishing between measures restricting or barring access to a specific market for goods or services and measures that only make it more difficult or expensive for goods or services to be exported to that market.[49]

D.   Government v Private Barriers

A fourth and final criterion for distinguishing between different types of trade barriers is based on the "source" of the barrier itself. According to this criterion, barriers can be described as "governmental" or "private" depending on whether they have been instituted by the government or arise from private parties (usually business) practices.

All trade-restrictive measures that have so far been analysed (tariffs, quantitative restrictions, domestic regulations) are measures imposed and implemented by governments. However, by interfering with free market forces, business practices such as price-fixing or market-sharing can have the same trade restrictive effect as barriers imposed by governments.

The ITO Charter signed in Havana contained a chapter with nine Articles dealing with restrictive business practices. These provisions would have required contracting States to prevent business practices affecting international trade which restrained competition, limited access to markets or fostered monopolistic control, whenever such practices had harmful effects on the expansion of production or trade. This chapter, however, was not incorporated in the GATT and after the demise of the proposed ITO, the issue of restrictive business practices was soon forgotten.[50]

The Treaty of Rome instituting the EEC also contained strict provisions dealing with anti-competitive business practices, which affected trade between Member States. These provisions have played an important role in Community law, in particular with regard to the creation of the single European market.

---

[49] The expression "market access" is in fact often employed (and not only in WTO circles) in a very general sense as a synonym of "liberalisation". Cf A Beviglia Zampetti and P Sauvé, "New Dimensions of Market Access: an Overview", in A Beviglia Zampetti and P Sauvé (eds), *New Dimension of Market Access in a Globalising World Economy* (Paris, Organisation for Economic Co-operation and Development, 1996) at 15, "unimpaired market access refers to conditions of competition which provide foreign goods, services, service providers and investors opportunities to compete in a market on terms equal or comparable to those enjoyed by locally produced goods and services and locally established firms."
[50] J Jackson, *World Trade and the Law of GATT* (1969) at 522 *et seq.*

Although the issue of restrictive business practices has found its way into WTO law, in particular within the intellectual property and trade in services agreements,[51] there does not exist at the multilateral level enough material to attempt any sort of comparison with the much richer regional experience of the EC. Accordingly, the present analysis will mainly focus on the legal tools employed in our two systems of reference in dealing with trade restrictive barriers imposed by governments.[52]

3.   APPROACHES TO TRADE LIBERALISATION: "NEGATIVE V POSITIVE INTEGRATION", "JUDICIAL V LEGISLATIVE INTEGRATION" AND "SHALLOW V DEEP INTEGRATION"

There are several different ways of tackling trade barriers and liberalising international trade. These mostly depend on the objective pursued, which in turn is a function of the degree of political will to proceed with liberalisation. A government may, for example, decide 1) to eliminate or reduce progressively tariffs and/or quantitative restrictions; 2) to prohibit all trade restrictive measures, both border and domestic; 3) to eliminate all border measures and prohibit discriminatory domestic ones; 4) to avoid national regulatory peculiarities by adopting the principle of mutual recognition, according to which a product produced pursuant to the rules and requirements of a Member State will enjoy the right to be exported and sold in the territory of any other participating State (this principle may be "absolute" or "relative" depending on whether the "right to export" is absolute or subject to certain conditions); 5) to reduce the impact of trade restrictive regulations by harmonising certain basic general requirements and leaving the adoption of regulatory details to each individual State; or 6) to replace all trade restrictive national regulations with uniform rules. Clearly, one option does not preclude any other.

Before proceeding with the analysis of the various solutions adopted by the EC and the WTO for the liberalisation of international trade in goods between their respective Members, it is convenient to categorise these solutions according to their principal features. For these purposes, I will start by reviewing three inter-linked pairs of concepts usually employed by economists, political scientists and jurists alike in describing

---

[51] Cf Arts VIII and IX of GATS, respectively on "Monopolies and Exclusive Service Suppliers" and "Business Practices", or the Annex on Telecommunications and the Protocol on Basic Telecommunications. Cf OECD, "Market Access After the Uruguay Round: Investment, Competition and Technology Perspectives" (1996).

[52] For a recent analysis of existing competition rules in WTO law, see CD Ehlermann and L Ehring, "WTO Dispute Settlement and Competition Law: Views from the Perspective of the Appellate Body's Experience", *EUI Policy Papers* (No 12, 2002).

the general approaches to trade liberalisation: *negative v positive integration, judicial v legislative integration* and *shallow v deep integration.*

It should be noted that in this context the concept of *integration* is used broadly to encompass any form of coordination between countries, from pure trade liberalisation to economic and political union.[53] This concept reflects the existence of both pure trade and non-trade issues in every such attempt at economic coordination, the main difference being the degree of intensity of the conflict between trade liberalisation and other non-economic values. As will be demonstrated later, the more intense the degree of coordination (or integration), the more problematic the potential for conflict with non-trade values.

A.   Negative v Positive Integration

The distinction between negative and positive integration was first coined by Tinbergen in 1954.[54] Tinbergen used the term "negative integration" to refer to measures consisting of the abolition of a number of impediments to the proper operation of an integrated economic area. It primarily consisted of "the reduction of trade impediments between national economies, that is, the reduction of import duties or the expansion of quotas."[55] The same author defined "positive integration" as:

> [the] creation of new institutions and their instruments or the modification of existing instruments. [...] More generally, positive integration should consist of the creation of all the institutions required by the welfare optimum which have to be handled in a centralised way. For example, the institution in charge of the distribution of incomes required by welfare economics, particularly if its purpose is to effectuate a redistribution of incomes between countries. Another example is the regulation of unstable markets with a market area surpassing national frontiers. Most of European agricultural policy consists of such market regulations. A third example is the need for some planning agency at the supranational level. The sound preparation of economic policy, at all levels, requires a type of planning corresponding to the degree of intervention. A subject for positive integration may also be seen in a supervision of the measures taken by member countries for the development of their less developed regions.[56]

Tinbergen's definition of the two concepts is useful, though a clear product of the time in which they were developed. In referring to trade impediments,

---

[53] Cf B Horvat, *The Theory of International Trade—An Alternative Approach* (London, MacMillan, 1999) at 136 *et seq.*, listing the several "degrees of economic integration".
[54] J Tinbergen, *International Economic Integration* (Amsterdam, 1954).
[55] *Ibid.*, at 76.
[56] *Ibid.*, at 78–79.

Tinbergen was clearly thinking of border measures, in particular import duties and quotas, which at that time were perceived as representing the principal obstacles to international trade. Since these barriers had to be "reduced" or "eliminated" without any need for replacing them with something else, characterising such operation as "negative" integration made perfect sense. On the other hand, "positive" integration was used to describe those activities where institutions or legal instruments had actually to be "created" or "modified".[57]

In 1968, Pinder employed Tinbergen's terminology but changed his definitions "so as to make the terms as useful as possible, in the light of the experience of the [European] Community as it has evolved."[58] He used negative integration for that part of economic integration that consists of the removal of discrimination, and positive integration as the formation and application of coordinated and common policies in order to fulfil economic and welfare objective other than the removal of discrimination.[59]

In 1986, Pelkmans, citing both previous authors, stated that

> *negative* integration denotes the removal of discrimination in national economic rules and policies under joint and authoritative surveillance; *positive* integration refers to the transfer of public market-rule-making and policy-making powers from the participating polities to the union levels.[60]

Along these same lines, the dichotomy between negative and positive integration has also been widely employed, at times with some slight variations, by political scientists[61] and lawyers,[62] especially with regard to EC law, but recently also in relation to WTO law.[63]

---

[57] The actual examples given by Tinbergen evidence once more the political and economic perceptions of those times.

[58] J Pinder, "Positive Integration and Negative Integration: Some Problems of Economic Union in the EEC", 24 *World Today* (1968) at 90.

[59] *Ibid.*

[60] J Pelkmans, "The Institutional Economics of European Integration", in M Cappelletti, M Seccombe and JHH Weiler (eds) *Integration Through Law, Vol 1 Methods, Tools and Institutions* (Berlin/NewYork, Walter de Gruyter, 1986) at 321. Cf A El-Agran (ed), *International Economic Integration* (London, Macmillan, 1982), and M Jovanovic, *International Economic Integration* (London/New York, Routledge, 1998).

[61] Cf F Scharpf, "Balancing Positive and Negative Integration: the Regulatory Options for Europe", *Policy Papers Robert Schuman Centre* (No 4, 1997).

[62] Cf J Scott, "GATT and Community Law: Rethinking the 'Regulatory Gap'", in Shaw and More (eds), *New Legal Dynamics of EU* (1995) at 147 (the actual terms employed are "'negative' (market) and 'positive' (policy) integration"); A McGee and S Weatherill, "The Evolution of the Single Market: Harmonisation or Liberalisation", 53 *The Modern Law Review* (Sept 1990) at 581 (the authors refer to "judicial 'negative integration' and legislative 'positive integration'"); D Gerardin, "Trade and Environmental Protection: Community Harmonization and National Environmental Standards", 13 *Yearbook of European Law* (1993) at 151 (the author writes about *negative* and *positive harmonization*).

[63] EU Petersmann, "From 'Negative' to 'Positive' Integration in the WTO: Time for 'Mainstreaming Human Rights' into WTO Law?", 37 *CMLRev* (2000) at 1363; T Cottier and

In order to further clarify these concepts, I will consider the general principle contained in Article 28 (ex Article 30) EC and the European Council's approximation authority under Articles 94 and 95 (ex Articles 100 and 100a) EC, which are usually considered to represent the typical forms of "negative" and "positive" integration respectively. In order to make things easier, Article 28 EC will be employed here as embodying inter alia the principle of non-discrimination.[64]

What, then, is the difference between the non-discrimination principle embodied in Article 28 EC and a Community harmonising directive or regulation adopted under Articles 94–95 EC? I will in turn analyse three features of both instruments: their "function", "origin/nature" and "definition/implementation".

Let us start with the *function*.

Article 28 provides that "Quantitative restrictions on imports and all measures having equivalent effect *shall be prohibited* between Member States". Without getting into the details of this provision, let us just say that the European Court of Justice (ECJ) has interpreted this provision as prohibiting, among others, national measures discriminating on the basis of the origin or nationality of the product.

The non-discrimination principle in Article 28 has thus a dual function: (a) it invalidates any existing discriminatory national rule and (b) it prohibits the adoption of any national rule discriminating on grounds of origin or nationality. In the first of these functions, the principle of non-discrimination performs a *negative* function: it invalidates *ipso facto* discriminatory rules.[65] In its latter sense, the principle of non-discrimination performs a *positive* function inasmuch as it provides for a normative criterion which Member States must follow in enacting new regulation. For example, in enacting new labelling regulations for Genetically Modified Organisms (GMOs), Members have to ensure not only that such regulations *formally* apply to both domestic and foreign products (prohibition of de jure discrimination) but also that they do not have the *effect* of affording protection to domestic products (prohibition of de facto discrimination). In these terms, although the non-discrimination principle does not regulate any particular activity, it mandates a "standard"

P Mavroidis, "Regulatory Barriers and the Principle of Non-Discrimination in WTO Law: An Overview", in T Cottier and P Mavroidis (eds), *Regulatory Barriers and the Principle of Non-Discrimination in World Trade Organization Law* (Ann Arbor, University of Michigan Press, 2000) at 4; J Bourgeois, "On the Internal Morality of WTO Law", in A von Bogdandy, P Mavroidis and Y Mény (eds), *European Integration and International Co-ordination—Studies in Transnational Economic Law in Honour of Claus-Dieter Ehlermann* (The Hague/London/New York, Kluwer Law International, 2002) at 40.

[64] For the several normative functions of Art 28 EC see below ch 4 on the Reasonableness Rule.

[65] In EC law this is certainly more evident after the transitional period and mostly with the application of the "direct effect" theory.

to be followed by the Member States in exercising their regulatory prerogatives.

Accordingly, the "negative" attribute does not quite do justice to the principle of non-discrimination on the grounds of nationality. This is confirmed by simply looking at the corresponding principle in WTO law. Article III:4 GATT provides that "the products of the territory of any contracting party imported into the territory of any other contracting party *shall be accorded treatment no less favourable* than that accorded to like products of national origin in respect of all laws, regulations and requirements affecting their internal sale, offering for sale, purchase, transportation, distribution or use". In pure descriptive terms, by mandating the treatment to be granted to foreign products, Article III:4 takes a positive approach rather than a negative one in imposing on Members the non-discrimination obligation. Contrary to Article 28 EC, Article III.4 GATT emphasises the *positive* function of the principle of non-discrimination.[66]

The positive function of the general prohibition of discriminatory measures (in both EC and WTO law) is even more evident if one takes into consideration the existence and operation of the general exception provisions, like Article 30 (ex Article 36) EC and Article XX GATT, which limit and qualify the application of the general non-discrimination principles. In brief, pursuant to these exceptions, Member States may adopt discriminatory measures if these are "suitable" or "necessary" to further a more or less broad set of legitimate public policies. As will be discussed in detail in subsequent chapters, the criteria employed to determine whether or not a measure is "suitable" or "necessary" to achieve a legitimate public policy goal represent in positive terms nothing other than the standards which national regulatory bodies must follow in order for their discriminatory measures to comply with EC or WTO law.

Let us now consider the function of an EC directive or a regulation taken pursuant to Articles 94 or 95 EC for the establishment of the common/internal market. Directives are the preferred instruments of harmonisation of national legislation, since they are binding on Member States as to the result to be achieved, but leave the choice of form and methods to Member States. On the other hand, regulations are directly applicable and generally require less implementation by Member States at a legislative level. While in the legislative practice of the Community the distinction between these two instruments of positive integration is not as clear-cut as it might appear,[67] it is evident that directives and

---

[66] Another fundamental distinction between Art 28 EC and Art III.4 GATT is the direct effect of the former. Accordingly, individuals do not have to wait for Member States to actually eliminate discriminatory measures, but can have such measures directly annulled by the judiciary.

[67] P Eeckhout, "The European Court of Justice and the Legislature", 18 *Yearbook of European Law* (1998) 1 at 5.

regulations do regulate specific activities by providing more or less detailed rules. Although they also have the effect of invalidating and preempting non-complying national regulations (negative function), their principal focus is to create "new instruments", to give uniform regulatory answers to market failures (positive function).

Following this perspective, it seems that the difference between the prohibition of discrimination and a harmonising directive (or regulation) is that the former, in its positive function, provides exclusively for a very general "standard" or "criterion", while the latter provides for a more or less detailed "rule" or "discipline". In other words, it is here submitted that the real difference between the two (or three) instruments is in their degree of "precision": general principle (non-discrimination), specified objective (directive), detailed provisions (regulation).

Let us now examine the *origin* or *nature* of the three above-mentioned instruments.

Borrowing the terminology of national legal systems, the principle of non-discrimination could be seen as embodying a "constitutional" principle, while directives and regulations could be seen as representing "legislative" enactment. This distinction is based not only on the fact that the former stems directly from the founding Treaty while the latter is a product of Community institutions. More interestingly, it is based on the perception that, in substantive terms, the principle of non-discrimination constitutes an indispensable pillar in the construction of any kind of transnational legal system.[68] The differences in procedural terms,[69] it is suggested, are actually rather minimal.

In connection with the nature of the instrument, one aspect should be noted. The dichotomy between negative and positive integration may also represent a distinction between free trade and the pursuit of non-economic public policy objectives. While the reduction or elimination of border measures as well as of discriminatory domestic regulations (generally referred to as "negative integration") might be perceived as instruments in pursuit of pure liberalisation objectives, the enactment of harmonising directives or regulations (generally referred to as "positive integration") might be seen as counterbalancing tools to safeguard and further other legitimate public policies.[70]

---

[68] G de Búrca, "Unpacking the Concept of Discrimination in EC and International Trade Law", in J Scott and C Barnard (eds), *The Law of the Single Market: Unpacking the Premises* (Oxford, Hart Publishing, 2002) at 181 *et seq.*

[69] Such as the body that adopts the general principle and which directives or regulations, as well as the relevant voting requirements.

[70] Cf J Scott, "GATT and Community Law: Rethinking the 'Regulatory Gap'", in Shaw and More (eds), *New Legal Dinamics of EU* (1995) at 147, who discusses the "relationship between 'negative' (market) and 'positive' (policy) integration". F Scharpf, "Balancing Positive and Negative Integration: the Regulatory Options for Europe", *Policy Papers Robert Schuman Centre* (No 4, 1997) at 3–4, "Requirements of 'negative integration' are derived from the

There is certainly some truth in this perception. It may in fact be appropriate to characterise negative integration instruments as mostly pursuing trade liberalisation policies. In fact, even taking into account the existence of a general exception provision that limits the scope of the provisions prohibiting trade barriers (such as Articles 30 EC or XX GATT), it is true that the overall balance between trade liberalisation objectives and public policy goals is tilted in favour of the former. There is no doubt that the relationship between Articles 28 and 30 EC, as well as between Articles III and XX GATT, has always been described as a relationship of rule and exception. However, I disagree with this conceptual characterisation; trade liberalisation is not "negative" per se and it would be unfair and misleading to employ this terminology simply to express a value judgement.[71] Even the most relentless critics of the WTO do not appear to be against the process of trade liberalisation in itself but mostly the manner in, and the extent to, which the process of liberalisation is carried out.[72]

Moreover, it is doubtful that "positive integration" instruments (directives, regulations and the like) only further non-economic public policies. This is so even despite the adoption by the EC in the wake of the ECJ decision in *Cassis de Dijon* of the so called "new approach to harmonisation" that focused on the removal of barriers imposed in pursuance of legitimate public policies and complying with the strict proportionality test envisioned by the Court.[73] For example, a national regulation setting a high level of safety for cars which complies with the proportionality test will need to be addressed by Community-level harmonisation, since that regulation may still constitute a barrier to trade (other countries provide for different levels of safety). In order to set the "appropriate" level of safety, Community institutions will have to make a political decision, the

commitment, contained in the original Treaties and reinforced by the Single European Act, to the free movement of goods, services, capital and workers, and to undistorted competition throughout the Community. [...] As a consequence, national policy makers now find themselves severely constrained in the choice of policy instruments [...]. At the same time, there is now a deep scepticism regarding the original hopes, in particular on the part of unions and the parties associated with them, that regulatory capacities lost at the national level could be re-established through 'positive integration' at the European level."

[71] M Jovanovic, *International Economic Integration* (London/New York, Routledge, 1998) at 5, noting that the use of the distintion between negative and positive integration by Tinbergen had "introduced some confusion since freedom was described as 'negative', while coercion was regarded as a 'positive' move!"

[72] S George, *Remettre l'OMC à sa Place* (Mille et nuits, département de la Librairie Arthème Fayard, 2001); G Dunkley, *The Free Trade Adventure, the WTO, the Uruguay Round and Globalism—A Critique* (London/New York, Zed Books, 2000).

[73] "The Commissiom's work of harmonisation will henceforth have to be directed mainly at national laws having an impact on the functioning of the common market where barriers to trade to be removed arise from national provisions which are admissible under the criteria set by the Court." Commission Practice Note on Import Prohibition, Communication from the Commission concerning the consequences of the Judgment given by the Court of Justice on 20 Feb 1979 in Case 120/78 ("*Cassis de Dijon*") [OJ 1980, No C256/2].

outcome of which may be considered as furthering either liberalisation objectives or public policy goals depending on what one considers to be the "appropriate" level of car safety.

Finally, let us examine the further distinction based on the *definition/implementation* of the "principle", "directive" or "regulation". How, and mostly by whom, are they defined and implemented? While in theory all three instruments are to be implemented principally by the Member States, the practice changes according to the *normative content* of the instrument itself. The principle of non-discrimination, at least in its more intense form (ie extending to de facto discrimination), is quite a general and complex norm and Member States thus enjoy broad discretionary powers in its application. A directive, though binding with regard to the result to be attained, leaves the Member States some freedom in relation to the choice of form and methods to be employed in pursuing the given objective. A regulation, on the other hand, directly and thoroughly regulates a specific subject, possibly requiring Member States' implementation only at the administrative level.

It follows from this that the more or less general the character of the normative instrument, the more or less controversy will arise with regard to its proper definition and/or implementation. In other words, the less a norm is defined, the more it will be up to the judiciary to specify and clarify its content. Accordingly, while the "non-discrimination principle" appears to be "managed" mainly by courts, "directives" and, even more so, "regulations" are adopted and implemented by the EC and Member States legislatures. This is the reason why some authors have referred to *"judicial* 'negative' integration" and *"legislative* 'positive' integration".[74] One could wonder whether or not the use of both adjectives— judicial/negative and legislative/positive—implies subconsciously, once again, some sort of value judgement on the type of instruments employed for the liberalisation of trade.

A few concluding remarks can now be advanced on the dichotomy of negative *v* positive integration. First of all, it is believed that the term "negative integration" should best be employed in its most original and limited meaning. Following what appears to be Tinbergen's original definition, "negative integration" should refer only to those instruments that prohibit the use or require the phasing out of a particular type of trade-restrictive measure. For example, a rule providing for the *abolition* or *reduction* of tariffs and quotas should be characterised as a form of negative integration. It follows that the use of the concept of "negative integration" is inappropriate with regard to the non-discrimination principle, as well as other general principles, such as the "reasonableness" principle.

---

[74] A McGee and S Weatherill, "The Evolution of the Single Market: Harmonisation or Liberalisation", 53 *The Modern Law Review* (Sept 1990) at 581.

Such principles do not in fact require the abolition or reduction of a specific type of government measure but simply mandate that all government measures (affecting trade) comply with certain general norms like "non-discrimination" and "reasonableness". As previously explained, characterising these norms as forms of *negative* integration has two unwanted results; it does not properly emphasise the *positive* function of these instruments and it may give cause for misunderstandings with regard to their underlying "values". In conclusion, both general principles (such as the non-discrimination or reasonableness principles) and more detailed rules and disciplines (such as an EC directive or regulation) should be viewed as forms of "positive integration", since they all provide for positive normative standards that Members must follow in exercising their regulatory prerogatives.

B. Judicial v Legislative (positive) Integration

Having restricted the notion of "negative integration" and broadened that of "positive integration", there is the need to distinguish further between the several instruments which now fall within the latter category. In this regard, it is here suggested that a distinction be drawn between "judicial" and "legislative" integration. This second dichotomy should point to the organ which is principally charged with the task of defining and/or implementing these types of (positive) integration instruments.

As has just been noted, although both the principle of non-discrimination and an EC directive or regulation provide for "positive" rules limiting Members' regulatory prerogatives, these rules differ in the *specificity* of their normative content. In other words, in its positive function, the non-discrimination principle provides exclusively for a very general "standard" or "criterion", while directives and regulations provide for more or less detailed "rules" or "disciplines". By adopting this perspective, it has been argued that the real difference between these three instruments is just in their degree of "precision".

Furthermore, the organ principally in charge of defining and/or implementing these norms will change according to the degree of precision of the respective norm. The less defined the norm, the more it will be up to the judiciary to specify and clarify its content. Accordingly, while general principles such as "non-discrimination" or "reasonableness" appear to be "managed" mainly by courts,[75] more detailed disciplines like

---

[75]Cf D Edward, "Competition and National Rule-Making" in A von Bogdandy, P Mavroidis and Y Mény (eds), *European Integration and International Co-ordination—Studies in Transnational Economic Law in Honour of Claus-Dieter Ehlermann* (The Hague/London/New York, Kluwer Law International, 2002) at 133, noting however that the judiciary's task of "filling the gap" (like that of the European Court of Justice) stems not only from the lack of sovranational legislation but also when such legislation is "imprecise".

"EC directives" and, even more so, "EC regulations" are adopted and implemented by legislatures. This is the reason why I would suggest distinguishing between instruments of "*judicial* integration" and those of "*legislative* integration".[76]

Accordingly, under "judicial integration" one would place all those instruments whereby the transnational legal system imposes on its Members certain general principles for whose definition or implementation recourse to the judiciary is indispensable (for example, the principle of non-discrimination and the principle of reasonableness).

On the other hand, the concept of "legislative integration" (or "positive integration *stricto sensu*") should encompass those instruments which are adopted at the transnational level and which are sufficiently detailed to avoid having to recourse, at least on a constant basis, to adjudicatory bodies for their implementation.[77] The specific character of these instruments will usually imply that they refer to a more or less specific subject matter. Furthermore, borrowing the terminology of private international law, these instruments will include a range of options which can be generally classified on the basis of the two following categories: (a) "uniform applicable law" rules (providing for the private or public "system of law" that regulates the case at hand) and (b) "uniform material law" rules (ie strict harmonisation). Clearly, there will be often mixed forms of "legislative integration" instruments, which will be characterised by both types of rules.[78]

Although, as will be explained shortly, instruments of "legislative integration" (or "positive integration *strictu senso*") do not form part of the present analysis, it might be worthwhile to spend a very few words on the issue in this introductory chapter. While instruments of this type occupy a clear place in EC law and have been the subject of detailed studies over past decades,[79] instruments of "positive integration" have

---

[76] Cf A McGee and S Weatherill, "The Evolution of the Single Market: Harmonisation or Liberalisation", 53 *The Modern Law Review* (Sept 1990) at 581; G Davies, *European Union Internal Market Law* (London/Sydney, Cavendish, 2001) at 145 *et seq*.

[77] Mayes affirmed that the definitions of negative and positive integration "are not comprehensive as there are many barriers in the form of language, social customs and habits, standards, taxation and others whose removal or circumvention whiles not necessarily constituting positive integration is certainly 'non negative'. The positive/negative distinction is an important behavioral categorisation and the two parts present different problems in quantification." Mayes, "The problems of quantitative estimation of integration effects", in A El-Agraa (ed), *International Economic Integration* (London, Macmillan, 1982) at 29.

[78] Note, for example, the minimum harmonisation approach followed by the EC and the TBT or SPS agreements within the WTO. In the systems established by the TBT and the SPS Agreements, one can find forms of "judicial integration" as well.

[79] Among many see CD Ehlermann, "The Internal Market Following the Single European Act", 24 *CMLRev* (1987) 361; A McGee and S Weatherill, "The Evolution of the Single Market—Harmonisation or Liberalisation", 53 *The Modern Law Review* (Sept 1990) 578; D Geradin, "Trade and Environmental Protection: Community Harmonisation and National

only recently been a feature of WTO law. There are at least two specific instruments employed in WTO law for the liberalisation of trade which, while still at their embryonic stage, may be referred to as forms of "legislative integration" or "positive integration *stricto sensu*".

The first is the reference in both the Agreement on the Application of Sanitary and Phytosanitary Measures (SPS Agreement) and the Agreement on Technical Barriers to Trade (TBT Agreement) to "international standards".[80] In both these sectorial Agreements, it is mandated that Members base their sanitary/phytosanitary measures as well as their technical regulations on relevant international standards, guidelines or recommendations.[81] When Members enact legislation in conformity with such standards, both Agreements establish a presumption of consistency with *either* the relevant provisions of the sectorial Agreement as well as the GATT (Article 3.2 SPS) *or* the necessity principle (Article 2.5 TBT). Members are, in any event, allowed to adopt sanitary or phytosanitary measures and technical regulations which are not based on existing international standards when such standards would be ineffective or inappropriate in light of the chosen level of protection or to fulfil the legitimate objectives pursued.[82]

Instead of directly adopting more specific disciplines in the fields of sanitary, phytosanitary or technical standards, WTO Members have employed an external source of transnational regulation in order to provide a harmonised, if not common, set of rules capable of limiting trade barriers stemming from divergent national laws.[83] Clear parallels may be drawn between these provisions and EC directives as well as the entire approach characterising Articles 94–95 EC on the approximations of laws within the European Community.

The second instrument employed in WTO law that may be described as representing a form of "positive integration *stricto sensu*" is found in Article VI:4 of the General Agreement on Trade in Services (GATS), which provides inter alia for a normative mandate to the Council for Trade in Services to develop any necessary disciplines in order to ensure that measures relating to qualification requirements and procedures, technical standards and licensing requirements do not constitute unnecessary

---

Environmental Standards", 13 *YEL* (1993) 151; M Dougan, "Minimum Harmonisation and the Internal Market", 37 *CMLRev* (2000) 853.

[80] See also such a reference in the General Agreement on Trade in Services (GATS), Art VI.
[81] Cf respectively, Art 3 SPS and Art 2.4 TBT.
[82] Cf respectively, Art 3.3 SPS and Art 2.4 TBT. Similar reference to international standards may also be found in Art VI of the General Agreement on Trade in Services (GATS). See on the interpretation of Art 2.4 TBT, the recent Panel and Appellate Body Reports on *European Communities—Trade Description of Sardines* (*EC–Sardines*), WT/DS231/R and WT/DS231/AB/R, respectively circulated on 29 May and 26 Sept 2002, adopted 23 Oct 2002. On the *Sardines* dispute see below ch 4.
[83] Art 3 SPS is entitled "Harmonisation".

barriers to trade in services.[84] Although this provision has so far only been applied once (with regard to the accountancy sector),[85] it is the first WTO provision which envisages on a permanent basis a sort of positive normative power to adopt specific disciplines dealing with "unnecessary" (and not simply discriminatory) restraints on international trade stemming from domestic regulation.[86] It is once again their *specificity* with regard to both "subject matter" and "normative content" that distinguish future disciplines adopted under Article VI:4 GATS from the "reasonableness" or "proportionality" principle. As evidenced in both the financial and telecommunication services negotiations carried out in the last eight years within the GATS framework, liberalisation of trade in services, even more than in the case of goods, requires the adoption of ad hoc approaches with regard to each type of service, in particular when one moves from more shallow to deeper forms of integration.

C.   Shallow v Deep Integration

While the previous distinctions are mostly based on the characteristics of the several legal instruments employed in the liberalisation of trade, the distinction at hand, it is here submitted, has to do with level of "intrusiveness" of these instruments in Members' regulatory prerogatives.

Although the terms "shallow integration" and "deep integration" are increasingly being employed by scholars,[87] their predominant definition does not appear to be satisfactory. For example, according to Kahler, there seems to be an equivalence between "border barriers" and "shallow integration", on the one hand, and "domestic barriers" and "deep integration", on the other. While shallow integration is "based on the removal of barriers to exchange at the border and limited coordination of national policies", deep integration deals with "a multitude of formerly

---

[84] Art VI:4 GATS provides moreover that "such disciplines shall aim to ensure that such requirements are, *inter alia*: (a) based on objective and transparent criteria, such as competence and the ability to supply the services; (b) not more burdensome than necessary to ensure the quality of the service; (c) in the case of licensing procedures, not in themselves a restriction on the supply of the service".

[85] *Disciplines on Domestic Regulation in the Accountancy Sector*, S/L/64, adopted by the Council for Trade in Services on 14 Dec 1998.

[86] Cf the work carried out within the WTO first by the Working Party on Professional Services (S/WPPS) and currently by the Working Party on Domestic Regulation (S/WPDR).

[87] M Kahler, *International Institutions and the Political Economy of Integration* (Washington DC, The Brookings Institution, 1995); J Pelkmans, "Removing Regulatory Access Barriers: the Case of 'Deep' Integration", OECD paper (1996); B Hoekman and C Primo Braga, "Protection and Trade in Services: A Survey", *World Bank paper* (March 1997); B Hoekman and D Konan, "Deep Integration, Nondiscrimination, and Euro-Mediterranean Free Trade", paper presented at the Conference Regionalism in Europe: Geometries and Strategies After 2000, Bonn, 6–8 Nov 1998.

neglected differences among nations' domestic (or behind-the-border) policies".[88]

Although there is some truth in the equivalence professed by Kahler, I would argue that the concept of shallow *v* deep integration should not be based solely on the nature or characteristics of trade barriers (border *v* domestic measures), but should instead reflect the conflict between trade liberalisation objectives and national regulatory prerogatives. This conflict arises from the simple fact that in order to reduce and eliminate barriers to trade (trade liberalisation, in its purest meaning), it is usually necessary to eliminate, modify or substitute national regulatory measures which often pursue legitimate public policy objectives stemming from specific political choices. In theory, it should not matter whether the trade restrictive national measure takes the form of a tariff, a quota, an internal tax or a health standard. What should matter is the *existence* and *relevance* of the public policy objective underlying the national measure.

Accordingly, since tariffs as well as quotas cannot usually be justified by any relevant long-term public policy objective, their reduction or elimination might indeed be characterised as "shallow integration", while tackling national health or safety standards might be characterised as "deep integration" in light of the fact that these standards fulfil important public policy functions that cannot simply be neglected in the name of free trade.

Kahler's definitions should also be qualified in two further respects. First of all, in light of the contingency of public policies underlying national regulatory measures, determining the level of integration (shallow or deep) depends heavily on an element of time (as well as space). While immediately after World War II a reduction of tariffs to single-digit level might have been perceived as "deep integration", nowadays that same reduction is characterised as "shallow integration". The same may be said if one takes into account the different level of development characterising the different countries of the world.

Moreover, if in general there are different ways to liberalise international trade, there are also different ways to tackle any given set of trade-restrictive measures. For example, tariffs can be eliminated altogether or progressively reduced (even in the case of reduction, this could take place at a fast or slow pace). Restrictions on trade may be prohibited as such or tolerated if they do not discriminate between products or services on the basis of nationality (even in this latter case, the non-discrimination principle could be limited to de jure discrimination or expanded to include de facto discrimination).

---

[88] M Kahler, *International Institutions and the Political Economy of Integration* (Washington DC, The Brookings Institution, 1995) at 2 and 22.

In conclusion, the shallow/deep integration dichotomy, reflecting the underlying conflict between trade liberalisation objectives and national regulatory prerogatives, focuses on the level of "intrusiveness" into Members' sovereignty of the legal instruments employed to tackle trade barriers. The key balancing factors to play in this calculation are, on the one hand, the strength of the *economic* theories underlying multilateral liberalisation instruments (or policies) and, on the other, the strength of the *political* interests underlying national trade restrictive measures. Depending on the outcome of this calculation, one can distinguish between shallow integration instruments (or policies) which are easier to pursue, and deep integration instruments (or policies) which involve more problematic issues. In any case, it must be noted, this dichotomy should not be read as representing two clear-cut stages in the process of liberalising international trade. All instruments or approaches employed in the liberalisation of trade sit rather on a continuum that starts at one end with very high barriers to trade among nations and ends at the other extreme with total regulatory harmonisation.[89]

It should be observed in this regard that a similar characterisation has been attributed to the negative/positive integration dichotomy, where negative integration is easier to advance than positive integration.[90]

---

[89] Kahler speaks of deep*er* integration. *Ibid.* Cf G Verhoosel, *National Treatment and WTO Dispute Settlement: Adjudicating the Boundaries of Regulatory Autonomy* (Oxford, Hart Publishing, 2002) at 4 *et seq.*; A Stone Sweet and W Sandholz, "Integration, Supranational Governance and the Institutionalization of the European Polity" in A Stone Sweet and W Sandholz (eds), *European Integration and Supranational Governance* (Oxford, OUP, 1998) at 7–10.

[90] Pinder, "Positive Integration and Negative Integration: Some Problems of Economic Union in the EEC", *The World Today* (March 1968) at 98, "The policies which have a strong chance of being implemented are those that deal with negative integration, while those with a weaker chance are those concerned with positive integration [...] It is not difficult to provide in a treaty for the removal of discrimination, which is relatively simple to define and to enforce. But it is much harder to ensure by means of a treaty that an effective common policy will be formed; for a policy might take any one of a thousand forms [...] In short, a treaty can more easily make effective the 'thou shalt not' commandments than the 'thou shalt' ones." See also A El-Agraa, "Policy Directives, Overall Conclusions and Prognostications on the Future for International Economic Integration" in A El-Agraa (ed), *International Economic Integration* (London, Macmillan, 1982) at 265–66, "A very significant overall conclusion is that the global experience of economic integration has clearly demonstrated the ease with which negative integration can be achieved and the difficulties involved in making progress, if at all, in terms of positive integration. This should not be surprising, however, since the dismantling of tariff barriers and import quota restrictions is easy, particularly in a world where these have been gradually reduced through multilateral negotiations (the Kennedy and Tokyo Rounds conducted under the auspices of GATT) and the GSP whereby certain industrial exports by developing nations are granted preferential treatment in certain advanced countries. Positive integration, on the other hand, is mainly about non-tariff barriers and here harmonisation is of paramount importance. However, harmonisation is a positive act which requires not only concerted action but also, in a number of areas, a certain degree of political commitment which implication s for the sensitive issue of sovereignty as, for example, is the case in fiscal harmonisation, monetary integration and the coordination of employment policies." Cf M Jovanovic, *International Economic Integration* (London/New York, Routledge, 1998) at 5.

It appears to be more appropriate to refrain from this characterisation in light of the fact that, as previously argued, the negative/positive integration dichotomy does not accurately describe all the instruments employed for the liberalisation of trade. Moreover, although it is true that negative integration (in its strict meaning, ie reduction/prohibition of tariffs and quotas) is generally easier to achieve than positive integration (in its strict meaning, harmonisation/unification of domestic regulation), there might be instances where this may not be the case.[91] Accordingly, it seems more correct to employ the dichotomy between negative and positive integration exclusively to describe the structural characteristics of the legal instruments employed in the liberalisation of trade, and that between shallow and deep integration in describing the level of "intrusiveness" into Members' sovereignty of these instruments, and thus whether they are more or less easy to implement.

Before setting forth the actual structure and content of this comparative study, the following table should clarify to the reader the above findings with regard to the three different approaches to trade liberalisation (negative *v* positive, judicial *v* legislative, shallow *v* deep).

Table 1.   Approaches to Trade Liberalisation

Instrument	*Function*	*Definition/ Implementation*	*Level of Intrusiveness*
Reduction/Abolition of border measures	Negative	(Judicial)	Shallow
Non-discrimination	Negative/Positive	Judicial	Shallow/(Deep)
Proportionality/ Reasonableness	Positive/Negative	Judicial	(Shallow)/Deep
EC directive/regulation	Positive	Legislative	Deep

4.   STRUCTURE OF THE RESEARCH

It is now time to advance a tentative structure for our comparative analysis of a few basic legal instruments which have been employed in EC and WTO law for the liberalisation of trade in goods among their respective Members. Once again I take inspiration from the words of Zweigert and Kötz:

> The next step [once the reports on the different legal systems have been completed] in the process of comparison is to build a system. For this one

[91] Compare for example the total abolition of tariffs with an international agreement disciplining the content and the manner in which technical standards are adopted by national governments.

needs to develop a special syntax and vocabulary, which are also in fact necessary for comparative researches on particular topics. The system must be very flexible, and have concepts large enough to embrace the quite heterogeneous legal institutions which are functionally comparable.[92]

The analysis will cover only a few basic instruments of "negative" and "judicial" integration. Restraints of time and space have not permitted the inclusion into the present study of instruments of "legislative integration" (or "positive integration" *stricto sensu*), which in WTO law are in any event at the embryonic stage. Moreover, taking into account the above described distinction between shallow and deep integration, the following analysis will subdivide instruments of "judicial integration" into three layers depending on the level of intrusiveness into Members' regulatory prerogatives of each general legal principle considered. This subdivision should emphasise once again that all instruments or approaches employed in the liberalisation of trade sit on a continuum that starts at one end with zero integration and ends at the other extreme with full integration.

The study is divided in two main parts.

Part I deals with instruments of "shallow integration" found in both EC and WTO law for the liberalisation of trade. In particular, in chapter 1 the analysis focuses on those rules whose emphasis is on the "elimination" of a particular type of trade-restrictive governmental measure, ie rules of "negative integration *stricto sensu*". Section 1 examines EC and WTO rules mandating the reduction/elimination of customs duties and other charges having equivalent effect (Articles 23 and 25 (ex 9 and 12) EC and Articles II and VIII GATT, respectively). Section 2 focuses on EC and WTO rules prohibiting quantitative restrictions and other measures restricting importation and exportation of goods (Articles 28–30 (ex 30 and 34) EC and Article XI GATT respectively). This first chapter is called "Negative integration *stricto sensu*: the elimination of border measures".

Chapter 2 examines the National Treatment principle, focusing in particular on the prohibition of de jure discrimination based on the origin or nationality of the product as it is applied to both fiscal charges and non-fiscal regulations restricting trade in goods. Since both EC and WTO law employ different provisions for applying the National Treatment principle depending on whether the measure is a "tax" or a "regulation", section 1 focuses on the prohibition of formal discrimination with regard to fiscal measures (Article 90 (ex 95) EC and Article III:2 GATT), while section 2 focuses on the prohibition of formal discrimination with regard to non-fiscal regulation (Article 28 (ex 30) EC and Article III:4 GATT). This chapter is called "Judicial integration—first layer: the National Treatment principle and the prohibition of *de jure* discrimination".

---

[92] K Zweigert and H Kötz, *Introduction to Comparative Law* (Oxford, OUP 1998) at 44.

Part II tackles instruments of "deep integration" in both EC and WTO law. Chapter 3 examines once again the National Treatment principle, this time focusing on the prohibition of de facto discrimination as it is applied to both fiscal charges and non-fiscal regulations restricting trade in goods. Once again, section 1 examines the prohibition of material discrimination with regard to fiscal measures (Article 90 (ex 95) EC and Article III:2 GATT), while section 2 focuses on the prohibition of material discrimination with regard to non-fiscal regulation (Article 28 (ex 30) EC and Article III:4 GATT). In the latter section, with particular regard to EC law, the analysis focuses on the legal approach stemming from the *Keck* jurisprudence of the European Court of Justice (ECJ) imposing a prohibition of de facto discrimination on grounds of the product's nationality with regard to marketing standards or "selling arrangements". This chapter is called "Judicial integration—second layer: the National Treatment principle and the prohibition of *de facto* discrimination".

The fourth and final chapter examines the requirement that national measures affecting trade in goods be "reasonable" or "proportionate" as it is applied in the context of both EC and WTO law. In particular, the legal approach stemming from the *Dassonville–Cassis de Dijon* jurisprudence of the ECJ dealing with "indistinctly applicable measures" is compared to that embodied in the two WTO sectorial agreements on Technical Barriers to Trade (TBT) and Sanitary and Phytosanitary Measures (SPS). Chapter 4 is called "Judicial integration—third layer: the reasonableness rule".[93]

A few preliminary points should be emphasised at this stage. First of all, the "legal instruments" or "rules" employed in EC and WTO law for the liberalisation of trade in goods chosen for the present comparative analysis are examined by focusing on the following three features: (a) *"normative content"*, (b) *"objective element"*, and (c) *"exceptions or justification options"*. This subdivision allows for a clearer exposition of each legal instrument or rule by clarifying (a) what each rule actually requires, (b) the types of governmental measures that are caught by each rule, and (c) the circumstances in which a violation of such a rule may be (exceptionally) justified.

With regard to the third feature ("exceptions" or "justification options"), it should furthermore be noted that both EC and WTO law employ the principle of proportionality as the main tool for limiting the availability of the public policy exceptions provided for in Article 30 (ex 36) EC and Article XX GATT. In particular, a national measure that is found

---

[93] Within Part II on Deep Integration, a further chapter on instruments of 'legislative' integration (or "positive integration *stricto sensu*") could examine those legal instruments which (a) directly provide for the substantive regulation of a specific area and (b) determine the law applicable to it. However, as noted above, problems of time and space have not permitted the inclusion of such a chapter into the present analysis. I reserve such an examination for the future.

to violate, for example, the prohibition of quantitative restrictions or the non-discrimination principle may be justified on the basis of the general exception provision if the infringing Member is able to establish that such measure is *suitable* and/or *necessary* to achieve one of the public policy objectives listed in Article 30 EC or Article XX GATT. The proportionality principle, however, is also employed as the principal normative standard imposed on Members under the "reasonableness rule". As will be further explained in chapter 4, there is a distinct doctrinal difference between proportionality employed within the ambit of the "public policy exception" and proportionality which constitute the normative content of the "reasonableness rule". While in the former instance, the measure's proportionality is assessed in order to justify an otherwise prohibited measure (whether because it is a border measure or it violates the non-discrimination principle), in the latter instance, the measure's proportionality operates as the principal normative standard, ie the "primary norm". In order to emphasise this distinction between proportionality as the "exception" and proportionality as the "rule", I have preferred to examine them in separate chapters.

It should not be too difficult to understand why the third feature ("exceptions" or "justification options") does not exist in the case of the requirement that national measures affecting trade in goods be "reasonable" or "proportionate". As the examination in chapter 4 will show, the reasonableness rule does not contain a "justification option" since the reasonableness principle embodies within its "normative content" the safety valves which are usually provided for in exception clauses.

Always with reference to the above mentioned three features, the reader should note that, while with regard to certain rules the analysis will give preference to the "objective element" (for example, in the case of the reduction/elimination of custom duties and quantitative restrictions), with regard to other rules the focus will principally or even exclusively be on the "normative content" (eg the National Treatment obligation). This is due both to the nature of each single "instrument" or "rule" as well as to the need to reduce to a minimum any unnecessary repetition.

Secondly, the present framework, which has been devised to analyse and compare the general legal instruments for the liberalisation of trade in EC and WTO law, should not be understood as a straightjacket. This is true first of all for both the dichotomy between shallow v deep integration as well as for the concepts of negative integration and judicial integration. As will be clarified in the subsequent chapters, this conceptual framework should only be taken as providing a *"chiave di lettura"* of the several basic legal instruments employed in EC and WTO law for the liberalisation of trade as well as emphasising the inherent *evolutionary* nature of "integration".

Finally, the present study does not pretend to take into consideration every tool employed in EC and WTO law in order to *tackle* barriers to international trade.[94] Rather, it is limited to a few basic legal instruments employed in both systems in order to liberalise trade in goods among their respective Members with the aim of showing the different types of issues that arise, depending on the nature and feature of the specific instrument considered.

---

[94]Specific areas such as antidumping, subsidies, safeguards, etc. are excluded, as well as other more general principles like the Most Favoured Nation (MFN) principle.

Part I

Shallow Integration

AS NOTED IN the introductory chapter, the dichotomy between shallow and deep integration reflects the underlying conflict between trade liberalisation objectives and national regulatory prerogatives and thus focuses on the level of "intrusiveness" in Members' sovereignty of the legal instruments employed to tackle trade barriers.

Two fundamental pillars in EC and WTO law relating to the liberalisation of international trade are (1) the obligation to reduce or eliminate quantitative restrictions and tariffs, and (2) the obligation not to discriminate directly on the basis of product's nationality or origin (prohibition of formal or de jure discrimination). These two fundamental obligations may be described as instruments of shallow integration, since the economic theories on which they are based are stronger than the political interests underlying the measures which they are supposed to prohibit or regulate (ie quantitative restrictions, tariffs, discriminatory regulations). For example, it is generally accepted that the economic benefits of a ban on import quotas favouring the opening of national markets are on the whole greater than the benefits stemming from protecting those same markets from foreign competition.

Despite their different features, these two obligations share one peculiar trait; their underlying aim is to further the creation of a level playing field for any good independently of the place of manufacture or sale. By imposing these two obligations, the Member States (whether of the EC or the WTO) demonstrate their willingness to prohibit measures which (a) *apply at the border on imported products only* (ie border measures) and (b) *formally discriminate on the basis of the product's nationality or origin* (ie de jure discriminatory measures).

Chapter 1 analyses the obligations to reduce and/or eliminate custom duties and quantitative restrictions on trade in goods, while chapter 2 examines the prohibition of formal or de jure discrimination as embodied in the National Treatment principle. As noted above, the term "National Treatment" will be employed since it better emphasises the "positive" character of this latter principle.

1

Negative Integration Stricto Sensu: The Elimination of Border Measures

T
WO ISSUES THAT figured prominently in the trade liberalisation agendas of both the GATT and the EEC were "customs duties" and "quantitative restrictions" imposed by Member States on the importation and exportation of goods into and out of their territory. In the preamble to the GATT, the GATT Contracting Parties specified that the Agreement was first of all directed to the "substantial reduction of tariffs and other barriers to trade". Similarly, Article 3 EEC included as the first Community activity "the elimination, as between Member States, of customs duties and of quantitative restrictions on the import and export of goods, and of all other measures having equivalent effect".

While a customs duty or tariff is a charge imposed at the border on imported or exported goods, a quantitative restriction (usually in the form of a quota) is a measure restricting the import or export of a given product simply by reference to a specific amount or value. These measures are usually administered by means of a licensing system, whereby a government agency formally authorises particular traders to import (or export) stated quantities of goods. Both measures fall within the broader category of *"border measures"* since they apply *"at the border"*, ie on the importation of foreign products or exportation of domestic products to foreign markets.

Both measures also constitute clear restrictions on the importation and exportation of products. The fact that they apply at the border as a condition of the importation or exportation of products serves to demonstrate their "negative" effect on international trade. It is thus hardly surprising that the rules dealing with both customs duties and quantitative restrictions were quite strict in both the GATT and the EEC Treaty,[1] envisioning their outright prohibition[2] or at least substantial reduction.[3] As mentioned in the introductory chapter, this general approach towards tariffs

---

[1] JH Jackson, *World Trade and the Law of GATT* (New York, The Bobs-Merrill Co, 1969) at 309; *Rapport des Chefs de Délégation aux Ministres des Affaires Etrangère* (Spaak Report) (1956) at 35. Cf D Wyatt and A Dashwood, *The Substantive Law of the EEC* (London, Sweet & Maxwell, 1980) at 97.
[2] EC Customs duties, and EC and GATT quantitative restrictions.
[3] GATT customs duties.

and quotas may be characterised as "negative integration *stricto sensu*", since the emphasis is on the ultimate elimination of a specific type of trade restrictive, governmental measure. In later chapters, a different regulatory approach is examined, the aim of which is not to eliminate a certain type of measure, but rather to require compliance with general criteria (ie the "judicial integration" instruments examined in chapters 2–4).

Within this general "negative" approach, at least within the GATT, tariffs were treated in a manner slightly different from that reserved to quotas. Although subject to multilateral negotiation directed at their substantial reduction, tariffs were (and still are) permitted (although today very much reduced), while quantitative restrictions were (and still are) prohibited.[4] This difference can be explained by noting that from the beginning there has always been little doubt that quotas negatively affect international trade to a greater extent than tariffs. During the GATT preparatory session in London in 1947, the United States Government perceived quantitative restrictions as the worst of all forms of restriction ever devised by the mind of man,[5] for the following reasons:

> In the case of tariff the total volume of imports can expand with the expansion of trade. There is flexibility in the volume of trade. Under a quota system, the volume of trade is rigidly restricted, and no matter how much more people may wish to buy or consume, not one single more unit will be admitted than the controlling authority thinks fit.
>
> In the case of tariff, the direction of trade and the sources of import can shift with changes in quality and cost and price. Under a quota system the direction of trade and the sources of imports is rigidly fixed by public authority without regard to quality, cost or price. Under a tariff, equality of treatment of all other states can be assured. Under a quota system, no matter how detailed our rules, no matter how carefully we police them, there must almost inevitably be discrimination as amongst other states. If these rules were further to be relaxed, we should emerge from this meeting with nothing more than a multilateral agreement to fasten bilateralism on world trade.
>
> Finally, quantitative restriction makes all international commerce a matter of political negotiation—goods move, not on the basis of quality, service and trade, but on the basis of deals completed country by country, product by product, and day by day between public officials. All economic relations between nations are moved into the area of political conflict.[6]

---

[4] In reality, in light of the several exceptions provided within the Agreement or de facto permitted by Contracting Parties with regard to quantitative restrictions, the general prohibition of Art XI GATT was also subject to a so called de facto progressive implementation.

[5] See US Government's view expressed at the GATT preparatory session in London in 1947, cited in JH Jackson, *World Trade and the Law of GATT*, above n 1, at 309.

[6] UN Doc EPCT/A/PV.22, at 16–17 (1947), cited in JH Jackson, *World Trade and the Law of GATT*, above n 1, at 309–10. During the early post-war years, quotas were also unpopular because they had been employed in the 1930s as a disguised means of restricting imports

Notwithstanding the focus on tariffs and quotas, as evidenced in the text of the GATT and the EC Treaty,[7] there are also other measures similar to tariffs and quotas equally restrictive of international trade as the traditional "border" measures. Consequently, the "negative integration" rules of Articles II and XI GATT apply respectively not just to customs duties or quotas but also to "all other duties or charges of any kind imposed on or in connection with the importation" and to "restrictions instituted or maintained on the importation or exportation of any product". Similarly, Article 23 (ex Article 9) EC and Articles 28–29 (ex 30 and 34) EC apply not just to customs duties or quantitative restrictions but also to "all charges having equivalent effect" and "all measures having equivalent effect" respectively.

While tariffs and quotas are fairly easy to define, concepts such as "all other duties or charges of any kind imposed on or in connection with the importation" or "all measures having equivalent effect to quantitative restrictions" raise a few more interpretative problems. The relevance of defining these concepts, however, depends on whether or not trade restrictive measures are subject to different rules. For example, in the EC context, the treatment of "pecuniary measures" differs depending on whether a measure falls within the category of "charges having equivalent effect to customs duties" of Article 23 EC or the category of "internal taxes" of Article 90 EC.[8] In the WTO context, there is a clear distinction between the provisions dealing with pecuniary and non-pecuniary *border* measures (Articles II and XI GATT) and the provisions dealing with pecuniary and non-pecuniary *internal* measure (Article III:2 and 4).

The implications of a dual normative approach should not be underestimated. For example, in EC law a charge deemed to constitute a "charge having equivalent effect to a customs duty" will be caught by the rule of

without breaching tariffs-reducing international agreements. See Panel Report on *Turkey–Textiles*, WT/DS34/R, which stated as follows:

> "The prohibition on the use of quantitative restrictions forms one of the cornerstones of the GATT system. A basic principle of the GATT system is that tariffs are the preferred and acceptable form of protection.[…] Two fundamental obligations contained in Part II are the national treatment clause and the prohibition against quantitative restrictions. The prohibition against quantitative restrictions is a reflection that tariffs are GATT's border protection 'of choice'. Quantitative restrictions impose absolute limits on imports, while tariffs do not. In contrast to MFN tariffs which permit the most efficient competitor to supply imports, quantitative restrictions usually have a trade distorting effect, their allocation can be problematic and their administration may not be transparent." *Ibid.*, para 9.63.

[7] For example, Art XI of the GATT is titled "General elimination of *quantitative restrictions*", and the whole ch 2 of the Treaty of Rome (of which Arts 30 and 34, now Arts 28–29, are part) is titled "Elimination of Quantitative Restrictions between Member States".

[8] As the analysis will show, although "non-pecuniary measures" restricting trade in goods fall under the same Treaty provisions (Arts 28–30, former 30–36 EC), they are in fact regulated by different rules. See below s 2 on Arts 28–30 EC.

"negative integration *stricto sensu*", and thereby prohibited (Article 23 EC). On the other hand, a charge deemed to constitute an "internal tax" will simply need to comply, under a "judicial integration" type of rule, with specific general criteria, such as the non-discrimination principle (A 90 EC).[9]

In this chapter, the analysis focuses on both WTO and EC rules the emphasis of which is on the (progressive) "elimination" of a particular type of trade-restrictive, governmental measure, ie rules of "negative integration *stricto sensu*". Section 1 examines EC and WTO rules mandating the reduction or elimination of customs duties and other charges having equivalent effect (Articles 23 and 25 (ex 9 and 12) EC and Articles II and VIII GATT respectively), while section 2 focuses on EC and WTO rules prohibiting quantitative restrictions and other measures restricting the importation and exportation of goods (Articles 28–30 (ex 30 and 34) EC and Article XI GATT respectively).

1.1   REDUCTION/ELIMINATION OF CUSTOMS DUTIES AND OTHER CHARGES HAVING EQUIVALENT EFFECT

As previously pointed out, one of the first issues in the liberalisation agendas of both the GATT and the EEC was to deal with all duties and charges which each Member State imposed at the border on the importation (and exportation) of goods into (and out of) its territory. These duties are generally referred to as *"pecuniary border measures"*.

Accordingly, Article 3 of the EEC Treaty provided for the "elimination, as between Member States, of customs duties [...] and of all other measures having equivalent effect", while the GATT preamble expressed the Contracting Parties' allegiance "to the substantial reduction of tariffs and other barriers to trade".

---

[9] In the more modern field of trade in services, there appears to exist, at least within WTO law, a similar dual approach (negative *v* judicial integration). As with the treatment of tariffs and quotas by the GATT, the General Agreement in Trade in Services (GATS) provides under Art XVI ("Market Access") a stricter treatment to a pre-determined and mainly "quantitative" set of measures. Art XVII GATS, on the other hand, imposes a National Treatment obligation on all other national measures restricting trade in services. Market access restrictions listed in Art XVI GATS include limitations on (a) the number of service suppliers; (b) the total value of services transactions or assets; (c) the total number of services operations or the total quantity of service output; (d) the total number of natural persons that may be employed in a particular sector; etc. The only category which is not of a quantitative nature is listed under sub-paragraph (e) and refers to limitations on specific types of legal entity through which a service can be supplied. Like Arts II and XI GATT, the rule in Art XVI GATS may be characterised as "negative integration *stricto sensu*", since the emphasis is once again on the ultimate elimination of a specific set of measures restricting trade in services. However, the approach under Art XVI GATS differs to a certain extent to the parallel one under Arts II and XI GATT, since Art XVI seems to prohibit any measures listed therein notwithstanding their "border" or "internal" nature. Cf A Mattoo, "National Treatment in the GATS: Corner-Stone or Pandora's Box?", 31 *JWT* (1997) 113.

As noted in the Introduction, the analysis of the relevant provisions in EC and WTO law dealing with "pecuniary border measures" is premised on the distinction between three main features of both rules: (a) "normative content", (b) the "objective element", and (c) the "exceptions". This section will deal with each of these features in turn, and will draw some conclusions in sub-section (d).

A. Normative Content

Although the long-term objectives of the two entities were different—the EEC aimed at the *elimination* of pecuniary border measures while the GATT aimed at their *substantial reduction*—in practical terms the real difference between the two is mostly one of timing. Where the EEC took approximately a decade to reduce and eliminate all pecuniary border measures, the GATT has taken 50 years to bring the level of tariffs and other charges from the high percentage rate in the post-war period to the low single-digit average of today. In the next few pages, I will focus on the normative content of the rule applicable to pecuniary border measures in both EC and WTO law.

1. Articles 25–27 EC

Even the original Members of the EEC could not "eliminate" custom duties with a snap of their fingers. Several of the original Articles of the Treaty of Rome in the section dealing with the "elimination of customs duties between Member States" provided for a detailed timetable of successive reductions of customs duties imposed both on imports and exports.[10] This timetable was supplemented by a standstill provision, which mandated the Member States to refrain from introducing between themselves any new customs duties on imports or exports or any charges having equivalent effect, and from increasing those that they already were applying in their trade with each other.[11] In its judgment of 14 December 1962, in the *Gingerbread* case,[12] the ECJ gave a strict interpretation to the Article 12 EEC standstill provision.[13]

In accordance with Article 16 of the EEC Treaty, customs duties on *exports* and equivalent charges were abolished at the end of the first stage

---

[10] Arts 13–17 EEC Treaty.
[11] Art 12 EEC Treaty.
[12] Joined Cases 2 and 3/62, *Commission v Luxembourg and Belgium* (*Gingerbread*) [1962] ECR 425.
[13] The defendants had claimed the Commission's application inadmissible, since the Commission had "prevented the rectification of the situation under consideration by improperly demanding the suspension of the measures criticized before deciding upon the requests for derogation put forward by them both under Art 226 of the Treaty and under a regulation adopted by the Council of Ministers on 4 April 1962, pursuant to Art 235.

on 31 December 1961. Following a so-called acceleration decision by the Council pursuant to Article 15 EEC, duties and charges on *imports*, which were to be abolished at the end of the transitional period (31 December 1969), were in fact eliminated in July 1968.[14] Accordingly, after a decade of high-paced "reduction" of customs duties and [measures of equivalent effect], the normative content of the EEC general rule dealing with pecuniary border measures since then has been unproblematic: customs duties and charges having equivalent effect are "prohibited".[15]

2.   Article II GATT

By contrast, the GATT never referred to the "elimination" of tariffs, but merely to their substantial reduction. As a matter of fact, in its original text, the only express reference to the reduction of customs duties and other charges was to be found in one of the recitals of the Preamble. There was not even any set timetable to be followed in the implementation of this latter objective.

Even with the adoption of Article XXVIII bis on Tariff Negotiations, as a result of agreements reached during the Review Session of 1954–1955, no new obligations were imposed on the Contracting Parties, which retained the right to decide whether or not to engage in negotiations or participate in a tariff conference.[16] Nevertheless, Article XXVIIIbis:1 recognises that "customs duties often constitute serious obstacles to trade" and

> thus negotiations on a reciprocal and mutually advantageous basis, directed
> to the substantial reduction of the general level of tariffs and other charges
> on imports and exports and in particular to the reduction of such high

---

By 'abusing its powers and by adopting an excessively legalistic attitude' and by failing to decide as a matter of urgency upon the requests, as it was obliged to do, the Commission has in the defendants' submission, lost the right to take proceedings against the defendants for infringement of the Treaty." *Ibid*. at 429. The Court rejected the defendants' arguments stating as follows: "as the Commission is obliged by Art 155 to ensure that the provisions of the Treaty are applied, it cannot be deprived of the right to exercise an essential power which it holds under Art 169 to ensure that the Treaty is observed. If it were possible to prevent the application of Art 169 by a request for rectification, that Art would lose all its effect." *Ibid*. at 430. Moreover, "a request for derogation from the general rules of the Treaty—in this case, moreover, made at a very late date—cannot have the effect of legalizing unilateral measures which conflict with those rules and cannot therefore legalize retroactively the initial infringement." On the merits, the Court concluded "that the 'special import duty' on gingerbread, increased and extended in Belgium and Luxembourg after the treaty entered into force, contains all the elements of a charge having equivalent effect to a customs duty referred to in Arts 9 and 12. It must therefore be declared and adjudged that the decisions to increase or extend this duty, taken after 1 Jan 1958, constituted infringements of the Treaty." *Ibid*.

[14] Council Decision 66/532/EEC on 26 July 1966, in GUCE n 165 of 21 Sept 1966, at 2971.
[15] See below for the few exceptions to this general rule.
[16] GATT, *Analytical Index: Guide to GATT Law and Practice*, 6th edn (1994) at 912.

tariffs as discourage the importation even of minimum quantities [...] are of great importance to the expansion of international trade.

For this purpose, the last sentence of the same Article recites as follows: "contracting parties may therefore sponsor such negotiations from time to time."

Accordingly, since 1947, eight "rounds" of multilateral tariff and trade negotiations have been completed within GATT, with the result that tariffs are now set on average at single-digit levels.

The central obligation of GATT over the years has been the "tariff concession", which is a commitment by a GATT Contracting Party to levy no more than a specified duty on a particular item.[17] Tariffs concessions, which are negotiated on a reciprocal and mutually advantageous basis during trade rounds, are inserted in each Contracting Party's Schedule of concessions (or commitments). The Schedules annexed to the Agreement become integral part the Agreement itself.[18]

Article II, under the heading *"Schedules of Concessions"*, sets forth disciplines with regard to pecuniary border measures. Paragraph (a) of Article II:1 contains a general prohibition against according treatment less favourable to imports than that provided for in a Member's Schedule,[19] and the two sentences in paragraph (b) prohibit two specific kinds of practices that will always be inconsistent with paragraph (a):

1. the application of "ordinary customs duties" in excess of those provided for in the Schedule with regard to the products (or items) described therein, and subject to the terms, conditions or qualifications set forth therein,[20] and

2. the application of "all other duties or charges of any kind" in excess of those imposed on the date of this Agreement, always with regard to the products (or items) described in the Schedule relating to any Contracting Party.[21]

---

[17] JH Jackson, W Davey and A Sykes, *Legal Problems of International Economic Relations: Cases and Materials* (St. Paul Minnesota, West Publishing Co, 1995) at 384; JH Jackson, *World Trade and the Law of GATT*, above n 1, at 201.

[18] Art II:7 GATT.

[19] Appellate Body Report on *Argentina—Measures Affecting Imports of Footwear, Textiles, Apparel and Other Items (Argentina–Textile)*, WT/DS56/AB/R, circulated 27 March/20 April 1998, adopted 22 April 1998, para 45. Art II:1(a) reads as follows: "Each Contracting Party shall accord to the commerce of the other contracting parties treatment no less favourable than that provided for in the appropriate Part of the appropriate Schedule annexed to this Agreement".

[20] Art II:1(b), first sentence, reads as follows: "The products described in Part I of the Schedule relating to any Contracting Party, which are the products of territories of other contracting parties, shall, on their importation into the territory to which the Schedule relates, and subject to the terms, conditions or qualifications set forth in that Schedule, be exempt from ordinary customs duties in excess of those set forth and provided therein".

[21] Art II:1(b), second sentence, reads as follows: "Such products shall also be exempt from all other duties or charges of any kind imposed on or in connection with the importation in excess

Following the Uruguay Round, the Understanding on the Interpretation of Article II:1(b) was included in the General Agreement on Tariffs and Trade 1994 as a clarification of the rule in Article II:1 relating to "other duties or charges". It provides inter alia that (i) in order to ensure transparency of the legal rights and obligations deriving from paragraph 1(b) of Article II, the nature and level of any "other duties or charges" levied on bound tariff items, as referred to in that provision, shall be recorded in the Schedules of concessions annexed to GATT 1994 against the tariff item to which they apply; (ii) the date as of which "other duties or charges" are bound, for the purposes of Article II, shall be 15 April 1994 [...] "other duties or charges" shall therefore be recorded in the Schedules at the levels applying on this date; and (iii) "other duties or charges" omitted from a Schedule at the time of deposit of the instrument incorporating the Schedule in question into GATT 1994 [...] shall not subsequently be added to it and any "other duty or charge" recorded at a level lower than that prevailing on the applicable date shall not be restored to that level unless such additions or changes are made within six months of the date of deposit of the instrument.

In short, the rule set out in Article II GATT with regard to pecuniary border measures is very much similar to that of Article 12 EEC. Although both Articles impose a standstill obligation, they do differ slightly in one respect. Whereas Article 12 EEC prohibits the EEC Member States from introducing any new customs duties or equivalent charges and from increasing those which they were already applying in their trade to each other, the prohibition in Article II GATT is limited to (i) the customs duties and charges set out in each Member's Schedule of Concessions and (ii) the items described therein.[22]

For example, if State A has agreed to reduce its tariff level on apples to 5 per cent, State A cannot apply a custom duty equal to 5.5 per cent on the importation of apples from any other Contracting Party (Article II:1(b), first sentence). On the other hand, if State A is not bound with regard to imports of tuna, State A may increase the tariff level on such imports without violating Article II.

With regard to "other duties and charges of any kind", State A will not be able to apply any other charges on the importation of apples in excess of those recorded in its Schedule of Concessions (Article II.1(b), second sentence and Understanding). On the other hand, no such prohibition can

---

of those imposed on the date of this Agreement or those directly and mandatorily required to be imposed thereafter by legislation in force in the importing territory on that date."

[22] There appears to be a slight difference between the two rules in Art II.1(b). While Art II implicitly mandates the reduction through successive rounds of "ordinary customs duties", it seems only to prescribe that "all other duties or charges of any kind" be kept at the level where they are. This perception might have changed following the adoption of the Understanding. Nevertheless, this apparent distinction in the original text of Art II would still not impede the inclusion of this latter type of pecuniary border measure in future rounds of negotiations.

be imposed on State A with regard to other duties and charges on imports of tuna, since tuna is not a bound item.[23]

Given the relevance of the content of each Member's Schedule, GATT panel practice as well as WTO jurisprudence has had to face and clarify a few issues relating to the effect, interpretation and scope of application of tariff concessions.

With regard to the effect of tariff concessions, it is settled case law that the commitments of WTO Members may not violate other WTO law obligations. In *EC–Bananas III*,[24] addressing the question of the consistency with Article XIII GATT of the allocation of tariff quotas as inscribed in a Schedule, the Appellate Body discussed whether the tariff concessions for agricultural products could deviate from Article XIII GATT. The Appellate Body limited the validity of tariff concessions as follows:

> With respect to concession contained in the Schedules annexed to the GATT 1947, the panel in *United States—Restrictions on Importation of Sugar* ("*United States–Sugar Headnote*") found that:
>
>> Article II permits contracting parties to incorporate into their Schedules acts yielding rights under the General Agreement but not acts diminishing obligations under that Agreement.[25]
>
> This principle is equally valid for the market access concessions and commitments for agricultural products contained in the Schedules annexed to the GATT 1994. The ordinary meaning of the term "concession" suggests that a Member may yield rights and grant benefits, but it cannot diminish its obligations.[26]

---

[23] It should be noted that a Member's commitment may be subject to the "terms and conditions" as referred to in Art II:1(b). See Panel Report on *Korea—Measures Affecting Imports of Fresh, Chilled and Frozen Beef* (*Korea—Beef*), WT/DS161/R and WT/DS169/R, circulated 31 July 2000, adopted 10 Jan 2001, para 609.

[24] *European Communities—Regime for the Importation, Sale and Distribution of Bananas* (*EC–Banana III*), WT/DS27, brought 12 Feb 1996.

[25] [Fn original] adopted on 22 June 1989, BISD 36S/331, para 5.2.

[26] Appellate Body Report on *EC–Bananas III*, WT/DS27/AB/R, circulated 9 Sept 1997, adopted 25 Sept 1997, para 154. The Appellate Body cited para 3 of the Marrakesh Protocol, which provides that "[t]he implementation of the concessions and commitments contained in the schedules annexed to this Protocol shall, upon request, be subject to multilateral examination by the Members. This would be without prejudice to the rights and obligations of Member under Agreements in Annex 1A of the WTO Agreement". *Ibid.* para 154. In *European Communities—Measures Affecting Importation of Certain Poultry Products* (*EC–Poultry*), WT/DS69, brought 4 March 1997, the Appellate Body, addressing a complaint against the allocation of tariff quotas for certain poultry products by the EC, confirmed its finding in *EC–Bananas III* and stated that "the concessions contained in Schedule LXXX pertaining to the tariff-rate quota for frozen poultry meat must be consistent with Art I and XIII of the GATT 1994." Appellate Body Report on *EC–Poultry*, WT/DS69/AB/R, circulated 13 July 1998, adopted 23 July 1998, paras 98–99. Cf Panel Report on *Argentina—Measures Affecting Imports of Footwear, Textiles, Apparel and Other Items* (*Argentina–Textile*), WT/DS56/R, circulated 25 Nov 1997, adopted 22 April 1998, para 6.81.

This principle has also been confirmed by the Understanding on the Interpretation of Article II:1(b) of the GATT 1994, where paragraph 5 provides that:

> the recording of "other duties or charges" in the Schedules is without prejudice to their consistency with rights and obligations under GATT 1994 [...]. All Members retain the right to challenge, at any time, the consistency of any "other duty or charge" with such obligations.

It is clear however that this principle applies for other GATT obligations which are applicable to the specific measure at issue (for example, while the MFN principle applies across the board, the NT principle applies only to internal measures).[27]

With regard to the issue of interpretation of tariff concessions, in *EC–Computer Equipment*,[28] the Appellate Body stated that, in light of the fact that tariff concessions provided for in a Member's Schedule are made an integral part of the GATT 1994 by Article II:7, the only rules which may be applied in interpreting the meaning of a concession are the general rules of treaty interpretation set out in the Vienna Convention.[29] Moreover, the Appellate Body disagreed with the Panel that the maintenance of the security and predictability of tariff concessions allowed the interpretation of a concession in the light of the "legitimate expectations" of exporting Members, ie their subjective views as to the meaning of the agreement reached during tariff negotiations.[30] Accordingly, the Appellate Body also limited the relevance of prior practice on tariff classification of only one of the parties, since the purpose of treaty interpretation is to establish the common intention of the parties to the Treaty.[31]

With regard to the scope of application of tariff concessions, it should be noted that each Member's concessions only constitute the maximum level of tariffs that can be levied on a particular product, without limiting a Member's freedom to impose a tariff *lower* than that specified in its Schedule. Article II:1(b) prohibits the imposition of ordinary customs duties and other charges "in excess of" those provided for in a Member's Schedule. In *Argentine–Textile*,[32] where the issue was whether certain minimum specific import duties were in violation of the tariff

---

[27] For a further discussion on this issue, see below the section on the "objective element" of Art II GATT.

[28] *European Communities—Customs Classification of Certain Computer Equipment* (*EC–Computer Equipment*), WT/DS62, brought 14 Nov 1996.

[29] Appellate Body Report on *EC–Computer Equipment*, WT/DS62/AB/R, circulated 5 June 1998, adopted 22 June 1998, para 84.

[30] *Ibid.*, para 82.

[31] *Ibid.*, para 93.

[32] *Argentina—Measures Affecting Imports of Footwear, Textiles, Apparel and Other Items* (*Argentina–Textile*), WT/DS56, brought 15 Oct 1996.

concession made by Argentina on an *ad valorem* basis, the Appellate Body explained that:

> A tariff binding in a Member's Schedule provides an upper limit on the amount of duty that may be imposed, and a Member is permitted to impose a duty that is less than that provided for in its Schedule.[33]

The Appellate Body then concluded that:

> The application of a type of duty different from the type provided for in a Member's Schedule is inconsistent with Article II:1(b), first sentence, of the GATT 1994 *to the extent that it results* in ordinary customs duties being levied in excess of those provided for in that Member's Schedule [emphasis added].[34]

In other words, the tariff applied by a Member may even be different in form compared to the one specified in its Schedule of concessions, as long as there is no possibility that its application will accord treatment less favourable than that guaranteed in that Schedule.[35]

B. Objective Element

The second feature of the rules employed by EC and WTO law to deal with pecuniary border measures is the "objective element" of those rules, or in other words, the types of measures which fall within the scope of application of the relevant rule. The following pages will define more precisely the scope of application of Article 25 EC and Article II GATT and in particular the meaning of the term "pecuniary border measures" with regard to both EC and WTO law.

1. *Article 25 EC*

Two issues are considered in this section: first, the meaning of the "customs duties" and "charges having equivalent effect" and secondly, the so-called "compensation exception".

---

[33] Appellate Body Report on *Argentina–Textile*, WT/DS56/AB/R, circulated 27 March/20 April 1998, adopted 22 April 1998, para 46.

[34] *Ibid.*, para 55.

[35] Already in the Panel Report on *Argentina–Textile*, it was noted that a "potential" violation is enough to demonstrate a breach of a GATT obligation, since "any measure which changes the competitive relationship of Members nullifies any such Member's benefits under the WTO Agreement." Panel Report on *Argentina–Textile*, above n 26, para 6.45. Cf Panel Report on *United States—Import Measures on Certain Products from the European Communities*, WT/DS165/R, circulated 17 July 2000, adopted 10 Jan 2001, paras 6.51–52 and Report of the *Panel on Newsprint*, L/5680, adopted on 20 Nov 1984, BISD 31S/114.

(a)   The meaning of "customs duties" and "charges having equivalent effect"   In its updated form, Article 25 (ex Article 12) EC simply states that "Customs duties on imports and exports and charges having equivalent effect shall be prohibited between Member States."[36] While the normative content of this provision, as previously analysed, is an absolute ban, the objective element includes both "customs duties" and "charges having equivalent effect". The reason for subjecting both types of burden to the prohibition of Article 25 is quite obvious. In the words of Craig and de Búrca:

> Member States are not stupid. If this phrase had been omitted from the Treaty then it would have been open to those who were minded not to play the Community system fairly to comply with the abolition of customs duties *stricto sensu*, but to reach the same protectionist goal through measures with created, in economic terms, a similar barrier against imported goods.[37]

With the gradual abolition of financial barriers to inter-State trade, the practical importance of this rationale has slightly decreased. The justification for the prohibition of charges having equivalent effect appears to lie more in the more basic assumption that "any pecuniary charge, however small, imposed on goods by reason of the fact that they cross a frontier constitutes an obstacle to the movement of goods, which is aggravated by the resulting administrative formalities."[38] This is after all the justification for the prohibition of customs duties.[39]

After an initial phase in which the ECJ interpreted the concept of charges of equivalent effect especially considering the effect of the challenged measures,[40] beginning with its judgment in the *Statistical Levy*

---

[36] Art 25, last sentence, specifies as follows: "This prohibition shall also apply to customs duties of a fiscal nature".

[37] P Craig and G de Búrca, *EU Law* (Oxford, OUP, 1998) at 554. See Joined Cases 2 and 3/62, *Commission v Luxembourg and Belgium (Gingerbread)* [1962] ECR 425, where the Court stated as follows: "Art 9 being placed at the beginning of the Title relating to 'free movement of goods', and Art 12 at the beginning of the Section dealing with the 'elimination of customs duties'—is sufficient to emphasize the essential nature of the prohibitions which they impose. The importance of these prohibitions is such that, in order to prevent their evasion by different customs or fiscal practices, the Treaty sought to forestall any possible breakdown in their application". *Ibid.*, at 432. Case 24/68, *Commission v Italy (Statistical Levy)* [1969] ECR 193, para 8, "The extension of the prohibition of customs duties to charges having an equivalent effect is intended to supplement the prohibition against obstacles to trade created by such duties by increasing its efficiency."

[38] R Barents, "Charges of Equivalent Effect to Customs Duties", 15 *CMLRev* (1978) 415 at 420, citing Case 46/76, *Bauhuis v The Netherlands* [1977] ECR 5, para 8.

[39] In the earlier judgment in the *Statistical Levy* case, the ECJ had employed the exact same argument with regard to the prohibition of customs duties. "The justification for this prohibition is based on the fact that any pecuniary charge, however small, imposed on goods by reason of the fact that they cross a frontier constitutes an obstacle to the movement of such goods." Case 24/68, *Statistical Levy* [1969] ECR 193, para 7.

[40] Joined Cases 2 and 3/62, *Commission v Luxembourg and Belgium (Gingerbread)* [1962] ECR 425 and Joined Cases 52 and 55/65, *Germany v Commission* [1965] ECR 159. The expression charges that having equivalent effect to customs duties "is evidence of a general intention to

case,[41] the Court has adopted a more strict and objective definition of charges having equivalent effect. At issue in that case was a charge levied at an equal rate on imported and exported goods the purpose of which was to finance the collection of statistical data on Italy's foreign trade. The amount of the levy was insignificant: ten lire on every 100 kilograms or every metric ton of goods or on every animal or vehicle. Abandoning the criterion based on the protectionist effect, the ECJ qualified, in more or less "positive" terms, a charge of equivalent effect as

> any pecuniary charge, however small and whatever its designation and mode of application, which is imposed unilaterally on domestic or foreign goods by reason of the fact that they cross a frontier, and which is not a customs duty in the strict sense [...] even if it is not imposed for the benefit of the State, is not discriminatory or protective in effect and if the product on which the charge is imposed is not in competition with any domestic product.[42]

This definition is without any doubt quite broad, especially considering the three negative qualifications in the last part of the above-mentioned paragraph. In the determination of the scope of application of Article 25, what counts is not the "effect" of the pecuniary measure, but that it is imposed on imported (or exported) goods by reason of the fact that they cross a frontier.

However, the Court's task could not end there. Foreshadowing what was to become one of the central issues in future litigation over pecuniary measures, the Court qualified, this time in "negative" terms, the concept of charges having equivalent effect in Part 2, chapter I, section I on the *Elimination of Customs Duties* in light of the similar phenomenon of *Internal Taxation*, which was regulated by the provisions in Part 3, chapter 2 of the EEC Treaty (Articles 95–99; today, Articles 90–93). It was not just a matter of an accurate "division of labour" between the several parts of the Treaty. Classifying a pecuniary imposition as a charge having an effect equivalent to a customs duty or as an internal tax, had one grave consequence: while in the latter case it would be prohibited only if discriminatory, in the former case the charge would be per se prohibited.[43] The Court explained the issue in these terms:

> [...] it follows from Articles 95 *et seq.* that the concept of a charge having equivalent effect does not include taxation which is imposed in the same

---

prohibit not only measures which obviously take the form of the classic customs duty but also all those which, presented under other names or introduced by the indirect means of other procedures, would lead to the same discriminatory or protective results as customs duties." Joined Cases 2 and 3/62, *Gingerbread* [1962] ECR 425, at 433.

[41] Case 24/68, *Statistical Levy* [1969] ECR 193.
[42] *Ibid.*, para 9.
[43] JHH Weiler, "The Constitution of the Common Marketplace: Text and Context in the Evolution of the Free Movement of Goods", in P Craig and G de Búrca (eds), *The Evolution of EU Law* (Oxford, OUP, 1999) at 355.

way within a state on similar or comparable domestic products, or at least falls, in the absence of such products, within the framework of general internal taxation, or which is intended to compensate for such internal taxation within the limits laid down by the treaty.[44]

From this statement, it is evident that the definition of internal taxation plays a central role in the determination of the scope of the per se prohibition of Article 25. In more substantive terms, the Court's definition of the two concepts ("charge having equivalent effect" and "internal taxation") seems to focus on two elements: (i) whether the charge on goods is imposed "by reason of the fact that they cross a frontier" or "within a state"; and (ii) whether or not the charge applies "in the same way [...] on similar or comparable domestic products". While the first element deals with the geographical "location" of the pecuniary measure, the second element focuses on the objective "scope of application" of that measure.

Although reference to each of the two elements may be found in several instances in the case-law of the ECJ with regard to the above-mentioned complementary concepts,[45] the central feature in drawing the dividing line between Article 25 and Article 90 relates principally to the general scope of application of the pecuniary measure (ie the second element). Accordingly, if the charge applies *exclusively* to imported (or exported) products, then the charge falls within the per se prohibition of Article 25. On the other hand, if the charge applies *indistinctly* to both imported (or exported) and domestic products, then it is caught under the net of Article 90 and is prohibited only if discriminatory.[46]

---

[44] Case 24/68, *Statistical Levy* [1969] ECR 193, para 11. This definition of charges having equivalent effect continues to be cited in the most recent cases as encapsulating the essential elements. See, for example, Joined Cases C–485 and 486/93, *Simitzi v Municipality of Kos* [1995] ECR I–2655, para 15, and Case C–45/94, *Cámara de Comercio, Industria y Navegación, Ceuta v Municipality of Ceuta* [1995] ECR I–4385, para 28.

[45] Case 10/65, *Waldemar Deutschmann v Germany* [1965] ECR 469, at 474, "This being so, Art 95, which lays down a different time-table for the progressive abolition of the obstacles referred to therein, cannot relate to a charge which is imposed either by reason of, or at the time of, importation and which, being imposed specifically upon a product imported from a member state to the exclusion of a similar domestic product, has, by altering its price, the same effect upon the free movement of goods as a customs duty." Case 29/87, *Dansk Denkavit ApS v Danish Ministry of Agriculture* [1988] ECR 2965, para 33, "[T]he Court has consistently held that the prohibition laid down in Art 9 of the Treaty of any customs duty and charge having an equivalent effect in relations between Member States covers any charge levied on the occasion or by reason of importation specifically affecting an imported product to the exclusion of a similar domestic product. Such a charge however does not fall within that classification if, as in the present case, it relates to a general system of internal dues applied systematically and in accordance with the same criteria to domestic products and imported products alike, in which case it does not come within the scope of Art 9 but within that of Art 95 of the Treaty."

[46] See Case C–90/94, *Haahr Petroleum Ltd v Åbenrå Havn and Others* [1997] ECR I–4085; G Tesauro, *Diritto Comunitario* (Padova, Cedam, 1995) at 262.

The geographical location of the charge (ie the first element) has not much been employed by the Court,[47] except at times as an indication that the charge applied exclusively to imports. For example, in *Waldemar Deutschmann v Germany*,[48] the Court found that charges levied upon the issuing of import licences (that is, on the occasion of importation) were imposed solely on imported products, since similar national products were *naturally* exempt from the licence requirement.[49]

The significance of the scope of application of the pecuniary measure under review has been clearly stressed in a series of cases beginning with *Steinike und Weinlig v Germany*,[50] in which the Court added to the *Statistical Levy* definition the following statement:

> The essential characteristic of a charge having an effect equivalent to a customs duty, which distinguishes it from internal taxation, is that the first is imposed exclusively on the imported product whilst the second is imposed on both imported and domestic products.[51]

For purposes of this determination, the Court will not take the individual pecuniary measure at issue in isolation. In particular, the ECJ has advanced a formula in order to appraise whether a pecuniary measure should be considered as an internal tax or as a charge of equivalent effect. This formula turns around the *general* and *abstract* character of the measure itself.[52] A charge does not come within the scope of Article 25, but rather within that of Article 90, if "it relates to a general system of internal dues applied systematically and in accordance with the same criteria to domestic products and imported products alike."[53]

---

[47] It could be argued that this criterion, as broadly employed by the ECJ, has lost its practical relevance. The often-used expression "by reason of importation" may in fact comprehend *any* measure which is imposed on imported goods, since such a measure would be in a way imposed by reason of importation. Compare this expression with the stricter terms "at the time of importation" or "on the occasion of importation".

[48] Case 10/65, *Waldemar Deutschmann v Germany* [1965] ECR 469.

[49] "It follows from the wording of the question put that it concerns charges imposed on the issue of import licences, that is, on the occasion of importation, the similar national product being naturally exempt from the licence. The charges referred to are thus imposed solely on imported products." *Ibid.*, at 473.

[50] Case 78/76 [1977] ECR 595, para 28.

[51] Case 78/76 *Steinike und Weinlig v Germany* [1977] ECR 595, para 28; see also Case 15/81 *Schul v Inspecteur der Invoerrechten en Accijnzen* [1982] ECR 1409, para 19; Case 193/85 *Co-Frutta v Amministrazione delle Finanze dello Stato* [1987] ECR 2085, para 9; Opinion of Advocate General Tesauro in Case C–45/94 *Cámara de Comercio, Industria y Navegación, Ceuta v Municipality of Ceuta* [1995] ECR I–4385; Joined opinion of Advocate General Jacobs in Case C–90/94 *Haahr Petroleum Ltd v Åbenrå Havn and Others* [1997] ECR I–4085, para 42.

[52] G Tesauro, *Diritto Comunitario*, (Padova, Cedam, 1995) at 262.

[53] Case 87/75, *Bresciani v Amministrazione Italiana delle Finanze* [1976] ECR 129, para 11; Case 46/76, *Bauhuis v The Netherlands* [1977] ECR 5, para 11; Case 29/87, *Dansk Denkavit ApS v Danish Ministry of Agriculture* [1988] ECR 2965, para 33.

Accordingly, the Court will not content itself with a formal reading of the measure under review. For example, a charge which is formally imposed on *any* product, but is in practice borne by imported products only (because there is no identical or similar domestic product), does not constitute a charge having equivalent effect but internal taxation within the meaning of Article 90 only if it relates to a general system of internal dues applied systematically to categories of products in accordance with objective criteria irrespective of the origin of the products.[54]

Clearly, determining whether or not a similar charge relates to a general system of internal dues in accordance with objective criteria will often depend on a case-by-case analysis of the several features of the pecuniary measure under review.[55]

Similarly, the Court would treat a duty within the general system of internal taxation applying systematically to domestic and imported products as a "charge having an effect equivalent to customs duty on imports" when it is intended exclusively to support activities specifically benefiting the taxed domestic product.[56] In these cases, the dividing line between Articles 25 and 90 EC will depend upon whether the charges imposed on the domestic product are "completely" or "partially" compensated. If the former (complete compensation), then the tax will be treated under Article 25, the rationale being that what in effect exists is a charge which is being levied on the imported product only. If, however, the charge is compensated only partially, directly or indirectly, the matter will fall to be assessed under Article 90, the rationale here being that the partial refund in effect means that there could be a discriminatory tax.[57]

The Court's willingness to go beyond the mere formal appearance of the measure under review may also work in the opposite direction. Take for example the *Bresciani* case,[58] where the Italian authorities had imposed a charge for veterinary and public health inspections carried out on imported raw cowhides. Although the specific measure at

---

[54] This sentence is taken *verbatim* from the ECJ judgment in Case 193/85, *Co-Frutta v Amministrazione delle Finanze dello Stato* [1987] ECR 2085, para 10.

[55] In Case 193/85 *Co-Frutta v Amministrazione delle Finanze dello Stato* [1987] ECR 2085, para 12, the Court examined inter alia, the rate of the tax, the basis of assessment and the manner in which the tax was levied.

[56] Case 77/72, *Capolongo v Maya* [1973] ECR 611, para 14: "In the interpretation of the concept 'charge having an effect equivalent to a customs duty on imports', the destination of the financial charges levied must be taken into account. In effect, when such a financial charge or duty is intended exclusively to support activities which specifically profit taxed domestic products, it can follow that the general duty levied according to the same criteria on the imported product and the domestic product nevertheless constitutes for the former a net supplementary tax burden, whilst for the latter it constitutes in reality a set-off against benefits or aids previously received." *Ibid.*, para 13. Cf Case C–72/92, *H Scharbatke GmbH v Germany* [1993] ECR I–5509.

[57] P Craig and G de Búrca, *EU Law*, above n 37, at 576.

[58] Case 87/75, *Bresciani v Amministrazione Italiana delle Finanze* [1976] ECR 129.

hand clearly applied on its face exclusively to imports, the Italian Government had argued that domestic production was subjected to similar burdens. The Court justified its findings that the Italian charge at issue was indeed a charge having equivalent effect to a customs duty in these terms:

> The fact that the domestic production is, through other charges, subjected to a similar burden matters little unless those charges and the duty in question are applied according to the same criteria and at the same stage of production, thus making it possible for them to be regarded as falling within a general system of internal taxation applying systematically and in the same way to domestic and imported products.[59]

In conclusion, the Court's determination of what constitutes a charge having equivalent effect to a customs duty will focus not simply on the geographical location of the measure but principally on whether or not the charge applies *exclusively* to imported products. Accordingly, the scope of application of Article 25 EC and thus the concept of "pecuniary border measures" has been limited to measures that apply (i) at the border and (ii) to imported products only. In other words, Article 25 EC applies to "inherently discriminatory" pecuniary measures, ie measures that by their very nature and characteristics may only be imposed on imported (and exported) products.

For purposes of this determination, however, the Court is willing to go beyond the mere formal appearance of the pecuniary measure under review, and investigate whether the measure actually applies to imported products only or whether it could not be considered to fall within a general system of internal taxation applying systematically and in the same way to both domestic and imported products. Accordingly, cases like *Bresciani v Amministrazione Italiana delle Finanze* and *Capolongo v Maya* show that the Court is willing to examine the measure under challenge not in isolation but together with other provisions imposing similar charges on domestic products or fully refunding such charges to domestic producers. It should also be noted that the Court's inquiry into whether a charge falls within a general system of internal taxation is carried out

---

[59] *Ibid.*, para 11. See also Case 84/71, *Marimex v Amministrazione Italiana delle Finanze* [1972] ECR 80, "Pecuniary charges imposed for reasons of public health examination of products when they cross the frontier, which are determined according to special criteria applicable to them, which are not comparable to the criteria for determining the pecuniary charges affecting similar domestic products, are to be regarded as charges having an effect equivalent to customs duties." Cf Case 29/87, *Dansk Denkavit ApS v Danish Ministry of Agriculture* [1988] ECR 2965, where a pecuniary imposition on importers was deemed to relate to a general system of internal dues applied systematically and in accordance with the same criteria to domestic products ad imported products alike, and thus fell within the scope of application of Art 90.

according to quite strict criteria, in particular where the charge under review formally applies only to imported products (as in *Bresciani*).

(b)   The "compensation for services" exception   A question connected with the "objective element" of the EC provisions dealing with pecuniary border measures relates to whether or not a pecuniary charge imposed on imported (or exported) products in consideration for administrative tasks or services (such as clearing procedures, sanitary inspections, or the delivery of certificates) should be considered as a charge having equivalent effect to a customs duty. The argument, at times advanced by Member States, is that in these cases one cannot talk about a "charge", but only of consideration for services rendered. For example, in the *Statistical Levy* case, the Italian Government defended its pecuniary imposition by arguing that "the disputed charge constitutes the consideration for a service rendered and as such cannot be designated as a charge having equivalent effect."[60] In that case, as in many others,[61] the Court dismissed this line of reasoning, arguing that, although importers (and exporters) do benefit by the services rendered, the benefit is so general and so difficult to assess that the charge cannot be regarded as a consideration for an actual and definite benefit.[62]

Next to the requirement that the charge be a consideration for a service actually rendered by the administration to the individualised benefit of a specific operator and not to the generalised public, the Court case-law has also indicated that the charge must not exceed either the value or the cost of that service.[63] In light of the strict nature of these conditions,[64] it is rare to find cases where the so-called "compensation exception" has been successfully claimed.[65]

---

[60] Case 24/68, *Statistical Levy* [1969] ECR 193, para 15, "According to the Italian Government the object of the statistics in question is to determine precisely the actual movements of goods and, consequently, changes the state of the market. It claims that the exactness of the information thus supplied affords importers a better competitive position in the Italian market whilst exporters enjoy a similar advantage abroad and that the special advantages which dealers obtain from the survey justifies their paying for this public service and moreover demonstrates that the disputed charge is in the nature of a *quid pro quo*."

[61] Case 39/73, *Rewe Zentralfinanz v Direktor der Landwirtschaftskammer Westfalen-Lippe* [1973] ECR 1039; Case 63/74, *Cadszky v Istituto Nationale per il commercio estero* [1975] ECR 281; Case 87/75, *Bresciani v Amministrazione Italiana delle Finanze* [1976] ECR 129.

[62] Case 24/68, *Statistical Levy* [1969] ECR 193, para 16.

[63] Cf R Barents, "Charges of Equivalent Effect to Customs Duties", 15 *CMLRev* (1978) 415 at 423; G Tesauro, *Diritto Comunitario* (Padova, Cedam, 1995) at 257.

[64] Emblematic is the Court's "concession" in the *Statistical Levy* case: "Although it is *not impossible* that in certain circumstances a specific service actually rendered may form the consideration for a possible proportional payment for the service in question, this may only apply in specific cases which cannot lead to the circumvention of the provisions of Arts 9, 12, 13 and 16 of the Treaty" [emphasis added]. Case 24/68, *Statistical Levy* [1969] ECR 193, para 11.

[65] See Case 142/77, *Statenskontrol* [1978] ECR 1543 and Case 32/80 *Kortmann* [1981] ECR 251.

2.   *Article II GATT*

Moving to the objective element of the rule dealing with pecuniary border measures affecting trade in goods within WTO law, the interpreter faces many of the same issues that have been encountered with regard to the respective rule in EC law. First of all, the distinction between customs duties and equivalent charges, on one hand, and internal taxes, on the other, is also found within the context of WTO law. Secondly, the so-called "compensation exception" is expressly embodied in the text of the GATT. Let us examine these two issues, in turn.

(a)   The meaning of "ordinary customs duties" and "charges of any kind"   As previously noted, Article II:1(b) GATT, as complemented by its Understanding on Interpretation annexed to GATT 94, provides that the products included in each Member's Schedule of Concessions shall be exempt from (i) ordinary customs duties (first sentence), as well as (ii) all other duties or charges of any kind imposed on or in connection with the importation (second sentence), *in excess of* those set forth and provided in that Schedule.

While the term "ordinary customs duties" is intended to cover regular tariff rates shown in the columns of the schedules (in French: "*droits de douane proprement dit*"), the term "charges of any kind" applies to various supplementary duties and charges imposed on imports.[66] It is clear that the expression employed in Article II:1(b), second sentence, is meant to be all-inclusive ("*all other* duties or charges of any kind"),[67] the reason being the willingness to preserve the value of tariff concessions negotiated by a Member with its trading partners.[68]

As seen in EC law, in determining whether a measure is a duty or charge imposed on or in connection with importation within the meaning of Article II GATT, the interpreter inevitably has to take into consideration other GATT provisions relating to internal taxation. Article III GATT basically prohibits WTO Members from applying internal taxes and other internal charges to any imported or domestic like product so as to afford protection to domestic production. Given the different normative content

---

[66] GATT, *Analytical Index: Guide to GATT Law and Practice*, 6th Edn (1994) at, 75.
[67] JH Jackson, *World Trade and the Law of GATT*, above n 1, at 209.
[68] In its original text, Art II:1(b), second sentence, merely required Contracting Parties to exempt bound items from all other duties or charges in excess of those imposed on the date when the concessions were made with regard the item to which the other duties or charges referred. Other duties or charges were not usually subject of negotiation and thus were not included in each Party's Schedule of Concessions. As previously mentioned, this changed after the Uruguay Round, with the adoption of the Understanding on Interpretation of Art II of GATT 94, which provides for the recording of any other duties or charges in the Schedule of concessions.

of the two provisions, "the distinction between import duties and internal charges is of fundamental importance."[69]

The first time a Panel examined whether a measure was a duty or charge pursuant to Article II or an internal tax within the meaning of Article III was in the *Belgian Family Allowances* case.[70] At issue in that case was a Belgian law providing for the levy of a charge on foreign goods purchased by public bodies when these goods originated in a country whose system of family allowances did not meet specific requirements. In focusing on the methods of collection of the charge under review, the Panel took a very formalistic reading of the Belgian levy. It noted first that "the 7.5 per cent levy was collected only on products purchased by public bodies for their own use and not on imports as such" and, secondly, that "the levy was charged, not at the time of importation, but when the purchase price was paid by the public body."[71] In light of these circumstances, the Panel concluded that the levy was to be treated as an "internal charge" within the meaning of Article III and not as an import charge within the meaning of Article II.[72]

In 1978, the Panel Report on *EEC—Measures on Animal Feed Proteins* examined the consistency with Articles II and III of an EEC Regulation requiring domestic producers or importers of oilseeds, cakes and meals, dehydrated fodder and compound feeds to purchase a certain quantity of surplus skimmed milk powder held by intervention agencies, or, in the alternative, present a security deposit.[73] From the drafting history of Articles II and III GATT, which was reviewed by the Panel with the particular aim of ascertaining the relationship between these two Articles, it was emphasised that a charge should be considered an import duty for purposes of Article II and not an internal tax when (a) it is "collected at the time of, and as a condition to, the entry of the goods into the importing country," *and* (b) it applies "exclusively to imported products without being related in any way to similar charges collected internally on like domestic products."[74] According to the Panel, this was confirmed by the Interpretative Note Ad Article III, which provides that:

> [a charge] which applies to an imported product and to the like domestic product and is collected or enforced in the case of the imported product at

[69] See Panel Report on *EEC—Regulation on Imports of Parts and Components*, L/6657, adopted on 16 May 1990, BISD 37/S132, para 5.4.
[70] Panel Report on *Belgium—Family Allowances (Allocations Familiales)*, G/32, adopted on 7 Nov 1952, BISD 1S/59.
[71] *Ibid.*, para 2.
[72] *Ibid.* The measure was however found inconsistent with the provisions of Art I (and possibly with those of Art III, para 2), and was furthermore "based on a concept which was difficult to reconcile with the spirit of the General Agreement." *Ibid.*, para 8.
[73] Panel Report on *EEC—Measures on Animal Feed Proteins*, L/4599, adopted on 14 March 1978, BISD 25S/49.
[74] *Ibid.*, para 4.16, citing the Sub-Committee at the Havana Conference (Havana Reports at 62–63, paras 42–43, E/CONF.2/C.3/A/W.30 at 2).

the time of importation, is nevertheless to be regarded as an internal tax or other internal charge, [...] and is accordingly subject to the provision of Article III.[75]

In light of its own findings that (a) the EEC measures applied to both imported and domestically produced vegetable proteins (except in the case of corn gluten), (b) the EEC measures basically instituted an obligation to purchase a certain quantity of skimmed milk powder and (c) the EEC security deposit and protein certificate were enforcement mechanisms for the purchase obligation, the Panel concluded that the EEC measures should be examined "as internal measures under Article III and not as border measures under Article II."[76]

This same line of reasoning was followed by subsequent GATT panels, where the classification between Articles II and III focused once again on the two following issues: (1) is the charge imposed on imported products only or does it apply to both imported and domestic products, and (2) is the charge levied at the time of, or as a condition of, importation?[77]

Both GATT and WTO Panels appear to content themselves with a very formalistic interpretation of the pecuniary measures under review. In the *Belgium–Family Allowances* case, for example, although the Belgian levy was not formally collected on imports as such, but rather on products purchased by public bodies, and was charged, not at the time of importation, but when the purchase price was paid, in practical terms it applied exclusively to imports. Similarly, in *EEC—Regulation on Imports of Parts and Components*, although the charges under review were formally imposed on the finished products assembled or produced in the EEC

[75] Panel Report on *EEC—Measures on Animal Feed Proteins*, above n 73, para 4.16 lett b). The Panel also based its findings on the exception to Art II:1 provided for in Art II:2, which reads: "Nothing in this Art shall prevent any Contracting Party from imposing at any time on the importation of any product: (a) a charge equivalent to an internal tax imposed consistently with the provisions of para 2 of Art III [...]." The Panel noted that "the wording of Art II:2(a) which refers to 'charges equivalent to internal taxes' is different from that of Art III:2 which refers to 'internal taxes and other charges of any kind', but it appeared to be the common understanding of the drafters of these Articles that their scope should be the same as to the kind of measures being covered." *Ibid.*, para 4.16 lett c).

[76] *Ibid.*, paras 4.17–18.

[77] See the Panel Report on *Canada—Measures Affecting the Sale of Gold Coins*, L/5863, unadopted, dated 17 Sept 1985, para 50, "The Panel noted that the Ontario retail sales tax is levied at the time of retail sale of goods within the province, not at the time of importation into Canadian territory. The Ontario measure thus affects the internal retail sale of gold coins rather than the importation of Krugerrands as such. The Panel therefore considered that the tax was an "internal tax" to be considered under Art III and not as an "import charge" to be considered under Art II." See the Panel Report on *EEC—Regulation on Imports of Parts and Components*, above n 69, para 5.5, "The Panel noted that the anti-circumvention duties are levied, according to Art 13:10(a), 'on products that are introduced into the commerce of the Community after having been assembled or produced in the Community'. The duties are thus imposed, as the EEC explained before the Panel, not on imported parts or materials but on the finished products assembled or produced in the EEC. They are not imposed conditional upon the importation of a product or at the time or point of importation."

(ie on domestic products), they were levied on those products because they contained *foreign* parts and components, which, if imported in a finished state, would have been subject to antidumping duty.[78]

In conclusion, notwithstanding the formalistic interpretation of the pecuniary measures under review adopted by GATT panel practice, the emphasis on both the geographical location and the objective scope of application of the measure shows that the "objective element" of Article II GATT focuses, as in EC law, on "inherently discriminatory" pecuniary measures.

(b)   Do Articles II (and XI) and III overlap?: the Indonesia–Auto *and* EC–Bananas III *disputes.*   The recent dispute concerning certain Indonesian measures affecting the automotive industry emphasises how the issue of whether Articles II and III GATT overlap remains controversial.

The *Indonesia–Auto*[79] dispute concerned various decrees and regulations implementing several Indonesian car programmes that inter alia provided for customs duty advantages on imports of parts and components to be used in finished motor vehicles using a certain percentage value of local content.[80] Japan, the EC and the United States complained that the Indonesian measures violated inter alia the provisions of Article III since only parts and components that originate in Indonesia contributed to the satisfaction by a National Car producer of the local content requirement upon which Indonesia conditioned the duty free treatment of the

---

[78] Panel Report on *EEC—Regulation on Imports of Parts and Components*, above n 69, para 5.5. For a discussion on the meaning of "border measures" and "ordinary customs duties" (although with regard to Art 4.2 of the Agreement on Agriculture), see recently, Panel Report on *Chile—Price Band System and Safeguard Measures Relating to Certain Agricultural Products* (*Chile—Price Band*), WT/DS207/R, circulated 03 May 2002, adopted 23 Oct 2002, para 7.25 ("The Chilean PBS applies exclusively to imported goods and is enforced at the border by Chilean customs authorities. It is therefore clear that the Chilean PBS is a border measure") and paras 7.48–65 respectively. Chile's Price Band System (PBS), contained in Law 18.525 on the Rules on the Importation of Goods, provides inter alia the methodology for the calculation of the price bands for purposes of imposing the relevant import duties. It is expressly stated that the purpose of the PBS is to ensure a reasonable margin of fluctuation of domestic wheat, oil-seeds, edible vegetable oils and sugar prices in relation to the international prices for such products. Accordingly, specific duties are then established in US dollars per tariff unit, or *ad valorem* duties, or both, as well as rebates on the amounts payable as *ad valorem* duties established in the Customs Tariff, which could affect the importation of such goods. The amount of these duties and rebates, established in accordance with the procedure laid down in the same Law, are determined annually by the President of the Republic, in terms which, applied to the price levels attained by the products in question on the international markets, and make it possible to maintain a minimum cost and a maximum import cost for the said products during the internal marketing season for the domestic production.

[79] *Indonesia—Certain Measures Affecting the Automobile Industry* (*Indonesia–Auto*), WT/DS54, WT/DS55, WT/DS59 and WT/DS64, brought 14, 10, 15 Oct, 5 Dec 1996.

[80] They also provided for tax advantages on finished motor vehicles using a certain percentage value of local content.

remaining imported parts and components used to assemble the National Car. In other words, the duty free treatment was biased towards domestic products.[81] In its reply, Indonesia argued that its customs import duties schedules for automotive companies, although using differing levels of domestic content, were consistent with Article III GATT because the schedules were border measures which are not subject to Article III GATT.[82] The defending Member argued as follows:

> Complainants erroneously contend that Indonesia's subsidized customs import duties are within the scope of Article III:4 of the General Agreement. They claim that the issue is "not the reduction of duties, as such, but conditioning such reduction on the purchase of domestic parts and components." The flaw in complainants' position is fundamental—the scope of Article III is limited to internal laws, regulations and requirements; subsidized customs import duties are border measures, not internal laws, regulations or requirements. No WTO or GATT precedent supports expanding the scope of Article III to cover border measures.[83]

Despite the apparent strength of the Indonesian argument, the Panel basically avoided addressing it by focusing its inquiry on the TRIMs Agreement (which does however refers to Article III GATT) and concluded that

> the local content requirements of the 1993 and of the 1996 February car programmes to which are linked [...] (ii) customs duty benefits for imported parts and components used in finished motor vehicles incorporating a certain percentage value of domestic products or used in National Cars violate the provisions of Article 2 of the TRIMs Agreement.[84]

Leaving the issue of the TRIMs Agreement aside for the moment, it would appear that any customs duty benefit, even if premised on local content requirement, should be reviewed under Article II rather than under Article III GATT. Under WTO law, customs duties are in principle allowed and there does not appear to exist, aside from the MFN principle (Article I GATT), an obligation that they apply in a non-discriminatory manner. Accordingly, in the particular case, I believe that the customs duty benefits, even if granted by the Indonesian Government on criteria which discriminated between imported and domestic products, did not appear to violate the GATT as long as they met Indonesia's tariff commitments (an issue which had not been even raised).

---

[81] Panel Report on *Indonesia–Auto*, WT/DS54/R, WT/DS55/R, WT/DS59/R and WT/DS64/R, circulated 2 July 1998, adopted 23 July 1998, paras 5.64–127.
[82] *Ibid.*, paras 5.395–5.409.
[83] *Ibid.*, paras 5.401–5.402.
[84] *Ibid.*, para 15.1.

I believe this reading conforms with the division of labour between GATT provisions dealing with border measures (II and XI) and GATT provisions dealing with internal measures (III:2 and 4).

It may be argued that the Panel's finding in *Indonesia–Auto* was premised on the perception that the TRIMs Agreement has attributed a broader scope to Article III:4 (through the inclusion of the illustrative list). The following paragraph is interesting in this regard:

> We need now to decide whether these [...] customs duty benefits are "advantages" in the meaning of the chapeau of paragraph 1 of that Illustrative List. In the context of the claims under Article III:4 of GATT, Indonesia has argued that the reduced customs duties are not internal regulations and as such cannot be covered by the wording of Article III:4. We do not consider that the matter before us in connection with Indonesia's obligations under the TRIMs Agreement is the customs duty relief as such but rather the internal regulations, ie the provisions on purchase and use of domestic products, compliance with which is necessary to obtain an advantage, which advantage here is the customs duty relief. The lower duty rates are clearly "advantages" in the meaning of the chapeau of the Illustrative List to the TRIMs Agreement and as such, we find that the Indonesian measures fall within the scope of the Item 1 of the Illustrative List of TRIMs.[85]

It would appear that this broad reading of the TRIMs Agreement (and indirectly of Article III GATT) is not at all convincing basically for the same reasons noted above. Tariffs and other border charges are only subject to the provisions of Article II (as well as Article I) and not to Article III GATT. The TRIMs Agreement, which is clearly based on the GATT framework, cannot change this clear division.

The panel statements in the *Indonesia–Auto* report quoted above are actually paraphrasing an earlier statement found in the Appellate Body Report on *EC–Bananas III*[86] with regard to the scope of Article III in connection with the EC bananas licensing requirements. In that report, notwithstanding the recognition that Article XI GATT imposing a ban on import restrictions such as import licences applied to the EC bananas import regime, the Appellate Body noted the following:

> At issue in this appeal is not whether *any* import licensing requirement, as such, is within the scope of Article III:4, but whether the EC procedures and requirements for the *distribution* of import licences for imported bananas among eligible operators *within* the European Communities are within the scope of this provision [...]. These rules go far beyond the mere import

[85] Panel Report on *Indonesia–Auto*, above n 81, para 14.89.
[86] Appellate Body Report on *European Communities—Regime for the Importation, Sale and Distribution of Bananas* (*EC–Bananas III*), WT/DS27/AB/R, circulated 9 Sept 1997, adopted 25 Sept 1997.

licence requirements needed to administer the tariff quota [...]. These rules are intended, among other things, to cross-subsidize distributors of EC (and ACP) bananas and to ensure that EC banana ripeners obtain a share of the quota rents. As such, these rules affect "the internal sale, offering for sale, purchase,... " within the meaning of Article III:4, and therefore fall within the scope of this provision. Therefore, we agree with the conclusion of the Panel on this point.[87]

Such a reading appears to be incorrect. As will be confirmed in the later section on the Elimination of quantitative restrictions and other measures restricting the importation and exportation of goods, Articles III and XI are two mutually exclusive provisions and thus cannot overlap. A measure is either a border measure within the meaning of Article II (pecuniary border measure) or Article XI (non-pecuniary border measure) *or* an internal measure within the meaning of Article III (covering both fiscal and non-fiscal measures). There is in fact not much sense in imposing a National Treatment requirement on a type of measure (such as a licensing requirement) which is *inherently* discriminatory vis-à-vis imported products.

In practical terms, this incorrect reading of Article III does not have any relevant impact in the realm of non-pecuniary border measures, since Article XI requires in principle the *elimination* of all restrictions on importation and exportation. The only unwanted practical consequence might possibly be that subjecting a non-pecuniary border measure to the unnecessary assessment under Article III GATT would run counter to the principle of judicial economy.[88]

On the contrary, in the realm of pecuniary border measures (such as tariff), this reading is capable of tilting the scale between a finding of conformity and one of violation as shown in the *Indonesia–Auto* dispute.

(c)   The "compensation for services" exception   As seen with regard to EC law, an analysis of the "objective element" of the rule dealing with pecuniary border measures has to take into account the issue of fees for services rendered by customs authority (the so-called, "compensation for services" exception).

There are a few provisions dealing with such services fees in the GATT. First, Article II:2 provides that

---

[87] Appellate Body Report on *EC–Bananas III*, WT/DS27/AB/R, circulated 9 Sept 1997, adopted 25 Sept 1997, para 211.

[88] For an even more recent case where the *EC–Bananas III* incorrect reading of Arts III and XI GATT was employed see the Panel Report on *India—Measures Affecting the Automotive Sector (India–Auto)*, WT/DS146/R and WT/DS175/R, circulated 21 Dec 2001, adopted 5 April 2002. In that case, the Panel reviewed an essentially border measure (India's licensing requirement) under Art III:4 because India subject the granting of certain import licenses inter alia on "indigenisation" conditions (ie local content requirements). The Panel then did not examine these same measures under Art XI GATT simply on judicial economy grounds.

> Nothing in this Article shall prevent any Contracting Party from imposing at any time on the importation of any product: [...] (c) fees or other charges commensurate with the cost of services rendered.

Secondly, Article VIII:1 states that

> All fees and charges of whatever character (other than import and export duties and other than taxes within the purview of Article III) imposed by contracting parties on or in connection with importation or exportation shall be limited in amount to the approximate cost of services rendered and shall not represent an indirect protection to domestic products or a taxation of imports or exports for fiscal purposes.

Moreover, Article VIII:4 specifies that

> The provisions of this Article shall extend to fees, charges [...] imposed by governmental authorities in connection with importation and exportation, including those relating to: (a) consular transaction, [...]; (b) quantitative restrictions; (c) licensing; (d) exchange control; (e) statistical services; (f) documents, documentation and certification; (g) analysis and inspection; and (h) quarantine, sanitation and fumigation.

For purpose of analysing the main features of Article II:2 and Article VIII:1 and 4, and their relationship, it is necessary to discuss the GATT Panel Report on *US–Customs User Fee*.[89] At issue in that case were several complaints by Canada and the EEC concerning the "merchandise processing fee". This was an *ad valorem* charge levied by the US Customs Services for the processing of commercial merchandise entering the United States, which was used to fund certain "commercial activities" performed by three Customs Service programmes known as "Inspection and Control", "Tariff and Trade", and "Investigations", as well as a pro rata share of certain "Executive Management" and "Administration" expenses deemed allocatable to these activities.[90]

Ibid., paras 7.206–7.208. Here again, the correct approach would have been to review India's licensing regulation at issue exclusively on the basis of Art XI GATT.

[89] Panel Report on *United States–Customs User Fee*, L/6264, adopted on 2 Feb 1988, BISD 35S/245.

[90] With regard to *Inspection and Control*, "commercial operations" include inspection and release of cargo (including the initial processing and clearance of cargo manifests supplied by carriers) and half the cost of airport passenger processing.

With regard to *Tariff and Trade*, "commercial operations" comprise the entire programme, including: (a) Appraisement and Classification: Establishing the value and particular tariff classification of merchandise, collecting antidumping and countervailing duties pursuant to outstanding antidumping or countervailing orders, and providing commodity expertise to the importing public; (b) Laboratories: Technical support for classification of merchandise and investigations of "commercial fraud" (fraudulent non-compliance by commercial importers with customs laws and other legal requirements pertaining to entry); (c) Regulatory

In its Report, the Panel first of all clarified the general meaning of Articles II:2(c) and VIII:1(a) and their relationship to each other. It noted that while Article VIII:1(a) provides for a rule applicable to all charges levied at the border (except tariffs and charges which serve to equalise internal taxes) whether or not there is a tariff binding on the product in question, Article II:2(c) is a provision somewhat narrower in scope, since it permits governments to impose non-tariff border charges on products which are subject to a bound tariff.[91]

Examining the origins and the drafting history of the two provisions, the Panel explained the existence of the two Articles by noting a difference in their original form. When the GATT was first adopted in 1947, the requirements of Article VIII:1(a) were merely hortatory, reading "should" rather than "shall", while Article II:2(c) was included in the original 1947 text in its present form. Only later, in the Review Session amendments to Part II of the General Agreement, which were adopted in March 1955 and which entered into force in October 1957, was Article VIII:1(a) made mandatory.[92]

With regard to the content of the two provisions, the Panel believed that despite their different wording there was no real difference in meaning between the two "cost of services" limitations of Article II:2(c) and Article VIII:1 (ie "commensurate with the cost of services rendered" and "limited in amount to the approximate cost of services rendered").[93] Moreover, with regard to the type of fees that should be incorporated within the basic concept of "services rendered" in both Articles, the Panel took a very open approach and concluded that the drafters of Articles II and VIII were clearly not employing the term "services" in the economic sense, but in

> [a] more artful political sense, ie, government activities closely enough con-
> nected to the processes of customs entry that they might, with no more than
> the customary artistic licence accorded to taxing authorities, be called a
> "service" to the importer in question.[94]

Audits: Facilitating entry processing by post-entry audits of importers, and providing support for detection of commercial fraud; and (d) Legal Rulings: Issuing decisions and rulings and promoting uniformity in application of customs laws.

With regard to *Investigations*, the activities classified as "commercial operations" are commercial fraud investigations.

With regard to the category of general expenses called *Executive Management*, "commercial operations" include approximately 60 % of the cost of all functions under this heading, which is the best estimate of the percentage that "commercial operations" bears to the entire operating budget of the US Customs Service. The functions listed under this category of expenses are Executive Management, International Affairs, Internal Affairs and Chief Counsel. *Ibid.*, paras 11–15.

[91] *Ibid.*, paras 69–70.
[92] *Ibid.*, para 74.
[93] *Ibid.*, para 75.
[94] *Ibid.*, paras 76–77. According to the Panel, "No other interpretation can make Arts II:2(c) and VIII:1(a) conform to their generally accepted meaning." *Ibid.*

The principal issue raised by Canada and the EEC focused on whether the structure of the US merchandise processing fee, which had the form of an *ad valorem* charge without upper limits, was consistent with the "cost of services" limitation in Articles II and VIII. Although the United States had argued that the "cost of services" limitation did not require exact conformity between fees and costs, but only that the fee be "commensurate with" the cost (Article II:2(c)), or limited to the "approximate" cost (Article VIII:1(a)),[95] the Panel concluded as follows:

> the term "cost of services rendered" in Articles II:2(c) and VIII:1(a) must be interpreted to refer to the cost of the customs processing for the *individual* entry in question and accordingly that the *ad valorem* structure of the United States merchandise processing fee was inconsistent with the obligations of Articles II:2(c) and VIII:1(a) to the extent that it caused fees to be levied in excess of such costs. [emphasis added].[96]

Employing the above-mentioned conclusion, the Panel examined whether or not the various costs included in the "commercial operations" budget of the US Customs Service could be considered "services rendered" to those commercial importers who were required to pay the fee. The Panel found that the US merchandise processing fee, as applied in Fiscal Year 1987 and as established for Fiscal Year 1988, exceeded the "cost of services rendered" within the meaning of Articles II:2(c) and VIII:1(a) only to the extent that it included charges for the cost of some activities, which could not be considered "services rendered" to the *individual* commercial importers paying the merchandise processing fee.[97]

With regard to other activities, such as investigations of customs fraud and counterfeit goods, the collection of antidumping and countervailing duties, technical laboratories and the service of providing legal rulings on

---

[95] *Ibid.*, para 79. The United States had "argued that, stated in these terms, the "cost of services" requirements would be satisfied if the total revenues from the fee did not exceed the total cost of the government activities in question, and if the fee were otherwise fair and equitable in its application. The United States had stressed that the *ad valorem* structure of the merchandise processing fee was the most equitable and least protective method by which such a fee could be imposed." *Ibid.*

[96] *Ibid.*, para 86. Canada and the EEC had argued in fact "that 'cost of services rendered' should be interpreted to mean the cost of the customs processing activities ('services') actually rendered to the individual importer with respect to the customs entry in question, or, at least, the average cost of such processing activities for all customs entries of a similar kind. Both complainants had stressed that the normal practice with respect to service fees was to require persons to pay only for the services rendered to them." *Ibid.*, para 80.

[97] The Panel's findings referred to the following activities of the US Customs Service: (i) airport passenger processing; (ii) collecting and forwarding of export documentation; (iii) the International Affairs item in the "commercial operations" budget; (iv) customs processing of imports exempt from the merchandise processing fee; (v) all activities within the present definition of "commercial operations" for the first two months of Fiscal Year 1987. *Ibid.*, para 125.

customs matters, the Panel, stressing the highly centralised customs processing in the United States,[98] was satisfied that the challenged activities were of sufficient "proximity" to the normal process of customs clearance, and of sufficiently "general applicability", that their costs could be allocated among all commercial importers and did not have to be charged solely to the specific importers who happened to be beneficiaries of their "services" at the time in question.[99]

From the Panel Report on *US–Customs User Fee*, the following conclusions may be advanced. First, Article II:2(c) and Article VIII:1, though differing in scope, respond to the same objective and are usually employed interchangeably. Secondly, the term "services" should be read in its non-economic sense to include all government activities closely enough connected to the processes of customs entry. Thirdly, although the term "cost of services rendered" must be interpreted to refer to the cost of customs processing for the *individual* entry in question,[100] it appears that, in order to meet this standard, a party will simply need to demonstrate that the challenged activity is sufficiently proximate to the normal customs activities and sufficiently general in its application.[101]

C. Exceptions

In order to more fully comprehend the rules dealing with pecuniary border measures in EC and WTO law, one should take into consideration

---

[98] "In reaching these conclusions, the Panel gave considerable weight to the United States explanation that customs processing in the United States had increasingly moved away from hands-on processing of incoming shipments, towards a highly centralised process which focused on identifying problem transactions and concentrating on them. Under such a system, centralised and specialised activities far removed from the ordinary importer were in fact an essential ingredient to the more rapid handling of the ordinary entry, the ultimate objective of the 'service' that importers were being made to pay for." *Ibid.*, para 103.

[99] *Ibid.*

[100] In determining whether the fees exceeded the "approximate cost of services rendered", reference is often made to the practical purposes of the charge itself. In a complaint brought against France in 1952, the United States maintained that the French "statistical and customs control" tax on imports and exports infringed Art VIII:1 since the proceeds of this tax were also used for funding social security benefits to farmers. France acknowledged the infringement and subsequently abolished the tax. In another complaint brought against France in 1955, the United States contended that the French stamp tax violated both Arts II:1 and VIII:1 since proceeds from this tax were used for financing agricultural family allowance and exceeded the "appropriate cost of services rendered". The stamp tax was subsequently reduced. Cf GATT, *Analytical Index*, above n 56, at 253. See also Panel Report on *Argentina–Textile*, above n 26, paras 6.70–6.80, where it was concluded that Argentina's statistical tax of three % *ad valorem* was in violation of Art VIII:1(a) of GATT to the extent it results in charges being levied in excess of the approximate cost of the services rendered as well as being a measure designated for fiscal purposes.

[101] See the Panel Report on *EEC—Programme of Minimum Import Prices, Licenses and Surety Deposits for Certain Processed Fruits and Vegetables*, L/4687, adopted on 18 Oct 1978, BISD 25S/68, para 4.2, where the panel reviewed inter alia interest charges and costs in

the possibility for Members to claim the existence and application of an exception that may justify the border charge under review.

1. No Justification Provision in EC Law

In its early case law the European Court of Justice rejected attempts by Member States to argue that an unlawful duty or charge could be defended on the basis of Article 30 (ex Article 36) EC, the general exception provision. Article 30 EC, first sentence, states, in part, that,

> the provisions of Articles 28 and 29 shall not preclude prohibitions or restrictions on imports, exports or goods in transit justified on grounds of public morality, public policy or public security; the protection of health and life of humans, animals or plants; the protection of national treasures possessing artistic, historic or archaeological value; or the protection of industrial and commercial property.[102]

In *Commission v Italy*,[103] the Italian Government tried to justify a charge on the export of artistic, historical, and archaeological items by arguing that the purpose of the charge was not to raise revenue but to protect the artistic and historic heritage of the country. The Court rejected the Italian claim for the following two sets of reasons. First, the application of Article 25 EC depends upon the "effect" of the duty or charge and not on its "purpose". Secondly, the general public policy exception included in Article 30 EC can only be used as a defence in relation to quantitative restrictions and equivalent measures which are caught by Articles 28 and 29 EC.[104]

connection with the lodging of the security associated with an import certificate requirement. In examining the argument that these charges and costs were imposed contrary to Art VIII:1(a), "[t]he Panel also noted the contention by the Community representative that the incidence of these charges did not exceed 0.005 per cent. The Panel considered that these interest charges and costs were limited in amount to the approximate costs of administration. The Panel further considered that the term 'cost of services rendered' in Art VIII:1(a) would include these costs of administration. Therefore the Panel concluded that the interest charges and costs associated with the lodging of the security were not inconsistent with the Community's obligations under Art VIII:1(a)." Cf Panel Report on *Argentina–Textile*, above n 26, paras. 6.70–6.80, where the Panel rejected Argentina's claim that an *ad valorem* tax of three % on imports covered the cost of providing statistical services, which were not rendered to any individual importer, or to the specific importer associated with a particular operation, but to foreign trade operators in general and foreign trade as an activity per se. This finding was not appealed.

[102] Art 30, second sentence, conditions the availability of the exception as follows: "Such prohibitions or restrictions shall not, however, constitute a means of arbitrary discrimination or a disguised restriction on trade between Member States." See below section on "Exceptions" with regard to the "Elimination of quantitative restrictions and other measures restricting the importation and exportation of goods".
[103] Case 7/68, *Commission v Italy* [1968] ECR 423.
[104] P Craig and G de Búrca, *EU Law* (Oxford, OUP, 1998) at 552–53. Cf Joined Cases 2 and 3/62, *Commission v Luxembourg and Belgium* (*Gingerbread*) [1962] ECR 425, at 433, "That the

In the *Diamantarbeiders* case,[105] in which the Belgian Government attempted to defend a 0.33 per cent *ad valorem* levy imposed on all importers of uncut diamonds to be contributed to the diamond worker's social benefit fund, the ECJ confirmed the irrelevance of the purpose of the incriminated charge. The Court stated:

> It follows from the system as a whole and from the general and absolute nature of the prohibition of any customs duty applicable to goods moving between Member States that customs duties are prohibited independently of any consideration of the purpose for which they were introduced and the destination of the revenue obtained therefrom.[106]

Besides the so called "compensation exception", which has been examined with regard to the objective element, the only other derogation to the prohibition of Article 25 EC concerns charges imposed by a State to cover the cost of a mandatory inspection required by EC law[107] or imposed pursuant to an international convention favouring the free movement of goods.[108]

2. Articles II, III, VI, VIII and XX GATT

With regard to WTO law, although in theory Article II (as well as Article VIII) may be justified by the general public policy exception found in Article XX, apparently there exists no case where the issue was even taken into consideration.[109]

In this connection, it should also be emphasised that according to established panel practice the purpose of the pecuniary border measure is irrelevant in determining whether the charge is in violation of Article II. In one of the early cases, where the French Government had tried to

---

prohibition of new customs duties, linked with the principles of the free movement of products, constitutes an essential rule and that in consequence any exception, which moreover is to be narrowly interpreted, must be clearly stipulated."

[105] Joined Cases 2 and 3/69, *Sociaal Fonds voor de Diamantarbeiders v SA Ch. Brachfeld & Sons* [1969] ECR 211.
[106] *Ibid.*, paras 11–14.
[107] Case 46/76, *Bauhuis v The Netherlands* [1977] ECR 5. This exception applies only where the Community imposed inspection is mandatory, whereas it would not apply if such inspections are merely permitted by EC law. Nevertheless, the fees should in any case not exceed the actual costs of the inspection in connection with which they are charged. Cf Case 18/87 *Commission v Germany* [1988] ECR 5427.
[108] Case 89/76, *Commission v The Netherlands* [1977] ECR 1355.
[109] In Panel Report on *EEC—Regulation on Imports of Parts and Components*, L/6657, adopted on 16 May 1990, BISD 37S/132, para 3.2, the EEC had argued that even if the duties imposed under Art 13:10 of Council Reg (EEC) No 2423/88 were inconsistent with Arts I, II and VI of the General Agreement, such inconsistency was justifiable under Art XX(d). Since the EEC charge was deemed to constitute internal taxation for purposes of Art III, the Panel did not examine whether Art XX justified a violation of Art II.

justify a charge on imports in violation of Article II by stating inter alia that the charge was designed to facilitate the removal of quantitative restrictions on imports, the Contracting Parties ruled that "whatever may have been the reasons which motivated the French Government's decision, and whatever may have been the French Government's interpretation of the relevant provisions of the General Agreement in respect of many of the goods affected, the tax has increased the incidence of customs charges in excess of maximum rates bound under Article II".[110]

Within the GATT, the irrelevance of the purpose of pecuniary measures is reinforced by the requirement of Article VIII:1 according to which all fees and charges (other than import and export duties) imposed on or in connection with importation or exportation shall not represent a taxation of imports or exports for "fiscal purposes".[111]

As will be explained later when dealing in detail with the general exception provision of Article XX GATT, given the inherently or per se discriminatory nature of pecuniary *border* measures, it is very difficult that a violation of Article II could be justified under Article XX.

With regard to other specific exceptions to Article II GATT, the same Article includes a list of exceptions, many of which relate to other provisions of GATT, like the exception in paragraph 2(a) in the case of a charge equivalent to an internal tax on a like product (see Article III), the exception in paragraph 2(b) for antidumping and countervailing duties (see Article VI and the specific Agreement), and the exception in paragraph 2(c) for services fees (see Article VIII).[112] It should be noted that in the words of an explanation of Article II:2 contained in a 1980 proposal by the Director-General,[113] the policy justification for the three types of border charges permitted by Article II:2 was that they did not "discriminate against imports".[114] Moreover, given the importance assigned by the General Agreement to the protection of the commercial value of tariff bindings,[115] any such exceptions should be interpreted in a strict manner.[116]

---

[110] Decision on *French Special Temporary Compensation Tax on Imports*, taken on 17 Jan 1955, BISD 3S/26. Cf GATT, *Analytical Index*, above n 56, at 76.

[111] In a complaint brought against France in 1952, the United States maintained that the French "statistical and customs control" tax on imports and exports infringed Art VIII:1 since the proceeds of this tax were also used for funding social security benefits to farmers. France acknowledged the infringement and subsequently abolished the tax. In another complaint brought against France in 1955, the United States contended that the French stamp tax violated both Arts II:1 and VIII:1 since proceeds from this tax were used for financing agricultural family allowance and exceeded the "appropriate cost of services rendered". The stamp tax was subsequently reduced. Cf GATT, *Analytical Index*, above n 56, at 253.

[112] JH Jackson, *World Trade and the Law of GATT*, above n 1, at 210.

[113] BISD 27S/24.

[114] See Panel Report *US—Customs User Fee, above* n 89, para 84.

[115] "A basic purpose of GATT 1994, as reflected in Art II, is to preserve the value of tariff concessions negotiated by a Member with its trading partners, and bound in that Member's Schedule." Appellate Body Report on *Argentina–Textiles*, above n 33, para 47.

[116] Panel Report *US—Customs User Fee*, above n 89, para 84.

Furthermore, several provisions in Article II are designed to protect the value of the concession from encroachment by other governmental measures, such as new methods of valuing goods (paragraph 3),[117] reclassification methods (paragraph 5) and currency revaluations (paragraph 6). Moreover, Article II:4 specifies limits on the protection against imports of a particular product, which can be afforded by the use of an import monopoly.[118]

D. Conclusions

It has been stressed how the real difference in the normative content of the rules dealing with pecuniary border measures in the EC and in the GATT is a reflection of the different pace which has characterised the respective experiences of the organisations. Where the EEC took approximately a decade to reduce and eliminate all pecuniary border measures, the GATT has taken 50 years to bring the level of tariff and other border charges from the post-war high percentage to a low single-digit average of today. Nevertheless, the GATT obligation to respect tariff levels as specified in each Member's schedule of commitments inevitably encounters several problems in application, which were disposed of quite quickly by the quasi-absolute prohibition on all customs duties and equivalent charges in Community law. For example, GATT panel practice as well as WTO jurisprudence have had to face and clarify issues relating to the effect, interpretation and scope of application of tariff concessions, rendering the whole stance on pecuniary border measures weaker than the EC one.

With regard to the objective element, although the concepts of "charges having equivalent effect" (Article 25 EC) and "all other duties or charges of any kind" (Article II:1(b), second sentence) are on the same theoretical wavelength,[119] there appear to be certain differences in their practical application. In defining the two above mentioned concepts, both legal systems focus on the same key issue: whether or not the charge applies to imported products only. If it does, then one is confronted with a so-called "pecuniary *border* measure", at least in its stricter meaning. If it does apply, even only formally, to both imported and domestic products, then

---

[117] "No Contracting Party shall alter its method of determining dutiable value or of converting currencies so as to impair the value of any of the concessions provided for in the appropriate Schedule annexed to this Agreement." Art II:3.
[118] JH Jackson, WJ Davey, AO Sykes, *International Economic Relations*, above n 17, at 385.
[119] Cf A Comba, *Il Neo Liberismo Internazionale* (Milano, Giuffré Editore, 1995) at 110–11; G Tesauro, *Il Diritto Comunitario* (Padova, Cedam, 1995) at 253, fn 27; JHH Weiler, "The Constitution of the Common Marketplace: Text and Context in the Evolution of the Free Movement of Goods" in P Craig and G de Búrca (eds), *The Evolution of EU Law* (Oxford, OUP, 1999) at 355.

the charge will be examined as an *internal* charge or tax (or "pecuniary *internal* measure").[120]

The dichotomy between "border" and "internal" measures has been employed in order to capture this fundamental difference: a border measure can only apply to imported goods, since domestic goods do not have to be "imported" into the market. An internal measure, on the other hand, at least formally, applies to any product, whether or not produced domestically or imported from abroad. Clearly, this internal measure may treat domestic products more favourably than imported ones, for example by explicitly providing a higher rate in the case of imports (direct or formal or de jure discrimination), or by indirectly affording protection to domestic production (indirect or factual or de facto discrimination).

As previously examined, reference to the "geographical location" of the pecuniary measure may be found in both EC and WTO law. However, the analysis of both the ECJ case law and the GATT panel practice has shown that the "geographical location" is not the decisive factor in drawing the line between Article 25 EC and Article II GATT, on the one hand, and Article 90 EC and Article III GATT, on the other. The geographical location is more often employed as a mere indication of whether the pecuniary measure under review applies to imported products only or to both imported and domestic ones.

As will be clarified in later chapters, the particular nature of the measures at issue should be read in conjunction with the different normative content of the rules dealing with border and internal measures. Since pecuniary (and non-pecuniary) *border* measures are inherently greatly discriminatory against imported products, they are disciplined by the stricter provisions of Article 25 EC and Article II GATT. On the other hand, pecuniary (and non-pecuniary) *internal* measures are not per se discriminatory and thus fall within the purview of the more relaxed provisions of Article 90 EC and Article III GATT.[121]

It should be noted, however, that GATT panels have applied this definition in a slightly more formalistic fashion, treating apparent border charges as internal taxation, thus expanding the scope of application of Article III GATT. Although in practical terms this formalistic interpretation of the pecuniary measures under review does not have any particular consequence (since the charge is usually found to violate the National Treatment obligation of Article III), there appears to be a certain bias for the non-discrimination principle embodied in Article III vis-à-vis the per se prohibition of Article II.[122] This approach can certainly be contrasted

---

[120] For purposes of this classification it is presumed that a pecuniary measure constitutes in itself a trade-restrictive measure.

[121] See below discussion in ch 2.

[122] Professor Weiler distinguishes between an obstacle-based regime with regard to customs duties and charges having an equivalent effect with a discrimination-based test with regard

with the one taken by the ECJ in the interpretation of the relationship between Articles 25 and 90 EC. Although maintaining intact the central feature distinguishing a charge of equivalent effect from an internal tax, the Court has certainly showed a clear willingness to expand the scope of application of the per se prohibition of Article 25 vis-à-vis the non-discrimination principle of Article 90. From a practical point of view, even with regard to the ECJ preferential treatment toward the per se prohibition, there appears to be no dramatic consequences: if every pecuniary measures deemed to be a charge of equivalent effect were to be assessed under Article 90, it would be found in one way or another to be in breach of the non-discrimination principle.[123]

A similar difference may also be encountered by comparing the EC "compensation exception" with Articles II:2(c) and VIII:1 GATT. While both derogations require that the cost for the services rendered (i) reflects an individualised benefit to a specific operator and (ii) does not exceed either the value or the cost of that service, the practical applications differ in the two legal systems. In the EC, following a strict interpretation of these requirements, it is rare to find cases in which the so-called "compensation exception" has been successfully claimed. In GATT, on the contrary, as exemplified in the *US–Customs User Fee* case, the same criteria have been more loosely interpreted, allowing the costs for several general services to be allocated among all commercial importers, even if not all of these importers are the specific beneficiaries of those services.

These differences clearly stem from differences not in the legal texts embodying the rules dealing with the particular trade barrier at issue, but in the broader contexts in which these rules are placed. The need to establish a European market, comprising an area without internal frontiers, is at the core of the hard-line approach toward pecuniary border measures adopted by Community organs. This approach is actually better explained by the even more intransigent stance with regard to non-pecuniary border measures, such as inspection. Charges imposed for services rendered at customs are hardly ever accepted, not so much because of the higher costs that they place on imported goods, but because they are imposed as compensation for activities that themselves constitute real barriers to trade. In other words, the real target is not the "cost of service" but the "service" itself. This explains the existence of a more relaxed derogation for charges imposed by a State to cover the cost of a mandatory inspection required by EC law. On the other hand, in GATT,

---

to taxation. JHH Weiler, "The Constitution of the Common Marketplace: Text and Context in the Evolution of the Free Movement of Goods" in P Craig and G de Búrca (eds), *The Evolution of EU Law* (Oxford, OUP, 1999) at 354 and 358.

[123] This is also due to the fact that a violation of Art 90 may not, at least in principle, be justified for public policy reasons (see below ch 2).

where no formal common market is being established and where national frontiers must still perform their ordinary functions, the approach with regard to pecuniary border measures is not as aggressive.

1.2   ELIMINATION OF QUANTITATIVE RESTRICTIONS AND OTHER IMPORT RESTRICTIVE MEASURES

Next to tariffs and other pecuniary border measures, the liberalisation agendas of both the GATT and the EEC had to deal with "quantitative restrictions", mainly in the form of quotas, which were perceived to be the worst of all forms of trade restriction ever devised by the mind of man.[124] Accordingly, it is hardly surprising that the outright elimination of quantitative restrictions was expressly included in both the GATT and the EEC Treaty[125] in Article XI (entitled "General elimination of quantitative restrictions") and in the whole chapter 2 of the Treaty of Rome (entitled "Elimination of Quantitative Restrictions between Member States"), respectively.

However, focusing on quotas was not enough, as there are also other non-pecuniary border measures that restrict international trade as much as the infamous traditional measures. Article XI GATT applies in fact not just to quotas but also to "restrictions instituted or maintained on the importation or exportation of any product". Similarly, Articles 28–29 EC apply not just to quantitative restrictions but also to "all measures having equivalent effect".

Along similar lines followed in the analysis with regard to tariffs and charges of equivalent effect, in the next few pages the "normative content", "objective element", and "exceptions" of both EC and WTO rules dealing with "non-pecuniary border measures" will be examined.

A.   Normative Content

The normative content of both WTO and EC rules dealing with "quantitative restrictions" is uncontroversial. Article XI GATT and Articles 28–29 EC clearly mandate the prohibition of quantitative restrictions on importation and exportation of goods.

---

[124] See the view of the US Government expressed at the GATT preparatory session in London in 1947, cited in JH Jackson, *World Trade and the Law of GATT*, above n 1, at 309.
[125] *Ibid.*; *Rapport des Chefs de Délégation aux Ministres des Affaires Etrangère* (Spaak Report) (1956) at 35; D Wyatt and A Dashwood, *The Substantive Law of the EEC* (London, Sweet & Maxwell, 1980) at 97.

Article XI:1 GATT provides that

> No prohibition or restriction other than duties, taxes or other charges whether made effective through quotas, import or export licenses or other measures, shall be instituted or maintained by any Contracting Party on the importation of any product of the territory of any other Contracting Party or on the exportation or sale for export of any product destined for the territory of any other Contracting Party.

Similarly, while Article 28 EC mandates that "Quantitative restrictions on imports and all measures having equivalent effect shall [...] be prohibited between Member States", Article 29 EC extends such prohibition to "quantitative restrictions on exports".

As for customs duties and other charges having equivalent effect, the EEC Treaty provided a strict, detailed timetable for the abolition of quantitative restrictions: in the case of imports, this was to be completed by the end of the transitional period;[126] and in the case of exports, by the end of the first stage.[127] A standstill provision prevented Member States from introducing new quantitative restrictions or measures having equivalent effect, or making more restrictive those measures already in existence at the time the Treaty entered into force. With Council's Decision of 12 May 1960, Member States decided to accelerate the date for implementing old Articles 30–34 EEC and provided for the elimination of all quantitative restrictions on imports of industrial products of the Member States by 31 December 1961.

While the general prohibition of Article XI:1 GATT was not subject to any transitional period, as were the corresponding EC principles, Articles XI:2, XII and XIV contain elaborate exception clauses, principally covering agricultural and fisheries products (Article XI:2(c)) and balance-of-payments cases (Article XII and XIV). Article XIII, however, provides for a series of principles and rules which attempt to regulate the use of quotas in cases where they are exceptionally allowed, principally imposing a non-discrimination obligation.[128]

Notwithstanding the clear prohibition against quantitative restrictions as provided for in Article XI GATT, for several years GATT contracting parties failed to respect completely this obligation. From early in the GATT, in sectors such as agriculture or textiles and clothing, quantitative restrictions were maintained and at times even increased. Certain Contracting Parties

---

[126] Arts 30, 32, and 33 EEC.
[127] Art 34 EEC.
[128] In particular Art XIII contains (i) a Most-Favoured-Nation obligation; (ii) certain rules for the manner in which quantitative restrictions are applied, designed to achieve an equitable distribution of import permissions among various contracting parties; and (iii) a series of obligations requiring notification and consultation. JH Jackson, *World Trade and the Law of GATT*, above n 1, at 322.

even believed that quantitative restrictions had gradually been tolerated and accepted as negotiable and that Article XI could not and had never been considered to be a provision prohibiting such restrictions irrespective of the circumstances specific to each case. This argument was however rejected in the Panel Report on *EEC–Imports from Hong Kong*.[129]

The need to restrict the use of quantitative restrictions became central to the Uruguay Round negotiations, where the participants recognised the need to devise mechanisms to phaseout quantitative restrictions in sectors such as agriculture and textiles and clothing. This recognition is reflected in the GATT 1994 Understanding on Balance-of-Payments Provisions,[130] the Agreement on Safeguards,[131] the Agreement on Agriculture where quantitative restrictions were eliminated;[132] as well as in the Agreement on Textiles and Clothing (further discussed below) according to which restrictions derived from the 1974 Arrangement Regarding International Trade in Textiles or Multifibre Arrangement ("MFA") are to be completely eliminated by 2005.[133]

B.   Objective Element

The most problematic feature of the rules adopted by EC and WTO law dealing with quantitative restrictions (and measures having equivalent effect) relates again to the "objective element" of those rules, or in other words, on the type of measures which fall within the scope of application of the general prohibitions incorporated in Articles 28–29 EC and Article XI GATT. In light of the peculiar interpretation given by the ECJ to Article 28 EC in particular, I propose this time to begin the present analysis with WTO law and jurisprudence on the scope of application of Article XI GATT. Hopefully, this should contribute to the reconstruction and understanding of what was indeed the original nature and purpose of the

---

[129] Panel Report on *EEC—Quantitative Restrictions Against Imports of Certain Products from Hong Kong*, L/5511, adopted on 12 July 1983, BISD 30S/129.

[130] See, for example, paras 2 and 3 of the GATT 1994 Understanding on the Balance-of-Payments Provisions, which provide that Members shall *seek* to avoid the imposition of new quantitative restrictions for balance-of-payments purposes.

[131] The Agreement on Safeguards also evidences a preference for the use of tariffs. Art 6 provides that provisional safeguard measures "should take the form of tariff increases" and Art 11 prohibits the use of voluntary export restraints.

[132] Under the Agreement on Agriculture, notwithstanding the fact that for over 48 years the Contracting Parties had been relying a great deal on import restrictions and other non-tariff measures, the use of quantitative restrictions and other non-tariff measures was prohibited and Members had to proceed to a "tariffication" exercise to transform quantitative restrictions into tariff based measures.

[133] This last paragraph and related footnotes are taken from the analysis carried out in the Panel Report on *Turkey—Restrictions on Imports of Textile and Clothing Products* (*Turkey–Textiles*), WT/DS34/R, circulated 31 May 1999, adopted 19 Nov 1999, paras 9.63–9.65.

Article 28 prohibition. Furthermore, the analysis will principally be focusing on *import* restrictions.

1. *Article XI GATT*

The difficulty in ascertaining the precise scope of application of Article XI GATT stems initially from an apparent contrast between its heading "General Elimination of *Quantitative Restrictions*" and the actual wording of its basic obligation in paragraph 1, which reads as follows:

> No prohibition or restriction other than duties, taxes or other charges whether made effective through quotas, import or export licenses or other measures, shall be instituted or maintained by any Contracting Party on the importation […] or on the exportation […] of any product […].

While the reference to "quantitative restrictions" in the heading appears to limit the scope of application of Article XI to quotas, the language of the first paragraph is in itself quite broad, providing for a general ban on import and export restrictions or prohibitions made effective through, not just quotas and import or export licences, but also *any other measure*.[134]

In order for a measure to be caught by Article XI, two distinct requirements must be met: (1) the measure must be a "restriction" and (2) the measure must be "on the importation".

(a) "Restriction" With regard to the first requirement, GATT panel practice and WTO case law have employed a *broad* interpretation of the term "restriction" by taking into consideration the effects of the measure under review. Thus, notwithstanding the emphasis on a particular type of measure in its heading, the Article XI prohibition has been read as being directed not simply at quotas or import/export licences but at *any restriction* on the importation (or exportation) of any product, where "the scope of the term 'restriction' is broad, as seen in its ordinary meaning, which is 'a limitation on action, a limiting condition or regulation'".[135] In other words, a quota or an import or export licence will violate Article XI only if it constitutes a "prohibition" or at least a "restriction" on the importation of any product of the territory of a Contracting Party or on the exportation of any product destined for the territory of a Contracting Party.

---

[134]See Panel Report on *India—Quantitative Restrictions on Imports of Agricultural, Textile and Industrial Products* (*India–Quantitative Restrictions*), WT/DS90/R, circulated 6 April 1999, adopted 22 Sept 1999, para 5.128. Arts 28–29 EC teach us something on this point (see below).
[135]*Ibid.*, para 5.128.

Panel reports dealing with import and export licences clearly illustrate this point. For example, the 1978 Panel Report on *EEC—Programmes of Minimum Import Price, Licences and Surety Deposits for Certain Processed Fruits and Vegetables*[136] found that the import certificate system operated by the Community, according to which import certificates were to be issued on the fifth working day following that on which the application was lodged, was not inconsistent with the Community's obligation under Article XI:1, because "automatic licensing did not constitute a restriction of the type meant to fall under the purview of Article XI:1".[137]

More recently, the 1999 Panel Report on *India–Quantitative Restrictions*,[138] citing previous GATT panel practice, found that the import licensing system maintained by India, being a discretionary import licensing system, in that licences were not granted in all cases, but rather on unspecified "merits", operated as a restriction on imports within the meaning of Article XI:1. Employing the same approach, ie, focusing on the restrictive effects of the measure under review, the same Panel also found that (a) the canalisation of imports through government agencies, (b) the Special Import Licence (SIL) system and (c) the Actual User requirement all *operated* as restrictions on imports within the meaning of Article XI:1.[139]

The inquiry into whether a measure constitutes a prohibition or a restriction on importation or exportation for the purposes of Article XI:1 does not, however, depend exclusively on the actual trade effects that the measure has in the specific case at hand. It is well-established in WTO law that Article XI:1 (like Articles I, II and III) GATT protects competitive

---

[136] L/4687, adopted on 18 Oct 1978, BISD 25S/68.

[137] *Ibid.*, para 4.1. See also the Panel Report on *Japan–Trade in Semi-conductors*, L/6309, adopted on 4 May 1988, BISD 35S/116, para 118, where the Panel found that "export licensing practices by Japan, leading to delays of up to three months in the issuing of licences for semi-conductors destined for contracting parties other than the United States, had been non-automatic and constituted restrictions on the exportation of such products inconsistent with Art XI:1". In the Panel Report on *Thailand—Restrictions on Importation of and Internal Taxes on Cigarettes (Thai Cigarettes)*, DS10/R, adopted on 7 Nov 1990, BISD 37S/200, para 67, noting that Thailand had not granted licences for the importation of cigarettes for the past 10 years, the Panel found that Thailand had acted inconsistently with Art XI:1.

[138] Panel Report on *India–Quantitative Restrictions*, WT/DS90/R, circulated 6 April 1999, adopted 22 Sept 1999.

[139] "It should be noted however, that the mere fact that imports are effected through state trading enterprises would not in itself constitute a restriction. Rather, for a restriction to be found to exist, it should be shown that the operation of this state trading entity is such as to result in a restriction." *Ibid.*, para 5.134. Accordingly, "canalization per se will not necessarily result in the imposition of quantitative restrictions within the meaning of Art XI, since an absence of importation of a given product may not always be the result of the imposition of a prohibitive quantitative restriction." *Ibid.*, para 5.135. However, in that case, the evidence submitted by the United States (canalization resulted in zero imports) led the Panel to conclude that the "canalization" measures operated as a restriction on imports within the meaning of Art XI. *Ibid.*, para 5.136. For the other two measures see *ibid.*, paras 5.138 and 5.143.

opportunities of imported products, not trade flows.[140] Consequently, in order to establish whether a measure infringes Article XI:1, one needs not prove actual trade effects, but simply "potential" trade effects. This is clearly seen with regard to quotas[141] and in particular with regard to import or export ban (ie, zero-quotas),[142] which are usually deemed to constitute per se restriction or prohibition on importation or exportation in violation of Article XI:1.[143]

The focus on the restrictive effect of the measure under review and thus the breath of application of Article XI can also be observed in the Panel's treatment of non-binding measures. In *Japan–Trade in Semi-conductors*,[144] the Japanese Government claimed that its measures were not restrictions in the sense of Article XI because they were not legally binding or mandatory. The panel found however that the wording of Article XI (which does not refer to laws or regulations but more broadly to measures) clearly indicates that any measure instituted or maintained by a Contracting Party which restricts the importation or exportation of products is covered by this provision *irrespective of the legal status of the measure*.[145] However, the Panel conditioned a finding of violation of Article XI on the following two essential criteria:

First, there were reasonable grounds to believe that sufficient incentives or disincentives existed for non-mandatory measures to take effect. Secondly, the operation of the measures to restrict export of semi-conductors at prices

---

[140] Panel Report on *Argentina—Measures Affecting the Export of Bovine Hides and the Import of Finished Leather (Argentina–Bovine Hides)*, WT/DS/155R, circulated 19 Dec 2000, adopted 16 Feb 2001, para 11.20.

[141] See Panel Report on *EEC—Quantitative Restrictions against Imports of Certain Products from Hong Kong*, L/5511, adopted on 12 July 1983, BISD 30S/129; Panel Report on *Japanese Measures on Imports of Leather*, L/5623, adopted on 15–16 May 1984, BISD 31S/94; Panel Report on *Japan—Restrictions on Imports of Certain Agricultural Products*, L/6253, adopted on 2 Feb 1988, BISD 35S/163; Panel Report on *Turkey–Textile*, above n 133, para 9.66: "The measures at issue, on their face, impose quantitative restrictions on imports and are applicable only to India. We consider that, given the absence of a defence by Turkey to India's claims […], India has made a prima facie case of violation of Arts XI and XIII of GATT."

[142] See Panel Report on *Canada—Measures Affecting Exports of Unprocessed Herring and Salmon*, L/6268, adopted on 22 March 1988, BISD 35S/98, para 4.1; Panel Report on *Canada—Measures prohibiting or restricting importation of certain periodicals (Canada–Periodicals)*, WT/DS31/R, circulated 14 March 1997, adopted 30 July 1997, para 5.5, "since the importation of certain foreign products into Canada is completely denied under Tariff Code 9958, it appears that this provision by its terms is inconsistent with Art XI:1 of GATT 1994."

[143] See also the cases of minimum import or export prices, which are usually found to constitute per se restrictions on importation or exportation. Cf Panel Report on *EEC— Programme of Minimum Import Prices, Licences, and Surety Deposits for Certain Processed Fruits and Vegetables*, L/4687, adopted on 18 October 1978, BISD 25S/68, para 4.9; Panel Report on *Japan–Trade in Semi-conductors*, L/6309, adopted on 4 May 1988, BISD 35S/116, para 105.

[144] L/6309, adopted on 4 May 1988, BISD 35S/116.

[145] *Ibid.*, para 106.

below company-specific costs was essentially dependent on Government action or intervention.[146]

(b)   "On importation"   While the term "restriction" has been given a *broad* interpretation, the term "on importation" has generally been interpreted in a *strict* manner, limiting the scope of application or "objective element" of Article XI:1.

Corresponding to the distinction between customs duties and internal taxes, the existence of a provision like Article III GATT, dealing with internal regulations, limits the scope of application of Article XI GATT. Article III applies inter alia to "laws, regulations and requirements *affecting* the internal sale, offering for sale, purchase, transportation, distribution or use of products, and internal quantitative regulations requiring the mixture, processing or use of products in specified amounts or proportions."

The problematic relation between Article III and Article XI stems from the broad language employed in these two Articles. Both Articles could easily be interpreted to cover measures that might be deemed to fall within the scope of application of the other. Any measure, even a purely border measure like a quota, may be deemed to *affect* the internal sale of an imported product, if one interprets the term "affect" broadly enough. Equally, any type of measure, even of a purely internal nature (such as product standards), may be deemed to *restrict* the importation of a product, if one interprets the term "restrict" as a synonym of "negatively affect".

As already noted in the section dealing with pecuniary border measures, it is of fundamental importance to delimit precisely the fields of application of these two provisions. While Article III:4 simply prohibits discriminatory or protectionist regulations, Article XI embodies a far-sweeping per se prohibition on import (and export) restrictions.

As a matter of fact, the possibility of conflict in the application of Article III:4 and Article XI was already envisaged in the GATT and it was solved in favour of the former. In the Note Ad Article III, the drafters specified that

> any law, regulation or requirement of the kind referred in paragraph 1 which applies to an imported product and the like domestic product and is [...] enforced in the case of the imported product at the time or point of importation, is nevertheless to be regarded as [...] a law, regulation or requirement of the kind referred to in paragraph 1, and is accordingly subject to the provisions of Article III.

---

[146] *Ibid.*, para 109. "The Panel considered that if these two criteria were met, the measures would be operating in a manner equivalent to mandatory requirements such that the difference between the measures and mandatory requirements was only one of form and not of substance, and that there could be therefore no doubt that they fell within the range of measures covered by Art XI.1." *Ibid.*

Although the note appears to refer only to the case of a *single* measure that is applied or enforced in different places depending on whether the products are imported or domestic, its rationale is clear enough to include the case of *two apparently distinct* measures applying a similar standard respectively to domestic products and imported products.[147]

On the basis of the Note Ad Article III, stressing the differing wording of the two Articles and implicitly adopting the same distinction between border and internal measures that was shown to exist in relation to the rules dealing with pecuniary measures, GATT panel practice and WTO jurisprudence have generally interpreted Article XI:1 as applying *only* to measures affecting the "importation" of products, while Article III regulates measures affecting "imported products".[148]

It should be noted at this stage that Article XI:1 covers every measures that restricts *exports* because there is no equivalent Article III:4 with regard to export restrictions. Accordingly, in order for a measure regulating the export of products to another Member to fall under Article XI:1, it needs only to constitute a "restriction" in the above-mentioned sense.[149]

In order to determine whether a measure affects the *importation* of a product for the purposes of Article XI:1, one must assess the "object" and "scope of application" of the measure itself: respectively, (1) does the measure *directly regulate* the importation of the product into the territory of the Member, and (2) does the measure *apply exclusively* to imported products or to both imported and domestic ones?

With regard to the first criterion, the 1984 Panel Report on *Canada— Administration of the Foreign Investment Review Act* (also known as the

---

[147] See Panel Report on *European Communities—Measures Affecting Asbestos and Asbestos Containing Products (EC–Asbestos)*, WT/DS135R, circulated 18 Sept 2000, adopted 5 April 2001. See more below.

[148] Panel Report on *Canada—Administration of the Foreign Investment Review Act (FIRA)*, L/5504, adopted on 7 Feb 1984, BISD 30S/140, para 5.14: "If Art XI:1 were interpreted broadly to cover also internal requirements, Art III would be partly superfluous. Moreover, the exceptions to Art XI:1, in particular those contained in Art XI:2, would also apply to internal requirements restricting imports, which would be contrary to the basic aim of Art III. The Panel did not find, either in the drafting history of the General Agreement or in previous cases examined by the Contracting Parties, any evidence justifying such an interpretation of Art XI." For a different view on the scope of application of Art XI GATT, JHH Weiler, "The Constitution of the Common Marketplace: Text and Context in the Evolution of the Free Movement of Goods", in P Craig and G de Búrca (eds), *The Evolution of EU Law* (Oxford, OUP, 1999) at 355–58.

[149] See Panel Report on *Japan–Trade in Semi-Conductors*, L/6309, adopted on 4 May 1988, BISD 35S/116; Panel Report on *Argentina–Bovine Hides*, above n 140, para 11.55. See also the Final Report of the Panel Under ch 18 of the Canada-United States Free Trade Agreement on *Lobsters from Canada*, USA 89–1807–01, dated 25 May, 1990, para 7.19: "Art XI:1 applies to imported and exported goods. With regard to imported goods, it covers measures (QRs) that apply at the border; with regard to exported goods, it covers measures (QRs) that apply at the border and internally." On the *Lobster* report see more below.

FIRA case)[150] found that purchase undertakings giving preferential treatment to domestic products imposed by the Canadian Government as a condition for foreign direct investment in Canada were not inconsistent with Article XI since they did "not prevent the importation of goods as such".[151] However, the Canadian measures were found to be inconsistent with Article III:4.[152]

With regard to the second criterion, the 1992 Panel Report on *Canada—Import, Distribution and Sale of Certain Alcoholic Drinks by Provincial Marketing Agencies (Canada Alcohol II)*,[153] in assessing the US claim that minimum prices maintained for beer in certain provinces of Canada were inconsistent with the General Agreement, examined whether such measures fell under Article XI:1 or Article III:4. The Panel noted in particular that the Interpretative Note Ad Article III provides that a regulation is subject to the provisions of Article III if it "applies to an imported product and to the like domestic product" notwithstanding the fact that it is "enforced in case of the imported product at the time or point of importation". Consequently, as the minimum prices were applied to both imported and domestic beer, the panel concluded that the Canadian measure under consideration fell within the scope of Article III.[154]

In the 1992 Panel Report on the *United States Measures on Importation and Distribution of Alcoholic and Malt Beverages*,[155] a very distinguished panel,[156] after having found that neither of the two above-mentioned criteria had been met, concluded that listing and delisting state practices regulating the sale and distribution of wine and beer in the United States

---

[150] Panel Report on *Canada—Administration of the Foreign Investment Review Act (FIRA)*, L/5504, adopted on 7 Feb 1984, BISD 30S/140.

[151] *Ibid.*, para 5.14.

[152] See ch 2 on the prohibition of de jure discrimination.

[153] DS17/R, adopted on 18 Feb 1992, BISD 39S/27. The first case was the Panel Report on *Canada—Import, Distribution and Sale of Alcoholic Drinks by Provincial Marketing Agencies (Canada Alcohol I)*, L/6304, adopted on 22 March 1988, BISD 35S/37.

[154] *Ibid.*, para 5.28. Cf Panel Report on *EEC—Programme of Minimum Import Prices, Licences, and Surety Deposits for Certain Processed Fruits and Vegetables*, above n 143, where the EEC measure setting minimum import prices was deemed to fall within Art XI. However in that case, the critical factor in the GATT Panel's determination that some aspects of the EEC programme were inconsistent with Art XI was the use of an import certificate and of an 'additional security' as condition for the issuance of the import certificate and thus as a condition for importation. In fact, the measures under review in that case were discussed by both parties under GATT provisions on 'border' measures, Arts II and XI. Art III was never an issue. See Final Report of the Panel Under ch 18 of the Canada–United States Free Trade Agreement on *Lobsters from Canada*, USA 89–1807–01, dated 25 May, 1990. Cf G Peabody, "The Lobster Size Conflict: Use of United States–Canada Free Trade Agreement Dispute Resolution Procedures", 1 *Territorial Sea Journal* (1991) 273.

[155] Panel Report on the *United States — Measures on Importation and Distribution of Alcoholic and Malt Beverages (Malt Beverages)*, DS23/R, adopted on 19 June 1992, BISD 39S/206.

[156] Ambassador Lacarte-Muro (later to be a Member of the Appellate Body) and Professor Ernst-Ulrich Petersmann were two of the three panel members.

were covered by Article III:4 rather than Article XI:1. The relevant passage reads as follows:

> Having regard to the past panel decisions and the record in the instant case, the present Panel was of the view that the listing and delisting practices here at issue *do not affect importation as such* into the United States and should be examined under Article III:4. The Panel further noted that the issue is not whether the practices in the various states affect the right of importation as such, in that they clearly *apply to both domestic* (out-of-state) *and imported wines*; rather, the issue is whether the listing and delisting practices accord less favourable treatment—in terms of competitive opportunities—to imported wine than that accorded to the like domestic product. Consequently, the Panel decided to analyse the state listing and delisting practices as *internal measures* under Article III:4 [emphasis added].[157]

With regard to the first criterion (the "object" of the measure), the apparent references to the measure's "effects" on importation in the *Malt Beverages* report (ie the measure does not "prevent" or "affect" importation) should not be taken as suggesting that the scope of application of Article XI GATT depends upon whether the measure under review has a "negative effect" on the importation of a specific foreign product. It has already been emphasised that using such a test would expand the scope of application of Article XI to include even purely internal regulations. Those references should only be taken as part of the panel's determination of the object or subject-matter of the measure under challenge. Accordingly, the question is not so much whether the measure negatively affects importation, but whether *it directly regulates importation*.

Moreover, the *broad* interpretation of the term "restriction" should not be confused with the *strict* reading of the term "on importation". As previously stated, a measure will be caught by Article XI if it is a (1) "restriction" (2) "on the importation". Two recent panel reports have to some extent confirmed this point.

In *India—Quantitative Restrictions on Imports of Agricultural, Textile and Industrial Products*,[158] the panel had to examine the GATT compatibility of India's so-called "Actual User" requirement according to which import licences were generally available only to an "industrial" or "non-industrial actual user". This was defined to be a person who utilises the imported goods respectively (a) for manufacturing in his own industrial unit or manufacturing for his own use in another unit including a jobbing unit and (b) for his own use in any commercial establishment, laboratory or service industry. Having determined that the requirement at issue was

---

[157] See Panel Report on *Malt Beverages*, above n 155, para 5.63.
[158] WT/DS90, brought 22 July 1997.

indeed "a restriction" for purposes of Article XI, the panel noted, albeit in a footnote, that "the restrictions at issue, although related to distribution, are *on importation*".[159]

In *Korea—Measures Affecting Imports of Fresh, Chilled and Frozen Beef (Korea–Beef)*,[160] Australia and the United States had argued for a broad interpretation of Article XI, according to which "it is sufficient that [the measure under review, for example a measure restricting availability of end-point sale for imported products] has an effect on importation" for it to have the effect of quantitative restrictions prohibited by Article XI GATT.[161] The complainants argued as follows: "Given that 'restriction' has a broad scope, Article XI applies to any measure which has the *practical* effect of restricting imports".[162] However, the panel rejected the argument stating that restrictions on the distribution of imported beef are laws, regulations and requirements affecting the internal sale, offering for sale, purchase, distribution or use of domestic or imported beef for purposes of Article III:4 GATT. Consequently, recalling that similar restrictions on the internal distribution of domestic beef did not exist, the Panel found that Korea had violated Article III:4.[163]

The strict interpretation of the second element (*on importation*) also conforms with the strict interpretation given of the concept of pecuniary border measure for purposes of Article II GATT. Notwithstanding this basic similar approach, if one were to compare the two criteria employed in the determination of whether a pecuniary measure falls within Article II or Article III:2 ("geographical location" and "scope of application" of the charge) with the two corresponding criteria employed in order to determine the respective "objective element" of Articles XI and III:4 ("object" and "scope of application" of the measure), it is not too difficult to capture the slight difference. While the criterion of the "scope of application" of the measure plays an equally fundamental role in both tests, panel practice dealing with Article XI does not focus on the "geographical location" of the measure under review (whether it applies at the border or internally), but rather seems to look at the "object" or "subject-matter" of the measure itself (whether or not it directly regulates importation). This slight difference, perhaps stemming from the non-pecuniary nature of the measures

---

[159] Panel Report on *India—Quantitative Restrictions* above n 138, para 5.142, fn 338 [emphasis added]. The Panel's intent was to distinguish its case with that examined in Panel Report on *Canada Alcohol I*, above n 153, where restrictions on importation and distribution were considered as being within the meaning of "other measures" under Art XI, even though they might have also be examined under Art III:4.

[160] WT/DS161 and WT/DS169, brought respectively 4 Feb and 19 April 1999.

[161] Panel Report on *Korea—Measures Affecting Imports of Fresh, Chilled and Frozen Beef (Korea–Beef)*, WT/DS161/R and WT/DS169/R, circulated 31 July 2000, adopted 10 Jan 2001, para 114.

[162] *Ibid.*

[163] *Ibid.*, paras 702–05.

falling under Article XI,[164] does not however appear to influence in any substantial way the outcomes of the two sets of determinations.

(c)   The historical antecedent: the 1927 Convention   A further confirmation of the meaning and purpose of Article XI may be gained by looking at the historical antecedent to the GATT, the 1927 Convention for the Abolition of Import and Export Prohibitions and Restrictions.[165] Article 2 of the 1927 Convention provided for the abolition within a period of six months from the date of the coming into force of the Convention of all import and export prohibitions or restriction, defined in Article 1 as "prohibitions and restrictions imposed on the importation […] and exportation of goods".[166] However, Article 4 listed eight classes of prohibitions and restrictions, which were not subjected to the general obligation of Article 2. Next to prohibitions or restrictions inter alia "relating to public security",[167] "imposed on moral or humanitarian grounds"[168] and "imposed for the protection of public health or for the protection of animals or plants against disease, insects and harmful parasites",[169] Article 4, note 7, of the 1927 Convention excluded from the general obligation of Article 2,

> prohibitions or restrictions designed to extend to foreign products the regime established within the country in respect of the production of, trade in, and transport and consumption of native products of the same kind.[170]

This exclusion was clearly meant to cover those restrictions, which, although applied at the border as a condition for importation, were mere extensions to imported products of internal regulations imposed on domestic products. In other words, if a country wanted to prohibit the manufacture of pornographic dolls throughout the national territory, a prohibition *on the importation* of pornographic dolls, which applied at the border (and, by definition, exclusively on foreign goods), would not have

---

[164] It probably makes more sense to refer to "charges imposed at the border" than to non-pecuniary regulations imposed at the border.

[165] International Convention for the Abolition of Import and Export Prohibitions and Restrictions, signed at Geneva on Nov 8, 1927, League of Nations Doc C.559, M.201 1927.IIB (1927), reproduced in 46 US Statute at Large 2461. The Convention was signed and ratified by 28 countries including Germany, United Kingdom, Italy, France, United States of America, Japan, India and Egypt.

[166] Art 1 stated as follows: "The provisions of the present Convention shall apply to prohibitions and restrictions imposed on the importation into the territories of any High Contracting Party of goods, the produce or manufacture of the territories of any other High Contracting Party, and to prohibitions and restrictions imposed on the exportation of goods from the territories of any High Contracting Party to the territories of any other High Contracting Party."

[167] Art 4, n 1.

[168] Art 4, n 2.

[169] Art 4, n 4.

[170] Art 4, n 7.

been caught by the general obligation of Article 2, since it represented the "border arm" of an internal measure. It follows thus that if the obligation to abolish import and export restrictions contained in the 1927 Convention did not apply to *border* measures, which were mere extensions of internal regulations, it was also never meant to cover *internal* measures in the first place.

This strict reading of the term "prohibitions or restrictions imposed on importation" employed in the 1927 Convention is confirmed by another provision of that Convention, which subjected what appeared to be specific types of *border* provisions to a more relaxed standard than that of Article 2. Article 3, in fact, provided that in the case the contracting parties, in pursuance of their legislation, subjected the importation or exportation of goods to certain regulations in respect of the manner, form or place of importation or exportation, or the imposition of marks, or to other formalities or conditions, they undertook that such regulations should not be made a means of disguised prohibition or arbitrary restriction. Although these measures appear to be border measures, they are referred to as "regulation" and are prohibited only in as far as they constitute *disguised* prohibition or *arbitrary* restriction. It would thus be illogical to subject internal measures to the unqualified obligation of Article 2 whereas certain (border) regulations need to comply with the looser standard of Article 3.

It is however relevant to emphasise that the drafters of the 1927 Convention appeared to be concerned also by other measures, which might not have been considered as purely border measures imposed on importation. A note to Article 4, note 7, explained that the contracting parties interpreted the paragraph in question as

> prohibiting recourse to any system of classifying or defining products which is employed as an indirect means of restricting the importation of foreign products or of subjecting importation to a regime of unfair discrimination.[171]

Thus, the Convention, albeit in a note, covered any system of classifying or defining products that might have been applicable to both imported and domestic products. However, such a system was deemed to fall outside of the express exclusion of Article 4, and thus within the general prohibition of Article 2, only if it was employed as an *indirect* restriction on importation or if it constituted *unfair discrimination* against imported products.[172]

---

[171] Ad Art 4 (b) ad No 7.
[172] It is not clear whether the Note refers to "discrimination" between products of other Contracting States (MFN) or to discrimination between foreign and domestic products (NT).

Without going into any more detailed analysis of the 1927 Convention, it should already be clear that even the historical antecedent of Article XI GATT was principally aimed at abolishing the more outrageous *border* measures prohibiting or restricting importation or exportation of goods. Moreover, although the Contracting Parties were worried by other forms of restrictions on importation or exportation, which may still be categorised for the most part as *border* measures (ie, measures applying on the importation of foreign products), they did not subject them to the strict per se prohibition of Article 2, but conditioned the application of this provision to the further additional requirement that these measures be "disguised", "arbitrary", "indirect", or "discriminatory" restrictions on importation or exportation. Thus, for example, a product classification system, even if imposed exclusively on the importation of foreign products, was necessary in order to manage other legitimate border measures, such as customs duties, and thus could not be prohibited unless it was employed as an indirect means of restricting imports.

This diversification between different types of border measures shows quite clearly at least two points: first, the unqualified general prohibition of "restrictions on importation" did not apply to internal measures, and secondly, the normative content of the liberalising rule changed according to the function of the trade restrictive measure.

As will be clarified more amply in the chapters dealing with the principle of National Treatment, the themes that had surfaced in the 1927 Convention were later picked up and further developed by the General Agreement on Tariff and Trade, which clearly subjected border and internal measures to different normative standards.

(d) Process-standards: the dissonant view? Although the "object" and "scope of application" of the measure should constitute the two guiding criteria in the determination of whether a restriction is imposed on the importation of goods for the purposes of Article XI, it appears that GATT/WTO panel practice has somehow taken a contrasting approach with regard to import prohibitions based on "process standards" (ie those standards that regulate the manner or method in which products are produced or manufactured).

The issue was for the first time raised in the two famous Panel Reports on *United States–Restrictions on Imports of Tuna*,[173] which concerned a US measure prohibiting (a) the "taking" (harassment, hunting, capture, killing or attempt thereof) of marine mammals incidental to harvesting of yellowfin tuna in the Eastern Tropical Pacific Ocean (ETP), and (b) the

---

[173] Panel Report on *United States—Restrictions on Imports of Tuna (Tuna I)*, DS21/R, unadopted, BISD 39S/155 and Panel Report on *United States—Restrictions on Imports of Tuna (Tuna II)*, DS29/R, unadopted, reprinted in ILM 842.

importation of yellowfin tuna and tuna products harvested in the ETP noting using fishing techniques designed to reduce the incidental taking of dolphins. While the complainants had argued that the US import prohibition constituted a quantitative restriction on importation within the meaning of Article XI GATT, the United States had counter-argued that they were internal regulations enforced at the time or point of importation under Article III:4 and the Note Ad Article III. In other words, the US prohibition of imports of tuna and tuna products merely constituted the "border arm" of the US laws regulating the harvesting of (domestic) tuna.

Employing the two above-mentioned criteria ("object" and "scope of application" of the measure), it would appear that Article III:4, and not Article XI, should have applied to the case at hand, since the measure at issue, although in a sense a restriction "on importation", was applicable to both imported and domestic products.

However, both panels rejected the applicability of Article III:4 advanced by the US Government on the basis that "Article III covers only measure affecting products as such".[174] Since the measures at hand could not be regarded as being applied to products as such, because they did not directly regulate the sale of tuna and could not possibly affect tuna as a product, the Panel found that the US import prohibition on certain yellowfin tuna and tuna products did not constitute internal regulations covered by Article III, as interpreted by the Note Ad Article III.[175]

Left with only Article XI, both panels briefly noted that the US measures constituted import prohibitions since they banned the import of tuna or tuna products from any country not meeting certain policy conditions and concluded that those measures were inconsistent with Article XI:1.[176]

Independently of what might have been the policy objectives underlying the *Tuna* Panel Reports (possibly, a willingness to apply the stricter standard of Article XI to "extraterritorial" environmental measures), the panel's reading of Article III:4 is simply incorrect.[177] Article III:4 does not

---

[174] Panel Report on *Tuna I*, above n 173, paras 5.10–5.16, "Art III:4 refers solely to laws, regulations and requirements affecting the internal sale, etc of *products*. This suggests that Art III covers only measures affecting products as such. Furthermore, the text of the Note Ad Art III refers to a measure 'which applies to an imported *product* and the like domestic *product* and is collected or enforced in the case of the imported *product* at the time or point of importation". [emphasis original] See also the Panel Report on *Tuna II*, above n 173, paras 5.8–5.9.

[175] Panel Report on *Tuna I*, above n 173, para 5.14. Interestingly enough, the Panel further concluded that, even if the provision at issue were regarded as regulating the sale of tuna as a product, the US import prohibition would not meet the requirements of Art III. *Ibid.*, para 5.15.

[176] Panel Report on *Tuna I*, above n 173, paras 5.17–5.18, and Panel Report on *Tuna II*, above n 173, para 5.10.

[177] R Howse and D Regan, "The Product/Process Distinction: An Illusory Basis for Disciplining 'Unilateralism' in Trade Policy", 11 *European Journal of International Law* (2000) 249 and J Wiers, *Trade and Environment in the EC and the WTO: A Legal Analysis* (Amsterdam, Europa Law Publishing, 2002) at 277–78.

cover "only measures affecting products as such", but it explicitly covers laws and regulations *affecting the internal sale of product*. In enunciating its scope of application, Article III:1 refers to

> internal taxes and other internal charges, and laws, regulations and require-ments *affecting* the internal sale, offering for sale, purchase, transportation, distribution or use of products.

This is clearly a broader concept than that advanced by the two *Tuna* panels. In the words of a famous panel,

> the selection of the word "affecting" would imply [...] that the drafters of the Article intended to cover in paragraph 4 not only the laws and regulations which directly governed the conditions of sale or purchase but also any laws or regulations which might adversely modify the conditions of competition between the domestic and imported products on the internal market.[178]

The broad definition of the term "affecting" has also been recognised by more recent WTO jurisprudence.[179] In *EC–Bananas III*,[180] the Panel exam-ined whether the EC procedures and requirements for the allocation of import licences for foreign products to eligible operators were measures included in the notion of "all laws, regulations and requirements affecting their internal sale, offering for sale, purchase [...]" in the meaning of Article III:4. The Panel held that "the word 'affecting' suggests a coverage of Article III:4 beyond legislation directly regulating or governing the sale of domestic and like imported products".[181] On appeal, the Appellate Body confirmed this broad reading of the scope of application of Article III

---

[178] Panel Report on *Italian Discrimination Against Imported Agricultural Machinery* (*Italian Agricultural Machinery*), L/833, adopted on 23 Oct 1958, BISD 7S/60, para 12. Cf Panel Report *United States—Section 337 of the Tariff Act of 1930* (*Section 337*), L/6439, adopted on 7 Nov 1989 BISD 36S/345, para 5.10, where the measure at issue was the US mechanism for enforcement of US patent law vis-à-vis imported products, thus a regulation which clearly did not affect the products as such.

[179] See above section on the "objective element" of Art II for a criticism of the Panel's and Appellate Body's reading of the relationship between Arts III and XI GATT in *EC–Bananas III*.

[180] Panel Report on *European Communities—Regime for the Importation, Sale and Distribution of Bananas* (*EC–Bananas III*), WT/DS27/R, circulated 22 May 1997, adopted 25 Sept 1997.

[181] *Ibid.*, para 7.175, citing the following GATT Panel practice: Panel Report on *Italian Agricultural Machinery*, above n 178, paras 11–12; Panel Report on *Section 337*, above n 178, para 5.10; Panel Report on *EEC–Parts and Components*, BISD 37S/132, paras. 5.20–5.21. The Panel Report on *Italian Agricultural Machinery*, above n 173, para 12, adopted a broad defini-tion of the term "affecting": "In addition, the text of para 4 referred both in English and French to laws and regulations and requirements *affecting* internal sale, purchase, etc., and not to laws, regulations and requirements governing the conditions of sale or purchase. The selection of the word 'affecting' would imply, in the opinion of the Panel, that the drafters of the Art intended to cover in paragraph 4 not only the laws and regulations which directly governed the conditions of sale or purchase but also *any laws or regulations which might adversely modify the conditions of competition between the domestic and imported products* on the internal market" [emphasis added].

by noting that the ordinary meaning of the word "affecting" implies a measure that has "an effect on", and is thus wider in scope than such terms as "regulating" or "governing".[182]

Both *Tuna* Panels reached the conclusion that Article III covered only measures affecting products as such by confusing the language employed to define the "objective element" with that describing the "normative content" of Article III. With regard to the objective element, internal taxes and regulations are caught by Article III if they *affect* the internal sale, purchase, distribution, etc, of products. For purposes of this determination, as previously emphasised, the scope of application of Article III is quite broad, practically covering any kind of national regulation that has an effect, even indirect, on the competitive conditions of products. With regard to the normative element, internal taxes and regulations should not be *applied* to imported or domestic products so as to afford protection to domestic production. This should simply be read as imposing on Members an obligation to regulate their markets without discriminating between *products* on the basis of their origin or nationality (the so-called National Treatment obligation). In this context, the reference to products as such should be viewed as a specification of the subject-matter of the GATT, just as *services* are the subject-matter of the GATS.[183]

It follows that once a measure is deemed to be, for example, an internal regulation *affecting* the internal sale of tuna products (because it prohibits the use of dolphin-unfriendly nets for catching tuna), then, it must be determined whether or not the measure is applied to imported or domestic *products* in a discriminatory manner. It is a mistake to mix the terms employed with regard to two distinct features of the same provision. Once again, the Article III *normative* requirement that the measure be *applied* to products in a non-discriminatory manner should not be

---

[182] Appellate Body Report on *EC–Bananas III*, WT/DS27/AB/R, circulated 9 Sept 1997, adopted 25 Sept 1997, para 220. These statements were made with regard to the similar worded provision in Art I GATS. See also Panel Report on *Canada—Certain Measures Affecting the Automotive Industry* (*Canada–Auto*), WT/DS139/R and WT/DS142/R, circulated 11 Feb 2000, adopted 19 June 2000, paras. 10.80–10.85: "In light of our interpretation of the word 'affecting' in Art III, we consider that a measure which provides that an advantage can be obtained by using domestic products but not by using imported products has an impact on the conditions of competition between domestic and imported products and thus affects the 'internal sale, [...] or use' of imported products, even if the measure allows for other means to obtain the advantage, such as the use of domestic services rather than products".

[183] R Howse and D Regan, "The Product/Process Distinction: An Illusory Basis for Disciplining 'Unilateralism' in Trade Policy", 11 *European Journal of International Law* (2000) 249 at 254, "it should be obvious that the repeated reference to 'products' tells us nothing about the product/process distinction. It merely reflects the fact that GATT is about trade in goods, not about trade in services or the movement of capital or labour." *Contra* JH Jackson, "Comments on *Shrimp/Turtle* and the Product/Process Distinction", 11 *European Journal of International Law* (2000) 303.

confused with Article III *objective* requirement that the internal regulation *affect* the internal sale of the products.[184]

Unfortunately, the *Tuna* Panels approach was followed, though only implicitly, by the WTO panel in *United States—Import Prohibition of Certain Shrimp and Shrimp Products (US–Shrimp* or *Shrimp/Turtle).*[185] There, a measure virtually identical to the above-mentioned import ban on tuna, this time a ban on imports of shrimp or shrimp products from any country not meeting certain policy conditions similar to those applying to domestic products, was also deemed to violate Article XI:1.[186] As will be discussed in the relevant section in the chapter on the principle of National Treatment, the US environmental measure regulating the manner in which shrimps are caught should have been reviewed under Article III:4 as representing a case of formal discrimination vis-à-vis imported products.

The dubious approach followed by the panels in *Tuna* and *Shrimp/Turtle* with regard to import restrictions based on "process standards" cannot be easily reconciled with a recent panel report dealing with an import restriction based on "product standards". In *European Communities—Measures Affecting Asbestos and Asbestos Containing Products*,[187] the panel was confronted with a French decree prohibiting the import, sale and use of asbestos. Canada had argued that the decree at issue should be examined in the light of both Articles III:4 and XI:1 because, on the one hand, it included internal regulations prohibiting the sale and use of asbestos in a manner incompatible with Article III:4, and on the other, it prohibited imports of asbestos in a manner incompatible with Article XI:1.[188] The EC countered by arguing that either the measure was an internal regulation, in which case it was covered by Article III:4, or it only concerned the import of products, in which case it had to be

---

[184] Note Ad Art III clearly adopts the broad definition of Art III:1, "of the kind referred to in paragraph 1" (ie, affecting the internal sale of products). See Howse and Reagan's thorough and convincing arguments supporting the inclusion of "process standards" within the scope of application of Art III GATT in R Howse and D Regan, "The Product/Process Distinction: An Illusory Basis for Disciplining 'Unilateralism' in Trade Policy", 11 *European Journal of International Law* (2000) 249 at 253–57.

[185] WT/DS58/R, circulated on 15 May 1998, adopted 6 Nov 1998.

[186] Panel Report on *United States—Import Prohibition of Certain Shrimp and Shrimp Products (US–Shrimp* or *Shrimp/Turtle),* WT/DS58/R, circulated on 15 May 1998, adopted 6 Nov 1998 above, para 7.17. However, the US Government had not argued this time that the measure imposed on imports of shrimp and shrimp product fell under Art III. It relied solely on an Art XX justification. Notwithstanding the US admission, the Panel found that "the wording of the measure under review and the interpretation made of it by the Court of International Trade (CIT) are sufficient evidence that the United States imposes a 'prohibition or restriction' within the meaning of Art XI:1".

[187] *European Communities—Measures Affecting Asbestos and Asbestos Containing Products (EC–Asbestos),* WT/DS135, brought 3 June 1998.

[188] Panel Report on *EC–Asbestos,* WT/DS135/R, circulated 18 Sept 2000, adopted 5 April 2001, para 8.84.

assessed in the light of Article XI:1. According to the EC, the French decree was necessarily covered by Article III:4 only, since the measure applied both to domestic and imported products, even if it was imposed on imported products at the time or place of importation.[189]

The panel agreed with the arguments advanced by the EC, and in particular it drew attention to the Note Ad Article III, which specifically covers a situation in which a law, regulation or requirement applies both to an imported product and to the like domestic product and is enforced in the case of the imported product at the time or point of importation. The panel thus rejected Canada's strict reading of Note Ad Article III, according to which the Note was not applicable to the case at hand, since the explicit import ban did not apply to domestic products. The panel argued, first of all, that regulations applicable to domestic products and foreign products led to the same result: the halting of the spread of asbestos and asbestos-containing products on French territory. Secondly, the wording of Note Ad Article III[190] as well as relevant GATT practice[191] did not support Canada's approach that an *identical* measure must be applied to the domestic product and the like imported product if the measure applicable to the imported product were to fall under Article III.[192] For the foregoing reasons, the panel concluded that Article III:4 GATT applied to the ban on importing asbestos and asbestos-containing products imposed by the decree.[193]

---

[189] *Ibid.*, para 8.85.

[190] "The word 'and' does not have the same meaning as 'in the same way as', which can be another meaning for the word 'comme' in the French text. We therefore consider that the word 'comme' cannot be interpreted as requiring an identical measure to be applied to imported products and domestic products if Art III is to apply." *Ibid.*, para 8.94.

[191] "In *United States—Section 337 of the Tariff Act of 1930*, the Panel had to examine measures specifically applicable to imported products suspected of violating an American patent right. In this case, referring to Note Ad Art III, the Panel considered that the provisions of Art III:4 did apply to the special procedures prescribed for imported products suspected of violating a patent protected in the United States because these procedures were considered to be 'laws, regulations and requirements' affecting the internal sale of the imported products, within the meaning of Art III of the GATT. It should be noted that in this case the procedures examined were not the same as the equivalent procedures applicable to domestic products." *Ibid.*, para 8.95.

[192] *Ibid.*, para 8.93. The panel also noted: "[C]onsider that an internal charge applied to a domestic product must also be imposed on an imported product. Nevertheless, if it is deemed appropriate to impose the charge at the border rather than waiting until the imported product is actually marketed, the same logic applies in the case of a regulatory measure prescribing a ban on marketing. Is it not equally preferable from the administrative point of view and in the interest of the importers themselves to prevent the entry of the like product into the country applying the measure rather than waiting until it is placed in a warehouse before banning its sale?" *Ibid.*, para 8.96.

[193] *Ibid.*, para 8.99. For a very interesting and insightful analysis of the relationship between Art III and Art XI GATT, see the Final Report of the Panel Under ch 18 of the Canada–United States Free Trade Agreement on *Lobsters from Canada*, USA 89–1807–01, dated 25 May, 1990, which concerned US legislation prohibiting the importation of lobsters smaller than the US federal minimum size (ie, an import ban based on product standards, which formally applied equally to both domestic and imported products). After a detailed analysis of

The Panel Report in *Asbestos* confirms that the dividing line between Article III and Article XI GATT is drawn on the basis of whether or not the measure under review is simply part of a broader regulatory framework applicable to both imported and domestic products, even if not in an identical manner.[194] At the same time, it implicitly contrasts with the erroneous, strict reading of the scope of application of Article III followed in the two *Tuna* reports and the *Shrimp/Turtle* report.

In conclusion, the *texts* of Article XI and Article III, as interpreted by the Note, as well as the *object and purpose* of Article XI, as confirmed both by the identical approach with regard to the treatment of pecuniary measures in Article II and III and by the 1927 Convention, show quite clearly the following: (1) the "objective element" of Article XI is and should be limited to trade restrictive measures that directly regulate the importation of products and apply exclusively to imported products; and (2) the "objective element" of Article III is and should be to review any measure affecting the sale or use of products that is part of a broader regulatory scheme applicable to both imported and domestic products, even if not in an identical manner. Within this calculation, whether the measure at hand is a process-standard or a product-standard should not matter since both types of regulation may be considered as falling either under Article XI or Article III.[195] For example, an import ban on shrimps caught without using TEDs (a process-standard) or an import ban on asbestos (a product-standard) may be caught *either* by Article XI if they are applied *only* to imported products *or* by Article III if similar requirements are also imposed on domestic products.[196] This approach respects the fundamental

---

GATT precedent, the five member panel, by a three-two margin, characterised the US measure as an "internal" measure under Art III:4 rather than an import restriction pursuant to Art XI. The principal basis for this finding was that the measure applied to both US and Canadian lobsters. *Ibid.*, para 7.22. The minority opinion, on the other hand, adopting a different reading of Art XI, concluded that Art XI was applicable because the measure at issue "prevented" Canadian lobsters from entering the US market. *Ibid.*, para 8.5. Cf M Trebilcock and R Howse, *The Regulation of International Trade* (London/New York, Routledge, 1999) at 402–3. Also JHH Weiler, "The Constitution of the Common Marketplace: Text and Context in the Evolution of the Free Movement of Goods" in P Craig and G de Búrca (eds), *The Evolution of EU Law* (Oxford, OUP, 1999) at 358, who argues, along the lines of the minority opinion in the *Lobster* case, that Art XI GATT *should* cover point of entry measures barring market access, while Art III GATT *should* regulate internal market regulation measures, where both process and product standards would fall in the former category and marketing arrangements in the latter.

[194] Cf J Wiers, *Trade and Environment in the EC and the WTO: A Legal Analysis* (Amsterdam, Europa Law Publishing, 2002) at 176–77.
[195] On the other hand, "marketing-standards", which regulate the manner in which goods are sold, will always be considered as "internal regulations" reviewable under Art III GATT.
[196] The consistency of a process-standard applicable to both imported and domestic products with the National Treatment obligation of Art III GATT will depend on whether the internal legislation accords to imported products treatment "no less favourable" than that accorded to "like" domestic products. This question will be examined in ch 2 and 3.

division of labour between "negative integration" and "judicial integration" type of rules.

2.   Articles 28 and 29 EC

The similar terminology employed, on the one hand, in Articles 28 and 29 EC and, on the other hand, in Article 25 EC would seem to suggest also a similar structure. Next to a ban on a specific type of trade measure, "quantitative restrictions" (or "customs duties" in Article 25), Articles 28 and 29 in fact also prohibit "all measures having equivalent effect" (or "charges having equivalent effect" in Article 25).

However, while the concept of "charges having equivalent effect to customs duties", even in its broadest reading given by the ECJ, has found a limit in the independent concept of "internal taxation" of Article 90 EC, the seemingly parallel concept of "measures having equivalent effect to quantitative restrictions" under Articles 28 and 29 apparently encountered no external limitation whatsoever. Consequently, it has been broadly interpreted as including, in the words of the classic definition set out in *Procureur du Roi v Dassonville*, "all trading rules enacted by Member States, which are capable of hindering, directly or indirectly, actually or potentially, intra-Community trade".[197]

Notwithstanding the jurisprudential evolution in the scope of application of Article 28 EC, it is suggested here that both in their original structure, as well as in their very early interpretation, as with Article XI GATT, the prohibitions of Articles 28 and 29 EC had been envisioned to cover mainly *border measures*.

In this section, by recounting the story of former Article 30 EEC (a story which will continue in all the remaining chapters), I will try to demonstrate this point and, at the same time, advance a plausible explanation for the apparent lack in the Treaty of Rome of a dual normative approach towards non-pecuniary measures restricting trade in goods that distinguishes between border and internal measures.[198]

(a)   The original structure of the EEC Treaty   Contrary to the current consolidated version of the Treaty establishing the European Community (EC) as provided for by the Treaty of Amsterdam, the original Treaty establishing the European Economic Community (EEC) was divided in six parts.[199] While the eight Articles in part One enunciated the *Principles* of the EEC, part Two laid out the *Foundations of the Community* including

---

[197] Case 8/74, *Procureur du Roi v Benoit and Gustave Dassonville* [1974] ECR 837.
[198] In WTO law, it is the dual approach embodied in Arts XI and III:4 GATT respectively.
[199] While the current version is still divided in six parts, Part Three now covers all *Community Policies*, including *Free Movement of Goods* (Title I) and *Common Rules on Competition, Taxation and Approximation of Laws* (Title VI).

four Titles, dealing respectively with the *Free Movement of Goods* (ex Articles 9–37), *Agriculture* (ex Articles 38–47), *Free Movement of Persons, Services and Capital* (ex Articles 48-73) and *Transport* (ex Articles 74–84). The Title on the free movement of goods was comprised of a first chapter on the *Customs Union*, which provided in section I for the *Elimination of Customs Duties Between Member States* (ex Article 12–17) and in section II for the *Setting up of the Common Customs Tariff* for trade with third countries (ex Article 18–29), and a second chapter on the *Elimination of Quantitative Restrictions Between Member States* (ex Articles 30–37). As clearly evidenced in the *Rapport des Chefs de Délégation aux Ministeres des Affaires Etrangères* of 1956 (the so-called Spaak Report),[200] in line with the 1947 GATT philosophy, the principal requirements for the "fusion des marchés" were "the elimination of customs duties within the common market" and "the elimination of quotas."[201] Accordingly, Articles 12 and 30 EEC, much like Article II and XI GATT, prohibited customs duties and quantitative restrictions respectively.[202] However, adopting an original term, the Treaty drafters included in both Articles an identical prohibition on any charges or measures "having equivalent effect". Although the definition of the new term was not included in the Treaty and could not be easily determined,[203] it appears that, at least in the minds of the original drafters the prohibition on any charge or measure having equivalent effect to a customs duty or a quantitative restriction was intended to cover only border measures, or at most all measures that were expressly imposed on imported products only (de jure discriminatory measures). The prohibition of discrimination on grounds of nationality was also provided for in the Treaty of Rome as a general principle in old Article 7 (then 6, now 12).[204]

Internal measures, such as taxation and regulation, were in principle dealt with in Part III of the EEC Treaty on the *Policy of the Community*, which in its first title laying out certain *Common Rules* provided for *Rules on Competition* (chapter I, ex Articles 85–94), *Tax Provisions* (chapter II, ex Articles 95–99), and *Approximation of Laws* (chapter III, ex Articles 100–102). Leaving aside the chapter on competition rules, the second and third chapters covered "internal taxation" and "provisions laid down by law, regulation or administrative action in Member States" respectively.

---

[200] Comité Intergouvernemental Créé par la Conférence de Messine, Bruxelles, 21 avril 1956.
[201] Spaak Report, above n 125, at 27 and 35.
[202] As previously emphasised, Art II GATT does not simply provide for the elimination of tariff but it regulates the process of reducing them through progressive multilateral negotiating rounds.
[203] Cf RC Béraud, "Les mesures d'effet équivalent au sens des Arts 30 et suivants du Traité de Rome", *Revue Trimestrelle de Droit Européen* (1968) 265 at 266–67.
[204] On the residual character and thus on the "gap-filling function" of the general prohibition of discrimination on grounds of nationality see T Tridimas, *The General Principles of EC Law* (Oxford, OUP, 1999) at 77 *et seq.*

Contrary to the general prohibition characterising the title on the free movement of goods (an instrument of "negative integration *stricto sensu*"), the two chapters dealing with "internal taxation" and "regulation" did not preclude Member States from employing such regulatory instruments but rather (1) subjected the former to the non-discrimination principle (a form of "judicial integration") and (2) subjected the latter to the Community's harmonisation prerogatives ("legislative integration" or "positive integration *stricto sensu*").

Without being able at this point to analyse this issue in much detail, it can be said that the difference in the normative content of the rules dealing with internal *pecuniary* and *non-pecuniary* measures (non-discrimination with regard to the former, and harmonisation with regard to the latter) can only be explained by the sensitivity of the field of internal taxation. This is clearly evidenced for example in both the Spaak report, which dealt with both taxation and regulation under the same chapter (addressing market distortions and suggesting a harmonisation solution),[205] as well as the express exclusion of taxation from the scope of application of Article 100A, the new harmonisation provision inserted into the EEC Treaty by the 1986 Single European Act.

Accordingly, the fundamental difference between the approaches adopted by the GATT and the EEC Treaty with regard to *border* and *internal* measures restricting trade in goods did not originally reside in the broader "objective element" of Article 30 EEC vis-à-vis Article XI GATT; but rather in the different "normative content" of Articles 100–02 EEC vis-à-vis Article III:4 GATT. As will be examined in more details in the following chapters, while Article III:4 "simply" imposed on Members a National Treatment obligation, Articles 100–02 aimed at the more ambitious (perhaps too ambitious) goal of harmonising those of the Member States' internal regulations that affected the establishment or functioning of the common market. As noted above, the prohibition of discrimination on grounds of nationality was also provided for in EC law, inasmuch as old Article 7 EEC (now Article 12 EC) affirmed that "any discrimination on grounds of nationality shall be prohibited". However, following the broad interpretation of Article 28 EC, which will be described in later chapters, that provision was mainly employed outside the realm of the free movement of goods.[206]

This explanation for the apparent lack of a dual approach in EC law with regard to non-pecuniary measures may be confirmed by looking at the early approaches of the ECJ and the Commission towards Article 30 EEC (now Article 28 EC).[207]

---

[205] Spaak Report, above n 125, Title 2, ch 2 (*"La Correction des Distorsions et le Rapprochement des Législations"*) at 60.

[206] Cf T Tridimas, *The General Principles of EC Law* (Oxford, OUP, 1999) at 77 *et seq.*

[207] On the history of Art 28 EC, see also J Wiers, *Trade and Environment in the EC and the WTO: A Legal Analysis* (Amsterdam, Europa Law Publishing, 2002) at 46 *et seq.*

(b)   The ECJ early approach towards Article 28 EC   In its first ten years, the Court of Justice never really seemed to apply the general prohibition of old Article 30 EC beyond pure border measures. This may be because, having been presented only with clear cases of border measures, such as import bans,[208] quantitative restrictions,[209] import restrictions,[210] or import licences,[211] the Court did not have the opportunity fully to test the potential of old Article 30. However, in contrast to the application within the GATT of Article XI, the ECJ from the very beginning applied prohibition of border measures in old Article 30 in quite a strict manner, for example including within its scope of application a Member State's import licence requirement even where the licence was granted *automatically* and the Member State concerned did not purport to reserve the right to withhold a licence.[212]

The Court's strict reading of the general public policy exception embodied in Article 36 EEC (now Article 30 EC) seemed also to lend support to a limited scope of application of the general prohibition of Article 30 EEC. It would in fact have been difficult to extend the scope of the general prohibition without admitting the possibility for Members to pursue legitimate public policy objectives. In its judgment of 14 December, 1968 in *Salgoil*,[213] the Court expressly excluded an extensive interpretation of the public policy exception of old Article 36 by stating as follows:

> Articles 36, 224 and 226 of the Treaty do not provide any argument to the contrary, because these clauses, which attach particular importance to the interests of Member States, concern, it would be noted, exceptional

---

[208] Case 7/61, *Commission v Italy* [1961] ECR 317, where the measure at issue was the re-establishment of a provisional suspension of imports of pigmeat in order for the Italian Government to remedy the artificially low prices prevailing in the national pigmeat sector.
[209] Case 13/68, *SpA Salgoil v Italian Ministry of Foreign Trade* [1968] ECR 453.
[210] Case 20/64, *SARL Albatros v Société des Pétroles et des Combustibles Liquides (Sopéco)* [1965] ECR 40, where the measures at issue were the rules governing the importation of petroleum which derive from the provisions of the French Law of 30 March 1928. Even the Belgian measure under review in the famous *Dassonville* case was none other than a border measure restricting the parallel importation of Scotch Whisky. Cf Case 8/74, *Procureur du Roi v Benoit and Gustave Dassonville* [1974] ECR 837.
[211] Joined Cases 51 to 54/71, *International Fruit Company NV and Others v Produktschap Voor Groenten en Fruit* [1971] ECR 1107. Case 62/70, *Werner A. Bock v Commission* [1971] ECR 897, where the case focused on an application for the partial annulment of Commission Decision No 70/446/EEC of 15 Sept 1970 authorising Germany to exclude from Community treatment, and subject to a licence requirement, prepared and preserved mushrooms under heading no 20.02 of the common customs tariff originating in China and in free circulation in the Benelux countries.
[212] Joined Cases 51 to 54/71, *International Fruit Company NV and Others v Produktschap Voor Groenten en Fruit* [1971] ECR 1107, "Apart from the exceptions for which provision is made by Community law itself, Arts 30 and 34 preclude the application to intra-Community trade of a national provision which requires, even as a pure formality, import or export licences or any other similar procedure." *Ibid.*, para 9.
[213] Case 13/68, *SpA Salgoil v Italian Ministry of Foreign Trade* [1968] ECR 453.

hypothetical cases, which are well defined and do not lend themselves to any extensive interpretation.[214]

The limited scope of application of old Article 30 EEC (now Article 28 EC) may be inferred also from the Court's early cases dealing with pecuniary measures. As already examined, in the *Gingerbread* case,[215] the Court found that the duty on gingerbread introduced in Belgium and Luxembourg fell under the prohibition of Article 12 EEC (now Article 25 EC) and not under the non-discrimination obligation of 95 EEC (now Article 90 EC), because the duty was "levied at the time and on the occasion of the importation of the products in question and imposed solely on these products by reason of their importation".[216] The Court further noted that

> the application of Article 95, with which chapter 2 of Part Three of the Treaty dealing with "tax provisions" begins, cannot be extended to every kind of charge, [since] in the present case the duty in dispute does not appear, either by its form or by its clearly proclaimed economic purpose, to be a tax provision capable of coming within the scope of Article 95.[217]

In *Firma Fink-Frucht GmbH v Hauptzollamt München-Landsbergerstrasse*,[218] the Court quite clearly appeared to limit the scope of application of the Article 30 prohibition. Having found that the German charge was to be considered as internal taxation for the purposes of Article 95 EEC, the ECJ also excluded the application of Article 30, advancing the following explanation:

> Nor does internal taxation imposed under the conditions set out above come within the prohibition on quantitative restrictions and measures having equivalent effect, within the meaning of Article 30 of the Treaty. Such restrictions, which are intended to limit the quantities imported, are in fact different both in their purpose and the way in which they operate from measures of a fiscal nature.[219]

Further confirmations may be found in the Court's statements in *Commission v Italy*,[220] once again with regard to the strict scope of

---

[214] *Ibid.*, at 463. Cf W Van Gerven, "The Recent Case Law of the Court of Justice Concerning Arts 30 and 36 of the EEC Treaty", *CMLRev* (1977) 5 at 10–11.
[215] Joined Cases 2 and 3/62, *Commission v Luxembourg and Belgium (Gingerbread)* [1962] ECR 425.
[216] *Ibid.*, at 433.
[217] *Ibid.*
[218] Case 27/67, *Firma Fink-Frucht GmbH v Hauptzollamt München-Landsbergerstrasse* [1968] ECR 223.
[219] *Ibid.*, at 231.
[220] Case 7/68, *Commission v Italy* [1968] ECR 423.

application of the general exception of Article 36 EEC and the functional relationship between the prohibition of "customs duties and charges having equivalent effect", on the one hand, and the prohibition of "quantitative restrictions and any measure having equivalent effect", on the other. Noting that old Article 36 formed part of the chapter relating to the Elimination of Quantitative Restrictions, both by its position and by an express reference to Articles 30 to 34, the Court first stated that "the subject of that chapter is state intervention in intra-Community trade by measures in the nature of prohibitions, total or partial, on import, export or transit, according to circumstances".[221] Secondly, the Court emphasised the parallel functions of this latter chapter and that on the Customs Union, stating as follows:

> The provisions of Title 1 of Part Two of the Treaty introduced the fundamental principle of the elimination of all obstacles to the free movements of goods between Member States by the abolition of, on the one hand, customs duties and charges having equivalent effect and, on the other hand, quantitative restrictions and measures having equivalent effect. Exceptions to this fundamental rule must be strictly construed.[222]

The Court's early case law regarding the provisions contained in Title 1 on the *Free Movement of Goods* shows that the original aim of those provisions was to eliminate clear instances of restrictions imposed on the importation (and exportation) of goods from one Member State to another. The cases brought before the Court, as well as the Court's statements with regard to (a) the relationship between old Articles 12 and 30, (b) the scope of application of old Article 95 and (c) the strict interpretation of old Article 36 exceptions, seem to suggest that, at least during those early years, the interpretation of the concept of "measures having equivalent effect to quantitative restrictions" was directed principally towards the more limited category of border measures.

(c)   The Commission's early approach towards Article 28 EC   Although it evolved more quickly, the Commission's initial view of the reach of Article 30 EEC was also in line with that of the ECJ. In its 1962 Memorandum on the Community Action Programme for the Second Stage,[223] the Commission clearly showed a difference in approach with regard to "measures having equivalent effect to quantitative restrictions", on the one hand, and "technical regulations", on the other. While it proposed (in paragraph 14) adopting further measures in order to eliminate

---

[221] *Ibid.*, at 430.
[222] *Ibid.*
[223] *Memorandum della Commissione sul Programma della Comunità nella seconda tappa* (Bruxelles, 1962).

the former (including so-called "administrative obstacles"),[224] the Commission then proposed a different solution for dealing with technical regulations (in paragraph 15). Noting that these regulations, imposed for purposes of general interest and for consumer protection, were often very different in each Member State and thus rendered more difficult the movement of goods in the common market,[225] the Commission proposed:

> to harmonise and even in several cases unify in a system of European law [...] the provisions dealing with quality, composition, packaging, origin and control of agricultural and pharmaceutical products, phytosanitary protection, animal health, etc.[226]

In line with the Treaty's original "division of labour", the Commission clearly adopted a different approach towards measures having equivalent effect to quantitative restrictions and internal technical regulations. While it subjected the former to the general prohibition set out in Article 30 EEC, the latter were dealt with by the harmonisation prerogatives of Articles 100–102 EEC. The Commission's timid reading of the general prohibition of old Article 30 is confirmed in its further proposal that

> Member States undertake a "standstill" obligation, which would include notification of any new proposal for a technical regulation that may have an effect on trade.[227]

---

[224] According to the Commission "administrative obstacles" were "represented by the several administrative checks carried out at the time of crossing the frontiers and which may have an effect similar to that of measures having equivalent effect of quotas." [author's translation from the Italian version of the Commission Memorandum].

[225] *Ibid.*, at 18. The original section dealing with "technical regulations" stated in relevant part as follows: "La commercializzazione di numerosi prodotti è disciplinata da disposizione emanate dalle pubbliche autorità sui mercati interni per motivi di interesse generale e per la protezione del consumatore. Tali regolamentazioni sono spesso molto divergenti, ciò che è fonte di difficoltà per la circolazione delle merci all'interno del mercato comune. Inoltre esse possono non soltanto comportare delle disparità nei costi, ma anche impedire o disturbare la produzione di massa a condizioni economiche, e falsare anche la concorrenza nei mercati della Comunità. Di conseguenza occorre armonizzare e addirittura, in numerosi case, unificare in un sistema di diritto europeo queste disposizioni degli Stati membri. Ci si riferisce, in particolare, alle disposizioni concernenti la qualità, la composizione, l'imballaggio, la denominazione ed il controllo delle derrate alimentari dei prodotti farmaceutici, la protezione fitosanitaria, la legislazione veterinaria, le semenze, ecc. Data la complessità delle disposizioni di cui trattasi e la necessità di ottenere l'accordo degli Stati membri, i lavori di ravvicinamento si protrarranno certamente per tutto il periodo transitorio. [...]" See Opinion of the Social and Economic Committee of 28 may 1963 regarding the principal features of the EEC Commission Memorandum on the Community Action Programme for the Second Stage [1963] *GU* 3019 at 3020–21.

[226] *Memorandum della Commissione*, above n 223, at 18 [author's translation].

[227] *Memorandum della Commissione*, above n 223, at 19 [author's translation]. The original text read as follows: "In attesa della realizzazione di questi programmi di ravvicinamento, la Commissione, fatta salva l'applicazione delle disposizioni del Trattato relative alle misure di effetto equivalente a delle restrizioni quantitative, chiederà algi Stati membri di sottoscrivere un accordo di 'standstill', che comporterebbe la comunicazione preventiva di tutti i

If technical regulations were indeed covered by the concept of "measures having equivalent effect" set out in Article 30 EEC, proposing a "standstill" obligation on those same regulations would have overlapped with the already existing standstill obligation in Article 31 EEC.

Perhaps because of political difficulties in bringing about harmonisation,[228] the Commission's attitude towards Article 30 soon evolved, and in the second part of the 1960s it appeared to take a bolder approach with respect to this provision than in previous years.

Replying to parliamentary questions asked by Mr Deringer in March and May 1967,[229] the Commission defined the measures falling under the "mysterious" concept of Article 30 as,

> all laws, administrative provisions and administrative practices which hinder imports or exports which could otherwise take place, including those provisions and practices which make importation or exportation more difficult or costly than the disposal of domestic production. [Moreover,] provisions, which are equally applicable to domestic and imported products, do not as a rule constitute measures having equivalent effect to quantitative restrictions.

It was convincingly argued at the time that this reading of the scope of application of Article 30 EEC was neither so broad as to include any measure simply *affecting* inter-state trade, nor limited exclusively to rules *regulating* inter-state trade (as the earlier approach might have indicated).[230] Nevertheless, the Commission was indeed showing that it recognised that the potential reach of the new concept in Article 30 EEC could have been broader than that attributed to Article XI GATT, including measures imposed on importation or exportation (border measures), measures openly discriminating against imported products (de jure discriminatory measures), and even those measures equally applicable to both imported and domestic products (indistinctly applicable measures). However, as evidenced in the second sentence in the passage cited above, the Commission was willing to expand the per se prohibition in Article 30 to "equally applicable measures" only in certain circumstances. In other

progetti di regolamentazione a carattere tecnico che possano avere un'incidenza sugli scambi, ed una procedura di consultazione su richiesta della Commissione." Cf E Fanara, "Art 30" in R Quadri, R Monaco, A Trabucchi (eds), *Commentario al Trattato Istitutivo della Comunità Economica Europea* Vol 1 (Milano, Giuffré Editore, 1965) at 177.

[228] Note also that the ECJ in the famous *Costa v Enel* judgment expressly excluded that the Treaty harmonisation provisions were "capable of creating individual rights which national courts must protect". Case 6/64, *Flaminio Costa v ENEL.* [1964] ECR 585, para 5.

[229] Written questions No 118 8 Dec 1966, [1967] JO 122 and No 64 11 May, 1966, [1967] JO 11.

[230] A Meij and J Winter, "Measures Having an Effect Equivalent to Quantitative Restrictions", *CMLRev* (1976) 79 at 82–83.

words, the Commission was aware that it could not have applied *sic et sempliciter* the general prohibition of Article 30 EEC to equally applicable measures, since this would have meant a general prohibition of all national provisions regulating national markets. Reliance on the exceptions in Article 36 EEC could not have represented a sufficient counterbalance to such a sweeping approach. Nevertheless, the Commission did not foreclose its prerogative to employ the concept of "measures having equivalent effect" as the liberalising tool with regard to equally applicable measures, although it subjected this latter type of measures to a somewhat different approach from the per se prohibition of Article 30 EEC.

Writing in 1968, René Béraud, legal counsellor of the Commission, put forward what he believed were the conditions according to which "equally applicable measures" might be subjected to Community law. Although he denied that these measures should fall within the scope of application of Article 30 EEC,[231] Béraud believed that the concept of "abuse de droit" might afford a viable legal standard in deciding when a national market regulation violates the principles of free movement of goods. According to this author, the Member States' right to regulate the market should not be abused in the sense that (a) the right should be exercised only in the pursuit of a public policy objective and (b) the regulation must be necessary and not disproportionate vis-à-vis its objective.[232]

As will be further explained in the chapter dealing with the non-discrimination principle, Béraud's two conditions were to constitute the core of the Commission's official interpretation of the Article 30 EEC prohibition on "measures having equivalent effect",[233] as well as soon

---

[231] R Béraud, "Les mesures d'effet équivalent au sens des Arts 30 et suivants du Traité de Rome", *Revue Trimestrelle de Droit Européen* (1968) 265 at 289, "[…] ces mesures [que s'appliquent indistinctement aux produits nationaux et aux produits importés] sont d'une toute autre nature. Alors que l'objectif de l'Etat qui instaura une restriction quantitative est de protéger la production natinale, l'objectif poursuivi par ces réglementations est bien différent: il s'agit, en effet le plus souvent, non pas de la défense dees producteurs, mais de celle des consommateurs et c'est pourquoi de telle mesures doivent nécessairement s'appliquer, pour ne pas être inopérantes, à la production nationale comme aux importations. Dès lors, qualifier ces dispositions de mesures d'effect équivalent en tant qu'elles affectent les importations e par conséquent exiger leur élimination à l'égard des seuls produits imortés reviendrait à constester aux Etats membres le droit de réglementer le c ommerce. Or, nous ne trouvons ni dans les travaux préparatoires, ni dans le Traité, de fondements à cette contestation."
[232] *Ibid.*, at 290. The two conditions imposed on the Member States' right to regulate the market were the following: "La première est que ce droit ne saurait être utilisé que pour atteindre les objectifs—tels que sécurité publique, ordre public, mais aussi qualité, standardisation des produits,.. —en vue desquels il s'est développé dans nos Etats. La seconde est que la réglementation doit être à la fois nécessaire et suffisante ou, si l'on veut, efficace et non excessive à cette fin. L'Etat membre qui userait de ce droit en dehors de ces limites en gênant davantage les importations que la production nationale poursuivrait en réalité le même objectif qu'en instaurant un contingent."
[233] Commission Directive 70/50 of 22 Dec 1969, OJ L 13 (1970) 29. See below ch 2.

thereafter the pillars of the new jurisprudential doctrine of the Court of Justice concerning equally (or indistinctly) applicable *internal* measures.[234]

There being today only one norm regulating both non-pecuniary border measures and de jure discriminatory internal regulations,[235] there has not been much need for the Court to distinguish between "border" and "internal" measures (the real distinction resides between the judge-made concepts of "distinctly" and "indistinctly" applicable measures).[236] All these measures would fall, at least formally, under the prohibition of Articles 28 and 29 EC.[237] This is even more true with regard to the distinction within border measures between "quantitative restrictions" and "measures having equivalent effect", as the ECJ case-law clearly confirms. If numerical quotas, as well as absolute prohibitions on imports or exports, have been generally found to be "quantitative restrictions",[238] all other measures, even if technically they were "quantitative restrictions", have been deemed to constitute either measures of equivalent effect or more simply a violation of Articles 28–29 EC.[239]

However, notwithstanding the sometimes inaccurate descriptions given by the Court of Justice, it is clear that border measures as such are prohibited by Articles 28 and 29 and, as it will be emphasised shortly, may be justified only by reference to the list of public policy objectives in Article 30.[240]

C.   Exceptions

Contrary to what has been noted in relation to pecuniary border measures, both EC and WTO law maintain general exceptions which enable a Member to justify a violation of the general prohibition of quantitative restrictions.[241] Article 30 (ex 36) EC and Article XX (and Article XXI)

---

[234] *Dassonville-Cassis de Dijon* jurisprudence. See below chs 2–3.

[235] On the prohibition of de jure discrimination see below ch 2.

[236] See below ch 2.

[237] P Oliver, *Free Movement of Goods in the European Community* (London, Sweet & Maxwell, 1996) at 68, where it is however pointed out that "whereas quantitative restrictions were to be abolished as between the original Member States in 1966, this did not occur for measures of equivalent effect until 1 Jan, 1970."

[238] Case 34/79, *Regina v Maurice Donald Henn and John Frederick Ernest Darby* [1979] ECR 3795, although a similar restriction was imposed on like domestic products. See below section on "exceptions". Cf the ECJ *dicta* in Case 2/73, *Geddo v Ente Nazionale Risi* [1973] ECR 865, at 879, "the prohibition on quantitative restrictions covers measures which amount to a total or partial restrain of, according to the circumstances, imports, exports or goods in transit".

[239] P Oliver, *Free Movement of Goods in the European Community* (London, Sweet & Maxwell, 1996) at 66 and cases cited therein. Cf E White, "In Search of the Limits to Arts 30 of the EEC Treaty" 26 *CMLRev* (1989) 235 at 241 *et seq.*; G Tesauro, *Diritto Comunitario* (Padova, CEDAM, 1995) at 274 *et seq.*

[240] Cf Case 124/81, *Commission v United Kingdom* [1983] ECR 203.

[241] As previously discussed, EC law does not provide for a general exceptions with regard to the prohibition on customs duties and measures having equivalent effect. WTO law, at least formally, does.

GATT provide respectively that Articles 28–29 EC and XI GATT, though subject to certain significant conditions, do not prevent the adoption or enforcement by any Contracting Party of restrictions on imports or exports justified inter alia on grounds of public morality, or public security; the protection of health and life of humans, animals or plants.[242]

Premised on the belief that the (economic) interests of free trade cannot automatically override other (strictly non-economic) interests guaranteed by national measures, these two Articles provide for the justification option not only for the prohibition on quantitative restrictions embodied in Article 28 (ex 30) EC and Article XI GATT, but also for other EC and WTO trade-liberalisation rules (as for example the National Treatment principle). Although there will be other occasions during the course of the present analysis where the interpretation and application of these two provisions will be examined, it may be appropriate at this point to note a few relevant differences in the text of the two provisions in particular with regard to the "conditions" to which EC and WTO law subject the availability of the general public policy exception.

Article 30 EC states as follows:

> The provisions of Articles 28 and 29 shall not preclude prohibitions or restrictions on imports, exports or goods in transit *justified on* grounds of public morality, public policy or public security; the protection of health and life of humans, animals or plants; the protection of national treasures possessing artistic, historic or archaeological value; or the protection of industrial and commercial property. Such prohibitions or restrictions shall not, however, constitute a means of *arbitrary discrimination* or a *disguised restriction* on trade between Member States. [emphasis added]

Article XX GATT, on the other hand, states as follows:

> Subject to the requirement that such measures are not applied in a manner which would constitute a means of *arbitrary or unjustifiable discrimination* between countries where the same conditions prevail, or a *disguised restriction* on international trade, nothing in this Agreement shall be construed to prevent the adoption or enforcement by any Contracting Party of measures: [...]
>
> (a) *necessary to* protect public morals;
> (b) *necessary to* protect human, animal or plant life of health;
> (c) [..]
> (d) *necessary to* secure compliance with laws or regulations [...];
> (e) [..]

---

[242] Furthermore, in WTO law, Art XI:2 and Art XII provide for certain specific exceptions to the "General Elimination of Quantitative Restrictions" rule of Art XI:1, for examples for critical shortages of essential products or balance of payments purposes.

(f) *imposed for* the protection of national treasures of artistic, historic or archaeological value;

(g) *relating to* the conservation of exhaustible natural resources if such measures are made effective in conjunction with restrictions on domestic production or consumption;

(h) [..]

(i) [..]

(j) *essential to* the acquisitions or distribution of products in general or local short supply [...]. [emphasis added]

It cannot be doubted that Article 30 EC was drafted with Article XX GATT clearly in mind.[243] This is evidenced not only by the circumstance that certain of the public policy interests to be protected in Article XX GATT are reproduced *verbatim* in the first sentence of Article 30 EC, but more significantly, by the fact that the introductory clause of Article XX GATT, usually referred to as the "Chapeau", finds its almost identical replica in the second sentence of Article 30 EC.[244]

However, the two Articles differ in two important respects. First of all, with regard to the number of public policies listed in the two provisions at issue, Article XX GATT covers a larger sets of interests compared to those covered by Article 30 EC. Secondly, the "connection" between the particular public policy interest (ie the protection of public health) and the national measure which needs to be justified (like a quota) is quite different in the respective texts of Article 30 EC and Article XX GATT. While pursuant to Article 30 EC an import or export restriction complies with Articles 28 and 29 simply if it is *justified on* one of the public policy grounds expressly provided in Article 30, Article XX GATT requires that such restrictions, which are found to violate a GATT obligation, be either *necessary, essential* or *related to* one of the public policy justifications listed in subparagraphs (a) to (j). Although there is a range of "connectors" in Article XX GATT,[245] it could be argued that in general it is easier for national governments to successfully claim that a measure is *justified on grounds of,* for example, public health (according to Article 30 EC) than to

---

[243] J Scott, "Mandatory or Imperative Requirements in the EU and the WTO" in C Barnard and J Scott (eds), *The Law of the Single European Market: Unpacking the Premises* (Oxford, Hart Publishing, 2002) at 286.

[244] Note however that in Art 30 EC, contrary to Art XX GATT, there is no reference to *unjustifiable* discrimination.

[245] It may be suggested that, rather than on the different strength of the policy objectives listed in Art XX, the difference in the intensity of the several "connectors" of Art XX is based on the different scope of the several subparagraphs of Art XX. Thus, for example, "protection of human, animal or plant life or health" covers potentially a wider spectrum of national measures compared to those adopted for "conservation of exhaustible natural resources" (at least in its original meaning). See below in ch 2 on the prohibition of de jure discrimination the section dealing with the justification option.

prove that that same measure is *necessary to protect* human health (according to Article XX(b) GATT).

This non-alignment has to some extent been remedied (and in certain respects reversed) by the Court of Justice which, as already indicated in the previous section, construed the public policy exception of Article 30 in a quite strict manner from the very beginning. As the Court held in *Bauhuis v The Netherlands*,[246] Article 30,

> constitutes a derogation from the basic rule that all obstacles to the free movement of goods between Member States shall be eliminated and must be interpreted strictly.[247]

The Court's rigorous interpretation of Article 30 may be noted not only in the fact that (a) this provision is exclusively "directed to eventualities of a *non-economic* kind"[248] and (b) the list of public policy exceptions provided for in Article 30 is of an *exhaustive* nature,[249] but moreover in the circumstance that (c) the concept of "a justified restriction" within the meaning of Article 30 means that a trade restriction is permitted only if it is "*necessary* for attainment of its objective".[250] In brief, whenever a Member invokes Article 30 in order to justify a violation of the prohibition of border measures contained in Article 28, the Court of Justice requires not simply that the national measure at issue be somehow connected with ("justified on grounds of") one of the relevant public policies listed in Article 30, but, more rigorously, that that same measure comply with the

---

[246] Case 46/76, *Bauhuis v The Netherlands* [1977] ECR 5.

[247] *Ibid.*, para 12.

[248] Case 7/61, *Commission v Italy* [1961] ECR 317, [emphasis added]. Cf Case 288/83, *Commission v Ireland* (*Potato Imports*) [1985] ECR 1761, where Ireland required licences in respect of the import of potatoes originating in third countries and in free circulation in another Member State, prohibiting imports of such potatoes in the absence of such a licence.

[249] In line with the strict interpretation of Art 30 EC, the Court has rejected arguments, for example, that the term "public policy" can embrace concerns for consumer protection. Cf P Craig and G de Búrca, *EU Law* (Oxford, OUP, 1998) at 597 and cases cited therein.

[250] Case 251/78, *Firma Denkavit Futtermittel GmbH v Minister für Ernähung, Landwirtschaft und Forsten des Landes Nordrhein-Westfalen* [1979] ECR 3369, para 21, [emphasis added]: "Having regard to the foregoing considerations it is necessary, with reference to the question put by the national court, to ascertain next whether the restrictions of the kind laid down by the Viehseuchenverordnung 1957 keep within the restrictions placed by Art 36 [now 30] of the Treaty on the exceptions to the free movement of goods permitted by that provision. In fact it is clear from the wording thereof that the prohibitions or restrictions which it permits must be justified, that is to say necessary for attainment of its objective and may not constitute a means of arbitrary discrimination or a disguised restriction on trade between Member States." Cf Case 12/78, *Eggers v Freie Hansestadt Bremen* [1978] ECR 1935, para 30, where the Court held that "Art 36 [now 30] is an exception to the fundamental principle of the free movement of goods and must, therefore, be interpreted in such a way that its scope is not extended any further than is necessary for the protection of those interests which it is intended to secure". Cf P Oliver, *Free Movement of Goods in the European Community* (London, Sweet & Maxwell, 1996) at 185 and T Tridimas, *The General Principles of EC Law* (Oxford, OUP, 1999) at 133 *et seq*.

so-called "proportionality principle". Employed in this manner as a tool for limiting the availability of the public policy exception,[251] the application of the principle of proportionality usually entails the following three-part test: first, it must be established whether the measure is suitable or effective to achieve a legitimate public policy aim (the "suitability" test); secondly, it must be established whether the measure is necessary to achieve that aim, namely, whether there are other less restrictive means capable of producing the same result (the "least restrictive alternative" or "necessity" test); and thirdly, even if there are no less restrictive means, it must be established that the measure does not have an excessive or disproportionate effect on trade (the test of proportionality *stricto sensu*).[252]

The practical result of this reading by the Court of Justice is that the several tests constituting the proportionality principle have become the central requirements in an Article 30 analysis, the conditions provided for in the second sentence of Article 30 having been practically absorbed by the proportionality test and only very rarely constituting a further ground of appraisal.[253] By contrast, as will be examined in more detail in the next chapter, both GATT and WTO jurisprudence has had to reconcile two distinct aspects of Article XX GATT: on the one hand, the several and different "connectors" qualifying the public policy interests found in Article XX, subparagraphs (a) to (j) (ie "necessary", "related to", "essential", etc) and, on the other hand, the general requirements of the Chapeau of Article XX (ie prohibition on "arbitrary and unjustifiable discrimination" and "disguised restrictions on international trade").[254]

While several of these issues will be further examined in the subsequent chapters, this section will simply emphasise the inherent difficulty in justifying border measures on non-economic public policy grounds. Indeed, notwithstanding the existence of the above mentioned general exceptions, in practical terms, it is very rare to find an inherently discriminatory measure that is justified on one of the public policy grounds found in either Article 30 EC or Article XX GATT. This section examines a few cases in both EC and GATT/WTO case-law which illustrate this point.

---

[251] See below ch 4 on the "Reasonableness rule", where it will be shown how and where the proportionality principle is employed as the "primary norm".
[252] For more on the proportionality principle see E Ellis (ed), *The Principle of Proportionality in the Laws of Europe* (Oxford, OUP, 1999) and G de Búrca, "The Principle of Proportionality and its Application in EC Law", 13 YEL (1994) 105. For a detailed analysis of the proportionality principle employed as "primary norm" see below ch 4.
[253] J Snell, *Goods and Services in EC Law—A Study of the Relationship Between the Freedoms* (Oxford, OUP, 2002) at 181, noting that "there will be few, if any, measures that pass the proportionality test but still constitute arbitrary discrimination or a disguised restriction on trade."
[254] See more below in chs 2 and 3, the sections on the "justification options" of the prohibition of de jure and de facto discrimination.

1.   Article 30 EC

The inherent difficulty of justifying border measures on non-economic public policy grounds is evidenced in the jurisprudence of the European Court of Justice dealing, for example, with the "public morality" and "animal health" exceptions.

(a)   The "public morality" exception: Henn & Darby *and* Conegate   In *Regina v Henn & Darby*,[255] defendants Henn and Darby were convicted for importing Danish sex films and magazines in the UK in violation of a 1876 customs law, as amended in 1952, which forbade the import of "indecent or obscene articles". The defendants argued that the relevant UK laws were contrary to Article 28 EC and could not be justified by Article 30 EC since (a) the constituent territories of the UK differed significantly from one another with respect to their statutory and common law rules on what constituted "indecent or obscene" materials (non-uniformity of domestic laws) and, more important, (b) UK customs law was more severe than some of the constituent territories' rules governing similar domestic materials (different treatment between domestic and imported materials).

The Court first held that the total ban on imported goods constituted a quantitative restriction prohibited by Article 28, and then dealt with the question of whether or not the UK import ban was justified on grounds of public morality pursuant to Article 30 EC. The Court rejected the defendants' first argument for the following reasons:

> Each Member State is entitled to impose prohibitions on imports justified on grounds of public morality for the whole territory, as defined in Article 227 [now 299] of the Treaty, whatever the structure of its constitution may be and however the powers of legislating in regard to the subject in question may be distributed. The fact that certain differences exist between the laws enforced in the different constituent parts of a Member State does not thereby prevent that State from applying a unitary concept in regard to prohibitions on imports imposed, on grounds of public morality, on trade with other Member States.[256]

With regard to the second argument, the Court noted that there existed certain differences between the prohibition on importing the goods in question and the laws in force in the various constituent parts of the UK: while the former was absolute, the latter appeared to be less strict, in the sense that the mere possession of obscene articles for non-commercial purposes did not constitute a criminal offence anywhere in the UK and that,

---

[255] Case 34/79, [1979] ECR 3795.
[256] *Ibid.*, para 16.

even if it was generally forbidden, trade in such articles was nevertheless subject to certain exceptions, notably those in favour of articles having scientific, literary, artistic or educational interest. Having regard to those differences, it had been argued by the defendants that the UK import ban might not come within the second sentence of Article 30, according to which restrictions on imports justified on public policy grounds may not "constitute a means of arbitrary discrimination or a disguised restriction on trade between Member States".

The Court noted that the function of the provision in the second sentence of Article 30 is to prevent restrictions on trade based on the grounds mentioned in the first sentence of the same Article from being diverted from their proper purpose and used in such a way as either to create discrimination in respect of goods originating in other Member States or indirectly to protect certain national products. The Court decided that this was not the purport of a prohibition, such as that in force in the United Kingdom, on the importation of indecent or obscene articles.[257] The Court stated as follows:

> Whatever may be the differences between the laws on this subject in force in the different constituent parts of the United Kingdom, and notwithstanding the fact that they contain certain exceptions of limited scope, these laws, taken as a whole, have as their purpose the prohibition, or at least, the restraining, of the manufacture and marketing of publications or articles of an indecent or obscene character. In these circumstances it is permissible to conclude, on a comprehensive view, that there is no lawful trade in such goods in the United Kingdom.[258]

Thus, although the prohibition on domestic products on public morality grounds was not as strict as that imposed on imported products, the Court believed that "as a whole" the two regimes shared the same purpose and partially the same effect (no lawful trade in the UK).

This case may usefully be compared with the later case of *Conegate*,[259] in which the measure under review was again the UK ban on imports of indecent or obscene goods, in this case applied to imports of life-size dolls from Germany. The UK court asked the ECJ whether a prohibition on imports could be justified on grounds of public morality even though the State did not ban the manufacture or marketing of the same product within its national territory. The ECJ stated that it was for each Member State to determine the standards of public morality which prevailed in its territory, but rejected the public morality argument advanced by the British Government on the grounds that the protection of public morality

---

[257] *Ibid.*, para 21.
[258] *Ibid.*
[259] Case 121/85, *Conegate Ltd. v Commissioners of Customs and Excise* [1986] ECR 1007.

did not constitute a valid justification for treating differently the same products exclusively on the basis of their origin.[260] Following the approach taken in *Henn & Darby*, the Court specified the relevant criteria in these terms:

> Although it is not necessary [...] that the manufacture and marketing of the products whose importation has been prohibited should be prohibited in the territory of all the constituent parts, it must at least be possible to conclude from the applicable rules, taken as a whole, that their purposes is, in substance, to prohibit the manufacture and marketing of those products.[261]

The Court noted that, in the case at hand, the UK allowed the goods in question to be manufactured freely and marketed subject only to certain restrictions, namely an absolute prohibition on the transmission of the goods by post, a restriction on their public display and, in certain areas of the UK a system of licensing of premises for the sale of those goods to customers aged 18 years and over. The Court concluded that "such restrictions cannot however be regarded as equivalent in substance to a prohibition on manufacture and marketing."[262]

Notwithstanding the fact that the ECJ reached two different results in these two "public morality" cases, it appears that, at least on a formal level, the Court followed a uniform approach. A Member State is entitled to adopt a restriction on the importation of indecent or obscene materials into its territory on the grounds of public morality *only if* it also maintains an *equivalent* restriction on the manufacture and marketing of the same materials within its territory. Moreover, the domestic restriction may differ according to the different constituent parts of a Member State depending on the structure of its constitution and, more importantly, need not be as strict as the import restriction, as long as, taken as a whole, its purpose is, in substance, to prohibit the manufacture and marketing of like domestic products. In other words, while it may be possible to justify an absolute ban on both imported and domestic "indecent or obscene articles" for the protection of public morality (*Henn & Darby*), it is not enough to claim such public policy to justify a ban *exclusively* on imports (*Conegate*).

In GATT terminology, the measure at issue in *Henn & Darby* would probably fall within the scope of application of Article III:4, while the measure in *Conegate* would fall within Article XI. In the former case, the UK restrictions on importation of Danish sex films and magazines was

---

[260] *Ibid.*, para 16: "[A] Member State may not relay on grounds of public morality to prohibit the importation of goods from other Member States when its legislation contains no prohibition on the manufacture or marketing of the same goods on its territory."
[261] *Ibid.*, para 17.
[262] *Ibid.*, para 18.

supplemented by *similarly strict* restrictions on like domestic products. In the latter case, the UK restrictions on importation of German life-size dolls was not matched by *similarly strict* restrictions on like domestic goods. Notwithstanding the fact that one might not agree with the ECJ's evaluation in these two cases, it is evident that the question whether or not an import restriction finds a domestic parallel is clearly a factual determination to be carried out on a case-by-case basis. If one were to compare this factual determination with the one carried out in the *Asbestos* panel report in order to establish whether Article III:4 or Article XI applied to the French import ban on asbestos and asbestos containing products, it would not be too difficult to appreciate a high degree of similarity. If in both *Henn & Darby* and *Asbestos* the regulations applicable to domestic and foreign products led to the same result (the prohibition of trade in sex films and magazines on UK territory and the halting of the spread of asbestos and asbestos-containing products on French territory respectively), in *Conegate* the purpose of the rules applicable to domestic products was not, in substance, equivalent to that of the prohibition on the importation of life-size dolls.

This parallel is simply to emphasise the initial assumption that measures falling within the scope of application of Article XI (border measures which apply exclusively to imported products) are only very rarely justified by one of the public policy grounds found in Article 30 EC and Article XX GATT. In *Connegate* the "inherently discriminatory" nature of the measure under review was used by the Court as the ground for denying the very existence of a public policy justification. Prohibiting *only* the importation of indecent or obscene material, while allowing, albeit with some limitations, the manufacture and marketing of a domestic like product, cannot rationally be justified by claiming the purported goal of protecting public morality.

(b) *"Animal health" protection:* German crayfish *and* Bluhme   Two further cases also serve to illustrate in what exceptional circumstances import restrictions may be justified on public policy grounds. Here, contrary to the two previously discussed cases, the rigid approach of the Court of Justice with regard to border restrictions is evidenced in the strict application of the proportionality principle employed as a tool for limiting the availability of the public policy exception.

In the so-called *German crayfish* case,[263] the Court was called on to determine whether the German ban on imports of live European freshwater crayfish from Member States or from non-Member countries in free circulation in other Member States could be justified on the basis of Article 30 EC in order to prevent the risks of crayfish plague and faunal distortion

---

[263] Case C–131/93, *Commission v Germany* [1994] ECR I–3303.

within the German territory. Although the Court recognised that, in the absence of Community rules on the matter, it was for the Member States to decide upon the level at which they wished to protect the health and life of animals, the Court conditioned such freedom on the requirements of the free movement of goods.[264] In particular, while it noted that the purpose of the national measure in question—to protect the health and life of native crayfish—was not disputed, the Court eventually found that the environmental measure failed the principle of proportionality (in particular the "necessity" test) because the German Government could have adopted "less restrictive measures".[265] The Court stated that,

> [...] instead of simply prohibiting imports of all species of live freshwater crayfish, the Federal Republic of Germany could have confined itself to making consignments of crayfish from other Member States or already in free circulation in the Community subject to health checks and only carrying out checks by sample if such consignments were accompanied by a health certificate issued by the competent authorities of the dispatching Member State certifying that the product in question presented no risk to health, or instead confined itself to regulating the marketing of crayfish in its territory, in particular by subjecting to authorization only the restocking of national waters with species likely to be carrying the disease and restricting release of animals into the wild and restocking in areas in which native species are to be found.[266]

Since the defending government had not convincingly shown that such alternatives, involving less serious restrictions for intra-Community trade, were incapable of effectively protecting the interests pleaded, the Court found the import prohibition at issue in breach of EC law.[267]

---

[264] *Ibid.*, para 16.

[265] The Federal Government had argued that "a total ban on importing live freshwater crayfish was the only way of effectively protecting native crayfish against aphanomycosis since not only animals from non-member countries but also species originating from other Member States are capable of carrying the crayfish plague virus. Furthermore, the rules in question were necessary to limit as much as possible the proliferation of non-indigenous species in natural stretches of water in Germany so as to protect the genetic identity of local populations of crayfish against faunal distortion which occurs upon the introduction in national territory of animals of the same species but of different origin." *Ibid.*, para 20.

[266] *Ibid.*, para 25.

[267] The Court noted, moreover, the following: "the conditions which importers are required to observe under the authorization system applied by the German authorities so as to mitigate the harshness of the import ban laid down by the Federal legislation, which require the traders concerned to comply with all health measures, to use imported crayfish in a way which prevents them from being released into the environment and to ensure that the water in which they are kept is disinfected, show that the defendant Government itself considers that those means, less restrictive of intra-Community trade than a total import ban, are sufficient for achieving the objective of protecting native crayfish against crayfish plague and faunal distortion." *Ibid.*, para 27.

In *Bluhme*,[268] the fifth chamber of the Court of Justice had to decide whether a prohibition on the importation or the keeping of bees on the Danish island of Læsø so as to protect an endangered native species (*Apis mellifera mellifera*, more commonly known as Læsø brown bee) complied with Articles 28–30 EC Treaty. It found that such a regulation constituted a measure having an effect equivalent to a quantitative restriction within the meaning of Article 28, but held that such a measure had to be regarded as justified, under Article 30, on the ground of the protection of the health and life of animals. The Court's decision in *Bluhme* is interesting not only for the ultimate result (import ban found to comply with EC law), but for both its broad reading of the traditional scope of the "human, animals, plants" exception in Article 30 and for its reliance on international environmental law in determining the "proportionality" of the incriminated measure. With regard to the former, the Court seemed to incorporate within the scope of Article 30 more modern notions on biological diversity and ecosystem protection when it noted that,

> measures to preserve an indigenous animal population with distinct characteristics contribute to the maintenance of biodiversity by ensuring the survival of the population concerned [and thus] are capable of being justified under Article 30 of the Treaty.[269]

With regard to the proportionality review, the Court expressly availed itself of the Rio Convention in order to establish the reasonableness of the relation between the specific measure at issue and its purported environmental objective. The Court stated as follows:

> Conservation of biodiversity through the establishment of areas in which a population enjoys special protection, which is a method recognised in the Rio Convention, especially Article 8a thereof, is already put into practice in Community law [in particular, by means of the special protection areas provided for in Council Directive 79/409/EEC of 2 April 1979 on the conservation of wild birds (OJ 1979 L 103, p. 1), or the special conservation areas provided for in Directive 92/43].[270]

---

[268] Case C–67/97, *Criminal Proceedings Against Ditlev Bluhme* [1998] ECR I–8033.
[269] *Ibid.*, para 33. Cf D French, "The Changing Nature of 'Environmental Protection': Recent Developments Regarding Trade and the Environment in the European Union and the World Trade Organisation", 47 *Netherlands International Law Review* (2000) 1, at 19–20. The Court added that "From the point of view of such conservation of biodiversity, it is immaterial whether the object of protection is a separate subspecies, a distinct strain within any given species or merely a local colony, so long as the populations in question have characteristics distinguishing them from others and are therefore judged worthy of protection either to shelter them from a risk of extinction that is more or less imminent, or, even in the absence of such risk, on account of a scientific or other interest in preserving the pure population at the location concerned." Case C–67/97, *Bluhme*, above n 268, para 34.
[270] *Ibid.*, para 36. The Court determined moreover that the threat of the disappearance of the Læsø brown bee was "undoubtedly genuine." *Ibid.*, para 37.

In conclusion, even these two more recent cases should give an idea of the circumstances in which a measure openly restricting the importation of goods may be justified on public policy grounds according to Article 30 EC. In particular, the decision in *Bluhme* shows that, even when the impact on intra-Community trade is minimal, an import restriction will be held to comply with EC law only when the regulating State is able to demonstrate that there are indeed no other less-restrictive alternatives capable of pursuing the specific public policy objective.

2. *Article XX GATT*

According to the practice of GATT panels, the general public policy exception of Article XX is not a positive rule establishing obligations in itself, but a list of general exceptions to obligations otherwise assumed by WTO Members. For this reason, the provisions of Article XX, just like the provisions of all other exceptions in WTO law, have to be construed narrowly,[271] thus indicating a ranking of interests in favour of free trade.[272] However, there is evidence in WTO jurisprudence, in particular in Appellate Body's reports, of a willingness to adopt a less clear-cut, more nuanced approach, which tries to balance the right of a Member to invoke a general exception under Article XX, on the one hand, and the substantive rights of the other Members provided for by the GATT, on the other hand, with due regard to the interests at stake.[273]

The list of general public policy justifications contained in Article XX GATT, like the list in Article 30 EC, is regarded as an exhaustive list. On the other hand, as mentioned above, contrary to Article 30 EC, the "necessity requirement" is expressly provided for in the text of Article XX, albeit not with regard to all justification grounds.[274]

Once again, while the specific features of the general exception provision of Article XX GATT will be dealt in greater details in the chapters dealing with the National Treatment principle, in this section I propose once again to focus simply on the inherent difficulty in justifying

[271] Cf A Mattoo and P Mavroidis, "Trade, Environment and the WTO: the Dispute Settlement Practice Relating to Art XX of GATT", in EU Petersmann (ed), *International Trade Law and the GATT/WTO Dispute Settlement System* (London, Kluwer Law International, 1997) at 334. For a critical view on establishing a hierarchy between the obligations under the GATT and the exceptions to those obligations see D McRae, "GATT Art XX and the WTO Appellate Body", in M Bronkers and R Quick (eds), *New Directions in International Economic Law* (London, Kluwer Law International, 2000) at 232.
[272] M Hilf, "Power, Rules and Principles—Which Orientation for WTO/GATT Law?", 4 *JIEL* (2001) 111 at 128.
[273] *Ibid.*, citing both the Appellate Body Reports on *US–Shrimp*, WT/DS58/AB/R, circulated 12 Oct 1998, adopted 6 Nov 1998 above, para 156 and *EC–Hormones*, WT/DS48/AB/R, circulated 16 Jan 1998, adopted 13 Feb 1998, above para 104.
[274] See below sections on "Justification options" in chs 2 and 3 dealing with the National Treatment principle.

"border measures" on non-economic, public policy grounds, as evidenced in two GATT panel reports dealing respectively with the issues of "animal" and "human health" protection.

(a) "Animal health" protection and the GATT Panel Report in Canadian Tuna
One of the first reports, if not the first one, in which a GATT panel had to apply the general exception provision of Article XX was the *US— Prohibition of Imports of Tuna and Tuna Products from Canada*, adopted in 1982.[275] In this case, the Canadian Government complained that the US prohibition on imports of tuna and tuna products from Canada was contrary to Articles I, XI and XIII GATT. The US ban had followed the seizure of 19 fishing vessels and the arrest by Canadian authorities of a number of US fishermen engaged in fishing for albacore tuna within 200 miles of the West Coast of Canada without authorisation by the Canadian Government, in waters regarded by Canada as being under its fisheries jurisdiction and regarded by the United States as being outside any State's tuna fisheries jurisdiction. The Panel found without much discussion that the US ban constituted a prohibition in terms of Article XI:1 (and was not justified under any of the exceptions specifically provided for in Article XI:2).[276]

The Panel then examined whether the US measure could be justified under Article XX(g), which provides that, subject to the additional requirements of the Chapeau, the General Agreement does not prevent the adoption or enforcement by any Contracting Party of measures relating to the conservation of exhaustible natural resources if such measures are made effective in conjunction with restrictions on domestic production or consumption.

In its finding that the US representative had not provided sufficient evidence that the import prohibition complied with the requirements of Article XX(g), the Panel focused on whether the US import ban (1) had been made effective in conjunction with restrictions on domestic production or consumption and (2) actually related to the conservation of tuna.

With regard to the first requirement, the panel noted that, although there had been indirect restrictions on the "production" in the United States of Pacific and Atlantic yellowfin tuna, bluefin and bigeye tuna, no restrictions had been applied to the catch or landings of any other species of tuna, such as albacore (the only tuna found within the territorial waters of Canada). Moreover, no domestic measures were applied in the United States, which restricted the domestic consumption of tuna and tuna products. Accordingly, the Panel concluded that the US ban on imports of all tuna and tuna products from Canada had not been made effective

---

[275] Panel Report on *United States—Prohibition of Imports of Tuna and Tuna Products from Canada* (*Canadian Tuna*), L/5198, adopted on 22 Feb 1982, BISD 29S/91.
[276] *Ibid.*, paras 4.4 and 4.6.

in conjunction with restrictions on US domestic production and consumption on all tuna and tuna products.[277]

With regard to the second and most contested issue,[278] the panel noted that the US prohibition of imports of all tuna and tuna products from Canada had been imposed in response to the Canadian arrest of US vessels fishing albacore tuna, and indicated, rather obscurely, that it "could not find that this particular action would in itself constitute a measure of a type listed in Article XX."[279]

Notwithstanding the fact that the circumstances in which the import ban was adopted showed that such measure had not really been taken for conservation purposes and that Article XX(g) specifically requires the existence of an equivalent restriction on domestic production or consumption, the Panel's emphasis on the great regulatory disparity between domestic and Canadian production and consumption of tuna and tuna products demonstrates the difficulty in justifying a "restriction on importation" in violation of Article XI.

(b)   "Human health protection" and the GATT Panel Report in Thai Cigarettes
In *Thailand—Restrictions on Importation of and Internal Taxes on Cigarettes* (also known as the *Thai Cigarettes* dispute),[280] the panel noted that

---

[277] *Ibid.*, para 4.12.
[278] The US Government had argued that, although Art XX(g) did not require that the exclusive motivation or effect of the measure under review necessarily be conservation, its effect was consistent with the international management approach to conservation of tuna. The United States, in fact, claimed that the Canadian seizure of US vessels and the arrest of US fishermen constituted a unilateral measure, which significantly impaired the international management approach of the Inter-American Tropical Tuna Commission (IATTC) aimed at the conservation of global tuna stocks. Accordingly, the prohibition on the importation of tuna from Canada had been taken to promote and encourage international co-operation in conservation of tuna, and to dissuade other countries from claiming unilaterally 200-mile jurisdiction over tuna stocks and from seizing US tuna vessels under such claims.
Canada had replied that, although the United States had a genuine interest in the conservation of tuna stocks (and Tuna, Canada agreed, indeed was an "exhaustible natural resource"), the specific event, which triggered the import prohibition, was not a general concern on the part of the United States about Canadian policies and actions related to the conservation of tuna, but more simply the seizure of a number of commercial fishing vessels and the arrest of US fishermen. Observing that the United States and one other country were standing alone in not recognising coastal State jurisdiction over tuna, Canada claimed that the import ban (as well as the US legislation upon which such measure was based, in particular s 205 of the Fishery Conservation and Management Act), was in effect intended to be a lever to dissuade Canada and other nations from enforcing their domestic laws to the detriment of commercial interests of the US tuna industry. In fact, Canada added, the import prohibition was lifted, not when Canadian conservation policies changed, but when Canadian and United States authorities reached an interim understanding providing reciprocal access for tuna fishermen of each country to waters under the fisheries jurisdiction of the other beyond the 12-mile limit as well as other provisions related to access to ports. There was nothing in the arrangement that related in any way to conservation of albacore or any other tuna species. *Ibid.*, paras 3.7–3.20.
[279] *Ibid.*, para 4.13.
[280] Panel Report, DS10/R, adopted on 7 Nov 1990, BISD 37S/200.

Thailand had not granted licences for the importation of cigarettes during the past 10 years, and consequently found that Thailand had acted inconsistently with Article XI. Thailand claimed that, if contrary to Article XI, its import restriction were justified by Article XX(b), which provides an exception for measures "necessary to protect human, animal or plant life or health". The principal health objectives advanced by Thailand to justify its import restrictions were to protect the public from harmful ingredients in imported cigarettes (quality concerns) and to reduce the consumption of cigarettes in Thailand (quantity concerns).

Referring to previous GATT panel practice, the Panel stated that the Thai import restrictions could be considered to be "necessary" in terms of Article XX(b) *only if* there were no alternative measure consistent with the General Agreement, or less consistent with it, which Thailand could reasonably be expected to employ to achieve its health policy objectives.[281]

With regard to the quality concerns, the Panel found that a non-discriminatory regulation implemented on a national treatment basis in accordance with Article III:4 requiring complete disclosure of ingredients, coupled with a ban on unhealthy substances, would be an alternative measure consistent with the General Agreement in order to address the quality-related policy objectives currently pursued by Thailand through an import ban on all cigarettes whatever their ingredients.[282]

With regard to the quantity concerns, the Panel first noted the views expressed by the World Health Organisation (WHO) that the demand for cigarette was influenced by cigarettes advertisements and that bans on advertising could therefore curb such demand. It then found that a ban on the advertisement of cigarettes of both domestic and foreign origin would normally meet the requirements of Article III:4 GATT.[283] Moreover, upon examination of the resolutions of the WHO on smoking, the Panel noted that the health measures recommended by the WHO in these resolutions were non-discriminatory and concerned all, not just imported, cigarettes.[284] The Panel also observed that a common consequence of import restrictions was the promotion of domestic production and the fostering of interests in the maintenance of that production.[285]

The panel therefore found that there existed various measures consistent with the General Agreement which were reasonably available to Thailand to control the quality and quantity of cigarettes smoked and which, taken together, could achieve the health policy goals that the Thai Government pursued by restricting the importation of cigarettes inconsistently with Article XI:1, and held that Thailand's practice of permitting the sale of

---

[281] *Ibid.*, para 75.
[282] *Ibid.*, para 77.
[283] *Ibid.*, para 78.
[284] *Ibid.*, para 80.
[285] *Ibid.*

domestic cigarettes while not permitting the importation of foreign cigarettes was an inconsistency with the General Agreement not "necessary" within the meaning of Article XX(b).[286]

Once again, the "inherently discriminatory" nature of the Thai measures under review constituted the principal ground for the Panel's finding that those measures were *not* necessary to protect human life or health. If the objective is to ensure the quality and reduce the quantity of cigarettes sold in a country, banning the importation of foreign cigarettes while permitting the sale of domestic ones can hardly represent a measure which is taken in pursuance of that objective, or at least, of that objective alone. It is in fact more probable that that measure is taken principally in order to afford protection to domestic products.

As a matter of fact, the Thai Government had advanced at least two grounds in order to justify the necessity of an inherently discriminatory measure. First of all, Thailand argued that cigarettes manufactured in the United States were more harmful than Thai cigarettes because of unknown chemicals placed by the United States cigarette companies in their cigarettes, partly to compensate for lower tar and nicotine levels. Secondly, Thailand argued that while competition had desirable effects in international trade in goods, this did not apply to cigarettes, where competition leads to the use of better marketing techniques (including advertising), a wider availability of cigarettes, a possible reduction of prices, and perhaps improvements in their quality. Moreover, as evidenced by WHO reports, once a developing country market in cigarettes was opened, the US cigarette industry would exert great efforts to force governments to accept terms and conditions which undermined public health. This would leave governments with no effective tool to carry out public health policies since advertising bans were easily circumvented and modern marketing techniques were used to boost sales.[287]

As previously indicated, the Panel correctly rejected the argument that US cigarettes were more harmful than Thai cigarettes on the basis that the Thai Government could have required, on a national treatment basis, complete disclosure of ingredients, coupled with a ban on unhealthy substances. If the objective was to avoid certain unhealthy substances in cigarettes, a non-discriminatory ban on such substances would have been as effective as a discriminatory ban on foreign cigarettes.[288]

---

[286] *Ibid.*, para 81.
[287] *Ibid.*, paras 27–28. WHO experts testified before the Panel that "if the multilateral tobacco companies entered the market, the poorly-financed public health programmes would be unable to compete with the marketing budgets of these companies, as had been the case in other Asian countries whose markets had been opened. As a result, cigarette consumption and, in turn, death and disease attributable to smoking would increase." *Ibid.*, para 52.
[288] More complex would have been to demonstrate whether any substance contained by foreign cigarettes were indeed "unhealthy". See below discussion in ch 4 on the SPS Agreement and the *EC–Hormones* case.

The argument based on the strength of multinational "marketing" techniques, advanced by Thailand and strongly backed up by WHO experts, seemed worthy of more consideration than was attributed to it by the Panel.[289] Noting how Thailand might restrict the supply of cigarettes in a manner consistent with the General Agreement by maintaining governmental monopolies on the importation and domestic sale of cigarettes, the Panel stated merely that it could not accept Thailand's argument that "competition between imported and domestic cigarettes would necessarily lead to an increase in the total sales of cigarettes and that Thailand therefore had no option but to prohibit cigarette imports".[290]

The Panel's disposal of this latter argument confirms once again the strong presumption under WTO law against the justifiability of an import ban or an inherent discriminatory measure, even if the alleged public policy behind the measure at issue deals with an important policy such as public health.

As will be more fully discussed in later chapters, the *Thai Cigarettes* dispute also illustrates (1) how there may exist several forms or layers of discrimination between imported and domestic products and (2) how these several forms are treated differently for the purposes of the public policy justifications. While an import ban on foreign cigarettes, such as that applied by the Thai government, fell under Article XI:1 and could not be justified on the basis of public health, a general ban on all cigarette advertising, according to the *Thai Cigarettes* Panel, would have been consistent with the National Treatment principle of the General Agreement. Although such an advertising ban might create "unequal competitive opportunities" between the existing Thai supplier of cigarettes and new, foreign suppliers and be therefore contrary to Article III:4 (a case of material or de facto discrimination), it would have been regarded as "unavoidable and therefore necessary within the meaning of Article XX(b) because additional advertising rights would risk stimulating demand for cigarettes."[291] Notwithstanding the fact that both an import ban on foreign cigarettes and a general ban on all cigarette advertising may be characterised as having protectionist or discriminatory effects, the former is only very exceptionally justifiable on public policy grounds because of its

---

[289] Cf R Howse, "Managing the Interface between International Trade Law and the Regulatory State: What Lessons Should (and Should Not) Be Drawn from the Jurisprudence of the United States Dormant Commerce Clause" in T Cottier and P Mavroidis (eds), *Regulatory Barriers and the Principle of Non-Discrimination in World Trade Law* (Ann Arbor, University of Michigan Press, 2000) at 147–48, "The Panel completely ignored this real world context—it simply assumed that a regulatory state of the level of development, and under the constraints, that characterized Thailand would have the capacity to bring US multinationals effectively under its regulatory control."

[290] Panel Report on *Thai Cigarettes*, above n 137, para 79. Cf J Kurtz, "A General Investment Agreement in the WTO? Lessons from ch 11 of NAFTA and the OECD Multilateral Agreement on Investment", *Jean Monnet Working Paper* (NYU School of Law, 2002) at 34–5.

[291] Panel Report on *Thai Cigarettes*, above n 137, para 78.

inherently discriminatory nature and direct negative effect on trade. By contrast, the protectionist effects of the latter measure (advertising ban) are only indirect and do not affect trade as negatively as an import ban. This makes the advertising ban an easier candidate for justification on grounds of public health.

D.   Conclusions

Notwithstanding the similarity in the "normative content" of EC and WTO rules dealing with quantitative restrictions, both mandating the outright prohibition of this type of measures, in practical terms, while the EEC was able to eliminate them within the first 15 years, the GATT Contracting Parties and now WTO Members have taken a relatively long time in effectively implementing the Article XI original mandate. This is not to say that the GATT Contracting Parties should have followed the Community's pace in eliminating quantitative restrictions, since clearly it would not have been feasible, let alone appropriate, for the majority of them to do so. This is just to put things into perspective and to explain why two similarly worded provisions (Article 28 EC and Article XI GATT) have been employed in different manners.[292]

It is thus not very difficult to understand why, in EC law, quotas and other non-pecuniary border measures have not attracted much attention. First, the Member States were able to quickly dispose of these barriers. Secondly, a dispute similar to the one in GATT/WTO law between non-pecuniary border *v* internal measures does not exist within the EC context principally because Articles 28–29 EC were soon interpreted to "regulate" *any* measure restricting trade, independently of their border/internal or quantitative/qualitative nature. However, this does not mean that in EC law there do not exist different normative approaches depending on the type of governmental measure restricting trade among Member States. As will be examined in the next chapters, the Court of Justice has employed the prohibition of "quantitative restrictions and measures having equivalent effect" in Article 28 EC in order to regulate different categories of national rules in different manner.[293] Such a multi-normative function of Article 28 EC in the jurisprudence of the Court of Justice may be explained by the original "division of labour" of the Treaty of Rome. As suggested above, the Community had perhaps too ambitiously relied on harmonising legislation as the principal tool for dealing with

---

[292] This is true even taking into consideration the existence in the GATT of specific exceptions to the general prohibition on import and export restrictions. See Arts XI:2 and XII.
[293] See below chs 2, 3 and 4.

market barriers stemming from (apparently) origin-neutral regulation (of a non-fiscal nature).[294]

In the GATT/WTO context, on the other hand, the original dual normative approach to non-pecuniary measures restricting trade in goods has been preserved: on the one hand, the "negative integration" rule of Articles XI (requiring the elimination of border measures) and, on the other, the "judicial integration" rule of Article III:4 (requiring that internal measures do not discriminate on the basis of the product's nationality or origin). Given the different normative content of these two rules and the fact that quotas and other non-pecuniary border measures were still heavily used to regulate and restrict trade, disputes over the scope of application of Article XI (and consequently Article III:4) have frequently been brought before panels.

An analysis of GATT panel practice and WTO jurisprudence shows that, in accordance with the wording of Article XI, a measure will fall within the scope of application of Article XI, rather than Article III, if it constitutes a "restriction on importation or exportation". First of all, it is necessary to take into consideration the *trade restrictive effects* of the measure under review. However, in order to establish an infringement of Article XI:1, one needs not prove "actual" trade effects, but simply "potential" trade effects. Secondly, and only with regard to restrictions on importation, Article XI:1 will catch trade restrictive measures which *directly regulate* the importation of products from another Contracting Party and *apply exclusively* to imported products. If the measure does not affect importation as such or it applies, albeit not in an identical manner, to both domestic and imported products, the measure will be caught by Article III:4, rather than Article XI:1. Accordingly, on the one hand, the term "restrictions on importation and exportation" has been interpreted *broadly* to include measures other than quotas and import or export licences, as well as non-binding governmental measures. At the same time, however, with regard to restriction on importation only, the same term has been interpreted *strictly* to exclude both internal measures and measures that are part of a broader regulatory scheme applying to both domestic and imported products.

Like the two criteria employed in EC and WTO law in order to distinguish between pecuniary border measures and pecuniary internal measures (is the charge imposed at the border + does the charge apply to imported products only), the two criteria employed in WTO law to determine whether a non-pecuniary measure is covered by Article XI show that the measures prohibited by Article XI are "inherently discriminatory measures." With the dubious exception of import prohibitions based on process standards, the general approach of both GATT panel practice and

---

[294] See above section on "Arts 28–29 EC" and below ch 2.

WTO jurisprudence clearly focuses on the non-discrimination principle of Article III:4, limiting the applicability of the general prohibition of Article XI to a restricted set of non-pecuniary border measures.

Notwithstanding the existence in EC and WTO law of general exceptions, in practical terms, it is very rare to find a measure of the type covered by Article XI GATT (ie an inherently discriminatory measure) justified (or even justifiable) on one of the public policy grounds found in Article 30 EC and Article XX GATT.

The only difference between the two regimes that is worthy of notice may be that in WTO case-law there appears to be, unfortunately only at the formal level, more deference towards Member's regulatory prerogatives. Even if the measure under review is of an inherently discriminatory nature, Panels do examine the arguments advanced by the defending Member and explain the reasoning behind the finding that the measure at hand is not justified on public policy grounds. In EC jurisprudence, on the contrary, the mere existence of an inherent discriminatory measure is usually enough for the Court to reject the defence based on public policy. This difference stems not only from differences in the perceived legitimacy of the EC and WTO adjudicating bodies, but also from the existence of several layers of social, economic and cultural diversities between the national communities of the two systems. Thailand's argument, based on the strength of multinational "marketing" techniques, holds some value only if one takes into consideration the level of economic and cultural development which characterises that country, in particular in light of the scarce resources available to the Thai Government to contrast the powerful US cigarette industry. This same argument would probably not even be taken into account if raised in a dispute between EC Members.

2

Judicial Integration—First Layer: The National Treatment Principle and the Prohibition of De Jure Discrimination

LTHOUGH THE HISTORY of the non-discrimination principle concerning international economic matters extends back for centuries, it is generally believed that customary international law does not impose a non-discrimination obligation on nations in the conduct of their international trading relationships, these latter having always been regarded as free to regulate their economic and monetary affairs internally and externally as they see fit.[1] Without having to assess the merit of this contention, it is sufficient to underline that in light of the many reciprocal international (bilateral and multilateral) agreements in which the non-discrimination principle appears, it plays today an unquestionably prominent role in the field of international economic law, and in particular in the regulation (and liberalisation) of international trade.[2] Thus, unsurprisingly, the principle of non-discrimination constitutes a fundamental pillar in both WTO and EC law.

The principle of non-discrimination, as applied in the context of international economic law, generally encapsulates two types of non-discrimination norms: the Most-Favoured-Nation (MFN) principle and the National-Treatment (NT) principle. In its broadest terms, the first norm requires "nation A to give equal treatment to economic transactions originating in, or destined for, other countries entitled to the benefit of the norm" and the second norm requires "that a nation treat within its own borders, goods, services, persons, etc, originating from outside its borders,

---

[1] P Malanczuk, *Akehurst's Modern Introduction to International Law* (London and New York, Routledge, 1997) at 223; J Jackson, *World Trade and the Law of GATT* (New York, The Bobs-Merrill Co, 1969) and *The Jurisprudence of GATT and the WTO* (Cambridge, CUP, 2000); E Laing, "Equal Access/Non-discrimination and Legitimate Discrimination in International Economic Law", *Wisconsin International Law Journal* (Spring, 1996) 246.

[2] EU Petersmann, *Constitutional Functions and Constitutional Problems of International Economic Law: International and Domestic Foreign Trade Law and Foreign Trade Policy in the United States, the European Community and Switzerland* (Fribourg, University Press, 1991).

in the same manner that it treats those which are of domestic origin".[3] As will be later explained, both norms forbid the use of the *"nationality"* of the economic transaction as the regulatory criterion. In other words, the nationality of the good or service is considered as an *"illegitimate criterion"* in the exercise of regulatory powers.

Contrary to the broad principle of equality, which requires, in very simple terms, that "like" should be treated in "like manner" and "unlike" in "unlike manner", the scope of application of both the MFN and NT principles is, at least in their purest form, much limited, banning only the use of *nationality* as the regulatory criterion.[4] However, as will be explored in particular in chapter 3, this scope will greatly increase when the NT (and MFN) principles are given a broad definition extending to more subtle and indirect forms of discriminations based on nationality.

The present analysis will be confined to the second of the two types of non-discrimination rules based on nationality, namely the National Treatment principle as employed in WTO and EC law. There are at least two reasons for this limitation. First, the two types of non-discrimination norms share for the most part many similar concepts (ie "origin of the product", "like product", "less favourable treatment", "public policy justification") and thus in several instances their analysis would be repetitive. Secondly, it is the National Treatment principle which is the more controversial obligation. In fact, between the two non-discrimination principles—MFN and NT—the former constitutes for the Member States a less "restrictive" or "intrusive" obligation compared to the latter, since only under the National Treatment obligation is a Member State not allowed to grant special protection to goods manufactured or services provided by its *own nationals*. This is certainly evidenced in EC law where the MFN principle has rarely been invoked.[5] In WTO law, the less intrusive nature of the MFN obligation vis-à-vis the NT obligation can be clearly noted in the General Agreement on Trade in Services (GATS): while the MFN obligation applies across the board with regard to any measure affecting trade in services (Article II.1), albeit subject to temporally limited exceptions (Article II.2), the NT obligation applies only in the service sectors which have been listed in the Member's schedule of commitments and are subject to the conditions inscribed therein (Article XVII.1). In other words,

---

[3] J Jackson, *The Jurisprudence of GATT and the WTO* (Cambridge, CUP, 2000), ch 5 "Equality and discrimination in international economic law: the General Agreement on Tariffs and Trade", at 57.

[4] This is a central point which is at times overlooked in both legal writings and case-law. For an example of the former, G More "The Principle of Equal Treatment: From Market Unifier to Fundamental Right?", in P Craig and G de Búrca (eds), *Evolution of EU Law* (Oxford, OUP, 1999) 517; and for one of the latter, Panel Report on *EC—Measures Affecting Asbestos and Asbestos Containing Products* (*EC–Asbestos*), WT/DS135R, circulated 18 Sept 2000, adopted 5 April 2001. See more in ch 3 on the National Treatment principle and the prohibition of de facto discrimination.

[5] Cf old Art 33 with regard to "goods" and Art 54 (ex 65) with regard to "services".

under the GATS, while MFN is a general obligation, NT is a specific obligation. In the continuum line between shallow and deep integration, the MFN principle clearly sits on the *shallower* side, while the NT principle on the *deeper* side.

As explained above, the general principle of non-discrimination as employed in WTO and EC law should not be characterised as a "negative integration" norm. Its principal function is in fact to impose a *positive* criterion (or standard), which Member States must comply with when exercising their regulatory authority. Contrary to rules of "negative integration *stricto sensu*", which restrict or prohibit the use by Member States of specific types of measures (such as tariffs or quotas), the non-discrimination principle "simply" requires Member States to make sure that any measure adopted for regulatory purposes affects in the same manner, in law and fact, the marketing of domestic and imported products. In other words, as long as imported products are not treated less favourably than domestic products, Member States are at liberty to adopt, implement and enforce *any* type of measure regulating any aspect of the life of a product, from the manner in which a product is manufactured or produced (process standards), to its characteristics (product standards) and the way in which it is sold in the marketplace (marketing standards).

I have proposed to define the non-discrimination principle as a form of "judicial integration", since, in light of its general nature, it is usually up to the "judiciary" to manage its application and, most importantly, as the subsequent analysis will show, to define its normative content. In this regard, the role of the European Court of Justice within the EC and the Appellate Body within the WTO has been, and will continue to be critical.

In this chapter, the analysis will focus exclusively on the purest, and thus clearest, form of the National Treatment principle, the prohibition of formal or de jure discrimination.[6] Such a prohibition represents a straightforward norm, whether one uses the more technical WTO-style definition—each Member State shall accord to goods (and services) of other Member States treatment no less favourable than that it accords to its own like goods (and services),[7] or the more general EC-style definition—discrimination on grounds of nationality shall be prohibited.[8]

---

[6] Ch 3 will in turn address the more intricate discrimination norm, that is the prohibition of de facto discrimination.

[7] I have paraphrased from the most recent definition of the National Treatment obligation as found in Art XVII of the General Agreement on Trade in Services (GATS), "In the sectors inscribed in its Schedule, and subject to any conditions and qualifications set out therein, each Member State shall accord to services and service suppliers of any other Member, in respect of all measures affecting the supply of services, treatment no less favourable than that it accords to its own like services and service suppliers."

[8] See the "wondering" Art 12 (ex Art 6 EC, ex Art 7 EEC), "Within the scope of application of this Treaty, and without prejudice to any special provisions contained therein, any discrimination on grounds of nationality shall be prohibited".

This apparently simple norm fits perfectly within a construct for the liberalisation of international trade. Much like the rules requiring the elimination of border measures,[9] the prohibition of formal discrimination based on nationality is nothing other than a prohibition on the very negation of the concept of trade among States. A national measure which discriminates on the sole basis of the foreign origin (import) or destination (export) of the good (or service), thus affording protection to domestic production, clearly represents a blatant obstacle to international trade, as generally defined as the movement of goods and services across State boundaries. For example, the case of a higher tax or a stricter safety standard imposed on imported cars compared to domestic cars, where the only regulatory criterion differentiating between the products in question—cars—is their "nationality" or more precisely their foreign "origin", constitutes the classical example of formal discrimination based on nationality. This type of discrimination is also known as de jure or direct discrimination based on nationality.[10]

A case of de jure discrimination based on nationality is rather easy to identify, since it is the challenged measure itself that differentiates between products on the basis of their nationality or origin. In the above-mentioned example, it is the tax measure itself that imposes a rate of 25 per cent on imported cars and one of 15 per cent on domestic cars. Since the products regulated by the national measure under review are considered, by the measure itself, identical (except for their origin, that is), in order to establish the existence of this type of discrimination, an applicant will only need to show that (a) the national measure employs nationality as the regulatory criterion and (b) the treatment afforded by the national measure to the foreign product is less favourable compared to the treatment afforded to the domestic one.

Accordingly, the search for discrimination does not go beyond the mere text of the measure under review. In the above-mentioned example, the applicant must simply prove that according to the letter of the fiscal legislation or safety regulation (a) cars are differentiated on the basis of their foreign origin (or nationality) and (b) imported (foreign) cars are afforded less favourable treatment (higher tax or stricter safety standard) compared to domestic cars.

It should be emphasised at this point that with regard to the case of import of goods, the "nationality" of a product is usually equivalent to its "origin": an imported product is in fact in the great majority of cases[11]

---

[9] See above ch 1.

[10] Also the terms "overt" and "express" discrimination may be found in the literature and jurisprudence.

[11] Eg the case of re-imports, where a product manufactured in Country A returns to Country A after having being initially exported to Country B: nationality (Country A) would differ from origin (Country B).

a "foreign" product and at the same time it originates in a "foreign" country. Both nationality and origin of a product usually refer to the place of production or manufacture. In the case of export of goods, on the other hand, the only relevant criterion is the "destination" of the product in question and not its nationality: a national measure regulating the export of a domestic product directly violates the non-discrimination obligation, when it discriminates, rather than on grounds of the product's nationality (the product will usually be a domestic product), on the basis of the foreign *destination* of the product itself. Returning to the above example, a tax or a safety standard imposed on domestically manufactured cars will be deemed to constitute de jure discrimination if the tax or safety standard is formally higher or stricter depending on whether the cars are exported abroad or sold in the domestic market. Accordingly, while in the case of imports the prohibited regulatory criteria are both the "nationality" and "origin" of the product, in the case of exports, it is only the product's "destination".

As noted in the introduction, the prohibition of de jure discrimination has been described as the "first layer" of "judicial integration" in order to distinguish it from more advanced and problematic instruments of judicial integration such as the prohibition of de facto discrimination and the "reasonableness" principle. These other "layers" of judicial integration will be dealt in chapter 3 and chapter 4 respectively.[12]

However, it should once more be emphasised that the several types of integration instruments (whether "negative", "judicial" or "legislative") employed in both EC and WTO law should be understood not as completely disconnected from one another, but, on the contrary, as part of the same overall structure aimed at the liberalisation/regulation of trade. The coexistence of different types of instruments of integration influences both the design and the application of these instruments. For example, although in theory it could be applied to any form of national regulation, the principle of non-discrimination is usually applied in both EC and WTO law principally with regard to "internal measures" only. This is because "border measures" are expressly regulated by other instruments of integration, like the obligation to reduce or eliminate customs duties and quantitative restrictions.

---

[12] Although the division between de jure and de facto discrimination does not usually find an express basis in the founding legal texts of GATT/WTO and EC law, it has been affirmed by legal commentators as well as the jurisprudence of both systems. More than a practical way to organise the analysis of a complex topic, this division should help the reader to understand the real nature and purpose of the National Treatment principle. See recently, G Verhoosel, *National Treatment and WTO Dispute Settlement: Adjudicating the Boundaries of Regulatory Autonomy* (Oxford, Hart Publishing, 2002) and L Ehring, "*De Facto* Discrimination in WTO Law: National Treatment and Most-Favoured-Nation Treatment—or Equal Treatment?", *Jean Monnet Working Paper* (NYU School of Law, 2002); C Hilson, "Discrimination in Community free movement law" 24 *ELRev* (1999) 445 and J Usher, *General Principles of EC Law* (London, Longman, 1998). Cf J Schwarze, *European Administrative Law* (London, Sweet and Maxwell, 1997) at 618.

At the same time, however, the absence of an effective instrument to deal with a specific type of measure restricting trade among States may also cause an expansion in the reach of an instrument whose original function had been more limited. For example, in EC law, the difficulty of applying the harmonisation approach with regard to internal measures restricting intra-Community trade was, as noted earlier, the principal cause for the broad interpretation of the prohibition of "quantitative restrictions and measures having equivalent effect" found in Article 28 (ex 30) EC. As will be further explained in this chapter in the section dealing with the evolution of Article 28 EC, that prohibition was almost immediately interpreted to cover all "distinctly applicable measures", ie both *border* measures and formally discriminatory *internal* measures. This development was indeed possible because both "border" and "formally discriminatory internal" measures maintain one common feature, they clearly discriminate against imported products.

As already noted in the chapter dealing with border measures, EC and WTO law employ different provisions to impose the National Treatment principle depending on whether the measure is a "tax" or a "regulation". Accordingly, while the non-discrimination obligations with regard to fiscal measures are provided for in Article 90 (ex 95) EC and Article III:2 GATT, the non-discrimination obligations with regard to non-fiscal regulations are found in Article 28 (ex 30) EC and Article III:4 GATT. In light of certain differences in both the language and application of the non-discrimination provisions dealing with fiscal and non-fiscal measures, I would propose to examine the respective sets of obligations separately, beginning with fiscal measures (section 1) and continuing with non-fiscal measures (section 2).

Following the simple analytical approach outlined in the introduction, in both sections I will examine (a) the legal standards employed in WTO and EC law for the prohibition on de jure discrimination (ie "normative content") and (b) the exceptions, which are provided for in both legal systems in order for Members to justify violations of this obligation on public policy grounds (ie "justification options").

In the present chapter, as well as in the subsequent chapter on de facto discrimination, the issue of the scope of application (ie "objective element") of the National Treatment obligations in WTO and EC law will not be covered in any great detail.[13] This matter has already been discussed in the chapter dealing with the "elimination of border measures".[14] The main findings of the analysis there were the following: (1) rules imposing

---

[13] The only exception is the discussion in the ch on the National Treatment principle and the prohibition of de facto discrimination on "selling arrangements" within the ECJ jurisprudence following the decision in *Keck*. As will be explained in the relevant section, the prohibition of material discriminatory non-fiscal regulations (affecting imports) applies in EC law exclusively with regard to "selling arrangements". See below ch 3.

[14] This applies in substance also to the more peculiar approach that EC law reserves to non-pecuniary measures, which are all dealt with by Art 28 (ex 30) EC.

the reduction or elimination of "customs duties", "quantitative restrictions" and "other similar measures" (rules of "negative integration *stricto sensu*") have been applied with regard to measures which are *imposed on* importation and *apply exclusively* to imported products (ie "border" measures), (2) non-discrimination obligations (rules of "judicial integration") will *a contrariis* catch those measures, which do not affect importation as such or apply, albeit not in an identical manner, to both domestic and imported products (ie "internal" measures).[15] Accordingly, National Treatment obligations in both EC and WTO law are employed to deal with the broad category of "internal measures".

2.1 PROHIBITION OF DE JURE DISCRIMINATION AND FISCAL CHARGES

The prohibition of de jure discrimination based on nationality applies first of all in the realm of fiscal measures affecting trade in goods. In light of the fact that the relevant provisions in WTO and EC law follow an almost identical design, it is appropriate to commence this comparative analysis with the case of formally discriminatory "internal taxation".

A. Normative Content

1. *Article III:2 GATT*

Following a general recognition in the first paragraph of Article III GATT that "internal taxes and other internal charges [...] affecting the internal sale [...] of products [...] should not be applied to imported or domestic products so as to afford protection to domestic production", the first sentence of Article III.2 GATT provides as follows:

> The products of the territory of any contracting party imported into the territory of any other contracting party shall not be subject, directly or indirectly, to internal taxes or other internal charges of any kind in excess of those applied, directly or indirectly, to like domestic products.[16]

---

[15] Any type of rule dealing with the liberalisation/regulation of international trade, whether falling within the category of "negative integration" or "judicial integration", will deal only with *public* or *governmental* measures and not with *private* acts. Although the concept of "public measure" has been interpreted in a broad manner in both EC and WTO law, this dichotomy constitutes a clear limitation to the scope of application of "integration rules".

[16] The second sentence of Art III.2 GATT, which is not relevant for purposes of understanding the concept of de jure discrimination, reads as follows: "Moreover, no contracting parties shall otherwise apply internal taxes or other internal charges to imported or domestic products in a manner contrary to the principles set forth in para 1". This second sentence will be analysed in the next chapter that examines de facto discriminatory measures.

There has never been any doubt that an internal tax formally discriminating on the basis of the nationality (or origin) of the product would be in violation of the National Treatment obligation of Article III. Since the early days of GATT panel practice, the principal purpose of this provision, which imposes a non-discrimination obligation with regard to both fiscal measures (paragraph 2) and non-fiscal regulations (paragraph 4), has been to assure equal conditions of competition between imported and domestic goods once imports have been cleared through customs.[17]

In *United States—Taxes on Petroleum and Certain Imported Substances*, more commonly known as the *Superfund* case,[18] Canada, the EEC and Mexico claimed that a US excise tax on petroleum and a tax on certain imported substances produced or manufactured from taxable feedstock chemicals violated Article III.2 of the GATT. The tax on petroleum, which had previously been imposed at the rate of 0.79 cent per barrel for both domestic and imported products, was increased to 8.2 cents per barrel for "crude oil received at a United States refinery" and 11.7 cents a barrel for "petroleum products entered into the United States for consumption, use or warehousing." The term "crude oil" was defined to include crude oil condensate and natural gasoline. The term "petroleum products" was defined to comprise not only the products defined as "crude oil" but also refined gasoline, refined and residual oil, and certain other liquid hydrocarbon products. The tax increases went into effect on 1 January 1987.

Although the different tax rates were applied to two apparently different products (crude oil and petroleum products), the tax, as indicated by its name and by the products' definitions therein, was effectively imposed on one product only, namely "petroleum".[19] The differential treatment was thus exclusively based on the origin of the product in question: domestic

---

[17] Panel Report on *Italian Discrimination against Imported Agricultural Machinery*, BISD 7S/60, para 11. The Panel Report on *United States—section 337 of the Tariff Act of 1930 (section 337)*, L/6439, adopted on 7 Nov 1989, BISD 36S/345, para 5.10, noted that "the purpose of Art III [..] is to ensure that internal measures "not be applied to imported or domestic products so as to afford protection to domestic production" (Art III:1)". Cf J Jackson, *World Trade and the Law of GATT* (1969) at 276–7. In *Japan—Taxes on Alcoholic Beverages*, WT/DS8/AB/R, circulated 4 Oct 1996, adopted 1 Nov 1996, at 16–7, the Appellate Body endorsed GATT panel practice in this regard and clarified that "although the protection of negotiated tariff concessions is certainly one purpose of Art III [...] the sheltering scope of Art III is not limited to products that are the subject of tariff concessions under Art II, [the National Treatment obligation clearly extending] also to products not bound under Art II."

[18] L/6175, adopted on 17 June 1987, BISD 34S/136. The tax measures under review in that case were prescribed in the US "Superfund Amendments and Reauthorization Act" or, briefly, the "Superfund Act" of 1986. The Superfund Act authorised a programme to clean up hazardous waste sites and dealt with public health programmes caused by hazardous waste. It provided for excise and corporate income taxes and appropriations to pay for the cost of these programmes.

[19] This was true at least for "crude oil", "crude oil condensates" and "natural gasoline". The Panel found that "The domestic products subject to the tax are: crude oil, crude oil condensates, and natural gasoline. The imported products subject to the tax are: crude oil, crude oil

petroleum was taxed at 8.2 cents a barrel while imported petroleum was taxed at 11.7 cents a barrel. Without explicitly referring to the tax at issue as a case of de jure discrimination, the Panel quickly reached the conclusion that the measure violated Article III:2 once it had determined that the two products were (a) "either identical or, in the case of imported liquid hydrocarbon products, serve substantially identical end" and (b) "the rate of tax applied to the imported products is 3.5 cents per barrel higher than the rate applied to the like domestic products."

It is interesting to note that the United States did not submit to the Panel any argument to support a legal conclusion different from that reached by the Panel. Instead, it merely contended that the tax differential was so small that its trade effects were minimal or nil and that the tax differential—whether or not it conformed to Article III:2, first sentence— did not nullify or impair benefits accruing to the complainants under the General Agreement as required by Article XXIII GATT. Although the Panel was convinced that the presumption that illegal measures cause nullification or impairment pursuant to Article XXIII had in practice operated as an irrefutable presumption, it nevertheless examined the *de minimis* argument advanced by the United States. The Panel forcefully rejected this argument on the basis that for the purposes of the National Treatment obligation the level of trade effects is irrelevant, the objective of such a provision being "to establish certain competitive conditions for imported products in relation to domestic products".[20]

A similar scenario can be found in the *Malt Beverages* case,[21] where a GATT Panel had been asked to rule on some 27 different state and federal taxes and regulations affecting beer and wine imports. With regard to the fiscal measures, both the federal government and several States had for the most part either imposed lower excise taxes on certain domestically produced wine and beer[22] compared to imported foreign wine and beer or

condensates, natural gasoline, refined and residual oil, and certain other liquid hydrocarbon products. The imported and domestic products are thus either identical or, in the case of imported liquid hydrocarbon products, serve substantially identical end-uses." Panel Report on *Superfund*, above n 18, para 5.1.1.

[20] *Ibid.*, para 5.1.9.
[21] Panel Report on *United States—Measures Affecting Alcoholic and Malt Beverages* (*Malt Beverages*), DS23/R, adopted on 19 June 1992, BISD 39S/206.
[22] The more favourable treatment was accorded on the basis of (a) the size or annual production of the domestic producer (the federal excise tax on domestic beer, the federal excise tax credit on domestic wine and cider, the excise tax exemptions and reductions to beer and wine of the states of New York, Oregon, Rhode Island and the Commonwealth of Puerto Rico, the excise tax credits to breweries accorded by the states of Kentucky, Ohio, Wisconsin and (possibly Minnesota)), (b) the origin of the product (the excise tax rates on wine of the states of Alabama, Georgia, Nebraska and New Mexico), (c) the wine's ingredients (the excise tax on wine of the states of Michigan, Ohio and Rhode Island), or for the purpose of (d) purchase of manufacturing equipment (the excise tax credit on beer of the state of Pennsylvania).

provided for excise tax credits exclusively for the former. These measures, which were formally discriminating between domestic and imported products[23] and could not be justified on the basis of Article III:8(b),[24] were all found to violate the National Treatment provision. Once again, noting that Article III protects competitive conditions between imported and domestic products but does not protect expectation on export volume, the Panel considered it "irrelevant" that the lower taxes and tax credits benefited only a very small proportion of United States production of beer and wine (respectively, 1.5 and 4 per cent).[25] The Panel also considered irrelevant the fact that many of the state provisions at issue in that dispute provided the same treatment to products of other states of the United States as that provided to foreign products, since it held that the National Treatment provisions require contracting parties to accord to imported products treatment no less favourable than that accorded to any like domestic product, whatever the domestic origin. In other words, in the Panel's view, Article III requires treatment of imported products no less favourable than that accorded to the *most favoured* domestic product.[26]

One relatively clear case of de jure discriminatory tax measures is also represented by the recent case of *Indonesia—Certain Measures Affecting the Automobile Industry*,[27] where Japan, the EEC and the United States complained that a series of measures adopted by Indonesia with respect to motor vehicles and parts and components violated inter alia the provisions of Article III:2, first sentence, by exempting from a luxury sales tax the sale of

[23] Panel Report *Malt Beverages*, above n 21, para 5.23. On the other hand, since the Minnesota excise tax credit to "small" breweries appeared to be available to both domestic and imported beer, it did not constitute a case of de jure discrimination (but possibly one of de facto discrimination). Likewise, it did not represent a case of de jure discriminatory tax measure Mississippi lower tax rate to wines in which a certain variety of grape was used, since the "tax provision in Mississippi was *applicable to all qualifying wine* produced from the specified variety of grape, *regardless of the point of origin*." [emphasis added]. See below the section on fiscal measures in ch 3 on the prohibition of de facto discrimination.

[24] Art III:8(b) reads in relevant part: "The provisions of this Article shall not prevent the payment of subsidies exclusively to domestic producers, including payments to domestic producers derived from the proceeds of internal taxes or charges applied consistently with the provisions of this Article." According to the Panel this provision was not applicable to the case at hand since "the specific reference to 'payments ... derived from the proceeds of internal taxes ... applied consistently with the provisions of this Article' relates to after-tax-collection payments and also suggests that tax credits and reduced tax rates inconsistent with Art III:2, which neither involve a 'payment' nor result in 'proceeds of internal taxes applied consistently with ... this Article', are not covered by Art III:8(b)." *Ibid.*, para 5.8.

[25] Panel Report on *Malt Beverages*, above n 21, paras 5.6 and 5.15: "The prohibition of discriminatory taxes in Art III:2, first sentence, is not conditional on a 'trade effects test' nor is it qualified by a *de minimis* standard".

[26] *Ibid.*, para 5.17.

[27] *Indonesia—Certain Measures Affecting the Automobile Industry (Indonesia–Auto)*, WT/DS54, WT/DS55, WT/DS59 and WT/DS64, brought 14, 10, 15 Oct, 5 Dec 1996.

several categories of motor vehicles which were "manufactured domestically" and/or had a specific "level of local content".[28]

While trying to establish the likeness of the products involved, as required by Article III:2, both Japan and the EEC emphasised the irrelevance of the likeness issue within the context of an allegedly de jure discriminatory measure. Japan argued that,

> in this present case, it is almost meaningless to discuss "likeness", because, even if vehicles identical in all aspects (including the end-uses, properties, nature and quality) with [domestic cars] are manufactured abroad (for example, in Japan) and imported, they would still be treated differently from [domestic cars].[29]

Along the same lines, the EC noted that the tax exemptions granted by Indonesia were all based either exclusively or partially on the country of manufacture of the products, thus "motor vehicles manufactured in Indonesia are not, *by definition*, 'unlike' motor vehicles manufactured in the territory of any other Member."[30]

Although the Panel first examined and resolved in the affirmative the question of whether the imported products affected by the Indonesian measure were like domestic products,[31] it further emphasised that in a case of a measure *formally* discriminating on the basis of origin or nationality the likeness of the products at issue is implicit in the formal discriminatory nature of the measure itself, with the effect that under the tax regime at issue, any imported like products would necessarily be taxed in excess of domestic like products. Stressing the difference from a previous

---

[28] The exempted categories were: motor vehicles (i) domestically manufactured motor cycles with engines of 250 cc or less; (ii) combines, minibuses, vans and pick-ups using gasoline as fuel which are manufactured domestically and have a local content of more than 60%; (iii) combines, minibuses, vans and pick-ups using diesel oil as fuel which are manufactured domestically and have a local content of more than 60%; (iv) domestically manufactured buses; (v) domestically manufactured sedans and stations wagons of less than 1,600 cc with a local content of more than 60%; (vi) National Cars assembled in Indonesia by pioneer companies; and (vii) imported National Cars. For the purposes of exemption (vi) and exemption (vii) a motor vehicle is deemed to be a "National Car" if it satisfies the conditions enumerated in Art 1 of Decree 31/96, which provides that National vehicles shall be those which: (a) are *domestically produced* by using facilities owned by national industrial companies or Indonesian statutory bodies with total shares belonging to Indonesian citizens; and (b) use trade marks created by relevant industrial companies themselves and not yet registered by other parties in Indonesia and owned by Indonesian citizens; and (c) are developed with technology, designs and engineering on the basis of national capacity to be realised in phases. Panel Report on *Indonesia–Auto*, WT/DS54/R, WT/DS55/R, WT/DS59/R and WT/DS64/R, circulated 2 July 1998, adopted 23 July 1998, paras 5.24–5.28.

[29] *Ibid.* para 5.7.
[30] *Ibid.*, para 5.29 [emphasis added]. "Similarly, there is nothing which, a priori, makes Indonesian manufactured parts and components for the assembly of motor vehicles 'unlike' Community manufactured parts and components." *Ibid.*, para 5.30.
[31] *Ibid.* paras 14.110–14.111.

WTO case involving an origin-neutral tax, where identical products (not considering brand differences) were taxed identically notwithstanding their origin,[32] the Panel stated that in the case at hand:

> The distinction between the products, which results in different levels of taxation, is not based on the products per se, but rather on such factors as the nationality of the producer or the origin of the parts and components contained in the product. As such, an imported product identical in all respects to a domestic product, except for its origin or the origin of its parts and components or other factors not related to the product itself, would be subject to a different level of taxation.[33]

The Panel concluded that, in accordance with the broad purposes of Article III:2, such an origin-based distinction in respect of internal taxes was sufficient in itself to violate Article III:2. It was unnecessary for the complainant to demonstrate the existence of actually traded like products.[34]

In the more recent Panel Report on *Argentina—Measures Affecting the Export of Bovine Hides and the Import of Finished Leather* (*Argentina– Bovine Hides*),[35] the EC claimed that the Argentine system of pre-payment of

---

[32] Cf Panel Report on *Japan—Taxes on Alcoholic Beverages* (*Japan–Alcohol II*), WT/DS8/R, WT/DS10/R and WT/DS11/R, circulated on 11 July 1996, adopted 1 Nov 1996. See below discussion in ch 3 on the National Treatment principle and the prohibition of de facto discrimination.

[33] Panel Report on *Indonesia–Auto*, above n 28, para 14.112.

[34] *Ibid.*, para 14.113 [emphasis added]. It should also be noted that in a fn, the Panel suggested that its finding accorded with a number of previous panel reports concluding that "differences in producers' characteristics, which do not affect the products' characteristics, cannot justify a different tax treatment of the products involved." The Panel cited the following GATT/WTO reports: Panel Report on *Malt Beverages*, above n 21, para 5.19 ("beer produced by large breweries is not unlike beer produced by small breweries"), Panel Report on *United States—Standards for Reformulated Conventional Gasoline* (*Reformulated Gasoline*), WT/DS2/R, circulated 29 Jan 1996, adopted 20 May 1996, para 6.11 ("Art III:4 of the General Agreement deals with the treatment to be accorded to like products; its wording does not allow less favourable treatment dependent on the characteristics of the producer"), and Panel Report on *United States—Measures Affecting the Importation, Internal Sale and Use of Tobacco*, DS44/R, adopted 4 Oct 1994, para 97 ("The Panel thus considered that the system for calculation of the BDA on imported tobacco itself, not just the manner in which it was currently applied, was inconsistent with Art III:2 because it carried with it the risk of discriminatory treatment of imports in respect of internal taxes"). It is submitted that the Panel erroneously confused a measure differentiating on the basis of origin or nationality with one employing a criterion that does not affect the product's characteristics. The former constitutes a case of de jure discrimination where products are identical by definition, while the latter involves the case of an (at least apparently) origin-neutral differentiating criterion, which may or may not be taken into consideration for the purposes of determining the likeness of the products (generally it will not, since it does not affect the products' characteristics). This latter differentiation will be deemed to violate the prohibition of de facto discrimination on the grounds of nationality only if the complaining Member is able to establish a prejudicial effect on imported foreign products compared to domestic like products. For a detailed analysis of these issues, see below the section analysing the *Asbestos* dispute in ch 3 on the National Treatment principle and the prohibition of de facto discrimination.

[35] WT/DS155/R, circulated on 19 Dec 2000, adopted 16 Feb 2001.

part of the applicable value-added tax (*Impuesto al Valor Agregado* or *IVA*)[36] and income tax (*Impuesto a las Ganacians* or *IG*)[37] was inconsistent with Article III:2, first sentence, since the pre-payments on imports required by Argentinean legislation (RG 3431 for IVA and RG 3543 for IG) exceeded the pre-payments to be made on internal sales of goods, with the consequence that importers bore a heavier financial cost than buyers of like domestic goods. Although its complaint was not intended to question Argentina's right to require the pre-payment of taxes, the EC noted its concern with the additional financial cost imposed on importers, which was the consequence of applying two formally different systems for the pre-payment of part of the IVA and the IG, which was more burdensome for importers.

Having found, in line with previous WTO jurisprudence, that in order to show an infringement of Article III:2, first sentence, there is no requirement to establish, separately or otherwise, the presence of a protective application,[38] the Panel addressed in turn the questions whether (1) the imported and domestic products subject to the collection mechanisms at issue in the present case were "like" and whether (2) the tax burden on imported products was "in excess" of the tax burden on like domestic products, there is an infringement within the meaning of Article III:2, first sentence.

With regard to the first question, the Panel agreed with the EC claim that in the specific case at hand, it was not incumbent upon it to compare specific products or address the criteria relevant to determine likeness. It noted that,

[i]n circumstances such as those confronting us in this case no comparison of specific products is required. Logically, no examination of the various criteria relevant to determining likeness is then called for either.[39]

---

[36] The types of transactions subject to the IVA include, inter alia, the sale of goods inside Argentina's territory and the definitive importation of goods into its territory. With respect to imports, the IVA is collected together with any applicable import duties. With respect to internal sales, sellers must charge the IVA to the purchasers and then pay the amounts so collected to the tax administration on a monthly basis, after deducting there-from any IVA paid on their own purchases and imports during the same period. The IVA is applied to both imports and internal sales at a general rate of 21% *ad valorem*. Lower rates apply to transactions involving certain specified products, including live bovine animals, offal of bovines as well as fresh fruit and vegetables. Law No 23349/97 (Exhibit EC II.1), as last amended by Law No 25239/99 (Exhibit EC II.3) (hereafter the "IVA Law"). Panel Report on *Bovine Hides*, above n 35, para 11.105.

[37] The IG applied to both natural and juridical persons and was levied on all sources of income, including the profits derived from the sale of domestic and imported goods. Its principal legal basis was the Law on the IG as codified in Decree No 649/97 (Exhibit EC II.2) and last amended by Law No 25239/99 (Exhibit EC II.3) (hereafter the "IG Law"). *Ibid.*, paras 11.116–11.117.

[38] *Ibid.*, para 11.138. See the discussion below in the section on the prohibition of de facto discrimination and fiscal measures in ch 3.

[39] *Ibid.*, para 11.168.

Recalling the similar approach followed in *Indonesia–Auto*, the Panel noted that the Argentine system of pre-payments differentiated on the basis of the origin of the products (and not on the basis of their physical characteristics or end-uses) and thus stated that it was therefore "inevitable" that like products would be subject to different provisions.[40]

With regard to the second question, the Panel noted that, in light of its purpose, which is to ensure "equality of competitive conditions between imported and like domestic products", Article III:2, first sentence, is not concerned with taxes or charges as such, or the policy purposes Members thereby pursue, but rather with economic impact of these taxes or charges on the competitive opportunities of imported and like domestic products. Following a thorough examination of the relevant legislation at issue, the Panel concluded that the Argentine system of pre-payments not only imposed higher nominal rates on imported products vis-à-vis domestic ones,[41] but also provided for several exceptions to the pre-payment obligation only with regard to domestic products.[42] Accordingly, the Panel concluded that imported products were taxed *in excess of* domestic products in violation of Article III:2, first sentence.

It is clear from these few cases that whenever a tax measure *formally* discriminates on the basis of the product's origin or nationality, the likeness of the products at issue is implicit in the formally discriminatory nature of the measure itself. A violation of the National Treatment obligation will thus be found if the measure at issue upsets the competitive conditions in favour of domestic production. For purposes of this determination, the level of actual trade effects is irrelevant. In other words, a national fiscal measure will be found to violate Article III:2 even if the higher burden on imported products is minimal (ie no *de minimis* exception) or the imported

---

[40] *Ibid.*, para 11.169. "The European Communities have demonstrated this to our satisfaction, and, in our view, this is all it needs to establish in the present case as far as the 'like product' requirement contained in Art III:2, first sentence, is concerned." The Panel further noted that "the European Communities can challenge RG 3431 even if no trade involving like imported products actually exists. [...] Art III provides protection not only to those EC producers who are actually contesting the Argentinean internal market, but also to those who are planning on contesting it or are preparing to do so. As to whether like products can exist, we confine ourselves to noting that, in our view, the European Communities, like other Members, is a potential producer and exporter of a wide range of products which are like Argentinean products, even considering the narrow definition of likeness appropriate in the context of Art III:2, first sentence." *Ibid.*, para 11.169, fn n 465.

[41] With regard to the IVA, under RG 3431 imports were subject, upon importation, to pre-payment of the IVA at a rate of 10% or 12.7% *ad valorem*. Under RG 3543, the IG had to be pre-paid on imports at a rate of 3% or 11% *ad valorem*. *Ibid.*, paras 11.174–11.284.

[42] Always with regard to the IVA, for example, no pre-payment of the IVA or additional IVA payment was required on *internal* sales to non-registered taxable persons. Likewise, no pre-payment was required on (i) *internal* sales transactions involving registered taxable persons as both sellers and purchasers and (ii) *internal* sales transactions between non-registered taxable sellers and registered taxable purchasers. Similar findings were reached with regard to the system of pre-payment of the IG. *Ibid.*

products potentially disadvantaged by such a measure are but a few (ie it is enough to show that potentially a *single* imported product may be taxed in excess of a domestic one).

2. Article 90 EC

It has been said that "the founding fathers of the Community must have been greatly inspired by the GATT, and by its Article III:2, when they drafted Article 95 [now Article 90] of the Treaty of Rome".[43] The first paragraph of Article 90 reads as follows:

> No Member State shall impose, directly or indirectly on the products of other Member States any internal taxation of any kind in excess of that imposed directly or indirectly on similar domestic products.

Even if the first paragraph of Article 90 employs the term "similar", which appears to be broader than the corresponding term "like" in the first sentence of Article III:2,[44] the two provisions are indeed virtually identical. With regard to its purpose, although the supplementary function of Article 90 EC in relation to the elimination of customs duties and charges having equivalent effect has at times been emphasised,[45] the broader mandate of Article 90,

> is to ensure free movement of goods between the Member States in normal conditions of competition by the elimination of all forms of protection which result from the application of internal taxation which discriminates against products from other Member States [and thus to] guarantee the complete neutrality of internal taxation as regard to competition between domestic products and imported products.[46]

[43] P J Kuyper, "Booze and Fast Cars: Tax Discrimination under GATT and the EC" in *Legal Issues of European Integration* (1996) 129 at 130.
[44] *Ibid.*, where the author suggests that "the explanation for the difference may be that the translators into English of Art 95 of the EEC Treaty did not care to look up the French and English texts of Art III:2 of GATT, where 'like' and 'similaire' are equivalent and thus translated the latter word as 'similar'."
[45] This is especially true in the early ECJ case law. See Case 21/79, *Commission v Italy (Regenerated Petroleum Products)* [1980] ECR 1, para 15: "The first paragraph of Art 95—the purpose of which is to ensure that the treaty provisions relating to the abolition of customs duties and charges having equivalent effect cannot be evaded or rendered nugatory by the introduction of internal taxation discriminating against imported products in comparison with domestic products—implements a fundamental principle of the common market." Cf Case 168/78, *Commission v France (Tax Arrangements Applicable to Spirits)* [1980] ECR 347, para 4: "[Art 90] provisions supplement, within the system of the Treaty, the provisions on the abolition of customs duties and charges having equivalent effect."
[46] Case 168/78, *Commission v France (Tax Arrangements Applicable to Spirits)* [1980] ECR 347, at para 4. Cf Joined Cases C–367/93 to C–377/93, F G. *Roders BV and Others v Inspecteur der Invoerrechten en Accijnzen* [1995] ECR I–2229, para 16 and Case C–47/88, *Commission v Denmark* [1990] ECR I–4509, para 9.

It is thus clear that, as in the case of the National Treatment obligation in Article III:2 GATT, an internal tax formally discriminating on the basis of the nationality (or origin) of the product would be deemed to violate the non-discrimination obligation of Article 90 EC.

In the *Regenerated Petroleum Products* case,[47] the ECJ found that the Italian Republic had failed to fulfil its obligations under Article 90 (ex 95) EC by affording a tax advantage to domestic regenerated petroleum products, which was denied to regenerated petroleum products imported from the other Member States.[48] The Court clearly emphasised the formally discriminatory nature of the Italian tax scheme at issue by noting that imported and home-produced regenerated oils are not only like products but are even identical so that the relationship between them is undeniably covered by the first paragraph of Article 90 of the Treaty.[49]

Whenever a national measure differentiates between two products exclusively on the basis of their origin, those two products must be considered "like" or "similar" products for the purposes of Article 90, since it is the measure itself that considers them identical (except for their origin). In this regard, a distinction should be drawn as to whether the (domestic and imported) products are *physically* or *legally* identical. In the case of an origin-based measure, only the latter concept is relevant.

In *Commission v Greece*,[50] the application of two different methods for calculation of the basis of assessment of the tax according to whether the cars were imported or manufactured in Greece was found to infringe Article 90 of the Treaty, since that system favoured cars assembled in Greece at the expense of those imported from other Member States.[51] Interestingly, the Court placed on the defending government the burden of proving that the system in question did not engender any discriminatory effects, principally in light of the fact that the measure *formally* discriminated on the basis of the origin of the products in question. The Court stated that,

> where a system like that created by the contested legislation applies rules to domestic products which differ from those applied to products imported from

[47] Case 21/79, *Commission v Italy (Regenerated Petroleum Products)* [1980] ECR 1.
[48] Under Italian law, an "imposta interna di fabbricazione"' (internal production tax), fixed at a certain amount of lire per quintal, which varied according to the products, was chargeable on mineral oils and processed products derived from them. A similar tax called "sovraimposta di confine" (frontier surcharge) was chargeable on similar foreign products when they crossed the frontier. With a view to encouraging, on both economic and ecological grounds, the recovery and re-use of used oils, Art 12 of Italian Law No 1852 of 31 Dec 1962 introduced a series of measures regulating the collection, recovery and re-use of petroleum products and granting the undertakings which engage therein on Italian territory *tax advantages as far as the imposta di fabbricazione is concerned.*
[49] Case 21/79, *Regenerated Petroleum Products*, above n 47, para 19.
[50] Case C–327/90, *Commission v Greece* [1992] ECR I–3033.
[51] The Commission had argued that "the discrimination derives mainly from the fact that a flat-rate increase of 21% or 23% of the basis of assessment of the tax is prescribed for

other Member States and lacks transparency and precision, the defendant government must furnish proof that the system of which the Commission complains could not in any circumstances have a discriminatory effect (see in that regard the decisions of the Court in Case C–152/89 *Commission v Luxembourg* [1991] ECR I–3141 and Case C–153/89 *Commission v Belgium* [1991] ECR I–3171).[52]

Furthermore, as the Court has pointed out on several occasions, the Article 90 prohibition of discrimination based on origin or nationality covers not only the rate of taxation but also the various provisions concerning the basis of assessment and the detailed rules for levying taxes. The decisive comparative criterion for the application of Article 90 was the *actual impact* of each tax on the domestic product, on the one hand, and on the imported product, on the other.[53]

B. Justification Options

1. *Article XX GATT*

Any violation of Article III:2 may in theory be justified on the basis of the general exception of Article XX GATT. Thus, even a *formally* discriminatory internal tax may be found to comply with WTO law if the Member exercising its fiscal authority is able to demonstrate that the discriminatory tax has been enacted in order to achieve one of the public policy objectives listed in Article XX. It appears, however, that this option has only very rarely been raised by Member States and/or considered by Panels at least with regard to a tax formally discriminating on the basis of the origin or nationality of the product.[54]

imported cars, whereas those assembled in Greece are taxed on the basis of actual data, namely the ex-factory price." *Ibid.*, para 7.

[52] *Ibid.*, para 20. In the two cases cited by the Court, the Belgian and Luxembourg legislation constituted de jure discrimination based on origin of the products since it took the hot wort as the basis for duty to be levied on *beer produced locally* but, for *beer imported from other Member States*, took the volume of the finished product, plus a flat-rate adjustment of 5%. See also the Opinion of Advocate-General Tesauro delivered on 28 Jan 1992 in Case C–327/90, *Commission v Greece* [1992] ECR I–3033, para 5.

[53] See Case 55/79 *Commission v Ireland* [1980] ECR 481, para 8, where although the tax itself applied to all goods irrespective of origin, domestic producers were treated more leniently as regard to payment, being allowed more time before payment was actually demanded, whereas importers had to pay the duty directly on importation. P Craig and G de Búrca, *EU Law* (Oxford, OUP, 1998) at 561–62.

[54] In Panel Report on *Canada—Import, Distribution and Sale of Certain Alcoholic Drinks by Provincial Marketing Agencies (Canada Alcohol II)*, DS17/27, adopted on 18 Feb 1992, BISD 39S/27, the United States claimed that the tax levied by the Canadian provinces of Manitoba and Ontario on beverage alcohol containers, which were not part of a deposit/return system, as well as the tax imposed by Nova Scotia on containers, which were shipped to the liquor

The only instance where the Article XX defence has been discussed by a WTO panel in this context is the recent *Argentina–Bovine Hides* dispute[55] concerning the GATT compatibility of the Argentine system of pre-payment of part of the IVA (value-added tax) and the IG (income tax), which formally discriminated between imports and domestic products.[56] The Panel determined that the Argentine pre-payment system violated Article III:2, first sentence, and went on to examine whether such system was (1) justified under Article XX(d) as "necessary to secure compliance with" Argentinean tax laws[57] and (2) complied with the requirements of the introductory clause of Article XX (ie that "measures are not applied in a manner which would constitute a means of arbitrary or unjustifiable discrimination between countries or a disguised restriction on international trade").[58] As will be further explained in the section dealing with "justification options" for de jure discriminatory *non-fiscal* measures, the Panel correctly applied the two-tiered justification test laid down by the Appellate Body: first, "provisional justification" by reason of characterisation of the measure under one of the paragraphs of Article XX taking into account the exhaustive *regulatory goals* listed in lett (a)–(j) and the varying *connections* between the regulation and the regulatory objective specified therein; secondly,

---

board for distribution, were inconsistent with Art III. Although these taxes on alcohol containers were apparently origin-neutral, the United States noted that according to Canadian legislation only domestic producers were entitled to establish their own *distribution systems* and the establishment of a separate container *collection system* for imported beer was therefore prohibitively expensive. Accordingly, while the taxes imposed by Manitoba and Ontario were only *materially* discriminatory, those imposed by Nova Scotia constituted a case of *formally* discriminatory taxation. Noting that it was not the charges on containers as such that the United States considered to be inconsistent with Art III but rather their application in a situation where different systems for the delivery of beer to the points of sale applied to imported and domestic beer, the Panel considered that its previous finding that the restrictions on delivery systems for imported beer containers were inconsistent with Art III also covered this matter. *Ibid.*, para 5.33. Although Canada had claimed that the incriminated levies were justified on the basis of Art XX(b) and (d) to protect the environment (*ibid.*, paras 4.73 and 4.90), the Panel did not even address this argument. Cf Panel Report on *EEC—Regulation on Imports of Parts and Components*, L/6657, adopted on 16 May 1990, BISD 37S/132, para 6.1

[55] Panel Report on *Argentina—Bovine Hides*, above n 35.
[56] See above section dealing with the "normative content" of Art III:2 GATT.
[57] Argentina contended that the contested mechanisms for the collection at source of the IVA and IG, ie RG 3431 and RG 3543, were put in place in order to avert actions which are illegal under the terms of the IVA Law and IG Law, such as failure to declare or pay the IVA or IG. Argentina argued, therefore, that those mechanisms were specifically designed to secure compliance with the IVA Law and IG Law respectively. Panel Report on *Argentina–Bovine Hides*, above n 35, para 11.292.
[58] Art XX provides relevantly that "[s]ubject to the requirement that such measures are not applied in a manner which would constitute a means of arbitrary or unjustifiable discrimination between countries, where the same conditions prevail, or a disguised restriction on international trade, nothing in this Agreement shall be construed to prevent the adoption or enforcement by any contracting party of measures: [...] (d) necessary to secure compliance with laws or regulations which are not inconsistent with the provisions of this Agreement, including those relating to [...] the protection of patents, trade marks and copyrights, and the protection of

"further appraisal" of the measure under the introductory clauses of Article XX, the so-called Chapeau.[59]

However, when it came to interpret the relevant "connector" in Article XX(d) (ie *necessary* to secure compliance) the Panel's analysis followed a somewhat original structure, which arguably does not conform to either previous GATT Panel practice or current WTO jurisprudence.[60] Probably on the basis of the earlier Appellate Body jurisprudence with regard to the *differently* worded Article XX(g),[61] the Panel interpreted "necessary" under the "provisional justification" as simply meaning "relating to" or "aimed at", while it transferred the more rigorous "necessity" test (ie "least trade-restrictive" or "less GATT inconsistent" test) to the ambit of the introductory clause of the Chapeau.[62] Accordingly, while the Panel was satisfied that Argentina had shown that the contested measures, in their general design and structure, were "necessary" on the basis that Argentina had stressed that "tax evasion is common in its territory",[63] it eventually rejected Argentina's Article XX defence on the grounds that the origin-based pre-payment system constituted "avoidable" and thus

---

deceptive practices". See above discussion on Art XX GATT in ch 1 on the Elimination of Border Measures.

[59] Cf Appellate Body Report, *United States—Standards for Reformulated and Conventional Gasoline (Reformulated Gasoline)*, WT/DS2/AB/R, circulated 29 April 1996, adopted 20 May 1999, para 21.

[60] The Report was never appealed before the Appellate Body and thus it was adopted as it was circulated by the panel.

[61] This is clearly confirmed by the Panel's statement in fn 564 which reads as follows: "It is true that the European Communities disputes that the higher rates applied to imported products pursuant to RG 3431 and RG 3543 are 'necessary' in order to secure compliance with the IVA Law and IG Law (see eg EC First Oral Statement, at paras 79, 82 and 84). We consider that this contention goes to the question of whether Argentina makes improper use of the exception set out in Art XX(d) and not to the question of whether RG 3431 and RG 3543, in light of their general design and structure, fall within the terms of Art XX(d). We therefore address the justifiability of applying higher rates to imported products when we appraise RG 3431 and RG 3543 under the chapeau of Art XX. This approach is in accordance with that followed by the Appellate Body Report [on *Reformulated Gasoline*], at 19 and 25–29)." Panel Report on *Argentina–Bovine Hides*, above n 35, para 11.306.

[62] As will be explained further in the section dealing with "justification options" of de jure discriminatory *non-fiscal* regulation, the "necessity" test under Art XX(d) (as well as Art XX(b)) has been interpreted in the sense that a contracting party cannot justify a measure inconsistent with another GATT provision as "necessary" in terms of Art XX(d) if an *alternative measure* which it could reasonably be expected to employ and which is *not inconsistent* with other GATT provisions is available to it. By the same token, in cases where a measure consistent with other GATT provisions is not reasonably available, a contracting party is bound to use, among the measures reasonably available to it, that which entails the *least degree of inconsistency* with other GATT provisions. Cf Panel Report on *section 337*, above n 17, para 5.26.

[63] "We are satisfied that Argentina has adduced argument and evidence sufficient to raise a presumption that the contested measures, in their general design and structure, are 'necessary' even on the European Communities' reading of that term. Argentina stresses the fact that tax evasion is common in its territory and that, against this background of low levels of tax compliance, tax authorities cannot expect to improve tax collection primarily through the pursuit of repressive enforcement strategies (eg aggressive criminal prosecution of tax offenders).

"unjustifiable discrimination" within the meaning of the Chapeau of Article XX, since there existed *other less inconsistent alternatives* capable of securing compliance with domestic tax laws.[64]

Although its approach was thus formally flawed,[65] the Panel's analysis and conclusion in *Bovine Hides* with regard to the merits of Argentina's defence under Article XX was in substance correct. Moreover, the *Bovine Hides* Report showed once more that, in order to justify a de jure discriminatory measure on public policy grounds, the defendant Member has to satisfy the very heavy burden of proving that such discrimination is indeed unavoidable.

2. Border Tax Adjustment in WTO Law

When reviewing justification options with regard to de jure discriminatory fiscal measures, it is necessary to consider the concept of "border tax adjustment".[66] The concept of border tax adjustment is employed as an instrument to guarantee "trade neutrality" in that a tax is expressly imposed on imported products only in order to compensate an equivalent tax imposed on similar domestic products.

In the *Superfund* case,[67] the Panel accepted the United States' claim that a US tax imposed on imported substances did not violate the National Treatment obligation in view of the fact that those substances were produced

In those circumstances, Argentina maintains, tax authorities must direct their efforts towards preventing tax evasion from occurring in the first place. According to Argentina, this is precisely what RG 3431 and RG 3543 are designed to accomplish. […] The European Communities does not dispute that, in the circumstances of the present case, collection and withholding mechanisms are necessary to combat tax evasion. Nor has the European Communities submitted other arguments or evidence which would rebut the presumption raised by Argentina in respect of the 'necessity' of RG 3431 and RG 3543." Panel Report on *Argentina–Bovine Hides*, above n 35, paras 11.305–11.306.

[64] The Panel noted that one alternative course of action available to Argentina would have been to reimburse importers for the additional interest foregone or paid. Similarly, Argentina could have provided for the additional interest lost or paid to be creditable against the tax liability arising from the IVA Law and IG Law. Furthermore, Argentina could have eliminated the rate differentials themselves. The Panel observed that Argentina had not convincingly demonstrated why these other alternatives were indeed not viable in order to secure compliance of its tax laws. *Ibid.*, paras 11.325–11.329.

[65] Cf A Desmedt, "Proportionality in WTO Law", 4 *JIEL* (2001) 441, at 465–69, where it is correctly noted that under GATT panel practice and WTO jurisprudence, the "necessary to" requirements of Art XX(b) and (d) has been interpreted as containing both a "causal connection" requirement (ie a sort of "suitability" test) and a "least inconsistent" or "least trade-restrictive measure" test. According to this author, the *Bovine Hides* Panel failed to perform the second, more rigid examination.

[66] Cf OK Fauchald, *Environmental Taxes and Trade Discrimination* (London, Kluwer Law International, 1998) at 164; T Schoenbaum, "International Trade and Protection of the Environment: The Continuing Search for Reconciliation" 91 *Am J Int'l L* (April, 1997) 268, at 307 *et seq.*

[67] Panel Report on *United States—Taxes on Petroleum and Certain Imported Substances (Superfund)*, L/6175, adopted on 17 June 1987, BISD 34S/136.

from chemicals that in the United States were subject to an excise tax. The Panel found that such tax adjustment was in compliance with the National Treatment requirement of Article III:2, first sentence, since the tax rate on the imported substance was determined, in principle, in relation to the amount of the chemicals used and not in relation to the value of the imported substance. It was thus in principle equivalent to the tax borne by domestic substances.[68]

It should noted that border tax adjustment can only take place in the case of a de jure discriminatory measure (ie a measure that formally employs the "origin" or "nationality" of the products as the differentiating criterion), since by definition a border tax adjustment is required to compensate for the higher fiscal burden imposed on the domestic product compared to that of the imported product. Thus, it follows that the concept of border tax adjustment is employed only when the domestic and imported products concerned are, at least for purposes of the national fiscal regime, identical. If the products were only "similar", then there would be no case of formal discrimination and accordingly no need to claim the necessity of the tax adjustment. In this case, in fact, the "neutrality" issue would be absorbed by the determination of whether or not the tax measure constitutes a de facto discrimination between domestic and imported like products.

3. Judge-Made Public Policy Exception in EC Law

Contrary to the National Treatment obligation of Article III GATT, the non-discrimination principle in Article 90 EC is not subject to any express exception. As already noted in the section on border measures, Article 30 EC applies only to non-pecuniary restrictions. However, the Court has on several occasions recognised a *"de facto derogation clause"* according to which Member States may plead any social policy as a justification for violating the non-discrimination principle in the field of internal taxation.[69]

---

[68] The Panel examined the case where the tax on certain imported substances would not necessarily be equal to the tax on the chemicals used in their production, in light of the penalty tax of 5% of the appraised value of the imported substance where an importer failed to furnish the information necessary to determine the amount of tax to be imposed. Since the tax on certain chemicals subjected some of the chemicals only to a tax equivalent to 2% of the 1980 wholesale price of the chemical, the 5% penalty tax could have been much higher than the highest possible tax that the importer would have had to pay had he provided sufficient information, thus breaching the equivalence requirement. The Panel saved the penalty rate provisions by noting that the tax authorities had the regulatory power to eliminate the need for the imposition of the penalty rate and recommended the Contracting Parties to take note of the statement by the United States that the penalty rate would in all probability never be applied. *Ibid.*, para 5.2.9.

[69] JHH Weiler, "The Constitution of the Common Marketplace: Text and Context in the Evolution of the Free Movement of Goods" in P Craig and G de Búrca (eds), *Evolution of EU Law* (Oxford, OUP, 1999) at 365.

This justification option has been employed also with regard to origin-based fiscal measures (ie de jure discriminatory taxes).

For example, in the *Regenerated Petroleum Products* case,[70] the Court considered the Italian Government argument that a tax exemption was justified by the very high production cost of regenerated oils, with the result that without the tax reduction at issue these oils could not compete with oils of primary distillation. Although the Court agreed with the defendant Government that reductions of the fabrication tax are in principle justified by the high cost of regeneration compared to primary distillation, it rejected this argument in the present case, noting that,

> the more favourable tax treatment is not in any way jeopardised by the obligation to apply it with due regard to Article 95 [now 90] of the Treaty [or in other words] the tax reductions which thus accrue to undertakings engaged in the regeneration of mineral oil are not in fact endangered by the obligation to allow regenerated oils imported from the other Member States to benefit from them.[71]

While a distinction between oils of primary distillation and regenerated oils with regard to their tax burden seems to be permitted by Article 90,[72] a Member State is not allowed to discriminate between imported and domestic regenerated oil. If, in the exercise of their discretion in the field of internal taxation, Member States decide to allow regenerated oils to benefit from more favourable tax treatment, they must accept the consequences of that choice and ensure that the system chosen complies with the fundamental principle laid down in Article 90 of the Treaty that there be no tax discrimination against imported products.[73]

The Italian government advanced a further argument to justify retention of the rules disqualifying imported regenerated oils from the benefit of the lower rates of tax allowed on home-produced regenerated oils. It stated that, since it is impossible to distinguish, by means of the experimental testing methods, regenerated oils from oils of primary distillation, the government had decided to exclude regenerated oils imported from other Member States from the tax advantages at issue in order to prevent likely tax evasion when the products in question are imported.[74] The Court did not accept this argument as a justification for the alleged differential treatment, noting that there were other ways to avoid tax evasion. The Court stated:

---

[70] Case 21/79, *Commission v Italy (Regenerated Petroleum Products)* [1980] ECR 1.
[71] *Ibid.*, para 24.
[72] See below ch 3 on the prohibition of de facto discrimination for an analysis of the basis of this finding (whether the two products at issue were dissimilar or whether the discrimination was justified on the basis of economic policy).
[73] Case 21/79, *Regenerated Petroleum Products*, above n 47, para 26.
[74] *Ibid.*, para 20.

It is for the importers of mineral oils from the other Member States who wish to qualify for the reduced rate to produce evidence that the oils imported by them into Italy are regenerated oils and the Italian administration, without being able nonetheless to set a higher standard of proof than is necessary, is entitled to require in particular that the evidence be adduced in a form that removes the risk of tax evasion, for example by producing certificates from the authorities or other appropriate bodies of the exporting Member State permitting the regenerated oil to be identified as from the premises where it was regenerated.[75]

Similarly, in *Commission v Greece*,[76] the Court of Justice took into consideration Greece's argument that the de jure discriminatory flat-rate system of taxation in that case was intended to prevent the tax evasion to which imports of cars were susceptible in view of the high rate of tax.[77] The Court categorically dismissed the defendant's claim, holding that the impossibility of carrying out the requisite controls and investigations concerning imported cars cannot justify the introduction of a flat-rate system of taxation for imported cars alone.[78] Interestingly, the Advocate-General, in reaching the same conclusion, added that there existed *other ways* to tackle tax evasion which did not violate the non-discrimination principle of Article 90. Apparently employing a sort of "least-trade restrictive test" in his analysis, he stated that,

> as rightly observed by the Commission, it is not entirely clear why it should not be possible to avoid the risk of under-declared invoice prices by using *non-discriminatory* systems for calculation of the basis of assessment, based for example on catalogue prices, as is the practice in other countries which have similar special consumption taxes.[79]

The defendant also advanced a further argument to justify its different and less favourable system for calculation of the basis of assessment for imported cars. It stated that, in light of the fact that in Greece the automobile industry was not highly developed and that car manufacturers usually sold their products directly to the final consumer without recourse to

---

[75] *Ibid.*, para 21. The Court added that "The practice in the Community, especially in relation to the discontinuance of public health inspections at the frontiers between Member States, offers numerous examples of such forms of permissible inspection." *Ibid.*
[76] Case C–327/90, *Commission v Greece* [1992] ECR I–3033.
[77] *Ibid.*, para 9, "Such evasion takes the form of under-declaration of the invoice price so as to reduce the amount of tax paid. Proof of this is provided by the fact that lorries, which are subject to a lower rate of tax and are therefore less susceptible to evasion of that kind, are taxed, without distinction as to origin, on the basis of the transaction value."
[78] *Ibid.*, para 24. Cf Case 45/75, *Rewe-Zentrale v Hauptzollamt Landau/Pfalz* [1976] ECR 181, para 15.
[79] AG Tesauro Opinion, para 8 [emphasis added].

intermediaries, the manufacturer's selling price, which served as the basis for calculating the tax on cars assembled in Greece, was equivalent to the retail price, which included marketing expenses. The government argued therefore that it was necessary to add to the foreign manufacturer's price the marketing costs incurred by the importer, such as promotional, advertising and after-sales-service expenses, in order to restore equality between cars manufactured in Greece and imported cars.[80]

Thus, the different method for calculation of the basis of assessment of the tax on imported cars was predicated on the grounds of *substantial equality* between domestic and imported cars. According to the defendant, the apparently less favourable treatment reserved to imported cars was in fact necessary in order to guarantee effective equality between cars manufactured in Greece (Greek cars) and imported cars.

The Court did not accept the "substantial equality" argument advanced by the Hellenic government for principally two sets of reasons. First, rejecting the facts on which the argument was based, the Court stated that "marketing expenses are often included, at least in part, in the ex-factory price of imported cars."[81] Secondly the Court attacked the *ability* of the alternative method to guarantee substantive equality. The Court noted that,

> as is apparent from the documents before the Court, the flat-rate increase of 21% or 23.2% was based on an average which was itself determined by reference to company balance-sheets. A flat-rate evaluation of that kind *cannot ensure that the imported product is never subjected to a heavier tax burden than the corresponding domestic product.*[82]

Although treated within the same framework, it should be clear that from a technical point of view the two justifications examined and rejected by the Court in *Commission v Greece* refer to two distinct issues. On the one hand, the "substantial equality" argument deals with the question of whether the tax measures in question affords *less favourable treatment* to imported than to domestic products, and aims at demonstrating that, though formally different, the two methods for calculating the basis of assessment in reality do not favour domestic products. In considering

---

[80] Case C–327/90, *Commission v Greece* [1992] ECR I–3033, para 8. The Greek government argued moreover that "as regard to the addition of 23.2%, which applies when imported cars are bought not direct from the manufacturer but from a foreign distributor, it is intended to cover that intermediary's profit as well." *Ibid.*

[81] *Ibid.*, para 17.

[82] *Ibid.*, para 18 [emphasis added]. The Court added that "The same applies to the 7% addition which is intended to cover the costs of transport and insurance. It must be observed, moreover, that, whilst insurance costs may vary according to the value of the product, transport costs are more closely related to its weight and dimensions and the distance over which it is carried." *Ibid.*, para 19.

whether the differential treatment meets the substantial equality test, the Court took into account both the factual circumstances justifying such treatment as well as the capability of the different treatment of imported products to guarantee substantive equality (much like the "suitability limb" of the proportionality principle). In light of its nature and function, I prefer to refer to this type of justification as a type of *"internal justification"*.

On the other hand, the "tax evasion" argument, presupposing a less favourable treatment towards imported products, functioned as a form of *external justification* for de jure discriminatory treatment. Accordingly, only with regard to this latter argument can one speak of a judge-made "exception" to the non-discrimination principle of Article 90. Moreover, as with the general exception provision in Article 30 EC, the Court will review the validity of the public policy objectives (in both of the above-mentioned cases, for example, tax evasion was the alleged purpose of the de jure discriminatory treatment) taking into account whether there exist other ways to achieve those objectives without violating the non-discrimination obligation of Article 90. This criterion resembles the "necessity" or "least-trade restrictive" limb of the proportionality test (which will be further examined in a subsequent section of this chapter). However, despite the resemblance in the criteria employed by the Court in evaluating the validity of the arguments brought under these two types of justification, one should not confuse the different nature and function of "internal" and "external" justifications.

C. Conclusions

With regard to the field of internal taxation, both EC and WTO law include a prohibition on de jure discrimination, which requires Members not to employ the origin or nationality of a product as a criterion for drawing regulatory distinctions in a manner such as to improve competitive conditions for domestic production. When dealing with de jure discriminatory or origin-based measures, the central focus of the dispute is mainly on the question whether or not the differential treatment between *identical* imported and domestic products violates the National Treatment obligations in EC and WTO law.

A fiscal measure formally differentiating on the basis of the product's origin or nationality is deemed to violate Article 90 (ex 95) EC and Article III:2 GATT whenever the imported product is taxed *in excess of* the tax on the domestic product. The prohibition of discrimination on the basis of origin or nationality contained in these two Articles covers not only the rate of taxation but also the various provisions concerning the basis of assessment and the rules for levying taxes. Accordingly, the prohibition of de jure discrimination includes, for example, the imposition of a higher tax rate on imported petroleum compared to that on domestic petroleum,[83] as well as the application of two different methods for calculating the basis of assessment of the tax according to whether cars are imported or manufactured.[84] For purposes of determining whether a fiscal measure discriminates between domestic and imported products, the level of actual trade effects is irrelevant and thus the prohibitions in Articles 90 EC and III:2 GATT may not be qualified by a *de minimis* standard.[85]

Especially in EC law, there appears to be a "presumption of illegality" when Member States employ origin or nationality as the differentiating criterion in the field of taxation. The burden of proving that the fiscal *differentiation* does not entail discrimination thus rests on the defending Member State, which may rebut this presumption by demonstrating that in reality the differential treatment does not really afford less favourable treatment to imported products or that such a treatment is justified in order to afford domestic products *substantially equal treatment* (this has been described as a form of "internal justification").[86] In this latter case, the Court will take into account the facts of the case as well as the "suitability" (and also "necessity") of the measure for achieving such equality.

Nevertheless, if "rules" have their "exceptions", a violation of the prohibition of de jure discrimination may be avoided by arguing that an origin-based measure is justified on public policy grounds. Where the GATT provides for such an option in the case of discriminatory fiscal measures, there is no equivalent in the EC Treaty (the public policy exception in the EC Treaty—Article 30 EC—is applicable only in order to justify non-fiscal regulations). However, the ECJ has on several occasions recognised a "*de facto* derogation clause" according to which Member States may plead any social policy in order to justify an origin-based fiscal measure found to violate the non-discrimination principle of Article 90 EC.

Notwithstanding this structural difference, it is interesting to note that in EC law more attention seems to be given to the possibility of justifying *fiscal* measures on public policy grounds even when there is a direct discrimination on the basis of the product's nationality, compared to WTO law, where the matter is very rarely even raised.[87]

---

[83] Panel Report on *United States—Taxes on Petroleum and Certain Imported Substances*, L/6175, adopted on 17 June 1987, BISD 34S/136.

[84] Case C–327/90, *Commission v Greece* [1992] ECR I–3033.

[85] Panel Report on *Malt Beverages*, above n 21, paras 5.6 and 5.15.

[86] Case C–327/90, *Commission v Greece* [1992] ECR I–3033.

[87] The only instance in which Art XX defence has been discussed by a WTO panel in this context is the recent Report on *Argentina–Bovine Hides*, above n 35, concerning the GATT compatibility of the Argentinean system of pre-payment of part of the IVA (value-added tax) and the IG (income tax), which formally discriminated between imports and domestic products.

2.2 PROHIBITION OF DE JURE DISCRIMINATION AND NON-FISCAL REGULATIONS

The prohibition of de jure discrimination on the basis of nationality applies also to the realm of non-fiscal regulations affecting trade in goods. However, contrary to the non-discrimination provisions dealing with fiscal measures, WTO and EC provisions imposing the National Treatment obligation with regard to non-fiscal regulations do not follow an identical design. The EC Treaty did not include a specific provision prohibiting discriminatory non-fiscal regulations. The only general obligation in the section on the free movement of goods was, and still is, the ban on "quantitative restrictions and measures having equivalent effect" included in Article 28 EC. However, as already noted in the chapter on "negative integration", Article 28 has been interpreted as going beyond a mere prohibition on border measures restricting the importation of goods and including, inter alia, a prohibition on de jure discriminatory non-fiscal measures.

Following the same scheme employed above with regard to fiscal measures, in this section I propose to analyse first the "normative content" and then the "justification options" of the National Treatment obligations in WTO and EC law as they are applied to origin-based non-fiscal internal regulations.

A. Normative Content

1. Article III:4 GATT

As evidenced in both its heading and introductory paragraph, Article III GATT covers, in addition to internal taxation, also *non-fiscal internal regulations*, or more specifically "all laws, regulations and requirements affecting the internal sale, offering for sale, purchase, transportation, distribution or use of products."

Article III:4 specifically provides that,

> The products of the territory of any contracting party imported into the territory of any other contracting party shall be accorded treatment no less favourable than that accorded to like products of national origin in respect of all laws, regulations and requirements affecting their internal sale, offering for sale, purchase, transportation, distribution or use.[88]

---

[88] Art III:4 also adds that "The provisions of this paragraph shall not prevent the application of differential internal transportation charges which are based exclusively on the economic operation of the means of transport and not on the nationality of the product."

The great majority of cases in both GATT and WTO jurisprudence that have dealt with this provision, involved internal measures which *formally* discriminated on the basis of the nationality (or origin) of the products (ie de jure discriminatory measures).

As already noted in the previous section dealing with fiscal measures, when confronted with a regulation that discriminates on a de jure basis, the focus of an Article III inquiry will mainly be on whether or not the differential treatment between *identical* imported and domestic products violates the non-discrimination obligation of that Article.[89] In the case of a non-fiscal regulation, a Panel will have to determine whether such differential treatment violates the "no less favourable treatment" standard of Article III:4. Accordingly, since a measure formally discriminating on the basis of the product's nationality presupposes by definition that the regulated products are, for purposes of that same measure, *identical* (that is identical except for their different origin or nationality), an examination of the products' relationship is not, or at least should not be, an issue in the case of de jure discriminatory internal regulations. The present examination will thus focus in particular on the meaning of the "no less favourable treatment" standard in both GATT panel practice and WTO jurisprudence.

(a)   GATT Panel Practice: from Italian Agricultural Machinery *to* Malt Beverages   One of the first internal measures falling within the net of Article III:4 was the Italian Law of 25 July 1952, which established a revolving fund enabling the Ministry of Agriculture and Forestry to grant special credit terms inter alia for the purchase of Italian agricultural machinery. The Panel found that this measure violated Article III:4 since the credit facilities provided under the Italian Law were not available to purchasers of imported tractors and other agricultural machinery, and therefore these products did not enjoy an *equality of treatment*.[90] Interestingly, the Italian delegation's defence was based entirely on the argument that the scope of application of Article III:4 should not be construed in a broad manner, since such an interpretation would have prevented the Italian government from taking the necessary measures to assist the economic development of the country and to improve the conditions of employment in Italy. The Panel rejected this line of argument noting, inter alia, that,

---

[89] Once again, within the scope of de jure discriminatory measures, the identity of the products is a "legal" not a "factual" one. If a Member State imposes an noise-reduction requirement on "car engines", and then provides for an exception for domestic "car engines", the specific regulation of that Member State does not distinguish whether car engines are 500 cc or 3000 cc. For purposes of that specific measure all car engines are "identical" and are treated differently only on the basis of their origin.

[90] Panel Report on *Italian Discrimination Against Imported Agricultural Machinery (Italian Agricultural Machinery)*, L/833, adopted on 23 Oct 1958, BISD 7S/60, para 5.

it was not the intention of the General Agreement to limit the right of a contracting party to adopt measures, which appeared to it necessary to foster its economic development or to protect a domestic industry, provided that such measures were permitted by the terms of the General Agreement [and] the GATT offered a number of possibilities to achieve these purposes through tariff measures or otherwise.[91]

In *EEC Measures on Animal Feed Proteins*,[92] the Panel found that an EC regulation subjecting the purchase of imported corn gluten to several requirements (to purchase denatured skimmed milk powder and to produce a protein certificate or a security deposit), while the purchase of domestic corn gluten was not, did not comply with the "less favourable treatment" standard provided for in Article III:4. Likewise, in *Canada—Administration of the Foreign Investment Review Act* (the so-called *FIRA* case),[93] the Panel found that several undertakings concluded between foreign investors and the Canadian government, according to which investors agreed to purchase goods of Canadian origin and goods from Canadian sources, were in violation of the National Treatment obligation embodied in Article III:4.[94]

The application of the National Treatment obligation of Article III:4 with regard to origin-based (or de jure discriminatory) internal regulations was further developed in the famous Panel Report on *United States—Section 337 of the Tariff Act 1930* (the so-called *Section 337* case).[95]

The *Section 337* Panel, whose members included the learned Professor Andreas Lowenfeld and Justice Pierre Pescatore, for the first time emphasised that the requirement of "no less favourable" treatment in Article III:4 calls for *effective* equality of opportunities for imported and domestic products, and thus does not mandate formally identical treatment

---

[91] Panel Report on *Italian Discrimination Against Imported Agricultural Machinery (Italian Agricultural Machinery)*, L/833, adopted on 23 Oct 1958, BISD 7S/60, para 16: "The Panel did not appreciate why the extension of the credit facilities in question to the purchasers of imported tractors as well as domestically produced tractors would detract from the attainment of the objectives of the Law, which aimed at stimulating the purchase of tractors mainly by small farmers and co-operatives in the interests of economic development. If, on the other hand, the objective of the Law, although not specifically stated in the text thereof, were to protect the Italian agricultural machinery industry, the Panel considered that such protection should be given in ways permissible under the General Agreement rather than by the extension of credit exclusively for purchases of domestically produced agricultural machinery." For a discussion of the Panel's broad reading of Art III:4 scope of application based on a textual interpretation, see above section dealing with the "objective element" of Art XI GATT in ch 1.
[92] Panel Report on *EEC Measures on Animal Feed Proteins*, L/4599, adopted on 14 March 1978, BISD 25S/49.
[93] Panel Report on *Canada—Administration of the Foreign Investment Review Act (FIRA)*, L/5504, adopted on 7 Feb 1984, BISD 30S/140.
[94] *Ibid.*, paras 5.4–11.
[95] Panel Report on *United States—section 337 of the Tariff Act of 1930 (section 337)*, L/6439, adopted on 7 Nov 1989, BISD 36S/345.

between imported and domestic products in every case. The EEC claimed in that instance that the United States had failed to carry out its obligations under Article III:4 of the General Agreement since, in patent infringement suits, it applied to *imported* products the stricter, and thus "less favourable", requirements of Section 337 of the United States Tariff Act of 1930, while goods of *national origin* enjoyed the more favourable treatment accorded by US federal procedures.

The *Section 337* Panel recognised that Members may apply to imported products different formal legal requirements if doing so would accord imported products more favourable treatment.[96] Accordingly, the mere fact that imported products were, in that particular case, subject under Section 337 to legal provisions that were *different* from those applying to products of national origin was in itself not conclusive in establishing inconsistency with Article III:4.[97] In such cases, it has to be assessed whether or not such differences in the applicable legal provisions accord to imported products less favourable treatment compared to that granted to domestic ones. The Panel furthermore specified that, in such cases, it is incumbent on the contracting party applying differential treatment to show that, in spite of such differences, the no less favourable treatment standard of Article III is met.[98]

In the *Section 337* report, the Panel also clarified that such a determination could not be made on the basis of an examination of the *actual results* of past cases where the incriminated measure had been applied, as suggested by the United States. Such an interpretation would not serve the general purpose of Article III, which is to protect *expectations* on the competitive relationship between imported and domestic products. A law, regulation or requirement could then only be challenged in GATT after the event as a means of rectifying less favourable treatment of imported products rather than as a means of forestalling it.[99] Accordingly, in order to establish whether the "no less favourable" treatment standard of Article III:4 is met, the Panel held that, in accordance with previous GATT Panel practice, it had to assess whether or not Section 337 in itself may lead to the application to imported products of treatment less favourable than that accorded to products of United States origin.

---

[96] *Ibid.*, para 5.11.
[97] The panel expressly envisaged extending the scope of application of Art III:4 to cover cases of de facto discrimination, when it also recognised that "there may be cases where application of formally identical legal provisions would in practice accord less favourable treatment to imported products and a contracting party might thus have to apply different legal provisions to imported products to ensure that the treatment accorded them is in fact no less favourable." *Ibid.* See below ch 3 on the National Treatment principle and the prohibition of de facto discriminatory measures.
[98] Panel Report on *section 337*, above n 17, para 5.11.
[99] *Ibid.*, paras 5.12–5.13.

The *Section 337* Panel report added moreover that the "no less favourable" treatment requirement of Article III:4 had to be understood as applicable to each individual case of imported products, thus rejecting "any notion of balancing more favourable treatment of some imported products against less favourable treatment of other imported products."[100]

The approach enunciated in the Panel Report in the *Section 337* case has been endorsed in subsequent GATT Panel practice and WTO jurisprudence, at least with regard to cases of de jure discriminatory internal measures.[101] For example, in the two *Alcohol* cases at the beginning of the 1990s, both GATT Panels expressly followed the teachings of the *337 Section* Panel report.

In *Canada—Import, Distribution and Sale of Certain Alcoholic Drinks by Provincial Marketing Agencies* (*Canada Alcohol II*),[102] the Panel stated that, although the liquor boards of several Canadian provinces[103] prohibited the private delivery of imported beer to the points of sale while they accorded domestic brewers the right to deliver their products to the point of sale, this difference was not, in itself, conclusive in establishing inconsistency with Article III:4 of the General Agreement.[104] The panel stated that it was up to Canada to demonstrate that, in spite of the application of different transportation regulations to imported and domestic beer, imported beer was accorded no less favourable treatment in this respect, and found, in fact, that the practices of the Canadian provincial liquor boards were indeed inconsistent with Article III:4.[105]

---

[100] *Ibid.*, para 5.14: "If this notion were accepted, it would entitle a contracting party to derogate from the no less favourable treatment obligation in one case, or indeed in respect of one contracting party, on the ground that it accords more favourable treatment in some other case, or to another contracting party. Such an interpretation would lead to great uncertainty about the conditions of competition between imported and domestic products and thus defeat the purposes of Art III."

[101] While in dealing with facially origin-neutral non-fiscal regulations the principal focus also rests on "effective equality of competitive opportunities" between imported and domestic products, the relevance of the measure's "actual trade effects", the "burden of proof" and the role of the "notion of balancing" may indeed be quite different from that seen in the case of origin-based measures. *See* below chapter 3 on de facto discriminatory measures.

[102] Panel Report on *Canada—Import, Distribution and Sale of Certain Alcoholic Drinks by Provincial Marketing Agencies* (*Canada Alcohol II*), DS17/R, adopted on 18 Feb 1992, BISD 39S/27.

[103] It was the case of the provinces of Alberta, British Columbia, Manitoba, New Brunswick, Newfoundland, Nova Scotia, Ontario and Quebec.

[104] Panel Report on Canada Alcohol II, above n 102, para 5.12.

[105] *Ibid.*, para 5.12–5.14: "The Panel noted that [the levy imposed for the delivery of imported beer to cover the costs actually incurred by the liquor boards] did not necessarily correspond to the cost that the liquor board would incur for the delivery of imported beer if it delivered not only imported but also domestic beer. It could reasonably be assumed that it would, in that case, make economies of scale from which also imported beer could benefit. Nor did such a levy necessarily correspond to the cost of private delivery of imported beer. It could reasonably be assumed that the structure and efficiency of private delivery systems would

In *United States—Measures Affecting Alcoholic and Malt Beverages* (*Malt Beverages*),[106] another distinguished Panel emphasised once again that the requirement of Article III:4 to accord imported products treatment no less favourable than that accorded to domestic products should be interpreted as requiring *effective equality of competitive opportunities* between imported and domestic products, without there being a need to establish actual adverse effects on imported products. In the case at hand, several states in the United States imposed a requirement that imported beer and wine could be sold only through in-state wholesalers or other middlemen, while permitting some in-state like products to be sold directly to retailers, and in some cases at retail on producers' premises.

Having considered as irrelevant to the examination under Article III:4 the fact that many—or even most—in-state beer and wine producers "preferred" to use wholesalers rather than market their products directly to retailers, the Panel found that the difference in treatment accorded to imported and domestic wine and beer nevertheless violated Article III:4 GATT. The Panel noted as follows:

> The Article III:4 requirement is one addressed to relative competitive opportunities created by the government in the market, not to the actual choices made by enterprises in that market. Producers located in the states in question have the opportunity to choose their preferred method of marketing. The Panel considered that it is the very denial of this opportunity in the case of imported products which constitutes less favourable treatment.[107]

(b)   WTO Jurisprudence: from Reformulated Gasoline *to* Korea–Beef   The first WTO panel applying Article III:4 in a case of de jure discrimination also

---

be different from the systems operated by the liquor boards." In *Canada Alcohol II*, the Panel also found that two other de jure discriminatory requirements were inconsistent with Art III:4. They were (a) the requirement imposed by Canada in the province of Ontario that imported beer be sold in the six-pack size, while in certain stores no such requirement was imposed on domestic beer; and (b) the restrictions maintained by Canada in all provinces except Prince Edward Island and Saskatchewan on access of imported beer to points of sale available to domestic beer. *Ibid.*, paras 5.4–5.7.

[106] Panel Report on *Malt Beverages*, above n 21.
[107] *Ibid.*, para 5.31. The Panel also found the following de jure discriminatory measures inconsistent with Art III:4 GATT: (a) the requirements in the states of Arizona, California, Maine, Mississippi and South Carolina that imported beer and wine be transported into these states by common carrier, which requirements do not exist for the in-state like products; (b) the application of a higher licensing fee for imported beer and/or wine in the states of Alaska (beer and wine) and Vermont (beer only) than for the like domestic products is, in the case of Alaska, in view of the wholesaler requirement applicable to imported beer and wine; (c) the exemption by the state of Mississippi of domestic in-state wine, but not the like imported product, from decisions to prohibit the sale of alcohol within political subdivisions of the state; (d) the application by the states of Massachusetts and Rhode Island of price

made reference to the *Section 337* report. At issue in *United States—Standards for Reformulated and Conventional Gasoline* (also known as the *Reformulated Gasoline* dispute)[108] was the US Clean Air Act and its implementing regulations ("the Gasoline Rule"), which was enacted by Congress in order to reduce air pollution in the United States. The Act basically permitted only gasoline of a specified cleanliness ("reformulated gasoline") to be sold in areas of high air pollution, while in other areas it permitted only gasoline no dirtier than that sold in the base year of 1990 ("conventional gasoline"). The Gasoline Rule applied to US refiners, blenders and importers of gasoline and it required that certain chemical characteristics of the gasoline in which they dealt respected, on an annual average basis, defined levels. While some of these levels were expressly fixed by the Gasoline Rule, others were expressed as "non-degradation" requirements, according to which each domestic refiner had to maintain, on an annual average basis, the relevant gasoline characteristics at levels no worse than its "individual baseline"— that is, the annual average levels achieved by that refiner in 1990.

To establish an individual baseline, a (domestic) *refiner* had to show evidence of the quality of gasoline produced or shipped in 1990 ("Method 1"). If that evidence was not complete, then it had to use data on the quality of blendstock produced in 1990 ("Method 2"). If these two methods did not result in sufficient evidence, the refiner had to use data on the quality of post-1990 gasoline blendstock or gasoline ("Method 3").

However, although *importers* were also required to use an individual baseline, they could do that *only* in the unlikely case that they were able to establish the individual baseline using Method 1 data. Unlike domestic refiners, importers were not allowed to establish an individual baseline by using the secondary or tertiary data specified in Methods 2 and 3. Accordingly, if an importer could not produce Method 1 data, then it had to use a "statutory baseline", which was established by law and derived from the average characteristics of all gasoline consumed in the United States in 1990.[109]

---

affirmation requirements for imported beer and wine, which requirements are not applicable to the like domestic products; (e) the listing and delisting practices maintained by the liquor control boards in the states of Idaho, Mississippi, New Hampshire, Pennsylvania, Vermont and Virginia, which accord to imported wine less favourable treatment than that accorded to the like domestic product.

[108] Panel Report on *United States—Standards for Reformulated and Conventional Gasoline (Reformulated Gasoline)*, WT/DS2/R, circulated on 29 Jan 1996, adopted 20 May 1996.
[109] *Ibid.*, paras 6.1–6.3. Some other domestic entities (such as refiners with only partial or no 1990 operations, and blenders with insufficient Method 1 data) were also assigned the statutory baseline. Exceptionally, importers that imported in 1990 at least 75% of the production of an affiliated foreign refinery were treated as domestic refiners for the purpose of establishing baselines. Since this dispute concerns only the Gasoline Rule's non-degradation requirements, and not reformulated and conventional gasoline as such, the Panel referred generally to "gasoline" in the course of its findings.

Although the Panel was not really clear on this point, the Gasoline Rule represented a quite evident example of de jure discrimination on the basis of the product's origin. The fact that the US measure applied to "refiners" and "importers" of gasoline, rather than to domestic and imported gasoline, should not cloud the formally discriminatory nature of the measure at issue in that case. By distinguishing between the gasoline standards to which refiners and importers were subject ("individual baseline" established according to Methods 1, 2 and 3, for the former; "individual baseline" according to Method 1 or "statutory baseline", for the latter), the Gasoline Rule *on its own terms* accorded different treatment to domestic and imported gasoline, since non-US gasoline could enter the US market only through importers and was thus directly affected by the standards imposed on them by the Gasoline Rule.

This reading is implicitly confirmed by the Panel's finding that imported and domestic gasoline were indeed chemically *identical* and thus met Article III:4 preliminary requirement of whether the products at issue were "like products".[110] By its terms, the Gasoline Rule did not employ a differentiating criterion based on the characteristics of the gasoline, but on whether the gasoline was sold by domestic refiners or importers, thus clearly envisaging a case of formal discrimination. Moreover, Venezuela and Brazil, the two complaining Members, which produced gasoline at a level of quality below the statutory baseline, invoked the National Treatment principle only in as far as imported gasoline was excluded from the perceived more favourable "individual baseline system". The only remedy that they were asking for was simply for their gasoline to be included in that system, or in other words, to enjoy what they perceived was the more favourable system applicable to domestic gasoline.[111]

Having determined that the Gasoline Rule afforded imported gasoline *formally different treatment* than to domestic gasoline, the Panel focused on the issue of whether the different treatment accorded to imported gasoline

---

[110] *Ibid.*, para 6.9. Moreover, the Panel observed that the United States did not argue that imported gasoline and domestic gasoline were not like per se, but rather that with respect to the treatment of the imported and domestic products, the situation of the parties dealing in the gasoline must be taken into consideration.

[111] R Hudec, "The Product-Process Doctrine in GATT/WTO Jurisprudence", in M Bronckers and R Quick (eds), *New Directions in International Economic Law* (London, Kluwer Law International, 2000) at 208. Venezuela and Brazil argued that by denying foreign refiners the possibility of establishing an individual baseline, the Gasoline Rule violated Art III:4 because it accorded less favourable treatment to imported gasoline, both reformulated and conventional, than to US gasoline. The Gasoline Rule required imported gasoline to conform with the more stringent statutory baseline when US gasoline had to comply only with a US refiner's individual baseline. Practically, this meant that imported gasoline with certain parameter levels above the statutory baseline could not be directly sold in the US market whereas gasoline with these same qualities produced in a US refinery could be freely sold on the US market provided that it conformed with that refiner's individual baseline.

was indeed *less favourable* than that accorded to like gasoline of national origin. The Panel observed that domestic gasoline benefited in general from the fact that the seller, who is a refiner, used an individual baseline, while imported gasoline did not. The Panel believed that this difference resulted in less favourable treatment for the imported product, as illustrated by the case of a batch of imported gasoline which was chemically identical to a batch of domestic gasoline that met its refiner's individual baseline, but not the statutory baseline levels. Recalling the interpretation given by the *Section 337* panel report of the term "treatment no less favourable", the Panel found that imported gasoline was indeed treated less favourably than domestic gasoline since, under the baseline establishment methods, imported gasoline was effectively prevented from benefiting from sales conditions as favourable as those afforded to domestic gasoline by an individual baseline tied to the producer of a product.[112]

The United States had offered two lines of defence against the claim that the Gasoline Rule was in violation of the national treatment obligation of Article III:4. First of all, the US refusal to permit foreign suppliers to employ the individual baseline option (at least to its full extent) did not constitute less favourable treatment of foreign suppliers but, on the contrary, was merely the even-handed application of a regulation applicable to both domestic and foreign suppliers. In other words, according to the United States, the Gasoline Rule denied the option of using individual baselines Methods 2 and 3 to *any* supplier (not just to importers) that could not provide sufficient data to calculate the cleanliness of the gasoline produced or sold in 1990.[113] Its second argument was that the treatment accorded to gasoline imported under a statutory baseline was *on the whole* no less favourable than that accorded to domestic gasoline under individual refiner baselines, since the statutory baseline (by the nature of its calculation) and the average of the sum of the individual baselines both corresponded to average gasoline quality in 1990, and thus domestic and imported gasoline was treated in overall terms equally.

With regard to the second argument, the Panel noted that it amounted to claiming that less favourable treatment of particular imported products in some instances would be *balanced* by more favourable treatment of particular products in others. Recalling the rejection by the *Section 337* Panel Report of any notion of balancing more favourable treatment of some imported products against less favourable treatment of other

---

[112] Panel Report on *Reformulated Gasoline*, above n 34, para 6.10.
[113] *Ibid.*, para 6.11: "According to the United States, the difference in treatment between imported and domestic gasoline was justified because importers, like domestic refiners with limited 1990 operations and blenders, could not reliably establish their 1990 gasoline quality, lacked consistent sources and quality of gasoline, or had the flexibility to meet a statutory baseline since they were not constrained by refinery equipment and crude supplies."

imported products, the Panel concurred with the reasoning of the previous Panel Report and consequently rejected the US argument.[114]

With regard to the first argument, the Panel could have easily dismissed it by noting that it was exactly the a priori inclusion by the Gasoline Rule of all *importers* within the category of suppliers excluded from enjoying the more favourable individual baseline system that violated the national treatment principle of Article III:4. Even if the Gasoline Rule did assign the less favourable statutory baseline to a few domestic entities (such as refiners with only partial or no 1990 operations and blenders with insufficient Method 1 data), by affording to the great majority of domestic refiners (and thus domestic gasoline) the possibility of employing the more flexible individual baseline system, while a priori excluding from this system practically all importers (and thus all imported gasoline), the United States had afforded, on a very formal level, imported products *less favourable treatment* than domestic products.

The Panel, however, chose a more controversial route and rejected the US argument on the basis of the so-called "product-process" doctrine.[115] Noting that the distinction in the Gasoline Rule between refiners, on the one hand, and importers and blenders, on the other, was related to certain differences in the *characteristics* of refiners, blenders and importers, and the nature of the data held by them, the Panel found that such differentiation was a priori not permitted by Article III:4. The Panel argued as follows:

> Article III:4 of the General Agreement deals with the treatment to be accorded to like products; its wording does not allow less favourable treatment dependent on the characteristics of the producer and the nature of the data held by it. [...] Apart from being contrary to the ordinary meaning of the terms of Article III:4, any interpretation of Article III:4 in this manner would mean that the treatment of imported and domestic goods concerned could no longer be assured on the objective basis of their likeness as products.

[114] *Ibid.*, paras 6.14–6.15. The Panel observed moreover that even considered from the point of view of imported gasoline as a whole, treatment was generally less favourable: "Importers of gasoline had to adapt to an assigned average standard not linked to the particular gasoline imported, while refiners of domestic gasoline had only to meet a standard linked to their own product in 1990. Statistics on baselines bore out this difference in treatment. According to the United States, as of Aug 1995, approximately 100 US refiners, representing 98.5% of gasoline produced in 1990, had received EPA approval of their individual baselines. Only three of the refiners met the statutory baseline for all parameters. Thus, while 97% of US refiners did not and were not required to meet the statutory baseline, the statutory baseline was required of importers of gasoline, except in the rare case (according to the parties) that they could establish a baseline using Method 1." *Ibid.*, para 6.15.

[115] As explained by Hudec, the effect of this doctrine would be to "make prima facie GATT-illegal for governments to impose tax or regulatory disadvantages on imported products because of the way they were produced—except where the manner of production had some impact on the characteristics of the product itself." R Hudec, "The Product-Process Doctrine in GATT/WTO Jurisprudence", in M Bronckers and R Quick (eds), *New Directions in International Economic Law* (London, Kluwer Law International, 2000) at 187.

Rather, imported goods would be exposed to a highly subjective and variable treatment according to extraneous factors. This would thereby create great instability and uncertainty in the conditions of competition as between domestic and imported goods in a manner fundamentally inconsistent with the object and purpose of Article III.[116]

The profound consequences for national regulatory freedom of such statements, quite clearly declaring regulatory distinctions linked to a producer to be per se inconsistent with Article III, have been emphasised, quite rightly, by a few commentators.[117] However, I believe it more appropriate to postpone a thorough analysis of this issue when dealing with de facto discrimination, since it is in that instance that the product-process doctrine shows all its potential "negative" effects.

There have been other Article III:4 cases in which the internal measures at issue represented, though not always very clearly, instances of formal discrimination on the basis of the product's origin and in which the Panel and Appellate Body did not really struggle to find a violation of the National Treatment obligation.

A clear case of de jure discrimination may be found in *Canada—Certain Measures Concerning Periodicals*,[118] where Canadian postal rates for magazines were openly discriminatory and in contravention of Article III:4, since Canada Post, a Canadian Government entity, was charging domestic magazines lower rates (either "commercial" or "funded" depending on the magazine) than it charged imported magazines that were mailed in Canada,[119] as well as offering also certain discounts only to domestic magazines. It was so clear a case of discrimination on the basis of the product's origin that there was no disagreement between the parties that domestic and imported periodicals were "like products" and that Canada Post was applying "higher" postal rates to imported periodicals than to

---

[116] Panel Report on *Reformulated Gasoline*, above n 34, paras 6.11–6.12. The Panel noted that in the *Malt Beverages* case, a tax regulation according less favourable treatment to beer on the basis of the size of the producer was found to violate Art III:2. Cf Panel Report on *Malt Beverages*, above n 21.

[117] S Charnovitz, "The WTO Panel Decision on US Clean Air Act Regulations", *International Environment Reporter* (6 March 1996); R Zedalis, "Product v Non-Product Based Distinctions in GATT Art III Trade and Environment Jurisprudence: Recent Developments", *European Environmental Law Review* (April, 1997).

[118] Panel Report on *Canada—Certain Measures Concerning Periodicals (Canada–Periodicals)*, WT/DS31/R, circulated on 14 March 1997, adopted 30 July 1997.

[119] *Ibid.*, para 2.11. The Canada Post's three categories of mail postal rates for publications were as follows: the "funded" publications rates and the commercial "Canadian" and commercial "International" publications rates. The first two categories apply to periodicals published and printed in Canada. "Funded" rates were rates subsidised by the Canadian Government and commercial rates were for publications ineligible for "funded" rates. "Canadian" rates were commercial rates available to Canadian publications and "International" commercial rates applied to all foreign publications mailed in Canada.

domestic periodicals, which clearly affected the sale, transportation and distribution of imported periodicals.[120]

More recently in *Korea—Measures Affecting Imports of Fresh, Chilled and Frozen Beef* (*Korea–Beef*),[121] there was a question concerning Korean legislation requiring the existence of two distinct systems for the distribution and sale of beef: one system for the retail sale of domestic beef and another system for the retail sale of imported beef.[122] The Panel found that the Korean measure violated Article III:4, emphasising that the Korean dual retail system formally distinguished on the basis of the origin of the product (ie the measure was a clear case of de jure discrimination). The Panel stated as follows:

> Any regulatory distinction that is based exclusively on criteria relating to the nationality or the origin of the products is incompatible with Article III and this conclusion can be reached even in the absence of any imports (as hypothetical imports can be used to reach this conclusion) confirming that there is no need to demonstrate the actual and specific trade effects of a measure for it to be found in violation of Article III.[123]

Although it reached the same conclusion, the Appellate Body corrected the Panel's reasoning by noting that Article III:4 does not require formal identical treatment of domestic and imported products, but only "that a measure

---

[120] *Ibid.*, para 5.33. Canada's defence was on the contrary entirely based on the argument that since Canada Post was a privatised agency (a Crown corporation) with a legal personality distinct from the Canadian Government, the "commercial Canadian" or "international" rates it charged for the delivery of periodicals were out of the Government's control and did not qualify as "regulations" or "requirements" within the meaning of Art III:4. Although Canada lost this argument before the Panel, it successfully argued that the postal rates advantages were nevertheless permitted under Art III:8(b). See *ibid.*, paras 5.34–5.39 and 5.40–5.48. The United States appealed the Art III:8(b) findings and the Appellate Body reversed them. See Appellate Body Report on *Canada—Certain Measures Concerning Periodicals* (*Canada–Periodicals*), WT/DS31/AB/R, circulated on 30 June 1997, adopted 30 July 1997, at 33–36.

[121] *Korea—Measures Affecting Imports of Fresh, Chilled and Frozen Beef* (*Korea–Beef*), WT/DS161 and WT/DS169, brought 4 Feb 1999.

[122] A small retailer (that is, a non-supermarket or non-department store) which is a "Specialized Imported Beef Store" could sell any meat *except domestic beef*; any other small retailer could sell any meat *except imported beef*. A large retailer (that is, a supermarket or department store) could sell both imported and domestic beef, as long as the imported beef and domestic beef were sold in separate sales areas. A retailer selling imported beef was required to display a sign reading "Specialized Imported Beef Store". The essential features of the Korean dual retail system for beef were found in the *Guidelines Concerning Registration and Operation of Specialized Imported Beef Stores*, (61550-81) 29 Jan 1990, modified on 15 March 1994; and the *Regulations Concerning Sales of Imported Beef*, (51550-100), modified on 27 March 1993, 7 April 1994, and 29 June 1998. On 1 Oct 1999, these two instruments were replaced by the *Management Guideline for Imported Beef*, (Ministry of Agriculture Notice 1999–67), which maintained, however, the basic principles of the dual retail system. Panel Report on *Korea—Measures Affecting Imports of Fresh, Chilled and Frozen Beef* (*Korea–Beef*), WT/DS161/R and WT/DS169/R, circulated 31 July 2000, adopted 10 Jan 2001.

[123] *Ibid.*, para 627.

accord treatment to imported products that is 'no less favourable' than that accorded to like domestic products."[124] Recalling extensively the findings of the *Section 337* Panel Report, the Appellate Body noted that a measure according formally *different* treatment to imported products does not per se, that is, necessarily, violate Article III:4, as long as that measure does not modify the conditions of competition in the relevant market to the detriment of imported products.[125]

Accordingly, since it held that portions of the Panel's analysis of the conditions of competition in the Korean market for beef appeared "problematic",[126] the Appellate Body re-examined the issue *de novo*. The Appellate Body noted that at the time beef was first imported into Korea in 1988, the new product simply entered into the pre-existing distribution system that had been handling domestic beef, and emphasised that the introduction of the dual retail system in 1990, according to which existing small retailers had to choose whether to sell domestic *or* imported beef, meant, so far as imported beef was concerned, the sudden cutting off of access to the previously existing distribution outlets through which the domestic product continued to flow to consumers in the urban centres and countryside.[127] As the vast majority of the small meat retailers chose to sell only domestic beef, the Appellate Body further noted that, in 1998, when the case began, eight years after the dual retail system was first enacted, the consequent reduction of *commercial opportunity* for imported beef was reflected in the much smaller number of specialised imported beef shops (approximately 5,000 shops) as compared with the number of retailers (approximately 45,000 shops) selling domestic beef. On this basis, the Appellate Body concluded that the treatment accorded to imported beef, as a consequence of the dual retail system established for beef by Korean law and regulation, was less favourable than the treatment given to like domestic beef and was, accordingly, not consistent with the requirements of Article III:4.[128]

---

[124] Appellate Body Report on *Korea–Beef*, WT/DS161/AB/R and WT/DS169/AB/R, circulated 11 Dec 2000, adopted 10 Jan 2001, para 135.

[125] *Ibid.*, paras 136–37: "[Although] the Korean measure formally separates the selling of imported beef and domestic beef [...], that formal separation, *in and of itself*, does not necessarily compel the conclusion that the treatment thus accorded to imported beef is less favourable than the treatment accorded to domestic beef. To determine whether the treatment given to imported beef is less favourable than that given to domestic beef, we must, as earlier indicated, inquire into whether or not the Korean dual retail system for beef modifies the *conditions of competition* in the Korean beef market to the disadvantage of the imported product." *Ibid.*, para 144.

[126] *Ibid.*, para 141: "For instance, while limitation of the ability to compare visually two products, local and imported, at the point of sale may have resulted from the dual retail system, such limitation does not, in our view, necessarily reduce the opportunity for the imported product to compete "directly" or on "an equal footing" with the domestic product."

[127] *Ibid.*, para 145.

[128] *Ibid.*, paras 145–48. The Appellate Body confirmed indirectly the irrelevance of the measure's actual trade effects by noting that the fact that the WTO-consistent quota for beef had,

In conclusion, since the National Treatment obligation in Article III:4 GATT requires that Members guarantee effective equality of opportunities for imported and domestic products, it has been recognised by GATT panel practice and WTO jurisprudence that Members may apply to imported products formally different legal requirements if doing so would not accord imported products less favourable treatment than that accorded to domestic products.[129] Although it is for the complaining Member to prove the existence of a "competitive imbalance" stemming from the formal differential treatment, it appears that establishing a prima facie case of violation of Article III is relatively unproblematic. In such cases, there almost seems to be a reversal of the burden of proof with the Member applying differential treatment on the basis of the product's origin having to show that, in spite of such differences, the no less favourable treatment standard of Article III is met.[130] This is confirmed, moreover, by both GATT panel practice and WTO jurisprudence that have interpreted the "no less favourable treatment" requirement of Article III:4 in a strict manner.[131] For example, they have denied defending Members the

save for two years, been fully utilised did not detract from the lack of equality of competitive conditions entailed by the dual retail system. Moreover, the Appellate Body rejected any argument that the disparities in retail opportunities had been determined by commercial decisions by stating that, although the reduction in number of retail outlets for imported beef followed from the decisions of individual retailers, the legal necessity of making a choice between domestic or imported beef was, however, imposed by the Korean measure itself. Accordingly, even the intervention of some element of private choice did not relieve Korea of responsibility under the GATT 1994 for the resulting establishment of competitive conditions less favourable for the imported product than for the domestic product. Cf Panel Report on *Canada—Certain Measures Affecting the Automotive Industry (Canada–Auto)*, WT/DS139/R and WT/DS142/R, circulated on 11 Feb 2000, adopted 19 June 2000, where the Panel found inter alia that Canada acted inconsistently with Art III:4 of the GATT 1994, as a result of the application of value added requirements and that the European Communities and Japan failed to demonstrate that Canada acted inconsistently with Art III:4 of the GATT 1994, as a result of the application of the production-to-sales ratio requirements. These issues were not raised on appeal. Cf moreover, Panel Report on *European Communities—Regime for the Importation, Sale and Distribution of Bananas (EC–Bananas III)*, WT/DS27/R/USA, circulated on 22 May 1997, adopted 25 Sept 1997, where EC procedures and requirements for (1) the distribution of licences for importing bananas among eligible "operators" within the European Communities and (2) the issuance of hurricane licences to mitigate or remedy the consequences of natural disasters, were (erroneously) reviewed under Art III:4 GATT and found to constitute instances of de jure discrimination. For a critical assessment of the Panel (as well as Appellate Body) approach to the issue of the division of labour between Art III and Art XI, see above discussion in ch 1.

[129] Panel Report on *section 337*, above n 17, para 5.11; Appellate Body Report on *Korea–Beef*, above n 124, paras 136–37 and 144.
[130] *Ibid.*
[131] For a recent example of the strict application of the prohibition of de jure discrimination on the basis of nationality outside the GATT see Appellate Body Report on *United States—s 211 Omnibus Appropriations Act of 1998 (Havana Club)*, WT/DS176/AB/R, circulated 2 Jan 2002, adopted 1 Feb 2002, where the Appellate Body in interpreting the National Treatment provision of the TRIPs Agreement (Art 3), held that "the *possibility* [even if small] that non-United States successors-in-interest face two hurdles is *inherently less favourable* than the undisputed fact that United States successors-in-interest face only one." *Ibid.*, para 265.

possibility of *balancing* more favourable treatment of some imported products against less favourable treatment of other imported products.[132] Furthermore, in order to establish that the "no less favourable treatment" standard of Article III:4 has been met, a panel shall not take into consideration *actual* trade effects, but whether or not the origin-based regulation *in itself* may lead to the application to imported product(s) of treatment less favourable than that accorded to domestic product(s).[133]

2. Article 28 EC and "Distinctly Applicable Measures"

As previously noted, contrary to the case of fiscal internal measures, the Treaty of Rome establishing the European Economic Community did not include a specific provision expressly imposing a National Treatment obligation with regard to non-fiscal internal regulations. Article 12 EC (ex 6, and 7 EEC) indeed prohibited "any discrimination on grounds of nationality", but only in a very general manner. In the original structure of the EEC Treaty, as well as in its early applications by the Commission and the ECJ, while the principal focus of Article 30 (now 28) EC was on non-pecuniary *border* measures, the provisions regulating non-fiscal *internal* measures were supposed to be the articles on "approximation of laws" included in Part III of the EEC Treaty on *Policy of the Community* (ex Articles 100–102). In other words, the prohibition of "measures having equivalent effect to quantitative restrictions" was supposed to cover other types of border measures which, like quotas were imposed at the border exclusively on imported products.

What then was the fate of internal regulations formally discriminating on the basis of the product's origin or nationality? Several options were available: (a) they could be caught by the general non-discrimination principle of Article 12 (ex 6) EC, (b) they could fall within the concept of "measures having equivalent effect" and thus be prohibited by Article 28 EC (and exceptionally justified on the basis of Article 30 EC), or (c) they could be dealt with exclusively through the harmonisation instruments of Articles 94–97 (ex 100–102) EC.

Continuing to recount the evolution of Article 28 EC, in this section I propose to sketch the manner in which the prohibition of measures having equivalent effect to quantitative restrictions was expanded to cover any trade-restrictive measures (ie border and internal regulations) *formally discriminating* against imported products.

(a)   The Commission's Official Broad Reading of Article 28 EC: Directive 70/50
Although the Commission had already indicated its willingness to expand the notion of "measure having equivalent effect" in its 1967

---

[132] *Ibid.*, para 5.14; Panel Report on *Reformulated Gasoline*, above n 34, paras 6.14–6.15.
[133] Panel Report on *section* 337, above n 17, paras 5.12–5.13.

replies to Mr Deringer's questions,[134] it was only with its Directive of 22 December 1969 on *"The abolition of measures which have an effect equivalent to quantitative restrictions on imports and are not covered by other provisions adopted in pursuance of the EEC Treaty"*, also known as *Directive 70/50*, that the Commission put forward its official *broad* interpretation of old Article 30 (now 28) EC.

Exercising its prerogatives under Article 33(7) of the EEC, the Commission adopted Directive 70/50 with the precise aim of identifying those "measures having equivalent effect" to quantitative restrictions which Member States were required to abolish at the latest by the end of the transitional period. In line with its bolder approach evidenced in the replies to Mr Deringer, the Commission distinguished between measures which expressly discriminated against imported products (distinctly applicable measures) and measures equally applicable to both domestic and imported products (equally or indistinctly applicable measures).

With regard to distinctly applicable measures, Article 2, paragraph 1, provided that the Directive covered and thus Member States had to abolish

> measures, other than those applicable equally to domestic or imported products, which hinder imports which could otherwise take place including measures which make importation more difficult or costly than the disposal of domestic production.

Article 2, paragraph 2, specified moreover that these were

> measures which make imports or the disposal, at any marketing stage, of imported products subject to a condition—other than a formality—which is required in respect of imported products only, or a condition differing from that required for domestic products and more difficult to satisfy. Equally, it covers, in particular, measures which favour domestic products or grant them a preference, other than an aid, to which conditions may or may not be attached.

Article 2, paragraph 3, listed a large number of examples of measures expressly discriminating against imported products including measures which "lay down, for imported products only, minimum or maximum prices", "make access of imported products to the domestic market conditional upon having an agent or representative in the territory of the importing Member State", "subject imported products only to conditions,

---

[134] Written questions No 118 of 8 Dec 1966, [1967] JO 122 and No 64 of 11 May 1966, [1967] JO. 11. See above ch 1.

in respect, in particular of shape, size, weight, composition, presentation, identification or putting up, or subject imported products to conditions which are different from those for domestic products and more difficult to satisfy", "prohibit or limit publicity in respect of imported products only, or totally or partially confine publicity to domestic products only", and "confine names which are not indicative of origin or source to domestic products only".

On the other hand, with regard to indistinctly applicable measures, Article 3 provided that the Directive also covered and thus Member States had to abolish,

> measures governing the marketing of products which deal, in particular with shape, size, weight, composition, presentation, identification or putting up and which are equally applicable to domestic and imported products, where the restrictive effect of such measures on the free movement of goods exceeds the effects intrinsic to trade rules. This is the case, in particular where:
> — the restrictive effects on the free movement of goods are out of proportion to their purpose;
> — the same objective can be attained by other means which are less of a hindrance to trade.

Two points should be stressed about Directive 70/50. By adopting a distinction between *distinctly* and *indistinctly* applicable measures, Directive 70/50 first of all muted the distinction between border and internal measures. As the illustrative list in Article 2, paragraph 3, shows, distinctly applicable measures included both measures which apply to imports at the border (border measures) and measures which are imposed internally once goods have crossed the border (internal measures). However, from that same list as well as from the other relevant Articles, it appears quite clearly that with regard to internal measures the concept of "distinctly applicable measures" referred exclusively to those internal measures which *formally* discriminate against imported products, either because they apply to imported products *only* or because they subject imported products to conditions which are *different* from those for domestic products and *more difficult* to satisfy.[135] The rationale for the Commission's decision to interpret Article 30 EEC as covering both "border measures" and "de jure discriminatory internal measures" may be that both types of measures afford on their face less favourable treatment to imported products vis-à-vis domestic products, clearly disrupting trade among Member States.

---

[135] P Oliver, *Free Movement of Goods in the European Community* (London, Sweet & Maxwell, 1996) at 89.

Secondly, drawing ample inspiration from the approach suggested by Béraud in his 1968 article,[136] Directive 70/50 introduced a *different* normative approach in relation to indistinctly applicable measures. While distinctly applicable measures were prohibited once they had been found to discriminate formally against imported products, indistinctly applicable measures fell within the scope of application of old Article 30 and thus had to be abolished *only if* their restrictive effects on the free movement of goods exceeded the effects intrinsic to trade rules. As expressly specified by Article 3, this was the case in particular where (a) the restrictive effects on the free movement of goods were out of proportion to their purpose and (b) the same objective could be attained by other means which are less of a hindrance to trade.

As will be analysed in more details in both chapters 3 and 4, by shifting the focus from the "discriminatory nature" of a measure to its "reasonableness", the Commission, consciously or unconsciously, advanced a different normative approach with regard to measures which were, at least formally, equally applicable to domestic and imported products (indistinctly applicable or facially origin-neutral measures).[137]

(b)   The Court of Justice's endorsement of the broad interpretation of Article 28 EC: an introduction to the Dassonville–Cassis de Dijon *jurisprudence*
While the approach embodied in Directive 70/50 expressed only one of the views which legal commentators were proposing in those early years as to the meaning of the concept of "measures of equivalent effect",[138] the Court of Justice eventually sided with the Commission's position and developed the so-called *Dassonville–Cassis de Dijon* jurisprudence. This can be summarised as follows: although all trading rules capable of hindering, directly or indirectly, actually or potentially, intra-Community trade are to be considered as measures having an effect equivalent to quantitative restrictions for purposes of the prohibition in Article 28 (the *Dassonville* limb), in the absence of Community harmonisation, *indistinctly applicable measures* must be accepted in so far as they are *necessary* in order to satisfy *mandatory requirements* relating inter alia to the effective of fiscal

---

[136] See above ch 1.

[137] As correctly noted by Oliver, while de jure discriminatory measures were automatically considered to be measures of equivalent effect under Art 2 of Directive 70/50, Art 3 of that directive provided for a presumption that "indistinctly applicable measures" were compatible with old Art 30, which could be rebutted by showing that the measure's restrictive effects exceeded the effects intrinsic to trade rules. Cf P Oliver, *Free Movement of Goods in the European Community* (London, Sweet & Maxwell, 1996) at 89.

[138] For insightful analysis of the several views expressed by legal authors during those times, see C-D Ehlermann, *Das Verbot der Wassnahmen gleicher Wirkung in der Rechtsprechung des Gerichthofes: Festschrift für Ipsen* (1985); P Oliver, *Free Movement of Goods in the European Community* (London, Sweet & Maxwell, 1996) at 90 *et seq.*; and A Meij and J Winter, "Measures Having an Effect Equivalent to Quantitative Restrictions", *Common Market Law Review* (1976) 79 at 84 *et seq.*

supervision, the protection of public health, the fairness of commercial transaction and the defence of the consumer (the *Cassis de Dijon* limb).[139]

Although both decisions will be further examined in subsequent sections, it is necessary to emphasise at this point the basic features of the *Dassonville–Cassis de Dijon* jurisprudence. Like Directive 70/50, the *Dassonville-Cassis de Dijon* jurisprudence abandoned any reference to the distinction between "border" and "internal" measures and adopted instead the dichotomy of distinctly and indistinctly applicable measures.[140] According to such jurisprudence, while the latter fall within the provisional prohibition of Article 28 EC only if they do not conform to the requirements of the "mandatory requirements" doctrine, the former are directly included within the concept of "measures having equivalent effect" and as such are thus provisionally prohibited by that Article.

The Court's different approach with regard to "distinctly" and "indistinctly" applicable measures entails two consequences. From a pure theoretical perspective, the "mandatory requirements" doctrine is employed by the Court in order to determine whether or not an "indistinctly applicable measure" is indeed a measure having equivalent effect to a quantitative restriction which is prohibited by Article 28 EC. In other words, if an indistinctly applicable measure is *necessary* to satisfy mandatory requirements (ie any legitimate public policy), that measure falls outside the scope of application of Article 28 altogether (ie it is not deemed to constitute a "measure having equivalent effect to quantitative restrictions"). On the other hand, distinctly applicable measures are automatically caught by the prohibition of Article 28 independently of an analysis of their public policy objectives. Nevertheless, these measures may subsequently be justified under the exhaustive list of public policy exceptions expressly provided for in Article 30 EC.[141]

---

[139] The connection between Directive 70/50 and Cassis de Dijon jurisprudence is widely recognised in the legal literature. Cf P Craig and G de Búrca, *EU Law* (Oxford, OUP, 1998) at 605; S Weatherill and P Beaumont, *EC Law* (London, Penguin Books, 1995) at 494. Note however that the Court made the link between *Dassonville* and *Cassis* de Dijon for the first time in the post-*Cassis* decision in Case 788/79, *Gilli & Andres* [1980] ECR 2071. Cf D Chalmers, "Repackaging the Internal Market—the Ramifications of the Keck Judgement", 19 ELRev (1994) 385, at 386.

[140] By adopting the distinction between "distinctly" and "indistinctly" applicable measures (ie origin-based and origin-neutral measures), the Court was able to get rid of the problematic concept of de facto discrimination.

[141] Several authors have criticised the approach followed by the ECJ in distinguishing between the exception provisions of Art 30 (as well as Art 46 or 55) and "mandatory or imperative requirements", at least from a perspective of theoretical clarity. Cf JHH Weiler, "Epilogue: Towards a Common Law of International Trade" in JHH Weiler (ed), *The EU, the WTO and the NAFTA: Towards a Common Law of International Trade?* (Oxford, OUP, 2000) at 220, who refers to the Court of Justice doctrinal distinction as mere "formalist sophistry"; and P Oliver, *Free Movement of Goods in the European Community* (London, Sweet & Maxwell, 1996) at 110 *et seq*. See below discussions on the distinction between "distinctly" and "indistinctly" applicable measures in the next section as well as on the Court of Justice Keck doctrine in ch 3.

From a more practical perspective, it follows that while distinctly applicable measures may be justified exclusively by reference to the scarce exhaustive list of public policy objectives included in Article 30 EC, indistinctly applicable measures enjoy the more generous open-ended list of public policy justifications provided for by the "mandatory requirements" doctrine.[142] As will be seen more clearly in the discussion below, there may be cases where this doctrinal difference does entail relevant practical consequences, in particular where a national measure deemed to constitute a prima facie violation of Article 28 is taken in order to pursue a public policy objective, such as consumer or environmental protection that is not included in the exhaustive list of Article 30.

(c)   Defining the boundaries between "distinctly" and "indistinctly" applicable measures: still an open question?   Notwithstanding the relevance of the distinction between distinctly and indistinctly applicable measures, several authors have recently noted that neither in the Court's case-law nor in the literature on free movement is there the consistency of terminology which, given the age of the subject matter at issue, one might have expected.[143] These authors refer as an example to the differences in terminology between two of the leading English language textbooks on EC law—Craig and de Búrca and Weatherill and Beaumont. For example, although the former employ the terms "discriminatory" and "indistinctly applicable" rules, they use "discriminatory" to cover not only rules which are discriminatory in law (distinctly applicable or de jure discriminatory), but also rules which appear indistinctly applicable but where, as in the 1985 *UK Origin Marking* case,[144] there is arguably an obvious *protectionist intent* on the part of the regulating Member States.[145] On the other hand, the latter use three categories in relation to goods: in addition to "distinctly" and "indistinctly" applicable measures, they add a third category of "indirectly discriminatory" measures which includes the case of perhaps obvious indirect or de facto discrimination, similar to the 1980 *French Alcohol Advertising* case.[146]

---

[142] JHH Weiler, "Epilogue: Towards a Common Law of International Trade" in JHH Weiler (ed), *The EU, the WTO and the NAFTA: Towards a Common Law of International Trade?* (Oxford, OUP, 2000) at 220; N Bernard, "Discrimination and the Free Movement in EC Law", 45 ICLQ (1996) 82 at 93; D Martin, "'Discrimination', 'entraves' et 'raisons impérieuses' dans le traité CE: trois concept en quête d'identité", CDE (1998) 261 at 275 *et seq.*

[143] C Hilson, "Discrimination in Community free movement law", 24 *ELRev* (1999) 445 at 448, who cites J Scott, *EC Environmental Law* (London, Longman, 1998) at 73. More recently J Scott, "Mandatory or Imperative Requirements in the EU and the WTO" in C Barnard and J Scott (eds), *The Law of the Single European Market: Unpacking the Premises* (Oxford, Hart Publishing, 2002).

[144] Case 207/83, *Commission v United Kingdom (UK Origin Marking)* [1985] ECR 1201.

[145] P Craig and G de Búrca, *EU Law—Text, Cases and Materials* (Oxford, OUP, 1998) at 588.

[146] Case 152/78, *Commission v France (French Alcoholic Advertising)* [1980] ECR 2299. See S Weatherill and P Beaumont, *EC Law* (London, Penguin, 1995) at 444.

It is here submitted that the relevant distinction for the purposes of determining whether to apply the per se prohibition of Article 28 or the "mandatory requirements" doctrine enunciated in *Cassis de Dijon* is and should be between, on the one hand, "*formally* discriminatory" measures and, on the other hand, "indistinctly applicable" measures, where the latter category includes both materially discriminatory and non-discriminatory measures (what may be referred to as de jure and de facto indistinctly applicable measures).[147] Before examining the Court's case-law with the view of demonstrating that this distinction *is* the relevant distinction predominantly, albeit at times obscurely, employed by the Court, it appears necessary to advance at least in general terms the principal reasons why materially discriminatory measures *should* be subject to the softer *Cassis de Dijon* approach.

As the EC free movement jurisprudence in general demonstrates,[148] the concept of de facto or material discrimination may take us so far as to include even the (only) apparently non-discriminatory minimum alcohol requirement at issue in *Cassis de Dijon* itself. In light of the strictures which characterise the per se rule of Article 28 (in particular, the limited justification options under Article 30), adopting a broad definition of the term "distinctly applicable" would thus entail unacceptable results with regard to national regulatory prerogatives.

Moreover, there is a fundamental difference between de jure and de facto discrimination: while the former is embodied in the terms of the measure itself (ie by adopting the product's origin or nationality as *the* differentiating criterion), the latter does not appear from the text of the measure but only through an analysis of the measure's potential effects in the relevant market(s). Thus, the fact that an origin-neutral regulation may have discriminatory effects against foreign products which were not intended by the legislator, or may be clearly justified on the basis of a legitimate public policy ground, should entail a more deferential treatment towards origin-neutral measures vis-à-vis origin-based measures. As will be shown in later sections, it is harder for Member States to justify de jure discriminatory measures than de facto discriminatory measures on public policy grounds. There are indeed very few valid reasons why a regulator needs to distinguish between two identical products only on the basis of their different origin.

Furthermore, any attempt to expand the concept of "distinctly applicable" measures to include those measures which, although apparently

---

[147] Cf J Wiers, *Trade and Environment in the EC and the WTO: a Legal Analysis* (Groningen, Europa Law Publishing, 2002) at 317; Joined Opinion AG Tesauro in Cases C–120/95 *Decker* and C–158/96 *Kohll* [1998] ECR I–1831.

[148] In particular, see the (earlier) case law on the free movement of services and persons.

origin-neutral, show a "clear" *protectionist intent*[149] should be avoided both because of the practical difficulties in assessing "intent" and, even more, because of the politically sensitive concerns which a finding of "hidden" protectionist intent may involve in terms of the institutional balance between judiciary and legislative powers, as well as between Community institutions and the Member States.

Let us now turn to the Court's case-law. The inconsistency in the terminology employed to describe the Court's approach with regard to obstacles to the free movement of goods, which has been noted above, appears to be the direct consequence of the Court's at times convoluted application of its own jurisprudential doctrines.[150] It is thus appropriate to begin the present analysis with the two cases previously mentioned, which are among those that seem to puzzle even experienced EC lawyers.

In the *French Alcohol Advertising* case,[151] the Commission had brought a complaint against French regulations on the advertising of alcoholic drinks which placed different drinks into different categories and accorded to them different treatment ranging from a total ban to an absolute freedom of advertising. The Commission argued that, although facially origin-neutral, the classification set out in the French regulation disadvantaged many imported products, as far as advertising was concerned, compared to the competing national products. For example, while rums and spirits obtained from the distillation of wines, ciders, perriers or fruits (typically domestic products), enjoyed unrestricted advertising, numerous competing products, notably grain spirits like whisky and geneva (nearly all of which were imported), were covered by a prohibition on advertising.[152] Although this was a post-*Cassis de Dijon* decision, the Court appeared to consider whether or not the French regulation discriminated, albeit only indirectly or de facto, against imported products as the essential issue in ascertaining whether that regulation constituted a "measure having equivalent effect" for purposes of Article 28. In its analysis of the application of Article 28, the Court as a preliminary point noted the following:

---

[149] Cf C Hilson, "Discrimination in Community free movement law", 24 *ELRev* (1999) 445 at 447 and 450; P Craig and G de Búrca, *EU Law—Text, Cases and Materials* (Oxford, OUP, 1998) at 588.

[150] Addressing the issue of whether mandatory requirements may justify measures which are indirectly discriminatory, Scott observes that "the language deployed by the European Court is not conclusive in respect of this question." According to this author, the Court refers to "measures which apply *without distinction* to imported and domestic goods", as well as to "measures which do not discriminate", or "which apply without discrimination", thus begging the indirect discrimination question. J Scott, "Mandatory or Imperative Requirements in the EU and the WTO" in C Barnard and J Scott (eds), *The Law of the Single European Market: Unpacking the Premises* (Oxford, Hart Publishing, 2002) at 275.

[151] Case 152/78, *Commission v France (French Alcoholic Advertising)* [1980] ECR 2299.

[152] *Ibid.*, paras 6–9.

[T]here is no dispute between the parties on whether a restriction on freedom of advertising for certain products *may* constitute a measure having an effect equivalent to a quantitative restriction within the meaning of Article 30 of the Treaty. Although such a restriction does not directly affect imports it is however capable of restricting their volume owing to the fact that it affects the marketing prospects for the imported products. The *issue in point* is therefore whether the prohibitions and restrictions on advertising laid down by the French legislation place a *handicap* on the importation of alcoholic products from other Member states.[153]

Having rejected the French government's argument that its system had the effect of subjecting also *some* national products to prohibitions or restrictions on advertising,[154] the Court concluded that,

even though it is conceded that an appreciable number of national products are subject to the prohibitions and restrictions on advertising [...], nevertheless the fact remains that the classifications which determine the application of those provisions put products imported from other member states at a disadvantage compared to national products and *consequently* constitute a measure having an effect equivalent to a quantitative restriction prohibited by Article 30 of the Treaty.[155]

The Court's apparent disregard of the *Cassis de Dijon*'s violation test based on the measure's trade-restrictive effects, the lack of any reference to the dichotomy between "distinctly" and "indistinctly" applicable measures, and its willingness to base a finding of a violation of Article 28 on a discriminatory-effect test confirm the impression regarding the Court's, at times, unclear case-law. It should be emphasised that, first of all, it had been only one and a half years since the famous French liqueur case and the Court, at least not the entire Court, had perhaps not yet digested all the implications of the *Cassis de Dijon* decision. Secondly, and more likely, the Court might have been influenced in that particular instance by the parallel decision on the French de facto discriminatory tax system of alcoholic drinks, which was based on the pure non-discrimination principle of Article 90 EC.

However, the *French Alcohol Advertising* case should not stand as even potentially an example in which the Court has included within the category of "distinctly applicable measures" a regulation which was, at least on its face, origin-neutral.[156] Such a proposition would run counter to the

---

[153] *Ibid.*, para 11 [emphasis added].
[154] *Ibid.*, para 13. Note that the Court expressly made reference to the findings in its decision on the parallel dispute regarding the French de facto discriminatory taxes on alcoholic drinks in Case 168/78.
[155] *Ibid.*, para 14 [emphasis added].
[156] S Weatherill and P Beaumont, *EC Law* (London, Penguin, 1995) at 444; C Hilson, "Discrimination in Community free movement law", 24 *ELRev* (1999) at 450 fn 38.

underlying logic of the distinction between "distinctly" and "indistinctly" applicable measures, and it would also contradict the great majority of the Court's case-law subjecting facially origin-neutral measures to the "mandatory requirements" doctrine, *even if* they showed clear discriminatory effects vis-à-vis imported products.[157] The fact that the Court went on in that case to examine the French Government's argument that its regulation was nevertheless justified on grounds of the protection of public health pursuant to Article 30, and not on the basis of "mandatory requirements", is not conclusive evidence that the Court indeed treated the French regulation as a "distinctly applicable measure" caught by the per se prohibition of Article 28 and justifiable *exclusively* on the basis of one of the public policy justifications of Article 30.[158]

Similar conclusions, though for different reasons, can be reached by examining the Court's decision in the *UK Origin Marking* case, which is usually and, and I believe incorrectly, categorised as a case falling outside of the mandatory requirements doctrine (ie an instance of "distinctly applicable measure").[159]

In this case, the Commission brought an Article 169 action against the United Kingdom, arguing that UK legislation requiring that certain goods not be sold in retail markets unless they were marked with their country of origin was a measure having equivalent effect to a quantitative restriction

---

[157] Cf Case 193/80, *Commission v Italy (Italian Vinegar)* [1981] ECR 3019, in which the Court applied the "mandatory requirements" doctrine to a clear case of a facially origin-neutral measure with de facto discriminatory effects against *similar* imported products (Italian legislation prohibited describing as "vinegar" any product other than that obtained from the acetic fermentation of wine and the marketing or importing fermented vinegar obtained from a product other than wine). The Court stated that "even if national legislation on the marketing of a product applies to national and imported products alike, it does not escape the prohibition enacted in Art 30 of the Treaty, if it in fact produces protective effects by favouring a typically national product and to the same extent putting various categories of products from other Member States at a disadvantage". *Ibid.*, at para 20. However, the Court then examined whether the Italian requirements were necessary in order to satisfy mandatory requirements such as consumer protection or fair trading. It found that they were not. *Ibid.*, at paras 21–23. It is interesting to note how the Court read the Italian requirements as, on the one hand, allowing vinegar made from wine and, on the other, prohibiting all other vinegar of agricultural origin. It appears that the Court implicitly believed that all types of vinegar made from agricultural products (whether wine or apple) were to be treated alike, or in other words that they were similar products. Cf G Marenco, "Pour une interpretation traditionnelle de la notion de mesure d'effet equivalent à une restriction quantitative", 20 *CDE* (1984) at 306, who includes both *Cassis* de Dijon and the *French Alcohol Advertising* cases within the same category of "*réglementation indistinctement applicable avec une discrimination matérielle*".

[158] Cf C Hilson, "Discrimination in Community free movement law", 24 *ELRev* (1999) at 450, fn 38.

[159] *Ibid.*; P Craig and G de Búrca, *EU Law* (Oxford, OUP, 1998) at 588; J Scott, "Mandatory or Imperative Requirements in the EU and the WTO" in C Barnard and J Scott (eds), *The Law of the Single European Market: Unpacking the Premises* (Oxford, Hart Publishing, 2002) at 277; L Gormley "Actually or Potentially, Directly or Indirectly? Obstacles to the Free Movement of Goods", 9 *YEL* (1989) 197 at 198.

and thus in breach of Article 28. The United Kingdom argued in its defence that (a) the legislation under review applied equally to imported and national products, (b) its effects on trade between Member States were uncertain, if not non-existent, and (c) this information was in any case of importance in order for consumers to be able to assess the quality of the goods.

In assessing the possible effect of the contested measure on intra-Community trade, the Court noted two points. First of all, the origin marking obligation, imposed on the retailer, had the potential also to affect wholesale trade and even manufacture.[160] Secondly, the origin-marking requirement not only made the marketing in a Member State of goods produced in other Member States in relevant sectors more difficult; it had also the effect of slowing down economic interpenetration in the Community by handicapping the sale of goods produced as the result of a division of labour between Member States.[161] Employing thus the very hardcore *telos* of *Cassis de Dijon*, the Court concluded that the UK legislation was likely to have the effect of increasing the production costs of imported goods and making it more difficult to sell them on the UK market.

The Court then considered whether the contested legislation, applicable without distinction to domestic and imported products, was necessary in order to satisfy imperative (or mandatory) requirements relating to consumer protection.[162] Although the Court rejected the consumer protection argument, it did not appear to do so for reasons of principle. In other words, it did not do so because the measure was *not* "indistinctly applicable" and thus could *not* be saved by the "mandatory requirements" doctrine.[163] The Court did note that the requirements relating to the indication of origin of goods were applicable without distinction to

---

[160] Case 207/83, *UK Origin Marking*, above n 144, para 16: "[...] in order to escape the obligations imposed on him by the legislation in question the retailer will tend, as the Commission has rightly pointed out, to ask his wholesalers to supply him with goods which are already origin-marked. That tendency has been confirmed by complaints received by the Commission. Thus, it emerges from the documents before the Court that [...] French manufacturers of domestic appliances who wish to sell their products on the United Kingdom market have had to mark such products systematically in response to pressure brought to bear on them by their distributors."

[161] *Ibid.*, para 17. The Court recognised in this regard that "the purpose of indications of origin or origin-marking is to enable consumers to distinguish between domestic and imported products and that this enables them to assert any prejudices which they may have against foreign products." *Ibid.*

[162] *Ibid.*, para 19. The United Kingdom noted that "a survey carried out amongst United Kingdom consumers has shown that they associate the quality of certain goods with the countries in which they are made. They like to know, for example, whether leather shoes have been made in Italy, woollen knitwear in the United Kingdom, fashion-wear in France and domestic electrical appliances in Germany." *Ibid.*

[163] Consumer protection is one of the public policy justifications which is not expressly included in the exhaustive list of Art 30 but which was mentioned by the Court in *Cassis de Dijon* as being one of the grounds on which an "indistinctly applicable measure" could be justified.

domestic and imported products "only in form", because, by their very nature, they were intended to enable the consumer to distinguish between those two categories of products.[164] However, the Court concluded that "Community law did not recognise any ground of justification" for the UK measure, observing that (a) consumer protection was not really the true purpose of the measure, (b) if the national origin of goods brought certain qualities to the minds of consumers, it would have been in the manufacturers' interests to indicate it themselves on the goods, and (c) consumer protection was sufficiently guaranteed by rules which enabled the use of false indications of origin to be prohibited.[165] In conclusion, it appears that the Court rejected the consumer protection argument *on the facts of the case*, or, in other words, because the UK rules on origin were deemed to be not truly necessary to satisfy any imperative requirement.[166]

Notwithstanding the somewhat unclear language employed by the Court, it would appear that in the *UK Origin Marking* case the Court indeed subjected the facially origin-neutral measure under review to the "mandatory requirements" doctrine, because the measure at issue, albeit "only in form", applied indistinctly to domestic and imported products. Once again, the Court's emphasis on the de facto discriminatory effects of the measure for the purposes of both establishing a prima facie violation of Article 28 and rejecting the justification argument based on consumer protection should not be taken as evidence that the Court, under certain circumstances, applies the strict approach reserved to "distinctly applicable" measures even to facially origin-neutral ones.[167]

The fact that the facially origin-neutral measure appeared, in that particular case, as an instance of "obvious intentional protectionism" should not justify treating that same measure as "distinctly applicable".[168] The Court's apparent willingness to keep the concept of "distinctly applicable measures" as flexible as possible, in order to be able to subject certain types of "protectionist" measures to the strict per se prohibition of Article 28 might appear comprehensible under a strict market integration perspective. However, in light of the more limited public policy exceptions available under Article 30 and the uncertainty in determining whether the purpose (or, even worse, the intent) of a measure is obviously

---

[164] Case 207/83, *UK Origin Marking*, above n 144, para 20.
[165] *Ibid.*, paras 21–22.
[166] Cf J Scott, *EC Environmental Law* (London, Longman, 1998) at 74–75.
[167] For the opposing view, according to which the Court characterised the apparently non-discriminatory national measures as in reality having the effect of promoting national products at the expense of imported products in order to escape from any need to analyse the alleged consumer protection arguments in favour of origin marking, *see* L Gormley "Actually or Potentially, Directly or Indirectly? Obstacles to the Free Movement of Goods", 9 *YEL* (1989) 197 at 198.
[168] Cf C Hilson, "Discrimination in Community free movement law", 24 *ELRev* (1999) at 450; P Craig and G de Búrca, *EU Law* (Oxford, OUP, 1998) at 588.

protectionist or not, it would certainly be wiser for the Court to apply the stricter approach exclusively to measures which formally discriminate against imported products (ie origin-based or de jure discriminatory measures).

Besides a few controversial cases similar to the two just examined,[169] and very few others where the Court followed a somewhat different path[170] or simply stuck its head in the sand,[171] there exist many examples in the Court's case-law where only *formally* discriminatory measures,

---

[169] See also Case 21/84, *Commission v France (Postal Franking Machines)* [1985] ECR 1356, where the Court considered the compatibility with Art 28 of a French requirement that domestic and imported postal franking machines obtain official approval. Although the measure was at least in appearance "indistinctly applicable", the case may be correctly considered to be an example of *formal discrimination* because at issue in that case was not really the measure as such but its administrative application. In particular, the Court found substantial evidence that a leading British manufacturer had met obstruction over a number of years in its attempts to secure approval for the use of its machines in France. Noting that Art 28 should include also "a systematically unfavourable attitude towards imported machines, either by allowing considerable delay in replying to applications for approval or in carrying out the examination procedure, or by refusing approval on the grounds of various alleged technical faults for which no detailed explanations are given or which prove to be inaccurate", the Court concluded that "the conduct of the French postal administration constitutes an impediment to imports contrary to Art 30 of the EEC Treaty". *Ibid.*, paras 11–14. Cf S Weatherill and P Beaumont, *EC Law* (London, Penguin, 1995) at 439, and for a recent overview of the most controversial cases see J Scott, "Mandatory or Imperative Requirements in the EU and the WTO" in C Barnard and J Scott (eds), *The Law of the Single European Market: Unpacking the Premises* (Oxford, Hart Publishing, 2002). Scott has noted that in Case 6/81, *BV Industrie Diensten Groep v JA Beele Handelmaatschappij BV* [1982] ECR 707, before concluding that the measure under review could be deemed to apply *without* distinction, the Court went beyond an examination of the legal form of the measure and looked to its substance in terms of its impact on imported goods. I believe, however, that in that case the Court's emphasis on the measure's discriminatory *effects* may perhaps be interpreted as a mere confirmation of the Court's previous finding that the measure was indeed *not* based on the products' origin. The relevant paragraph reads as follows: "Although the main action concerns the protection of a product manufactured in a non-Member country against the marketing of a product manufactured in a Member State, according to the national court the application of case-law does not depend on country of origin of the product imitated and country of origin of the imitation. *What is more*, there is nothing in the judgement of the national court from which it may be inferred that that case-law is applied in a manner adapted to the specific needs of national products thereby putting imported products at a disadvantage. Therefore it must be assumed that the case-law referred to by the national court applies without distinction to national and imported products." *Ibid.*, para 8 [emphasis added].

[170] Cf Case 229/83, *Association des Centres Distributeurs Édouard Leclerc and Others v SARL "Au blé vert" and Others* [1985] ECR 1, described as "puzzling" by J Scott, "Mandatory or Imperative Requirements in the EU and the WTO" in C Barnard and J Scott (eds), *The Law of the Single European Market: Unpacking the Premises* (Oxford, Hart Publishing, 2002) at 276.

[171] In Case C–379/98, *PreussenElektra AG v Schhleswag AG* [2001] ECR I–2099, the Court seems simply to have ignored the formally discriminatory nature of the national measure under review. At issue in that case was a German law obliging electricity suppliers to purchase the electricity produced in their area of supply from renewable sources of energy, which the Court found to be justified apparently on grounds of environmental protection (ie mandatory requirements) as well as the protection of health and life of human, animal and plant (ie Art 30 EC). Avoiding having to deal with the formally discriminatory

whether "border" or "internal" in nature, have been *explicitly* considered to be "distinctly applicable measures" and thus subject to the per se prohibition of Article 28.[172]

For a case of discriminatory *border measure* one can look at the dispute on the German legislation on the importation of vermouth.[173] The background of the so-called *Vermouth* case was that, while Italian law required that the alcoholic content of vermouth marketed in Italy be at least 16 per cent by volume, weaker vermouth could be made in Italy provided that it was destined only for export. German law, by contrast, imposed no minimum limit on the alcohol content of vermouth. However, by requiring that wine-based beverages produced abroad may be imported into Germany only if they conformed with the rules applicable in the country of production, German law resulted in a ban on the importation into Germany of Italian vermouth with an alcoholic content of less than 16 per cent, even though an *identical* German-made vermouth could lawfully be sold. The Court noted that the provision applied only to imported products, and affirmed that in the present case it was not possible to plead consumer protection to exclude Article 30 as the Court had stated in *Cassis de Dijon*, since the same protection was not given in relation to the national products.[174]

In *Allen and Hanburys Ltd v Generics (UK) Ltd*,[175] one of the questions submitted to the Court of Justice was whether old Articles 30 and 36 of the Treaty must be interpreted as precluding the courts of a Member State from granting a legal remedy to prevent the importation from another Member State of a product that infringed a patent, while no such remedy could be granted in the same circumstances against an infringer who

---

features of the law, the Court found the German measure "not incompatible" with Art 28 simply noting the usefulness of measures aimed at encouraging the use of renewable energy. Case 379/98, *PreussenElektra*, paras 72–5. Cf J Wiers, *Trade and Environment in the EC and the WTO: a Legal Analysis* (Groningen, Europa Law Publishing, 2002) at 98–9.

[172] There are others instances in which the Court has only *implicitly* applied the "distinctly applicable measure" approach to formally discriminatory regulations. Cf Case 72/83, *Campus Oil Ltd. v Minister for Industry and Energy (Campus Oil)* [1984] ECR 2727; Case 249/81, *Commission v Ireland (Buy Irish)* [1982] ECR 4005; Case 251/78, *Firma Denkavit Futtermittel GmbH v Minister für Ernährung, Landwirtschaft und Forsten des Landes Nordrhein-Westfalen* [1979] ECR 3369, where at para 6 the Court stated that the national measures under review "are measures having an effect equivalent to quantitative restrictions within the meaning of Art 30 of the Treaty, the dispute only being concerned with the question whether those restrictions are covered by the exception provided for in Art 36 of the Treaty according to which the provisions of Arts 30 to 34 shall not preclude restrictions on imports justified on grounds of the protection of health and life of humans and animals, provided that these restrictions do not however constitute a means of arbitrary discrimination or a disguised restriction on trade between Member States".
[173] Case 59/82, *Schutzverband gegen Unwesen in der Wirtschaft v Weinvertriebs-GmbH (Vermouth)* [1983] ECR 1217.
[174] *Ibid.*, para 11.
[175] Case 434/85, *Allen and Hanburys Ltd v Generics (UK) Ltd.* [1988] ECR 1245.

manufactured the product in the national territory. Thus the measure at issue was an *internal measure* formally discriminating between imported and domestically manufactured products. The Court found that the measure at issue fell within the scope of application of old Article 30 and could not be justified under old Article 36, but then asked whether the UK measure could nevertheless be justified on the grounds of imperative requirements relating to consumer protection and fair trading, as recognised by the court in its *Cassis de Dijon* jurisprudence. Noting that the national legislation relating to licences of right was not applicable without distinction to manufacturers established in the national territory and to importers,[176] the Court stated that,

> it is only where national rules apply without distinction to both domestic and imported products that they do not fall under the prohibition laid down by Article 30 of the Treaty if they are necessary in order to satisfy imperative requirements relating in particular to consumer protection or fair trading.[177]

The fact that both "border" and "formally discriminatory internal" measures fall within the per se prohibition of Article 28 (ex 30) and are similarly excluded from the "benefits" of the *Cassis de Dijon* jurisprudence, can be seen in the even earlier *Irish Souvenirs* case.[178]

In that case, the Commission challenged two separate Irish measures before the Court. The first was Statutory Instrument No 306, also referred to as "the sale order", which prohibited the sale or exposure for sale of imported articles of jewellery depicting motifs or possessing characteristics which suggested that they were souvenirs of Ireland (for example an Irish character, event or scene, wolfhound, round tower, shamrock). Secondly, Statutory Instrument No 307, also referred to as "the importation order", prohibited the importation of such articles unless they bore an indication of their country of origin or the word "foreign". While the importation order was a clear case of an import restriction, the sale order represented a clear case of de jure discriminatory internal regulation.

The Court nevertheless applied exactly the same approach with regard to both measures. The Court first of all rejected the Irish government's argument that the measures at issue were justified under Article 30 (ex 36) EC in the interests of consumer protection and fairness in commercial transaction between producers. This was because, in the Court's view, Article 30 could not be extended to cover cases which are not specifically laid down therein.[179] The Court then examined whether on the basis of those same public policy grounds it was possible to argue that the Irish

---

[176] *Ibid.,* para 34.
[177] *Ibid.,* para 35.
[178] Case 113/80, *Commission v Ireland (Irish Souvenirs)* [1981] ECR 1625.
[179] *Ibid.,* paras 5–8.

orders were not measures having an effect equivalent to quantitative restrictions on imports in light of the *Cassis de Dijon* jurisprudence. The Court noted that the Irish orders were *not* applicable to domestic products and to imported products without distinction, but were rather a set of rules applicable only to imported products and were therefore formally discriminatory in nature, and concluded that those measures were not covered by the above-mentioned jurisprudence, which relates exclusively to provisions that regulate in a uniform manner the marketing of domestic products and imported products.[180]

The *Irish Souvenirs* case is interesting for a further argument advanced by the Irish government. Although it recognised that the contested measures applied solely to imported Articles, the Irish government maintained that the difference in the treatment awarded to home produced Articles and to imported Articles did not constitute discrimination on the ground that the products at issue were indeed *different*. The Irish government noted that the appeal of "souvenirs" lay essentially in the fact of their being manufactured in the place where they were purchased and consequently, the requirement that all imported "souvenirs" covered by the two orders had to bear an indication of origin was justified and in no way constituted discrimination "because the articles concerned are different on account of the differences between their essential characteristics."[181]

Although the Court found it necessary to consider whether the contested measures were indeed discriminatory or whether they constituted "discrimination in appearance only", upon closer examination it found that the provisions contained in the sale order and importation order indisputably constituted discriminatory measures since,

> the essential characteristic of the souvenirs in question is that they constitute a pictorial reminder of the place visited, which does not by itself mean that a souvenir, as defined in the orders, must necessarily be manufactured in the country of origin.[182]

Although in the end it proved unsuccessful, the argument advanced by the Irish government shows that for any finding of discrimination it is necessary to establish a certain "relationship" between the products which are allegedly discriminated against and those which are favoured or protected. In the case at hand, the Irish government tried to argue that, even if domestic and imported souvenirs were *physically identical*, their different place of production constituted a significant distinguishing element, which would have excluded the comparability of their respective

---

[180] *Ibid.*, para 11.
[181] *Ibid.*, para 12.
[182] *Ibid.*, paras 14–15.

treatment and thus a finding of discrimination. In other words, the *Irish Souvenirs* case seems to show that it is possible for a Member State to claim that an apparently distinctly applicable measure may indeed be discriminatory in appearance only when in reality the "disfavoured" imported products are different from the "favoured" domestic ones.

To my knowledge, there appears to exist only one case where this argument has indeed been successful, at least in the case of origin-based non-fiscal regulations. In the *Walloon Waste* case,[183] the Walloon region of Belgium had imposed a ban on the import of, inter alia, non-hazardous waste from other regions of Belgium and from other Member States (interestingly, the Belgian measure deemed waste not produced in the Walloon region as "foreign").[184] Although it determined that waste (whether recyclable or not) had to be regarded as "goods" for the purposes of the Treaty provisions on free movement and that any restriction on its circulation (such as effected by the measure at issue) was a violation of Article 28,[185] the Court also reached the conclusion that the contested legislation met imperative requirements relating to environmental protection and thus conformed with EC law.[186]

The Court had however to tackle the Commission's argument that, because it was distinctly applicable, the measure at issue fell within the per se prohibition of Article 28 and could only be justified on the basis of Article 30, which does not include environmental protection as one of its justification grounds.[187] It should be noted in this regard that the fact that the Walloon restriction applied equally to "non-Walloon Belgian" and "non-Belgian" waste was not sufficient to establish the "indistinctly" nature of the restriction at issue. According to previous ECJ case law,

---

[183] Case C–2/90, *Commission v Belgium (Walloon Waste)* [1992] ECR I–4431.

[184] The 1985 decree of the Walloon regional government also prohibited the importation of hazardous waste, which the Court eventually found in violation of the EC directive 84/631 dealing specifically with transborder movements of hazardous waste. Cf S Walker, *Environmental Protection Versus Trade Liberalisation: Finding the Balance* (Bruxelles, Faculté Universitaires Saint-Louis, 1993) at 68 *et seq.*

[185] Case C–2/90, *Walloon Waste* [1992] ECR I–4431, para 28.

[186] *Ibid.*, para 32. The Court noted that "[w]ith respect to the environment, […] waste is matter of a special kind. Accumulation of waste, even before it becomes a health hazard, constitutes a danger to the environment, regard being had in particular to the limited capacity of each region or locality for waste reception. In the instant case the Belgian government argued, without being contradicted by the Commission, that in view of the abnormal large-scale inflow of waste from other regions for tipping in Wallonia, there was a real danger to the environment, having regard to the limited capacity of that region." *Ibid.*, paras 29–31.

[187] Hilson correctly argues that Art 30 would not have enabled an environmental justification to be put forward. He states that "[w]hile Art 30 refers to human health and to life of animals or plants, the former would probably remain unaffected by non-hazardous waste and the latter appears to require a direct interference." C Hilson, "Discrimination in Community free movement law", 24 *ELRev* (1999) at 461–62 and fn 98, citing J Scott, *EC Environmental Law* (London, Longman, 1998) at 78 and Krämer, "Environmental Protection and Art 30 EEC Treaty" 30 *CMLRev* (1993) at 111.

regional restrictions of this sort were in fact to be considered as distinctly applicable measures.[188]

Although it confirmed the validity of its previous case-law excluding distinctly applicable measures from the mandatory requirements doctrine, the Court noted that "in assessing whether or not the barrier in question is discriminatory, account must be taken of the particular nature of waste".[189] Recalling the principle that environmental damage should, as a matter of priority be remedied at source, as provided by Article 174(2) (ex 130r (2)) EC, and consistently with the principles of self-sufficiency and proximity set out in the Basel Convention of 22 March 1989 on the control of trans-boundary movements of hazardous wastes and their disposal (to which the Community is a signatory), the Court concluded that,

> having regard to the differences between waste produced in different places and to the connection of the waste with its place of production, the contested measures cannot be regarded as discriminatory.[190]

Following the same reasoning, which had been unsuccessfully advanced by the Irish government in the previously mentioned *Irish Souvenirs* case, the Court of Justice decided that the Walloon ban was not discriminatory, on the basis that Walloon-produced and non-Walloon-produced waste were indeed *not* like products. Accordingly, the differential treatment of these products could not amount to (either formal or material) discrimination. This finding allowed the Court to submit the measure under review to the *Cassis de Dijon* doctrine and, more specifically, to justify the ban on import of non-hazardous waste into the Walloon region on the basis of environmental protection.[191]

As is usually the case, the Court of Justice did not really explain on what basis it found that the goods at issue were indeed not like. By referring to the principle that environmental damage should be remedied at source, as well as to the other environmental principles of self-sufficiency and proximity, the Court seemed to emphasise the "place of production" of waste as the differentiating element between two otherwise identical goods. However, it is not clear whether this element could be deemed to be an element related to the physical characteristics of waste or to its

---

[188] Cf Joined Cases C–1/90 and C–176/90 *Aragonesa de Publicidad Exterior and Publivía* [1991] ECR I–4151.

[189] Case C–2/90, *Walloon Waste* [1992] ECR I–4431, para 34.

[190] *Ibid.*, para 36.

[191] Although in *Cassis* de Dijon the Court did not mention environmental protection as one of the mandatory requirements which may justify indistinctly applicable measures, in the 1985 case of *Bruleurs d'Huiles Usagées*, the Court expressly acknowledged environmental protection as a matter of general interest for purposes of the mandatory requirements doctrine. Cf C Hilson, "Discrimination in Community free movement law", 24 *ELRev* (1999) at 462; J Scott, *EC Environmental Law* (London, Longman, 1998) at 79.

processing methods. Moreover, one may doubt whether the two products at issue were really unlike having regard to their relevant end-uses or consumer perception.

It has been argued that the weakness of the argument put forward by the Court of Justice with regard to its finding of "unlikeness" legitimises a different reading of the *Walloon Waste* decision. Confronted with an apparently distinctly applicable measure that it believed was justified on the basis of environmental protection, in order to make available the open-ended list of mandatory requirements, the Court referred to the products' relationship to rebut the appearance or presumption of de jure discrimination, which would have otherwise condemned the Walloon measure.[192]

Notwithstanding the merits of this particular case, two things should be noted at this point. First, the *Walloon Waste* case clearly demonstrates the practical consequences of the Court's strict approach with regard to "distinctly applicable measures", which may only be justified by one of the public policy objectives included in Article 30 EC. There may be cases where a national regulation employing the product's origin as the differentiating criteria (ie an origin-based measure) will be deemed to violate Community law simply because Article 30 does not cover all possible public policy objectives. It should however be noted that this circumstance is indeed quite exceptional in at least two respects: first, as will be argued below, it is usually very difficult for a formally discriminatory measure to be justified on (any) public policy grounds;[193] secondly, it is only where Article 30 does not provide for a ground of justification that the Court's different treatment of distinctly and indistinctly applicable measures may result in unwanted outcomes.

Secondly, notwithstanding the motives behind the Court's conclusion with regard to the likeness issue, it is clear from the *Walloon Waste* case that a finding of discrimination always entails a certain relationship between the products allegedly affected by such discrimination. In particular, as

---

[192] Cf C Hilson, "Discrimination in Community free movement law", 24 *ELRev* (1999) at 462. It is worthwhile emphasising that the Court *first* found that the measure was justified on the basis of environmental protection under the mandatory requirements doctrine and *only then* took into consideration whether the measure could even be subject to such a doctrine. In this manner, the Court tried to strengthen its fundamentally weak argument that the goods at issue were different. For a harsher view on the Court's decision in the *Walloon Waste* case *see* N Bernard, "Discrimination and Free Movement in EC Law", 45 *ICLQ* (1996) 82 at 94, where the author openly states that "the case was clearly wrongly decided". Cf J Scott, "Mandatory or Imperative Requirements in the EU and the WTO" in C Barnard and J Scott (eds), *The Law of the Single European Market: Unpacking the Premises* (Oxford, Hart Publishing, 2002) at 273.

[193] As a matter of fact, the Court of Justice did not really subject the Walloon ban to any substantial proportionality review and simply noted that "[i]n the instant case the Belgian Government argued, without being contradicted by the Commission, that in view of the abnormal large-scale inflow of waste from other regions for tipping in Wallonia, there was a real danger to the environment, having regard to the limited capacity of that region." Case C–2/90, *Walloon Waste* [1992] ECR I–4431, para 31.

already noted, a determination of de jure discrimination by definition presupposes also a determination that the products at issue are (except for their origin or nationality) *identical* in all respects (at least for purposes of the measure under review). Take the case of a State imposing a higher tax on foreign waste than on locally-produced waste. On its own terms, that tax measure discriminates between two identical goods (foreign and local waste). However, if that State is able to establish that the goods at issue are, for some reason, different, the necessary basis for the comparison disappears and the tax is no longer discriminatory. In practical terms, and as a confirmation of the exceptionality of a case such as the *Walloon Waste*, the only way in which a (apparently) "distinctly applicable measure" may escape the per se prohibition of Article 28 is for the enacting Member State to demonstrate that the product's *origin* constitutes a valid criterion for differentiating otherwise apparently identical products. The *Walloon Waste* case aside, this appears to be a very arduous, if not heroic, task indeed.[194]

Going back to the issue of the correct meaning of the term "distinctly applicable", and keeping in mind the practical implications of expanding the strict per se prohibition of Article 28 evidenced in *Walloon Waste*, the recent opinion by AG Tesauro, as well as the subsequent Court's decision, in the joined cases of *Decker v Caisse de maladie des employés privés* and *Kohll v Union des caisses de maladie*[195] tend to confirm a strict scope of application of the concept of "distinctly applicable measures".

In *Decker* and *Kohll*, the question which had been referred to the Court of Justice was whether a national regulation, by making reimbursement of medical expenses incurred in another Member State—whether to purchase medicinal products or to obtain medical treatment—conditional on prior authorisation, was in violation of the EC free movement principles. Having determined that the measures in question inhibited, albeit indirectly, imports of medical products contrary to Article 28,[196] the Advocate-General examined whether those measures could nevertheless be justified on public policy grounds. Confirming the consistent, albeit at times unclear, approach followed by the Court with regard to distinctly applicable measures, the AG noted first of all that,

> [...] in order to determine what type of justification is permissible it first needs to be decided whether the contested measure is to be categorised as formally discriminatory or as indistinctly applicable. In the former case it

---

[194] Cf Case C–379/98, *PreussenElektra AG v Schhleswag AG* [2001] ECR I–2099, where the Court did not even try to distinguish between locally-produced and non-locally produced green electricity in order to justify an otherwise distinctly applicable measure on grounds of environmental protection. See above n 171.

[195] Joined Cases C–120/95 *Decker v Caisse de Maladie des Employés Privés (Decker)* and C–158/96, *Kohll v Union des Caisses de Maladie (Kohll)* [1998] ECR I–1831.

[196] Opinion of AG Tesauro in Joined Cases C–120/95 *Decker* and C–158/96 *Kohll* [1998] ECR I–1831, paras 37–9.

can be justified, and hence upheld as compatible with Community law, only if it comes within the scope of Article 36 (goods) [...], in other words, if it comes within one of the derogations expressly provided for by the Treaty, with the further consequence that no consideration may be given to economic aims pursued by means of the restrictive measure but only, in the present instance, to the protection of public health. In the latter case, on the other hand, there is a broader range of requirements pertaining to the general interest capable of justifying the measure.[197]

The AG also observed that, while the parties and the governments which had submitted observations referred without distinction both to the protection of public health (one of the derogations provided by Article 30) and to the safeguarding of the financial stability of the health-care system (a reason relating to the general interest, in the "mandatory requirements" doctrine), the Commission had advanced the following distinction: while the measures under review were discriminatory vis-à-vis foreign goods, since prior authorisation was not required to purchase the relevant products in the national territory, they were indistinctly applicable with regard to services, since the authorisation requirement, although applicable only where medical services were sought abroad, *applied* in the same manner to nationals and non-nationals alike.[198]

Rejecting the Commission's dual view, the AG determined that the measure in question, even though it favoured the purchase of products sold in the national territory, could not be deemed a "distinctly applicable measure" because the measure was not formally discriminatory. The AG argued as follows:

> Given that authorisation is required solely for the purpose of conferring a benefit and not for the purpose of importation, it must be recognised, however, that the measure in question does not lay down different rules for imported products, but rather entails a difference in the treatment of persons (the insured), all resident in the same Member State, according to whether they have chosen to purchase a particular product in their State of residence or in some other Member State. [...] the fact that the difference in the treatment of insured persons depends, albeit indirectly, on the place where the optician or pharmacist who supplies the products is established, is of no significance for the purposes of the rules on goods, even if it may be considered to constitute formal discrimination based on the place of establishment.[199]

---

[197] *Ibid.*, para 45.

[198] The AG thus agreed with the Commission's argument that "under the rules laid down for goods even measures which, while not prescribing any particular formalities for the purposes of importation as such, are likely to discourage imports, are discriminatory, whereas under the rules governing services only measures which involve different treatment based on nationality are discriminatory." *Ibid.*, para 46.

[199] *Ibid.*, para 47. Note moreover that with regard to services, the AG added the following: "I would first recall that the Court has consistently held that measures are formally

In other words, the AG adopted a very strict interpretation of the term "distinctly applicable", excluding from its scope the case of a measure which *on its terms* does not distinguish expressly between products according to their origin. It may be argued that the AG based his opinion on the ground that the Luxembourg measures under review, in theory, affected any products (even Luxembourg ones), which were purchased outside Luxembourg.

Moreover, under the assumption that the national measures under consideration were to be regarded as "indistinctly applicable", the AG examined whether both requirements relied upon by the defending government, namely the protection of public health and the maintenance of a balanced medical and hospital system, could indeed justify those measures. While with regard to the former the AG concluded rather quickly that the measure in question could not be regarded as "necessary" for the protection of health, with regard to the latter requirement the AG reached a more nuanced conclusion. On the one hand, he found that the contested measure was justified in relation to all benefits provided to insured persons in hospitals and, in general, to all benefits which the insured person wished to have paid or reimbursed in full by the competent social security institution. On the other hand, he noted that the measure was not justifiable in relation to the purchase of products or medical services provided by private practitioners.[200]

As the reasoned opinion of the AG in *Decker* and *Kohll* shows, the availability of public policy justifications additional to those expressly provided for in the Treaty may at times make the difference between a finding of violation and one of conformity. While the Court of Justice treated, albeit only implicitly, the measures under review as "indistinctly applicable measures" (subjecting them to the "mandatory requirements" doctrine), in the end, in partial contrast with the conclusions of the Advocate-General Tesauro, it found that the authorisation requirements could not be justified

---

discriminatory only where they prescribe different rules for non-nationals and/or for the provision of services "originating" in other Member States. It regard to as indistinctly applicable, on the other hand, measures capable of applying to all those who carry on a particular activity in the territory of a particular Member State, even if such measures expressly impose a requirement of residence or establishment which effectively makes it impossible for service providers established in another Member State to carry on the activity in question. The measure under consideration, it is worth noting, does not entail any discrimination based on nationality nor does it prescribe, at least not directly, separate rules for service providers established in another Member State. The difference in treatment concerns, at least formally, all those insured under the social security scheme in question. Bearing in mind, however, that different treatment depends on the choice of doctor or of hospital, it is quite clear that the difference in the way insured persons are treated depends on the place where the provider of the service is established." *Ibid.*, para 48 [original fns omitted].

[200] *Ibid.*, para 60.

under either the protection of public health or the maintenance of the financial balance of the social security system.[201]

In concluding this section on Article 28 and de jure discriminatory non-fiscal regulations, it may be useful to briefly sum up the main findings.

Following a broad reading of the obscure concept of "measures having equivalent effect", first the Commission and, shortly thereafter, the Court of Justice applied the prohibition of Article 28 to cover any trade-restrictive measures (ie border and internal regulations) formally discriminating against imported products. In other words, Article 28 has been interpreted as including, inter alia, a rule mandating the elimination of "border measures" (a "negative integration *stricto sensu*" rule) and a rule prohibiting de jure discriminatory internal regulations (a "judicial integration— first layer" rule). This step is rather uncontroversial since, as both "border" and "formally discriminatory internal" measures substantially maintain the same negative effect on trade, by *openly* discriminating against imported products, they clearly represent blatant obstacles to the movement of goods across State boundaries. The category of "distinctly applicable" measures should thus be interpreted in a strict manner as excluding (even only facially) origin-neutral regulation. This interpretation conforms with the limited justification options which the text of the Treaty as well as the jurisprudence of the Court of Justice recognises as reflecting the prerogative of Member States to pursuit public policy objectives.

B. Justification Options

1. *Article 30 EC*

As stated above, "distinctly applicable" or origin-based measures may be justified only on the basis of one of the public policy grounds included in Article 30 EC, since the additional justifications labelled "mandatory requirements" by the *Cassis de Dijon* jurisprudence may only be applied for "indistinctly applicable" (or origin-neutral) measures.[202]

---

[201] Joined Cases C–120/95 *Decker* and C–158/96 *Kohll* [1998] ECR I–1831, para 38–42: "It must be recalled that aims of a purely economic nature cannot justify a barrier to the fundamental principle of the free movement of goods. However, it cannot be excluded that the risk of seriously undermining the financial balance of the social security system may constitute an overriding reason in the general interest capable of justifying a barrier of that kind. But, as the Luxembourg government acknowledged in reply to a question from the Court, it is clear that reimbursement at a flat rate of the cost of spectacles and corrective lenses purchased in other Member States has no effect on the financing or balance of the social security system".

[202] After a recent decision in Case C–203/96, *Chemische Afvalstoffen Dusseldorp BV and Others v Minister van Volkshuisvesting (Dusseldorp)* [1998] ECR 4075, concerning a Dutch measure restricting the export of waste for recovery, which appeared to constitute a case of distinctly

The above chapter dealing with the elimination of border measures emphasised the difficulty for Member States to justify a measure imposed on importation (or exportation) on public policy grounds. This is due principally to the *inherent* discriminatory character of this type of measures. It should not be too difficult to extend this observation also to formally discriminatory *internal* measures, which are those at issue in this chapter. When it comes to justification, internal measures discriminating between products expressly and exclusively on the basis of their origin or nationality (origin-based or de jure discriminatory measures) encounter the very same obstacles as seen for (inherently discriminatory) border measures. It is thus not surprising that to find a case of straightforward de jure discrimination in recent EC case-law, let alone one which has been found to be justified on public policy grounds, constitutes a rather difficult task.

Before examining a couple of exemplary cases which confirm these observations, it is important briefly to remind the reader of the main findings of the discussion carried out in the preceding chapter on the interpretation of Article 30 EC in the context of the ban on quantitative restrictions.

In that discussion, it was noted that from the very beginning the Court of Justice had interpreted the public policy exception of Article 30 EC in quite a strict manner. This rigorous interpretation can be observed in three different respects: (a) Article 30 is exclusively "directed to eventualities of a *non-economic* kind",[203] (b) the list of public policy exceptions provided for in Article 30 is of an *exhaustive* nature,[204] and (c) the concept of "a justified restriction" within the meaning of Article 30 means that a trade restriction is permitted only if it is "*necessary* for attainment of its objective".[205]

In particular with regard to this latter issue, in order to avail itself of the justification option of Article 30, a Member State is required to establish

applicable measure (formally discriminatory), and where the Court, albeit not very clearly, seemed willing to consider "environmental protection" as a possible public policy justification, few authors have signalled the possibility of the Court overturning even its traditional jurisprudence distinguishing between distinctly and indistinctly applicable measures. Cf D French, "The Changing Nature of "Environmental Protection": Recent Developments Regarding Trade and the Environment in the European Union and the World Trade Organisation", 47 *Netherlands International Law Review* (2000) 1, at 22–25, also citing in support Case C–389/96, *Aher-Waggon GmbH v Germany* [1998] ECR 4473. For a more cautious reading of *Dusseldorp*, see J Jans, "Analysis", 11 *Journal of Environmental Law* (1999) at 159; and P Oliver, "Some Further Reflections on the Scope of Art 28–30 (Ex 30–36) EC", 36 *CMLRev* (1999) 783, at 805.

[203] Case 7/61, *Commission v Italy* [1961] ECR 317, [emphasis added]. Cf Case 288/83, *Commission v Ireland (Potato Imports)* [1985] ECR 1761, where Ireland required licences in respect of the import of potatoes originating in third countries and in free circulation in another Member State, prohibiting imports of such potatoes in the absence of such a licence.
[204] In line with the strict interpretation of Art 30, the Court has rejected arguments, for example, that the term "public policy" can embrace concerns for consumer protection. Cf P Craig and G de Búrca, *EU Law* (Oxford, OUP, 1998) at 597 and cases cited therein.
[205] Case 251/78, *Firma Denkavit Futtermittel GmbH v Minister für Ernährung, Landwirtschaft und Forsten des Landes Nordrhein-Westfalen* [1979] ECR 3369, para 21 [emphasis added].

not simply that the national measure violating Article 28 is taken in pursuit of (ie somehow connected with) one of the relevant public policies listed in Article 30, but more rigorously that that same measure complies with the so-called "proportionality principle", that is with the tests of "suitability", "necessity" and "proportionality *stricto sensu*".[206]

Moreover, it was also emphasised that as a result of this reading (a) the various tests constituting the proportionality principle have become the central requirements in an Article 30 analysis and (b) the conditions provided for in the second sentence of Article 30 (prohibiting in any event "arbitrary discrimination" and "disguised restriction on trade") have been practically absorbed by the proportionality test and only very rarely constitute a further ground of appraisal.[207]

This reminder is indispensable for two reasons. First of all, it explains in part why it is indeed very difficult for Member States to invoke successfully the public policy grounds of Article 30 EC to justify an internal regulation formally discriminating on the basis of the product's origin or nationality. If it is already difficult to put forward a valid reason for employing the product's origin or nationality as a legitimate criterion for regulatory distinctions, it is even more difficult to overcome the hurdles established by the proportionality principle.

Secondly, this reminder should also facilitate a comparison between the interpretation and application of Article 30 EC with that of Article XX GATT. As will be examined in more detail in the subsection on Article XX,

The original paragraph reads as follows: "Having regard to the foregoing considerations it is necessary, with reference to the question put by the national court, to ascertain next whether the restrictions of the kind laid down by the Viehseuchenverordnung 1957 keep within the restrictions placed by Art 36 [now 30] of the Treaty on the exceptions to the free movement of goods permitted by that provision. In fact it is clear from the wording thereof that the prohibitions or restrictions which it permits must be justified, that is to say necessary for attainment of its objective and may not constitute a means of arbitrary discrimination or a disguised restriction on trade between Member States." Cf Case 12/78, *Eggers v Freie Hansestadt Bremen* [1978] ECR 1935, para 30, where the Court held that "Art 36 [now 30] is an exception to the fundamental principle of the free movement of goods and must, therefore, be interpreted in such a way that its scope is not extended any further than is necessary for the protection of those interests which it is intended to secure". Cf P Oliver, *Free Movement of Goods in the European Community* (London, Sweet & Maxwell, 1996) at 185.

[206] First, it must be established whether the measure is suitable or effective to achieve a legitimate public policy aim (test of "suitability"). Secondly, it must be established whether the measure is necessary to achieve that aim, namely, whether there are other less restrictive means capable of producing the same result (the "least restrictive alternative" or "necessity" test). Thirdly, even if there are no less restrictive means, it must be established that the measure does not have an excessive or disproportionate effect on trade (test of proportionality *stricto sensu*). For a detailed analysis of the proportionality principle, albeit employed as the primary norm, see below ch 4.

[207] J Snell, *Goods and Services in EC Law—A Study of the Relationship Between the Freedoms* (Oxford, OUP, 2002) at 181, noting that "there will be few, if any, measures that pass the proportionality test but still constitute arbitrary discrimination or a disguised restriction on trade".

contrary to the above-mentioned ECJ approach, GATT panel practice as well as WTO jurisprudence have had to deal with, and reconcile, two distinct aspects of Article XX GATT: on the one hand, the several and different "connectors" qualifying the public policy interests found in Article XX, sub-letters (a) to (j) (ie "necessary", "related to", "essential", etc) and, on the other hand, the general requirements of the Chapeau of Article XX (ie prohibition on "arbitrary and unjustifiable discrimination" and "disguised restrictions on international trade").[208]

Let us now examine two cases where Article 30 (ex 36) EC has been employed in order to justify a non-fiscal regulation formally discriminating on the basis of the product's nationality. The aim is to show both the inherent difficulty in justifying formal discrimination on public policy grounds and the Court of Justice "unstructured" approach with regard to the requirements of Article 30 EC (ie the proportionality tests and the prohibition on "arbitrary and unjustifiable discrimination" and "disguised restrictions on international trade").

(a) The protection of intellectual property and Generics   In *Allen and Hanburys Ltd v Generics (UK) Ltd,*[209] the Court of Justice was confronted with the issue of whether Articles 28 and 30 (ex 30 and 36) of the Treaty precluded the courts of a Member State from granting a legal remedy to prevent the importation from another Member State of a product that infringed a patent, while no such remedy could be granted in the same circumstances against an infringer who manufactured the product in the national territory. The Court put forward the relevant law of Articles 28 and 30 in the following paragraph:

> It should be noted that the effect of the provisions of the treaty on the free movement of goods, in particular Article 30 [now 28], is to prohibit as between Member States restrictions on imports and all measures having equivalent effect. According to Article 36 [now 30], however, those provisions do not preclude prohibitions or restrictions on imports justified on grounds of the protection of industrial and commercial property. However, such prohibitions or restrictions must not constitute a means of arbitrary discrimination or a disguised restriction on trade between Member States.[210]

Implicitly assuming that the measure at issue constituted a "measure having equivalent effect" for purposes of the prohibition of Article 28 EC, the Court stated that the "measure" in question could have been justified

---

[208] See more below discussion on the "justification options" in WTO.
[209] Case 434/85, *Allen and Hanburys Ltd v Generics (UK) Ltd.* [1988] ECR 1245.
[210] *Ibid.*, para 9.

under the provisions of Article 30 EC on the protection of industrial and commercial property only if that prohibition had been necessary to ensure that the proprietor of such a patent had, vis-à-vis importers, the same rights as he enjoyed as against producers manufacturing the product in the national territory, that is to say the right to a fair return from his patent.[211] In other words, employing the language of proportionality (in particular, of the "necessity" test), the Court examined whether the legal remedy recognised to the proprietor of a patent endorsed "licences of right" (ie an injunction preventing the importation of products) was indeed *necessary* in order to guarantee the right attached to such a licence as provided by UK law (ie the right to obtain a fair return).

Although both the plaintiff and the UK government advanced several public policy arguments, the Court concluded that the measure under review was not "justified" within the meaning of Article 30 EC in essence because the parties had not satisfactorily put forward any valid explanation for the formally discriminatory treatment between domestic and foreign-manufactured products. For example, it was suggested that, in light of the fact that an importer may have no substantial presence in the importing Member State, an injunction prohibiting him from importing the product could be deemed to be justified (at least) until the patent proprietor was guaranteed actual payment of the sums due to him. The Court could not accept this argument, since under UK law a similar injunction was not provided for in the case of UK-based manufacturers that did not have adequate assets. In other words, if the rationale for the injunction at issue was the safeguard of the right of the patent proprietor to obtain a fair return, why was such an injunction envisioned only in the case of "infringing" importers and not in the case of "infringing" domestic manufacturers?

The United Kingdom also maintained that the injunction at issue was provided for only in the case of imported goods because of the difficulty of carrying out the checks on the origin and quantities of goods imported on the basis of which the royalties payable to the patent proprietor had to be calculated. The Court rejected this further argument on the same ground: it may also be difficult to check the quantity of goods even where they are manufactured within the national territory, and yet no injunction or interdict is possible in those circumstances.[212]

It is interesting to emphasise that the Court concluded its review by stating that,

an injunction issued against an importer-infringer in the circumstances described by the National Court would constitute *arbitrary discrimination*

---

[211] *Ibid.*, para 14.
[212] *Ibid.*, para 18. The Court also rejected the further argument that an injunction prohibiting imports may be justified in order to enable the patent proprietor to check on the quality of

prohibited by Article 36 [now 30] of the Treaty and could not be justified on grounds of the protection of industrial and commercial property.[213]

From this sentence it would appear that the previous analysis on the "justifiability" and "necessity" of the national regulation under review stems from the second sentence of Article 30 EC prohibiting, inter alia, arbitrary discrimination. It has, in fact, been argued in the literature that the proportionality principle, as a tool employed to limit the availability of the public policy exception, finds its roots in the requirements of Article 30, second sentence.[214]

It is not the time and place to resurrect this issue since the Court of Justice has indeed never really explained in clear terms its reading of Article 30. What should be emphasised is more pragmatically that the Court does not really distinguish between the requirement of Article 30, first sentence ("justified on") and the requirements of Article 30, second sentence ("arbitrary discrimination" and "disguised restriction"). With regard to a public policy claim based on Article 30, the Court's approach is indeed quite "unstructured".[215] Nevertheless, the substance of the Court's application of Article 30 focuses principally on the proportionality of the measure at issue and in particular on whether such a measure is indeed "necessary" to achieve the public policy objective allegedly pursued by the Member State. The above mentioned difficulty of justifying a formally discriminatory regulation stems from the nature of such a test. In the case of de jure discrimination, in order to avail itself of the public policy exception provided for in Article 30, a Member needs to explain why it is employing the product's nationality or origin as the regulatory differentiating criterion. Since in regulatory terms the choice of such a criterion is usually not easy to justify, national regulations expressly based on nationality often fail Article 30 test.[216]

(b)   Public security and Campus Oil   One of the few cases where a distinctly applicable (or de jure discriminatory) measure was indeed found to be justified on grounds of the public policy exception of Article 30 EC is

---

an imported medicine in the interests of public health, noting that "that consideration has nothing to do with protection of the exclusive rights of the patent proprietor and, therefore, may not be relied on in order to justify, on grounds of protection of industrial and commercial property, a restriction on trade between Member States." *Ibid.*, paras 20–21.

[213] *Ibid.*, para 22 [emphasis added].
[214] S Weatherill and P Beaumont, *EU Law* ((London, Penguin Books, 1995); MA Jarvis, *The Application of EC Law by National Courts—The Free Movement of Goods* (Oxford, OUP, 1998).
[215] See below ch 4 discussing "proportionality" within the ambit of the *Dassonville-Cassis de Dijon* "rule of reason" approach.
[216] In the recent *Pistre* judgement, the justification argument based on Art 30 was dismissed in no more than one sentence. Joined Cases C–321–324/94 *Criminal Proceedings Against Jacques Pistre* [1997] ECR I–2343.

Campus Oil.[217] In this case, the Court was asked to review an Irish law requiring importers of petrol into Ireland to buy 35 per cent of their requirements from a state-owned oil refinery at prices fixed by the Irish government. The Irish requirement constituted a facial discrimination because it distinguished between domestic and imported petroleum products, affording the former an advantage through the imposition of a purchase requirement and the fixing of the purchase price. It was for this reason caught by Article 28. In its defence Ireland sought to rely on the "public policy" and "public security" grounds of Article 30, arguing that the importance of oil for the life of the country meant that it was vital for Ireland to be able to maintain refining capacities of its own. Moreover, the Irish argument went, the challenged rule was the *only way* of keeping the Irish refinery in operation.

Campus Oil is interesting, not only in that it shows that in exceptional circumstances even a "distinctly applicable measure" may be justified on public policy grounds, but also in that the specific test which the incriminated measure is required to meet, at least on a formal level, is identical to the proportionality test employed by the *Cassis de Dijon* jurisprudence to determine whether an "indistinctly applicable measure" is caught by the "prohibition" of Article 28. As will be shown in detail in chapter 4, in the context of the "reasonableness rule" in both EC and WTO law, the application of the principle of proportionality may entail in effect the same three-part test based on the concepts of "suitability" (whether the measure is suitable or effective to achieve a legitimate public policy objective), "necessity" or "least trade restrictivness" (whether the measure is necessary to achieve that aim, namely, whether there are other less restrictive means capable of producing the same result), and "proportionality *stricto sensu*" (whether the measure has an excessive or disproportionate effect on trade).[218]

In *Campus Oil*, after having determined that Article 30 covered rules of the type laid down by the Irish measure, the Court examined (a) whether the concept of public security covers reasons such as those advanced by the Irish Government, (b) whether the system at issue was such as to enable the objective of ensuring supplies of petroleum products to be attained and (c) whether it complied with the principle of proportionality.

---

[217] Case 72/83, *Campus Oil*, above n 172.
[218] G de Búrca, "The Principle of Proportionality and its Application in EC law", 13 *YEL* (1994) 105, at 113. Cf T Tridimas, "Proportionality in Community Law: Searching for the Appropriate Standard of Scrutiny" in E Ellis (ed), *The Principle of Proportionality in the Laws of Europe* (Oxford, OUP, 1999) at 68. The ECJ has however never clearly endorsed this structured approach to the proportionality test, even when invited to do so by its Advocate-Generals (in particular Van Gerven). In the area of goods, see Opinion of the Advocate-General Van Gerven in Case C–169/89, *Criminal Proceedings Against Gourmetterie Van den Burg (Dead Red Grouse)* [1990] ECR I–2143, and in the area of services, see Opinion of Advocate-General Van Gerven in Case C–159/90 *SPUC v Grogan* [1991] ECR I–4685.

On the issue of the scope of the concept of "public security", although the Court emphasised its jurisprudence excluding the availability of Article 30 for matters of a purely economic nature,[219] the Court concluded that,

> in the light of the seriousness of the consequences that an interruption in supplies of petroleum products may have for a country's existence, the aim of ensuring a minimum supply of petroleum products at all times is to be regarded as transcending purely economic considerations and thus as capable of constituting an objective covered by the concept of public security.[220]

With regard to the second question, the Court concluded that the presence of a refinery on the national territory *could effectively contribute* to improving the security of supply of petroleum products to a state which does not have crude oil resources of its own, by reducing both the risk of an oil crisis and of an interruption in deliveries.[221]

On the compliance with the proportionality principle, the Court pointed out that a Member State may have recourse to Article 30 (ex 36) to justify a measure having equivalent effect to a quantitative restriction on imports only if no other measure, less restrictive from the point of view of the free movement of goods, is capable of achieving the same objective.[222] After reviewing each of the main features of the Irish system[223] under the necessity test, the Court concluded that,

> a Member State which is totally or almost totally dependent on imports for its supplies of petroleum products may rely on grounds of public security within the meaning of Article 36 [now 30] of the Treaty for the purpose of requiring importers to cover a certain proportion of their needs by purchases from a refinery situated in its territory at prices fixed by the competent minister on the basis of the costs incurred in the operation of that refinery, if the production of the refinery cannot be freely disposed of at competitive prices on the market concerned. The quantities of petroleum products covered by such a system must not exceed the minimum supply requirement without which the public security of the state concerned would be affected or the level of production necessary to keep the refinery's production capacity available in the event of a crisis and to enable it to continue to refine at all times the crude oil for the supply of which the state concerned has entered into long-term contracts.[224]

---

[219] Case 72/83, *Campus Oil*, above n 217, para 35: "A Member State cannot be allowed to avoid the effects of measures provided for in the Treaty by pleading the economic difficulties caused by the elimination of barriers to intra-Community trade."
[220] *Ibid.*
[221] *Ibid.*, para 41.
[222] *Ibid.*, para 44.
[223] The purchase requirement, the percentage of petroleum products whose marketing is ensured, and the price fixing.
[224] Case 72/83, *Campus Oil*, above n 172, para 51.

As previously noted, this case constitutes a rather good example of how the Court employs the proportionality principle in reviewing the validity of de jure discriminatory national measures within the ambit of Article 30 EC. Once it has been determined that a particular measure is caught by the prohibition of Article 28, the Court is left to determine whether that measure may be justified on one of the public policy grounds of Article 30. The first question to be addressed is whether the objective of the national measure falls within the scope of one of the public policy grounds of Article 30 (ie whether the aim of ensuring a minimum supply of petroleum products at all times represents a legitimate public policy ground). Secondly, the Court has to determine whether the measure is such as to enable that particular objective to be attained (ie whether the Irish system at issue is such as to enable the objective of ensuring supplies of petroleum products to be attained). Although the Court seemed to consider this question outside the proportionality principle, this analysis represents the first limb of the proportionality principle, the so-called "suitability test".

Next, the Court has to take into consideration whether the measure employed to attain the particular objective at issue is the least-restrictive alternative available to the Member State, ie the "necessity test" (ie whether, even if the operation of a refinery is justified in the interest of public security, it is necessary in order to achieve that objective). Although the plaintiffs and the Commission argued that the Irish system was not merely unnecessary but also "disproportionate",[225] possibly inviting the Court to apply the third limb of the proportionality test (the concept of "proportionality *stricto sensu*"), in this case the Court did not distinguish between the second and third limbs of the test.

With regard to this latter issue, as will be shown in chapter 4 when examining the principle of proportionality employed as the principal normative rule, the Court of Justice very seldom and perhaps only in an indirect way makes recourse to the "proportionality *stricto sensu*" limb of the test. This will be explained by emphasising that a review of the measure's proportionality in the strict sense involves a determination of whether the negative effects of a measure on intra-Community trade are *out of proportion* to its benefits in terms of a legitimate public policy objective. In other words, what is at stake under the "proportionality *stricto sensu*" test is whether the chosen level of public policy protection (and the measure necessary to reach it) is out of proportion with respect to the principle of free circulation of goods. With regard to the regulatory prerogatives of the Member States, this is undoubtedly the more intrusive and thus problematic

---

[225] The plaintiffs and the Commission had argued that "even if the operation of a refinery is justified in the interest of public security, it is not necessary in order to achieve that objective, and, in any event, it is disproportionate in relation to that objective, to oblige importers to satisfy a certain proportion of their requirements by purchase from the national refinery at a price fixed by the competent minister." *Ibid.*, para 42.

form of review, since it focuses on assessing the relative values of, on the one hand, non-economic, public policy objectives (such as public health, consumer protection or environmental protection), and, on the other, the aim of liberalising intra-Community trade.

Campus Oil is also indicative of the Court's very pragmatic approach to the issue of justification on public policy grounds. It has been said that from a purely doctrinal point of view the *Campus Oil*'s stance on the scope of the concept of "public security" and on the review of "necessity" could be criticised.[226] The "public security" argument advanced by the Irish government was clearly interwound with purely economic aspects, which could have easily "disqualified" it from the coverage of Article 30. Even more strongly, when it comes to the necessity of the Irish requirements, it may be argued that the Irish refinery could have been financed from the public purse (ie an alternative measure which is less trade-restrictive, albeit more expensive). Taking *Campus Oil* as an example, Snell has noted that in general "the Court has not been overly dogmatic, rather, its approach has been a pragmatic and mostly balanced response to the competing interests".[227]

As a final note, it is interesting to emphasise that in *Campus Oil*, contrary to the decision in *Allen and Hanburys Ltd v Generics (UK) Ltd* examined above, no mention is made of the requirements provided for in the second sentence of Article 30. This absence confirms the previous remarks on the overall "unstructured" approach followed by the Court of Justice in applying the public policy justification of Article 30.

2.   *Article XX GATT*

As stated above, any internal measure that is found to violate the National Treatment obligation of Article III GATT may eventually be deemed to conform with WTO law if it is found to be justified on one of the public policy grounds included in Article XX GATT. Contrary to the case of origin-based fiscal measures, in both GATT panel practice and WTO jurisprudence there exist several cases where Members have resorted to the general exception provision of Article XX GATT in order to "save" an origin-based non-fiscal measure that had been found to violate the non-discrimination obligation of Article III:4. However, there is practically no case in which a Member has been able to plead successfully the Article XX GATT defence with regard to a de jure discriminatory internal regulation.

In chapter 1, while discussing the use of the general exception provision in the context of measures violating the prohibition of quantitative

---

[226] J Snell, *Goods and Services in EC Law—A Study of the Relationship Between the Freedoms* (Oxford, OUP, 2002) at 175.
[227] *Ibid.*, at 175.

restrictions of Article XI GATT, it was noted that any GATT violation may be justified under Article XX GATT if several conditions specified in that Article are met. The Appellate Body has grouped these conditions in two different stages, thus laying down a two-tiered justification test:

(1) "provisional justification" by reason of characterisation of the measure under one of the paragraphs of Article XX taking into account the exhaustive *regulatory goals* listed in subparagraphs (a)–(i) and the varying *connections* between the regulation and the regulatory objective specified therein; and
(2) "further appraisal" of the measure under the introductory clauses of Article XX, the so-called Chapeau.[228]

In light of the fact that the language qualifying the connection between regulatory measure and regulatory objective varies widely between stricter terms such as "essential" or "necessary" and looser terms such as "involving" or "relating to",[229] measures formally discriminating on the basis of the product's origin have been found not to be justified on public policy grounds under Article XX GATT at times simply because they did not meet the requirements of the first step ("provisional justification" under one of the subparagraphs) and, in other circumstances, because they did not comply with the provisions of the second step ("further appraisal" under the Chapeau). For example, in the instances where Members have attempted to justify a de jure discriminatory regulation on the basis of the public policies listed in Article XX(b) and (d), they have failed to satisfy the strict "necessity" requirement that qualifies the connection between "regulatory measure" and "regulatory objective" in the context of those subparagraphs.[230] On the other hand, when Members have relied on the justification policy under Article XX(g), which provides for the looser connector of "relating to",[231] de jure discriminatory regulations have been found unjustified, not on the basis of the "provisional justification" limb, but in light of the requirements of the introductory clauses of Article XX (the "further appraisal" or "Chapeau" limb). In this sense, it might be said that the Chapeau of Article XX has effectively been employed as a tool to "harmonise" the *degree of connection* between the challenged regulation and the regulatory objective that is required in

---

[228] Appellate Body Report on *Reformulated Gasoline*, above n 34, para 21.
[229] As noted in ch 1, this difference appears to reflect the broader or stricter scope of each sub-paragraphs.
[230] While Art XX(b) permits measures "necessary to protect human, animal or plant life of health", Art XX(d) provides an exception for measures "necessary to secure compliance with laws or regulations which are not inconsistent with the provision of this Agreement".
[231] Art XX(g) permits measures "relating to the conservation of exhaustible natural resources if such measures are made effective in conjunction with restrictions on domestic production or consumption".

order to justify a measure under the general public policy exception of Article XX. However, in the following paragraphs, I will also try to emphasise the further role which the introductory clause of Article XX plays in preventing the abuse or misuse of the general public policy exception.

While examining the complementary role of the two types of justification requirements ("provisional justification" and "further appraisal"), this section will also stress the progressive development of the relevant conditions of Article XX GATT. From the very simplistic and mechanical applications of the early GATT panel reports, recent Appellate Body decisions show a much more refined and elaborated approach with regard to the legal tests employed under the general public policy exception of Article XX in order to balance efforts to liberalise trade with other public policy interests. As the following analysis will show, such a development is certainly not without its obstacles and still much in progress.

(a)   Justifying de jure discriminatory measures under article XX(d)   Article XX provides in relevant part that, subject to the requirements of the introductory paragraph thereof, the General Agreement does not prevent the adoption or enforcement by any Member of measures:

> (d) necessary to secure compliance with laws or regulations which are not inconsistent with the provisions of this Agreement, including those relating to [...] the protection of patents, trade marks and copyrights, and the protection of deceptive practices.

In this section, the focus will be on both GATT panel practice and WTO jurisprudence interpreting the various features of Article XX(d). To facilitate such examination, I propose to distinguish between the "functional" and "objective" connection requirements of Article XX(d); with the former I refer to the term "necessary", while the latter is used to describe the term "secure compliance with laws or regulations".

(i) "Necessary" as the "functional connection" requirement of Article XX(d) in Section 337 *and* Malt Beverages

In the *Section 337* case,[232] discussed above, the United States claimed that even if it were found that its Section 337 afforded less favourable treatment to imported products contrary to Article III:4, this provision was nevertheless justified under Article XX(d) on the basis that it was "necessary to secure compliance with" US patent laws.[233]

---

[232] Panel Report on *United States—s 337 of the Tariff Act of 1930*, L/6439, adopted on 7 Nov 1989, BISD 36S/345.

[233] For an earlier case where the Panel found that a measure inconsistent with Art III:4 was not justified on the basis of Art XX(d) see Panel Report on *Canada—Administration of the Foreign Investment Review Act (FIRA)*, L/5504, adopted on 7 Feb 1984, BISD 30S/140, paras 5.19–5.20: "Since Art XX(d) is an exception to the General Agreement it is up to Canada,

According to the Panel, in order for an inconsistency with a GATT provision to be justified under Article XX(d), Members must meet, inter alia, the following two conditions: (1) the "laws or regulations" with which compliance is being secured are themselves "not inconsistent" with the General Agreement and (2) the measures are "necessary to secure compliance" with those laws or regulations.[234]

Since the "laws or regulations" with which Section 337 secured compliance were the US substantive patent laws and the conformity of these laws with the General Agreement were not being challenged, the Panel began its analysis with the issue of whether the inconsistencies with Article III:4 could be considered "necessary" to secure compliance with these laws. Having noted that the United States and the European Community interpreted the term "necessary" differently,[235] the Panel

as the party invoking the exception, to demonstrate that the purchase undertakings are necessary to secure compliance with the Foreign Investment Review Act. On the basis of the explanations given by Canada, the Panel could not, however, conclude that the purchase undertakings that were found to be inconsistent with Art III:4 are necessary for the effective administration of the Act. The Panel is in particular not convinced that, in order to achieve the aims of the Act, investors submitting applications under the Act had to be bound to purchasing practices having the effect of giving preference to domestic products. It was not clear to the Panel why a detailed review of investment proposals without purchasing requirements would not be sufficient to enable the Canadian government to determine whether the proposed investments were or were likely to be of significant benefit to Canada within the meaning of s 2 of the Foreign Investment Review Act."

[234] Panel Report on *s 337*, above n 17, para 5.22. The Panel also added the further condition provided for in the introductory paragraph of Art XX GATT that the measures under review "not [be] applied in a manner which would constitute a means of arbitrary or unjustifiable discrimination between countries where the same conditions prevail, or a disguised restriction on international trade". *Ibid*. On the interpretation and application of these requirements see below the discussion of the Appellate Body Reports on *Reformulated Gasoline and Shrimp/Turtle*.

[235] The United States had claimed that "the 'necessary to secure compliance' requirement in Art XX(d), as applied to United States patent laws, meant that the measure at issue must serve to prevent circumvention of the United States patent regime. The requirement did not impose an obligation to use the least trade restrictive measure that could be envisaged; this would invite continuous disputes regarding measures that the Contracting Parties had clearly intended to exempt from the obligations of the General Agreement. The concept of necessity should be interpreted taking into consideration the overall effectiveness of the measure, the inherent characteristics of imports, and the need for flexibility in achieving the objective of securing compliance with laws and regulations consistent with the General Agreement." On the other hand, the Community had argued that "A contracting party could not make something 'necessary' by merely writing its legislation in such a way that one type of enforcement measure was applicable to imported goods and another was applicable to domestic goods in otherwise similar situations. If there were objective practical or legal reasons of the kinds indicated, a contracting party would be free to apply enforcement procedures to domestic goods that could not be applied, without modification, to imported goods at the moment of their arrival at the frontier. But, if it did, any difference between the two enforcement mechanisms that might be required to adapt the domestic measures to deal with imports must be confined to what discriminated least against imported goods. Since Art XX(d) was an exceptions provision and applicable only in so far as national rules infringed other rules of the GATT, each such infringing rule should be examined to see whether it was necessary or not." *Ibid*., paras 3.59–3.60.

accepted the stricter interpretation put forward by the latter and introduced in GATT law the notion of "least trade-restrictive" or "less GATT inconsistent" measure. The relevant paragraph reads as follows:

> It was clear to the Panel that a contracting party cannot justify a measure inconsistent with another GATT provision as 'necessary' in terms of Article XX(d) if an alternative measure, which it could reasonably be expected to employ and which is not inconsistent with other GATT provisions, is available to it. By the same token, in cases where a measure consistent with other GATT provisions is not reasonably available, a contracting party is bound to use, among the measures reasonably available to it, that which entails the least degree of inconsistency with other GATT provisions. The Panel wished to make it clear that this does not mean that a contracting party could be asked to change its substantive patent law or its desired level of enforcement of that law, provided that such law and such level of enforcement are the same for imported and domestically-produced products. However, it does mean that, if a contracting party could reasonably secure that level of enforcement in a manner that is not inconsistent with other GATT provisions, it would be required to do so.[236]

Accordingly, a measure is deemed to be "necessary" for the purposes of Article XX(d) only if neither a GATT consistent nor less GATT inconsistent measure is reasonably available in order for a Contracting Party to secure the desired level of enforcement. Although apparently a quite strict reading of the term "necessary", the inherent limits of the necessity test were clearly emphasised by the Panel. Requiring that Members employ the least-GATT inconsistent measure reasonably available to pursue a certain public policy objective did not mean that Members' discretion in setting the "desired level" of enforcement or compliance with that objective was impaired. In the particular case, if the United States wished to guarantee zero-risk of patent infringements, which implied the adoption of very strict regulatory measures, it could have done so. The only proviso put forward by the Panel in this regard is that the level of enforcement be the same for imported and domestically produced products. In other words, discrimination on grounds of nationality in the level of enforcement or compliance is not permitted.[237]

Following this approach, the *Section 337* Panel considered whether Section 337 of the US Tariff Act could be justified on the basis that it provided the *only* means of enforcement of US patent rights against imports of products manufactured abroad by means of a process patented in the United States. The Panel found that the system of determining allegations

---

[236] *Ibid.*, para 5.26.
[237] See below discussion of the Appellate Body Report on *Korea–Beef*, above n 124. For further discussion on the inherent limits of the necessity test see also ch 4 on the Reasonableness Rule in EC and WTO Law.

of violation of US patent rights under Section 337 could not be justified as necessary within the meaning of Article XX(d) essentially because the reasons advanced by the United States were not sufficient to explain its differential treatment of domestic and imported products. For example, the Panel considered the US argument that many of the procedural aspects of Section 337 reflected the need to provide expeditious prospective relief against infringing imports. The Panel understood this argument to be based on the notion that, in respect of infringing imports, there would be greater difficulty than in respect of infringing products of domestic origin in collecting awards of damages for past infringement. This was apparently the case because foreign manufacturers are outside the jurisdiction of national courts and importers might have little by way of assets. However, in the Panel's view, given the issues at stake in typical patent suits, this argument could only provide a justification for rapid provisional measures against imported products, combined with the necessary safeguards to protect the legitimate interests of importers in the event that the products prove not to be infringing. The tight time-limits for the conclusion of Section 337 proceedings, when no comparable time-limits applied in federal district court, and the other features of Section 337 inconsistent with Article III:4 that served to facilitate the expeditious completion of Section 337 proceedings (such as the inadmissibility of counterclaims) could not be justified as "necessary" on this basis.[238]

Similar arguments were advanced by the United States in the *Malt Beverages* case[239] in the context of supporting its claim that several of the federal and state regulations affecting the sale and distribution of alcoholic beverages in violation of the National Treatment provision of Article III:4 could nonetheless be justified on the basis of the general exception in Article XX(d). For example, the United States claimed that the requirement that imported beer be distributed through in-state wholesalers (which requirement was not imposed in the case of beer from in-state breweries) was justified under Article XX(d) as the only reasonable measure able to secure compliance with state excise taxes on beer.[240] Adopting the interpretation put forward by the *Section 337* Panel on the meaning of "necessary", the Panel rejected the US claim. It stated that

---

[238] Panel Report on *s 337*, above n 17, para 5.34. The Panel noted, moreover, that some of the inconsistencies with Art III:4 of individual aspects of procedures under s 337 could be justified under Art XX(d) in certain circumstances. *Ibid.*, paras 5.32–5.33.

[239] Panel Report on *Malt Beverages*, above n 21.

[240] *Ibid.*, para 5.42: "The Panel recalled the position of the United States that there was no reasonable alternative to the existing regulatory scheme in the various states which required out-of-state and imported beer to be distributed to retailers via in-state wholesalers while allowing in-state beer to be shipped directly from producers to retailers. The United States considered that the wholesaler was the only reasonable place for beer excise taxes to be collected for out-of-state and foreign products, but that there was no such necessity with respect to products from in-state producers that were, by definition, under the jurisdiction of the state."

the United States had not met its burden of showing that the specific inconsistency with Article III:4 of the discriminatory wholesaler requirements in the various states is the only reasonable measure available to secure enforcement of state excise tax laws. The Panel demonstrated that alternative measures for enforcement of state excise tax laws did indeed exist by observing that not all 50 states maintained discriminatory distribution systems and that hardly any domestic in-state breweries exercised the privilege of selling directly to retailers.[241]

Similar conclusions were reached by the *Malt Beverages* Panel with regard to the US argument that its requirement of using common carriers, which was imposed only on imported beer (deemed to violated Article III:4), was necessary for purposes of Article XX(d) in order to ensure independent record-keeping for shipments of out-of-state alcohol.[242] Noting once again that not all 50 states of the United States maintained common carrier requirements, the Panel found that the United States had not demonstrated that,

> the common carrier requirement is the *least trade restrictive enforcement measure* available to the various states and that less restrictive measures, eg record-keeping requirements of retailers and importers, are not sufficient for tax administration purposes.[243]

(ii) "To secure compliance to laws or regulations" as the "objective connection" requirement of Article XX(d) in EEC—Parts and Components *and* Reformulated Gasoline

In *United States—Standards for Reformulated and Conventional Gasoline*,[244] the Panel examined whether a US measure imposing different baseline establishment methods with regard to imported and domestic gasoline, in violation of Article III:4, could be justified as necessary to secure compliance with the US non-degradation requirements under Article XX(d). The Panel rejected the US defence on the basis of a quite strict interpretation of the policy objective of "securing compliance with consistent laws or regulations". The Panel found that the baseline establishment methods did not "secure compliance" with the baseline system since these methods were not an enforcement mechanism but were simply

---

[241] *Ibid.*, 5.43.
[242] The United States maintained that such an independent source of records was necessary because the state authorities did not have access to the out-of-state producers' shipping records with which to verify information provided by in-state wholesalers; that such independent verification was necessary in order to curb tax avoidance; and that because in-state producers were within the jurisdiction of the state tax authorities, there was no reason to require that their beer and wine be shipped by common carrier. *Ibid.*, para 5.51.
[243] *Ibid.*, para 5.52 [emphasis added].
[244] Panel Report on *Reformulated Gasoline*, above n 34.

rules for determining the individual baselines, and as such "they were not the type of measures with which Article XX(d) was concerned."[245]

The Panel based its strict reading of the term "to secure compliance" on the previous GATT panel report on *EEC–Parts and Components*,[246] where it was determined that Article XX(d) "covers only measures related to the enforcement of obligations under laws or regulations consistent with the General Agreement".[247] In that case, the relevant Article XX(d) issue was whether the imposition of anti-circumvention duties (which had been found to be inconsistent with Article III:2) was a measure "to secure compliance with" the EC general antidumping regulations and individual regulations imposing definitive antidumping duties. The *EEC–Parts and Components* Panel noted that the general antidumping regulation of the EC did not establish obligations that required enforcement, but merely established a legal framework for EC authorities. In the Panel's view, only the individual regulations imposing definitive antidumping duties gave rise to obligations that required enforcement, namely the obligation to pay a specified amount of antidumping duties. However, since the anti-circumvention duties did not serve to enforce the payment of antidumping duties, the Panel concluded that the anti-circumvention duties did not secure compliance with obligations under the EEC antidumping regulations for purposes of Article XX(d) exception.[248]

There are at least a couple of reasons why I do not believe that the term "to secure compliance" should be interpreted to mean exclusively "to enforce" as the Panels in *Reformulated Gasoline* and *EEC–Parts and Components* seem to have suggested.

First of all, I am not fully convinced of the arguments based on a pure literal interpretation of the term "to secure compliance", since the term appears to require a looser connection between the inconsistent measure (to justify) and "laws and regulations" (not inconsistent with the provisions of GATT), whose compliance the inconsistent measure has to secure (Article XX(d) "objective connection" requirement). Moreover, it does not appear that laws or regulations for purposes of Article XX(d) need to be

---

[245] *Ibid.*, para 6.33.
[246] Panel Report on *EEC Measures on Animal Feed Proteins*, L/4599, adopted on 14 March 1978, BISD 25S/49.
[247] *Ibid.*, para 5.18.
[248] *Ibid.* The Panel examined the alternative interpretations in the light of the purpose of Art XX(d) and said the following. "If the qualification 'to secure compliance with laws and regulations' is interpreted to mean 'to enforce obligations under laws and regulations', the main function of Art XX(d) would be to permit contracting parties to act inconsistently with the General Agreement whenever such inconsistency is necessary to ensure that the obligations which the contracting parties may impose consistently with the General Agreement under their laws or regulations are effectively enforced. If the qualification 'to secure compliance with laws and regulations' is interpreted to mean 'to ensure the attainment of the objectives of the laws and regulations', the function of Art XX(d) would be substantially broader." *Ibid.*, para 5.17.

exclusively those relating to "enforcement" (ie be enforcement mechanisms). On the contrary, following a literal reading of subparagraph (d) of Article XX, it is clear that "laws or regulations" include "those relating to [...] the protection of patents [...] and the prevention of deceptive practices."

Under a somewhat different perspective, it is here submitted that a broader interpretation of the "objective connection" requirement would arguably allow for Article XX(d) to function as the basis for including other legitimate policy objectives within the otherwise exhaustive list of Article XX.[249] As will be further discussed in chapter 3 in the sections on justification options for the prohibition of de facto discrimination, the (apparently) exhaustive nature of the list of public policy objectives provided for in Article XX GATT has been regarded by several commentators as a problematic issue in the debate concerning the appropriate balance between multilateral trade liberalisation and national regulatory prerogatives. A broad reading of Article XX(d) could represent a possible solution of such a problem.

Furthermore, such a more enlightened reading of Article XX, by means of a broad interpretation of the "objective connection" requirement of Article XX(d), should not be discarded by fears of Members abusing the general public policy exception. Any such risk would be prevented by the rigorous requirements that the inconsistent measure (1) be "necessary" to secure compliance (Article XX(d) "functional connection" requirement) and (2) comply with the provisions of the introductory clauses of Article XX.[250]

(iii) Article XX(d) and the more enlightened approach in Korea–Beef

The recent *Korea–Beef* dispute[251] seems to have afforded both the Panel and the Appellate Body with the opportunity to endorse the more enlightened approach with regard to Article XX(d) suggested above: while the Panel adopted a looser reading of the term "to secure compliance", the Appellate Body interpreted the term "necessary" for purposes of that same provision in quite a strict manner.

As already noted, both the Panel and the Appellate Body found in that case that Korean legislation requiring the existence of two distinct systems for the distribution and sale of imported and domestic beef violated inter alia the National Treatment obligation of Article III:4. However, Korea argued that its dual retail system was justified on the basis of Article XX(d) since such a system was necessary to secure compliance with the Korean *Unfair Competition Act*. The Panel thus began its analysis under Article XX(d) with the issue of whether the inconsistent measure

---

[249] This is provided that the other conditions stipulated in Art XX(d) have been met. Cf G Verhoosel, *National Treatment and WTO Dispute Settlement* (Oxford, Hart Publishing, 2002) at 35.

[250] Moreover, the original law would have to be in compliance with the GATT.

[251] Panel Report on *Korea–Beef*, above n 122; Appellate Body Report on *Korea–Beef*, above n 124.

was designed to "secure compliance" with laws or regulations consistent with the GATT. The Panel found that,

> despite … troublesome aspects, … the dual retail system was put in place, at least in part, in order to secure compliance with the Korean legislation against deceptive practices to the extent that it serves to prevent acts inconsistent with the *Unfair Competition Act*.[252]

The panel acknowledged that (a) the dual retail system was established at a time when acts of misrepresentation of origin were widespread in the beef sector and that (b) such system indeed appeared to reduce the opportunities and thus the temptation for butchers to misrepresent less expensive foreign beef as more expensive domestic beef, at least compared with the situation where all domestic and imported beef could officially be supplied to the same shop.[253]

Although the Panel noted that its interpretation of the "objective connection" requirement under Article XX(d) was not inconsistent with the approach taken by the Panel on *EEC–Parts and Components*,[254] it is clear that the Panel in *Korea–Beef* adopted a much looser definition of the term "to secure compliance". Focusing on whether the inconsistent measure was *aimed at* (Panel's above mentioned argument sub (a)), and *capable of* (sub (b)), securing compliance with the Korean legislation against deceptive practices, the Panel appeared not to require that the discriminatory dual retail system be deemed a mechanism for the *enforcement* of specific obligations stemming from the Korean *Unfair Competition Act*. In other words, the test applied by the Panel in *Korea–Beef* with regard to the "objective connection" requirement of Article XX(d) seems to come close to the so-called "suitability" limb of the proportionality test employed in EC law in similar context.[255]

Since the parties did not appeal these findings, the Appellate Body did not have the opportunity to pronounce on the correct interpretation of the "objective connection" requirement under Article XX(d) and thus simply limited its analysis to restating the grounds upon which the Panel had

---

[252] Panel Report on *Korea–Beef*, above n 122, para 658.
[253] *Ibid.*
[254] *Ibid.*, fn 363: "The interpretation given by the present Panel to the words 'measures to secure compliance … ' would be inconsistent with the *EEC–Parts and Components* only if one were to interpret the approach taken by the panel in that case as requiring that measures coming within the scope of Art XX(d) be technically part of the 'laws and regulations' themselves. The reading of the *EEC–Parts and Components* panel does not warrant such an interpretation and if it would, which is not the case, the present Panel would disagree with so narrow an interpretation of Art XX(d)".
[255] Cf D Osiro, "GATT/WTO Necessity Analysis: Evolutionary Interpretation and its Impact on the Autonomy of Domestic Regulation", 29 *Legal Issues of Economic Integration* (2002) 123 at 132.

based its findings.[256] However, emphasising the context of Article XX(d), for purposes of deciphering the term "necessary", the Appellate Body did note that Article XX(d) is susceptible of application in respect of a *wide variety* of laws and regulations to be enforced.[257]

Let us now turn to the Panel and, in particular, the Appellate Body's statements and findings with regard to the "necessity" requirement of Article XX(d).

Following the approach of the *Section 337* Panel Report,[258] the Panel found that the Korean dual retail system was not "necessary" to secure compliance with the Unfair Competition Law on two related grounds. First of all, the Panel noted that, in order to prevent similar cases of misrepresentation of origin from occurring in other sectors of its domestic economy, Korea did not deem it necessary to establish "dual retail systems" but instead employed traditional enforcement measures, consistent with WTO law, which included record-keeping, investigations, policing and fines. Moreover, the Panel noted that Korea had not satisfactorily shown that measures other than a dual retail system, compatible with the WTO law, were not sufficient to deal with cases of misrepresentation of origin involving imported beef.[259]

Korea appealed the Panel's conclusion arguing that (1) the Panel incorrectly interpreted the term "necessary" in Article XX(d) as requiring *consistency* among enforcement measures taken in related product areas and (2) the Panel neglected to take into account the *level of enforcement* that Korea sought with respect to preventing the fraudulent sale of imported beef.

As is usually the case, the Appellate Body first of all addressed in general terms the issue of the "ordinary meaning of the word "necessary", in its context and in the light of the object and purpose of Article XX, in accordance with Article 31(1) of the Vienna Convention" and subsequently reviewed the merits of Panel's findings on the basis of such a general approach and the Appellant's claims.

---

[256] Appellate Body Report on *Korea–Beef*, above n 124, para 158: "The Panel found, 'despite … troublesome aspects, … that the dual retail system was put in place, at least in part, in order to secure compliance with the Korean legislation against deceptive practices to the extent that it serves to prevent acts inconsistent with the *Unfair Competition Act*.' It recognised that the system was established at a time when acts of misrepresentation of origin were widespread in the beef sector. It also acknowledged that the dual retail system 'does appear to reduce the opportunities and thus the temptations for butchers to misrepresent [less expensive] foreign beef for [more expensive] domestic beef'."

[257] *Ibid.*, para 162.

[258] The Panel stated that "To demonstrate that the dual retail system is 'necessary', Korea has to convince the Panel that, contrary to what was alleged by Australia and the United States, no alternative measure consistent with WTO law is reasonably available at present in order to deal with misrepresentation in the retail beef market as to the origin of beef." Panel Report on *Korea–Beef*, above n 122, para 659.

[259] *Ibid.*, paras 660–74.

The Appellate Body began by noting that the word "necessary" normally denotes something "that cannot be dispensed with or done without, requisite, essential, needful".[260] At the same time, it observed that a standard law dictionary cautions that,

> [t]his word must be considered in the connection in which it is used, as it is a word susceptible of various meanings. It may import absolute physical necessity or inevitability, or it may import that which is only convenient, useful, appropriate, suitable, proper, or conducive to the end sought. It is an adjective expressing degrees and may express mere convenience or that which is indispensable or an absolute physical necessity.[261]

The Appellate Body held that, as employed in the context of Article XX(d), the reach of the word "necessary" is not limited to that which is "indispensable" or "of absolute necessity" or "inevitable". Noting that the term "necessary" refers to a range of degrees of necessity going from "necessary" understood as "indispensable" to "necessary" taken to mean as "making a contribution to", the Appellate Body considered that a "necessary" measure is, in this continuum, located significantly closer to the pole of "indispensable" than to the opposite pole of simply "making a contribution to".[262]

According to the Appellate Body, in appraising the "necessity" of a measure in these terms, it is useful to bear in mind the context in which "necessary" is found in Article XX(d). The measure at stake has to be "necessary to ensure compliance with laws and regulations ..., including those relating to customs enforcement, the enforcement of [lawful] monopolies..., the protection of patents, trade marks and copyrights, and the prevention of deceptive practices". In the Appellate Body's view, this provision is susceptible of application in respect of a wide variety of "laws and regulations" to be enforced, and thus,

> a treaty interpreter assessing a measure claimed to be necessary to secure compliance of a WTO-consistent law or regulation may, in appropriate cases, take into account the relative importance of the common interests or values that the law or regulation to be enforced is intended to protect. The more vital or important those common interests or values are, the easier it would be to accept as 'necessary' a measure designed as an enforcement instrument.[263]

---

[260] The Appellate Body drew this definition from *The New Shorter Oxford English Dictionary* (Clarendon Press, 1993), Vol II, at 1895. Appellate Body Report on *Korea–Beef*, above n 124, para 160.

[261] The Appellate Body drew this paragraph from *Black's Law Dictionary* (West Publishing, 1995) at 1029. Appellate Body Report on *Korea–Beef*, above n 124, para 160.

[262] *Ibid.*, para 161.

[263] *Ibid.*, para 162.

Furthermore, according to the Appellate Body, other aspects of the enforcement measure to be considered in evaluating that measure as "necessary" are (a) the extent to which the measure contributes to the realisation of the end pursued, the securing of compliance with the law or regulation at issue ("[t]he greater the contribution, the more easily a measure might be considered to be 'necessary'");[264] and (b) the extent to which the compliance measure produces restrictive effects on international commerce, that is, in respect of a measure inconsistent with Article III:4, restrictive effects *on imported goods* ("[a] measure with a relatively slight impact upon imported products might more easily be considered as 'necessary' than a measure with intense or broader restrictive effects").[265]

In sum, in the Appellate Body's view, a determination of whether a measure that is not "indispensable" may nevertheless be "necessary" within the context of Article XX(d) involves in every case a process of *weighing and balancing* a series of factors which prominently include the contribution made by the compliance measure to the enforcement of the law or regulation at issue, the importance of the common interests or values protected by that law or regulation, and the accompanying impact of the law or regulation on imports or exports.[266]

The general approach delineated by the Appellate Body in *Korea–Beef* with regard to the fundamental issue of the meaning of the term "necessary" within Article XX(d) clearly evidences the struggle in which the Appellate Body finds itself in attempting to put forward the appropriate balance between two diverging needs, "flexible application" and "legal certainty". If the Appellate Body recognises the inescapable and indispensable flexibility in applying concepts such as the "necessity" requirement, it also tries to provide the elements upon which to base a "necessity" determination. Although in doing so the Appellate Body does put forward certain new elements, which will need further elaboration, it would seem that this general approach does not differ substantially from that enunciated in the famous *Section 337* Panel Report. The several factors included in the weighing and balancing process are all to be employed in order to determine whether there exist an alternative measure that (1) is less restrictive than that found to violate one of the obligations of the GATT and (2) may equally secure compliance with the relevant "laws or regulations". In this regard, it is the Appellate Body itself that recognises that the "weighing and balancing" process outlined in its Report on *Korea–Beef* is comprehended in the standard described by the *Section 337* panel, or in other words:

---

[264] *Ibid.*, para 163.
[265] *Ibid.*
[266] *Ibid.*, para 164.

in the determination of whether a WTO-consistent alternative measure which the Member concerned could "reasonably be expected to employ" is available, or whether a less WTO-inconsistent measure is "reasonably available".[267]

Put it more bluntly, the "weighing and balancing" test advanced by the Appellate Body in *Korea–Beef* should not be equated to what in EC law terminology is the test of "proportionality *stricto sensu*", according to which the Court of Justice balances the national interest in pursuing a legitimate public policy against the Community interest in ensuring the free movement of goods. On the basis of this test, for example, it would be possible to strike down a national measure even if it is found to be "necessary" to pursue a legitimate aim like environmental protection, on the basis that, on balance, the measure's negative effects on trade are *disproportionate* to its benefits on the environment.

It is here submitted that the Appellate Body's reference to the *extent* of the *restrictive effects* on international commerce produced by the GATT-inconsistent compliance measure should not be regarded as introducing this type of "weighing and balancing", but simply as the necessary limb in the determination of the existence of a *less restrictive* measure which may equally secure compliance with the relevant "laws and regulations".[268]

Let us now turn to the Appellate Body's review of the Panel's findings on the issue of whether the Korean dual retail system was indeed "necessary" to secure compliance with the *Unfair Competition Act*, taking into consideration Korea's claims on appeal.

Korea claimed that the Panel had introduced an illegitimate "consistency test" into Article XX(d) by drawing conclusions from the absence of any requirement for a dual retail system in related product areas. The Appellate Body dismissed this line of argument without much ado, noting that the examination of enforcement measures applicable to the same illegal behaviour relating to like, or at least similar, products does not necessarily imply the introduction of a "consistency" requirement into the "necessary" concept of Article XX(d). On the contrary, in the Appellate Body's view, examining such enforcement measures may provide useful input in determining whether an alternative measure, which could be reasonably expected to be utilised, is indeed available or not.[269] Furthermore, the Appellate Body observed that the application by

---

[267] *Ibid.*, para 166.
[268] For a different reading of the Appellate Body Report on *Korea–Beef*, see G Marceau and J Trachtman, "The Technical Barriers to Trade Agreement, the Sanitary and Phytosanitary Measures Agreement, and the General Agreement on Tariffs and Trade: A Map of the World Trade Organization Law of Domestic Regulation of Goods", in 36 JWT (2002) 811, at 851–53.
[269] Appellate Body Report on *Korea–Beef*, above n 124, para 170.

a Member of WTO-*compatible* enforcement measures to the same kind of illegal behaviour—the passing-off of one product for another—for like or at least similar products, provides a "suggestive indication" that an alternative measure, in the above-mentioned sense, may well be available. Consequently, the application of such measures for the control of the same illegal behaviour for like, or at least similar, products raises doubts with respect to the objective *necessity* of a different, much stricter, and WTO-inconsistent enforcement measure.[270]

The other argument advanced by Korea on appeal—ie that the Panel had neglected to take into account the *level of enforcement* that Korea sought with respect to preventing the fraudulent sale of imported beef—proved much trickier and the Appellate Body's response is not at all convincing.

Korea had argued that under Article XX(d) a panel must examine whether a means reasonably available to the Member could have been used in order to reach the objective sought *without putting into question the level of enforcement pursued*. In other words, alternative measures must not only be reasonably available, but must also guarantee the level of enforcement sought which, in the case of the dual retail system, is the elimination of fraud in the beef retail market.

Korea's argument brilliantly exploits the inherent limits of the "necessity" or "least-restrictive measure" test: contrary to the weighing and balancing of the test of "proportionality *stricto senso*", the "necessity" test simply focuses on whether there exist other GATT-consistent or less-restrictive measures which, to take the example of Article XX(d), are capable of securing the *same level* of compliance as set by WTO Members. Under the "necessity" test, the Member's desired level of compliance or enforcement may not be subject to any judicial review.[271] As noted above, this was clearly emphasised also by the *Section 337* Panel Report.

Although it firmly recognised this fundamental feature of the "necessity" test by affirming that WTO Members "have the right to determine for themselves the level of enforcement of their WTO-consistent laws and regulations",[272] the Appellate Body indeed appears to improperly assess Korea's intended level of protection.

---

[270] *Ibid.*, para 172.

[271] A Mattoo and P Mavroidis, "Trade, Environment and the WTO: The Dispute Settlement Practice Relating to Art XX of GATT" in EU Petersmann (ed) *International Trade Law and the GATT/WTO Dispute Settlement System* (London, Kluwer Law International, 1997) at 338. D Osiro, "GATT/WTO Necessity Analysis: Evolutionary Interpretation and its Impact on the Autonomy of Domestic Regulation" 29 *Legal Issues of Economic Integration* (2002) 123, at 137 *et seq.*

[272] Appellate Body Report on *Korea–Beef*, above n 124, para 176. The Appellate Body noted moreover that "this has also been recognised by the panel in *US–s 337*, where it said: 'The Panel wished to make it clear that this [the obligation to choose a reasonably available GATT-consistent or less inconsistent measure] does not mean that a contracting party could

The Appellate Body did recognise that, in establishing the dual retail system, Korea could well have intended to secure a *higher* level of enforcement of the prohibition set out in the *Unfair Competition Act* of acts misleading the public about the origin of beef sold by retailers compared to the level of enforcement of the same prohibition with respect to beef served in restaurants, or the sale by retailers of other meat or food products, such as pork or seafood. However, it determined that this could not have been Korea's intention. The relevant paragraph reads as follows:

> We think it unlikely that Korea intended to establish a level of protection that *totally eliminates* fraud with respect to the origin of beef (domestic or foreign) sold by retailers. The total elimination of fraud would probably require a total ban of imports. Consequently, we assume that in effect Korea intended to *reduce considerably* the number of cases of fraud occurring with respect to the origin of beef sold by retailers. The Panel did find that the dual retail system 'does appear to reduce the opportunities and thus the temptations for butchers to misrepresent foreign beef for domestic beef'. And we accept Korea's argument that the dual retail system *facilitates* control and permits combating fraudulent practices *ex ante*. Nevertheless, it must be noted that the dual retail system is only an *instrument* to achieve a significant reduction of violations of the *Unfair Competition Act*. Therefore, the question remains whether other, conventional and WTO-consistent instruments can not reasonably be expected to be employed to achieve the same result. [emphasis original][273]

Korea's desired level of protection having been the "significant reduction" of fraud, rather than its "total elimination", the Appellate Body agreed with the Panel that Korea had not demonstrated that it could not achieve its desired level of enforcement of the *Unfair Competition Act* with respect to the origin of beef sold by retailers by using conventional WTO-consistent enforcement measures such as investigations, fines, record-keeping and policing.[274]

The Appellate Body's treatment of the "level of protection" argument may be interpreted in either of two ways. On the one hand, the Appellate Body's own assessment of Korea's actual desired level of protection may be regarded as implicitly operating the kind of "weighing and balancing" process between the national interest in combating fraud and the WTO interest in liberalising trade, which in EC law usually goes under the term of "proportionality *stricto sensu*". Seen in this perspective, it might be said that, in the Appellate Body's view, the restrictive effects on trade of a

---

be asked to change its substantive patent law or its desired *level of enforcement* of that law ....'." [emphasis added]. *Ibid.*

[273] *Ibid.*, para 178.
[274] *Ibid.*, paras 179–80.

rigorous policy against fraud (zero tolerance) were disproportionate to the actual benefits of such a policy. This interpretation would clearly take the "necessary" connector of Article XX(d) well beyond the traditional ambit of the "necessity" test, as well as contradicting what the Appellate Body itself had noted with regard to WTO Members' right to determine for themselves the level of enforcement of their laws and regulations.

The second possible interpretation of the approach followed by the Appellate Body in *Korea–Beef* would be to consider the Appellate Body's assessment of Korea's intended level of protection as simply a required step in determining whether other alternative measures were reasonably available in order to secure *that* level of compliance. In other words, in order to assess whether the compliance measure under review (the Korean dual retail system) met the terms of the necessity requirement of Article XX(d), the Appellate Body had to determine inter alia the level of protection that Korea wanted to pursue with regard to fraud occurring with respect to the origin of beef sold by retailers. It is only by knowing the "desired level of protection" that the treaty interpreter is able to establish whether other "less-restrictive measures" are indeed reasonably available. Following this perspective, it could be argued that the Appellate Body was not convinced that the dual retail system had originally been enacted to implement a policy of zero-fraud, as argued by Korea, but rather that the aim of that system was to achieve a "significant reduction" of violations of the *Unfair Competition Act*.

Now if this second interpretation is in line with the traditional application of the "necessity" test, I would still have liked the Appellate Body to explain on what basis it believed "unlikely" that Korea *intended* to establish a level of protection that totally eliminated fraud. Moreover, it is not altogether clear how the Appellate Body determined the actual level of protection that Korea was supposedly pursuing with its selling requirement. As the Appellate Body noted, the total elimination of fraud would probably have required a total ban of imports rather than the setting up of the dual retail system. On that basis, it could be argued that the actual level of protection which Korea was pursuing with its dual retail system was somewhere in-between a "zero-fraud policy" (implemented through a ban on imports) and a more relaxed policy of substantial fraud reduction (implemented through conventional mechanisms). This is simply to show that any attempt to assess the exact level of protection for purposes of reviewing the "necessity" of any given measure involves several thorny issues which the Appellate Body report in *Korea–Beef* did not really (want to) address.

Even assuming that, on the facts of the case, the Appellate Body was correct in its assessment of the *real* level of protection pursued by the Korean dual retail system, this approach does not solve more complicated scenarios. What if the Korean legislation enacting the dual retail system in the beef sector had *expressly* stated in its preamble that the objective of such a system was to implement a policy of zero-fraud with respect to the origin of beef sold by retailers in the Korean market? Would the Appellate Body have considered this sufficient to accept Korea's argument that the desired level of protection was indeed a total elimination of fraud and thus its dual-retail system in compliance with the "necessity" requirement?

It is believed that this more complicated scenario could and should be solved not solely on the basis of the "necessity" test, but rather within the context of the introductory clause of Article XX (the so-called "Chapeau" of Article XX), which subjects the application of the general public policy exception of that Article to the requirement that national measures be not applied in a manner which would constitute a means of *arbitrary or unjustifiable discrimination* between countries, where the same conditions prevail, or a *disguised restriction* on international trade.

As will be more fully examined in the following section, the Chapeau would be able to limit the use of the public policy justification in cases such as that mentioned above. Even if a panel were to find that a national measure inconsistent with Article III:4 (such as the Korean dual retail system) was indeed the least restrictive alternative reasonably available to attain the (very rigorous) desired level of protection (total elimination of fraud in the specific sector), such a measure might still be deemed to constitute a means of arbitrary or unjustifiable discrimination or a disguised restriction on international trade for purposes of the introductory clauses of Article XX.

For example, the existence of disparities in the "level of protection" with respect to situations involving *similar* deceptive practices—"zero-fraud policy" in the beef retail sector versus "substantial reduction of fraud" in the pork retail sector—could certainly constitute the basis for a finding of arbitrary discrimination or disguised restriction.[275]

Furthermore, another factor to be taken into consideration would be, in the words of the Appellate Body,

> that, through its dual retail system, Korea has in effect shifted all, or the great bulk, of these potential costs of enforcement (translated into a drastic reduction of competitive access to consumers) to imported goods and retailers of imported goods, instead of evenly distributing such costs between the domestic and imported products.[276]

In other words, the Appellate Body charged Korea with taking into consideration exclusively the interests of domestic beef producers without giving any relevance to the interests of imported beef producers.

---

[275] A similar standard has been expressly introduced into the SPS Agreement in Art 5.5. See below ch 4.

[276] Appellate Body Report on *Korea–Beef*, above n 124, para 181.

As will be discussed in the next section, this form of process-review fits well within the types of arguments which the Appellate Body jurisprudence has employed in order to attribute meaning to the requirements of the introductory clause of Article XX.[277]

As a possible justification for the approach followed by the Appellate Body in focusing its review *entirely* on the "provisional justification" limb, it may be argued that it is perhaps more difficult to reason under the "Chapeau" after having determined that a measure is indeed "necessary" to achieve a certain public policy objective under *littera* (b) or (d). As the ensuing analysis will show, the relationship between the review under the "Chapeau" and the review under one of the "provisional justifications" is smoother when one moves from the strict requirement of "necessity" to the looser connector of "related to" as found in Article XX(g).

(b)   Justifying de jure discriminatory measures under Article XX(g) and the relevance of the "chapeau" of Article XX GATT   With regard to the "provisional justification" step, it was noted earlier that the language qualifying the connections between "regulation" and "objective" varies widely, ranging from stricter terms such as "essential" or "necessary" to looser terms such as "involving" or "relating to". In light of this difference, the justification option for de jure discriminatory measures pursuing certain public policy goals may appear to be easier to invoke compared to similar measures taken for other legitimate aims. In other words, WTO Members appear to enjoy more leeway with regard to certain public policy interests compared to other ones.

However, this difference does not seem to depend on the perceived different degrees of importance of the various public policy objectives listed in Article XX. For example, the protection of natural resources under Article XX(g), which is subject to the looser standard of "relating to", does not appear any more fundamental than the protection of human health under Article XX(b), which, on the contrary, is subject to the stricter standard of "necessary". As suggested in chapter 1, the difference in the intensity of the several "connectors" seems to be based on the different scope of the several subparagraphs of Article XX rather than on the different strength of Article XX policy objectives. Thus, for example, "protection of human, animal or plant life or health" covers potentially a wider spectrum of national measures than "conservation of exhaustible natural resources" (at least in its original meaning).[278]

Notwithstanding the difference in the several "connectors", as will be shown in the following paragraphs, it appears that, at least in the realm of

---

[277] Cf J Scott, "On Kith and Kine (and Crustaceans): Trade and Environment in the EU and WTO", *Jean Monnet Working Paper* (Harvard Law School, 1999).

[278] See below on the evolutionary interpretation given by WTO jurisprudence to the term "exhaustible natural resources".

de jure discriminatory measures, the requirements included in the so-called Chapeau of Article XX have effectively been employed as a tool for harmonising the intensity of the review under Article XX with regard to all the public policy aims listed therein. This section will thus examine the manner in which the Appellate Body has interpreted the requirements of Article XX(g) and those of the introductory clause of Article XX.

(i) *The Appellate Body Report in* Reformulated Gasoline

In *United States—Standards for Reformulated and Conventional Gasoline*,[279] the Panel examined whether a US measure imposing different baseline establishment methods with regard to imported and domestic gasoline in violation of Article III:4 could be justified as "relating to the conservation of exhaustible natural resources" under Article XX(g). Although it held that the US policy to reduce the depletion of clean air was indeed a policy to conserve a natural resource within the meaning of Article XX(g), the Panel found that the baseline establishment methods were not "related to" the conservation of clean air, since in the Panel's view there was "no direct connection" between the formally discriminatory treatment of imported gasoline and the US objective of improving air quality in the United States.[280] Following an appeal by the United States, the Panel's finding with regard to Article XX(g) came under the scrutiny of the Appellate Body.

Although the Appellate Body agreed with the Panel that the term "relating to" should be interpreted to mean "primarily aimed at", as suggested in the GATT Panel Report on *Canada–Measures Affecting Exports of Unprocessed Herring and Salmon*,[281] it found at least two significant errors in the Panel's reasoning.[282]

First of all, in the Appellate Body's view, the Panel erred in focusing on whether the "less favourable treatment" of imported gasoline (rather than the measure as a whole) was "primarily aimed at" the conservation of natural resources. According to the Appellate Body, the proper approach is to examine whether the baseline establishment rules taken as a whole (that is, the provisions relating to establishment of baselines for domestic refiners, along with the provisions relating to baselines for blenders and importers of gasoline), are related to the "non-degradation" requirements set out elsewhere in the Gasoline Rule. Those provisions could scarcely be understood if scrutinised strictly by themselves, totally divorced from other sections of the Gasoline Rule constituting part of the context of these provisions.[283]

---

[279] Panel Report on *Reformulated Gasoline*, above n 34.
[280] *Ibid.*, para 6.40.
[281] Panel Report on *Canada—Measures Affecting Exports of Unprocessed Herring and Salmon*, L/6268, adopted on 22 March 1988, BISD 35S/98.
[282] Appellate Body Report on *Reformulated Gasoline*, above n 59, at 7 *et seq.*
[283] *Ibid.*, at 11.

Furthermore, the Appellate Body noted that the Panel erred in employing its conclusion under Article XX(b) that the baseline establishment rules were not "necessary" for the protection of human, animal or plant life for purposes of determining whether the US measure "related to" or was "primarily aimed at" the conservation of natural resources. In the Appellate Body's view, the Panel appeared to have applied the "necessity" test not only in examining the baseline establishment rules under Article XX(b), but also in the course of applying Article XX(g). Referring to the "General rule of interpretation" contained in Article 31 of the Vienna Convention on the Law of Treaties, the Appellate Body noted that Article XX uses different terms in enumerating the various categories of governmental acts, laws or regulations which WTO Members may carry out or promulgate in pursuit of differing legitimate state policies or interests outside the realm of trade liberalisation. It deduced therefrom that,

> [i]t does not seem reasonable to suppose that the WTO Members intended to require, in respect of each and every category, the same kind or degree of connection or relationship between the measure under appraisal and the state interest or policy sought to be promoted or realised.[284]

Reversing the Panel's findings, the Appellate Body concluded that the baseline establishment rules were indeed "related to" the conservation of natural resources in the meaning of Article XX(g). The Appellate Body noted as follows:

> The baseline establishment rules whether individual or statutory, were designed to permit scrutiny and monitoring of the level of compliance of refiners, importers and blenders with the 'non-degradation' requirements. Without baselines of some kind, such scrutiny would not be possible and the Gasoline Rule's objective of stabilizing and preventing further deterioration of the level of air pollution prevailing in 1990, would be substantially frustrated. The relationship between the baseline establishment rules and the 'non-degradation' requirements of the Gasoline Rule is not negated by the inconsistency, found by the Panel, of the baseline establishment rules with the terms of Article III:4. We consider that, given that *substantial relationship*, the baseline establishment rules cannot be regarded as merely incidentally or inadvertently aimed at the conservation of clean air in the United States for the purposes of Article XX(g).[285]

---

[284] *Ibid.*, at 17–18.

[285] *Ibid.*, at 19 [emphasis added]. Moreover, the Appellate Body noted that "in a particular case, should it become clear that realistically, a specific measure cannot in any possible situation have any positive effect on conservation goals, it would very probably be because that measure was not designed as a conservation regulation to begin with. In other words, it would not have been 'primarily aimed at' conservation of natural resources at all." *Ibid.*, at 21.

It thus follows from the Appellate Body statements that, in order for a measure to be considered as "relating to" the conservation of exhaustible natural resources within the meaning of Article XX(g), there is no need to demonstrate that the measure is "necessary" to pursue such policy goal. However, the Appellate Body is nevertheless not satisfied with the mere existence of *a* relationship between the measure and the policy goal, either, since it is expressly required that such relationship be *substantial*.

The Appellate Body next examined whether the other condition provided for in Article XX(g) had been met by the baseline establishment rules (ie whether the measures for which the exception was being invoked "are made effective in conjunction with restrictions on domestic production or consumption").

Following an examination of its ordinary meaning, the Appellate Body noted that, taken together, the second clause of Article XX(g) appears to refer to governmental measures like the baseline establishment rules being promulgated or brought into effect together with restrictions on domestic or consumption of natural resources. Put in a slightly different manner, the Appellate Body held that the relevant clause is appropriately read as a requirement that the measures concerned impose restrictions, not just in respect of imported gasoline but also with respect to domestic gasoline.[286] However, it specified that if this clause did not require identical treatment of domestic and imported gasoline, it certainly covered the case where *no* restriction on domestically produced like products is imposed at all and all limitations are placed upon imported products *alone*. In light of the fact that in the present case the baseline establishment rules did affect both domestic and imported gasoline, although in a different manner, the Appellate Body concluded that restrictions on the consumption or depletion of clean air by regulating the domestic production of "dirty" gasoline were established jointly with corresponding restrictions with respect to imported gasoline. Thus, the requirement of the second clause of Article XX(g) was met.[287]

Having concluded that the US regulation formally discriminating on the basis of the origin of gasoline in violation of Article III:4 was provisionally justified on the basis of Article XX(g) (the first step), the Appellate Body turned to the question of whether that regulation also met the requirements of the Chapeau of Article XX (the second step).

Since GATT panel practice on the meaning of the introductory clause of Article XX was relatively little and not altogether reliable,[288] the Appellate Body was faced in *Reformulated Gasoline* with the difficult task

---

[286] *Ibid.*, at 20–21.
[287] *Ibid.*
[288] Cf Panel Report on *United States—Prohibition of Imports of Tuna and Tuna Products from Canada (Canadian Tuna)*, L/5198, adopted on 22 Feb 1982, BISD 29S/91, para 4.8 and Panel Report on *United States—Imports of Certain Automotive Spring Assemblies*, L/5333, adopted

of interpreting quite ambiguous concepts.[289] As noted before, the introductory clause of Article XX requires that,

> measures are not applied in a manner which would constitute a means of arbitrary or unjustifiable discrimination between countries, where the same conditions prevail, or a disguised restriction on international trade.

Drawing from the drafting history of Article XX, the Appellate Body began by underscoring that the purpose and object of the introductory clauses of Article XX is generally the prevention of abuse of the general exception provision of Article XX. In the Appellate Body's view, the Chapeau is animated by the principle that, while the exceptions of Article XX may be invoked as a matter of legal right, they should not be so applied as to frustrate or defeat the legal obligations of the holder of the right under the substantive rules of the GATT. Accordingly, if those exceptions are not to be abused or misused, the measures falling within the particular exceptions must be applied *reasonably*, with due regard both to the legal duties of the party claiming the exception and the legal rights of the other parties concerned.[290]

The Appellate Body added, moreover, that the *burden of demonstrating* that a measure provisionally justified as being within one of the exceptions set out in the individual paragraphs of Article XX does not, in its application, constitute abuse of such exception under the Chapeau, rests on the party invoking the exception and that this is, of necessity, a *heavier task* than that involved in showing that an exception, such as Article XX(g), encompasses the measure at issue.[291]

The Appellate Body continued its general interpretation of the Chapeau by rejecting the notion that the provisions of the introductory clause of Article XX refer to the same standards that are used in determining that there has been a violation of the substantive rules of the GATT. This approach would both empty the Chapeau of its contents and deprive the exceptions in subparagraphs (a) to (j) of meaning, thus contradicting one of the corollaries of the "general rule of interpretation" in the Vienna Convention, according to which interpretation must give meaning and effect to all the terms of a treaty.

on 26 May 1983, BISD 30S/107, para 56, where the concept of "disguised restriction on international trade" was given a very literal interpretation putting the emphasis simply on the "publicity" of the measure.

[289] Cf T Schoenbaum, "International Trade and Protection of the Environment: the Continuing Search for Reconciliation," 91 *Am J Int'l L* (April, 1997) 268, at 274 *et seq.*; P Manzini, "Environmental Exceptions of Art XX GATT 1994 Revisited in the Light of the Rules of Interpretation of General International Law" in P Mengozzi (ed) *International Trade Law on the 50th Anniversary of the Multilateral Trade System* (Milano, Giuffré, 1999) at 846.
[290] Appellate Body Report on Reformulated Gasoline, above n 59, at 22.
[291] *Ibid.*

The Appellate Body furthermore noted that the three principal standards included in the Chapeau, "arbitrary discrimination", "unjustifiable discrimination" and "disguised restriction" on international trade, should be read side-by-side. In other words, the kinds of considerations pertinent to deciding whether the application of a particular measure amounts to "arbitrary or unjustifiable discrimination" may also be taken into account in determining the presence of a "disguised restriction" on international trade.[292]

Moving from the general to the specific, the Appellate Body stated that "there was more than one alternative course of action available to the United States in promulgating regulations implementing the Clean Air Act." For example, the imposition of statutory baselines without differentiation as between domestic and imported gasoline or making available individual baselines to foreign refiners as well as domestic refiners. These approaches, if properly implemented, could have avoided any discrimination on grounds of origin.[293]

The Appellate Body thus appeared to perform under the Chapeau a very similar version of the "necessity" review, which the Appellate Body had not permitted within the context of Article XX(g).[294] As a matter of fact, the Appellate Body based its findings with regard to the Chapeau on the very same arguments raised by the United States in its attempt to demonstrate that the baseline establishment rules were indeed *necessary* (ie least GATT inconsistent or least trade restrictive) to protect human health for purposes of Article XX(b). Upon closer examination, however, it would appear that the Appellate Body is actually doing something slightly different than reviewing the challenged measure on the basis of the "necessity" test.

The Appellate Body explained why it did not accept the US claim that it could not impose either statutory or individual baselines on both foreign and domestic refiners so as to avoid any (at least formal) discrimination.

With regard to the option of making individual baselines available to foreign refiners as well as domestic refiners, the Appellate Body noted that the alleged administrative difficulties concerning verification and subsequent enforcement, although real to some degree, were not sufficient to

---

[292] *Ibid.*, at 24.
[293] *Ibid.*
[294] Cf T Schoenbaum, "International Trade and Protection of the Environment: the Continuing Search for Reconciliation," 91 *Am J Int'l L* (April, 1997) 268, at 277 noting that "the standard of review in the chapeau is more deferential than the 'least trade restrictive' interpretation of 'necessary'"; P Manzini, "Environmental Exceptions of Art XX GATT 1994 Revisited in the Light of the Rules of Interpretation of General International Law" in P Mengozzi (ed) *International Trade Law on the 50th Anniversary of the Multilateral Trade System* (Milano, Giuffré, 1999) at 848; A Appleton, "GATT Art XX's Chapeau: A Disguised 'Necessary' Test?: The WTO Appellate Body's Ruling in *United States—Standards for Reformulated and Conventional Gasoline*", 6 *RECIEL* (1997) 131 at 134.

justify the denial to foreign refiners of individual baselines permitted instead to domestic refiners. In line with the findings of the Panel, the Appellate Body emphasised that there are established techniques for checking, verification, assessment and enforcement of data relating to imported goods, techniques which in many contexts are accepted as adequate to permit international trade to go on and grow.[295] In this regard, the Appellate Body noted that, although the United States must have been aware that for these established techniques and procedures to work, co-operative arrangement with both foreign refiners and the foreign governments concerned would have been necessary and appropriate, the United States had apparently not pursued the possibility of entering into these arrangements with the interested governments or, if it had, not to the point where it encountered governments that were unwilling to co-operate.[296]

With regard to the option of imposing statutory baselines to all refiners, domestic and foreign, the Appellate Body noted the US argument that application of the statutory baseline to domestic producers of reformulated and conventional gasoline in 1995 would have been physically and financially impossible because of the magnitude of the changes required in almost all US refineries. The Appellate Body, however, rejected this line of defence noting that,

> while the United States counted the costs for its domestic refiners of statutory baselines, there is nothing in the record to indicate that it did other than disregard that kind of consideration when it came to foreign refiners.[297]

While it moved from the underlying premise that other less restrictive, non-discriminatory alternatives were indeed available, the Appellate Body focused its review under the Chapeau not on an assessment of the technical *capability* of these alternatives to attain the (desired level of) environmental protection pursued by the Clean Air Act, but rather on an examination of the regulatory *process* that had brought to life the challenged baseline establishment rules. On the basis of this examination the Appellate Body could locate two omissions on the part of the United States: (1) to explore adequately means, including in particular co-operation with the governments of Venezuela and Brazil, of mitigating the administrative problems relied on as justification by the United States for rejecting individual baselines for foreign refiners and (2) to count the costs for foreign refiners that would result from the imposition of statutory baselines. The Appellate Body ended its reasoning by noting the following:

---

[295] Appellate Body Report on *Reformulated Gasoline*, above n 59, at 25.
[296] *Ibid.*
[297] *Ibid.*, at 25–6.

In our view, these two omissions go well beyond what was necessary for the Panel to determine that a violation of Article III:4 had occurred in the first place. The resulting discrimination must have been foreseen, and was not merely inadvertent or unavoidable. In the light of the foregoing, our conclusion is that the baseline establishment rules in the Gasoline Rule, in their application, constitute 'unjustifiable discrimination' and a 'disguised restriction on international trade.' We hold, in sum, that the baseline establishment rules, although within the terms of Article XX(g), are not entitled to the justifying protection afforded by Article XX as a whole.[298]

Although this part of the reasoning is not altogether clear, it appears that, in the Appellate Body's view, the failure to attempt to enter into cooperative arrangements with the interested governments, as well as the failure to take into consideration the costs incurred by foreign refiners, transformed what could have been considered "inadvertent or unavoidable" (thus justifiable) discrimination into "foreseen or avoidable" (and thus unjustifiable) discrimination. According to the Appellate Body, this type of discrimination falls within the concepts of "unjustifiable discrimination" and "disguised restriction on international trade" prohibited by the Chapeau of Article XX.[299]

In conclusion, the Appellate Body's assessment of the Gasoline Rule's compatibility with the requirements of the Chapeau of Article XX does appear to mix the features of the "necessity" review with those of the "regulatory process" review. While it refers to the *existence* of less restrictive or less GATT inconsistent measures that could attain the (desired level of) environmental protection pursued by the Clean Air Act, the Appellate Body appears to base its findings principally on the *deficiencies* in the regulatory process that brought the United States to adopt a measure in violation of the National Treatment obligation. Indeed, the Appellate Body concluded that the Gasoline Rule did not comply with the requirements of the Chapeau on the grounds that (1) the United States had not tried to pursue co-operation agreements with the interested governments which would have possibly enable the United States to extend the more favourable individual baselines methods also to foreign gasoline and thus avoided discrimination, and (2) the United States had not taken into account the interests of foreign refiners when it implemented the statutory baseline methods.

Taking this reasoning to its apparently logical conclusions, one might add that the Appellate Body would have been satisfied if, in similar circumstances, the United States had indeed pursued, even if without

---

[298] *Ibid.*, at 26.
[299] For a detailed, critical analysis of the Appellate Body applications of the Chapeau of Art XX in *Reformulated Gasoline* see L Bartels, "Art XX of GATT and the Problem of Extraterritorial Jurisdiction: The Case of Trade Measures for the Protection of Human Rights", 36 JWT (2002) 353.

success, the above mentioned international co-operation and had indeed taken into consideration foreign refiners' interests, even had it failed to arrive at a better solution than that actually embodied in the Gasoline Rule. In other words, although it would nonetheless have had to explain how and why international co-operation efforts did not succeed as well as how and why a "better solution" for foreign refiners could not be found, the United States might have been able to overcome the hurdle of the Chapeau by curing such deficiencies in the regulatory process.

I believe, however, that the Appellate Body findings in *Reformulated Gasoline* should not be interpreted too strictly, which is to say that, in order to comply with the Chapeau of Article XX, it is sufficient for a WTO Member to *attempt* to pursue international co-operation and to *take into account* all interested parties involved. The evident ambivalence in the reasoning underlying the *Reformulated Gasoline*'s findings is indicative of the Appellate Body's preference for a more flexible approach, which leaves open different interpretative options that may be employed in future disputes. Accordingly, depending on the different features of the disputed measure, the treaty interpreter will be able to make use of a broader range of tools in order to prevent any abuse or misuse of the general exception provision of Article XX.[300]

(ii) The Appellate Body Report in Shrimp/Turtle Recently hailed as one of the two most "profound" cases that have come through the WTO appellate process,[301] *Shrimp/Turtle* is a confirmation of the Appellate Body's preference for a flexible approach to Article XX and in particular to its Chapeau as it has just been suggested in the previous section.

The dispute at issue in *United States—Import Prohibition of Certain Shrimp and Shrimp Products (Shrimp/Turtle)*[302] arose against a backdrop of concerns in the United States about the incidental capture and drowning of sea turtles by shrimp trawlers, which scientific evidence shows constitutes the most significant risk to endangered species of sea turtles. In 1987, pursuant the 1973 Endangered Species Act ("ESA"), the United States issued regulations requiring all shrimp trawlers to use turtle excluder devices ("TEDs") or tow time restrictions in specified areas that had significant mortality of sea turtles. In 1989, the United States enacted Section 609 of US Public Law 101–62 ("Section 609") which required inter alia the following: (a) the US Secretary of State, in consultation with the US

---

[300] More on the Appellate Body Report on *Reformulated Gasoline* see C Maas, "Should the WTO Expand GATT Art XX: An Analysis of *United States—Standards for Reformulated and Conventional Gasoline*", 5 *Minn J Global Trade* (1996) 415.

[301] J Jackson, "Comments on *Shrimp/Turtle* and the Product/Process Distinction", 11 *European Journal of International Law* (2, 2000) 303, at 304. In the view of this author, the other case is the Hormones dispute.

[302] *United States—Import Prohibition of Certain Shrimp and Shrimp Products (Shrimp/Turtle)*, WT/DS58, brought 14 Oct 1996.

Secretary of Commerce, shall initiate negotiations for the development of bilateral or multilateral agreements aimed at the protection and conservation of sea turtles further legislation; (b) as of 1 May 1997, the importation of shrimp or shrimp products that have been harvested with commercial fishing technology likely to hurt sea turtles shall be prohibited. Such prohibition would not apply if the President annually certifies to the Congress that (i) the harvesting country concerned has a regulatory programme governing the incidental taking of such sea turtles that is comparable to that of the United States, (ii) the average rate of that incidental taking by the vessels of the harvesting country is comparable to the average rate of incidental taking of sea turtles by Unites States vessels in the course of such harvesting, or (iii) the fishing environment of the harvesting country does not pose a threat to sea turtles in the course of such harvesting.[303]

In 1993, the United States issued guidelines for comparing foreign regulatory programmes with the US programme. These guidelines limited the scope of application of Section 609 to the wider Caribbean/western Atlantic region and required, inter alia, a commitment that all shrimp trawlers use TEDs at all times. In 1996, following a ruling by the US Court of International Trade, the Department of States extended the reach of Section 609 to all countries and promulgated new guidelines which permitted the importation into the United States of shrimp or shrimp products declared to have been harvested with TEDs even if the exporting country could not be certified as having a regulatory programme comparable to that of the United States. Hence, at that time, US legislation *permitted* the importation of specific batches of shrimp from non-approved countries so long as that batch had been captured in a manner consistent with the relevant United States standards.[304] However, following further rulings by the US Court of International Trade in 1996, shrimp harvested with commercial fishing technology (ie shrimp not harvested by manual methods with no harm to sea turtles) were permitted access to the US market *only* in the event that it originated in a country which had been certified by the President according to Section 609.[305]

In 1997, at the requests of Malaysia, Thailand, Pakistan, and India, the Dispute Settlement Body of the WTO established three panels, which were later merged into one, in order to examine the GATT compatibility of the US ban on importation of certain shrimp and shrimp products

---

[303] Appellate Body Report on *Shrimp/Turtle*, WT/DS58/AB/R, circulated 12 Oct 1998, adopted 6 Nov 1998, paras 2–6.

[304] J Scott, "On Kith and Kine (and Crustaceans): Trade and Environment in the EU and WTO", *Jean Monnet Working Paper* (Harvard Law School, 1999).

[305] Although the 1996 orders by the US Court of International Trade were subsequently vacated by the US Court of Appeals of the Federal Circuit in 1998, the Appellate Body noted that "in practice, however, exemption from the import ban for TED-caught shrimp from non-certified countries remained unavailable while this dispute was before the Panel and before us". Appellate Body Report on *Shrimp/Turtle*, above n 303, para 5.

under Section 609 and the "Revised Notice of Guidelines for Determining Comparability of Foreign Programs for the Protection of Turtles in Shrimp Trawl Fishing Operations".[306]

Before proceeding to an examination of the Appellate Body's interpretation of the environmental exception provided for in Article XX(g) as well the introductory clause of Article XX, it is important to clarify why the US measure at issue in *Shrimp/Turtle* should have been treated as a case of *formally* discriminatory *internal* regulation inconsistent with the National Treatment obligation of Article III:4.

This issue has already been touched upon while examining the "objective element" (ie the scope of application) of the general prohibition on quantitative restrictions of Article XI GATT. There, it was argued that both regulations under consideration in the *Tuna/Dolphin* and *Shrimp/Turtle* disputes should have been reviewed under Article III:4, rather than Article XI, since they were "laws, regulations and requirements *affecting* the internal sale or use of products". By mixing the terms employed with regard to two distinct features of the National Treatment obligation, the unadopted GATT Panel reports in *Tuna/Dolphin*, first, and the WTO Panel report in *Shrimp/Turtle*, as a consequence,[307] confused Article III's *normative* requirement that a "measure *applies* to products" in a non-discriminatory manner, with the *objective* requirement that "internal regulation *affects* the internal sale of products". In that section, I concluded that the texts of Article XI and Article III, as interpreted by the Ad Note, as well as the object and purpose of Article XI (as confirmed both by the identical approach with regard to the treatment of pecuniary measures in Articles II and III and by the 1927 Convention for the Abolition of Import and Export Prohibitions and Restrictions), show quite clearly that (1) the "objective element" of Article XI *is* and *should be* limited to trade restrictive measures that directly regulate the importation of products and apply to imported products only, and (2) the "objective element" of Article III *is* and *should be* to review any measure affecting the sale or use of products that is applicable to both imported and domestic products, even if not in an identical manner. Within this calculation, it should not matter whether the measure at

---

[306] Cf D Ahn, "Environmental Disputes in the GATT/WTO: Before and After US-Shrimp Case", 20 *Mich J Int'l L* (Summer, 1999) 819; S Gaines, "The WTO's Reading of the GATT Art XX Chapeau: A Disguised Restriction on Environmental Measures", 22 *U Pa J Int'l Econ L* (Winter, 2001) 739; P Mavroidis, "Trade and Environment after the Shrimps-Turtles Litigation", 34 *JWT* (2000) 73.

[307] Panel Report on *Shrimp/Turtle*, WT/DS58/R, circulated on 15 May 1998, adopted 6 Nov 1998, para 7.17. However, the US government had not argued this time that the measure imposed on imports of shrimp and shrimp product fell under Art III, resting exclusively on Art XX justification. Notwithstanding the US admission, the Panel found that "the wording of the measure under review and the interpretation made of it by the Court of International Trade (CIT) are sufficient evidence that the United States imposes a 'prohibition or restriction' within the meaning of Art XI:1." This finding was not appealed before the Appellate Body.

hand is a process- or a product-standard, since both types of regulation may in theory fall under Article XI or Article III GATT.[308]

On the facts of both cases, it is clear that the battle over the GATT-legality of the environmental regulations protecting dolphins and sea turtles should have been fought on National Treatment grounds rather than within the context of the general prohibition of border measures. Both the import ban on yellowfin tuna and tuna products harvested other than by means of fishing techniques designed to reduce the incidental taking of dolphins and the import ban on shrimp and shrimp products caught using sea turtles unfriendly techniques represented the "external arms" of similar restrictions imposed by the United States on the national territory with regard to fishing carried out by domestic entities.[309] Accordingly, the correct legal dispute should have been in both cases on whether the US environmental regulations protecting dolphins and sea turtles afforded "less favourable treatment" to imported products in comparison with the treatment accorded to "like products" of national origin in the meaning of Article III:4 GATT.[310]

Limiting the following analysis to the *Shrimp/Turtle* dispute, I would argue that, considered as a whole (ie both the 1987 regulation requiring all US shrimp trawlers to use TEDs and the 1989 Section 609, as subsequently implemented by the relevant Guidelines and interpreted by the CIT, prohibiting the import of shrimp except if it originated in a country which had been certified as complying with US standard), the US legislation on the protection of sea turtles indeed violated Article III:4 since it formally discriminated between domestic and imported shrimps.[311]

By prohibiting imports of shrimp harvested by commercial shrimp trawl vessels using TEDs comparable in effectiveness to those required in the United States, if those shrimp originated in waters of countries not certified under Section 609, the US legislation indeed discriminated *on its terms* against imported shrimp. As was observed *incidenter tantum* in the

---

[308] On the other hand, "marketing-standards", which regulate the manner in which goods are sold, will always be considered as "internal regulations" reviewable under Art III GATT.
[309] With regard to the *Shrimp/Turtle* dispute, one should note the statements in Appellate Body Report with respect to the issue of whether the import ban had been made effective in conjunction with restriction on domestic production or consumption within the meaning of Art XX(g). Cf Appellate Body Report on *Shrimp/Turtle*, above n 303, para 144.
[310] Doubts on this point are expressed by de Búrca and Scott, "The Impact of the WTO on EU Decision-Making" in G de Búrca and J Scott (eds), *The EU and the WTO: Legal and Constitutional Aspects* (Oxford, Hart Publishing, 2001) at 17, fn 42.
[311] Since I would argue that it was a case of de jure discrimination, there is no need to determine whether the products at issue were indeed "like". As will be discussed in the section dealing with de facto discriminatory internal regulation (specifically the Appellate Body Report in *Asbestos*), it is usually very difficult, albeit not impossible, to demonstrate that two products that are *physically identical* may nevertheless be deemed to be *unlike* for purposes of the National Treatment obligation of the GATT on the basis of the *manner* in which they are produced or harvested (ie pure process-characteristics). See below ch 3 discussing the Appellate Body Report in *Asbestos*.

Appellate Body Report, shrimp caught using methods identical to those employed in the United States were excluded from the United States market solely because they have been caught in waters of countries that have not been certified by the United States.[312] In other words, identical shrimps were subject to different treatment solely depending on their origin.[313]

As already noted, following the US government's de facto admission that its import ban was a restriction in the sense of Article XI (in its view, justified by Article XX), the Panel did not struggle to conclude that it was indeed inconsistent with that Article.[314] Furthermore, the Panel rejected the US claim with regard to the availability of the general exception provision of Article XX, since the US measure at issue constituted "unjustifiable discrimination" within the meaning of the introductory clause of Article XX. Along the lines of some of the arguments advanced in the *Tuna/Dolphin* reports,[315] the Panel held that an interpretation of Article XX Chapeau that allowed a Member to take measures conditioning access to its market for a given product upon the adoption by the exporting Members of certain policies (such as that at issue in that case) would have undermined the security and predictability of the WTO multilateral trading system as a whole.[316]

[312] Appellate Body Report on *Shrimp/Turtle*, above n 303, para 165.

[313] For a further discussion on whether the US environmental legislation protecting sea turtles constituted also de facto discrimination in violation of Art III:4, see below ch 3.

[314] Panel Report on *Shrimp/Turtle*, above n 307, para 7.17. Given its conclusion with regard to Art XI, the Panel thus found that it was not necessary to review the allegations of the complainants with respect to Art I:1 and XIII:1. India, Pakistan, Thailand, and Malaysia had claimed that the US embargo was inconsistent with the Most-Favoured-Nation principle since initially affected countries had been given a phase-in period of three years, while newly affected nations generally had not received a similar period of time. *Ibid.*, paras 7.18–7.23.

[315] Panel Report on *United States—Restrictions on Imports of Tuna (Tuna I)*, DS21/R (unadopted), BISD 39S/155, para 5.27: "The Panel considered that if the broad interpretation of Art XX(b) suggested by the United States were accepted, each contracting party could unilaterally determine the life or health protection policies from which other contracting parties could not deviate without jeopardizing their rights under the General Agreement. The General Agreement would then no longer constitute a multilateral framework for trade among all contracting parties but would provide legal security only in respect of trade between a limited number of contracting parties with identical internal regulations".

[316] Panel Report on *Shrimp/Turtle*, above n 307, paras 7.44–7.45. It is interesting (as well as a confirmation that the dispute was indeed about an *internal* regulation) to note that some of the reasoning put forward by the Panel in its refusal to interpret the chapeau as allowing the US import ban resembles the "regulatory overlap" arguments underlying the *Dassonville–Cassis* de Dijon jurisprudence in EC law. Note the Panel's following statements: "if one WTO Member were allowed to adopt such measures [conditioning access to its market for a given product upon the adoption by the exporting Members of certain policies, including conservation policies], then other Members would also have the right to adopt similar measures on the same subject but with differing, or even conflicting, requirements. [...] Market access for goods could become subject to an increasing number of conflicting policy requirements for the same product and this would rapidly lead to the end of the WTO multilateral trading system." *Ibid.*, para 7.45. These issues will be addressed in the subsequent section addressing the jurisprudential evolution of Art 28 EC from *Cassis-de Dijon* to *Keck*, as well as in ch 4 dealing with the "reasonableness rule" in EC and WTO law.

The United States appealed only the Panel's findings with respect to Article XX and the Appellate Body indeed reversed such findings, noting that the interpretative analysis embodied therein constituted error in legal interpretation. In the Appellate Body's view, the Panel did not follow all of the steps necessary to an application of the "customary rules of interpretation of public international law" as required by Article 3.2 of the DSU: "examination of the ordinary meaning of the words of a treaty, read in their context, and in the light of the object and purpose of the treaty involved".

With regard to the "text", the Appellate Body stressed the fact that the Chapeau of Article XX addresses not so much the questioned measure or its specific contents as such, but rather *the manner* in which that measure is applied. Accordingly, within this context, focus on the design of the measure itself is misplaced.[317]

With regard to the "object and purpose", the Appellate Body noted that it is the object and purpose of the Chapeau, rather than that of the whole of the GATT 1994 and the WTO Agreement, that needs to be considered. As stated by the Appellate Body in *Reformulated Gasoline*, the purpose and object of the introductory clause of Article XX is generally the prevention of abuse or misuse of the general exception provision.[318]

Furthermore, the Appellate Body found fault in the sequencing of the Panel's analysis under Article XX. Instead of determining first whether the measure was "provisionally justified" on the basis of one of the subparagraphs of Article XX and only then whether it complied with the requirements of the Chapeau, the Panel skipped the first step and moved straight into the opening clause of Article XX. In the Appellate Body's view, changing the sequencing of the two-tier analysis renders very difficult, if not altogether impossible, the task of interpreting the Chapeau so as to prevent the abuse or misuse of the specific exemptions provided for in Article XX, since the specific exceptions threatened with abuse have not yet been identified and examined. Moreover, the Appellate Body noted that the standards established in the Chapeau are necessarily broad in scope and reach and thus their actual contours and contents may vary depending on the kind of measure (ie the type of policy justification) under examination.[319]

Finally, according to the Appellate Body, constructing an a priori test that purports to define a category of measures which, *ratione materiae*, fall outside the justifying protection of Article XX's Chapeau (ie measure conditioning access to a Member's domestic market upon the adoption by the exporting Members of certain policies) would render most, if not all,

---

[317] Appellate Body Report on *Shrimp/Turtle*, above n 303, para 115.
[318] *Ibid.*, para 116.
[319] *Ibid.*, paras 117–20.

of the specific exceptions of Article XX inutile since it is usually those type of measures that fall within the scope of the general exception provision of Article XX.[320]

The Appellate Body thus went on to complete the legal analysis in order to determine whether Section 609 indeed qualified for justification under Article XX.

Beginning with the first tier of the analysis ("provisional justification" under one of the subparagraphs of Article XX), the Appellate Body found that Section 609 met the requirements of Article XX(g), which covers measures "relating to the conservation of exhaustible natural resources if such measures are made effective in conjunction with restrictions on domestic production or consumption". The Appellate Body rejected first of all the strict reading advanced by the complainants with regard to the meaning of the term "exhaustible natural resource", according to which the term referred only to *finite* resources, such as minerals, and not to living, reproducing resources, like sea turtles. On the contrary, the Appellate Body endorsed an "evolutionary" interpretation of the term "exhaustible" (taking into account "contemporary concerns of the community of nations"), which embraces both living and non-living resources.[321] Invoking modern biological science and the international recognition of the sea turtles' endangered status, the Appellate Body concluded that sea turtles were indeed "exhaustible".

Moving next to the question of whether the challenged measure "related to" the conservation of exhaustible natural resources, the Appellate Body looked at the *relationship* between the general structure and design of the measure at stake (Section 609) and the policy goal it purported to serve (the conservation of sea turtles). Following an examination of the principal features of Section 609, the Appellate Body concluded that Section 609 was indeed a measure "relating to" the conservation of an exhaustible natural resources within the meaning of Article XX(g) GATT,[322] although it put forward several bases for reaching this conclusion. In the Appellate Body's view, the requirement that a country adopt a regulatory programme requiring the use of TEDs by commercial shrimp trawling vessels in areas where there is a likelihood of intercepting sea turtles is "directly connected with the policy of conservation of sea turtles", and the use of TEDs is an "effective tool for the preservation of sea turtles".[323] The Appellate Body, moreover, found that Section 609 *cum* implementing guidelines "is not disproportionately wide in its scope and reach in relation to the policy objective of protection and conservation of

---

[320] *Ibid.*, para 121.
[321] *Ibid.*, para 130.
[322] *Ibid.*, para 142.
[323] *Ibid.*, para 140.

sea turtle species", that "the means are, in principle, reasonably related to the ends", or in other words that,

> the means and ends relationship between Section 609 and the legitimate policy of conserving an exhaustible, and, in fact, endangered species, is observably a close and real one, a relationship that is every bit as substantial as that [...] found in *United States – Gasoline* between the EPA baseline establishment rules and the conservation of clean air in the United States.[324]

While it is clear that the Appellate Body was convinced that Section 609 *related to* the protection of sea turtles within the meaning of Article XX(g), it is also evident that the Appellate Body did not really clarify the exact legal standard on which it based this conviction. In the Appellate Body's view, if the specific instrument employed by the United States was both "effective" and "not disproportionate", the relationship between this instrument and the policy goal of protecting sea turtles was deemed to be "direct", "reasonable", "close", "real" and "substantial". The infelicitous use of this wide range of concepts may be indicative of the Appellate Body's willingness, on the one hand, to increase the threshold for meeting the "relating to" requirement (in particular, note the terms such as "disproportionate" and "reasonable") and, on the other, to recognise a broad discretion to the treaty interpreter in applying such a requirement to the particular case.

Nevertheless, despite the rigorous language, the Appellate Body's review in the *Shrimp/Turtle* case does not seem to be very strict in practice and, as in the earlier *Reformulated Gasoline* case, appeared to be basically limited to a determination of whether the US measure was indeed *capable* of protecting sea turtles (ie a sort of "suitability" test).[325]

Lastly, because the United States had already implemented equivalent measures for shrimp harvesting activities under US jurisdiction, the Appellate Body also found that the Section 609 embargo on shrimp also satisfied the Article XX(g) condition that the challenged measure be taken "in conjunction with" restrictions on domestic production and consumption of the same resource. The Appellate Body considered that in principle Section 609 "is an even-handed measure".[326]

---

[324] *Ibid.*, para 141.

[325] Concluding its examination of the US regulatory scheme, the Appellate Body stated that "In its general design and structure, therefore, s 609 is not a simple, blanket prohibition of the importation of shrimp imposed without regard to the consequences (or lack thereof) of the mode of harvesting employed upon the incidental capture and mortality of sea turtles." *Ibid.* This statement shows that the Appellate Body's assessment of the relationship between the regulatory scheme at issue and the alleged policy objective does not appear to be a very demanding one.

[326] *Ibid.*, paras 144–45. As previously noted, this statement strongly supports the argument that the measure at issue in this dispute should have been treated as an "internal regulation" for purposes of Art III:4, as interpreted by the relevant Ad Note.

Even the toughest critics of the Appellate Body report in *Shrimp/Turtle* have praised this part of the report "for its new-found sensitivity to environmental considerations and welcome reliance on sources of public international law outside the WTO."[327] Both the evolutionary interpretation of the term "exhaustible natural resources"[328] and the wide range of concepts employed in order to determine that the measure *related to* the protection of sea turtles constitute clear evidence of the Appellate Body's attempt to interpret GATT provisions in a more flexible and enlightened way. However, with regard to the interpretation of Article XX(g) connector, the Appellate Body's approach appears to foreshadow possible future increases of the threshold for meeting the "relating to" requirement, moving the bar from a mere "suitability" test to a more demanding "reasonableness" test.

Let us now move to the more controversial and complex interpretation and application in the Appellate Body Report in *Shrimp/Turtle* of the "second tier" of the analysis under Article XX, that is whether the challenged measure, provisionally justified under Article XX(g), satisfied the requirements of the introductory clause—the Chapeau—of Article XX.

As a preliminary matter, the Appellate Body rejected, I believe correctly, the US argument according to which the existence of a relationship between the incriminated measure and the legitimate public policy goal (as established under the subparagraph (g) of Article XX) was enough to satisfy the requirements of the Chapeau. Such interpretation would, in the Appellate Body's view, disregard the standards established by the Chapeau.[329]

Addressing the issue of the ordinary meaning of the Chapeau, the Appellate Body noted that the precise language of the Chapeau requires that a measure not be applied in a manner which would constitute a means of "arbitrary or unjustifiable discrimination between countries where the same conditions prevail" or a "disguised restriction on international trade". In the Appellate Body's view, there are thus three standards contained in the Chapeau: first, arbitrary discrimination between countries where the same conditions prevail; secondly, unjustifiable discrimination between countries where the same conditions prevail; and thirdly, a disguised restriction on international trade. Focusing on the first two, the Appellate Body added the following:

---

[327] S Gaines, "The WTO's Reading of the GATT Art XX Chapeau: A Disguised Restriction on Environmental Measures", 22 *U Pa J Int'l Econ L* (Winter, 2001) 739, at 772.

[328] Cf A Appleton, "Shrimp/Turtle: Untangling the Nets", 2 *JIEL* (1999) 477, emphasising the important political implications for the WTO and its dispute settlement system of the Appellate Body's decision in the *Shrimp/Turtle* case. More broadly on the evolutionary interpretation of WTO law see J Pauwelyn, "The Nature of WTO Obligations", *Jean Monnet Working Paper* (NYU School of Law, 2002) at 28 *et seq.*

[329] Appellate Body Report on *Shrimp/Turtle*, above n 303, para 149.

In order for a measure to be applied in a manner which would constitute 'arbitrary or unjustifiable discrimination between countries where the same conditions prevail', three elements must exist. First, the application of the measure must result in *discrimination*. As we stated in *United States— Gasoline*, the nature and quality of this discrimination is different from the discrimination in the treatment of products which was already found to be inconsistent with one of the substantive obligations of the GATT 1994, such as Articles I, III or XI. Secondly, the discrimination must be *arbitrary* or *unjustifiable* in character. We will examine this element of *arbitrariness* or *unjustifiability* in detail below. Thirdly, this discrimination must occur *between countries where the same conditions prevail*. In *United States–Gasoline*, we accepted the assumption of the participants in that appeal that such discrimination could occur not only between different exporting Members, but also between exporting Members and the importing Member concerned. Thus, the standards embodied in the language of the chapeau are not only different from the requirements of Article XX(g); they are also different from the standard used in determining that Section 609 is violative of the substantive rules of Article XI:1 of the GATT 1994.[330]

The Appellate Body next emphasised that the purpose and object of the introductory clauses of Article XX is generally the prevention of abuse of the exceptions of Article XX. More generally, according to the Appellate Body, the Chapeau embodies the recognition on the part of WTO Members of the need to maintain a balance of rights and obligations between the right of a Member to invoke one or another of the exceptions of Article XX, specified in subparagraphs (a) to (j), on the one hand, and the substantive rights of the other Members under the GATT 1994, on the other hand. Under a slightly different angle of vision, a balance must be struck between the *right* of a Member to invoke an exception under Article XX and the *duty* of that same Member to respect the treaty rights of the other Members.[331]

In the Appellate Body's view, the Chapeau of Article XX is, in fact, but one expression of the principle of good faith, which controls the exercise of rights by states. One application of this general principle prohibits the abusive exercise of a state's rights and enjoins that whenever the assertion of a right "impinges on the field covered by [a] treaty obligation, it must be exercised bona fide, that is to say, reasonably".[332] The Appellate Body concluded its "general considerations" on the Chapeau by noting that the

---

[330] *Ibid.*, para 150 [emphasis in original] [original footnotes omitted].
[331] *Ibid.*, para 156.
[332] *Ibid.*, para 158 citing B Cheng, *General Principles of Law as applied by International Courts and Tribunals* (Stevens & Sons, Ltd., 1953), ch 4, in particular, at 125 the author elaborates that "A reasonable and bona fide exercise of a right in such a case is one which is appropriate and necessary for the purpose of the right (ie in furtherance of the interests which the right is intended to protect). It should at the same time be *fair and equitable as between the parties* and not one which is calculated to procure for one of them an unfair advantage in the light of the

application of a measure may be characterised as amounting to an abuse or misuse of an exception of Article XX not only when the detailed operating provisions of the measure prescribe the arbitrary or unjustifiable activity, but also where a measure, otherwise fair and just on its face, is actually applied in an arbitrary manner. In other words, the standards of the Chapeau, in the Appellate Body's view, project both substantive and procedural requirements.[333]

Starting with the question of whether Section 609 had been applied in a manner constituting "*unjustifiable* discrimination between countries where the same conditions prevail", the Appellate Body put forward three main basis for finding the US measure not in compliance with this first requirement. In the Appellate Body's view, perhaps the most conspicuous flaw in the *application* of Section 609 related to its *intended* and *actual coercive effect* on the specific policy decisions made by foreign governments, Members of the WTO. The Appellate Body noted several differences between the measure itself (Section 609) and its application (1996 Guidelines and regulatory practice of administrators). For example, although the statutory provisions of Section 609 did not require that other WTO Members adopt essentially the same policy (together with an approved enforcement programme) as that applied to, and enforced on, US domestic shrimp trawlers, the implementing Guidelines did in effect mandate this. According to the Appellate Body, any flexibility that may have been intended by Congress when it enacted the statutory provision had been effectively eliminated in the implementation of that policy through the 1996 Guidelines promulgated by the Department of State and through the practice of the administrators in making certification determinations.

Moreover, although the 1996 Guidelines stated that, in making a *comparability* determination, the Department of State "shall also take into account other measures the harvesting nation undertakes to protect sea turtles", *in practice*, the competent government officials only looked to see whether there is a regulatory programme requiring the use of TEDs or one that comes within one of the extremely limited exceptions available to US shrimp trawl vessels. Other specific policies and measures that an exporting country may have adopted for the protection and conservation of sea turtles were not taken into account, *in practice*, by the administrators making the comparability determination.[334]

Elaborating on the failure to take into account the specific differences between the national and international spheres, the Appellate Body

---

obligation assumed. […]" [emphasis added by the Appellate Body]. Appellate Body Report on *Shrimp/Turtle*, above n 303, fn 156.

[333] *Ibid.*, para 160.
[334] *Ibid.*, paras 161–3.

observed the following: while it may be quite understandable and acceptable for governments, in enacting and implementing a domestic policy, to adopt a single standard applicable to all its citizens throughout its territory (regardless of the particular conditions existing in certain parts of the country), the same is not acceptable in international trade relations. In other words, in the Appellate Body's view, it is not acceptable for one WTO Member to use an economic embargo to require other Members to adopt essentially the same comprehensive regulatory programme, to achieve a certain policy goal, as that in force within that Member's territory, without taking into consideration different conditions which may occur in the territory of those other Members.[335] The Appellate Body said that discrimination results not only when countries in which the same conditions prevail are differently treated, but also when the application of the measure at issue does not allow for any inquiry into the appropriateness of the regulatory programme for the conditions prevailing in those exporting countries.[336]

According to the Appellate Body, another aspect of the application of Section 609 that bore heavily in any appraisal of justifiable or unjustifiable discrimination was the failure of the United States to engage the appellees, as well as other Members exporting shrimp to the United States, in serious, across-the-board negotiations with the objective of concluding bilateral or multilateral agreements for the protection and conservation of sea turtles, before enforcing the import prohibition against the shrimp exports of those other Members. In this regard, the Appellate Body noted the following points: (1) the US Congress expressly recognised the importance of securing international agreements for the protection and conservation of the sea turtles species in enacting Section 609; (2) as recognised by the WTO itself as well as in significant number of other international instruments and declarations, the protection and conservation of highly migratory species of sea turtles, that is, the very policy objective of the measure, demands concerted and co-operative efforts on the part of the many countries whose waters are traversed in the course of recurrent sea turtles migrations; and (3) the fact that the United States did negotiate and conclude one regional international agreement for the protection and conservation of sea turtles provides convincing demonstration that an alternative course of action was reasonably open to the United States for securing the legitimate policy goal of its measure, a course of action other than the unilateral and non-consensual procedures of the import prohibition under Section 609.[337]

---

[335] *Ibid.*, para 164.
[336] *Ibid.*, para 165.
[337] *Ibid.*, paras 166–71.

Thirdly, the Appellate Body based its finding of "unjustifiable discrimination" on the differential treatment among various countries desiring certification. While 14 countries in the wider Caribbean/western Atlantic region had a "phase-in" period of three years (from 1991 to 1994) during which their respective shrimp trawling sectors could adjust to the requirement of the use of TEDs, all other countries exporting shrimp to the United States (including the complainants/appellees) had only four months (from December 1995 to April 1996) to implement the above mentioned requirement. The Appellate Body rejected as "less than persuasive" the US defence that the longer time-period was justified by the then undeveloped character of TED technology, while the shorter period was later made possible by technological improvements. It noted that such explanation did not address the administrative and financial costs and the difficulties of governments in putting together and enacting the necessary regulatory programmes and "credible enforcement efforts", as well as in implementing the compulsory use of TEDs on hundreds, if not thousands, of shrimp trawl vessels. Moreover, the Appellate Body emphasised that differing treatment of different countries desiring certification was also observable in the differences in the *levels of effort* made by the United States in transferring the required TED technology to specific countries. Far greater efforts to transfer that technology successfully were made to certain exporting countries—basically the 14 wider Caribbean/western Atlantic countries cited earlier—than to other exporting countries, including the appellees.[338]

Moving next to the issue of whether Section 609 had been applied in a manner constituting *"arbitrary* discrimination between countries where the same conditions prevail", the Appellate Body first of all made a brief reference once again to the rigidity of the requirement imposed on countries wishing to export shrimp to the United States and furthermore noted several problematic aspects of the *certification processes* applied under Section 609. In this latter regard, the Appellate Body observed that (1) the certification processes were not "transparent" and "predictable", (2) there was no formal opportunity for an applicant country to be heard, or to respond to any arguments that may be made against it, (3) no formal written, reasoned decision is rendered on certification applications, (4) no specific notification as well as (5) no procedure for review of, or appeal from, a denial of an application is provided. In other words, in the Appellate Body's view, exporting Members applying for certification whose applications were rejected were in effect denied *basic fairness* and *due process* and are discriminated against, vis-à-vis those Members which are granted certification.[339]

---

[338] *Ibid.*, paras 173–5.
[339] *Ibid.*, paras 178–81.

Accordingly, having determined that the US measure is applied in a manner which amounts to a means not just of "unjustifiable discrimination", but also of "arbitrary discrimination" between countries where the same conditions prevailed, contrary to the requirements of the Chapeau of Article XX, the Appellate Body concluded that such measure is not entitled to the justifying protection of Article XX of the GATT 1994.

As already noted, it is this second tier of the Appellate Body's analysis under Article XX that has drawn most attention from legal commentators, and it is thus with regard to this part of the *Shrimp/Turtle* report that I would like to advance a few remarks.

First of all, as noted by Hilf, in *Shrimp/Turtle* the Appellate Body approached the issue of justification (and in particular the function of the introductory clause of Article XX GATT) in a nuanced manner, searching for a balance between the right of a Member to invoke a general exception under Article XX and the rights of other Members provided for by the GATT taking into proper consideration the interests at stake.[340] In other words, the Appellate Body seemed to distance itself from the traditional characterisation of Article XX as an exception to the various obligations provided, for example, by Articles III or XI GATT. Although this more balanced approach might be seen as excessively deferential in a case involving a formally discriminatory measure, this approach will show all its value when WTO adjudicating bodies start dealing more often with the issue of justifying apparently origin-neutral regulations.

Secondly, I would argue that the Appellate Body's strict interpretation of the term "applied" for purposes of determining the requirements provided for in the Chapeau is not altogether convincing, at least if the intention was indeed to foreclose other uses of the Chapeau. In reviewing the US legislation at issue in *Shrimp/Turtle*, the Appellate Body clearly distinguished three sets of regulations which come into play in applying Article XX: first, the measure's "design and structure" (ie Section 609 provisions), secondly, its "substantial" application or "detailed operating provisions" (ie 1996 Guidelines), and thirdly, the measure's "procedural" application (ie mere administrative practices). In the Appellate Body's view, while the first set of regulations is taken into consideration for the purposes of determining the measure's "provisional justification" under Article XX(g) (as well as whether it violates any of the substantive obligations of the GATT), the second and third are relevant in order to establish whether the measure is applied as a means of arbitrary or unjustifiable discrimination between countries where the same conditions prevail under the Chapeau of Article XX.[341]

---

[340] M Hilf, "Power, Rules and Principles—Which Orientation for WTO/GATT Law?", 4 *JIEL* (2001) 111 at 128.
[341] Appellate Body Report on *Shrimp/Turtle*, above n 303, para 160: "[T]he application of a measure may be characterised as amounting to an abuse or misuse of an exception of Art XX not only when the *detailed operating provisions* of the measure prescribe the arbitrary

This subdivision appears inappropriate since it makes the application of the introductory clause conditional upon the manner in which the national regulation under review is enacted. For example, if the "rigid" requirements embodied in the 1996 Guidelines as well as the "discriminatory" practices carried out by the administrators in charge of the certification process were directly provided for in Section 609, the Chapeau would not even have entered the picture, since those same "requirements" and "practices" would have been deemed to be part of the measure's design and structure, not of its application. Accordingly, I believe that the requirements of the introductory clause of Article XX should not be limited to the mere "application" or actual implementation of the measure under review.

On the contrary, Article XX's requirement that measures "not [be] *applied* in a manner which would constitute a *means* of arbitrary or unjustifiable discrimination or a disguised restriction on international trade" appears to denote a certain emphasis on the Member's *conduct* amounting to arbitrary or unjustifiable discrimination or disguised restriction. This may explain why under the Chapeau the Appellate Body has looked mostly at the more "subjective" features of the "regulatory process" giving life to the particular measure under review rather than simply at the more "objective" features of the "design and structure" of the measure. The function of the Chapeau is nevertheless broad enough to leave room for the treaty interpreter to consider both mentioned features, the only limitation being to avoid any duplication of the analysis carried out at different stages.

In particular, as noted by the Appellate Body in its reports on *Reformulated Gasoline* and *Shrimp/Turtle*, the requirements of the introductory clause should not constitute a repetition of the type of review which the treaty interpreter has to carry out under both any of GATT substantive obligations (such as Article III or Article XI) or any of the subparagraphs of Article XX. In both determinations, the interpreter will look at the measure's "design and structure" in order to establish respectively whether a national measure is in violation, for example, of the National Treatment obligation or whether that same measure is provisionally justified on the basis of one of the public policy objectives listed in subparagraphs (a)–(j). But it would be "illogical" to repeat either of those determinations within the introductory clauses of Article XX.[342] For example, if by looking at its "design and structure" a measure has been found to afford

---

or unjustifiable activity, but also where a measure, otherwise fair and just on its face, is *actually applied in an arbitrary manner*. In other words, the standards of the chapeau, in the Appellate Body's view, project both *substantive* and *procedural* requirements." [emphasis added].

[342] Citing its Report on *Reformulated Gasoline*, above n 59, at 23, the Appellate Body stated that: "The provisions of the chapeau cannot logically refer to the same standard(s) by which

"less favourable treatment" to imported products (in violation of Article III GATT) and to "relate to" the protection of exhaustible natural resources (within the meaning of Article XX(g)), a treaty interpreter subjecting the same measure to the Chapeau of Article XX should neither fail or pass it on the basis of those same findings (respectively, that it constituted "discrimination" in violation of Article III and that it was "directly connected to" the protection of exhaustible natural resources under Article XX(g)).

However, the need to avoid any duplication of the several analysis does not mean that "discrimination" for the purposes of the Chapeau must always be something different from "discrimination" for purposes of, for example, Article III. There is, in fact, a clear difference between the pure *non-discrimination* standard of Articles I and III and the requirement not to discriminate *arbitrarily* and/or *unjustifiably* provided for in the Chapeau of Article XX, which prevent any risk of duplicating the respective analysis. Accordingly, I would not exclude the possibility that the Chapeau might also be used as a mechanism to screen the "arbitrariness" and "unjustifiability" of discriminatory measures deemed to violate the GATT. In other words, there is no reason why a *formally* discriminatory measure that is found both to violate the National Treatment obligation of Article III and to be provisionally justified according to one of the subparagraphs of Article XX may not be subject to further review under the Chapeau to determine whether that discriminatory measure is indeed arbitrary and/or unjustifiable.

The Appellate Body's reference in *Shrimp/Turtle* to the general principle of good faith, interpreted in the specific context of Article XX as the "appropriate and necessary" and "fair and equitable" exercise of the right to invoke GATT exceptions, clearly confirms the Appellate Body's emphasis on legal standards that go beyond the mere non-discrimination principle, including both "substantive" (appropriate and necessary) as well as "procedural" (fair and equitable) type of mechanisms for reviewing the (discriminatory) measure at issue.

Taking this argument to its logical conclusion, it might be argued that the Chapeau may be employed inter alia as a tool to harmonise the *degree of connection* between the incriminated regulation and the regulatory objective that is required in order to justify a measure under the general public policy exception of Article XX. In other words, while in the case of Article XX(b) and (d), which mandate that the measure be "necessary" to achieve the public policy objectives specified therein, the requirements of the introductory clause would mainly be applied in order to review the measure's "regulatory process",[343] in those instances where a lower

---

a violation of a substantive rule has been determined to have occurred." Appellate Body Report on *Shrimp/Turtle*, above n 303, para 150 fn 138.

[343] See above the discussion on the Appellate Body reading of Art XX(d) in *Korea–Beef*.

degree of connection between the measure and the objective is required (such as for example in Article XX(g)), the Chapeau may be employed not only in order to review the "regulatory process" but also as a sort of "necessity" requirement.

This multifaceted reading of the functions of Article XX introductory clauses is in line with the interpretation of the Appellate Body Report in *Reformulated Gasoline* suggested above, where it was argued that the Appellate Body's ambivalent reasoning was indicative of its preference for a more flexible approach, which left open different interpretative options that could be employed depending on the peculiarities of each particular dispute.

This preference for a flexible approach is, furthermore, confirmed by the similarly "ambivalent" findings in *Shrimp/Turtle* as regard to the role played by the concept of unjustified or arbitrary discrimination.[344] However, in *Shrimp/Turtle* there is a further complication which needs to be taken into consideration in order to really comprehend the nature of the inquiry under the Chapeau.

As previously argued, in *Shrimp/Turtle* both the parties and the adjudicating bodies erroneously focused on Article XI rather than on Article III. In other words, in light of the fact that, considered as a whole, the US requirement to use TEDs applied, though not in identical manner, both to domestic and imported shrimp trawlers, the specific US measure under review in *Shrimp/Turtle* (Section 609 and implementing legislation) should have been treated as a case of *formally* discriminatory *internal* regulation inconsistent with the National Treatment obligation of Article III:4 rather than as an *import* restriction within the meaning of Article XI. If this had been the approach followed by the Panel, the US measure would have been deemed to violate the GATT only upon demonstrating that such measure afforded de jure or de facto less favourable treatment vis-à-vis imported products (ie the National Treatment obligation of Article III:4) or that it discriminated de jure or de facto among the products of different countries (ie the Most-Favoured-Nation Treatment obligation of Article I).

Accordingly, several of the arguments referred to by the Appellate Body in its findings that the US measure did not comply with the conditions set out in the introductory clause of Article XX should have been considered at the preliminary stage of determining the existence of *discriminatory* "design and structure" within the meaning of Article III:4 (and Article I). For example, in emphasising the excessive *rigidity* of the US measure (or in the words of the Appellate Body, its "actual application"), the Appellate Body clearly makes two points that could be employed in

---

[344] G de Búrca and J Scott, "The Impact of the WTO on EU Decision-Making" in G de Búrca and J Scott (eds), *The EU and the WTO: Legal and Constitutional Aspects* (Oxford, Hart, 2001) at 18.

order to find a violation of the National Treatment obligation of Article III:4. As noted earlier, by prohibiting imports of shrimp harvested by commercial shrimp trawl vessels using TEDs comparable in effectiveness to those required in the United States if those shrimp originated in waters of countries not certified under Section 609, the US legislation clearly constituted *formal* discrimination against imported shrimp.[345]

Moreover, the Appellate Body's findings with regard to the differential treatment among various countries desiring certification are based on *formal* discrimination between, on the one hand, the 14 countries in the wider Caribbean/western Atlantic region and, on the other, all other countries exporting shrimp. This may easily be said to constitute a violation of the Most-Favoured-Nation Treatment principle of Article I.[346]

If this had been the violation findings and thus the starting point of the review under Article XX, the Appellate Body's application of the requirements provided for in the introductory clauses of Article XX would have certainly been clearer. Leaving aside those "certain problematic aspects" of the certification process (to which I will turn shortly), there would only be one reason for the US measure failing the requirements of the Chapeau: the "excessive" and "avoidable" *unilateralism* of the US approach to sea turtles protection. *Excessive* because the US measure in its "design and structure" (for us) or in its "application" (for the AB) showed no real sensitivity to the peculiar conditions characterising foreign markets and thus the appropriateness of the regulatory programmes in those exporting countries (this is the argument based on the "lack of flexibility"). *Avoidable* because there was an alternative course of action reasonably open to the United States for securing the legitimate policy goal of its measure, a course of action other than the unilateral and non-consensual procedures of the import prohibition under Section 609 (this is the argument based on the alleged "failure to negotiate an international agreement" with the interested countries).

---

[345] Moreover, even assuming that the requirement imposed on domestic and foreign shrimp trawlers were formally identical (facially origin-neutral), failure to take into account different conditions which may occur in the territories of other Members may de facto result in discriminatory treatment of imported and domestic products. The Appellate Body's argument focusing on the United States' failure to take into consideration other specific policies and measures that an exporting country may have adopted for the protection and conservation of sea turtles recalls the "dual burden" reasoning in EC jurisprudence.

[346] The reader should note that in the ensuing Art 21.5 dispute, both elements of formal discrimination were deemed to have been corrected by the US government in particular with the adoption of the 1999 Guidelines. Cf Panel Report on *United States—Import Prohibition of Certain Shrimp and Shrimp Products, Recourse to Art 21.5 of the DSU (Shrimp–Art 21.5)*, WT/DS58/RW, circulated 15 June 2001, adopted 21 Nov 2001, paras 5.105–5.111 (prohibition of import of TED-caught shrimp from non-certified countries) and 5.112–5.120 ("phase-in periods" and "transfer of technology"); and Appellate Body Report on *Shrimp–Art 21.5*, WT/DS58/AB/RW, circulated 22 Oct 2001, adopted 21 Nov 2001, paras 94–96. See more below.

The type of arguments advanced by the Appellate Body in explaining why the US measure was not a "reasonable" exercise of the right to invoke Article XX(g) exception confirm the broad range of issues that may be employed in order to review a Member's measure under the introductory clause of Article XX. In both the Appellate Body's findings of "lack of flexibility" and "failure to negotiate an international agreement", there is a dual emphasis on both the measure's "design and structure" and its "regulatory process".[347] With regard to the finding of "lack of flexibility", the Appellate Body's arguments appear to imply both the "discriminatory" *character* of the US measure as well as the "unreasonableness" of the *regulatory process* that brought to life the shrimp import prohibition. The absence of a degree of discretion or flexibility in certification standards,[348] the failure to take into account other specific policies and measures adopted in exporting countries for the protection of sea turtles[349] and the general lack of any real consideration for the conditions prevailing in those exporting countries[350] may be taken at the same time as constituting forms of de facto discriminatory treatment as well as serious deficiencies in the regulatory process.[351]

Similarly, with regard to the finding concerning the "failure to negotiate an international agreement", the Appellate Body's arguments appear to include both that the US measure is not the least-trade restrictive measure capable to achieve the specific public policy goal and that the unilateral manner in which the measure came about underscores the unreasonableness of its regulatory process. Focusing on the measure's "design and structure" (ie whether the measure is *necessary* to achieve the policy objective), the Appellate Body appears to perform the type of analysis which is required, for example, in subparagraphs (b) and (d) of Article XX. As previously noted, the Appellate Body observed in this regard that the Inter-American Convention provides convincing demonstration that an *alternative* course of action was *reasonably* open to the United States in order to secure the legitimate policy goal of its measure.[352] On the other

---

[347] G de Búrca and J Scott, "The Impact of the WTO on EU Decision-Making" in G de Búrca and J Scott (eds), *The EU and the WTO: Legal and Constitutional Aspects* (Oxford, Hart Publishing, 2001) at 18 *et seq*, noting that "there is a tension inherent in the AB report. It shifts somewhat uneasily between recourse to standards which are not predicated upon an assessment of comparative treatment—basic fairness, just treatment, reasonableness—to notions of discrimination which by definition require a comparative perspective.

[348] Appellate Body Report on *Shrimp/Turtle*, above n 303, para 161.

[349] *Ibid.*, para 163.

[350] *Ibid.*, paras 164–5.

[351] It should be noted in this regard that, as EC law of free movement shows, the failure to take into proper consideration the peculiar conditions characterising foreign markets (and thus foreign products) may indeed be taken as constituting a form of de facto discriminatory treatment. Moreover, as noted in the *section 337* GATT Panel Report, formally identical treatment does not always imply that the measure complies with the National Treatment principle.

[352] Appellate Body Report on *Shrimp/Turtle*, above n 303, para 171.

hand, focusing on the measure's "regulatory process", the Appellate Body emphasises the principal consequence of the failure to engage several Members exporting shrimp in serious across-the-board negotiations, that is "the resulting unilateralism evident in the application of Section 609." In particular, the Appellate Body noted that,

> the policies relating to the necessity for use of particular kinds of TEDs in various maritime areas, and the operating details of these policies, are all shaped by the Department of State, *without the participation* of the exporting Members. The system and processes of certification are established and administered by the United States agencies *alone*. The decision-making involved in the grant, denial or withdrawal of certification to the exporting Members, is, accordingly, also *unilateral*. The unilateral character of the application of Section 609 heightens the disruptive and discriminatory influence of the import prohibition and underscores its unjustifiability.[353]

As noted earlier, it should not be relevant whether the deficiencies in the regulatory process occur at the stage of enacting the "measure" or at the later stage of its application or implementation. What is fundamental in this part of the Appellate Body's decision is its willingness to impose on WTO Members a duty to avoid unnecessary unilateral action by requiring them to pursue co-operation strategies at all regulatory stages. By imposing procedural requirements of this type, the Appellate Body is trying to balance the need to safeguard national regulatory prerogatives with the need to strengthen the multilateral approach to trade liberalisation,[354] or in the words of the Appellate Body,

> locating and marking out a line of equilibrium between the right of a Member to invoke an exception under Article XX and the rights of the other Members under varying substantial provisions of the GATT.[355]

Following its stance in *Reformulated Gasoline*, the Appellate Body in *Shrimp/Turtle* confirmed its preference for a flexible approach with regard to the requirements of the Chapeau of Article XX. Although the emphasis appears to be on a review of the reasonableness of the "regulatory process" that has brought to life the measure at issue, the Appellate Body does not seem to be willing to limit the Chapeau to any particular type of analysis.[356]

One final note. Notwithstanding the above-mentioned flaws, the Appellate Body's interpretation of Article XX, and in particular its introductory clause, demonstrates the positive normative function of WTO law.

---

[353] *Ibid.*, para 172 [emphasis added].
[354] P Mavroidis, "Trade and Environment after the Shrimps-Turtles Litigation", 34 *JWT* (2000) 73, at 81.
[355] Appellate Body Report on *Shrimp/Turtle*, above n 303, para 159.
[356] Cf CD Ehlermann, "Some Personal Experiences as Member of the Appellate Body of the WTO", *EUI Policy Papers* (N. 2, 2002) at 42, who, noting the weakness of the political arm of

It may be argued in fact that, at the end of the day, the Appellate Body struck down the US measure on the basis of a line of argument that in over-all terms does not seem to be very distant from that advanced by the Panel: unilateralism versus multilateralism. However, there is indeed a signifi-cant difference between the approach followed by the two adjudicating bodies. Contrary to the Panel, the Appellate Body did not simply limit itself to putting forward an a priori conclusion with regard to the unjustifi-ability of a type of national regulation. Instead, it explained in detail where the national regulator had indeed failed and how this failure should be remedied. It is the clear attempt to put forward certain normative criteria and standards which Members must and can follow in regulating their markets that characterises the Appellate Body Report on *Shrimp/Turtle*. This is in line with Article 19 of the Dispute Settlement Understanding (DSU) which, in requiring panels and the Appellate Body to recommend that the infringing Member bring its measures into conformity with WTO law, grants to the former the authority to suggest ways in which the Member concerned could implement the recommendations.

The subsequent dispute over the implementation by the United States of the DSB recommendations with regard to the US regime for the impor-tation of shrimp and shrimp products (the so-called *Shrimp – Article 21.5* dispute)[357] confirms this positive normative function. In that dispute, both the Panel and the Appellate Body found in favour of the United States by concluding that Section 609 of Public Law 101–62, as imple-mented by the Revised Guidelines of 8 July 1999 (modified following the adoption by the DSB of the reports of the original panel and the Appellate Body on *Shrimp/Turtle*) and as applied so far by the US authorities, was justified under Article XX because the United States had complied with the regulatory criteria established by the Appellate Body in its earlier report. In other words, the United States (a) had complied with the duty to make *serious good faith efforts to negotiate* with all interested parties a bilateral or multilateral solution for the protection and conservation of endangered sea turtle before the enforcement of a unilaterally designed import prohibition;[358] (b) had introduced a sufficient level of *flexibility* in the certification requirements which would make possible to take into account peculiar conditions prevailing in the interested exporting coun-tries;[359] (c) by modifying its guidelines and adjusting its practice so as to

---

the WTO, argues for the necessity for the Appellate Body to reason on a case-specific basis, avoiding sweeping statements.

[357] *United States—Import Prohibition of Certain Shrimp and Shrimp Products, Recourse to Art 21.5 of the DSU (Shrimp–Art 21.5)*, WT/DS58, brought 23 Oct 2000.

[358] Panel Report on *Shrimp–Art 21.5*, above n 346, paras 5.87–5.88. This finding was con-firmed in Appellate Body Report on *Shrimp–Art 21.5*, above n 346, para 134.

[359] Panel Report on *Shrimp–Art 21.5*, above n 346, para 5.104; Appellate Body Report on *Shrimp–Art 21.5*, above n 346, paras 135–52.

permit import of TED-caught shrimp from non-certified countries, had complied, as long as that situation remained unchanged,[360] with the DSB recommendations and rulings in this respect;[361] and (d) with regard to the certification process, had complied with *due process requirements.*[362]

It is interesting to note that, following the US modification to its Guidelines implementing Section 609, the *Shrimp – Article 21.5* dispute became a dispute over an (apparently) origin-neutral measure. As noted above, formal discrimination between identical domestic and imported products (National Treatment) was eliminated (TED-caught shrimp, whether domestic or imported from non-certified countries, could be sold in the US market) and formal discrimination between products of different WTO Members (Most-Favoured-Nation) was revised (differential treatment with regard to "phase-in periods", "transfer of technology" and "serious good-faith effort to negotiate an international agreement" was indeed corrected).[363]

The Appellate Body thus focused principally on two issues: "the nature and the extent of the duty of the United States to pursue international co-operation in the protection and conservation of sea turtles" and "the flexibility of the Revised Guidelines".

With regard to the first issue, the Appellate Body simply confirmed the panel reading of the Appellate Body original report in *Shrimp/Turtle,* according to which the duty to pursue international co-operation does not require the conclusion of an international agreement. The Appellate Body appears, moreover, to have reduced the value of such a duty to a mechanism for detecting the existence of (unjustifiable or arbitrary) *discrimination*, essentially by comparing the efforts of the United States to negotiate the Inter-American Convention with one group of exporting WTO Members with the efforts made by the United States to negotiate a similar agreement with another group of exporting WTO Members.

With regard to the second issue, the flexibility of the Guidelines, the analysis of the Appellate Body seems better inspired. The Appellate Body correctly noted the

---

[360] This condition refers to the pending litigation before the Court of Appeals on the correct interpretation of s 609. The CIT had in fact ruled that the interpretation given by the Department of State in the 1999 Guidelines was not compatible with the terms of s 609. The CIT, however, refrained from granting an injunction that the US Department of State modify its guidelines. This was the basis for the Panel and the Appellate Body to find that, at the time of the Art 21.5 litigation, US municipal law permitted importation of shrimp caught with TEDs even from non-certified countries. Cf Panel Report on *Shrimp–Art 21.5*, above n 346, paras 5.105–5.111 and Appellate Body Report on *Shrimp–Art 21.5*, above n 346, paras 94–6.

[361] Panel Report on *Shrimp–Art 21.5*, above n 346, para 5.111, confirmed in Appellate Body Report on *Shrimp–Art 21.5*, above n 346, paras 94–6.

[362] Panel Report on *Shrimp–Art 21.5*, above n 346, paras 5.126–5.137. Cf S Shaw and R Schwartz, "Trade and Environment in the WTO: State of Play", 36 *JWT* (2002) 129 at 148–49.

[363] Cf Panel Report on *Shrimp–Art 21.5*, above n 346, paras 5.105–5.111 and 5.112–5.120; and Appellate Body Report on *Shrimp–Art 21.5*, above n 346, paras 94–96 and 129–34.

important difference between conditioning market access on the adoption of essentially the same programme, and conditioning market access on the adoption of a programme *comparable in effectiveness*.[364]

The Appellate Body held that permitting an importing Member to condition market access on exporting Members putting in place regulatory programmes *comparable in effectiveness* to that of the importing Member gives sufficient latitude to the exporting Member with respect to the programme it may adopt to achieve the level of effectiveness required, allowing the exporting Member to adopt a regulatory programme that is "suitable" to the specific conditions prevailing in its territory.

Similar to the provision of the TBT Agreement establishing a preference for "performance" requirements rather than "design" or "descriptive" requirements,[365] the Appellate Body's statement with regard to the value of flexibility seems to make perfect regulatory sense. It is not just "fair" but also "reasonable" for a national regulator to impose its standards by simply specifying the aims pursued rather than requiring conformity with a pre-determined set of technical specification.

C. Conclusions

Following the broad interpretation of the ban on "quantitative restrictions and measures having equivalent effect" of Article 28 EC, it may easily be argued that, in the field of non-fiscal regulation, both EC and WTO law include the prohibition of de jure discrimination, which requires Members not to employ the origin or nationality of a product as the regulatory differentiating criterion in such a manner as to upset the competitive conditions in favour of domestic production. In the case of de jure discriminatory or origin-based measures, the focus of the dispute will mainly be on whether or not the differential treatment between *identical* imported and domestic products violates the National Treatment obligations in EC and WTO law.

Article III:4 GATT has mainly been invoked with regard to internal measures which *formally* discriminated on the basis of the nationality (or origin) of a product. As already noted, when confronted with a case of de jure discriminatory measures, a Panel's main focus will be on determining whether the differential treatment between domestic and imported products violates the "no less favourable treatment" standard of Article III:4. Accordingly, since a measure formally discriminating on the basis of the product's nationality presupposes *by definition* that the regulated

---

[364] Appellate Body Report on *Shrimp–Art 21.5*, above n 346, para 144 [emphasis original].
[365] See Art 2.8 TBT Agreement.

products are, for purposes of that same measure, *identical* (that is, identical except for their different origin or nationality), an examination of the "products relationship" is not, or at least should not be, an issue in the case of de jure discriminatory internal regulations.

Since the National Treatment obligation requires that Members guarantee effective equality of opportunities for imported and domestic products, it has been recognised by GATT panel practice and WTO jurisprudence that Members may apply to imported products different formal legal requirements if doing so would accord imported products more favourable treatment.[366] Although it is for the complaining Member to prove the existence of a "competitive imbalance" stemming from the formal differential treatment, it appears that establishing a prima facie case of violation of Article III is relatively unproblematic. In such cases, there almost seems to be a reversal of the burden of proof with the Member applying differential treatment on the basis of the product's origin having to show that, in spite of such differences, the no less favourable treatment standard of Article III is met.[367] This is confirmed, moreover, by both GATT panel practice and WTO jurisprudence that have interpreted the "no less favourable treatment" requirement of Article III:4 in a strict manner.[368] In particular, the "no less favourable" treatment requirement of Article III:4 is understood as applicable to each individual case of imported products, a defendant Member may not avoid a finding of discrimination by *balancing* more favourable treatment of some imported products against less favourable treatment of other imported products.[369] Furthermore, in order to establish that the "no less favourable" treatment standard of Article III:4 has been met, a panel shall not take into consideration *actual trade effects*, but whether or not the origin-based regulation *in itself* may lead to the application to imported products of treatment less favourable than that accorded to domestic products.[370]

Following the *Dassonville–Cassis de Dijon* jurisprudence, Article 28 (ex 30) EC has been interpreted as prohibiting not only *border* measures but also any *internal* measures which apply exclusively to, or formally discriminate against, imported products (so-called "distinctly applicable" measures). In

---

[366] Panel Report on *section 337*, above n 17, para 5.11; Appellate Body Report on *Korea–Beef*, above n 124, paras 136–7 and 144.

[367] Panel Report on *section 337*, above n 17, para 5.11.

[368] For a recent example of the strict application of the prohibition of de jure discrimination on the basis of nationality outside the GATT see Appellate Body Report on *United States—section 211 Omnibus Appropriations Act of 1998 (Havana Club)*, WT/DS176/AB/R, circulated 2 Jan 2002, adopted 1 Feb 2002, where the Appellate Body in interpreting the National Treatment provision of the TRIPS Agreement (Art 3), held that "the *possibility* [even if small] that non-United States successors-in-interest face two hurdles is *inherently less favourable* than the undisputed fact that United States successors-in-interest face only one." *Ibid.*, para 265.

[369] *Ibid.*, para 5.14; Panel Report on *Reformulated Gasoline*, above n 34, paras 6.14–6.15.

[370] Panel Report on *section 337*, above n 17, paras 5.12–5.13.

light of its peculiar features, contrary to the case of Article III:4, the formally discriminatory nature of the measure has been employed not in order to determine whether the formal *differential* treatment between domestic and imported products indeed constitutes *discrimination* against imported products, but mainly for purposes of determining whether the measure under review could be justified on the basis of the exhaustive list of public policy exception of Article 30 EC or the open-ended list of "mandatory requirements" (which is instead reserved to "indistinctly applicable" measures). It is nonetheless interesting to note how Member States have tried to avoid having their measures considered "distinctly applicable" by arguing that the product's origin constituted a valid criterion for differentiating otherwise apparently identical products (*Irish Souvenirs* and *Walloon Waste*).

Notwithstanding the fact that there appears to be in the Court's case-law as well as in the free movement literature a certain inconsistency of terminology with regard to the concepts of "distinctly" and "indistinctly" applicable measures, it has been submitted that the relevant distinction for purposes of determining whether to apply the per se prohibition of Article 28 or the "mandatory requirements" doctrine enunciated in *Cassis de Dijon* is and should be between, on the one hand, "*formally* discriminatory" measures and, on the other hand, "indistinctly applicable" measures, where the latter category includes both materially discriminatory and non-discriminatory measures (what I have also referred to as de jure and de facto indistinctly applicable measures).[371] Not only does this appear to be the prevalent, though at times convoluted, approach followed by the Court of Justice, it is also the better approach in defining the boundaries between the "per se prohibition" and the "reasonableness rule". As the EC free movement jurisprudence in general demonstrates, the concept of de facto or material discrimination may take us so far as to include even the (only) apparently non-discriminatory minimum alcohol requirement at issue in *Cassis de Dijon* itself. In light of the strictures characterising the per se rule of Article 28 (in particular, the limited justification options of Article 30), adopting a broad definition of the term "distinctly applicable" would thus entail unacceptable results with regard national regulatory prerogatives. Moreover, there is a fundamental difference between de jure and de facto discrimination: while the former is embodied in the terms of the measure itself (ie by adopting the product's origin or nationality as *the* differentiating criterion), the latter does not appear from the text of the measure but only through an analysis of the measure's *effects* in the relevant market. Thus, the fact that an origin-neutral regulation may have discriminatory effects against foreign products not

---

[371] Cf J Wiers, *Trade and Environment in the EC and the WTO: a Legal Analysis* (Groningen, Europa Law Publishing, 2002) at 317; Opinion of Advocate-General Tesauro in Joined Cases C–120/95, Decker and C–158/96, *Kohll* [1998] ECR I–1831.

intended by the legislator, or may be clearly justified on the basis of a legitimate public policy ground, and should require a more deferential treatment of origin-neutral measures vis-à-vis origin-based measures. Justifying de jure discriminatory measures on public policy grounds represents a clearly more difficult endeavour on the part of Member States compared to justifying de facto discriminatory measures. There are indeed very few valid reasons for which a regulator needs to distinguish between two identical products only on the basis of their different origin.

Furthermore, any attempt to expand the concept of "distinctly applicable" measures to include those measures which, although apparently origin-neutral, show "clear" *protectionist intent*[372] should be avoided both because of the practical difficulties of having to assess "intent" and, even more, because of the politically sensitive concerns which a finding of "hidden' protectionist intent" may involve in terms of the institutional balance between judiciary and legislative powers, as well as between Community institutions and the Member States.

Nevertheless, in both EC and WTO law a finding of formal discrimination may be justified on public policy grounds. Both Article 30 EC and Article XX GATT provide for an *exhaustive* list of public policy aims which Members may employ in order to justify a violation of the prohibition on origin-based or de jure discriminatory regulation.

Contrary to the case of origin-based *fiscal* measures, in both GATT panel practice and WTO jurisprudence there exist several cases where a Member has resorted to the general exception provision of Article XX GATT in order to "save" an origin-based *non-fiscal* regulation which had been found to violate the non-discrimination obligation of Article III:4.

It appears that, in the field of non-fiscal regulations, WTO adjudicating bodies are much more sensitive to the public policy objectives alleged by Members in order to justify the adoption of even formally discriminatory measures. For example, it is in a way surprising that in *Korea–Beef*, a case involving an internal measure *formally* discriminating between domestic and imported products, the Appellate Body got involved in a lengthy analysis of the "proportionality" of the origin-based dual-retail system in order to reject Korea's justification claim. With the exception of a very few cases (such as *Campus Oil*), ECJ jurisprudence shows, on the other hand, that the analysis over the justifiability of formal discriminatory non-fiscal regulations is usually dispensed with in a few lines (like in *Pistre*).

This more sensitive approach evidenced in both GATT panel practice and WTO jurisprudence may be explained once again by taking into consideration both the different nature of the integration processes characterising

---

[372] Cf C Hilson, "Discrimination in Community free movement law", 24 *ELRev* (1999) 445 at 447 and 450; P Craig and G de Búrca, *EU Law—Text, Cases and Materials* (Oxford, OUP, 1998) at 588.

the EC and the WTO and the different legitimacies of the respective adjudicating bodies. It is evident in WTO jurisprudence that even in cases of de jure discriminatory measures, panels and the Appellate Body need to address Members' public policy claims and examine whether these claims may indeed provide a justification for violating the National Treatment obligation of Article III:4.

With regard to the more technical issue of the type of review to which both the European Court of Justice and WTO adjudicating bodies subject a justification claim based on one of the public policy objectives listed respectively in Article 30 EC and Article XX GATT, a few remarks should here be noted.

From a very first look at the interpretation of the respective justifications available under EC and WTO law, the liberal and emancipated approach pursued by the ECJ may be contrasted with the rigorous, textually-faithful approach of GATT panel practice and WTO jurisprudence. In other words, while the Court of Justice has reinterpreted the requirements of Article 30 EC, first and second sentences, as providing for a public policy exception conditioned by a review of the proportionality of the national regulation at issue, WTO jurisprudence has demonstrated a willingness to follow more faithfully the text of the "general exception" provision distinguishing between, on the one hand, the specific requirements contained in the subparagraphs from (a) to (j) of Article XX and, on the other, the general requirements of the Chapeau of Article XX.

Perhaps the most evident sign of this difference in the general approach may be seen in the length of the examination which the respective adjudicating bodies have reserved to this issue: if the Court of Justice deals with the public policy justification claims in a few paragraphs, both WTO panels as well as the Appellate Body examine an Article XX defence throughout several pages.

The pros and cons of the two respective approaches are the following: while the liberal approach pursued by the Court of Justice enables a greater flexibility (and thus the ability to reach the right result in the specific case), it does not much help the cause of the "certainty of the law" (and thus the ability of the "rule" to provide a normative standard for national regulators to follow). On the other hand, while the more rigorous approach followed by WTO jurisprudence may improve the certainty and thus the positive normative function of the "rule", it may at the same time lose the flexibility necessary to finding the "appropriate" solution for each specific case.

However, upon closer examination, the Appellate Body's jurisprudence seems to have striven (and I believe with certain success) for the establishment of a more appropriate balance between "certainty" and "flexibility". In particular, while maintaining the textual distinctions between the several conditions specified in Article XX GATT ("provisional justifications", "connectors", and "further appraisal" or "Chapeau"), the Appellate Body has demonstrated in its early interpretation of Article XX a preference for a multifaceted and flexible approach which enables the treaty interpreter to review Members' measures under several perspectives.

Accordingly, although both systems have made use of the so-called "proportionality" principle, and in particular its "suitability" and "least-trade restrictive" limbs, in order to carry out the justification analysis, Article XX and in particular its introductory clause has been employed in WTO jurisprudence to impose on Members both "substantive" and "procedural" standards. For example, the Appellate Body found that the US measure regulating the manner in which shrimp are caught was not a "reasonable" exercise of the right to invoke the public policy exception of Article XX. As previously noted, in the Appellate Body's findings of "lack of flexibility" and "failure to negotiate an international agreement", there existed a dual emphasis on both the measure's "design and structure" and its "regulatory process".[373] With regard to the findings of "lack of flexibility", the Appellate Body's arguments implied both the "discriminatory" *character* of the US measure as well as the "unreasonableness" of the *regulatory process* that brought to life the shrimp import prohibition. Similarly, with regard to the finding concerning the "failure to negotiate an international agreement", the Appellate Body's arguments included (1) that the US measure is not the least-trade restrictive measure capable to achieve the specific public policy goal and (2) that the unilateral manner in which the measure came about underscores the unreasonableness of its "regulatory process". This dual approach may also be evidenced in the Appellate Body's earlier report in the *Reformulated Gasoline* dispute.

In sum, notwithstanding the apparent rigorousness of the approach to Article XX undertaken in WTO jurisprudence and the liberal approach followed by the ECJ with regard to Article 30, it is the former that has developed a broader sets of legal tests for purpose of assessing the public policy justifiability of formally discriminatory national regulations.

One final point. It may be asked what is the relevance of such a multifaceted approach when, as a practical matter, the outcome of the justification analysis in both EC and WTO law with regard to non-fiscal regulations in violation of the prohibition of de jure discrimination always goes in the same direction: formal discriminatory measures are very rarely (almost never) justified on public policy grounds. The answer, it is suggested, lies in the willingness of the WTO adjudicating bodies, and in particular the Appellate Body, to clarify the content of the "positive" normative standards provided for in Article XX GATT, stemming from the conscious or unconscious

---

[373] G de Búrca and J Scott, "The Impact of the WTO on EU Decision-Making" in G de Búrca and J Scott (eds), *The EU and the WTO: Legal and Constitutional Aspects* (Oxford, Hart, 2001) at 18 *et seq.*

awareness of the increasing relevance within the WTO legal system of these same standards.[374] As the discussion in Part II will show, when one moves from rules prohibiting forms of inherent or direct discrimination to rules dealing with more subtle forms of discrimination or rules simply requiring "reasonableness" or "proportionality", the meaning of, for example, the "necessity" requirement or the prohibition on "arbitrary and unjustifiable discrimination" becomes a much more important and sensitive issue in the underlying conflict between multilateral liberalisation efforts and national regulatory prerogatives.

[374] D McRae, "GATT Art XX and the WTO Appellate Body" in M Bronckers and R Quick (eds), *New Directions in International Economic Law* (London, Kluwer Law International, 2000) at 233.

Part II

Deep Integration

A
S NOTED IN the introductory chapter, the dichotomy between shallow and deep integration has been used in this study to describe the underlying conflict between the objectives of trade liberalisation and national regulatory prerogatives. It thus focuses on the degree to which the legal instruments employed to tackle trade barriers are more or less "intrusive" in Members' sovereignty. The key balancing factors in this calculation are, on the one hand, the strength of the *economic* theories underlying the instruments (or policies) for multilateral liberalisation and, on the other, the strength of the *political* interests underlying national trade restrictive measures. Depending on the outcome of this calculation, one can distinguish between instruments (or policies) of shallow integration, which are easier to pursue, and instruments (or policies) of deep integration, which involve more problematic issues. This dichotomy should not be read as representing two clear-cut stages in the liberalisation of international trade. All instruments or approaches employed in the liberalisation of trade sit rather on a continuum that starts at one end with very high barriers to trade among nations and ends at the other with total regulatory harmonisation.

When one moves away from the obligation to reduce or eliminate border measures and the prohibition of formal discrimination (ie instruments of "shallow integration"), and starts examining (a) the prohibition of material discrimination and (b) the requirement that national regulation be "reasonable" or "proportionate", then one gets into what I have described as instruments of *deep(er) integration*.

As anticipated in the introduction, instruments of "deep integration" also include instruments which are adopted at the supranational level and which provide directly for the substantive regulation of specific areas (what I have called instruments of "legislative integration" or "positive integration *strictu senso*"). However, constraints of time and space have not permitted the inclusion of such a further category of instruments of "deep integration" in the present analysis. This focuses exclusively on two further layers of instruments of "judicial integration": the National Treatment principle and the prohibition of de facto discrimination (chapter 3) and the "reasonableness" rule (chapter 4).

3

Judicial Integration—Second Layer: The National Treatment Principle and The Prohibition of De Facto Discrimination

A NATIONAL TREATMENT principle would not mean much if its scope were restricted to catching de jure discriminatory (ie origin-based) measures, only. A Member State would be able to comply with such a principle by simply avoiding the use of the product's origin or nationality as the differentiating criterion in imposing a tax or regulation, even if this measure had the *effect* of discriminating between imported and domestic products or services. Imagine a Member State with a high production of beer and very low production of wine that applies a higher tax on wine than on beer. Although the tax system would not formally discriminate on the basis of origin or nationality (ie it is origin-neutral), by favouring a typically domestic product (beer) compared to a *similar*, and typically imported, product (wine), this system would represent a classical example of material discrimination. In this circumstance, though origin-neutral, the criterion employed to distinguish the level of tax (in our hypothetical example of wine/beer) has the same *protectionist effect* as if the Member State had formally discriminated between domestic and imported beer. This type of discrimination is also known as de facto or indirect discrimination based on origin or nationality.[1]

In order for a (formally) origin-neutral tax or regulation to be equated in its *effects* to a measure formally discriminating on the basis of origin or nationality, the two elements which characterise a de jure discriminatory measure—"nationality criterion" and "less favourable treatment of imported products"—must somehow be reproduced.

---

[1] Also referred to in the literature and the jurisprudence as "implicit" or "disguised" or "covert" discrimination.

As examined in the previous chapter, in the case of de jure discrimination the products at issue are by definition "identical" and the "differentiation" between those products on the basis of their "origin or nationality" is inherent in the regulatory instrument itself. It follows that in the case of de jure discrimination the analysis will focus principally on whether the differentiation between identical products on the sole basis of the products' nationality or origin complies with the "less favourable treatment" standard, which mandates Member States to provide *effective* equality of competitive conditions for imported products in relation to domestic products. It should be remembered that both GATT panel practice and WTO jurisprudence have recognised that Members may apply to imported products different formal legal requirements as long as this would not accord imported products less favourable treatment compared to domestic products.

On the other hand, in the case of de facto discrimination, the national measure, again by definition, does not in its terms differentiate between products on the basis of origin or nationality. This is why it will be necessary to go behind the formal text of the origin-neutral measure under review and determine whether or not that measure has *in practice* the same protectionist effect of a measure formally discriminating on the basis of origin or nationality. In order to accomplish this task, next to a comparison of the actual treatment afforded to *identical* imported and domestic products, it may also be appropriate to examine how *similar* imported and domestic products are treated. Accordingly, an origin-neutral measure will be deemed to discriminate, albeit only in its effects, on the basis of the product's origin depending on (a) the relationship of the products or services at issue (whether identical, similar or competitive) *and* (b) the effect of the measure itself on domestic and imported products (whether discriminatory or protectionist).

Based on these two elements, one can distinguish at least two types of de facto discriminatory measures or, in other words, two types of origin-neutral measures that *materially* discriminate against imported products. First, a measure that treats identical products in exactly the same manner may be deemed to constitute de facto discrimination when it materially adversely affects imported products compared to identical domestic products (formally *identical* treatment of *identical* products with de facto discriminatory effects toward imported products (in WTO jurisprudence *Kodak–Fuji* or *Shrimp–Article 21.5* type of cases)). Secondly, a measure that treats differently two similar or competitive products may be deemed to constitute de facto discrimination when that differentiation materially adversely affects imported products compared to similar imported products (formally *different* treatment of *similar or competitive* products with de facto discriminatory effects toward imported products (in both

EC and WTO jurisprudence the several disputes involving taxes on alcoholic beverages).[2]

As in the case of the prohibition of de jure discrimination, once an ostensibly origin-neutral measure has been found to discriminate against imported products or to afford protection to domestic products, the regulating State may still claim the existence of a public policy justification in order to avoid a finding of violation of the National Treatment obligation. However, while the relationship between the non-discrimination obligation and the public policy justification is still one of "rule" to "exception", within the realm of de facto discrimination the dividing line between the "rule" and the "exception" becomes blurred. Neither the jurisprudence nor academic writings on the issue appear conclusive on whether the legitimate public policy purposes underlying an internal measure should be taken into account in determining the existence of discrimination contrary to the National Treatment obligation, or whether those same public policy purposes should function exclusively as grounds for justification once the measure has been found to violate this obligation.

As will be further developed in this chapter, it is suggested that there is at least a *physiological* reason for this uncertainty. The dividing line between establishing a prima facie case of de facto discrimination and providing for a public policy justification is not altogether clear because both determinations necessitate taking into consideration and evaluating practically the same features of the national measure under review. This explanation has to do with the concept of de facto discrimination and demonstrates that, with regard to both the findings of discrimination and the public policy justification, there is an important difference between the cases of de jure and de facto discrimination. If a de jure discriminatory tax or regulation by definition *intentionally* employs the product's origin as the differentiating criterion, a de facto discriminatory tax or regulation merely employs an origin-neutral criterion which nonetheless happens to have a discriminatory *effect* vis-à-vis imported products. In other words, contrary to the case of de jure discriminatory measures, within the realm of de facto discriminatory measures, discrimination is not *in* the law and thus must be determined on the basis of an analysis of the measure's features and effects. As will be explained in detail in this chapter, in the case of origin-neutral taxation or non-fiscal regulation, assessing whether the measure has a de facto

---

[2] There may even be a third type of de facto discrimination which is a combination of the first and second types described above. For example, a measure that treats similar or competitive products or services in exactly the same manner may be deemed to constitute de facto discrimination when it materially adversely affects imported products or services compared to similar or competitive domestic products or services (formally identical treatment of similar or competitive products with de facto discriminatory effects toward imported products).

protectionist effect benefiting domestic products vis-à-vis imported ones may involve some of the same issues which are at the basis of determining whether the same measure may be justified on public policy grounds.

This should be enough for the reader to start appreciating why I have chosen to describe the prohibition of de facto discrimination as the "second layer" of "judicial integration", and in particular the reason for distinguishing this category of instruments from the less problematic prohibition of formal discrimination ("first layer") and the more advanced principle of "reasonableness" ("third layer"). At issue is once again the different level of conflict between the objectives of trade liberalisation and national regulatory prerogatives characterising the several legal instruments employed in both EC and WTO law for the liberalisation and regulation of international trade.

As noted in the chapter on de jure discrimination, in both WTO and EC law there exist two sets of provisions requiring Members not to discriminate in law or in fact between domestic and imported products: one for fiscal charges and the other for all other non-fiscal regulations. Accordingly, this chapter will examine both sets in turn.

3.1   THE PROHIBITION OF DE FACTO DISCRIMINATION AND FISCAL CHARGES

Once again, in light of their almost identical design, the comparative analysis of the prohibition of de facto discrimination in WTO and EC law will begin with the respective provisions dealing with fiscal measures affecting trade in goods. Adopting a similar structure to that used in the previous chapter dealing with the prohibition of de jure discrimination, I will analyse (a) the legal standards employed in WTO and EC law in order to impose the prohibition of material discrimination ("normative content") and (b) the exceptions, which are provided for in both legal systems in order for Members to justify violations of the prohibition of material discrimination on public policy grounds ("justification options").

A.   Normative Content

1.   *Article III:2 GATT*

As examined above, the first sentence of Article III:2 GATT provides that

> The products of the territory of any contracting party imported into the territory of any other contracting party shall not be subject, directly or

indirectly, to internal taxes or other internal charges of any kind in excess of those applied, directly or indirectly, to like domestic products.

The second sentence of Article III:2 GATT adds that

Moreover, no contracting party shall otherwise apply internal taxes or other internal charges to imported or domestic products in a manner contrary to the principles set forth in paragraph 1.

Paragraph 1 of Article III GATT, it should be reminded, states that "internal taxes and other internal charges [...] affecting the internal sale [...] of products [...] should not be applied to imported or domestic products so as to afford protection to domestic production".

Moreover, the Ad Note to Article III GATT which authoritatively interprets paragraph 2, states that,

A tax conforming to the requirements of the first sentence of that paragraph could be considered to be inconsistent with the provisions of the second sentence only in those cases where competition was involved between, on the one hand, the taxed product and, on the other hand, a directly competitive or substitutable product which was not similarly taxed.

The text of Article III:2 has been interpreted as containing two distinct obligations depending on the nature of the relationship between the products at issue. If the imported and domestic products at issue are *"like products"*, the National Treatment provision prohibits any tax applied to the imported products that is *"in excess of"* those applied to the like domestic products (Article III:2, first sentence). On the other hand, if the imported and domestic products at issue are only *"directly competitive or substitutable products"*, the National Treatment provision prohibits a fiscal measure imposed by a Member if (a) the directly competitive or substitutable imported and domestic products are *"not similarly taxed"*, and (b) the dissimilar taxation of the directly competitive or substitutable imported and domestic products is *"applied so as to afford protection to domestic production"* (Article III:2, second sentence).[3]

Following the theoretical structure outlined above, this section will examine these two distinct obligations on the basis of the two elements characterising the "normative content" of the prohibition of de facto discriminatory measure: (i) the relationship of the products at issue (ie whether the products are identical, similar or competitive) and (ii) the

---

[3] Appellate Body Report on *Japan—Taxes on Alcoholic Beverages (Japan–Alcohol II)*, WT/DS8/AB/R, WT/DS10/AB/R, WT/DS11/AB/R, circulated 4 Oct 1996, adopted 1 Nov 1996, at 18 and 25.

effects of the measure itself on domestic and imported products (ie whether the effects are discriminatory or protectionist).

(a) Relationship between products   In order to determine whether the first or second sentence of Article III:2 applies it is first of all necessary to establish whether the products at issue are "like" or "directly competitive or substitutable" products.

(i) Like products

In *Japan–Alcohol II*,[4] the first case dealing with Article III:2 after the establishment of the WTO, the fiscal measure at issue concerned the Japanese taxation system of alcoholic beverages, which according to the EC, Canada and the US discriminated between domestic and imported like and/or directly competitive and substitutable products. In particular, the tax on imported vodka, whisky, brandy, rum, gin, genever, and liqueurs was either "in excess of" the tax imposed on domestic shochu or "applied as to afford protection to" domestic shochu.

Confronted with the issue of "likeness" in the first sentence of Article III:2, and drawing inspiration from previous GATT panel and working party practice, the Panel noted that the term "like product" should be interpreted on a case-by-case basis,[5] and that different criteria had so far been used in order to establish likeness, such as the product's properties, nature and quality, and its end-uses; consumers' tastes and habits, which change from country to country; as well as the product's classification in tariff nomenclatures.[6] In the Panel's view, although "like products" need not be identical in all respects, the term should be construed narrowly in the case of Article III:2, first sentence, in particular because Article III:2 distinguishes between "like" and "directly competitive or substitutable" products, the latter obviously being a much larger

---

[4] *Japan—Taxes on Alcoholic Beverages (Japan–Alcohol II)*, WT/DS8, WT/DS10, WT/DS11, brought 29 June and 17 July 1995.

[5] Panel Report on *Japan–Alcohol II*, WT/DS8/R, WT/DS10/R and WT/DS11/R, circulated 11 July 1996, adopted 1 Nov 1996, para 6.21 citing, for example, the Working Party Report on *Border Tax Adjustments*, L/3464, adopted on 2 Dec 1970, BISD 18S/97, at 102, para 18 (hereinafter "the 1970 Working Party Report"); Panel Report on *United States—Taxes on Petroleum and Certain Imported Substances (Superfund)*, L/6175, adopted on 17 June 1987, BISD 34S/136, at 154–5, para 5.1.1; Panel Report on *Japan—Customs Duties, Taxes and Labelling Practices on Imported Wines and Alcoholic Beverages (Japan—Alcohol I)*, L/6216, adopted on 10 Nov 1987, 34S/83 at 113–5, para 5.5–5.7; and Panel Report on *United States—Measures Affecting Alcoholic and Malt Beverages (Malt Beverages)*, DS23/R, adopted on 19 June 1992, BISD 39S/206, at 276–7, paras 5.25–26.

[6] See the 1970 Working Party Report, above n 5, para 18, the Panel Report on *Japan–Alcohol I*, above n 5, para 5.6, the Panel Report on *Superfund*, above n 5, para 5.1.1, the Panel Report on *EEC—Measures on Animal Feed Proteins*, L/4599, adopted on 14 March 1978, BISD 25S/49, para 4.3.

category of products than the former.[7] Giving a narrow meaning to "like products", the Panel argued, is also justified by the inescapability of violation in case of taxation of foreign products in excess of that of like domestic products.[8]

The Panel also examined Japan's argument according to which, in determining whether two products that are taxed differently are nonetheless "like products" for the purposes of Article III:2, a panel should examine not only the similarity in physical characteristics and end-uses, consumer tastes and preferences, and tariff classifications for each product, but also whether the tax distinction in question was "applied … so as to afford protection to domestic production"; that is, whether the *aim* and *effect* of that distinction, considered as a whole, was to afford protection to domestic production (the so-called *"aims-and-effects test"*).[9] Noting the inconsistency with the wording of Article III:2, first sentence,[10] the difficulty for the complainants to establish the multiplicity of aims of a particular measure,[11] and the risk of making the general exception

---

[7] "The wording of Art III and of the Interpretative Note ad Art III make it clear that a distinction must be drawn between, on the one hand, like, and, on the other, directly competitive or substitutable products. Such an approach is in conformity with the principle of "effective treaty interpretation" as laid down in the "general rule of interpretation" of the Vienna Convention on the Law of Treaties. The Panel recalled in this respect the conclusions of the Appellate Body in its report on *United States—Standards for Reformulated and Conventional Gasoline* where it stated that "an interpreter is not free to adopt a reading that would result in reducing whole clauses or paragraphs of a treaty to redundancy or inutility". In the view of the Panel, like products should be viewed as a subset of directly competitive or substitutable products. The wording ("like products" as opposed to "directly competitive or substitutable products") confirmed this point, in the sense that all like products are, by definition, directly competitive or substitutable products, whereas all directly competitive or substitutable products are not necessarily like products." Panel Report *Japan–Alcohol II*, above n 5, para 6.22.

[8] The Panel Report on *Superfund*, above n 5, para 5.1.9, made it clear that no *de minimis* defence can be raised in cases of taxation of foreign products in excess of domestic like products. The Panel agreed with this statement.

[9] Although its conclusions differed, the United States had also suggested the application of the *aims-and-effects* doctrine. See generally R Hudec, "GATT/WTO Constraints on Domestic Regulation: Requiem for an 'Aims and Effects' Test", 32 *The International Lawyer* (1998) 623.

[10] Panel Report *Japan–Alcohol II*, above n 5, para 6.16, "The Panel recalled that the basis of the aim-and-effect test is found in the words 'so as to afford protection' contained in Art III:1. The Panel further recalled that Art III:2, first sentence, contains no reference to those words."

[11] *Ibid.*, "Moreover, the adoption of the aim-and-effect test would have important repercussions on the burden of proof imposed on the complainant. The Panel noted in this respect that the complainants, according to the aim-and-effect test, have the burden of showing not only the effect of a particular measure, which is in principle discernible, but also its aim, which sometimes can be indiscernible. The Panel also noted that very often there is a multiplicity of aims that are sought through enactment of legislation and it would be a difficult exercise to determine which aim or aims should be determinative for applying the aim-and-effect test."

provision of Article XX GATT redundant,[12] the Panel rejected the aim-and-effect test proposed by Japan and the United States.[13]

Recalling the conclusion of the 1987 Panel Report on *Japan–Alcohol I* and its independent consideration of the issue, the Panel concluded that only vodka and shochu were like products for purposes of the first sentence of Article III:2, since only vodka, apart from commonality of end-uses, shared with shochu most physical characteristics, the only difference being in the media used for filtration.[14]

The Appellate Body, emphasising with a poetic touch the complexity of the likeness concept,[15] confirmed almost entirely the approach, as well as the findings, of the Panel on the issue. This same approach has also been applied in subsequent cases.[16]

---

[12] *Ibid.*, para 6.17, "The Panel further noted that the list of exceptions contained in Art XX of GATT 1994 could become redundant or useless because the aim-and-effect test does not contain a definitive list of grounds justifying departure from the obligations that are otherwise incorporated in Art III. The purpose of Art XX is to provide a list of exceptions, subject to the conditions that they 'are not applied in a manner which would constitute a means of arbitrary or unjustifiable discrimination between countries where the same conditions prevail, or a disguised restriction of international trade', that could justify deviations from the obligations imposed under GATT. Consequently, in principle, a WTO Member could, for example, invoke protection of health in the context of invoking the aim-and-effect test. The Panel noted that if this were the case, then the standard of proof established in Art XX would effectively be circumvented."

[13] The *aims-and-effects* doctrine will be analysed in detail in this chapter in the section dealing with the "justification options".

[14] Panel Report on *Japan–Alcohol II*, above n 5, para 6.23, "Substantial noticeable differences in physical characteristics exist between the rest of the alcoholic beverages at dispute and shochu that would disqualify them from being regarded as like products. More specifically, the use of additives would disqualify liqueurs, gin and genever; the use of ingredients would disqualify rum; lastly, appearance (arising from manufacturing processes) would disqualify whisky and brandy."

[15] Appellate Body Report on *Japan–Alcohol II*, above n 3, at 21–22, "The concept of 'likeness' is a relative one that evokes the image of an accordion. The accordion of 'likeness' stretches and squeezes in different places as different provisions of the WTO Agreement are applied. The width of the accordion in any one of those places must be determined by the particular provision in which the term 'like' is encountered as well as by the context and the circumstances that prevail in any given case to which that provision may apply. We believe that, in Art III:2, first sentence of the GATT 1994, the accordion of 'likeness' is meant to be narrowly squeezed."

[16] See Panel Report on *Korea—Taxes on Alcoholic Beverages* (*Korea–Alcohol*), WT/DS75/R and WT/DS84/R, circulated 17 Sep 1998, adopted 17 Feb 1999, paras 10.103–104, where the insufficiency of evidence in the record did not enable the Panel to establish that the products at issue were like. Such a finding was, however, not necessary since the Panel had already found those same products to be "directly competitive and substitutable". See also Panel Report on *Canada—Certain Measures Concerning Periodicals* (*Canada–Periodicals*), WT/DS31/R, WT/DS31/R, circulated 14 March 1997, adopted 30 July 1997, para 5.22–27, where the Panel found that imported "split-run" periodicals and domestic non "split-run" periodicals were like products. On appeal, the Appellate Body, having noted that the Panel had correctly enunciated, in theory, the legal test for determining 'like products' in the context of Art III:2, first sentence, as established in the Appellate Body Report on *Japan–Alcohol II*, reversed the Panel's finding on the issue of likeness for lack of proper legal reasoning based on inadequate factual analysis. Appellate Body Report on *Canada–Periodicals*, WT/DS31/AB/R, circulated 30 June 1997, adopted 30 July 1997, at 20–22.

(ii) Directly competitive or substitutable products

In *Japan–Alcohol II*, the Panel, having determined that only vodka and shochu were like products, examined next whether the other imported products (whisky, brandy, rum, gin, genever, and liqueurs) and shochu were at least directly competitive or substitutable products pursuant to Article III:2, second sentence.

Emphasising that the term "directly competitive or substitutable product", in accordance with its ordinary meaning, should be interpreted more broadly than the term "like product", the Panel noted that the same wording of the former did not suggest at all that physical resemblance is required in order to establish whether two products fall under this category. In the Panel's view, this impression was further supported by the use of the words "where competition exists" in the Interpretative Note; competition can and does exist among products that do not necessarily share the same physical characteristics. Thus, the Panel concluded, in order to determine whether two products are directly competitive or substitutable, the decisive criterion is whether they have common end-uses, inter alia, as shown by elasticity of substitution.[17] The Panel then added,

> In this context, factors like marketing strategies could also prove to be relevant criteria, since what is at issue is the responsiveness of consumers to the various products offered in the market. Such responsiveness, the Panel recalled, may vary from country to country, but should not be influenced or determined by internal taxation.[18] The Panel noted the conclusions in the 1987 Panel Report, that a tax system that discriminates against imports has the consequence of creating and even freezing preferences for domestic goods. In the Panel's view, this meant that consumer surveys in a country with such a tax system would likely understate the degree of potential competitiveness between substitutable products.[19]

The Panel reached the conclusion that the imported and domestic products at issue were indeed directly competitive and substitutable products on the basis of three elements. First, the 1987 Panel Report on *Japan—Alcohol I* had reached the same conclusion based essentially on the substitutability of the products in dispute as a result of "their respective prices, their availability

---

[17] Panel Report on *Japan–Alcohol II*, above n 5, para 6.22.

[18] [original footnote] "In this respect, note para 5.7 of the 1987 Panel Report 'since consumer habits are variable in time and space and the aim of Art III:2 of ensuring neutrality of internal taxation as regard to competition between imported and domestic like products *could not be achieved if differential taxes could be used to crystallize consumer preferences* for traditional domestic products, the Panel found that the traditional Japanese consumer habits with regard to shochu provided no reason for not considering vodka to be a like product' (emphasis added)." *Ibid.*, para 6.28.

[19] *Ibid.*

through trade and their other competitive inter-relationships".[20] Secondly, the ASI study submitted by the complainants had concluded that there was a high degree of price-elasticity between shochu, on the one hand, and five brown spirits (Scotch whisky, Japanese whisky, Japanese brandy, cognac, North American whisky) and three white spirits (gin, vodka and rum), on the other.[21] Thirdly, the evidence submitted by complainants concerning the 1989 Japanese tax reform which showed that whisky and shochu were essentially competing for the same market.[22]

The Appellate Body endorsed the analysis and conclusion of the Panel with regard to the competitive relationship of the products at issue, although it took time to underline that the examination of the "market place" as well as the "elasticity of substitution" are only two "among a number of means of identifying the broader category of products that might be described as 'directly competitive or substitutable'."[23]

Notwithstanding the more cautious approach suggested by the Appellate Body in *Japan–Alcohol II*, subsequent analyses of the "competitive relationship" issue have clearly focused on market characteristics. This is evident in the *Canada–Periodicals* case,[24] where the Appellate Body concluded that imported split-run periodicals and domestic non-split-run periodicals were directly competitive or substitutable products "in so far as they are part of the same segment of the Canadian market for periodicals",[25] as well as in *Korea–Alcohol*.[26]

In this latter case, the issue of whether domestic soju was directly competitive or substitutable to other imported distilled spirits such as whisky, brandy, vodka, rum, gin, afforded both the Panel and the Appellate Body a further chance to clarify the relevant approach. Stressing that the "key question" arising under Article III:2, second sentence, was "whether the products are *directly* competitive or substitutable,"[27] the Panel stated that

---

[20] See Panel Report on *Japan–Alcohol I*, above n 5, para 5.7.

[21] Panel Report on *Japan–Alcohol II*, above n 5, paras 4.171 *et seq.* of the Descriptive Part.

[22] *Ibid.*, para 6.30.

[23] Appellate Body Report on *Japan–Alcohol II*, above n 3, at 26.

[24] *Canada—Certain Measures Concerning Periodicals* (*Canada–Periodicals*), WT/DS31, brought 14 March 1996.

[25] Appellate Body Report on *Canada–Periodicals*, WT/DS31/AB/R, circulated 30 June 1997, adopted 30 July 1997, at 23–28. The Appellate Body had to analyse *ab initio* the issue of the competitive relationship between imported split-run and domestic non-split-run periodicals, since the Panel had erred in finding that those products were like for purposes of Art III:2, first sentence. The Appellate Body relied mainly on Canada's admission that the Canadian and foreign periodicals in question were directly competitive at least with regard to their advertising. See R Hudec, "The Product-Process Doctrine in GATT/WTO Jurisprudence", in M Bronckers and R Quick (eds), *New Directions in International Economic Law* (London, Kluwer Law International, 2000) at 215.

[26] Panel Report on *Korea–Alcohol*, above n 16.

[27] *Ibid.*, para 10.39 [emphasis original].

an assessment of whether there is a direct competitive relationship between two products or groups of products requires evidence that consumers consider or could consider the two products or groups of products as alternative ways of satisfying a particular need or taste.[28]

Accordingly, in the Panel's view, the focus should not exclusively be on the *quantitative* extent of the competitive overlap, but on the *methodological basis* on which a panel should assess the competitive relationship.[29] In other words, in analysing whether products are "directly competitive or substitutable", the emphasis should rest on the *nature* of competition and not on its *quantity*.[30] Moreover, the Panel clearly stated that its analysis of the products' relationship included both *actual* and *potential* competition. Noting that assessment of competition has a temporal dimension,[31] the Panel considered that

> panels should look at evidence of trends and changes in consumption patterns and make an assessment as to whether such trends and patterns lead to the conclusion that the products in question are either directly competitive now or can reasonably be expected to become directly competitive in the near future.[32]

This interpretation accords with the settled law that Article III protects competitive expectations not of any particular trade volume but rather of the equal competitive relationship between imported and domestic products.[33]

Following a detailed and thorough analysis of the physical characteristics, end-uses (including evidence of advertising activities), channels of distribution, and price relationships including cross-price elasticities, of the products at issue, the Panel found that there was sufficient unrebutted evidence to show both "*present* direct competition" and "a *strong potentially* direct competitive relationship" between these products, and thus concluded that the imported and domestic products were directly

---

[28] *Ibid.*, para 10.40.
[29] *Ibid.*, para 10.39. "[Q]uantitative analyses, while helpful, should not be considered necessary" and "quantitative studies of cross-price elasticity are relevant, but not exclusive or even decisive in nature." *Ibid.*, respectively para 10.42 and para 10.44.
[30] *Ibid.*, para 10.44, "… the question is not of the degree of competitive overlap, but its *nature*. *Is there a competitive relationship and is it direct?* …" [emphasis added]. See Appellate Body Report on *Korea–Alcohol*, WT/DS75/AB/R and WT/DS84/AB/R, circulated 18 Jan 1999, adopted 17 Feb 1999, para 133. In this latter report the Appellate Body also emphasised that "a determination of the precise extent of the competitive overlap can be complicated by the fact that protectionist government policies can distort the competitive relationship between products, causing the quantitative extent of the competitive relationship to be understated." *Ibid.*, para 109.
[31] Panel Report on *Korea–Alcohol*, above n 16, para 10.47.
[32] *Ibid.*, para 10.48.
[33] *Ibid.*, citing Appellate Body Report on *Japan–Alcohol II*, above n 5, at 16.

competitive or substitutable for purposes of Article III:2, second sentence.[34] The Appellate Body not only confirmed *in toto* the Panel's findings with regard to the competitive relationship between the products at issue, but, more importantly, fully endorsed the Panel's general approach.[35]

The breath of the scope of the term "directly competitive or substitutable" is evidenced in particular in two points raised by the Panel in its analysis of the products' end-uses, a particularly relevant factor for the issue of *potential* competition or substitutability. First, the Panel believed that it should not be required to draw "fine distinctions" in end-uses, for instance, by permitting significant differences in the application of the law based upon whether one beverage is used in the context of snacks or of other meals, as was suggested by the Korean Government.[36] Secondly, citing a similar approach developed in EC law,[37] the Panel rejected Korea's argument that it should use the same "strict" criteria for defining markets under Article III:2 as under competition law. Noting that, while antitrust law generally focuses on firms' practices or structural modifications which may prevent or restrain or eliminate competition,

---

[34] *Ibid.*, para 10.98.

[35] Appellate Body Report on *Korea–Alcohol*, above n 30, paras 108–45. "In view of the objectives of avoiding protectionism, requiring equality of competitive conditions and protecting expectations of equal competitive relationships, we decline to take a static view of the term 'directly competitive or substitutable.' The object and purpose of Art III confirms that the scope of the term 'directly competitive or substitutable' cannot be limited to situations where consumers *already* regard products as alternatives. If reliance could be placed only on current instances of substitution, the object and purpose of Art III:2 could be defeated by the protective taxation that the provision aims to prohibit." *Ibid.*, para 120. In Panel Report on *Chile—Taxes on Alcoholic Beverages* (*Chile–Alcohol*), WT/DS87/R and WT/DS110/R, circulated 15 June 1999, adopted 12 Jan 2000, para 7.88, the Panel followed almost verbatim the approach in *Korea–Alcohol* and found the products at issue "directly competitive and substitutable". It is noteworthy that in its appeal before the Appellate Body, Chile did not raise again the issue of the competitive relationship between the products.

[36] Panel Report on *Chile–Alcohol*, above n 35, para 10.76. The Panel recalled the examples of substitutable products offered by the drafters of Art III:2 and the Note Ad, which included "apples" and "oranges". See GATT, *Analytical Index: Guide to GATT Law and Practice*, 6th Edition (1994) at 145.

[37] Panel Report on *Chile–Alcohol*, above n 35, para 10.81, "For instance, under Art 95 of the Treaty of Rome, which is based on the language of Art III, distilled alcoholic beverages have been considered similar or competitive in a series of rulings by the European Court of Justice ('ECJ'). On the other hand, in examining a merger under the European Merger Regulation, the Commission of the European Communities found that whisky constituted a separate market. Similarly, in an Art 95 case, bananas were considered in competition with other fruits. However, under EC competition law, bananas constituted a distinct product market. We are mindful that the Treaty of Rome is different in scope and purpose from the General Agreement, the similarity of Art 95 and Art III, notwithstanding. Nonetheless, we observe that there is relevance in examining how the ECJ has defined markets in similr situations to assist in understanding the relationship between the analysis of non-discrimination provisions and competition law." [original footnotes omitted].

trade law addresses the issue of the potential for competition, the Panel stated that

> it is not illogical that markets be defined more broadly when implementing laws primarily designed to protect competitive opportunities than when implementing laws designed to protect the actual mechanisms of competition.[38]

(b) The Effects of the Measure   Depending on the nature of the relationship between the imported and domestic products at issue, the legal test to be met by the origin-neutral fiscal measure in order to conform with the National Treatment obligation of Article III:2 differs in the following manner. If the imported and domestic products are *"like products"*, the first sentence of Article III:2 prohibits any tax applied to imported products that is *"in excess of"* those applied to like domestic products. On the other hand, if the imported and domestic products are *"directly competitive or substitutable products"*, the second sentence of Article III:2, as authoritatively interpreted by the corresponding Note Ad Article III, prohibits a fiscal measure imposed by a Member if (a) the directly competitive or substitutable imported and domestic products are *"not similarly taxed"*, and (b) the dissimilar taxation of the directly competitive or substitutable imported and domestic products is *"applied so as to afford protection to domestic production"*.[39] Let us examine these three terms in turn.

(i) In excess of

Both GATT panel practice and WTO jurisprudence have consistently interpreted the benchmark in Article III:2, first sentence, in a very strict manner. As examined in the section dealing with the prohibition of de jure discriminatory fiscal measures, the prohibition of discriminatory taxes in Article III:2, first sentence, is not conditional on a "trade effects test" nor is it qualified by a *de minimis* standard.[40] In other words, as stated by the Panel in *Japan–Alcohol II*, "the phrase 'not in excess of those applied ... to like domestic products' should be interpreted to mean at least identical or better tax treatment."[41]

Arguments advanced in order to affirm that the term "in excess of" should be interpreted in a broader manner will be examined in the

---

[38] *Ibid.*
[39] Appellate Body Report on *Japan–Alcohol II*, above n 3, at 20 and 27.
[40] *Ibid.*, at 26, citing the following reports: *Malt Beverages*, above n 5, para 5.6; *Brazilian Internal Taxes*, GATT/CP.3/42, adopted on 30 June 1949, II/181, para 16; *Superfund*, above n 5, para 5.1.9; *Japan–Alcohol I*, above n 5, para 5.8.
[41] Panel Report on *Japan–Alcohol II*, above n 5, para 6.24.

section dealing with the term *"applied so as to afford protection to domestic production"*.

(ii) Not similarly taxed

In *Japan–Alcohol II*, the Appellate Body noted that in order to give due meaning to the distinctions in the wording of Article III:2, first sentence, and Article III:2, second sentence, the phrase "not similarly taxed" in the Note Ad Article III must not be construed so as to mean the same thing as the phrase "in excess of" in the first sentence. It thus agreed with the Panel that dissimilarity in taxation must be more than *de minimis*. In other words, there may be an amount *of excess taxation* that may well be more of a burden on imported products than on domestic "directly competitive or substitutable products" but may nevertheless not be enough to justify a conclusion that such products are "not similarly taxed" for the purposes of Article III:2, second sentence. Thus, to be "not similarly taxed", the tax burden on imported products must be heavier than on "directly competitive or substitutable" domestic products, and that burden must be more than *de minimis* in any given case.[42]

(iii) So as to afford protection to domestic production: the current approach

While the two previous terms have been interpreted without much controversy, the phrase contained in the first paragraph of Article III has raised quite a few concerns. Postponing the examination of the ill-fated *aim-and-effect* doctrine to the section dealing with the public policy "exception",[43] I propose to begin the analysis of the relevant term with the Appellate Body Report on *Japan–Alcohol II*, which constitutes the current legal standard with regard to Article III:2 violations. Once the current approach has been outlined, I will then advance two propositions for taking this approach two steps further in order for the two obligations in Article III:2 to conform fully with the nature and function of the National Treatment principle.

---

[42] Appellate Body Report on *Japan–Alcohol II*, above n 3, at 29–30.

[43] In a few cases at the beginning of the 1990s (Panel Report on *Malt Beverages*, above n 5 and Panel Report on *United States–Taxes on Automobiles*, DS31/R, unadopted, reprinted in 33 ILM 1397), panels considered that the "like product" determination under Art III:2 and 4 should have had regard to the *purpose* of Art III, which is, as enunciated in the first paragraph thereof, to ensure that internal taxation and regulation "should not be applied to imported or domestic products so as to afford protection to domestic production." Accordingly, in determining whether two products subject to different treatment are "like products" for purposes of Arts III:2 and 4, it would be necessary to consider whether such *product differentiation* is being made "so as to afford protection to domestic production". In practice, this test required panels to perform an examination of the *aim* and *effect* of the particular national internal measure at issue. In the section examining the "likeness" issue, it has already been mentioned that the so called "aim-and-effect" doctrine was eventually rejected with force by the Panel, and implicitly by the Appellate Body in the *Japan–Alcohol II* case. See *below* section on "Justification Options" for de facto discriminatory fiscal measures.

In *Japan–Alcohol II*, the Appellate Body stated that the general principle articulated in Article III:1—that internal measures should not be applied so as to afford protection to domestic production—informs the rest of Article III and constitutes

> a guide to understanding and interpreting the specific obligations contained in Article III:2 and in the other paragraphs of Article III, while respecting, and not diminishing in any way, the meaning of the words actually used in the texts of those other paragraphs.[44]

Accordingly, in light of the textual differences in the two sentences of Article III:2, the Appellate Body held that Article III:1 informs the first sentence and the second sentence of Article III:2 *in different ways.*[45]

With regard to Article III:2, first sentence, the Appellate Body was of the view that the absence of a specific invocation in this sentence of the general principle in Article III:1 requiring Members of the WTO not to apply measures "so as to afford protection" simply meant that the presence of a *protective application* need not be established independently of the specific requirements that are included in the first sentence in order to show that a tax measure is inconsistent with the general principle set out in that first sentence.[46] Recognising that the first sentence of Article III:2 is, in effect, an application of this general principle, the Appellate Body concluded that if the imported and domestic products are "like products", and if the taxes applied to the imported products are "in excess of" those applied to the like domestic products, then the measure is inconsistent with Article III:2, first sentence.[47]

With regard to the second sentence of Article III:2, the Appellate Body noted that this time the sentence specifically invokes Article III:1, and considered that here the general principle of Article III:1 operates expressly as a separate issue that must be addressed along with two other issues that are raised in applying the second sentence. Thus, next to the determination of whether the imported and domestic products are "directly competitive or substitutable" and whether these products are "not similarly taxed", a violation of the National Treatment obligation will be found

---

[44] Appellate Body Report on *Japan–Alcohol II*, above n 3, at 18.
[45] *Ibid.*, at 19.
[46] *Ibid.*, at 19–20, "Art III:1 informs Art III:2, first sentence, by establishing that if imported products are taxed in excess of like domestic products, then that tax measure is inconsistent with Art III. Art III:2, first sentence does not refer specifically to Art III:1. There is no specific invocation in this first sentence of the general principle in Art III:1 that admonishes Members of the WTO not to apply measures "so as to afford protection". This omission must have some meaning. We believe the meaning is simply that the presence of a protective application need not be established separately from the specific requirements that are included in the first sentence in order to show that a tax measure is inconsistent with the general principle set out in the first sentence."
[47] *Ibid.*

only if the dissimilar taxation of the directly competitive or substitutable imported domestic products is "applied... so as to afford protection to domestic production".[48]

According to the Appellate Body, the Panel applied correct legal reasoning in determining whether "directly competitive or substitutable" imported and domestic products were "not similarly taxed", but erred in blurring the distinction between that issue and the entirely separate issue of whether the tax measure in question was applied "so as to afford protection". The Appellate Body stated,

> [...] these are separate issues that must be addressed individually. If "directly competitive or substitutable products" are *not* "not similarly taxed", then there is neither need nor justification under Article III:2, second sentence, for inquiring further as to whether the tax has been applied "so as to afford protection". But if such products are "not similarly taxed", a further inquiry must necessarily be made.[49]

In putting forward the appropriate analysis under Article III:2, second sentence, the Appellate Body stated, on the one hand, that determining whether "directly competitive or substitutable products" are "not similarly taxed" *in a way that affords protection* is not an issue of *intent*. Thus, it is not necessary to sort through the many reasons legislators and regulators often have for what they do and weigh the relative significance of those reasons to establish legislative or regulatory intent.[50] As a matter of fact, in the Appellate Body's view, it is irrelevant whether protectionism was an intended objective of the particular fiscal measure at issue, if that same measure is nevertheless "applied to imported or domestic products so as to afford protection to domestic production".[51]

On the other hand, the Appellate Body considered that this determination is an issue of how the measure in question is *applied*, which thus requires a "comprehensive and objective analysis of the structure and application of the measure in question on domestic as compared to imported products."[52] While the aim of a measure may not be easily

---

[48] *Ibid.*, at 27.
[49] *Ibid.*, at 30.
[50] *Ibid.*
[51] *Ibid.* As clearly emphasised by Howse and Tuerk, the irrelevance of protectionist "intent" does not exclude consideration of evidence such as legislative history and ministerial statements, that apparently go to protectionist intent, since "an inquiry into the structure and design of the scheme may well be decisive with respect to whether it is protective, obviating the need for making sensitive judgements about intent, but this does not mean that in other cases evidence of intentional protection may well be relevant." Howse and Tuerk, "The WTO Impact on Internal Regulations—A Case Study of the Canada–EC Asbestos Dispute" in G de Búrca and J Scott (eds), *The EU and the WTO: Legal and Constitutional Aspects* (Oxford, Hart, 2001) at 299 n 56.
[52] Appellate Body Report on *Japan–Alcohol II*, above n 3, at 32.

ascertained, the Appellate Body was of the view that the measure's protective application can most often be discerned from "the design, the architecture, and the revealing structure of a measure."[53]

Next to these general statements, the Appellate Body specified that, while the very magnitude of the dissimilar taxation in a particular case may be evidence of such a protective application, most often there will be other factors to be considered as well. Thus, panels should give full consideration to all the relevant facts and all the relevant circumstances in any given case.[54] Emphasising the findings of the 1987 Panel Report on *Japan–Alcohol I*, according to which the application of considerably lower internal taxes by Japan on shochu than on other directly competitive or substitutable distilled liquors had trade-distorting effects affording protection to domestic production of shochu contrary to Article III:1 and 2, second sentence,[55] the Appellate Body concluded that the Japanese Liquor Tax Law was not in compliance with Article III:2. Although the Panel had blurred its legal reasoning in addressing clearly and separately the three elements of the second sentence of Article III:2, the Appellate Body agreed with the Panel that,

> through a combination of high import duties and differentiated internal taxes, Japan manages to "isolate" domestically produced shochu from foreign competition, be it foreign produced shochu or any other of the mentioned white and brown spirits.[56]

(iv) Taking the current approach two steps further

It is suggested here that the approach developed in *Japan–Alcohol II* must be taken two steps further in order for it to fully conform with the National Treatment principle. Thus, I would propose that

(1) the "protective application" of a fiscal measure as required by the principles set forth in Article III:1 is deemed to exist only in so far as the measure *predominantly favours* domestic products, and

---

[53] *Ibid.*

[54] *Ibid.*

[55] *Ibid.*, at 30–31, citing *Japan–Alcohol I*, above n 5, para 5.11. The factors examined by the 1987 Panel Report on *Japan–Alcohol I* to detect whether the taxation was protective included "the considerably lower specific tax rates on shochu than on imported directly competitive or substitutable products; the imposition of high *ad valorem* taxes on imported alcoholic beverages and the absence of *ad valorem* taxes on shochu; the fact that shochu was almost exclusively produced in Japan and that the lower taxation of shochu did "afford protection to domestic production"; and the mutual substitutability of these distilled liquors." *Ibid.*

[56] Appellate Body Report on *Japan–Alcohol II*, above n 3, at 35, citing the Panel Report on *Japan–Alcohol II*, above n 5, para 6.35.

(2) the difference in the role of the "principles" set forth in Article III:1 resides simply in the different structure of the burden of proof for purposes of establishing a violation of the first and second sentences of Article III:2.

These two prepositions, which will be in turn examined, are not at all revolutionary,[57] since they fully accord with the letter and objective of Article III and find partial confirmation in both GATT panel practice and WTO jurisprudence.

It is unanimously and correctly believed that the broad and fundamental purpose of Article III is to avoid "protectionism" in the application of internal tax and regulatory measures, and more specifically, as evidenced in the first paragraph of this Article, to ensure that internal measures must "not be applied to imported or domestic products so as to afford protection to domestic production". The emphasis on the "origin" or "nationality" of the products clearly shows that the aim of the National Treatment principle in Article III is to provide equality of competitive conditions for *imported* and *domestic* products, or, in other words, to prohibit discriminatory measures, both in law and in fact, on the basis of the "origin" or "nationality" of these product.

The two obligations found in Article III:2, respectively in the first and second sentence thereof, should be viewed (much as the obligation in Article III:4) as mere instruments for achieving this general purpose.

As examined in the previous section, the case of a de jure discriminatory measure is generally unproblematic since it is the measure itself that distinguishes between two "identical" products on the basis of origin or nationality, thus presumptively breaching the National Treatment principle of treating *imported* products less favourably than like domestic products.[58] In the case of de facto discrimination, on the other hand, the measure at issue is, at least formally, origin-neutral, so for a violation of the National Treatment obligation to be found, it is indispensable to establish that the measure *in its effects* discriminates in favour of *domestic* products. This is true whether the products are "identical", "similar" or only "competitive". As explained in the introductory section to this chapter,

---

[57] Cf W Davey and J Pauwelyn, "MFN Unconditionality: A Legal Analysis of the Concept in View of its Evolution in the GATT/WTO Jurisprudence with Particular Reference to the Issue of 'Like Product'", in T Cottier and P Mavroidis (eds), *Regulatory Barriers and the Principle of Non-Discrimination in World Trade Law* (Ann Arbor, The University of Michigan Press, 1999) at 38, who raise the question of whether there should be a discriminatory effects test applied in examination of claims under Art I and III. *See* also O Fauchald, *Environmental Taxes and Trade Discrimination* (London, Kluwer Law International 1998) at 220–21. More recently, L Ehring, "De facto Discrimination in WTO Law: National and Most-Favored-National Treatment—or Equal Treatment?", *Jean Monnet Working Paper* (NYU, 2002).
[58] The defendant may argue in its defence that the differentiation was justified in order to provide substantial equality.

a measure that taxes *identical* products in exactly the same manner may still have de facto discriminatory effects towards imported products. Likewise, a measure that taxes differently two *similar* or *competitive* products may be deemed to constitute de facto discrimination if that differentiation materially adversely affects imported products compared to similar imported products.

Accordingly, while the relationship between the products (whether identical, similar or competitive) and the difference in the tax burden (whether *de minimis* or more than *de minimis*) operate as the necessary prerequisites for performing the relevant "comparison", the central element for a finding of violation of the National Treatment obligation is the *material discrimination between imported and domestic products*. It is suggested here that such discrimination exists only in so far as the facially origin-neutral fiscal measure favours predominantly *domestic* products. In practical terms, the higher tax must be imposed in the majority of cases on imported products. Clearly, in this regard, evidence that a specific national measure *disfavours predominantly imported* products may be submitted in order to prove the so called "protective application" requirement (ie the higher tax is imposed in the majority of cases on imported products). This is my first proposition.

Although never clearly expressed by either GATT panel practice or WTO jurisprudence, this has been in practice the constant underlying element in determining whether a tax is "applied [...] so as to afford protection".

In the 1987 Panel Report on *Japan–Alcohol I*,[59] in addition to finding that (1) distilled liquors (whisky, brandy, gin, vodka) were directly competitive with shochu (the relationship between the products) and (2) shochu was not subject to *ad valorem* taxes and the specific tax rates on shochu were many times lower than the specific tax rates on whiskies, brandies and other spirits (difference in the tax burden), the Panel found that (3) shochu was *almost exclusively produced in Japan* and the lower taxation of shochu did "afford protection to domestic production" (protective application). In the Panel's view, these elements constituted sufficient evidence of fiscal distortions of the competitive relationship between imported distilled liquors and domestic shochu affording protection to the domestic production of shochu.[60]

It should be noted that Japan had argued in its defence that in line with its drafting history as well as with the case law of the EC Court of Justice

---

[59] Panel Report on *Japan–Alcohol I*, L/6216, adopted on 10 Nov 1987, 34S/83.
[60] *Ibid.*, para 5.11, "The Panel found that the following factors were sufficient evidence of fiscal distortions of the competitive relationship between imported distilled liquors and domestic shochu affording protection to the domestic production of shochu:

— the considerably lower specific tax rates on shochu than on imported whiskies, brandies and other spirits (see Annex III);
— the imposition of high *ad valorem* taxes on imported whiskies, brandies and other spirits and the absence of *ad valorem* taxes on shochu;

relating to Article 95 (now 90) of the EC Treaty,[61] a correct interpretation of Article III GATT would not require a Contracting Party to apply the same internal tax rate to all like products, if imported and almost identical domestic products were equally taxed and there was *substantial domestic production* of these almost identical products. Nor did Article III:2, second sentence, prohibit any favourable taxation on any domestic product which might be directly competitive with or substitutable for an imported product, if equal taxation was actually assured between the imported product and the like domestic product which was domestically produced in *substantial* quantities.[62] In other words, Japan argued that, since there was "substantial *domestic* production" of like products for all the EC products in question, there was no inconsistency with Article III:2, second sentence.[63]

However, emphasising the fact that the lower tax on shochu did "afford protection to domestic production", the Panel implicitly rejected Japan's argument that the mere existence of domestic products in the higher taxed category was enough to rebut a prima facie case of protective application. The fact that an essentially Japanese product[64] was taxed more favourably than any of the competitive imported products was by itself enough to

— the fact that shochu was almost exclusively produced in Japan and that the lower taxation of shochu did "afford protection to domestic production" (Art III:1) rather than to the production of a product produced in many countries (say, butter) in relation to another product (say, oleomargarine, as in the example referred to by Japan in para 3.11 above);
— the mutual substitutability of these distilled liquors, as illustrated by the increasing imports into Japan of 'Western-style' distilled liquors and by the consumer use of shochu blended in various proportions with whisky, brandy or other drinks."

[61] *Ibid.*, para 3.11, "Among the series of decisions given by the EC Court of Justice on distilled liquor taxes in 1980 in circumstances where distilled liquor taxes imposed by France, Italy and Denmark were lower on their domestic distilled liquor (brandy, grappa, acquavite, respectively) and were higher on imported distilled liquor (whisky, rum, etc), the following findings of the Court deserved attention in the view of Japan:

'the legitimacy of certain differentiations concerning the taxation of alcohol was only recognised for the purpose of enabling the maintenance of productions or enterprises which otherwise would no longer be profitable, owing to the increase of the cost of production; on the other hand, such tax exemption or tax reduction in favour of certain products are valid only if these measures do not hide a discrimination due to the origin of the products taxed or if they do not have a protective character [...] the Italian fiscal system is characterized by the fact that the most typical of the national products are in the most favoured fiscal category, while two sorts of products which are nearly entirely imported from other member states are more heavily taxed [...] This means that this practice in reality hides a discrimination against imported products'."

[62] *Ibid.*, para 3.11.
[63] *Ibid.*, "91 per cent of the whiskies consumed in Japan was domestically produced, and of the special grade whiskies, 83 per cent of that consumed in Japan was produced in Japan. Of the spirits which included vodka, gin, rum, etc. under the Japanese Liquor Tax Law, 94 per cent was produced in Japan."
[64] The EC had argued that *imported* shochu represented 0.4% of domestic production: *Ibid.*, para 3.5.

satisfy the protective application test, and thus establish a prima facie case of de facto discrimination between imported and domestic products.

In the sequel to the 1987 dispute, the Panel, in addressing the issue of protective application, took note of the statement by Japan that the 1987 Panel Report had erred when it concluded that shochu was essentially a Japanese product, since a shochu-like product is produced in various countries outside Japan, including the Republic of Korea, the People's Republic of China and Singapore. Although the Panel accepted the evidence submitted by Japan as true, it nonetheless rejected Japan's defence. In the Panel's view, what was at stake in determining whether the Japanese tax system afforded protection to domestic production was the market share of the shochu market in Japan that was occupied by Japanese-made shochu; the high import duties on foreign-produced shochu resulted in a significant share of the Japanese shochu market held by Japanese shochu producers.[65] It is thus clear that the Panel found the Japanese tax system in violation of the National Treatment obligation on the basis that the more favourable tax treatment accorded to shochu was *in fact* reserved *predominantly* to a *domestic* product.

As evidenced in subsequent cases, the "comprehensive and objective analysis of the structure and application of the measure" employed in order to determine the *protective application* of the national fiscal measure at issue for purposes of Article III:2, second sentence, clearly revolves around an inquiry of whether that measure affords protection to *domestic* products *in practice*.

In *Canada–Periodicals*, the Appellate Body noted that there was ample evidence that the very design and structure of the measure imposing dissimilar taxation between imported split-run periodicals and domestic non-split-run periodicals was to prevent the establishment of the former in Canada, thereby ensuring that Canadian advertising revenues flow to Canadian magazines.[66]

---

[65] Panel Report on *Japan–Alcohol II*, above n 5, para 6.35, "[…] the combination of customs duties and internal taxation in Japan has the following impact: on the one hand, it makes it difficult for foreign-produced shochu to penetrate the Japanese market and, on the other, it does not guarantee equality of competitive conditions between shochu and the rest of 'white' and 'brown' spirits. Thus, through a combination of high import duties and differentiated internal taxes, Japan manages to 'isolate' domestically produced shochu from foreign competition, be it foreign produced shochu or any other of the mentioned white and brown spirits." The Appellate Body agreed with this finding of the Panel, see Appellate Body Report on *Japan–Alcohol II*, above n 3, at 35.

[66] Appellate Body Report on *Canada–Periodicals*, above n 25, at 30–32, "We therefore conclude on the basis of the above reasons, including the magnitude of the differential taxation, the several statements of the Government of Canada's explicit policy objectives in introducing the measure and the demonstrated actual protective effect of the measure, that the design and structure of Part V1 of the Excise Tax Act is clearly to afford protection to the production of Canadian periodicals." Moreover, the Appellate Body's emphasis on comparing foreign split-run with domestic non-split-run seems to indicate that the Appellate Body was concerned with the protectionist effect of the tax measure (the example analysed by the

In *Korea–Alcohol*, the Appellate Body confirmed the Panel's conclusion that the Korean tax system on alcoholic beverages applied so as to afford protection to domestic production, noting, next to the very large differences in levels of taxation between competitive products, that the tax operated in such a way that the lower tax brackets covered almost exclusively domestic production (soju), whereas the higher tax brackets embraced almost exclusively imported products ("Western-style" alcoholic beverages like whiskies, brandies, cognac, rum, gin, tequila, and liqueurs). Quoting the Panel, the Appellate Body noted that this was evidenced by the fact that "in practice, '[t]here is virtually no imported soju so the beneficiaries of this structure are almost exclusively domestic producers'."[67]

The relevance of an inquiry on the *beneficiaries* of the tax system was emphasised in the last of the alcoholic beverage tax cases (*Chile–Alcohol*), where the Panel clarified the content of the "protective application" test for purposes of Article III:2, second sentence, in the following manner,

> In our view, an important question is who receives the benefit of the dissimilar taxation. This is implicit in the reference of the Appellate Body and previous panels to the magnitude of the tax differentials. For example, the magnitude of the differentials would not be particularly relevant if the products realizing the resulting benefits were imports. Furthermore, the Appellate Body's review of the results of the application of dissimilar taxation in the marketplace in *Canada–Periodicals* shows that the Appellate Body

Panel, which was rejected by the AB, presented in fact the case of a comparison between a domestic split-run and a domestic non-split-run). Cf R Hudec, "The Product-Process Doctrine in GATT/WTO Jurisprudence", in M Bronckers and R Quick (eds), *New Directions in International Economic Law* (London, Kluwer Law International, 2000). For a somewhat different view, see L Ehring, "De facto Discrimination in WTO Law: National Treatment and Most-Favoured-Nation Treatment—or Equal Treatment?", *Jean Monnet Working Paper* (NYU School of Law, 2002) at 17.

[67] Appellate Body Report on *Korea–Alcohol*, above n 30, para 150, citing Panel Report on *Korea–Alcohol*, above n 16, para 10.102 and noting "that we considered a similar finding by the panel in *Japan–Alcoholic Beverages*, at 31, to be relevant for the establishment of the third element of Art III:2, second sentence." Para 10.102 of the Panel Report on *Korea–Alcohol* reads in its entirety as follows: "In addition to the very large levels of tax differentials, we also note that the structures of the Liquor Tax Law and the Education Tax Law are consistent with this finding. The structure of the Liquor Tax Law itself is discriminatory. It is based on a very broad generic definition which is defined as soju and then there are specific exceptions corresponding very closely to one or more characteristics of imported beverages that are used to identify products which receive higher tax rates. There is virtually no imported soju so the beneficiaries of this structure are almost exclusively domestic producers. Thus, in our view, the design, architecture and structure of the Korean alcoholic beverages tax laws (including the Education Tax as it is applied in a differential manner to imported and domestic products) afford protection to domestic production." In a footnote to this paragraph, the Panel noted that "the only domestic product which falls into a higher category that corresponds to one type of imported beverage is distilled soju which represents less than one percent of Korean production."

was reviewing *who* had benefited from the tax rate differentials. This is only logical given the language of Article III itself.[68]

The tax system at issue in that case imposed taxes on all alcoholic beverages with an alcohol content of 35 degrees or below on a linear basis, at a fixed rate of 27 per cent *ad valorem*. Thereafter, the rate of taxation increased steeply, by four percentage points for every additional degree of alcohol content, until a maximum rate of 47 per cent *ad valorem* was reached. This fixed tax rate of 47 per cent applied, once more on a linear basis, to all beverages with an alcohol content in excess of 39 degrees, irrespective of how much in excess of 39 degrees the alcohol content of the beverage was. In the Panel's view, the "most persuasive evidence" that this system afforded protection to domestic production rested on the finding that,

> roughly 75% of domestic production will enjoy the lowest tax rate and that over 95% of current (and potential) imports will be taxed at the highest rate unless the imported products change their alcohol content and abandon their generic, familiar product names.[69]

After an examination of the design, architecture and structure of the "anomalous" Chilean tax system for alcoholic beverages,[70] the Appellate Body reached the conclusion that, as the Panel had found, the application of dissimilar taxation of directly competitive or substitutable products afforded protection to domestic production. The Appellate Body noted as follows:

> in practice, therefore, the New Chilean System will operate largely as if there were only two tax brackets: the first applying a rate of 27 per cent *ad valorem* which ends at the point at which most domestic beverages, by volume, are found, and the second applying a rate of 47 per cent *ad valorem* which begins at the point at which most imports, by volume, are found.[71]

---

[68] Panel Report on *Chile–Alcohol*, above n 35, para 7.123.
[69] *Ibid.*, para 7.158.
[70] Appellate Body Report on *Chile–Alcohol*, WT/DS87/AB/R and WT/DS110/AB/R, circulated 13 Dec 1999, adopted 12 Jan 2000, paras 63–65. In addition to the Panel's findings with regard the structure of the Chilean system, the Appellate Body also noted the following: "Moreover, according to figures supplied to the Panel by Chile, approximately *half* of all domestic production has an alcohol content of 35° and is, therefore, located on the line of the progression of the tax at the point *immediately before* the steep increase in tax rates from 27 per cent *ad valorem*. The start of the highest tax bracket, with a rate of 47 per cent *ad valorem*, coincides with the point at which most imported beverages are found." *Ibid.*, para 64.
[71] *Ibid.*, para 66. The Appellate Body also added that "the magnitude of the difference between these two rates is also considerable". *Ibid.*

Like the Panel,[72] the Appellate Body rejected Chile's argument that the tax system could not be found to be applied in a manner so as to afford protection to domestic production since there actually were more domestic products at the highest level of taxation than imports. The Appellate Body confirmed the approach taken by the GATT Panel in the 1987 *Japan–Alcohol I* case, and stated that the existence of domestic products taxed at the highest level did not by itself outweigh the fact that most of the domestic production was taxed at the lowest level while almost the totality of imported products are placed in highest tax-bracket.[73]

It should be noted that the Appellate Body Report on *Chile–Alcohol* quite clearly suggested that the *purposes* of the measure, as objectively manifested in the design, architecture and structure of the measure itself, are "intensely pertinent" to the task of evaluating whether or not that measure is applied so as to afford protection to domestic production.[74] The Appellate Body noted that Chile's explanations concerning the structure of its tax system of alcoholic beverages, in particular the truncated nature of the line of progression of tax rates, might have been helpful in understanding what prima facie appeared to be anomalies in the progression of tax rates. The Appellate Body concluded that, in the absence of countervailing explanations by Chile, the finding of protective application reached by the Panel "becomes very difficult to resist".[75] The possible implications of these statements will be analysed in more details in the section dealing with the public policy justification.

In conclusion, in light of the text and general purpose of Article III, as well as the relevant GATT panel practice and WTO jurisprudence, a national fiscal measure will be deemed to afford protection to domestic production as required by the principles set forth in Article III:1 only in so far as the complainant Member is able to establish that it predominantly favours domestic products. The Appellate Body's emphasis on the objective features of the measure under review, its design, architecture and structure, shows a willingness to base a finding of de facto discrimination (on the basis of the product's nationality) on the *objective features* of the measure, thus limiting as much as possible the risks involved in applying a pure effects-based analysis. It follows that, while the principal aim of the protective application calculation appears to be the determination of the protectionist *effect* of the measure under review (in line with the wording of Article III:1 GATT), this calculation must principally be focused on the protectionist (as well as the discriminatory) *features* of that same measure.

---

[72] Panel Report on *Chile–Alcohol*, above n 35, para 7.158.
[73] Appellate Body Report on *Chile–Alcohol*, above n 70, para 67.
[74] *Ibid.*, para 71.
[75] *Ibid.*

Thus, the "appropriate proportion" between *favoured* domestic products and *disfavoured* imported products will have to be determined on a case-by-case basis giving full consideration to all the relevant facts and all the relevant circumstances,[76] focusing in particular on the design, architecture and structure of the measure in question. Accordingly, the "magnitude" of dissimilar taxation between imported and domestic competitive products should play a relevant role, albeit complementary to a finding of protectionist effect. The greater the difference in the tax burden, the less the difference there will need to be in the proportion between favoured domestic products and disfavoured imported products in order to establish that the fiscal measure has a protective application.[77]

It should not be too difficult at this point to accept the second preposition that is here advanced. For purposes of establishing a violation of Article III:2, first and second sentences, I would argue that the difference in the role of the principle of "protective application" simply reflects a different structure of the burden of proof. Whereas to establish that a measure dissimilarly taxing directly competitive or substitutable products violates Article III:2, second sentence, the complainant needs to prove that the tax is applied "so as to afford protection to domestic production", a tax imposed on imported products in excess of that applied to like domestic products is *presumed* to violate Article III:2, first sentence, unless the defendant Member is able to establish that the measure at issue does not afford protection to its domestic production. In other words, the burden of proving the existence of the measure's "protective application" is on the complaining Member when the products at issue are "directly competitive or substitutable" and rests on the defending Member in the event that the products are "like".[78]

This interpretation would accord with the established notions that (a) the general principle in Article III:1 constitutes a guide to understanding and interpreting *both* obligations contained in Article III:2 and (b) the same general principle, in light of the textual differences in the two sentences of Article III:2, informs the first sentence and the second sentence

---

[76] Appellate Body Report on *Japan–Alcohol II*, above n 3, at 30.

[77] For an interesting analysis of the "geographical distribution of discriminatory effects" see O Fauchald, *Environmental Taxes and Trade Discrimination* (London, Kluwer Law International 1998) at 225–34. Cf L Ehring, "*De facto* Discrimination in WTO Law: National Treatment and Most-Favoured-Nation Treatment—or Equal Treatment?", *Jean Monnet Working Paper* (NYU School of Law, 2002) at 36–38.

[78] Cf O Fauchald, *Environmental Taxes and Trade Discrimination* (London, Kluwer Law International 1998) at 220–21, where the author raises the related "essential question [...] whether the contested tax arrangement violates the first sentence of Art III:2 once *one* imported product is subject to taxes 'in excess' of those applied to *any* like domestic product, or whether the arrangement only violates the provision when the relevant imported products are *as a whole* subject to taxes 'in excess' of those applied to like domestic products" [emphasis original]. *Ibid.*, at 220.

of Article III:2 *in different ways.*[79] Excluding Article III:2, first sentence, from the reach of the non-discrimination principle underlying the GATT National Treatment obligation would in practice and without justification extend such obligation beyond non-discrimination, prohibiting Members from taxing similar products differently.[80]

The difference in the burden of proof with regard to a measure's protective application would also accord with the distinction between the concept of "likeness" characterising the first sentence of Article III:2 and the concept of "direct competition and substitution", employed in the second sentence of Article III:2. The stronger relationship between two "like" products justifies a presumption, albeit rebuttable, that a tax distinction may in fact discriminate against imported products. This seems to be confirmed by a recent tendency in WTO jurisprudence to favour a narrow interpretation of the term "like product" in Article III:2, first sentence, thus clearly distinguishing like products from competitive products.

I am indeed aware that there are a few cases in which GATT Panels have openly disregarded the need to determine whether an origin-neutral tax discriminated between domestic and imported products. In the Panel Report on *United States—Measures Affecting Alcoholic and Malt Beverages*, Canada had argued that Minnesota's tax advantage for small beer producers violated the National Treatment obligation of Article III:2, first sentence, since imported beer from large producers was *like* beer from small domestic producers and that the former was taxed *in excess* of the latter. Although the Panel was not altogether clear whether the Minnesota's tax advantage was indeed available to foreign small beer producers (ie whether the measure at issue was origin-neutral or origin-based), it

---

[79] Appellate Body Report on *Japan–Alcohol II*, above n 3, at 19. The Appellate Body's reasoning in *Japan–Alcohol II* in fact appears contradictory. While the Appellate Body states that the omission in Art III:2, first sentence, of a reference to the general principle of Art III:1 simply means "that the presence of a protective application need not be established separately from the specific requirements that are included in the first sentence in order to show that a tax measure is inconsistent with the general principle set out in the first sentence", on the other hand, it seems to recognise a more positive role to such general principle with regard the first sentence of Art III by emphasising that "the general principle of Art III:1 does […] apply to this sentence."

[80] Cf W Davey and J Pauwelyn, "MFN Unconditionality: A Legal Analysis of the Concept in View of its Evolution in the GATT/WTO Jurisprudence with Particular Reference to the Issue of 'Like Product'", in T Cottier and P Mavroidis (eds), *Regulatory Barriers and the Principle of Non-Discrimination in World Trade Law* (Ann Arbor, The University of Michigan Press, 1999) at 38–39 and accompanying endnotes, where the authors advance the further proposition that a discriminatory effect requirement should be introduced into Art III:2, first sentence, at least for those cases where there is no de jure discrimination. The authors base their argument on the wording of both Art III:2, first sentence, which refers to *imported* and *domestic* products, and Art III:2, second sentence, where the words "moreover" and "otherwise" "make a clear link between, on the one hand, both the first and second sentence of Art III:2 and, on the other hand, Art III:1." While I fully endorse the arguments advanced by Davey and Pauwelyn as clear evidence that the general principle of Art III:1 "applies" to both obligations in Art III:2, I prefer to limit such application in the manner advanced in this section.

considered that, even if Minnesota were to grant the tax credits on a non-discriminatory basis to small breweries inside and outside the United States, there would still be an inconsistency with Article III:2, first sentence. The two reasons for such a findings were that (a) beer produced by large breweries is not unlike beer produced by small breweries and (b) imported beer from large breweries would be "subject ... to internal taxes ... in excess of those applied ... to like domestic products" from small breweries.[81] In other words, the Panel found the origin-neutral tax in violation of the National Treatment obligation without expressly considering the fiscal measure's protectionist impact.[82]

However, further confirmation that the "protectionist impact" related to origin constitutes the premise of the obligation of Article III:2, first sentence, may be found in the evidence that is analysed by some GATT/WTO tribunals in the course of determining whether there is a violation of this obligation, as well as in the language employed by these bodies in making such a determination.

In the 1987 Panel Report on *Japan–Alcohol I*, the Panel concluded that several of the Japanese internal taxes on whiskies, brandies, still wines, sparkling wines, spirits and liqueurs imported from the EC were in excess of those applied to like Japanese products contrary to Article III:2, first sentence, on the basis either explicitly or implicitly that, while the majority of imported products fell in the disadvantaged category, the majority of domestic products were placed in the advantaged category. For example, with regard to the difference in the tax rate between whiskies/brandies *special grade* and whiskies/brandies *first and second grade*, the Panel found that as a result of this differential taxation of "like products", *almost all* whiskies/brandies imported from the EC were subject to the higher rates of tax whereas *more than half of* whiskies/brandies produced in Japan benefited from considerably lower rates of tax.[83]

---

[81] Panel Report on *Malt Beverages*, above n 5, para 5.19.

[82] For a plausible reading of 'protectionist impact' in the *Malt Beverages* findings, see L Ehring, "*De facto* Discrimination in WTO Law: National Treatment and Most-Favoured-Nation Treatment—or Equal Treatment?", *Jean Monnet Working Paper* (NYU School of Law, 2002) at 17. In the *Malt Beverages* report, there was another instance of origin-neutral tax which Canada had claimed constituted a violation of Art III:2, first sentence. This was the case of the Mississippi lower tax rate on wines in which a certain variety of grape was used, which was *applicable to all qualifying wine* produced from the specified variety of grape, *regardless of the point of origin*. Panel Report on *Malt Beverages*, above n 5, para 5.23. However, contrary to the case of the Minnesota's tax credit, the Panel determined the GATT inconsistency of the Mississippi lower tax on wine on the basis of the *aims-and-effects* test. See below section on "Justification options".

[83] Panel Report on *Japan–Alcohol I*, above n 5, para 5.9(a), "The Panel concluded, therefore, that (special and first grade) whiskies/brandies imported from the EEC were subject to internal Japanese taxes 'in excess of those applied [...] to like domestic products' (i.e. first and second grade whiskies/brandies) in the sense of Art III:2, first sentence." With regard to the

Interestingly, while examining the legality of the Japanese tax system with Article III:2, first sentence, the Panel emphasised that the underlying purpose of the National Treatment obligation was not to prescribe any particular method or system of taxation but rather to prohibit discrimination on the basis of origin. The Panel stated that:

> [...] Article III:2 does not prescribe the use of any specific method or system of taxation. [...] there could be objective reasons proper to the tax in question which could justify or necessitate differences in the system of taxation for imported and for domestic products. The Panel found that it could also be compatible with Article III:2 to allow two different methods of calculation of price for tax purposes. Since Article III:2 prohibited only discriminatory or protective tax burdens on imported products, what mattered was, in the view of the Panel, whether the application of the different taxation methods *actually* had a *discriminatory or protective effect* against *imported* products.[84] [emphasis added]

This statement is especially relevant in light of the fact that in that particular circumstance the Panel was reviewing a de jure discriminatory measure, according to which Japan applied formally different methods to calculate the price for tax purposes in relation to imported and domestic products.[85]

Even more relevant is the quotation by the Appellate Body of this same paragraph from the earlier report when later enunciating in *Japan–Alcohol II* the proper approach with regard to Article III:2, *second sentence*.[86] Was the Appellate Body aware that the earlier panel was dealing in that instance with Article III:2, *first sentence*, and, for that matter, with a case of de jure discrimination? Did the Appellate Body

---

difference in taxation according to extract content, the Panel noted the EC argument that this type of taxation discriminated against imports contrary to Art III:2 because it ensured that *almost all Community liqueurs* were subject to the higher rate of specific tax whilst *some Japanese liqueurs are able to benefit from a lower specific rate* (one third of the rate on most Community liqueurs). *Ibid.* para 5.9(d).

[84] *Ibid.*, para 5.9(c).
[85] *Ibid.* The EC had argued that there existed different methods of calculating *ad valorem* tax for imported and domestic products. In the case of imports, the tax base was usually the CIF cost plus duty. Importers had no choice as to the method of calculation. For domestic products, there were two methods of which producers could choose the most favourable: the manufacturer's selling price to wholesalers, excluding tax, or the retail price less trade margins less tax (the so-called "fixed subtraction ratio system"). Although the latter method was officially described as a "special case", applicable when the retail price was known, in practice it was almost always used. This allowed domestic producers to choose effective tax values for domestic products which could lead to the application of more advantageous rates for domestic products when different *ad valorem* tax rates were provided as was the case for special grade brandy and whisky. See *ibid.*, para 3.2(d).
[86] Appellate Body Report on *Japan–Alcohol II*, above n 3, at 33.

extend its approval of the panel's reasoning with regard to both sentences of Article III:2?[87]

In conclusion, the relevance of taking the current approach two steps further as suggested in this section would have the following beneficial effects. With regard to the obligation in Article III:2, second sentence, it would serve to clarify what current Panels and the Appellate Body are already doing. With regard to the obligation in Article III:2, first sentence, it would avoid findings such as that concerning the Minnesota's tax credits, where the tax differentiated between the characteristics not of the *product* but rather of the *producer* (ie when identical or like products are treated differently on the basis of the producer's characteristics without any relevant protectionist/discriminatory impact on grounds of nationality or origin). Moreover, following the strict interpretation of the concept of "like products" in recent WTO jurisprudence, it would appear that tax distinctions based on the characteristics of products will generally be reviewed within the framework of the second sentence, where the "protective application" requirement is already a reality, while the first sentence will be mainly employed as a prohibition of de jure discriminatory measures.

2. *Article 90 EC*

It is now time to turn to the "normative content" of EC rules dealing with the non-discrimination obligation and internal taxation. As noted above, the EC provision dealing with fiscal measures follows a dual structure virtually identical to that in Article III GATT. While the first paragraph of Article 90 (ex 95) EC reads that no Member State shall impose, directly or indirectly on the products of other Member States, any internal taxation of any kind in excess of that imposed

---

[87] It should be noted that in *Japan–Alcohol II*, the Panel's approach was also not altogether linear on this point. Examining whether vodka was taxed "in excess of" the tax imposed on shochu under the Japanese Liquor Tax Law, the Panel initially noted that Art III:2 does not contain any presumption in favour of a specific mode of taxation, and that "[u]nder Art III:2, first sentence, WTO Members are free to choose any system of taxation they deem appropriate provided that they do not impose on foreign products taxes in excess of those imposed on like domestic products." Having next asserted that the Japanese taxes on vodka were higher than those imposed on shochu, thus 'in excess' for purposes of Art III:2, first sentence, the Panel went on to address the argument put forward by Japan that its legislation, by keeping the tax/price ratio "roughly constant", was indeed trade neutral and consequently no protective aim and effect of the legislation could be detected. Although the Panel rejected this further argument because the existence or non-existence of a protective aim and effect was *not relevant* in an analysis under Art III:2, first sentence, it nonetheless clarified that "even if it were to be a comparison of tax/price ratios of products could offset the fact that vodka was taxed significantly more heavily than shochu on a volume and alcoholic content basis, there were significant problems with the methodology for calculating tax/price ratios submitted by Japan, such that arguments based on that methodology could only be viewed as inconclusive." Panel Report on *Japan–Alcohol II*, above n 5, paras 6.24–25.

directly or indirectly on similar domestic products, the second paragraph states that,

> [f]urthermore, no Member State shall impose on the products of other Member States any internal taxation of such a nature as to afford indirect protection to other products.

Accordingly, the text of Article 90 has been interpreted as containing two obligations. While the first paragraph of Article 90 covers taxation imposed on domestic products and on imported products which may be classified as *similar*, the second paragraph of Article 90 deals with taxation of products which, without being similar within the meaning of the first paragraph, are nevertheless in *competition*, even partially, indirectly or potentially, with certain products of the importing country.[88] Moreover, while the criterion indicated in the first paragraph of Article 90 focuses on the *comparison of tax burdens*, whether in terms of the rate, the mode of assessment or other detailed rules for the application thereof, the second paragraph of that Article is based upon a more general criterion, which turns on the *protective nature* of the system of internal taxation.[89]

Once again, pursuant to the theoretical structure outlined above, this section will examine the two obligations in terms of a distinction between the two elements which characterise the prohibition of de facto discriminatory measure: (i) the relationship of the products at issue (ie whether the products are identical, similar or competitive) and (ii) the effects of the measure itself on domestic and imported products (ie whether the effects are discriminatory or protectionist).

(a) Relationship between products   In order to determine whether it is the first or second paragraph of Article 90 that applies, it is first of all necessary to establish whether the products at issue are "similar" or "competitive" products.

(i) Similar products

While in one of the first cases where the ECJ was asked for a ruling on the interpretation of the concept of "similar domestic products" in Article 90(1), the Court focused exclusively on whether the products concerned were normally (for tax, tariff or statistical purposes) placed in the same

---

[88] Case 168/78, *Commission v France (Tax Arrangements Applicable to Spirits)* [1980] ECR 347, para 5–6.
[89] *Ibid.*, para 7. Cf L Daniele, *Il diritto materiale della Comunità Europea* (Milano, Giuffré, 2000) at 42–43; P Craig and G de Búrca, *EU Law* (Oxford, OUP, 1998) at 566; PJ Kuyper, "Booze and Fast Cars: Tax Discrimination under GATT and EC", *Legal Issues of European Integration* (1996) at 139–40; D Wyatt and A Dashwood, *The Substantive Law of the EEC* (London, Sweet & Maxwell, 1980) at 90.

classification,[90] the subsequent and constant jurisprudence takes principally into account whether "products, at the same stage of production or marketing, have similar characteristics and meet the same needs from the point of view of consumers."[91] The Court has thus endorsed a broad interpretation of the concept of similarity, not limiting its assessment to whether the products at issue are strictly identical.[92]

As clearly stated in *John Walker & Sons Ltd v Ministeriet for Skatter og Afgifter*,[93] the Court has examined the issue of similarity according to the following two-prong analysis:

> In order to determine whether products are similar for purposes of Article 90(1) it is necessary *first* to consider certain objective characteristics of both categories of beverages, such as their origin, the method of manufacture and their organoleptic properties, in particular taste and alcohol content, and *secondly* to consider whether or not both categories of beverages are capable of meeting the same needs from the point of view of consumers.[94] [emphasis added]

From the Court's actual examination of the similarity issue in that case, it is possible to perceive the greater weight put by the Court on the products' objective characteristics (first prong) compared to the products' capability of meeting the same consumer's needs (second prong). Having found that the two categories of beverages at issue (fruit wine of the liqueur type and Scotch Whisky) exhibited manifestly different characteristics, in view of their different origins (fruit v cereal), methods of production (natural fermentation v distillation), and organoleptic properties,[95] the Court rejected the contention that Scotch Whisky might be consumed in the same way as fruit wine of the liqueur type, for example as an aperitif diluted with water or with fruit juice (ie same consumer's use or need). A similar use, even if it were established, would not be "sufficient

---

[90] Case 27/67, *Firma Fink-Frucht GmbH v Hauptzollamt München-Landsbergstrasse* [1968] ECR 223, at 232.

[91] Case 45/75, *Rewe-Zentrale des Lebensmittel-Grosshandels v Hauptzollamt Landau/Pfalz* [1976] ECR 181, para 12. The Court added that "[t]he fact that the domestic product and the imported product are or are not classified under the same heading in the common customs tariff constitutes an important factor in this assessment." *Ibid.*

[92] Case 168/78, *Commission v France (Tax Arrangements Applicable to Spirits)* [1980] ECR 347 and Case 216/81, *Cogis v Amministrazione delle Finanze dello Stato* [1982] ECR 2701.

[93] Case 243/84, *John Walker* [1986] ECR 875.

[94] *Ibid.*, para 11.

[95] *Ibid.*, para 12, "The fact that the same raw material, for example alcohol, is to be found in the two products is not sufficient reason to apply the prohibition contained in the first paragraph of Art 95. For the products to be regarded as similar that raw material must also be present in more or less equal proportions in both products. In that regard, it must be pointed out that the alcoholic strength of scotch whisky is 40% by volume, whereas the alcoholic strength of fruit wine of the liqueur type, to which the Danish tax legislation applies, does not exceed 20% by volume."

to render the scotch whisky similar to fruit wine of the liqueur type, whose intrinsic characteristics are fundamentally different."[96] The Court thus found that the two products at issue could not be regarded as similar products.[97]

The particular relationship between the "characteristics" and "uses" of a product for purposes of determining the "similarity" issue is emphasised in *Commission v Denmark (Wine)*,[98] where the Court based its assessment of whether wine made from grapes and wine made from other fruit (taxed differently under Danish law) met the same needs essentially on the basis of those products' objective characteristics. Having determined that grape wine and wine made from other fruit (of the table-wine type) share similar objective characteristics,[99] the Court stated that,

> [...] in view of their similar characteristics the two categories of beverages can meet the same needs from the point of view of consumers inasmuch as they can be consumed in the same way, namely to quench thirst, as refreshments and at meal times. [...] The question whether they meet the same needs must be assessed on the basis not of existing consumer habits but of the prospective development of those habits and, essentially, on the basis of objective characteristics which ensure that a product is capable of meeting the same needs as another product from the point of view of certain categories of consumers.[100]

Accordingly, in order to determine whether two products are similar for the purposes of Article 90(1), it is essential for the complainant to establish that the products at issue share certain objective characteristics. The product's capability of meeting the same consumer's needs, as well as the consumer's perception of the product's characteristics and uses, though possibly relevant in tilting the scale one way or another in grey-area cases, appears usually to be employed as an additional element confirming whatever finding has been reached on the basis of the product's objective characteristics.[101] The emphasis on the objective characteristics rather than on the capability of meeting the same consumer's needs conforms clearly with the existence, in the second paragraph of Article 90, of the

---

[96] *Ibid.*, para 13.
[97] *Ibid.*, para 14.
[98] Case 106/84, *Wine* [1986] ECR 833.
[99] *Ibid.*, para 14.
[100] *Ibid.*, para 15.
[101] See Case 184/85, *Commission v Italy (Bananas)* [1987] ECR 2013, para 10, where the ECJ held that the two categories of fruit in question (bananas and table fruit typically produced in Italy) were not similar within the meaning of the first paragraph of Art 90, having, first of all, determined that these two products had different organoleptic characteristics and water content (the higher water content of pears and other fruit typically grown in Italy gave them thirst-quenching properties which bananas did not possess), and having accepted, moreover, the observation advanced by the Italian Government that "banana is regarded, at least on the Italian market, as a foodstuff which is particularly nutritious, of a high energy content and well-suited for infants." Although avoiding the issue of similarity,

additional type of relationship between the products, which, as will be next examined, focuses on the latter factor.[102]

(ii) Competitive products

Although not expressly provided for in the text of Article 90(2), the Court soon came to interpret the prohibition contained therein on any form of taxation "of such a nature as to afford indirect protection to other products" as including the case of,

> an internal tax imposing a heavier burden on an imported product than on a domestic product with which the imported product is, by reason of one or more economic uses to which it may be put, in competition, even though the condition of similarity for the purposes of the first paragraph of Article 90 is not fulfilled.[103]

It should be noted that the Court's interpretation with regard the relationship between the relevant products to be employed in Article 90(2) stems directly from the content and purpose of that Article. In order for a tax to "afford protection" to a domestic product vis-à-vis a product of any other Member States (which is not similar to the domestic product), it is indispensable that the domestic and imported products be in some sort of competitive relationship. The lack of this relationship would clearly make a finding of "indirect protection", if not impossible, highly improbable.

The competitive relationship between products has also been interpreted broadly as covering the case where competition is only *partial, indirect or potential*.[104] In this regard the series of cases initiated by the Commission at the end of the 1970s against the taxes of several Member States on alcohol (the so-called "spirits cases") afford a fairly

Advocate-General Lenz noted nonetheless that "it is not possible to accept without reservation that bananas and other fruit are broadly comparable products. As the Italian Government has shown, they do not have exactly the same characteristics and do not fulfil the same needs; on the contrary, *some characteristics (flavour, water content) are markedly different.*" AG Opinion, para 12. Cf Case 277/83, *Commission v Italy (Marsala)* [1985] ECR 2049; Case 106/84, *Commission v Denmark (Wine)* [1986] ECR 833; Joined Cases C–367–377/93, *F G Roders et al. v Inspecteur der Invoerrechten en Accijnzen* [1995] ECR 2229; S Weatherill and P Beaumont, *EC Law* (London, Penguin Books, 1995) at 408; L Daniele, *Il diritto materiale della Comunità Europea* (Milano, Giuffré, 2000) at 42.

[102] Cf G Bermann, R Goebel, W Davey, E Fox, *Cases and Materials on European Community Law* (St. Paul, West Publishing, 1993) at 333, where the authors note that in certain cases like the *French Alcoholic Excise Tax* case the Court concentrated its analysis of "similar products" on the consumer's view, in other cases, like the *Danish Wine Tax* case, on the criterion of objective physical characteristics.

[103] Case 27/67, *Firma Fink-Frucht v Hauptzollamt München-Landsbergstrasse* [1968] ECR 223, at 232.

[104] Case 168/78, *Commission v France (Tax Arrangements Applicable to Spirits)* [1980] ECR 347, para 5–6.

good example of the Court's use of the concept of competitive products. In *Commission v United Kingdom I*,[105] for example, the Court, faced with the question of whether "beer" was in competition with "wine", emphasised the "dynamic" nature of the competitive relationship between the products at issue in the following terms:

> In order to determine the existence of a competitive relationship under the second paragraph of Article 95, it is necessary to consider not only the present state of the market but also the possibilities for development within the context of free movement of goods at the Community level and the further potential for the substitution of products for one another which may be revealed by intensification of trade, so as fully to develop the complementary features of the economies of the member states in accordance with the objectives laid down by Article 2 of the Treaty.[106]

Thus, the test of consumer substitutability must be analysed taking into consideration both present and future trends affecting the relevant market, since consumer resistance to a switch from one product to another (in the *Commission v UK* case, from beer to wine) may, in fact, be attributable to the higher price of wine, which is in turn the direct consequence of the different internal taxation on the two products.[107]

Emphasis on such factors as consumer substitutability or cross-elasticity of demand does not mean that the objective characteristics of the products at issue become completely irrelevant for purposes of Article 90, second paragraph. On the contrary, the existence of certain basic features common to the products under consideration constitutes one of the elements in the competitive relationship calculation.

In one of the "spirits cases", this time involving the French tax system differentiating inter alia between cognac and whisky, the Court's approach to the question of the relationship between the products seems to confirm this point.[108] In its analysis of the relationship between certain alcoholic beverages, the Court takes into account the following three "lines of thought". First of all, it is impossible to disregard the fact that all the products in question, whatever their specific characteristics in other respects, have *common generic features*; and thus it follows that, within the largest group of alcoholic beverages, spirits form an identifiable whole

---

[105] Case 170/78 [1980] ECR 417. See also Case 170/78 *Commission v United Kingdom II* [1983] ECR 2265.

[106] Case 170/78 *Commission v United Kingdom I* [1980] ECR 417, para 6.

[107] See S Weatherill and P Beaumont, *EC Law* (London, Penguin Books, 1995) at 412, where the authors note how the steady rise in British wine consumption after the amendments to the UK tax system following the Court's decision "demonstrates the truth of the Court's implied assumption that a latent wine-buying public existed in the United Kingdom, suppressed only by unfair tax rates."

[108] Case 168/78, *Commission v France (Tax Arrangements Applicable to Spirits)* [1980] ECR 347.

united by common characteristics.[109] Secondly, in spite of those common characteristics, it is possible to *distinguish* within spirits products which have their own more or less pronounced characteristics, depending on either the raw materials used or the manufacturing process or even the flavouring added.[110] Thirdly, it is impossible to disregard the fact that there are, in the case of spirits, in addition to well-defined products which are put to relatively *specific uses*, other products with *less distinct characteristics* and *wider uses*.[111] From this analysis, the Court concludes as follows:

> First, there is, in the case of spirits considered as a whole, an indeterminate number of beverages which must be classified as "similar products" within the meaning of the first paragraph of Article 95, although it may be difficult to decide this in specific cases, in view of the nature of the factors implied by distinguishing criteria such as flavour and consumer habits. Secondly, even in cases in which it is impossible to recognize a sufficient degree of similarity between the products concerned, there are nevertheless, in the case of all spirits, common characteristics which are sufficiently pronounced to accept that in all cases there is at least partial or potential competition. It follows that the application of the second paragraph of Article 95 may come into consideration in cases in which the relationship of similarity between the specific varieties of spirits remains doubtful or contested.[112]

Leaving to the next section the discussion of the possible policy reasons for, and important consequence of, "globalising" Article 90(1) and (2),[113] the link between the product's characteristics and the product's uses should be emphasised here. The existence of certain basic features common to the products under consideration represents evidence of a commonality of usages of those same products and vice-versa.[114]

(b) The effects of the measure   Depending on the nature of the relationship between the imported and domestic products at issue, the wording of Article 90 provides for two different legal standards which must be met by any national fiscal measure conforming to the non-discrimination provisions of that Article. If the imported and domestic products are "similar

---

[109] *Ibid.*, para 11, "All are the outcome of the distillation procedure; all contain, as a principal characteristic ingredient, alcohol suitable for human consumption at a relatively high degree of concentration."

[110] *Ibid.*

[111] *Ibid.*

[112] *Ibid.*, para 12. The Court restated this approach at the end of its analysis of the application of the contested tax system, finding it unnecessary to give a ruling on the question whether or not the spirituous beverages concerned are wholly or partly similar products within the meaning of the first paragraph of Art 90. *Ibid.*, paras. 39–40.

[113] This is the expression which Easson has employed to refer to the Court's attitude in avoiding a determination of "similarity" pursuant to Art 90(1) by a finding of at least a "competitive relationship" between the products at issue. A Easson, "Fiscal Discrimination: New Perspectives on Art 95 of the EEC Treaty", 18 *CMLRev* (1981) 521 at 535.

[114] Cf Case 112/84, *Humblot v Directeur des Services Fiscaux* [1986] ECR 1367, para 15, "In the absence of considerations relating to the amount of the special tax, consumers seeking

products", the first paragraph of Article 90 prohibits any tax applied to the imported products that is *"in excess of"* those applied to the similar domestic products. On the other hand, if the imported and domestic products are "competitive products", the second paragraph of Article 90 prohibits a fiscal measure imposed by a Member if it is of such a nature *"as to afford protection to"* the domestic products. Thus, in light of the two different terms employed in Article 90, the Court has stated that while the criterion indicated in the first paragraph consists of the comparison of tax burdens,

> the second paragraph is based upon a more general criterion, in other words the protective nature of the system of internal taxation.[115]

Notwithstanding this apparently clear language and the often contrary view of legal commentators,[116] an examination of the case-law shows that the essential factor in determining a breach of either of the obligations enunciated in Article 90 focuses on the issue of whether the internal taxation in question has the effect of protecting *domestic* products.[117] In other words, a prima facie case of violation of the non-discrimination principle embodied in Article 90, first and second paragraphs, will not be established unless the complainant demonstrates the *protective nature* of the fiscal measure under review. Thus the difference between the obligations in the first and second paragraphs of Article 90 rests simply on the level or magnitude of the protectionist effect of the measure; while in the first instance the Court

---

comparable cars as regard to such matters as size, comfort, actual power, maintenance costs, durability, fuel consumption and price would naturally choose from among cars above and below the critical power rating laid down by French law." In Case 184/85, *Commission v Italy (Bananas)* [1987] ECR 2013, although the Court found that the two products at issue (bananas and table fruit typically produced in Italy) were in partial competition on the sole basis that bananas afforded an alternative choice to consumers of fruit (para 12), Advocate-General Lenz reached the same conclusion noting however that "it would be hard to deny—even a layman could confidently make this judgment—that if not all the characteristics of bananas and other fruit at least a number of them (which is sufficient according to the case-law) are the same or similar and accordingly those products are largely comparable as regard to their use, and in certain cases are substitutes for each other as far as the consumer is concerned." AG Opinion, para 17.

[115] Case 168/78, *Commission v France (Tax Arrangements Applicable to Spirits)* [1980] ECR 347, para 7.
[116] Cf L Daniele, *Il diritto materiale della Comunità Europea* (Milano, Giuffré, 2000) at 42–43; P Craig and G de Búrca, *EU Law* (Oxford, OUP, 1998) at 566; PJ Kuyper, "Booze and Fast Cars: Tax Discrimination under GATT and EC", *Legal Issues of European Integration* (1996) at 139–40; G Bermann, R Goebel, W Davey, E Fox, *Cases and Materials on European Community Law* (St. Paul, West Publishing, 1993) at 325; D Wyatt and A Dashwood, *The Substantive Law of the EEC* (London, Sweet and Maxwell, 1980) at 90. For a more 'illuminated' view see Easson, "Fiscal Discrimination: New Perspectives on Art 95 of the EEC Treaty", 18 *CMLRev* (1981) 521 at 540. Also for a more cautious approach see G Tesauro, *Diritto Comunitario* (Padova, Cedam, 1995) at 264; S Weatherill and P Beaumont, *EC Law* (London, Penguin Books, 1995) at 408–09.
[117] What Easson terms the 'National Dimension', Easson, "Fiscal Discrimination: New Perspectives on Art 95 of the EEC Treaty", 18 *CMLRev* (1981) 521 at 540.

does not allow for even the smallest protectionist effect, in the second instance there exists a *de minimis* level under which the measure is not deemed to afford protection to domestic products.

Before turning to the issue of the "protective nature" of internal taxation, it is necessary to examine, albeit briefly, the issue of the "differential treatment" of products within a system of internal taxation.

(i) Differential treatment

As evidenced expressly in the first and implicitly in the second paragraph of Article 90, in order to establish a violation of either of the two obligations contained in those two paragraphs, it is first necessary to establish whether or not the products at issue are taxed differently, or, more precisely, whether the tax burden on one product is higher than that on the other.[118]

For purposes of this comparison, as expressly provided in the text of Article 90, the Court will take into account taxes imposed both "directly and indirectly" on a *product*, thus including in the calculation those taxes that are only apparently imposed on the *producer* but, in reality, represent indirect taxes on the product. The relevant criterion for distinguishing between taxes *indirectly* imposed upon a *product* and those which are truly imposed on the *producer* focuses on the relationship between the tax burden and the product. Accordingly, for example, while charges such as those for licences, motor vehicle registration or advertising fall outside the scope of Article 90,[119] a transportation tax applied to a load of gravel or a privilege given to producers of alcohol to defer payment of the excise duty on spirits, beer and wine are caught by Article 90 since they can clearly be attributed to a particular product (gravel in the first case, and alcoholic beverages in the second).[120]

Focusing on the relationship between the tax burden and the product, it is evident that most process-standard taxes will be considered to be imposed either directly or indirectly upon a product for the purposes of this determination, depending on whether they are imposed on the final product or on the producer.

Moreover, as the Court has pointed out on several occasions, the relevant comparison of tax burdens will take into consideration not only the rate of taxation but also the various provisions concerning the basis of assessment and the detailed rules for levying taxes, the decisive

---

[118] It is implicit for purposes of the differential treatment that the two products at issue are in one of the relevant relationships as examined in the previous section.

[119] Case 45/64, *Commission v Italy* [1965] ECR 857.

[120] A Easson, "Fiscal Discrimination: New Perspectives on Art 95 of the EEC Treaty", 18 *CMLRev* (1981) 521 at 527, citing Case 20/76, *Schöttle* [1977] ECR 247 and Case 55/79, *Commission v Ireland* [1980] ECR 481. Although both cases were instances of de jure discrimination, they clearly show the scope of the comparison pursuant to Art 90.

comparative criterion for the application of Article 90 being the *actual impact* of each tax upon the products in question.[121]

Accordingly, taking into consideration both above-mentioned aspects of a national tax system, the Court will be able to determine whether two products are taxed differently, or in other words whether the tax burdens on these two products are not identical.[122] The simplest scenario is when the tax system in question imposes a different amount or percentage of taxation on two products. An example would be a value added tax (VAT) on wine of 25 per cent, where the VAT rate on beer is 19 per cent, the percentage being calculated in both cases on the basis of the same criterion, the *price* of the alcoholic beverage.[123] Another would be where liqueur wines in general are subject to a consumption duty of FF6,795 per hectolitre of pure alcohol, but natural sweet wines are taxed at a rate of FF2,545 per hectolitre of pure alcohol.[124]

It should be emphasised that at this stage of determining the differential treatment between two products, the issue of the relationship between the products has already been answered in the affirmative. In the above examples, wine and beer, like liqueur wines and natural sweet wines, have already been established to be either similar or competitive products, in the sense explained above. Thus, at this stage, the Court is simply trying to determine whether the tax burden on one product is higher than that on the other.

It is clear, however, that differential treatment in this context means more than simply "formal identical treatment" and includes more complex cases such as when the tax burden on two products is calculated according to two distinct criteria (to take a similar example to the VAT one, where a tax on wine is calculated on the basis of its alcohol content, while the tax on beer is calculated on the basis of its volume) or when the tax burden on two products, although calculated on the basis of the same taxing criterion, differs in practice (for example, because the alcohol content of wine is higher than that of beer).

The Court was confronted with this latter scenario in the (in)famous case of the UK system of taxing wine and beer.[125] In its examination of the

---

[121] See Case 55/79 *Commission v Ireland* [1980] ECR 481, para 8, where although the tax itself applied to all goods irrespective of origin, domestic producers were treated more leniently as regard to payment, being allowed more time before payment was actually demanded, whereas importers had to pay the duty directly on importation. P Craig and G de Búrca, *EU Law* (Oxford, OUP, 1998) at 561–62.

[122] For purposes of this analysis it is irrelevant if the differential treatment is simply "in excess of" pursuant to Art 90(1) or "of such a nature as to afford indirect protection to other products" ex Art 90(2).

[123] Case 356/85, *Commission v Belgium* [1987] ECR 3299.

[124] Case 196/85, *Commission v France* [1987] ECR 1597.

[125] Cf Case 170/78, *Commission v United Kingdom I* [1980] ECR 417 and Case 170/78, *Commission v United Kingdom II* [1983] 2265.

tax system at issue in that case, the Court was confronted with a puzzling fiscal relationship between wine and beer. If the relative tax burdens were measured in terms of volume, the ratio between wine and beer was approximately five to one; if measured according to alcoholic strength, 1.6 to 1, and if measured, as the UK Government suggested, as a proportion of the retail price in supermarkets or by reference to the manner in which the two drinks were customarily consumed (a glass of wine v a pint of beer), the tax ratio was virtually one to one. Following an extended legal battle, the Court reached the conclusion that whatever criterion for comparison was used in that case (there being no need to express a preference for one or the other), it was apparent that wine was subject both in absolute and relative terms to a considerably higher tax burden than beer.[126]

This case shows how a determination of the "differential treatment" issue, which constitutes a necessary step towards a finding of violation of the non-discrimination principle of Article 90, might involve at times a rather complex analysis of the tax system in question, especially when the tax burden on the products at issue is calculated on the basis of formally identical criteria. Moreover, no particular criterion may be taken as the a priori appropriate basis of taxation, and thus any claim with regard to the "objectivity" of the taxing criteria will have to sustain a thorough review by the Court.

(ii) Protective nature

Let us now examine the proposition that the essential factor in determining a breach of either of the obligations enunciated in Article 90 should focus on the issue of whether the internal taxation in question has the effect of protecting domestic products.

In *Commission v Italy (Marsala)*,[127] the Italian tax system of liqueur wines was at issue. Although the Italian legislation imposed a tax on the manufacture of domestically produced wine distilled from alcohol (so-called "liqueur wines") and a frontier surcharge of the same amount

---

[126] Case 170/78, *Commission v United Kingdom* [1983] 2265, para 26. With regard to the volume of the two beverages the Court noted that "during the years to which these proceedings relate, namely 1976 and 1977, the taxation of wine was, on average, five times higher, by reference to volume, than the taxation of beer; in other words, wine was subject to an additional tax burden of 400% in round figures." *Ibid.*, para 19. As regards the criterion for comparison based on alcoholic strength, the Court noted "that in the United Kingdom during the period in question wine bore a tax burden which, by reference to alcoholic strength, was more than twice as heavy as that borne by beer, that is to say an additional tax burden of at least 100%." *Ibid.*, para 21. With regard to the criterion of the incidence of taxation on the price (net of tax), although the Court experienced considerable difficulty in forming an opinion, in view of the disparate nature of the information provided by the Commission, it nevertheless noted that it was clear that "all cheaper wines marketed in the United Kingdom are taxed, by reference to price, more heavily in relative terms than beer." *Ibid.*, para 25.
[127] Case 277/83, [1985] ECR 2049.

on imported alcohol distilled from wine and used in the production of liqueur wines imported from other Member States (ie an apparently origin-neutral tax), it also granted a reduction of 60 per cent on the rate of the tax payable in respect of the manufacture of liqueur wines which qualified for the designation of "Marsala" (a liqueur wine which was subject to special rules concerning, in particular, the geographical demarcation of vineyards, the quality of grapes which may be used in its manufacture and supervision of the production and marketing of such wine by the public authorities). In the Commission's view, the Italian law was in violation of Article 90 since all liqueur wines, including Marsala, were similar products for the purposes of the first paragraph of Article 90, and the tax system had the effect of placing imported liqueur wines at a disadvantage by according preferential treatment to Marsala liqueur wine, which accounted, amongst all liqueur wines with a registered designation of origin, for *over 90 per cent of Italy's domestically produced liqueur wines*.[128]

Having underlined the general aim of Article 90 as well as the basic rule contained in the first paragraph of that Article,[129] the Court fully accepted the Commission's argument noting the following:

> It cannot be disputed that liqueur wines constitute a range of homogeneous products with similar characteristics and that they have similar properties and meet the same needs from the point of view of consumers. Moreover, it is also quite clear that no imported liqueur wine can ever qualify for the preferential treatment accorded to Marsala and that imported liqueur wines accordingly suffer discrimination.[130]

The Court's reliance on the fact that the Italian preferential treatment accorded to Marsala was *in all effects* accorded exclusively to a *domestic* product (accordingly, a very clear case of de facto discrimination based on the origin of the product) should be emphasised in light of the Italian argument according to which there existed other domestically produced liqueur wines which were *not* also given a tax advantage.

The Court also rejected a further argument by the Italian Government based on the assumption that the reduction of the tax conferred only a very limited advantage on producers of Marsala (*de minimis* argument). The Court pointed out, in this regard, that the purpose of the first paragraph of Article 90, which is to eliminate all forms of direct and indirect

---

[128] *Ibid.*, paras. 6–7.

[129] "The aim of Art 95 is to ensure free movement of goods between Member States in normal conditions of competition by the elimination of all forms of protection which result from the application of internal taxation which discriminates against products from other Member States or which is protectionist in scope. The first paragraph of Art 95, which is based on a comparison of the tax burdens imposed on domestic products and on imported products which may be classified as 'similar', is the basic rule in this respect." *Ibid.*, para 12.

[130] *Ibid.*, para 13.

discrimination, could not be achieved if the advantages granted in respect of domestic products could escape the prohibition laid down by Article 90 by reason of their purportedly limited effect.[131] The Court concluded that even the case of a tax relief, the discriminatory effect of which is "slight", falls within the prohibition of Article 90. Thus, it clearly rejected, at least in the realm of the first paragraph of Article 90, a *de minimis* argument.

A similar approach, although with a different result, can be seen in *Commission v France*,[132] where the Commission had argued, much like in the previous case, that the French system taxing sweet wines produced in a "traditional and customary" fashion at a lower rate compared to liqueur wines was contrary to Article 90, since the relevant criterion, although it ostensibly applied without distinction to domestic products and to imports from other Member States, could be fulfilled *only by domestic products*.[133]

Following its consistent case law, the Court first of all noted that at its present stage of development Community law did not restrict the freedom of each Member State to lay down tax arrangements which *differentiate* between certain products, even products which are *similar* within the meaning of the first paragraph of Article 90, on the basis of objective criteria, such as the nature of the raw materials used or the production processes employed. The Court held that such differentiation is compatible with Community law if (a) it pursues objectives of economic policy which are themselves compatible with the requirements of the Treaty and its secondary legislation, and (b) the detailed rules are such as to avoid any form of discrimination, direct or indirect, in regard to imports from other Member States or any form of protection of competing domestic products.[134] More specifically, the Court added that Article 90 does not prohibit Member States, in pursuit of legitimate economic or social aims, from granting tax advantages to certain types of spirits or to certain classes of producers, provided that such preferential systems are extended without discrimination to imported products conforming to the same conditions as preferred domestic products.

The Court found that these criteria had been satisfied in the particular case in light of the fact that (a) the aims pursued by the contested tax

---

[131] *Ibid.*, para 17.

[132] Case 196/85 [1987] ECR 1597.

[133] *Ibid.*, para 4. It should be noted that the Commission's claim included not only the criterion of "traditional and customary" production methods, but also certain requirements imposed on imported wines in order to qualify for the preferential tax scheme (ie imported wines had to be subject to controls in the Member State of exportation which afforded guarantees equivalent to those required of natural sweet wines produced in France). Contrary to the opinion of Advocate-General Slynn, the Court also found this measure in compliance with Art 90.

[134] *Ibid.*, para 6, citing its most recent judgement of 4 March 1986 in Case 106/84, *Commission v Denmark (Wine)* [1986] ECR 833.

scheme (offsetting the more severe conditions under which the particular sweet wines at issue were produced) were compatible with the requirements of Community law,[135] and (b) there was nothing in the evidence before the Court to suggest that the application of the scheme *in fact* gave preference to *French* wines at the expense of wines with the same characteristics from other Member States.[136] With regard the latter issue, the Court furthermore noted that,

> [I]t has not been demonstrated that because of physical factors or patterns of production the tax advantage in question operates *solely*, or *even preponderantly*, to the benefit of the French product. It should be added that national provisions which cover both domestic and imported products without distinction cannot be regarded as contrary to Community law merely because they might lend themselves to discriminatory application, unless it is proved that they are actually applied in that way.[137]

The *French Sweet Wine Tax* case demonstrates that the existence of different levels of taxation is not in itself enough to establish a violation of Article 90, even where the two products at issue are similar.[138] In that case, it was not even an issue of *de minimis* effect, in as much as natural sweet wines produced in traditional and customary fashion were taxed at a relatively lower rate than other similar wines.[139] In the words of Advocate-General Slynn, what was lacking in the Commission's case was evidence that

> the areas with customary and traditional production in France were the *only* areas in the Community which could possibly benefit from the tax advantage.[140] [emphasis added]

---

[135] Case 196/85 [1987] ECR 1597, para 9. This issue will be further explored in the section addressing the 'Judge-made public policy exception'.
[136] *Ibid.*, para 10.
[137] *Ibid.*
[138] Cf Case 106/84, *Commission v Denmark (Wine)* [1986] ECR 833, para 21, where the Court examined the 'protective nature' of the Danish measure *only after* it had already established that wine made from grapes bore a *higher* fiscal burden than the same quantity of wine made from other fruit contrary to the first paragraph of Art 90. The Court, in fact, rejected the justification advanced by the Danish Government by stating that the differential taxation at issue "is incompatible with Community Law if the products most heavily taxed are, as in this case, *by their very nature*, imported products" [emphasis added].
[139] Case 196/85 [1987] ECR 1597, para 4. While liqueur wines in general were subject to a consumption duty of FF6,795 per hectolitre of pure alcohol and to a circulation duty of FF22 per hectolitre, the natural sweet wines were taxed at a rate of FF2,545 and FF54.80, respectively. Cf Opinion of Advocate-General Slynn in Case 196/85, *Commission v France* [1985] ECR 1597 at 1598 noting that "The current tax differential is substantial".
[140] AG Opinion, Case 196/85 [1987] ECR 1597.

Only in such circumstances might it have been that the apparently origin-neutral differentiating criterion employed by the French legislation ("traditional and customary" production methods) was in reality a "disguised form of protection or discrimination".[141] On the contrary, as clearly evidenced by Advocate-General Slynn, it was undisputed that, for example, sweet wine from Samos, Greece, was imported into France in substantial quantities and benefited from the tax advantages at issue in that case *and* that French wine makers in new vine-growing areas producing wines with comparable physical characteristics did not benefit from the lower tax.[142] Thus the "protective nature" of the French tax scheme had not been established, principally because the favoured category of wine was not exclusively or predominantly of French origin and the disadvantaged wines included as well domestic wines.[143]

Although I am conscious that one should not attribute too much weight to a few cases, it appears that the existence of a de facto discriminatory effect based on the product's origin is always a central factor, albeit not the only one,[144] in the Court's analysis under the first paragraph of Article 90.

This is further confirmed in the *Italian Ethyl Alcohol* cases,[145] in which the Court found that an Italian tax scheme imposing a higher charge on synthetic ethyl alcohol than on ethyl alcohol obtained from fermentation (two products which were considered almost "identical") was not at variance with the first paragraph of Article 90 since, although the rate of tax prescribed for synthetic alcohol resulted in restraining the importation of synthetic alcohol originating in other Member States,[146] it had an *equivalent economic effect* in the national territory in that it also hampered the establishment of profitable production of the same product by the Italian industry, that production being technically perfectly possible.[147] Likewise, in *Humblot v Directeur des Services Fiscaux*,[148] the Court struck down a French law imposing a tax gradually increasing to a maximum of

---

[141] *Ibid.*

[142] *Ibid.*

[143] Cf PJ Kuyper "Booze and Fast Cars", above n 116, at 134, fn 16.

[144] See below the section dealing with the exception to the non-discrimination obligation.

[145] Case 140/79, *Chemical Farmaceutici v DAF Spa* [1981] ECR 1, and Case 46/80, *Vinal Spa v Orbat Spa* [1981] ECR 77.

[146] *Ibid* para 8. The Commission's argument was as follows: "In the *absence of production of synthetic alcohol in Italy*, the difference in the rate of tax prescribed by Italian law for denatured synthetic alcohol, on the one hand, and denatured alcohol obtained by fermentation, on the other, has the result of preventing practically all imports of synthetic alcohol from other Member States and of directly favouring national production of alcohol by fermentation. The Commission thus considers that, being a product *similar* to denatured alcohol obtained by fermentation, denatured synthetic alcohol imported from other Member States should qualify for the same rate of tax as the former" [emphasis added]. *Ibid.*, para 9.

[147] Case 140/79, *Chemical Farmaceutici v DAF Spa* [1981] ECR 1, para 16; Case 46/80, *Vinal Spa v Orbat Spa* [1981] ECR 77, para 15. Italy had indeed a considerable production of ethylene, a petroleum derivative which is used in the manufacture of synthetic alcohol.

[148] Case 112/84 [1985] ECR 1367.

1,100 francs on cars below 16CV and a flat rate of 5,000 francs on cars above 16CV on the ground that this system manifestly exhibited discriminatory or protective features contrary to Article 90. This was because the power rating determining liability to the higher tax had been fixed at a level such that only imported cars, in particular from other Member States, were subject to the higher tax, whereas all the cars of domestic manufacture were liable to the distinctly more advantageous differential tax.[149]

The attentive reader will have noticed the difference in the Court's approach in assessing the protective nature of the national systems taxing ethyl alcohol and cars respectively. While in the former case the Court concluded that the Italian tax system complied with the non-discrimination obligation of Article 90 by reference to the fact that in Italy there existed at least a *potential* for production of the "disadvantaged" product, in the latter case the Court found a violation of that same obligation on the broader basis that the whole French *current* car production fell within the more "advantaged" product group. Were not the French "potentially" capable of manufacturing cars above 16CV in power? Why then was the Court satisfied with potential production in one case and not in the other?

In the section dealing with the exception to the non-discrimination obligation, I will try to put forward an explanation for this dual approach and, in particular, I will examine the role that the strength of the public policy underlying the measure under review plays with regard to the assessment of the protective or discriminatory nature of the measure.

Notwithstanding this dual approach and the Court's margin of discretion, two points should be emphasised at this stage. First, in order to establish a prima facie case of violation of the first paragraph of Article 90, the complainant needs to demonstrate the protective nature of the measure under review. In other words, this will require a demonstration that the internal fiscal measure, though formally origin-neutral, has the *effect* of favouring, in particular, national production (protective nature). For this purposes, evidence that a fiscal measure has the effect

---

[149] *Ibid.*, para 14. Although the Court did not clearly determine whether the products at issue were similar or competitive (ie whether it was applying the first or second para of Art 90), I believe that, at least with regard to cars sharing very similar characteristics and sitting just on the borderline of the critical power rating (16CV), the Court was dealing with "similar" products. This is evidenced in the following paragraph of the Court's decision: "In the absence of considerations relating to the amount of the special tax, consumers seeking *comparable* cars as regard to such matters as size, comfort, actual power, maintenance costs, durability, fuel consumption and price would naturally choose from among cars above *and* below *the critical power rating laid down by French law*" [emphasis added]. *Ibid.*, para 15. Cf P Demaret, "The Non-Discrimination Principles and the Removal of Fiscal Barriers to Intra-Community Trade" in T Cottier and P Mavroidis (eds), *Regulatory Barriers and the Principle of Non-Discrimination in World Trade Law* (Ann Arbor, The University of Michigan Press, 2000) at 183.

of disfavouring, in particular, products from other Member States (discriminatory nature) may be employed to establish the protective nature of that same measure.[150]

Secondly, reliance on the protectionist (and discriminatory) effect of the measure under review is merely the application of the uncontroversial purpose of Article 90, which is not to equalise internal taxation depending on the similarity of the products (all liqueur wines, ethyl alcohol or cars should be taxed equally), but to eliminate all forms of discrimination or protection, whether formal or material, *based on the product's origin*.[151] This is the difference between the Equality principle and the National Treatment principle.[152]

In line with the wording of Article 90,[153] the Court's own language confirms the correct reading of the meaning of the two non-discrimination obligations enunciated in that Article. In the first interlocutory judgement in the extended controversy between the Commission and the United Kingdom over the taxation of wine and beer, the Court stated as follows:

> It is true that the first and second paragraphs of Article 95 [now 90] lay down different conditions as regard to the characteristics of the tax practices prohibited by that Article. Under the first paragraph of that Article, which relates to products which are similar and therefore hypothetically broadly comparable, the prohibition applies where a tax mechanism is of such a nature as to impose higher taxation on *imported* products than on *domestic* products. On the other hand, the second paragraph of Article 95 [now 90], precisely in view of the difficulty of making a sufficiently precise comparison between the

---

[150] In this context, the discrimination/protection dichotomy thus emphasizes a mere difference in perspective, although the two "perspectives" are very much related to one another.

[151] This is implicitly evidenced also in the cases dealing with de jure discriminatory taxation, where the Court seemed to emphasise that, in order to comply with the non-discrimination principle, the fiscal measure must not discriminate between *domestic* and *imported* products, rather than simply treat differently like products. For example in Case 127/75, *Bobie Getränkevertrieb GmbH v Hauptzollamt Aachen-Nord* [1976] ECR 1079, para 10, the Court quite clearly stated that a tax differentiation based on the size and characteristics of the producer would comply with the first para of Art 90 as long as imported and domestic beer were taxed at the same rate. Thus beer produced by large breweries could be taxed more than beer from small breweries so long as this arrangement did not have the practical effect of predominantly discriminating against foreign-produced beer or favouring beer manufactured at home. Likewise, in the *Italian Regenerated Oil* case, the Court implicitly permitted the Member States to tax "regenerated oils" lower than "primary distillation oils" as long as this differentiation would not discriminate in law and in fact between imported and domestic products. Case 21/79, *Commission v Italy (Regenerated Petroleum Products)* [1980] ECR 1, para 22.

[152] L Ehring, "*De facto* Discrimination in WTO Law: National Treatment and Most-Favoured-Nation Treatment—or Equal Treatment?", *Jean Monnet Working Paper* (NYU School of Law, 2002).

[153] Art 90, first para, EC Treaty reads as follows: "No Member State shall impose, directly or indirectly, on the products of *other Member States* any internal taxation of any kind in excess of that imposed directly or indirectly on similar *domestic* products" [emphasis added].

products in question, employs a more general criterion, in other words the indirect protection afforded by a domestic tax system.[154]

Even with regard to the obligation in the first paragraph of Article 90, the Court cannot avoid referring to the fundamental nature of the principle contained in that Article, which is the prohibition of discrimination on the basis of the product's nationality or origin. The Court's emphasis on comparing the tax treatment of *imported* and *domestic* products manifestly demonstrates that, in order to breach the provision in the first paragraph of Article 90, the measure must be shown to be discriminating, albeit only indirectly or materially, on the ground of the *nationality* or *origin* of the products.

Turning now to the obligation of the second paragraph of Article 90, the need to establish the "protective nature" of the internal taxation measure is quite uncontroversial. In *John Walker*,[155] the Court, having emphasised the general aim pursued by the obligation in the second paragraph of Article 90, which is to guarantee *fiscal neutrality*, and seeking to ensure that Member States do not discriminate against products originating in other Member States by *favouring domestic products* under their national tax legislation,[156] upheld the validity of the Danish legislation at issue. It noted that a system of taxation which differentiates between certain beverages on the basis of objective criteria does not favour domestic producers if a *significant* proportion of domestic production of alcoholic beverages falls within each of the relevant tax categories.[157] In *Commission v Italy (Bananas)*,[158] the Court found a system of taxation in Italy that imposed a consumption tax on bananas amounting to almost half the import price, but that did not impose any similar tax on a range of other fruit, to violate the non-discrimination obligation in the second paragraph of Article 90 on the ground that "the tax rules in question are characterised by the fact that the relevant consumer tax does not apply to the most typical Italian-produced table fruit".[159]

---

[154] Case 170/78, *Commission v United Kingdom I* [1980] ECR 417 para 9.
[155] Case 243/84, *John Walker and Sons Ltd v Ministeriet for Skatter og Afgifter (John Walker)* [1986] ECR 875.
[156] *Ibid.*, para 20.
[157] *Ibid.*, para 23. The Court noted in fact that "it is clear from the documents forwarded by the national court and from the observations submitted to the Court of Justice that the product, which bears the lightest tax burden, is manufactured almost exclusively in Denmark and that whisky, which is exclusively an imported product, is taxed not as such but as an alcoholic beverage included in the tax category of spirits—that is to say beverages with a high alcohol content—which comprises other products, the vast majority of which are Danish." *Ibid.*, para 21.
[158] Case 184/85 [1987] ECR 2013.
[159] *Ibid.*, para 13. The Court elaborated further: "That the tax is protective is underscored by its rate of Lit 525 per kilogram, which is almost half the 1985 import price. Hence, that difference in taxation influences the market in the products in question by reducing the potential consumption of the imported products. That being so, the protective nature of the tax system criticized by the Commission clearly emerges." *Ibid.*

The "Spirits" cases clearly confirm the relevance of the "protective nature" of the national taxation at issue.[160] As eloquently noted by Easson,

> what was found offensive, in the "spirits" cases, was not that vodka was taxed more heavily than aquavit, or whisky more heavily than brandy, but that the tax systems in question were characterised by the fact that those products of essentially domestic manufacture came within the most favourable tax categories and almost all of those which were imported were subject to higher taxation, that is to say there existed an effective discrimination which possessed a "national dimension".[161]

It is interesting to note how in those early cases, the Court, emphasising the link between the provision in the second paragraph of Article 90 and the "nature" of the tax system in question, gave instructions on how to assess the protective effect of a given tax system. The Court noted the two following points: first of all, for purposes of the application of the second paragraph of Article 90, the complainant needs to show that "a given tax mechanism is likely, in view of its inherent characteristics, to bring about the protective effect referred to by the Treaty"; and secondly, without disregarding the importance of statistical evidence from which the effects of a given tax system may be measured, it is impossible to require in each case that the actual foundation of the protective effect of the tax system under review should be shown statistically.[162] Thus, the protective effect of a given tax system should be assessed *in vitro* on the basis of the "nature" of that system and in particular by reference to its "inherent characteristics", which may only prove the "capability" and "likelihood" for that tax system to afford protection to domestic products.[163]

As previously mentioned, these early "Spirits" cases also show the Court's efforts to avoid a determination of "similarity" pursuant to

---

[160] Case 168/78, *Commission v France* (*Tax Arrangements Applicable to Spirits*) [1980] ECR 347, para 41, "As the competitive and substitution relationships between the beverages in question are such, the protective nature of the tax system criticized by the Commission is clear. A characteristic of that system is in fact that an essential part of domestic production, in other words spirits obtained from wine and fruit, come within the most favourable tax category whereas at least two types of product, almost all of which are imported from other Member States, are subject to higher taxation under the "manufacturing tax". The fact that another domestic product, aniseed spirits, is similarly placed at a disadvantage does not rule out the protective nature of the system as regard to the treatment for tax purposes of spirits obtained from wine and fruit […]". Cf Case 170/78, *Commission v United Kingdom II* [1983] ECR 2265, para 27; Case 323/87, *Commission v Italy* (*Rum*) [1989] ECR 2275, para 13.
[161] A Easson, "Fiscal Discrimination: New Perspectives on Art 95 of the EEC Treaty", 18 *CMLRev* (1981) 521, at 544.
[162] Case 170/78, *Commission v United Kingdom I* [1980] ECR 417, para 10.
[163] Although enunciated with regard to the second para of Art 90, this approach has also been employed in order to review whether an internal fiscal measure indirectly discriminates on the basis of the product's origin in violation of the first para of Art 90.

Article 90(1) by finding that the products at issue are at least "competitive" for purposes of Article 90(2). This so-called "globalisation" of the two paragraphs of Article 90 may represent further evidence of the substantial similarity in the purpose and structure of the two obligations contained in those paragraphs respectively. The fundamental aim of Article 90 is to combat fiscal internal measures which discriminate, formally or materially, on the basis of the product's origin, thus imposing on Member States the duty to avoid tax differentiations which have the effect of protecting domestic production.

One important difference between the two obligations in the first and second paragraph of Article 90 is the existence with regard to the latter of a *de minimis* exception. In *Commission v Belgium*,[164] for example, the Court refused to hold a Belgian system of taxation that imposed a value added tax rate of 25 per cent on wine and a rate of only 19 per cent on beer incompatible with the second paragraph of Article 90 (the two products at issue, though not similar, were nonetheless in competition with each other), since the Commission had not established that the tax system in question actually had a protective effect.[165] The Court noted that, in light of the undisputed fact that Belgium did not produce wine but did produce a substantial quantity of beer, a *greater* tax burden was borne by the product for which internal demand was met almost entirely by *imports*, whereas the product of which substantial quantities were produced in Belgium bore a *lesser* tax burden.[166] However, the Court concluded that the system was not capable of having the required protective effect, since the difference between the respective prices for comparable qualities of beer and wine was so that the difference of 6 per cent between the VAT rates applied to the two products was not capable of influencing consumer behaviour.[167]

The Court's application of a *de minimis* approach with regard to Article 90(2), and not with regard to Article 90(1) serves to demonstrate that the difference between the two paragraphs dealing with internal taxation is in reality one of degree. The weaker the relationship between the products at issue, the greater is the need for the complainant to establish the magnitude of the differential tax treatment accorded to those products. Where the products at issue are almost identical in their objective characteristics and/or consumer's uses, a small difference in their respective tax burdens having the effect of protecting domestic production is enough to demonstrate a violation of the non-discrimination obligation of Article 90. Where, on the contrary, the products are not similar but are

---

[164] Case 356/85 [1987] ECR 3299.
[165] *Ibid.*, para 21.
[166] *Ibid.*, para 3.
[167] *Ibid.*, para 18. Cf Case 27/67, *Firma Fink-Frucht v Hauptzollamt München-Landsbergstrasse* [1968] ECR 223, at 233.

nonetheless in competition with each other, a violation of Article 90 will only be found if the differential treatment, although in theory applied so as to afford protection to domestic production in the sense explained above, is more than *de minimis*.[168]

B. Justification Options

Technically speaking, the concept of "justification" or "exception" comes into play once the fiscal measure has been found to violate, whether directly or indirectly, the non-discrimination obligation of either Article III:2 GATT or Article 90 EC. In the case of formal discrimination, as seen in the previous section, once it has been established that the measure expressly discriminates on the basis of the product's origin, the infringing State may still avoid a final finding of violation by arguing that such de jure discriminatory treatment is justified on public policy grounds. Likewise, in the case of material discrimination, once the measure has been found, albeit only covertly, to afford protection to domestic products, the regulating State may still claim the existence of a public policy justification, in order to avoid a finding of violation. In other words, the relationship between the non-discrimination obligation and the public policy justification is usually known as one of "rule" to "exception".

In practical terms, however, in both EC and WTO law the dividing line between establishing a prima facie case of discrimination (the "rule") and providing for a public policy justification (the "exception") is not altogether clear, in particular in the case of de facto discrimination. Both the jurisprudence and academic writings on the issue do not appear conclusive on whether the legitimate public policy purposes underlying an internal fiscal measure should be taken into account in determining the existence of discrimination contrary to Article III:2 GATT or Article 90 EC, or whether those same public policy purposes should function exclusively as justification grounds once the measure has been found to violate the above mentioned non-discrimination provisions.

The purpose of this section is thus to revisit this issue and to determine the actual role of the public policy objective of a fiscal measure in assessing its compatibility with the GATT and the EC Treaty. This time the analysis will start with EC law, since, as mentioned in the section dealing with

---

[168] Cf S Weatherill and P Beaumont, *EC Law* (London, Penguin Books, 1995) at 414, fn 81, where the authors, although they agree that the *Commission v Belgium* case "may be seen as an example of a *de minimis* approach to Art 95", suggest that it is "perhaps more accurately, [...] an illustration that minimal differences confer no protective effect and are therefore not caught by Art 95(2) at all". It is suggested here that while the two issues are closely related to one another (when the differential is *de minimis* there might also be no protective effect), they should be kept separate so that the interpreter does not lose the actual purpose and structure of the non-discrimination obligation of Art 90 EC.

de jure discrimination, the EC Treaty does not provide for any express exception to the non-discrimination obligation of Article 90 capable of addressing legitimate public policy objectives, thus making the issue of the overlap between the "rule" and the "exception" even more evident.

1. *Judge-made Public Policy Exception in EC Law*

Despite the absence of a public policy exception provision capable of justifying national fiscal measures which are found to violate Article 90 EC, the ECJ has always appeared very keen to emphasise each Member State's regulatory prerogatives. In one of its most commonly cited statements, the Court recalled that

> in its present stage of development Community law does not restrict the freedom of each Member State to lay down tax arrangements which differentiate between certain products on the basis of objective criteria, such as the nature of the raw materials used or the production processes employed.[169]

Indeed, differentiation of this kind may serve legitimate economic or social purposes, including the use of certain raw materials, the continued production of a particular high quality product, or the continuance of certain classes of undertakings.[170]

Notwithstanding these very general statements, the Court has at the same time qualified the relevance of the public policy objectives of a national fiscal measure with two further provisos: (a) the differentiation must pursue economic policy objectives which are themselves compatible with the requirements of the Treaty and its secondary law and (b) the detailed rules must be such as to avoid any form of discrimination, direct or indirect, in regard to imports from other Member States or any form of protection of competing domestic products.[171]

Following a pattern that is not original to the analysis under Article 90 EC,[172] the Court begins by recognising the Member States' freedom to exercise their regulatory prerogatives in the field of taxation, only to cut back on this by imposing a review of both the legitimacy of the public policy objectives underlying the tax measure and its discriminatory/protectionist nature. Notwithstanding the fact that in the Court's reasoning the balance between the non-discrimination principle and the public policy

---

[169] Case 46/80, *Vinal SpA v Orbat SpA* [1981] ECR 77, para 13.
[170] Case 148/77, *H. Hansen Jun. and O C Balle GmbH & Co. v Hauptzollamt de Flensburg* [1978] ECR 1787, para 16.
[171] Case 46/80, *Vinal SpA v Orbat SpA* [1981] ECR 77, para 13 and Case 148/77, *H. Hansen Jun. and O C Balle GmbH & Co. v Hauptzollamt de Flensburg* [1978] ECR 1787, para 17.
[172] See also the *Cassis de Dijon* jurisprudence with regard to Art 28 EC. Cf P Craig and G de Búrca, *EU Law* (Oxford, OUP, 1998) at 607.

justification is clearly tilted in favour of the former, it is undeniable that the public policy objectives of a tax measure do play a role in an analysis of Article 90. Since this role is not altogether clear in the Court's above mentioned statements, in order to effectively appreciate the real value of the public policy objectives underlying national tax systems it is indispensable to examine in practice the Court's treatment of the Member States' arguments on public policy.

The first cases that have been cited to show the Court's recognition of a "de facto derogation clause" according to which Member States may plead a social or economic policy as a justification for violating the non-discrimination principle in the field of internal taxation arose from the controversy surrounding the Italian taxation of ethyl alcohol.[173] As previously noted, in these cases the Court found that the Italian tax scheme imposing on synthetic ethyl alcohol a higher charge compared to the charge on ethyl alcohol obtained from fermentation was not at variance with the first paragraph of Article 90, even if the tax rate prescribed for synthetic alcohol resulted in a restraint on the importation of synthetic alcohol originating in other Member States,[174] because it had a *potentially equivalent economic effect* in the national territory.[175] In reaching its conclusion, the Court noted that the different taxation of synthetic alcohol and of alcohol produced by fermentation was the result of a *legitimate choice of economic policy* to favour the manufacture of alcohol from agricultural products and, correspondingly, to restrain the processing into alcohol of ethylene, a derivative of petroleum, in order to reserve that raw material for other more important economic uses.

It has been rightly suggested that, although the Court in the *Italian Ethyl Alcohol* cases predicated its acceptance of the Italian tax scheme on the basis that it did not result in any discrimination, whether direct or indirect,

---

[173] Case 140/79, *Chemical Farmaceutici v DAF Spa* [1981] ECR 1, and Case 46/80, *Vinal Spa v Orbat Spa* [1981] ECR 77. Cf JHH Weiler, "The Constitution of the Common Marketplace: Text and Context in the Evolution of the Free Movement of Goods", in P Craig and G de Búrca (eds), *The Evolution of EU Law* (Oxford, OUP, 1999) at 365–66.

[174] Case 46/80, *Vinal Spa v Orbat Spa* [1981] ECR 77, para 8. The Commission's argument was as follows: "In the *absence of production of synthetic alcohol in Italy*, the difference in the rate of tax prescribed by Italian law for denatured synthetic alcohol on the one hand and denatured alcohol obtained by fermentation on the other has the result of preventing practically all imports of synthetic alcohol from other Member States and of directly favouring national production of alcohol by fermentation. The Commission thus considers that, being a product *similar* to denatured alcohol obtained by fermentation, denatured synthetic alcohol imported from other Member States should qualify for the same rate of tax as the former" [emphasis added]. *Ibid.*, para 9.

[175] Case 140/79, *Chemical Farmaceutici v DAF Spa* [1981] ECR 1, para 16; Case 46/80, *Vinal Spa v Orbat Spa* [1981] ECR 77, para 15. Noting that Italy had indeed a considerable production of ethylene, a petroleum derivative which is used in the manufacture of synthetic alcohol, the Court believed that the tax scheme also hampered the establishment of profitable production of synthetic ethyl alcohol by Italian industry, that production being technically perfectly possible.

the ECJ's reasoning bears testimony to its willingness to accept objective justifications where the national policy is acceptable from the Community's perspective, even if this benefits domestic traders more than importers.[176]

In other words, the public policy purpose of the Italian tax scheme was employed, not as part of an autonomous assessment of whether the discriminatory measure was *justified* (the "exception" prong), but within the determination of whether the measure did indeed *discriminate* against imported products (the "rule" prong). This may be explained simply by emphasising that formally there does not exist an exception provision. However, the real issue is another one: in what way did the existence of a legitimate public policy objective influence the Court's assessment of discrimination?

I have already noted the difference in the Court's approach to the issue of "discriminatory effect" between the *Italian Ethyl Alcohol* cases, on the one hand, and the *Humblot* case, on the other.[177] On the facts of both cases, domestic production of the higher-taxed product (synthetic ethyl alcohol and cars above 16CV) was similarly non-existent. However, while in the former case the Court concluded that the Italian tax system complied with the non-discrimination obligation of Article 90 by reference to the fact that in Italy there existed at least a *potential* for production of the "disadvantaged" product, in the latter case the Court found a violation of that same obligation on the broader basis that the whole French *current* car production fell within the more "advantaged" product group. Employing the Court's reasoning in the *Italian Ethyl Alcohol* cases, the French Government could have easily argued that French car industry was certainly "potentially" capable of manufacturing cars above 16CV in power. Why then was the Court satisfied with potential production in one case and limited its analysis to current production in the other?

The only objective difference, and thus explanation, for the Court's dual approach in these two cases appears to be the nature of the public policy objective underlying the two fiscal measures under review; while the higher tax on synthetic ethyl alcohol in the Italian legislation was justified on the basis of an industrial policy decision to restrain the processing into alcohol of ethylene, a scarce resource, the French Government did not advance any specific public policy objective, other than raising revenues, to justify the different taxation of cars below and above 16CV in power.[178] Accordingly, it follows that the Court's assessment of the protective nature

---

[176] P Craig and G de Búrca, *EU Law*, above n 172, at 565.

[177] Case 112/84, *Humblot v Directeur des Services Fiscaux* [1985] ECR 1367, where the Court found that the French tax scheme differentiating between cars below and above 16CV exhibited discriminatory or protective features contrary to Art 90 since the power rating determining liability to the higher tax had been fixed at a level such that only imported cars were subject to the higher tax whereas all the cars of domestic manufacture were liable to the distinctly more advantageous differential tax.

[178] Cf S Weatherill and P Beaumont, *EC Law*, above n 168, at 402.

of an origin-neutral tax will be "stricter" in the case where the tax purpose is simply to raise revenues and "looser" when the tax is aimed at affecting the *behaviour* of market's participants.[179]

How "loose" is the Court's discrimination assessment of a "behavioural" tax system? The Court's willingness to take into consideration specific public policy objectives as part of its assessment of the measure's "protective nature" seems to find its limit in the level of discrimination characterising the measure itself. The Court's decision in the *Marsala* case manifestly illustrates this point.[180]

As previously noted, in this case the Italian Government had been called to defend its tax system of liqueur wines, which granted, although on formally origin-neutral terms, a reduction of 60 per cent on the rate of the tax payable in respect of the manufacture of liqueur wines that qualified for the designation of "Marsala". The Commission claimed that the Italian law violated Article 90 on the basis that all liqueur wines, including Marsala, were similar products and that Marsala liqueur wine accounted, amongst all liqueur wines with a registered designation of origin, for *over 90 per cent of Italy's domestically produced liqueur wines*.[181] According to the Italian Government, the rules concerning Marsala were not contrary to Article 90 since, taken as a whole, the provisions relating to Marsala lay down exceptional requirements, which were extremely strict and restrictive, for the production of all such wines. In other words, the tax relief granted by the Italian legislation was simply seeking to take into account the special position of producers of Marsala who were required to bear the additional charges resulting from this detailed regulatory system. The tax advantages granted to Marsala could be seen either as necessary in order for the Italian Government to impose on Marsala extremely demanding requirements or more simply as encouraging the production of a high quality product.

Having found that the products at issue were similar and that the Italian tax system discriminated exclusively against imported products (no imported liqueur wine could ever qualify for the preferential treatment accorded to Marsala), the Court considered whether that system was nevertheless compatible with the first paragraph of Article 90 in light of the reasons relied upon by the Italian Government to justify the differential tax treatment of alcohol distilled from wine and used in the manufacture of Marsala.[182] Without expressly mentioning the argument based

---

[179] Cf Case 184/85, *Commission v Italy (Bananas)* [1987] ECR 2013, where the Court assessed the discriminatory nature of the Italian tax scheme in the same strict fashion as in *Humblot* because the Italian Government did not advance any specific public policy objective justifying that scheme.

[180] Case 277/83, *Commission v Italy (Marsala)* [1985] ECR 2049.

[181] *Ibid.*, paras. 6–7.

[182] *Ibid.*, para 14.

on the extremely demanding requirements imposed on Marsala, the Court appeared to reject this argument by simply noting *once again* that

> liqueur wines from other Member States will never be able to satisfy the requirements laid down by the Italian rules in order to qualify for the designation Marsala and accordingly they can never qualify for the tax advantage granted in respect of Marsala.[183]

In addition, the Court rejected a further argument by the Italian Government, according to which the region in which Marsala was produced was underdeveloped, noting that discriminatory fiscal practices are not exempt from the application of Article 90 on the ground that they may be classified at the same time as a method of financing state aid.[184]

This case calls for a number of comments. First of all, it seems to represent an example of the Court's unsuccessful attempt to distinguish between a finding of "discrimination" and a finding of "justification". In the end, in fact, the Court, relying on both occasions on the discriminatory nature of the tax system (ie Marsala requirements could only be met by domestic products), appears to weaken the case for keeping the "rule" strictly separate from the "exception".

Secondly, and more importantly, the reason for not accepting the specific public policy objective submitted by the Italian Government (to encourage the production of a high-quality product in an underdeveloped area) seems to rest on the finding that the differentiating criterion employed by the Italian legislation (Marsala liqueur wine v other liqueur wine) was *inherently biased* toward domestic production. In other words, the Court's conviction that imported liqueur wines would never be able to satisfy the Marsala requirements and accordingly qualify for the tax advantages granted to Marsala constituted both the *evidence* of the protectionist impact of the Italian tax scheme and the *reason* for not accepting the public policy justifications pleaded by the Italian Government.

This conclusion is confirmed by comparing the decision in that case with that in the *Italian Ethyl Alcohol* cases. Although in both instances the *public policy objectives* underlying the tax schemes at issue were in principle similarly legitimate and the *effects* of those tax schemes were clearly discriminatory, only in the former case did the Court find the measure to be in violation of the non-discrimination principle of Article 90. The explanation for such a different result may be that in the *Marsala* case discrimination against imported products was *inherent* in the differentiating criterion. In the *Italian Ethyl Alcohol* cases, by contrast, the emphasis on the *potentially*

---

[183] *Ibid.*, para 15.
[184] *Ibid.*, para 16.

equivalent economic effect in the national territory[185] clearly shows that the Court upheld the Italian measure on the basis that the measure itself was not intrinsically discriminatory toward imported products; the fact that Italy *could* have produced synthetic ethyl alcohol was the evidence that the differentiating criterion was not *inherently* biased toward domestic production, and thus any effect prejudicial to imported goods was shown to be incidental and overridden by the scheme's legitimate purpose.

Notwithstanding their treatment under the discrimination assessment, these cases should not be confused with those instances in which the Court has found in favour of the taxing Member State on the basis that the fiscal measure at issue does not have any protectionist effects whatsoever.[186]

In the *French Sweet Wine* case,[187] for example, the Commission argued, much as in the *Marsala* case, that the French system taxing sweet wines produced in a "traditional and customary" fashion at a lower rate than liqueur wines was contrary to Article 90 since the relevant criterion, although it formally applied without distinction to domestic products and to imports from other Member States, could be fulfilled *only by domestic products*.[188] As previously noted, the Court rejected the Commission's claim, arguing that the public policy aims pursued by the French tax scheme (ie to offset the more severe conditions under which natural sweet wines were produced) were compatible with the requirements of Community law *and* that there was nothing in the evidence before the Court to suggest that the application of the scheme *in fact* gave preference to *French* wines at the expense of wines with the same characteristics from other Member States.[189]

Although the Court's decisions in both the *French Sweet Wine* and *Italian Ethyl Alcohol* cases were technically based on the identical conclusion that neither tax scheme discriminated, whether directly or indirectly, on the basis of the product's origin, this conclusion rested in practice on two different findings. While in the former case the conclusion that there was no discrimination was based on the finding that the French tax had no protectionist effects whatsoever, in the latter case the conclusion that there was no discrimination was predicated on the finding that the Italian tax was not "discriminatory" in the sense of Article 90 despite the fact that it demonstrated some discriminatory effects against imported synthetic ethyl alcohol. The measure was held to pursue a legitimate public policy objective

[185] Case 140/79, *Chemical Farmaceutici v DAF Spa* [1981] ECR 1, para 16; Case 46/80, *Vinal Spa v Orbat Spa* [1981] ECR 77, para 15.
[186] Case 196/85, *Commission v France* [1987] ECR 1597; Case 200/85, *Commission v Italy* [1988] ECR 3853; Case C–132/88, *Commission v Greece* [1990] ECR 1567; Case 243/84, *John Walker* [1986] ECR 875.
[187] Case 196/85, *Commission v France* [1987] ECR 1597.
[188] *Ibid.*, para 4.
[189] *Ibid.*, para 10. However, the *French sweet wine* case does give a sense of the inherent uncertainty in distinguishing between the discriminatory nature and the public policy

and the differentiating criterion was not inherently discriminatory. In other words, where the issue of justification on public policy grounds is relevant when the fiscal measure has some protectionist effects (as in the *Italian Ethyl Alcohol* cases), that same issue loses its relevance if the fiscal measure has, on the contrary, no such effect (as in the *French Sweet Wine* case).[190]

In conclusion, notwithstanding the ambivalent approach which the ECJ has been forced to follow in light of the absence in EC law of a provision capable of expressly justifying on public policy grounds a national fiscal measure that is found to violate Article 90, the Court seems to decide according to the following criteria: first of all, public policy arguments seem to play a role only where the internal fiscal measure under review is deemed to have some protectionist effects with respect to imported products, in the sense explained in the section dealing with the "normative content" of the non-discrimination obligation (*French Sweet Wine, Commission v Greece, John Walker*); secondly, pure fiscal policy objectives are not enough to justify a tax system that, albeit origin-neutral on its face, is found to discriminate in practice on the basis of the product's origin or nationality (*Humblot, Bananas*); and thirdly, where the tax system differentiates between products on the basis of more specific public policy purposes, the Court will be willing to take account of these purposes (albeit formally within its discrimination assessment) only if the differentiating criterion is not inherently discriminatory against imported products (*Italian Ethyl Alcohol, Marsala*).

justification in the case of (formally) origin-neutral measures. The French Government in fact defended its tax scheme by explaining the reasons for according preferential tax treatment to wine produced according to traditional and customary methods. The French Government argued, first of all, that the concept of "traditional and customary production" had both a *historical aspect*, alluding to time-honoured products closely associated with a particular locality, whose long ancestry was part of their fame, and a *technical meaning*, referring to oenological rules and practices which codify fair and traditional practices (para 5). Moreover, the French Government explained that natural sweet wines were made in regions characterised by low rainfall and relatively poor soil, in which the difficulty of growing other crops meant that the local economy depended heavily on their production. Although the Court did not analyse the likeness issue in that case, it is not difficult to see how with the first argument the French Government was trying to justify its measure by demonstrating the objectivity or legitimacy of the differentiating criterion: wine produced by traditional and customary methods had "historical" and "technical" peculiarities, which differentiated it from other types of wine. On the other hand, with the second argument the French Government was defending its measure by focusing on more general, social and economic issues affecting particularly poor regions, which were only indirectly related to wine produced by traditional and customary methods.

[190]This is even more apparent in Case C–132/88, *Commission v Greece* [1990] ECR 1567, where the Court found that the Greek system progressively taxing cars on the basis of their cylinder capacity (the progression distinguished three categories: up to 1200 cc, between 1201 and 1800 cc, and over 1800 cc) did not discriminate against imported products, because, notwithstanding the fact that all cars above 1800 cc were manufactured abroad, all the models in the range of cars having cylinder capacities between 1600 and 1800 cc (the next best alternative for consumers) were also of foreign manufacture. The Court reached the conclusion that the Commission had not shown how the system of taxation at issue might

2. *Article XX GATT and Alternative Ways to Justify De Facto Discriminatory Fiscal (and Non-fiscal) Measures on Public Policy Grounds*

As in the case of a de jure discriminatory tax, an apparently origin-neutral fiscal measure that is found to violate the National Treatment obligation of Article III:2 GATT may be justified under other provisions, including in particular those in Article XX GATT dealing with general public policy exceptions. Thus, contrary to EC law, WTO law does provide for a clear two-step analysis, according to which a tax is, first of all, strictly reviewed pursuant to the non-discrimination obligations of Article III, and then, only if it is deemed to transgress such obligations, may that same tax be justified on the basis of one of the public policies listed in Article XX, conditional upon observing the requirements specified in both the several paragraphs as well as in the introductory clause of Article XX.

As was noted with regard to formal discriminatory taxes, Article XX has similarly never really been applied in order to justify an origin-neutral tax found to have violated the National Treatment obligation of Article III:2. Once again, what is surprising is the fact that the general exception appears not to have even been raised as a defence of a de facto discrimination finding.

Nevertheless, commentators have eloquently voiced the potentially serious weakness of this two-step analysis, noting that Article XX lists only ten policy goals capable of justifying national measures deviating from GATT obligations, thus leaving outside the coverage of the exception a host of other (perhaps even more) important or legitimate policy goals.[191] The prospect of these objectives being broadened through political negotiation appearing not very likely, there have been several attempts within both GATT panel practice and academic writings to permeate the content of the non-discrimination "rule" with the features of

---

have the effect of favouring the sale of cars of Greek manufacture without taking into account the *weak* public policy purpose underlying the tax scheme. In that case, the Greek Government had in fact argued that the differential taxation of cars was objectively justified by the social circumstances prevailing in Greece and, to some extent, in Europe as a whole: cars of less than 1200 cc are for people with modest incomes; those with a cylinder capacity of between 1201 and 1800 cc are bought by people whose income is in the middle range; and those of above 1800 cc are, above all in Greece, only for people with very substantial incomes. *Contra* P Craig and G de Búrca, *EU Law*, above n 172, at 565.

[191] F Roessler, "Diverging Domestic Policies and Multilateral Trade Integration" in J Bhagwati and R E Hudec (eds), *Fair Trade and Harmonization: Prerequisites for Free Trade? Volume 2: Legal Analysis*, (Cambridge, MA, MIT Press, 1996) at 30; A Mattoo and A Subramanian, "Regulatory Autonomy and Multilateral Disciplines: The Dilemma and a Possible Resolution", 1 *JIEL* (1998) 303 at 313-14; R Howse and D Regan, "The Product/Process Distinction: An Illusory Basis for Disciplining "Unilateralism" in Trade Policy", 11 *European Journal of International Law* (2000) 249 at 253.

the public policy "exception", in a way similar to what the Court of Justice *had to* do with regard to the non-discrimination rule of Article 90 EC.

In this section, I will first of all examine the most prominent, though not the most convincing (and subsequently even rejected), attempt to introduce public policy objectives within the determination of discrimination, the so called *aims-and-effects* doctrine. This section will additionally investigate the few instances in the jurisprudence (outside the *aims-and-effects* doctrine) where the measure's purposes have indeed been taken into consideration in determining whether an internal fiscal measure was in violation of the National Treatment obligation. Lastly, it will briefly report on the arguments, recently advanced by a few authors, to integrate a determination under Article III with an "economic efficiency" criterion or "necessity" test.

(a) Aims-and-effects doctrine: Malt Beverages *and* US Taxes on Automobiles
The first and best known effort to bring the criteria governing WTO legal restraints on domestic regulatory measures closer to recognised GATT policy goals[192] is the so called *aims-and-effects* doctrine. This approach was proposed in a few Panel Reports, not all of them adopted by GATT Members, at the beginning of the 1990s, when panels began to be confronted with claims that apparently origin-neutral measures were indeed in violation of the National Treatment obligations.[193]

As previously mentioned, this doctrine attempted to redefine the "like product" concept of GATT Article III with regard to the *purpose* of Article III, which is to ensure that internal taxation and regulation "should not be applied to imported or domestic products so as to afford protection to domestic production." Accordingly, in determining whether two products subject to different treatment are "like products" for the purposes of Article III:2 (and 4), it would be necessary to consider whether such *product differentiation* is being made "so as to afford protection to domestic production" or for the purpose of pursuing policy purposes unrelated to the protection of domestic products.[194] Following this

---

[192] R Hudec, "GATT/WTO Constraints on Domestic Regulation: Requiem for an 'Aims and Effects' Test", 32 *The International Lawyer* (1998) 619.

[193] Panel Report on *Malt Beverages*, above n 5, and Panel Report on *US–Taxes on Automobiles*, above n 43.

[194] See Panel Report on *Malt Beverages*, above n 5, para 5.25: "The purpose of Art III is thus not to prevent contracting parties from using their fiscal and regulatory powers for purposes other than to afford protection to domestic production. Specifically, the purpose of Art III is not to prevent contracting parties from differentiating between different product categories for policy purposes unrelated to the protection of domestic production. The Panel considered that the limited purpose of Art III has to be taken into account in interpreting the term 'like products' in this Article Consequently, in determining whether two products subject to different treatment are like products, it is necessary to consider whether such product differentiation is being made 'so as to afford protection to domestic production'".

approach, the Panel in the 1992 *Malt Beverages* case found that the State of Mississippi's origin-neutral excise tax on wine made from a specified variety of grape, which was lower than the excise tax imposed on other types of wine (including Canadian imports), was inconsistent with Article III:2, first sentence. The Panel reasoned as follows:

> Applying the above considerations to the Mississippi wine tax, the Panel noted that the special tax treatment accorded in the Mississippi law to wine produced from a particular type of grape, which grows only in the south-eastern United States and the Mediterranean region, is a rather *exceptional basis* for a tax distinction. Given the limited growing range of the specific variety of grape, at least in North America, the Panel was of the view that this particular tax treatment *implies a geographical distinction* which affords protection to local production of wine to the disadvantage of wine produced where this type of grape cannot be grown. [...] The Panel noted that the United States did not claim any public policy purpose for this Mississippi tax provision other than to subsidize small *local* producers. The Panel concluded that unsweetened still wines are *like products* and that the particular distinction in the Mississippi law in favour of still wine of a local variety must be presumed, on the basis of the evidence submitted to the Panel, to afford protection to Mississippi vintners.[195] [emphasis added]

The Panel noted the "exceptional" basis as well as the "inherent discriminatory" nature of the Mississippi tax distinction (the specific type of grape grows only in the south-eastern United States and the Mediterranean region), and found first of all that the tax scheme afforded protection to domestic production, or in other words, that the *effect* of the tax differential was *protectionist*. Secondly, noting that the United States had not advanced any legitimate public policy purpose to explain the differentiating criterion, the Panel concluded that the only evident purpose of the product distinction was to "protect local producers": in other words, the *aim* of the tax differential was *protectionist*. Based on these findings, the Panel concluded that the two categories of wines were "like products" and thus had to be treated the same.[196]

The *aims-and-effects* doctrine was next applied and better elaborated in the unadopted 1994 Panel Report on *United States–Taxes on Automobile* (also known as the CAFE case). Here, the EC claimed inter alia that the US origin-neutral taxes on luxury and low fuel economy cars (Luxury Excise Tax and Gas Guzzler Tax respectively) violated Article III:2 principally because (a) cars below and above the $30,000 luxury threshold and the 22.5 mpg

---

[195] *Ibid.*, para 5.26.
[196] R Hudec, "GATT/WTO Constraints on Domestic Regulation: Requiem for an 'Aims and Effects' Test", 32 *The International Lawyer* (1998) 619 at 627. The Panel Report in the *Malt Beverages* case also applied the *aims-and-effects* doctrine with regard to Art III:4. This part of the Report will be analysed in the section dealing with non-fiscal internal measures. See below.

(miles per gallon) fuel economy threshold were like products, since they had the same end use, basic physical characteristics and tariff classification and (b) the product distinctions employed in these measures effectively targeted and thus discriminated against EC automobiles.[197]

Following the US argument, according to which the key criterion in judging "likeness" under Article III was whether the measure was applied "so as to afford protection to domestic production", the Panel, recalling the Report in the *Malt Beverages* case, examined both the *aim* and *effect* of the measures under review in order to determine whether the products at issue were indeed *like* for purposes of Article III.[198] The Panel explained the meaning of an aim-and-effect analysis in the following terms:

> A measure could be said to have the *aim* of affording protection if an analysis of the circumstances in which it was adopted, in particular an analysis of the instruments available to the contracting party to achieve the declared domestic policy goal, demonstrated that a change in competitive opportunities in favour of domestic products was a desired outcome and not merely an incidental consequence of the pursuit of a legitimate policy goal. A measure could be said to have the *effect* of affording protection to domestic production if it accorded greater competitive opportunities to domestic products than to imported products. The effect of a measure in terms of trade flows was not relevant for the purposes of Article III, since a change in the volume or proportion of imports could be due to many factors other than government measures.[199]

With respect to the issue of whether the $30,000 threshold distinction was drawn so as to afford protection to domestic production, the Panel found that neither the aim nor the effect of the Luxury Tax were protectionist. With regard to the *aim* of the measure under review, the Panel noted that (a) the aim of the legislation could not be based solely on statements by legislators suggesting that the measure had been intentionally targeted at foreign automobiles, but had to be based rather on the interpretation of the wording of the legislation as a whole, (b) the policy objective apparent in the legislation (to raise revenue from sales of perceived "luxury" products) was *consistent* with setting a price threshold, and setting it at a level at which only a small proportion of automobiles sold within the US market were taxed, (c) the fact that a large proportion of EC imports (but not necessarily a large proportion of imports from other countries)

---

[197] Panel Report on *US–Taxes on Automobiles*, above n 43, paras. 5.2 and 5.19 respectively.
[198] *Ibid.*, paras. 5.5–5.9. The Panel's justification for this approach was that the "primary purpose of the General Agreement was to lower barriers to trade between markets, and not to harmonize the regulatory treatment of products within them […] Art III could not be interpreted as prohibiting government policy options, based on products, that were not taken so as to afford protection to domestic production". *Ibid.*, para 5.8.
[199] *Ibid.*, para 5.10.

was affected by the measure did not demonstrate that the legislation was aimed at affording protection to domestic automobiles selling for less than $30,000, (d) the conditions of competition accorded to products just above the $30,000 threshold did not differ markedly from those just below the threshold, and (e) there was considerable uncertainty as to the proportion of foreign and domestic automobiles selling above and below the threshold.[200]

With regard to the *effect* of the threshold distinction in the luxury tax, the Panel based its decision on the assumption that the differentiating criterion was not inherently discriminatory vis-à-vis imported cars. First of all, the Panel noted that, even assuming the EC sales data figures showing a high proportions of EC cars affected by the tax were correct,[201] the luxury tax could not be deemed to afford protection to domestic production since there were other possible reasons explaining the higher level of adverse effect on EC cars, such as marketing and production decisions by EC manufacturers, their US or other foreign competitors, or the decisions of consumers in the market.[202] Considering evidence other than sales or trade flow data, the Panel noted more explicitly that "a selling price above $30,000 did not appear from the evidence to be inherent to EC or other foreign automobiles." According to the Panel, no evidence had been advanced demonstrating that EC or other foreign automobile manufacturers did not in general have the design, production, and marketing capabilities to sell automobiles below the $30,000 threshold, or that they did not in general produce such models for other markets. On the contrary, there was evidence that EC automobile manufacturers produced a wide range of automobiles that, if exported to the United States, could sell for below $30,000. Nor had evidence been advanced that US manufacturers did not have the capabilities to design, produce and market automobiles costing over $30,000.

Noting, moreover, that there was no sudden transition to a higher tax at the threshold, as well as that the threshold did not appear *arbitrary* or *contrived* in the context of the policies pursued, the Panel reached the conclusion that the regulatory distinction of $30,000 did not create conditions of competition that divided the products inherently into two classes, one of EC or other foreign origin, and the other of domestic origin.

---

[200] *Ibid.*, para 5.12.
[201] Noting the highly contradictory character of the sales data submitted by the parties, the Panel found that this data did not provide conclusive evidence of a change in the conditions of competition favouring US cars. "Just below the threshold, EC figures suggested that some 85 percent of automobiles sold in 1991 in the United States were domestic; the United States estimate was 42 percent. Just above the threshold, in the $30,000 to $33,000 range, the EC claimed that some 40 percent of automobiles sold in the United States in 1991 were domestic; the United States put the figure at 90 percent." *Ibid.*, para 5.13.
[202] *Ibid.*

In respect of the issue of whether the 22.5 mpg threshold was drawn so as to afford protection to domestic production, the Panel found that both the aim and the effect of the Gas Guzzler tax were once again not protectionist. With regard to the *aim* of the US tax, the Panel rejected the EC argument that the overall aim of the measure advanced by the United States (to conserve fossil fuels) could not be fulfilled, since the few cars affected by the measure could have only a very small effect on the overall consumption of fossil fuels in the United States. It observed that, although it was not the most economically efficient measure to reduce fuel consumption (for example in comparison with a fuel tax), the Gas Guzzler tax was nevertheless *capable* of contributing to that policy objective.[203] Moreover, picking up a clever argument submitted by the United States, the Panel also noted that when the Gas Guzzler tax was introduced in 1978, most domestic automobiles could not achieve the final threshold figure set out in the legislation, which reinforced the argument that the Gas Guzzler threshold figure had not been enacted to target foreign automobiles.[204]

With regard to the *effect* of the fuel economy threshold, the Panel used essentially the same reasoning it had employed in finding that the luxury threshold distinction did not have any protectionist effect. It noted that,

> the nature and level of the regulatory distinction made at the threshold of the gas guzzler measure were *consistent* with the overall purpose of the measure and did not appear to create categories of automobiles of *inherently* foreign or domestic origin.[205]

Without at all explaining the basis for the "consistency" finding, the Panel simply made reference to the availability of manufacturing technology in order to justify the latter finding.[206]

Professor Hudec has advanced two principal advantages offered by the *aims-and-effects* approach, which centred on a more favourable attitude towards public policy justifications. He stated,

---

[203] "The Panel observed that the threshold in the Gas Guzzler tax created an incentive in the United States market to purchase more fuel-efficient automobiles, and that this incentive would normally lead to increased conservation of fossil fuels. Although the overall economic efficiency of the measure with respect to the reduction of fuel consumption might be questioned when compared to, for example, a fuel tax, the Panel did not consider that this factor was by itself relevant in determining obligations under Art III." *Ibid.*, para 5.24.

[204] *Ibid.*

[205] *Ibid.*, para 5.25.

[206] *Ibid.*, "The technology to manufacture high fuel economy automobiles—above the 22.5 mpg threshold—was not inherent to the United States, nor were low fuel economy automobiles inherently of foreign origin, as the Panel noted from fuel economy figures submitted by the parties. Thus the fact that EC automobiles bore most of the burden of the tax did not mean that the measure had the effect of affording protection to United States production."

First, [the *aims-and-effects* doctrine] consigned the metaphysics of "likeness" to a lesser role in [Article III] analysis and instead made the question of violation depend primarily on the two most important issues that separate bona fide regulation from trade protection—the trade effects of the measure and the bona fides of the alleged regulatory purpose behind it; second, by making it possible for the issue of regulatory justification to be considered at the same time the issue of violation itself is being determined, the "aim and effects" approach avoided both the premature dismissal of valid complaints on grounds of "un-likeness" alone, and excessively rigorous treatment given to claims of regulatory justification under Article XX whenever the two products were ruled "like".[207]

It is interesting at this stage to focus on the several factors which both above mentioned Panels applying the *aims-and-effects* doctrine employed in order to determine whether the origin-neutral fiscal measures under review (and in particular their differentiating criteria or threshold distinctions) were indeed expressions of legitimate public policy objectives.

As a preliminary matter, it should be noted that, notwithstanding the attempt to distinguish between the assessment of the measure's aim and effect, these two issues were in practice two prongs of a "single analysis". This is evidenced first of all in the uniformity of the respective results: in the *Malt Beverages* case, both the aim and effect of the Mississippi tax were "protectionist"; and in the *US Taxes on Automobiles* case, both the aims and effects of the Luxury and Gas Guzzler Taxes were deemed "not protectionist".[208] Secondly, and more importantly, the interchangeability of the factors employed in the assessment of the measure's aims and effects confirms the "single analysis" theory: the measure's *consistency* with its policy objectives was noted in the assessment of the *aim* of the Luxury Tax as well as in determining the *effect* of the Gas Guzzler Tax; and, similarly, the *inherently* protectionist nature of the measure was noted in order to conclude that the *aim* of the Mississippi tax was protectionist and to determine that the *effects* of both the Luxury Tax and Gas Guzzler Tax were not.

Looking at it as a single analysis, a finding that the aims and effects of a fiscal measure were not protectionist basically focused on the three following elements: (1) the existence of a legitimate public policy objective, (2) the measure's suitability or capacity to contribute, even only partially,

---

[207] R Hudec, "GATT/WTO Constraints on National Regulation: Requiem for an 'Aim and Effects' Test" 32 *International Lawyer* 619 (1998) at 628.

[208] Hudec correctly notes how "the new 'aim and effects' approach was obviously not a finished legal standard" and that "cases where the various factors point in different directions (for example, where a product distinction has a bona fides regulatory purpose but also has protective market effects) would obviously require more complex balancing that would have to be worked out in subsequent litigation." R Hudec, "GATT/WTO Constraints on National Regulation: Requiem for an 'Aim and Effects' Test" 32 *International Lawyer* 619 (1998) at 628.

to that policy objective, and (3) the non-inherently protectionist nature of the relevant differentiating criterion.

These three elements show that in order to determine whether the aim and effect of the measure were protectionist, the two Panels relied on the *objective* characteristics of the incriminated measure itself. Legislators' statements, preparatory work, as well as pure disproportionate adverse effects on imported products were *not* decisive elements. What mattered was whether the measure was pursuing a legitimate policy objective, was consistent with its objective, and was not inherently discriminatory. The emphasis on the magnitude of the differential treatment between products below and above the chosen threshold distinction (ie products just above the $30,000 and below the 22.5 mpg thresholds did not differ markedly from those just below or above those thresholds), as well as on the market's conditions at the time of the enactment of the measure, confirm that the Panels' *aims-and-effects* analysis focused on the *objective features* characterising the measures under review.

Although there is some merit in the criticism voiced by Mattoo that the standards relied upon in the *US Taxes on Automobiles* case for establishing protectionist intent and effect were set "impossibly high",[209] it appears that the real deficiency in the two Panel Reports' application of the *aims-and-effects* doctrine was in the depth of their reasoning. For example, the panels never really explained why the Mississippi policy of encouraging a particular type of wine was not considered a *legitimate* public policy, or why the nature and level of the regulatory distinctions made at the threshold of the gas guzzler measure "were *consistent* with the overall purpose of the measure", as well as why the threshold distinction of the luxury tax "did not appear *arbitrary* or *contrived* in the context of the policies pursued."

This deficiency was never cured before the demise of the *aims-and-effects* approach as a whole. The Panel Report on *US–Taxes on Automobiles* was never adopted and, as has already been mentioned in the section examining the "likeness" issue, the *aims-and-effects* doctrine was eventually rejected with force by a WTO Panel, and implicitly by the Appellate Body, in *Japan–Alcohol II*. This rejection was principally premised on the doctrine's inconsistency with the wording of Article III:2, first sentence, the fact that complainants would find it too difficult to establish the multiplicity of aims of a particular measure, and the risk of making the general exception provision of Article XX GATT redundant.[210]

---

[209] A Mattoo and A Subramanian, "Regulatory Autonomy and Multilateral Disciplines: The Dilemma and a Possible Resolution", 1 *JIEL* (1998) 303 at 310.
[210] Panel Report on *Japan–Alcohol II*, above n 5, paras. 6.16–17.

Notwithstanding the fact that certain commentators continue to argue for a resuscitation of the *aims-and-effects* doctrine within the analysis of "likeness",[211] I agree with the rejection in *Japan–Alcohol II* of the doctrine on the grounds that, according to that doctrine, the assessment of the measure's aim and effect was carried out in order to determine whether the two products treated differently were indeed *like products*. While one can understand the objective of protecting national measures adopted in the pursuit of legitimate public policies (especially if not covered by one of the exceptions of Article XX), I find it difficult to comprehend why several of the proponents of the more enlightened approach to Article III have relied and still rely on the pillar of the National Treatment obligation focusing on the "relationship between products" rather than on the other, more important, pillar focusing on the "protectionist nature" of the measure.[212] The *Malt Beverages* and *US Taxes on Automobiles* cases show that both the purpose of, and the issues analysed under, the *aims-and-effects* doctrine are better considered in terms of the protective or discriminatory nature of a measure than in terms of "likeness". ECJ case law dealing with the lack of a general exception provision also demonstrates that public policy justifications influence the "protective nature" analysis and not the "product likeness" determination.

Accordingly, while I would not like to see the resuscitation of the *aims-and-effects* doctrine as it was originally employed (ie for purposes of determining likeness), I believe that several of its tenets may indeed become useful in the context of determining the measure's protectionist nature. I will come back to this issue when analysing the recent illuminating statements of the Appellate Body in *Asbestos* with regard to the true function and aim of the National Treatment obligation.

(b) Post-aims-and-effects WTO jurisprudence Before I proceed any further, it is necessary to examine the role, if any, of the public policy objectives of fiscal measures in WTO jurisprudence, subsequent to the demise of the *aims-and-effects* doctrine.

In the several disputes dealing with internal fiscal measures allegedly infringing Article III:2, there does not seem to be any case where the respondent State has invoked one of the general exceptions of Article XX GATT as a justification. This might in a way strengthen the argument that Article XX does indeed cover only a limited set of public policy objectives. For example, in the 1987 *Japan–Alcohol I* case, the Panel noted that the

---

[211] Cf R Howse and D Regan, "The Product/Process Distinction: An Illusory Basis for Disciplining 'Unilateralism' in Trade Policy", 11 *European Journal of International Law* (2000) 249 at 264 *et seq*; R Hudec, "GATT/WTO Constraints on Domestic Regulation: Requiem for an 'Aims and Effects' Test", 32 *The International Lawyer* (1998) 619 at 630 *et seq*.

[212] Cf R Howse and D Reagan, "The Product/Process Distinction: An Illusory Basis for Disciplining 'Unilateralism' in Trade Policy", 11 *European Journal of International Law* (2000) 249 at 264 *et seq*.

General Agreement did not provide for the possibility of justifying discriminatory or protective taxes inconsistent with Article III:2 on the ground that they had been introduced for the purpose of "taxation according to the tax-bearing ability" of domestic consumers of imported and directly competitive domestic liquors.[213]

Let us examine the few instances where the purposes of a measure have been taken into consideration in determining whether an internal fiscal measure was in violation of the National Treatment obligation.

In *Japan–Alcohol II*, Japan had argued that the purpose of its tax system of alcoholic beverages was trade-neutral, and thus guaranteed equality of competitive conditions, since it maintained a "roughly constant" tax/price ratio and no protective aim or effect of the legislation could be detected.[214] Recalling that it had already dismissed the *aims-and-effects* test put forward by Japan, the Panel nevertheless correctly considered Japan's "horizontal tax equity" claim as an argument going towards a denial of the existence of differential treatment between the relevant products. In other words, Japan argued that the apparent different treatment afforded to competitive products at issue was necessary in order to ensure *substantial* equality. The Panel rejected Japan's argument noting that (i) it is not at all clear that maintaining a "roughly constant" tax/price ratio avoids violating the "not similarly taxed" requirement of Article III:2, second sentence; (ii) the statistics on the tax/price ratio show that significant differences do indeed exist between shochu and the other directly competitive or substitutable products and that there are significantly different tax/price ratios within the same product categories;[215] and (iii) the lack of any mention in the contested legislation that its purpose was to maintain a constant tax/price ratio constitutes evidence that this was rather an *ex post facto* rationalisation by Japan and, at any rate, there are no guarantees in the legislation that the tax/price

---

[213] Panel Report on *Japan Alcohol I*, above n 5, para 5.13.

[214] *Ibid.*, para 6.34.

[215] The Panel noted also the following: "Moreover, as noted in paragraph 6.33 above, there were significant problems with the methodology for calculating tax/price ratios submitted by Japan, such that arguments based on that methodology could only be viewed as inconclusive. More particularly, although Japan had argued that the comparison of tax/price ratios should be done on a category-by-category basis, its statistics on which the tax/price ratios were based excluded domestically produced spirits and whisky/brandy from the calculation of tax/price ratios for spirits and whisky/brandy. Since the prices of the domestic spirits and whisky/brandy are much lower than the prices of the imported ones, this exclusion has the impact of reducing considerably the tax/price ratios cited by Japan for those products. In this connection, the Panel noted that one consequence of the Japanese tax system was to make it more difficult for cheaper imported brands of spirits and whisky/brandy to enter the market. Moreover, the Panel noted that the Japanese statistics were based on suggested retail prices and there was evidence in the record that these products were often sold at a discount, at least in Tokyo. To the extent that the prices were unreliable, the resultant tax/price ratios would be unreliable as well." *Ibid.*

ratio will always be maintained at a constant (or "roughly constant") level.[216]

In *Canada–Periodicals*, the purpose of the measure at issue was quite clearly to reserve advertising revenues to domestic periodicals. Whether this may or may not have been a legitimate public policy purpose, it could certainly not have been justified by any of the public policy exceptions listed in Article XX GATT. Thus, Canada tried to win its case on the question of whether or not the two products at issue (split-run v non-split run magazines) were "like" or "competitive". The Appellate Body relied on the stated objective of the measure (modification of the competitive relationship in the advertising market) in order to find, first, that the two products were indeed in competition with each other[217] and subsequently that there existed "protective application" contrary to Article III:2.[218]

In *Korea–Alcohol*, the purpose of the measure was not taken into consideration by the Korean Government, whose defence focused exclusively on the fact that the products at issue were different. Korea did however try to put forward an explanation for the structure of its internal tax system, emphasising the fact that for a long time the typical domestic product (soju) was the only spirit subject to liquor taxes and that only over time, other spirits were marketed, and as they appeared, new tax categories were created.[219] While the Panel ignored Korea's explanation for the structure of the law,[220] the Appellate Body correctly found that those reasons did not modify the conclusion that the measures were applied "so as to afford protection to domestic production".[221]

From these few cases, it is possible to gain some appreciation of the minimal role played by the policy purposes of a fiscal measure in an Article III:2 analysis. Besides the "substantial equality" argument, which as previously explained may be taken into consideration for the purpose of determining whether the tax treats two products differently (a function similar to that of the "border tax adjustment" mechanism), the objectives of a measure were only really considered in *Canada–Periodicals*, though as evidence of the products' competitive relationship and the measure's protective application.

---

[216] *Ibid.*
[217] Appellate Body Report on *Canada–Periodicals*, above n 25, at 26-28.
[218] *Ibid.*, at 32, "Canada also admitted that the objective and structure of the tax is to insulate Canadian magazines from competition in the advertising sector, thus leaving significant Canadian advertising revenues for the production of editorial material created for the Canadian market".
[219] Panel Report on *Korea–Alcohol*, above n 16, para 5.176.
[220] *Ibid.*, para 10.60.
[221] Appellate Body Report on *Korea–Alcohol*, above n 30, para 150, "Likewise, the reason why there is very little imported soju in Korea does not change the pattern of application of the contested measures."

*(c) Integrating an Article III determination with an "Economic Efficiency"
criterion or "Necessity" test*   In an attempt to remedy the excessive narrowness of the list of regulatory objectives in Article XX GATT, Mattoo and
Subramanian have proposed reading into the Article III determination the
kinds of disciplines—but not just those—contained in Article XX. Drawing
inspiration from the novel approach found in both the TBT and SPS
Agreements, where regulatory objectives and standards for determining
protectionism are part of the determination of the violation rather than being
invoked as part of an affirmative defence, these Authors have suggested a
two-stage test for evaluating whether a measure taken for regulatory reasons indeed discriminates against imported products or affords protection
to domestic products. While at the first stage "product likeness" will be
defined on the basis of a similarity of end uses and a clear relationship of
substitutability and direct competition based on market conditions (in a
manner not very different from the current interpretation of Article III), at
the second stage there would be a presumption in favour of the choice of the
economically optimal policy to achieve the legitimate objective pursued by
the Member.[222] In other words, if the measure in question is economically
the most optimal means of achieving a particular public policy objective,
then that measure would be presumed not to have been taken for protectionist purposes in violation of the National Treatment obligation of Article
III. On the other hand, if a country chooses to pursue an objective by an
instrument other than the economically first-best instrument, then it should
be obliged to demonstrate why instruments ranked above it in the hierarchy
of instruments were not chosen.[223] One of the advantages of this approach
would clearly be the recognition of WTO Members' right to invoke a wider
set of public policy objectives than those explicitly recognised as legitimate
in Article XX GATT.

Although the authors point out the similarity of their economic efficiency criterion with the necessity test (or the "least-GATT inconsistent
measure" test) as it has been applied within the context of Article XX,[224]
they also stress the "superiority" of the former on the basis that it provides clearer criteria for the choice of instruments and allows Members to
adopt any regulatory measures by simply showing the non-feasibility of
economically superior instruments.[225]

---

[222] A Mattoo and A Subramanian, "Regulatory Autonomy and Multilateral Disciplines: The
Dilemma and a Possible Resolution", *JIEL* (1998) 303, at 315.

[223] *Ibid.*, at 318.

[224] For example, they emphasise that "the 'consistent' application of a measure would be a
key aspect of the economic efficiency criteria. The right to take regulatory action entails a
responsibility to apply it consistently across products that are clearly covered by the objective that the government professes to uphold". *Ibid.*, at 319.

[225] They believe that (a) very few measures would pass the 'necessity test' ("frequently we
can conceive of a measure which could also achieve the relevant objective without being
inconsistent with a Member's obligations"), and (b) the necessity test as applied by GATT

In a more recent and in depth study, Verhoosel develops the argument that WTO adjudicators should apply an "integrated necessity test" under those provisions of both the GATT and the GATS that lay down their respective National Treatment obligations.[226] He argues that, for a proper line to be drawn between trade liberalisation and deep integration,

> de facto discrimination can only be revealed in an objective manner [...] by engaging in an analysis as to whether a particular regulatory instrument (1) specifically and adversely affects imported products or foreign services/service suppliers as compared with their like domestic counterparts, and (2) is necessary to achieve a purported legitimate policy goal, or, alternatively, whether other, less restrictive, regulatory means are available.[227]

Among the legal arguments put forward in his book to ground his proposition, the author points to both the Panel and Appellate Body Reports on *Chile–Alcohol*, where in order to determine whether the Chilean fiscal legislation violated the non-discrimination obligation of Article III:2, both WTO tribunals appeared to look at the "rational relationship" between the legislation under review and its purported public policy objectives. While the Panel considered the absence of a clear relationship between the stated objectives and the tax measure itself to be "evidence confirming the discriminatory design, structure and architecture of [the Chilean] measure,"[228] the Appellate Body stated, in a not altogether clear manner, that,

> a measure's purposes, objectively manifested in the design, architecture and structure of the measure, *are* intensely pertinent to the task of evaluating whether or not that measure is applied so as to afford protection to domestic production.[229]

Although the Appellate Body subsequently stated that "it would be inappropriate, under Article III:2, second sentence, of the GATT 1994, to examine whether the tax measure is *necessary* for achieving its stated objectives

---

panels does not provide clear rules for choosing the appropriate regulatory instrument ("the heart of the problem is that, in its exclusive concern with GATT-consistency, the interpretation of Art XX proposed by GATT panels does not explicitly address the issue of efficiency of measures." *Ibid.*, at 317. Cf A Mattoo and P Mavroidis, "Trade, Environment and the WTO: How Real is the Conflict?" in EU Petersmann (ed), *International Trade Law and the GATT/WTO Dispute Settlement System* (London, Kluwer Dordrecht, 1997).

[226] G Verhoosel, *National Treatment and WTO Dispute Settlement: Adjudicating the Boundaries of Regulatory Autonomy* (Oxford, Hart Publishing, 2002).
[227] *Ibid.*, at 2.
[228] Panel Report on *Chile–Alcohol*, above n 35, para 7.154.
[229] Appellate Body Report on *Chile–Alcohol*, above n 70, para 71.

or purposes",[230] the Author suggests that, despite their formally denying doing so, the Panel conducted and the Appellate Body condoned an in-depth necessity test as regard to domestic regulation under GATT Article III:2, second sentence.[231]

The particularly novel and audacious feature of Verhoosel's proposi-tion is in his argument that a finding of material discrimination not only *should* but *must* be based on an assessment of the regulatory measure's "necessity". In Verhoosel's view, there are very sound normative policy *and* legal arguments to suggest that National Treatment should and can *only* be defined by referring to the necessity of domestic regulation.[232] In other words, a measure which is deemed to be "necessary" or the "least-trade restrictive alternative" to achieve a legitimate public policy objec-tive must also be found to comply with the National Treatment principle. In this regard, taking inspiration and support from the *Hand Formula* in torts and a game theoretical model, the author develops a theory of opti-mal care in international trade arguing that, under an economic analysis of the non-discrimination principle, the good faith obligation not to cause unnecessary adverse effects on imports also constitutes the optimal level of care by a regulating WTO Member.[233]

If one were to derive a conclusion from the two above-mentioned proposals, it would be that there may be good reasons for abandoning the non-discrimination approach for a rule based on a different normative standard which involves taking into consideration the "rea-sonableness" of the relationship between the national measure and the pursuit of a legitimate public policy purpose. In fact, even if the concept of material discrimination, as the basis for the normative standard, were counterbalanced by a broad public policy exception, the central question would still be how to limit the availability of such an exception. In other words, under what criteria should a Member be allowed to adopt a regu-latory measure in the pursuit of a legitimate public policy, when it is established that that measure has discriminatory effects on imported products? Whether these criteria are found in the standard of "economic efficiency" or in the concept of "necessity", it is clear that the way for-ward must be somehow to replace the two-step approach based on the "non-discrimination" *rule* and the "public policy" *exception* with a single-prong approach that focuses directly on the "reasonableness" of the rela-tionship between the regulatory measure and its legitimate objective. This approach would have the benefit not only of avoiding having to determine whether a measure is indeed discriminatory in effect (in itself

---

[230] *Ibid.*, para 72.
[231] G Verhoosel, *National Treatment and WTO Dispute Settlement: Adjudicating the Boundaries of Regulatory Autonomy* (Oxford, Hart Publishing, 2002) at 29–30.
[232] *Ibid.*, at 7.
[233] *Ibid.*, ch 5.

quite an onerous task), it would also impose on national regulators more uniform and clear normative criteria. Although this approach might appear to constitute a further intrusion into national regulatory autonomy, it is so only in certain limited respects. As evidenced in the next chapter dealing with the prohibition of de facto discrimination with regard to non-fiscal regulations, as well as in the later chapter on the "reasonableness" rule, if correctly applied, an approach based on the "reasonableness" of the relationship between the measure and its objective, excluding the possibility of inquiring into the "proportionality" of the objective itself, would not represent an excessive depauperisation of Members' regulatory prerogatives.

3.2 THE PROHIBITION OF DE FACTO DISCRIMINATION AND NON-FISCAL REGULATIONS

The prohibition of de facto discrimination based on the product's nationality applies also to the realm of non-fiscal regulations affecting trade in goods.

Following the same scheme as employed with regard to origin-neutral fiscal measures, this section will analyse both the "normative content" and the "justification options" of the National Treatment obligations in WTO and EC law as they are applied to facially origin-neutral non-fiscal internal regulations.

A. Normative Content

1. Article III:4 GATT

As already mentioned, there exist only few cases where Article III:4 has been employed to review measures, which, although on their face applying equally to domestic and imported products (facially or formally origin-neutral measures), allegedly violate the National Treatment obligation. Contrary to the case-law dealing with hidden tax discrimination, de facto discrimination claims involving internal non-fiscal regulations have rarely been successful. Of the five instances where a formally origin-neutral regulation has been claimed to discriminate de facto on the basis of the product's origin in violation of Article III:4, only once has the complaining party been successful.

Before examining these cases in more detail, it is relevant to emphasise that two types of de facto discrimination claims have emerged so far from GATT/WTO practice. On the one hand, there are the claims according to which an origin-neutral measure is alleged to violate the

National Treatment obligation on the basis that its application de facto upsets the competitive relationship between domestic and imported "identical" products. One can refer to this type of claim as the case of "formally *identical* treatment of *identical* products with de facto discriminatory effects on imported products". In *Japan—Measures Affecting Consumer Photographic Film and Paper,*[234] for example, the United States claimed that the Japanese Government had negatively affected the competitive opportunities of imported photographic film and paper vis-à-vis domestic photographic film and paper through the application of several apparently origin-neutral "liberalisation countermeasures".

The second type of cases involves a claim that an origin-neutral measure, by affording different treatment to two similar products, in effect discriminates between domestic and imported "like" products. This is the case of "formally *different* treatment of *similar* products with de facto discriminatory effects on imported products".[235] In the recent *European Communities—Measures Affecting Asbestos and Asbestos-Containing Products* dispute,[236] for example, Canada claimed that the differential treatment by France of two similar products[237] altered the conditions of competition between domestic and imported like products. In particular, Canada argued that the French measure, although formally origin-neutral, was in practice discriminating between Canadian production of chrysotile fibre and French production of allegedly similar substitute fibres.[238]

As the following analysis will show, while the case of "formally *identical* treatment of *identical* products with de facto discriminatory effects on imported products" focuses exclusively on whether the identical treatment affects the competitive relationship between domestic and imported products, the case of "formally *different* treatment of *similar* products with de facto discriminatory effects on imported products" needs in the first instance to determine whether the products at issue are indeed similar.

---

[234] Panel Report on *Japan—Measures Affecting Consumer Photographic Film and Paper* (*Japan–Film*), WT/DS44/R, circulated 31 March 1998, adopted 22 April 1998.
[235] Cf L Ehring, "De facto Discrimination in WTO Law: National Treatment and Most-Favoured-Nation Treatment—or Equal Treatment?", *Jean Monnet Working Paper* (NYU School of Law, 2002) where the author seems to distinguish between the case of "vertical" and "horizontal asymmetry".
[236] Panel Report on *European Communities—Measures Affecting Asbestos and Asbestos Containing Products* (*EC–Asbestos*), WT/DS135R, circulated 18 Sep 2000, adopted 5 April 2001.
[237] While chrysotile fibre—also known as asbestos—and products containing it were banned, substitute fibres, such as PVA, cellulose or glass fibres, and products containing them were permitted)
[238] Panel Report on *EC–Asbestos*, above n 236, paras 3.12 and 8.151.

(a) GATT panel practice: EEC Animal Feed Protein, Malt Beverages *and* Canada Alcohol II   Of the three Article III:4 violation claims in GATT panel practice dealing with origin-neutral non-fiscal measures, two were eventually rejected on the basis that the products were not like,[239] while the third was accepted.[240] While the former involved cases of "formally *different* treatment of *similar* products", the latter was a case of "formally *identical* treatment of *identical* products".[241]

Let us start with the first ever case of a formally origin-neutral regulation reviewed under Article III:4. In *EEC Measures on Animal Feed Proteins*,[242] a panel examined the legality under GATT 1947 of certain EEC measures inter alia imposing on both domestic producers and importers of several vegetable protein feeds (such as oilseeds, cakes and meals, dehydrated fodder and compound feeds) the obligation to purchase a certain quantity of skimmed milk powder held by intervention agencies and to have it denatured for use as feed for animals other than calves.

In its complaint, the United States argued that even though the EEC purchase requirement applied to both domestic and imported vegetable proteins alike, the impact of the measure was nevertheless felt more directly by *imported* vegetable proteins. The US claim was based on the two following observations. First of all, the EEC purchase requirement did not apply to animal, marine and synthetic proteins, even though these proteins were, according to the United States, *substitutable* for vegetable proteins for use in feeds. Secondly, the reason for excluding animal, marine and synthetic proteins from the purchase requirement was that in the EEC there existed a *substantial* production of these types of proteins, while the EEC did not produce a *substantial* amount of its own domestic needs of vegetable proteins. Moreover, the United States maintained that, taking account of their generally higher protein content and certain technical advantages, the exclusion of animal, marine and synthetic proteins from the scope of the EEC measure could not be explained on the ground that animal, marine and synthetic proteins were not *like* vegetable proteins.[243]

---

[239] Panel Report on *EEC Measures on Animal Feed Proteins*, above n 6, and Panel Report on *Malt Beverages*, above n 5.

[240] Panel Report on *Canada—Import, Distribution and Sale of Certain Alcoholic Drinks by Provincial Marketing Agencies (Canada–Alcohol II)*, DS17/R, adopted on 18 Feb 1992, BISD 39S/27.

[241] On cases involving facially neutral measures with disparate effects *see* D Farber and R Hudec, "GATT Legal Restraints on Domestic Environmental Regulations", in J Bhagwati and R Hudec (eds), *Fair Trade and Harmonization: Prerequisites for Free Trade*, vol 2 (Cambridge, MA. MIT Press, 1996) at 70 *et seq.*

[242] Panel Report on *EEC Measures on Animal Feed Proteins*, above. n 6.

[243] *Ibid.*, paras 3.7 and 3.39. The United States also argued that the purchase of denatured skimmed milk powder required by the EEC measures clearly violated Art III:5, which prohibits regulations requiring, directly or indirectly, that any specified amount or proportion of a domestic product be mixed, processed or used. Even though the regulation did not expressly favour *domestic* skimmed milk powder over *imported* vegetable proteins, the United States maintained that the purpose and effect of the Council Regulation (EEC) No 563/76 was to require that a specified amount of skimmed milk powder from domestic

The US claim that the formally origin-neutral regulation constituted hidden discrimination between domestic and imported products within the meaning of Article III:4, was rejected by the Panel on the basis of a very strict interpretation of the likeness concept as employed in Article III:4. The Panel concluded that the non-application of the EEC measure to animal, marine and synthetic proteins did not violate Article III:4,[244] since, although technically substitutable in terms of their final use, the various protein products at issue could not be considered "like products" within the meaning of Article III:4.[245] The Panel's determination of unlikeness was premised on (a) the number of products and tariff items carrying different duty rates and tariff bindings, (b) the varying protein contents of the products at issue and (c) the different vegetable, animal and synthetic origins of the protein products.[246]

Although on the basis of a completely different approach to the likeness concept, the Panel Report on *United States—Measures Affecting Alcoholic and Malt Beverages*[247] also found that certain formally origin-neutral restrictions imposed by a number of states on beer depending on its alcohol content did not violate Article III:4 because high alcohol beer was not *like* low alcohol beer. In that particular case, Canada had argued that certain states restricted the location at which beer with *over 3.2 per cent* by weight (4 per cent by volume) alcohol content might be sold, while no restriction was imposed on the sale of beer *at 3.2 per cent* alcohol content or *lower*. Similarly, in some states, different labelling requirements were imposed on beer containing more than 3.2 per cent alcohol content than on lower alcohol content beer.[248] Arguing that all beers were "like products" irrespective of their alcohol content, Canada claimed that regulatory differences based on beer alcohol content with respect to distribution, points of sale and labelling treated imported like products less favourably and afforded protection to the US industry, contrary to Article III.[249]

The Panel began its examination by considering whether, in the context of Article III:4, low alcohol beer and high alcohol beer should be considered "like products". The Panel observed that the treatment of imported and domestic products as like products under Article III may have significant implications for the scope of obligations under the

intervention agencies stocks, which held *only domestically produced products*, be purchased and denatured and thereby used as a source of proteins in feeding stuffs, replacing imported vegetable proteins. *Ibid.*, paras 3.5–3.7.

[244] *Ibid.*, para 4.11.
[245] *Ibid.*, paras 4.2–4.3.
[246] *Ibid.*
[247] Panel Report on *Malt Beverages*, above n 5.
[248] *Ibid.*, para 2.32.
[249] *Ibid.*, para 3.120.

General Agreement and for the regulatory autonomy of Contracting Parties with respect to their internal tax laws and regulations. In particular, the Panel noted that

> once products are designated as like products, a regulatory product differentiation, eg for standardisation or environmental purposes, becomes inconsistent with Article III even if the regulation is not "applied ... so as afford protection to domestic production".[250]

Thus stressing that it was imperative that the like product determination in the context of Article III had to be made in such a way that it did not unnecessarily infringe upon the regulatory authority and domestic policy options of Contracting Parties, the Panel considered that it was essential that such determination were made not only in the light of such criteria as the products' physical characteristics, but also in the light of the purpose of Article III, which is to ensure that internal taxes and regulations "not be applied to imported or domestic products so as to afford protection to domestic production".[251]

Although it recognised that on the basis of their physical characteristics, low alcohol beer and high alcohol beer were indeed "similar", the Panel concluded that they could not be considered "like products" in terms of Article III:4 since the choice of the particular level of alcohol content did not have the *purpose* or *effect* of affording protection to domestic production.[252]

With regard to the effect of the beer alcohol content requirements, the Panel noted the following: (a) both Canadian and US beer manufacturers produced both high and low alcohol content beer, (b) the laws and regulations in question in the various states did not differentiate between imported and domestic beer as such, and (c) the burdens resulting from these regulations thus did not fall more heavily on Canadian than on US producers.[253] With regard to the purpose of the laws regulating the alcohol content of beer, the Panel noted that

> irrespective of whether the policy background to the laws distinguishing alcohol content of beer was the protection of human health and public morals [as argued by the United States] or the promotion of a new source of government revenue [as argued by Canada], both the statements of the parties and the legislative history suggest that the alcohol content of beer has not been singled out as a means of favouring domestic producers over foreign producers.[254]

---

[250] *Ibid.*, para 5.72.
[251] *Ibid.*, paras 5.71–72.
[252] *Ibid.*, paras 5.73–75.
[253] *Ibid.*, para 5.73.
[254] *Ibid.*, para 5.74.

As pointed out in the section dealing with internal taxation, the approach followed by the *Malt Beverages* panel introduced the so called *aims-and-effects* test to the likeness determination. Keeping in mind the findings with regard to claims of de facto discriminatory taxation, the arguments employed by the *Malt Beverages* panel in order to exclude the likeness of the two products at issue (high and low alcohol beer) focused principally on one issue: whether the regulatory distinction under review had the effect of predominantly protecting domestic products. The fact that both Canadian and US beer manufacturers produced high and low alcohol content beer was enough for the Panel to exclude that the burdens resulting from distribution and labelling regulations fell more heavily on Canadian than on US products. In other words, even assuming that high and low alcohol beers were indeed similar products, there was no evidence that the (origin-neutral) regulations at issue were indeed de facto discriminatory measures.

Contrary to the previous two cases, the Panel Report on *Canada—Import, Distribution and Sale of Certain Alcoholic Drinks by Provincial Marketing Agencies*, the so called *Canada–Alcohol II* case,[255] eventually found that the minimum price requirements imposed by the liquor boards of British Colombia, New Brunswick, Newfoundland and Ontario on both imported and domestic beer was in violation of Article III:4. Although the United States had based its claim on the argument that the minimum price requirements were in violation of Article XI, the Panel correctly reviewed the particular measure at issue under Article III:4 since the minimum prices (applied to both imported and domestic beer) were clearly internal measures and according to the Note Ad Article III were within the scope of application of that Article.[256]

The Panel was thus confronted with a different scenario compared to the EEC protein feed regulation and the US alcohol content requirements examined above. The minimum price requirements imposed by the Canadian provinces apparently applied "formally *identical* treatment to *identical* products".[257] The Panel, however, recalled the findings of the *Section 337* report, according to which there may be cases where application of formally identical legal provisions would in practice accord less

---

[255] Panel Report on *Canada—Import, Distribution and Sale of Certain Alcoholic Drinks by Provincial Marketing Agencies* (*Canada–Alcohol II*), DS17/R, adopted on 18 Feb 1992, BISD 39S/27.

[256] *Ibid.*, para 5.28.

[257] In reality it is not altogether clear from the Panel Report whether all these minimum price requirements were indeed origin-neutral. Canada maintained the following: in Newfoundland, the "floor price" was equal to the lowest-priced provincial beer (para 4.69); in New Brunswick the "floor price" applied through the linking of imported beer prices to prices of out-of-province beer prices (para 4.66); in Ontario the "reference price", which was also referred to as the "Non-discriminatory Reference Price" or NDRP, included the supplier quote, plus federal excise tax and duty and the liquor-board freight and in-store and out-of-store cost-of-service charges (para 4.60); and, in British Columbia the "reference price" for

favourable treatment to imported products and a contracting party might thus have to apply different legal provisions to imported products to ensure that the treatment accorded to them is in fact no less favourable.[258] It then found that the maintenance of a minimum price for an imported product at a level at which a directly competing, higher-priced domestic product was supplied was indeed inconsistent with Article III:4. The Panel argued that minimum prices, even if applied equally to imported and domestic beer, did not accord equal conditions of competition to imported and domestic beer whenever they prevented imported beer from being supplied at a price below that of domestic beer.[259] Expressly avoiding a general finding on the consistency of minimum prices with Article III:4, the Panel concluded that the minimum prices imposed by the liquor boards of the four Canadian provinces were inconsistent with Article III:4 *to the extent* that they were fixed in relation to the prices at which domestic beer was supplied.[260]

(b) WTO jurisprudence: Kodak–Fuji *and* Asbestos   A few years later, after the establishment of the WTO, in what was to become the *Kodak–Fuji* dispute, the same underlying argument developed in *Canada–Alcohol II* was at the basis of the US claim against several Japanese liberalisation "countermeasures" (*taisaku*), whose application, according to the United States, had for more than 30 years de facto inhibited the distribution and sale of imported consumer photographic film and paper in Japan.[261] The Japanese measures under review included; (1) distribution "measures", which allegedly encouraged and facilitated the creation of a market structure for photographic film and paper in which imports were excluded from traditional distribution channels;[262] (2) restrictions on large retail stores, which allegedly restricted the growth of an alternative distribution

---

draught beer appeared to be similar to the Ontario's NDRP (para 4.64). Although the Panel noted that there was "for neither British Columbia nor Ontario any indication given as to the criteria for setting the current level of the minimum price" (para 4.70), it appears that at least with regard to these two latter provinces the minimum price requirements were not formally based on the price level of domestic beer, or in other words they were at least facially origin-neutral measures.

[258] Panel Report on *United States—Section 337 of the Tariff Act of 1930* (*Section 337*), L/6439, adopted on 7 Nov 1989, BISD 36S/345, para 5.11, cited in Panel Report on *Canada–Alcohol II*, above n 255, para 5.29.
[259] Panel Report on *Canada–Alcohol II*, above n 255, paras. 5.29–531.
[260] *Ibid.*, para 5.31.
[261] Panel Report on *Japan—Measures Affecting Consumer Photographic Film and Paper* (*Kodak–Fuji*), WT/DS44/R, circulated 31 March 1998, adopted 22 April 1998.
[262] The essence of the US claim in respect of this type of distribution "countermeasures" was that Japan created vertical integration and single-brand distribution in the Japanese film and paper market through standardisation of transaction terms, systemisation and limitations on premiums to businesses. *Ibid.*, para 10.204.

channel for imported film;[263] and (3) promotion "measures", which allegedly disadvantaged imports by restricting the use of sales promotion techniques.[264] Next to the claim that all these measures nullified or impaired benefits accruing to the United States from tariff concessions made by Japan on black and white and colour photographic film and paper under Article XXIII:1 of the GATT (a so-called "non-violation" claim), the United States argued that the distribution "measures" were also inconsistent with Article III:4 of the GATT. The US case in this respect was based on two arguments: first, vertical integration or single-brand distribution in the photographic film and paper sector in Japan negatively affected imports more than domestic products; secondly, the Japanese Government was responsible for promoting and facilitating such vertical integration and single-brand distribution.

First of all, the Panel rejected Japan's argument that its distribution measures did not violate Article III:4 since they were neutral as to origin of the goods (none of them *formally* distinguishing between the imported and domestic products concerned). Correctly following GATT panel practice, the Panel stated that, even in the absence of de jure discrimination (measures which on their face discriminate as to origin), it may be possible for a complainant to show de facto discrimination (measures which have a disparate impact on imports).[265] In this regard, the Panel emphasised that the consistent focus of GATT panel practice and WTO jurisprudence had been on ensuring effective equality of competitive opportunities between imported products from different countries (Most Favoured Nation principle) and between imported and domestic products (National Treatment principle). Once again extensively referring to the *Section 337* report, the Panel noted that even formally identical treatment of domestic and imported products may constitute less favourable treatment for imported products for the purpose of Article III:4.[266] The Panel stated, however, that in such circumstances, the complaining party is called upon to make a detailed showing of any claimed disproportionate impact on imports resulting from the origin-neutral measure, and the burden of demonstrating such impact may be significantly more difficult where the relationship between the measure and the product is questionable.[267]

---

[263] The United States asserted that the application of the Large Stores Law had negatively affected the relative competitive position of imported film in the Japanese market because it restricted the spread of large stores, which the United States claimed, on the basis of survey evidence, were more likely to carry imported film. *Ibid.*, paras 10.224–10.226.

[264] *Ibid.*, para 10.22.

[265] *Ibid.*, para 10.85.

[266] *Ibid.*, para 10.379, "[The] standard of effective equality of competitive conditions on the internal market is the standard of national treatment that is required, not only with regard to Art III generally, but also more particularly with regard to the "no less favourable treatment" standard in Art III:4."

[267] *Ibid.*, para 10.85.

Following a thorough analysis, which focused more on the non-violation complaint than on the violation complaint, the Panel found in favour of Japan on all counts on the ground that the United States had not been able to show that the various "measures" at issue had indeed upset the competitive relationships between domestic and US film and paper in the Japanese market. In particular, with regard to the alleged violation of Article III:4 by Japan's distribution "countermeasures", the Panel noted the following: (1) single-brand distribution appeared to have occurred before and independently of those "measures", (2) the United States had not demonstrated that these "measures" were indeed directed at promoting vertical integration or single-brand distribution, and (3) single brand wholesale distribution was the common market structure— indeed the norm—in most major national film markets, including the US market.[268]

Although the Panel was not really convinced by the US argument that single brand distribution discriminated against imported products, the United States lost its case principally by failing to establish a cause-and-effect connection between the Japanese measures under review and the allegedly discriminatory market structure for photographic film and paper.

More recently, in *European Communities—Measures Affecting Asbestos and Asbestos-Containing Products*,[269] Article III:4 was employed to review a formally origin-neutral regulation, which by differentiating between two allegedly similar products was believed to constitute hidden discrimination on the basis of the origin of the products; once again, a case of "formally *different* treatment of *similar* products with de facto discriminatory effects on imported products".[270]

In the *Asbestos* dispute, Canada had in particular claimed that the differential treatment by France of two similar products (chrysotile fibre—also known as asbestos—and products containing it were banned, while substitute fibres, such as PVA, cellulose or glass fibres, and products containing them were permitted) altered the conditions of competition between domestic and imported like products. Canada argued that the French measure, although formally

---

[268] *Ibid.*, paras 10.204–10.208 and 10.381.

[269] Panel Report on *European Communities—Measures Affecting Asbestos and Asbestos-Containing Products* (*EC–Asbestos*), WT/DS135/R, circulated 18 Sep 2000, adopted 5 April 2001.

[270] As noted in the chapter dealing with the general prohibition of quantitative restrictions of Art XI, although the *Asbestos* dispute technically involved two measures, one banning imports of asbestos and asbestos-containing products into France and another prohibiting their production and use in France, the Panel correctly concluded that the two measures were part of one regulatory system. Similarly, the *Shrimp/Turtles* dispute should have been categorised, like the *Asbestos* dispute, as involving an internal regulation (implemented by two distinct measures with regard to imports and domestic products), which did not formally discriminate on the basis of the product's origin but which apparently afforded de facto less favourable treatment to imported products. *See* below section dealing with 'justification options' for de facto discriminatory non-fiscal regulations.

origin-neutral, was in practice discriminating between Canadian production of chrysotile fibre and French production of allegedly similar substitute fibres.[271]

The Panel examined Canada's claim under Article III:4, correctly distinguishing the "likeness" issue from the "less favourable treatment" requirement. With regard to the former, the Panel employed the standard criteria referred to in GATT/WTO jurisprudence for determining whether two products are "like" (ie consumers' tastes and habits, product's property, nature and quality, product's end uses and tariff classification), and found that the products at issue, chrysotile, PVA, cellulose and glass fibres and cement products containing them, were indeed like products for purposes of Article III:4.[272]

With regard to the "less favourable treatment" requirement, the Panel noted that the terms of the French measure at issue established in themselves less favourable treatment of chrysotile fibre as compared with substitute fibres, and found that de jure [that measure] treats imported chrysotile fibres and chrysotile-cement products less favourably than domestic PVA, cellulose and glass fibres and fibro-cement products.[273]

However, since the Panel eventually concluded that the French ban on asbestos and asbestos containing products was justified under the general exception provision of Article XX(b) for public health reasons,[274] Canada appealed the Panel Report to the Appellate Body, which for the first time had the opportunity to address a claim based on Article III:4 involving an origin-neutral measure.[275]

In light of the comprehensive analysis of the "likeness" issue and the revealing *obiter dictum* regarding the "less favourable treatment" requirement, it is necessary to examine the Appellate Body report in the *Asbestos* dispute in some detail.

(i) The Appellate Body Report on Asbestos *and likeness*

The analysis of the Appellate Body concerning the issue of "likeness" may be divided into three distinct parts: first, an elaboration of the general approach to the interpretation of "like products" as found in Article III:4; secondly, findings of error of law by the panel; and finally "completing

---

[271] Panel Report on *EC–Asbestos*, above n 236, paras 3.12 and 8.151.
[272] *Ibid.*, paras 8.112–8.150.
[273] *Ibid.*, para 8.155. The Panel appears to confuse the concepts of de jure and de facto discrimination. Compare the above-cited statement with the Panel's findings with regard to the introductory clause of Art XX in para 8.228.
[274] *Ibid.*, para 8.241.
[275] The Panel Report on *Kodak–Fuji* was never appealed. Cf Appellate Body Report on *European Communities—Measures Affecting Asbestos and Asbestos-Containing Products*, WT/DS155/AB/R, circulated 12 March 2001, adopted 5 April 2001

the analysis, where the Appellate Body applies Article III:4 to the facts of the case.[276]

With regard to the elaboration of the general approach, the Appellate Body began its analysis by delineating the meaning of the term "likeness" as employed in Article III:4.[277] Observing that the *textual* meaning leaves many interpretative questions open,[278] the Appellate Body turned to paragraphs 1 and 2 of Article III as the relevant *context* of Article III:4. It noted that while the "general principle" of Article III:1 is expressed in Article III:2 through two distinct obligations—the first lays down obligations in respect of "like products", and the second lays down obligations in respect of "directly competitive or substitutable" products—Article III:4 includes only an obligation applicable to "like products". Therefore, given the textual difference between Articles III:2 and III:4, the "accordion" of "likeness" stretches in a different way in Article III:4. In other words, the strict reading of "like products" in Article III:2 should not be replicated under Article III:4. According to the Appellate Body, this interpretation conforms with the purpose of Article III which is "to prevent Members from applying internal taxes and regulations in a manner which affects the competitive relationship, in the marketplace, *between the domestic and imported products involved*, 'so as to afford protection to domestic production'."[279] As products that are in a competitive relationship in the marketplace could be affected through treatment of *imports* "less favourable" than the treatment accorded to *domestic* products, the Appellate Body believed that the word "like" in Article III:4 was to be interpreted to apply to products that are in such a competitive relationship. In other words, a determination of "likeness" under Article III:4 is, fundamentally, a determination about the nature and extent of a competitive relationship between and among products. It would be, moreover, incongruous if, due to a significant difference in the product scope of paragraphs 2 and 4 of Article III, Members were prevented from using one form of regulation—for instance, fiscal—to protect domestic production of certain products, but were able to use another form of regulation—for instance, non-fiscal–to achieve those ends. Without ruling on the *precise* product scope of Article III:4, the Appellate Body concluded that,

---

[276] This division is taken from R Howse and E Tuerk, "The WTO Impact in Internal Regulations—A Case Study of the Canada—EC Asbestos Dispute" in G de Búrca and J Scott (eds), *The EU and the WTO: Legal and Constitutional Aspects* (Oxford, Hart Publishing, 2001) at 296.

[277] The Appellate Body noted that, although there had already been occasions to interpret other aspects of Art III:4 of the GATT 1994, it was the first time that the Appellate Body examined the meaning of the word "like" in Art III:4. Appellate Body Report on *EC–Asbestos*, above n 275, para 88.

[278] *Ibid.*, para 90, citing Appellate Body Report on *Canada—Measures Affecting the Export of Civilian Aircraft*, WT/DS70/AB/R, adopted 20 Aug 1999, para 153.

[279] Appellate Body Report on *EC–Asbestos*, above n 275, para 98 [emphasis original].

although broader than the *first* sentence of Article III:2, [the product scope of Article III:4] is certainly *not* broader than the *combined* product scope of the *two* sentences of Article III:2 of the GATT 1994.[280]

Making use of the purpose of the National Treatment obligation, the Appellate Body thus aligned the product scope of paragraphs 2 and 4 of Article III, and at the same time rejected the strict reading of the term "like product" in Article III:4 which had been put forward by the earlier Panel Report in *EEC Measures on Animal Feed Proteins*.[281] If the purpose of the National Treatment obligation is to protect the competitive relationship between and among domestic and imported products from all overt and hidden regulatory discriminations, it is necessary to extend the product scope of Article III:4 to cover, not just almost identical products, but also competitive or substitutable products.

The Appellate Body turned next to the issue of how a treaty interpreter should proceed in determining whether products are "like" under Article III:4, and recalled the four general criteria that had been followed by both GATT panel practice and WTO jurisprudence since the Report of the Working Party on *Border Tax Adjustments*.[282] The Appellate Body noted that these four criteria comprise four categories of "characteristics" that the products involved might share: (i) the physical properties of the products; (ii) the extent to which the products are capable of serving the same or similar end-uses; (iii) the extent to which consumers perceive and treat the products as alternative means of performing particular functions in order to satisfy a particular want or demand; and (iv) the international classification of the products for tariff purposes. Although they provide a framework for analysing the "likeness" of particular products on a case-by-case basis, in the Appellate Body's view, these criteria are simply tools to assist in the task of sorting and examining the relevant evidence, and they should not dissolve the duty or the need to examine, in each case, *all* of the pertinent evidence.[283] Moreover, emphasising once more that, under Article III:4, the term "like products" is concerned with competitive relationships between and among products, the Appellate Body stated that, whether the *Border Tax Adjustments* framework is adopted or not, it is important under Article III:4 to take account of evidence which

---

[280] *Ibid.*, para 99 [emphasis original].

[281] Panel Report on *EEC Measures on Animal Feed Proteins*, L/4599, adopted on 14 March 1978, BISD 25S/4.

[282] They were: (i) the properties, nature and quality of the products; (ii) the end-uses of the products; (iii) consumers' tastes and habits—more comprehensively termed consumers' perceptions and behaviour—in respect of the products; and (iv) the tariff classification of the products. Note, however, that the fourth criterion, tariff classification, was not mentioned by the Working Party on *Border Tax Adjustments*, but was included by subsequent panels (see, for instance, *EEC–Animal Feed*, above n 6, fn 58, para 4.2, and *Japan–Alcohol I*, above n 5, fn 58, para 5.6). Cf Appellate Body Report on *EC–Asbestos*, above n 275, para 101.

[283] Appellate Body Report on *EC–Asbestos*, above n 275, para 102.

indicates whether, and to what extent, the products involved are—or could be—in a competitive relationship in the marketplace.[284]

Although the Appellate Body did not seem to limit excessively the relevant evidence in determining whether two products are "like" for the purposes of Article III:4, it made no reference to the elements that the panel in the *Malt Beverages* case had taken into consideration in order to determine that high alcohol beer was *un*like low alcohol beer. In other words, following its earlier jurisprudence with regard to Article III:2, the Appellate Body report in the *Asbestos* dispute has, though only implicitly, rejected the *aims-and-effects* test, at least as a tool to be employed for purposes of determining the likeness issue.[285]

The Appellate Body then turned to the various findings of error of law by the panel. The Appellate Body first of all noted that, although the Panel had indeed adopted an approach based on the four criteria set forth in *Border Tax Adjustments*, it had quite blatantly erred by basing its findings on the assessment of the evidence relating to only one of the four criteria. On the contrary, in the Appellate Body's view, the Panel should have examined the evidence relating to *each* of those four criteria and, then, weighed *all* of that evidence, along with any other relevant evidence, in making an *overall* determination of whether the products at issue could be characterised as "like".[286]

In reviewing more closely the Panel's treatment of the four individual criteria, the Appellate Body revealed several other errors of law and at the same time put forward a few relevant considerations.

With regard to the relevance of the *physical properties* of the product, the Appellate Body noted generally that, although not decisive, the extent to which products share common physical properties may be a useful indicator of "likeness", and may also influence how the product can be used, consumer attitudes about the product, and tariff classification. In the Appellate Body's view, in reaching the conclusion that differences in physical properties between chrysotile asbestos fibres and substitute fibres were not of a kind and degree to make these products "unlike", the Panel had focused exclusively on assumptions about end-uses of the products. In other words, the Panel had erroneously conflated the analysis of physical properties with that of end-uses.

Moreover, reversing the Panel's findings in this respect, the Appellate Body held that evidence relating to the health risks associated with a

---

[284] *Ibid.*, para 102.
[285] Cf R Howse and E Tuerk, "The WTO Impact in Internal Regulations—A Case Study of the Canada—EC Asbestos Dispute" in G de Búrca and J Scott (eds), *The EU and the WTO: Legal and Constitutional Aspects* (Oxford, Hart Publishing, 2001) at 299. See below discussion with regard to the relevance of the *aims-and-effects* doctrine for purposes of the "less favourable treatment" requirement.
[286] Appellate Body Report on *EC–Asbestos*, above n 275, para 109.

product may be pertinent in an examination of "likeness" under Article III:4 under the existing criteria of both *physical properties* and *consumers' tastes and habits*. The Appellate Body noted that certain physical properties of chrysotile asbestos—their molecular structure, chemical composition and fibrillation capacity—were important because the microscopic particles and filaments of chrysotile asbestos fibres are carcinogenic in humans, following inhalation. Citing the Panel's statements regarding chrysotile asbestos fibres, the Appellate Body noted as follows:

> This carcinogenicity, or toxicity, constitutes, as we see it, a defining aspect of the physical properties of chrysotile asbestos fibres. The evidence indicates that PCG fibres, in contrast, do not share these properties, at least to the same extent. We do not see how this highly significant physical difference *cannot* be a consideration in examining the physical properties of a product as part of a determination of "likeness" under Article III:4 of the GATT 1994.[287]

The Appellate Body was also persuaded that evidence relating to consumers' tastes and habits would establish that the health risks associated with chrysotile asbestos fibres influence consumers' behaviour with respect to the different fibres at issue. In the Appellate Body's view, consumers' tastes and habits regarding fibres, even in the case of commercial parties (such as manufacturers), are very likely to be shaped by the health risks associated with a product that is known to be highly carcinogenic.[288] In this context, the Appellate Body also rejected Canada's claim that the criterion of consumers' tastes and habits was *irrelevant* in this dispute, because the existence of the French measure had disturbed normal conditions of competition between the products at issue. In such situations, the Appellate Body observed, a Member may submit "evidence of latent, or suppressed, consumer demand in that market, or it may submit evidence of substitutability from some relevant third market."[289]

The Appellate Body moreover noted that, although *consumers' tastes and habits* and *product's end uses* involve certain of the key elements relating to the competitive relationship between products and are thus

---

[287] *Ibid.*, para 114 [emphasis original]. Cf I Musselli, "Alla ricerca di un difficile equilibrio tra commercio e diritti sociali: la nozione di 'similarità' dei prodotti ex Art III del GATT", *Riv Dir Comm Int* (2001) 873.
[288] Appellate Body Report on *EC–Asbestos*, above n 275, para 122. Moreover, the Appellate Body did not share the Panel's view that considering evidence relating to the health risks associated with a product for purposes of establishing the likeness requirement under Art III:4 deprived the general exception in Art XX(b) of *effet utile*. In the Appellate Body's view, evaluating evidence relating to the health risks arising from the physical properties of a product does not prevent a measure which is inconsistent with Art III:4 from being justified under Art XX(b), and thus does not nullify the effect of this provision. *Ibid.*, para 125.
[289] *Ibid.*, para 123.

particularly important for purposes of a "likeness" determination,[290] in cases where the evidence relating to *physical properties* establishes that the products at issue are indeed quite different, a higher burden is placed on complaining Members to establish that, despite the pronounced physical differences, there is still a competitive relationship between the products such that *all* of the evidence, taken together, demonstrates that the products are "like" under Article III:4 of the GATT 1994.[291] Noting that the Panel's evaluation of the products' end-uses was far from comprehensive[292] and that the Panel had refused to examine evidence relating to consumers' tastes and habits,[293] the Appellate Body stated that, in such a situation, "there is no basis for overcoming the inference, drawn from the different physical properties of the products, that the products are not 'like'."[294]

From the Appellate Body's review of the Panel's analysis of the likeness issue, it appears that, except for the criterion of tariff classification, all other criteria are equally relevant in determining whether two products are "like" for the purposes of Article III:4. The Appellate Body's emphasis on consumers' perception of the health risks of chrysotile asbestos fibres clearly shows its willingness to consider consumers' preferences as an important factor in the determination of likeness.[295] I do not therefore share the view expressed by some commentators that in the *Asbestos* report the Appellate Body appears to privilege the investigation

---

[290] "Evidence of this type is of particular importance under Art III of the GATT 1994, precisely because that provision is concerned with competitive relationships in the marketplace. If there is—or could be—*no* competitive relationship between products, a Member cannot intervene, through internal taxation or regulation, to protect domestic production. Thus, evidence about the extent to which products can serve the same end-uses, and the extent to which consumers are—or would be—willing to choose one product instead of another to perform those end-uses, is highly relevant evidence in assessing the 'likeness' of those products under Art III:4 of the GATT 1994." Appellate Body Report on *EC–Asbestos*, above n 275, para 117 [emphasis original].

[291] *Ibid.*, para 118.

[292] Having noted that there was a 'small number of applications' for which the products at issue were substitutable, "the Panel did not explain, or elaborate in any way on, the 'small number of … applications' for which the various fibres have similar end-uses. Nor did the Panel examine the end-uses for these products which were not similar. In these circumstances, we believe that the Panel did not adequately examine the evidence relating to end-uses." *Ibid.*, para 119.

[293] "The Panel declined to examine or make any findings relating to the third criterion, consumers' tastes and habits, '[b]ecause this criterion would not provide clear results'." *Ibid.*, para 120.

[294] *Ibid.*, para 121.

[295] G de Búrca, "Unpacking the Concept of Discrimination in EC and International Trade Law" in C Barnard and J Scott (eds), *The Law of the Single European Market: Unpacking the Premises* (Oxford, Hart Publishing, 2002) at 193. Cf G Verhoosel, *National Treatment and WTO Dispute Settlement: Adjudicating the Boundaries of Regulatory Autonomy* (Oxford, Hart Publishing, 2002) at 57.

of physical differences as being of special and prior importance.[296] The Appellate Body seems to suggest, on the contrary, that for a finding of likeness *all* of the relevant criteria, not only have to be taken into account, but they need to point overall to "likeness".

The Appellate Body confirms this impression by emphasising that, if *any* of the relevant criteria suggests that the products are not like, the burden of proving likeness becomes quite heavy. In other words, in line with the relevant burden of proof, the Appellate Body appears to make more difficult the case for "likeness" than that for "unlikeness". For example, taking the case of two products sharing several or even all physical characteristics (ie being "like" with regard to the physical properties criterion), if for some reason consumers perceive those same two products as two very different products (ie they are "unlike" with regard to consumers' tastes and habits), the Appellate Body's report in *Asbestos* seems to stand for the conclusion that the two products would probably fail the "likeness" requirement of Article III:4.[297]

It is suggested that this reading may indirectly open the door, albeit in exceptional circumstances, for a finding that two products, although physically identical, may nevertheless be found to be unlike for purposes of Article III:4 in light of consumers' perceptions with regard to non-product related features, such as the characteristics of the producer or of the production methods. In other words, even purely process-based regulations *à la Shrimp/Turtle* may indeed fail the likeness test of Article III:4.

The recognition of the relevance of consumer preference for purpose of the likeness determination does indeed in a way "[bring] into the picture the kinds of regulatory interests, which had under the GATT been taken into account through the *aims-and-effects* doctrine."[298] Consumers may distinguish between physically similar products on the basis of a variety of factors that may or may not be related to pure product characteristics, for instance, differentiating between whether shrimps are caught with turtle-friendly or unfriendly nets, whether car engines produce environment-unfriendly gases or not, or whether roof tiles are carcinogenic or not. The important difference between the *Asbestos* report and the *aims-and-effects* doctrine is that, while the latter focused on the often nationally-biased perspective of the regulator, the former clearly adopts the more origin-neutral perspective of the consumer.[299]

---

[296] Cf R Howse and E Tuerk, "The WTO Impact in Internal Regulations—A Case Study of the *Canada—EC Asbestos* Dispute" in G de Búrca and J Scott (eds), *The EU and the WTO: Legal and Constitutional Aspects* (Oxford, Hart Publishing, 2001) at 304.

[297] Cf Appellate Body Report on *EC–Asbestos*, above n 275, paras 117–18.

[298] R Howse and E Tuerk, "The WTO Impact in Internal Regulations", above n 296 at 301.

[299] *Ibid.* Cf G Verhoosel, *National Treatment and WTO Dispute Settlement: Adjudicating the Boundaries of Regulatory Autonomy* (Oxford, Hart Publishing, 2002), where the author says that "although it seems, a priori, very laudable that such weight is given to consumer

Having thus reversed the Panel's conclusion that chrysotile fibres, on the one hand, and PVA, cellulose and glass fibres, on the other, were "like products" within the meaning of Article III:4,[300] in the third and last part of its Report, the Appellate Body completed the analysis on the basis of the factual findings of the Panel and of the undisputed facts in the Panel record. Having noted that (1) the evidence relating to physical properties indicated that chrysotile asbestos fibres and substitute fibres were *very different*, (2) the end-uses of chrysotile asbestos fibres and substitute fibres were the same *only* "for a small number" of applications, (3) Canada had presented *no* evidence on consumers' tastes and habits regarding the products at issue, and (4) chrysotile asbestos fibres and the various substitute fibres all had *different* tariff classifications,[301] the Appellate Body rather timidly concluded as follows:

> Taken together [...] all of this evidence is certainly far from sufficient to satisfy Canada's burden of proving that chrysotile asbestos fibres are "like" [substitutes] fibres under Article III:4 of the GATT 1994. Indeed, this evidence rather tends to suggest that these products are not "like products" for the purposes of Article III:4 of the GATT 1994.[302]

(ii) The Appellate Body Report on Asbestos *and less favourable treatment*

Although the Appellate Body could not examine the Panel's finding that Canadian chrysotile asbestos fibres had been accorded "less favourable treatment" than French substitute fibres in violation of Article III:4,[303] it nonetheless made some potentially important statements that may shed light on the future application of this crucial requirement.

It should be remembered that in order to determine whether "less favourable treatment" was accorded to imported "like products", the Panel apparently considered whether there were *any* imported products

---

preferences, arguably the closest proxy for cross-price elasticity, [the Appellate Body approach] basically allows a health risk evaluation by the consumer, which is void of any scientific underpinning, to justify a domestic regulation which specifically and adversely affects imports."*Ibid.*, at 57.

[300] The Appellate Body noted that the only evidence supporting the Panel's finding of "likeness" (ie the fibres at issue shared a "small number" of end-uses) was insufficient to justify such a finding. Appellate Body Report on *EC–Asbestos*, above n 275, para 126.

[301] *Ibid.*, paras 134–140.

[302] *Ibid.*, para 141.

[303] Contrary to what it is usually believed, the Appellate Body did not examine the Panel's finding on "less favourable treatment", not simply because it had reversed the Panel's preliminary finding on the "likeness" of the fibres at issue, but because the European Communities had not appealed this part of the finding. Reversing the Panel's finding on 'likeness' did not in fact stop the Appellate Body from reviewing the Panel's conclusions on Art XX(b), which for all practical purposes might appear unnecessary. See below for a discussion on the possible reasons for the Appellate Body's decision to review the Panel's Art XX(b) findings.

that were banned and *any* "like" domestic products that were permitted.[304] Adopting what Ehring has recently termed the "diagonal test" for the "less favourable treatment" requirement of Article III:4,[305] the Panel found that the French ban on asbestos on its own terms treated Canadian asbestos products less favourably than the like domestic substitutes. The Panel thus reached its finding without considering the "symmetric impact" of the French ban on French asbestos production capabilities or on Canadian production of substitute fibres. At least potentially, the French measure was negatively affecting *both* Canadian and French production of asbestos and asbestos-containing products, as well as favouring *both* French and Canadian production of PVA, cellulose and glass fibres and products containing them. In this regard, the fact that the European Communities did not appeal the Panel's finding on this issue is quite surprising and represents a clear indication that the European Communities apparently believed that the Panel's *diagonal* application of the "less favourable treatment" requirement was indeed the correct approach.

Nonetheless, in order to counterbalance its broad reading of the term "like product", the Appellate Body reminded the treaty interpreter of the existence of the "less favourable treatment" element that must be established before a measure can be held to be inconsistent with Article III:4. In doing so the Appellate Body added the following *obiter dictum* on the meaning of the "less favourable treatment" requirement:

> [...] even if two products are "like", that does not mean that a measure is inconsistent with Article III:4. A complaining Member must still establish that the measure accords to the group of "like" *imported* products "less favourable treatment" than it accords to the group of "like" *domestic* products. The term "less favourable treatment" expresses the general principle, in Article III:1, that internal regulations "should not be applied ... so as to afford protection to domestic production". If there is "less favourable treatment" of the group of "like" imported products, there is, conversely, "protection" of the group of "like" domestic products. However, a Member

---

[304] S Lester and K Leitner, *Dispute Settlement Commentary, European Communities—Asbestos (Appellate Body Report)* at 13 (2001), available at <http://www.worldtradelaw.net/dscsamples/index.htm>, visited 19 Feb 2003.

[305] L Ehring, "De facto Discrimination in WTO Law: National Treatment and Most-Favoured-Nation Treatment—or Equal Treatment?", *Jean Monnet Working Paper* (NYU School of Law, 2002) at 3. "Under the diagonal approach, one compares the treatment accorded to the disfavoured foreign goods with that enjoyed by the favoured domestic goods, eg domestic low-alcohol beer receives more favourable treatment than imported strong beer. This means that it is always possible to find a violation of Art III:4, as long as the disfavoured type is (potentially) imported and the favoured type exists domestically. Even when imported products overwhelmingly receive the better treatment and most domestic goods fall in the less advantageous category, there is still a violation."

may draw distinctions between products which have been found to be "like", without, for this reason alone, according to the group of "like" *imported* products "less favourable treatment" than that accorded to the group of "like" *domestic* products. In this case, we do not examine further the interpretation of the term "treatment no less favourable" in Article III:4, as the Panel's findings on this issue have not been appealed or, indeed, argued before us.[306]

Although I agree that this statement by the Appellate Body does not resolve the matter entirely,[307] it certainly is a clear indication that the obligation embodied in Article III:4 has to reflect the purpose and nature of the National Treatment principle. By ignoring the *overall* impact on *all* domestic and imported like products, the Panel's simplistic diagonal approach went well beyond the scope of the principle of non-discrimination on the basis of the product's origin or nationality, introducing implicitly the broader and unqualified principle of equal treatment.[308] The Appellate Body's emphasis on a comparison between the "group of like imported products" and the "group of like domestic product" quite clearly stands as a rejection of the Panel's assumption that, in order for a violation of the National Treatment obligation to be found, a complaining Member simply needs to establish that *some* imported products are treated less favourably than *some* like domestic products. As emphasised by Ehring,

> [f]ollowing an aggregate comparison, it makes perfect sense that a distinction between like products does not necessarily result in less favourable treatment of the entire group of imports, although some like imported products (necessarily) do receive worse treatment than some like domestic goods.[309]

Accordingly, there is clearly no breach of the National Treatment obligation if the negative impact on the *group* of like imported products as a whole is equivalent to or less than the negative impact on the *group* of like domestic products as a whole. The Appellate Body's use of italics to emphasise the origin of goods further supports a reading that the burden must specifically affect *imported* products more than *domestic* products, so that it is possible to conclude that the formally origin-neutral regulation

---

[306] Appellate Body Report on *EC–Asbestos*, above n 275, para 100 [emphasis original].
[307] S Lester and K Leitner, *Dispute Settlement Commentary, European Communities—Asbestos (Appellate Body Report)* at 15 (2001), available at <http://www.worldtradelaw.net/dscsamples/index.htm>, visited 19 Feb 2003.
[308] L Ehring, "De facto Discrimination in WTO Law: National Treatment and Most-Favoured-Nation Treatment—or Equal Treatment?", *Jean Monnet Working Paper* (NYU School of Law, 2002) at 27, 29, 31.
[309] *Ibid.*, at 19.

does indeed indirectly or de facto discriminate on the basis of the product's origin.[310]

Although one can quite comfortably argue that both the *text* and the *context* of Article III:4 allow for such a reading of the "less favourable treatment" requirement,[311] the decisive element rejecting the Panel's simplistic diagonal approach stems from the *object and purpose* of that provision. Article III:4, specifically, like Article III, more generally, embodies the principle according to which Members shall not discriminate, in law or in fact, on the basis of the product's origin. As GATT panel practice and WTO jurisprudence have repeatedly noted, the purpose of the National Treatment principle is to provide equal competitive conditions for imported products in relation to domestic products. In the case of a facially origin-neutral measure, discrimination on the basis of the product's origin will not be deemed to be found simply because one imported product is or may be treated less favourably than one domestic like product. The National Treatment principle will be breached only if imported products, on the whole, are treated less favourably than domestic products, in a way that affords protection to domestic production.

The reader will have noticed that the "aggregate comparison" approach enunciated by the Appellate Body in the *Asbestos* dispute recalls quite strongly the notion of "balancing" more favourable treatment of some imported products against less favourable treatment of other imported products, which the *Section 337* Panel Report expressly rejected.[312]

---

[310] *Ibid.*, where the author also notes that "This interpretation accords well with the semantic equivalence the Appellate Body gives to 'less favourable treatment' and 'protection to domestic production'," the paradigms of GATT Art III:4 and Art III:1, respectively. In particular, the Appellate Body again speaks of "'protection' of the group of 'like' domestic products", "ie the entire group of all foreign goods meeting the requirement of likeness". Cf R Howse and E Tuerk, "The WTO Impact in Internal Regulations—A Case Study of the *Canada—EC Asbestos* Dispute" in G de Búrca and J Scott (eds), *The EU and the WTO: Legal and Constitutional Aspects* (Oxford, Hart Publishing, 2001) at 297–98; S Lester and K Leitner, *Dispute Settlement Commentary, European Communities—Asbestos (Appellate Body Report)* at 15 (2001), available at <http://www.worldtradelaw.net/dscsamples/index.htm>, visited 19 Feb 2003.

[311] L Ehring, "De facto Discrimination in WTO Law: National Treatment and Most-Favoured-Nation Treatment—or Equal Treatment?", *Jean Monnet Working Paper* (NYU School of Law, 2002) at 30 *et seq*; W Davey and J Pauwelyn, "MFN Unconditionality: A Legal Analysis of the Concept in View of its Evolution in the GATT/WTO Jurisprudence with Particular Reference to the Issue of 'Like Product", in T Cottier and P Mavroidis (eds), *Regulatory Barriers and the Principle of Non-Discrimination in World Trade Law* (Ann Arbor, University of Michigan Press, 2000) at 40.

[312] Panel Report on *Section 337*, above n 258, para 5.14, "If this notion were accepted, it would entitle a contracting party to derogate from the no less favourable treatment obligation in one case, or indeed in respect of one contracting party, on the ground that it accords more favourable treatment in some other case, or to another contracting party. Such an interpretation would lead to great uncertainty about the conditions of competition between imported and domestic products and thus defeat the purposes of Art III."

There is however no conflict between the two rulings. As correctly noted by several commentators, the *Section 337* case dealt with an overt or de jure discriminatory measure and the issue was whether the facially differential treatment of imports might nevertheless have been "no less favourable". On the other hand, the *Asbestos* dispute dealt with an origin-neutral measure and the issue was whether such a measure nevertheless constituted "less favourable" treatment of imports.[313] It follows that in the case where the terms of the measure itself differentiate on the basis of the product's origin (origin-based measure), the defending State may not plead that in *some* circumstances imported products are afforded no less favourable treatment: in such a case, the defending State may avoid a finding of "less favourable treatment" *only if* it demonstrates that in *all* circumstances imported products are not afforded less favourable treatment. On the contrary, when one is faced with a case of an origin-neutral measure, in order for the measure to be deemed to constitute indirect or de facto discrimination against imported products, the complaining State will need to show that *as a whole* imported products are afforded less favourable treatment than like domestic products.

If there is no doubt of the Appellate Body's rejection in *Asbestos* of the diagonal approach to the "less favourable treatment" requirement of Article III:4, that report does not quite delineate all the relevant contours of the correct approach. Future disputes will certainly afford the opportunity to perform this task. Nevertheless, it might be useful at this point to advance a few preliminary observations on the details of the new approach.

There appear to be two quite different ways in which the Appellate Body's new reading of the "less favourable treatment" requirement may be applied. According to one perspective, a measure may be found in violation of the National Treatment obligation as set in Article III:4 if it negatively affects imports more than domestic products considered as a whole. In other words, while it will still be necessary to show an overall imbalance between the measure's impact on the group of like domestic products (the majority of which fall within the more favoured sub-group of like products) and the group of like imported products (the majority of which falls within the more disfavoured sub-group of like products), it will be sufficient to prove, under a *pure discriminatory effect test*, that such

---

[313] R Howse and E Tuerk, "The WTO Impact in Internal Regulations—A Case Study of the *Canada—EC Asbestos* Dispute" in G de Búrca and J Scott (eds), *The EU and the WTO: Legal and Constitutional Aspects* (Oxford, Hart Publishing, 2001) at 297, fn 55; L Ehring, "De facto Discrimination in WTO Law: National Treatment and Most-Favoured-Nation Treatment—or Equal Treatment?", *Jean Monnet Working Paper* (NYU School of Law, 2002) at 21; S Lester and K Leitner, *Dispute Settlement Commentary, European Communities—Asbestos (AppellateBody Report)* at 15 (2001), available at <http://www.worldtradelaw.net/dscsamples/index.htm>, visited 19 Feb 2002.

imbalance has occurred in the past, is currently present or may happen in the future.

Let us take for example the *Asbestos* dispute and imagine for the sake of the argument that the Appellate Body had actually found that chrysotile fibres and substitute fibres were indeed "like products". Canada could have established that its products were *not* accorded treatment no less favourable than that accorded to like products of French origin in violation of Article III:4 by showing that Canada produced (even simply at the time of the dispute) exclusively or prevalently chrysotile asbestos products (which were banned by the French measure), while France produced exclusively substitute fibres (which were permitted).

Under the second perspective, a violation of Article III:4 will be found only if it is established that the measure under review *inherently* discriminates against imported products as a whole. According to this approach, which borrows partially from the rationale of the *aims-and-effects* doctrine, the existence of an overall imbalance between domestic and imported like products would not be enough for a violation of the National Treatment obligation unless it is not also supported by a finding that, under an *inherent discriminatory nature test*, the structural characteristics of the measure itself constitute the principal and direct cause for that imbalance.[314] To use the *Asbestos* dispute once more, Canada could have established that its products were *not* accorded treatment no less favourable than that accorded to like products of French origin in violation of Article III:4 *only if* it showed that the imbalance between the "prohibited" Canadian fibres and the "permitted" French fibres was inherent to the regulatory criterion employed by the French measure (ie chrysotile v substitute fibres). For example, Canada could have demonstrated that France does not have the raw material or the know-how with which to produce chrysotile asbestos fibres.

I believe that the correct approach to be followed in determining whether a given measure affords no less favourable treatment sits halfway between the two above-mentioned perspectives. While a finding that an origin-neutral measure is inherently discriminatory in nature should clearly be enough for a violation of the National Treatment principle, a mere demonstration of an overall imbalance between imported and domestic like products should not.

As a preliminary matter, it is suggested that the interpreter should focus principally on the *object and purpose* of Article III:4, as specifically

---

[314] This appears to be the view proposed by the supporters of the *aims-and-effects* doctrine, who tend to limit as much as possible any intrusion into national legitimate regulatory prerogatives. Cf R Howse and E Tuerk, "The WTO Impact in Internal Regulations—A Case Study of the *Canada—EC Asbestos* Dispute" in G de Búrca and J Scott (eds), *The EU and the WTO: Legal and Constitutional Aspects* (Oxford, Hart Publishing, 2001) at 297, fn 55.

enunciated in Article III:1. As previously noted, the first paragraph of Article III states in relevant part that "internal regulations [...] should not be applied to imported or domestic *products* so as to afford *protection* to domestic production". Accordingly, the ultimate aim of determining whether an origin-neutral internal measure affords less favourable treatment to imported products, should be to pin-point measures which afford *protection* to domestic products. It follows that an origin-neutral measure that differentiates between two like products will be deemed to violate Article III:4 if it is found *predominantly* to favour domestic products considered as a whole.

Moreover, in order to determine whether the measure predominantly favours domestic products, a Panel should, in line with current WTO jurisprudence, focus on all the relevant evidence pertaining to the case at hand on a case-by-case approach. In particular, this evidence should include the following elements: (1) past, current and potential *ratio* of *domestic* favoured and disfavoured like products, as well as the ratio of *imported* favoured and disfavoured like products, (2) past, current and potential *ratio* of domestic and imported *favoured* products, as well as the ratio of domestic and imported *disfavoured* products, (3) past, current and potential *size* of both domestic and imported products, which are negatively affected by the national measure at issue, (4) past, current and potential imports from other *third-party Members*, (5) the *magnitude* of the differential treatment between like products.[315]

In this regard, previous GATT panel practice employing the *aims-and-effects* doctrine may represent a useful, albeit only indicative, reference in examining some of these elements.

2. *Article 28 EC and the* Keck *doctrine*

In light of the broad interpretation given by both the Commission and the European Court of Justice to the prohibition of "measures having equivalent effect" of Article 28, respectively in Directive 70/50 and in the *Dassonville–Cassis de Dijon* jurisprudence, for many years the concept of de facto discrimination on the basis of the product's origin or nationality played a very limited role in the law of the free movement of goods, at least on a purely formal level.[316] But since the Court's seminal ruling in

---

[315] Cf L Ehring, "De facto Discrimination in WTO Law: National and Most-Favored-National Treatment—or Equal Treatment?", *Jean Monnet Working Paper* (NYU, 2002).
[316] Next to the taxation field, which we have previously examined, there are at least two types of non-fiscal internal measures which the Court continued to review according to the non-discrimination principle: export restrictions and price controls. Neither of these will be considered in much detail here, as export restrictions have basically been struck down only where they formally discriminated on the basis of the destination of the products (de jure discrimination) and price controls now seem to fall within the scope of application of the new *Keck* doctrine relating to 'selling arrangements'. For a case of pre-*Keck* de facto

Keck & Mithouard,[317] this statement seems to be no longer accurate. In this case, the Court expressly excluded from the scope of application of Article 28 those provisions restricting or prohibiting certain selling arrangements that affect in the same manner, in law and fact, the marketing of domestic products and those from other Member States.[318] Before examining the meaning of the concept of "certain selling arrangements" (the "objective element" of the *Keck* doctrine) and the precise features of the non-discrimination conditions (*Keck*'s "normative content"), this section will briefly examine the historical antecedents to the Court's most recent interpretive developments.

(a) From Cassis de Dijon *to* Keck   Following the jurisprudential reformulation of Article 28 during the 1970s, while de jure discriminatory measures (in the ECJ language, "distinctly applicable measures") were caught by the per se prohibition of Article 28 and could exceptionally be saved only on the basis of one of the public policy objectives of Article 30, the Court subjected all other internal regulations (so called "indistinctly applicable measures") capable of hindering, directly or indirectly, actually or potentially, intra-Community trade to the more relaxed "mandatory requirements" doctrine, independently of whether these measures were in fact discriminatory or not.

Despite the fact that there have been attempts, most notably by Marenco,[319] to explain the Court's case-law on Article 28 in terms of the non-discrimination principle, I tend to agree with the majority of commentators who have argued that the approach of the Court, both in principle and in practice, clearly went beyond the concept of non-discrimination.[320]

From the *Cassis de Dijon* decision onward, the Court of Justice subjected to its "proportionality" review any indistinctly applicable measure that showed a mere indirect or potential restrictive effect on trade between the

---

discriminatory price controls see Case 82/77, *Openbaar Ministerie v Van Tiggele* [1978] ECR 25, paras. 13–14, where the Court noted that "[w]hilst national price-control rules applicable without distinction to domestic products and imported products cannot in general produce such an effect [hinder, directly or indirectly, actually or potentially, imports between Member States] they may do so in certain specific cases. Thus imports may be impeded in particular when a national authority fixes prices or profit margins at such a level that imported products are placed at a disadvantage in relation to identical domestic products either because they cannot profitably be marketed in the condition laid down or because the competitive advantage conferred by lower cost prices is cancelled out."

[317] Joined Cases C–267 and 268/91, *Keck & Mithouard* [1993] ECR 6097.
[318] *Ibid.*, para 16.
[319] G Marenco, "Pour une interprétation traditionelle de la notion de mesure d'effet équivalent à une restriction quantitative", 20 *CDE* (1984) 291.
[320] Cf P Eeckhout, "Constitutional Concepts for Free Trade in Services" in G de Búrca and J Scott (eds), *The EU and the WTO: Legal and Constitutional Aspects* (Oxford, Hart, 2001) at 225–26.

Member States, without really inquiring into whether the measure constituted indirect discrimination against imported products or protection in favour of domestic production. In *Cassis de Dijon* itself, for example, the Court found that the German law requiring spirits to have a minimum alcohol content fell within the concept of "measures having an effect equivalent to quantitative restrictions on imports" set out in Article 28 and was thus prohibited because it could *not* be justified under either consumer protection or public health grounds, and not because, as suggested by Marenco, the measure contained "une discrimination matérielle".[321] As will be analysed in the next chapter, *Cassis de Dijon* clearly shifted the focus from the discriminatory nature of the measure under review to its reasonableness and proportionality.

However, the broad interpretation of the concept of "measures having equivalent effect" as well as the general debate about the true meaning of the *Cassis de Dijon* doctrine of "mandatory requirements" cannot really be understood without focusing on the underlying issues which the Court was trying to address in that case. As the Commission had emphasised since its 1962 Action Programme,[322] Member States' rules governing the marketing of products which deal inter alia with shape, size, weight, composition, presentation (the so-called "product standards") and apply (at least on their face) equally to domestic and imported products might have a restrictive effect on the free movement of goods. This results from the *inherent disparities* between the rules applied by Member States in this respect. It is the issue of the so-called "regulatory overlap". The mere existence of several regulatory authorities with limited territorial competencies (the Member States) can impede or severely restrict the free circulation of goods within the greater market (the Common Market) by imposing different product requirements within their respective jurisdictions.

In *Cassis de Dijon*, the Court of Justice was confronted with precisely this issue: while Germany provided for a specific minimum alcohol content requirement for certain types of spirit, France did not. The practical effect of such disparity was that the French liqueur, Cassis de Dijon, could not be marketed in Germany as it was produced and marketed in France because it did not comply with the German alcohol content requirement. It is no surprise that in *Cassis de Dijon* the Court began its analysis under Article 28 by recognising the existence of "[o]bstacles to movement within the

---

[321] G Marenco, "Pour une interprétation traditionelle de la notion de mesure d'effet équivalent à une restriction quantitative", 20 *CDE* (1984) 291 at 306, who stated that "Légiférer en matière de qualité de ces boissons en ne prenant pour base que des traditions qui se sont développées sur le marché interne désavantage automatiquement les importations." Cf OA Torgersen, "The Limitations of the Free Movement of Goods and the Freedom to Provide Services—In Search of a Common Approach", *European Business Law Review* (Sept/Oct 1999) 371, at 372.

[322] *Memorandum della Commissione sul Programma della Comunità nella seconda tappa* (Bruxelles, 1962). See above the discussion in ch 1 in the section dealing with the objective element of Art 28 EC.

Community resulting from disparities between the national laws relating to the marketing of products".

The Court's emphasis on the negative effects of this type of national regulation should also be noted. Having concluded that the German requirements relating to the minimum alcohol content of alcoholic beverages did not serve a public interest objective that may take precedence over the requirements of the free movement of goods, the Court noted the following:

> [i]n practice, the principle effect of requirements of this nature is to promote alcoholic beverages having a high alcohol content by *excluding* from the national market products of other Member States which do not answer that description.[323]

In other words, the Court viewed the disparities in national product requirements as having the effect of *preventing*, and not merely *impeding*, the free circulation of goods among the several Member States.

In light of the nature of the problem (regulatory overlap) and the magnitude of the adverse effects on the free circulation of goods within the common market (possible exclusion from the Member States' markets), the solution found by the Court of Justice in *Cassis de Dijon* made perfect sense. As correctly interpreted by the Commission in its communication following the Court's judgment, *Cassis de Dijon* introduced the so called principle of "mutual recognition" (recently defined by Weiler as "functional parallelism"),[324] according to which

> any product imported from another Member State must in principle be admitted to the territory of the importing Member State if it has been lawfully produced, that is, conforms to the rules and processes of manufacture

---

[323] Case 120/78, *Rewe-Zentral AG v Bundesmonopolverwaltung für Branntwein* (*Cassis de Dijon*) [1979] ECR 649, para 14 [emphasis added]. Marenco points to this statement as evidence that the true reason for the Court's finding of violation was that the German requirements were materially discriminatory against imported products. Cf G Marenco, "Pour une interprétation traditionelle de la notion de mesure d'effet équivalent à une restriction quantitative", 20 *CDE* (1984) 291, at 306. It is suggested here, however, that the Court's statement with regard to the practical effect of the German requirements should be viewed rather as a general statement applicable to any equally applicable market regulation. In other words, the Court did not find that the German indistinctly applicable requirements had in that particular case the effect of affording protection to domestic products, but simply that requirements such as the German requirements at issue *in general* constituted obstacles to trade resulting from disparities between national laws regulating the marketing of products, and as such were incompatible with the Treaty free movement principles unless justified by *exigence imperatives*.

[324] JHH Weiler, "The Constitution of the Common Marketplace: Text and Context in the Evolution of the Free Movement of Goods" in P Craig and G de Búrca (eds), *The Evolution of EU Law* (Oxford, OUP, 1999) at 365, where the expression is actually attributed to Alan Dashwood. See below in ch 4, the discussion of the *Dassonville–Cassis de Dijon* doctrine.

that are customarily and traditionally accepted in the exporting country, and is marketed in the territory of the latter. [...] Only under very strict conditions does the Court accept exceptions to this principle [...].

By establishing a *rebuttable presumption* that the product and process-standards imposed by the exporting Member State are functionally equivalent to those imposed by the importing Member State,[325] the Court considerably reduced market barriers stemming from the Member States' regulatory disparities and at the same time furthered the creation of a unified market.[326]

Although this principle applied relatively smoothly in all cases in which the national measure at issue concerned the *product itself*,[327] problems arose when that same principle was extended to measures relating to *commercial arrangements* (ie rules regulating the circumstances in which goods may be sold or used).[328] The jurisprudence on this latter type of national regulations did not appear settled. While in some cases the application of Article 28 was excluded regardless of whether the rules were justified or not, in other, quite similar, cases, commercial arrangements were brought within the ambit of Article 28 and were subjected to the *Dassonville–Cassis de Dijon* proportionality review.[329] In *Cinétheque*,[330] for example, the Court was called on to review whether a French law applying equally to domestic and imported products and banning the sale or hire of videos of films during the first year in which the film was released violated Article 28. The measure at issue was thus unrelated to the product's characteristics but simply imposed restrictions on *when* those products could be sold on the French market.

---

[325] P Oliver, *Free Movement of Goods in the European Community* (London, Sweet and Maxwell, 1996) at 110 *et seq.*

[326] E White, "In search of the Limits to Art 30 of the EEC Treaty", in 26 *CML Rev* (1989) 235, at 245 *et seq*, where it is noted that "the different legal and economic environment of the Member State of origin finds its expression in the different *characteristics* of an imported product compared with the national product. Consequently, as the judgment of the Court in *Cassis de Dijon* clearly shows, Member States are not entitled to require that imported products have the same *characteristics* as are required of, or are traditional in, domestic products unless this is strictly necessary for the protection of some legitimate interest." On the *Dassonville–Cassis de Dijon* 'rule of reason' doctrine, see below the discussion in ch 4 on the reasonableness principle.

[327] For example, the German requirement that beer be manufactured only from specific ingredients (Case 178/84, *Commission v Germany*, [1987] ECR 1227), the Italian requirement that pasta be made only from durum wheat (Case 407/85, *Glocken GmbH v USL Centro-Sud*, [1988] ECR 4233) or the French prohibition on the sale of any milk powder or milk concentrate made entirely from non-dairy ingredients (Case 216/84, *Commission v France*, [1988] ECR 793).

[328] G Tesauro, "The Community's Internal Market in light of the Recent Case-Law of the Court of Justice" in *YEL* (1995) 1, at 4.

[329] *Ibid*. Cf Opinion of Advocate-General Jacobs in Case C–412/93, *Société d'Importation Edouard Leclerc-Siplec v TF1 Publicité SA and M6 Publicité SA*. [1995] ECR I–0179, paras 27–33.

[330] Joined Cases 60 and 61/84, *Cinéthèque SA v Fédération Nationale des Cinémas Francais* [1985] ECR 2605.

Although it eventually justified the French selling requirement on the need to protect or enhance artistic works, the Court had previously concluded, in light of its *Cassis de Dijon* jurisprudence, that the French measure could have created barriers to intra-Community trade in video-cassettes incompatible with the principle of the free movement of goods (and thus it fell foul of Article 28 unless it was justified).[331]

In *Quietlynn*,[332] on the contrary, the Court rejected a claim that an English licence requirement for sex shops violated Article 28, noting that the English legislation (a) did not constitute an absolute prohibition on the sale of the products in question, (b) did not render any more difficult the marketing of imported products than domestic products, (c) did not have any connection with intra-Community trade (since the products covered by the Act could have been marketed through licensed sex establishment and other channels) and (d) were not of such a nature as to impede trade between Member States.[333]

The divergent case-law with regard to the applicability of Article 28 to indistinctly applicable measures relating to commercial arrangements may be briefly explained in these terms: the cases where the Court extended the concept of measures having equivalent effect to cover

[331] *Ibid.*, para 22. Note the contrasting view of Advocate-General Slynn in his opinion in *Cinéthèque*. In *Torfaen v B & Q*, where B & Q was prosecuted in England for violation of the Sunday trading laws which prohibited retail shops from selling on Sundays, subject to exceptions for certain types of products, it was argued that these laws constituted a violation pursuant to Art 28, since the effect of the law was to reduce total turnover by about 10%, with a corresponding decrease of imports from other Member States. Although Advocate-General van Gerven suggested that a restriction on Sunday trading did not constitute a measure of equivalent effect within the meaning of Art 28 at all, unless it discriminated against imports or 'screened off' the domestic market (and this was not the case in the dispute at hand), the Court, following its earlier ruling in *Cinétheque*, rejected the AG approach and found that the English laws fell within the scope of Art 28. Nevertheless, the Court went on to save those same laws since their objectives were indeed justified from the perspective of Community law in accordance with *Cassis de Dijon* jurisprudence ("national rules governing the opening hours of retail premises [...] reflect certain political and economic choices in so far as their purpose is to ensure that working and non-working hours are so arranged as to accord with national ore regional socio-cultural characteristics". *Ibid.*, para 14). Cf P Oliver, *Free Movement of Goods in the European Community* (London, Sweet & Maxwell, 1996) at 97–98.
[332] Case C–23/89, *Quietlynn v Southend Borough Council* [1990] ECR 3059. Similarly in Case 75/81, *Blesgen* [1982] ECR 1211, paras. 8–9, the Court held that Art 28 did not apply to a Belgian law which prohibited the sale and consumption of spirits in public places since the restrictive effect of this measure on imports did not exceed that intrinsic to trade rules and no distinction was made based on nature or origin. Although the Belgian law on the sale of spirits in cafés undoubtedly led to a reduction of consumption and therefore restricted imports of spirits and certainly came under the *Dassonville* formula, the Court concluded that the measure had "in fact no connection with the importation of the products and for that reason is not of such a nature as to impede trade between Member States". Cf E White, "In search of the Limits to Art 30 of the EEC Treaty", in 26 *CML Rev* (1989) 235, at 249 *et seq*; P Oliver, *Free Movement of Goods in the European Community* (London, Sweet and Maxwell, 1996) at 96 *et seq*.
[333] For extensive analysis of the controversial cases cf P Craig and G de Búrca, *EU Law* (Oxford, OUP, 1998) at 610 *et seq*.; P Oliver, *Free Movement of Goods in the European Community* (London, Sweet and Maxwell, 1996) at 96 *et seq*.; S Weatherill and P Beaumont, *EC Law* (London, Penguin Books, 1995) at 532 *et seq*.

measures merely regulating in a general and neutral manner the circumstances in which goods may be sold rested on a literal interpretation of the *Dassonville–Cassis de Dijon* reformulation of Article 28 (if capable of restricting, directly or indirectly, actually or potentially, intra-Community trade, *any measure* fell within the prohibition of Article 28, unless justified by mandatory requirements).[334] The cases where the Court excluded very similar measures from the scope of application of Article 28 were based on a teleological interpretation of the same jurisprudential doctrine (selling requirements do not involve any "regulatory overlap" and do not tend to "exclude" products from the Common Market).

Confronted with the momentous question whether Article 28 should be interpreted as a provision with the purpose of liberalising trade between the Member States, or more broadly to liberalise the pursuit of economic activities within a Member State as well (even where there was no link with either "trade" or "market integration"),[335] the Court in *Keck & Mithouard*[336] chose the former and subjected "certain selling arrangements" to the less intrusive non-discrimination test.[337] In that particular case, the defendants had been prosecuted for selling goods below their purchase price, contrary to the provisions of French law, and the French court hearing the case asked the Court of Justice whether such legislation was contrary to the EC Treaty.

With the clear intent of somehow limiting the need to review the proportionality of almost any internal regulation,[338] in *Keck* the Court

---

[334] Cf E White, "In search of the Limits to Art 30 of the EEC Treaty", in 26 *CML Rev* (1989) 235, at 279. It should be noted in this regard that in the *Cassis de Dijon* judgment the Court's broad reading of Art 28 was not based even indirectly on the *Dassonville* formula and only referred to restrictions on the *characteristics* of a product. Only later did the Court of Justice make the connection between *Dassonville* and *Cassis de Dijon*, opening the door for the eventual overextension of the jurisprudential doctrine. Cf D Chalmers, "Repackaging the Internal Market—The Ramifications of the *Keck* Judgment", 19 *ELRev* (1994) 385, at 386.

[335] This is in brief the question which was put to the Court by Advocate-General Tesauro in his opinion in Case C–292/92, *Hünermund v Landesapothekerkammer Baden-Württemberg*, [1993] ECR I–6787, para 28. "In short, I am persuaded that the *Dassonville* test neither can nor should be so construed as to include in the definition of measures having equivalent effect even those national laws which, because they affect supply and/or demand and therefore, but on that account alone, may bring about a reduction in the volume of sales, that is to say, where there exists no obstacle whatsoever to the movement within the Community of the products concerned and no connection whatsoever with the disparity between the laws in question. I consider that the purpose of Art 30 is to ensure the free movement of goods in order to establish a single integrated market, eliminating therefore those national measures which in any way create an obstacle to or even mere difficulties for the movement of goods; its purpose is not to strike down the most widely differing measures in order, essentially, to ensure the greatest possible expansion of trade." Cf G Tesauro, "The Community's Internal Market in light of the Recent Case–Law of the Court of Justice", *YEL* (1995) 1, at 5.

[336] Joined Cases C–267 and 268/91, *Keck & Mithouard* [1993] ECR 6097.

[337] C Barnard, "Fitting the Remaining Pieces into the Goods and Persons Jigsaw", 26 *ELRev* (2001) 35, text at notes 54–56.

[338] The Court also stated that "in light of the increasing tendency of traders to invoke Art 30 of the Treaty as a means of challenging any rules whose effect is to limit their commercial

rendered once again an "authoritative interpretation" of the famous prohibition of "measures having equivalent effect" of Article 28: while *product requirements* fall within the established *Dassonville–Cassis de Dijon* jurisprudence, certain *selling arrangements*, contrary to what has previously been decided, are caught by the prohibition of Article 28 *only if* they discriminate, in law or in fact, between domestic and imported products.[339] The relevant paragraphs read as follow:

> 15 It is established by the case-law beginning with *Cassis de Dijon* [...] that, in the absence of harmonization of legislation, obstacles to free movement of goods which are the consequence of applying, to goods coming from other Member States where they are lawfully manufactured and marketed, rules that lay down requirements to be met by such goods (such as those relating to designation, form, size, weight, composition, presentation, labelling, packaging) constitute measures of equivalent effect prohibited by Article 30. This is so even if those rules apply without distinction to all products unless their application can be justified by a public-interest objective taking precedence over the free movement of goods.

> 16 By contrast, contrary to what has previously been decided, the application to products from other Member States of national provisions restricting or prohibiting certain selling arrangements is not such as to hinder directly or indirectly, actually or potentially, trade between Member States within the meaning of the *Dassonville* judgement [...], so long as those provisions apply to all relevant traders operating within the national territory and so long as they affect in the same manner, in law and in fact, the marketing of domestic products and of those from other Member States.

> 17 Provided that those conditions are fulfilled, the application of such rules to the sale of products from another Member State meeting the requirements laid down by that State is not by nature such as to prevent their access to the market or to impede access any more than it impedes the access of domestic products. Such rules therefore fall outside the scope of Article 30 of the Treaty.[340]

Both the rationale for and the normative content of the new doctrine enunciated in *Keck* are clear. On the basis of an a priori judgement on the different effect and nature of two categories of national measures, the Court introduced a distinction between "rules relating to product characteristics" (so-called "product requirements") and "rules relating to selling arrangements". While product requirements are "by nature" capable of

---

freedom even where such rules are not aimed at products from other Member States, the Court considers necessary to re-examine and clarify its case law on this matter." Joined Cases C–267 and 268/91, *Keck & Mithouard* [1993] ECR 6097, para 14 Cf JHH Weiler, "Epilogue: Towards a Common Law of International Trade", in JHH Weiler (ed), *The EU, the WTO and the NAFTA: Towards a Common Law of International Trade?* (Oxford, OUP 2000) at 226–29.

[339] P Oliver, "Some Future Reflections on the Scope of Art 28–30 (Ex 30–36) EC", 36 *CMLRev* (1999) 783, at 793–94.

[340] Joined Cases C–267 and 268/91, *Keck & Mithouard* [1993] ECR 6097, paras. 15–16.

hindering intra-Community trade because they normally impose on imported goods burdens in addition to those stemming from similar requirements existing in the country of exportation (or home country), selling arrangements are not "by nature" such as to prevent their access to the market or to impede access any more than it impedes the access of domestic products, since they normally impose an equal burden on the marketing of all products, whether domestic or imported.[341]

It is interesting to note how *Keck* has revealed that the *Dassonville–Cassis de Dijon* doctrine is based on nothing other than a general assumption: product requirements hinder intra-Community trade.[342]

Moreover, the difference in the "assumed" effect and nature of the two types of measures is reflected in the different *normative content* of the two doctrines; while product requirements are caught by the prohibition of Article 28 unless they are justified on the basis of a mandatory requirement (*Dassonville–Cassis de Dijon* doctrine), selling arrangements are excluded from the reach of Article 28 provided that they affect in the same manner, in law and fact, the marketing of domestic and imported products or are justified on public policy grounds (*Keck* doctrine). Although the justification option is the same with regard both forms of regulation, the threshold of violation is higher in the case of selling arrangements than in the case of product requirements.[343]

The *Keck* decision has spurred, to say the least, a very lively debate among the extended circle of EC lawyers, not just on the specific contours of the new doctrine on "selling arrangements", but more generally on the broader implications of the Court's latest turn on the entire law of the free movement. While the focus here will be mainly on the former debate, a few words on *Keck*'s broader implications are nevertheless indispensable.

---

[341] P Craig and G de Búrca, *EU Law* (Oxford, OUP, 1998) at 618.

[342] Cf Case C–470/93, *Verein gegen Unwesen in Handel und Gewerbe Köln e.V v Mars GmbH*, [1995] ECR I–1923, paras 13–14, "Although it applies to all products without distinction, a prohibition such as that in question in the main proceedings, which relates to the marketing in a Member State of products bearing the same publicity markings as those lawfully used in other Member States, *is by nature such to hinder intra-Community trade*. It may compel the importer to adjust the presentation of his products according to the place where they are to be marketed and consequently to incur additional packaging and advertising costs. Such a prohibition therefore falls within the scope of Art 30 of the Treaty" [emphasis added]. As it will be discussed in the ch dealing with the proportionality principle, contrary to the *Keck*'s assumption, the *Cassis de Dijon* one is subject to rebuttal where the Member States is able to demonstrate that the effect on intra-Community trade is "uncertain and indirect".

[343] Barnard has also suggested that the two approaches differ in respect of presumptions and the burden of proof. "If the measure is classified as a certain selling arrangement then the presumption is that it does not hinder access to the market (the per se legal approach) and the trader will need to work hard to rebut this presumption, possibly by producing statistical or other evidence to prove actual hindrance rather than merely relying on the potential effect on trade. If, on the other hand, the measure is classified as a product requirement, it is presumed that there is an impediment to access to the market (Cassis) (the per se illegal approach)." C Barnard, "Fitting the Remaining Pieces into the Goods and Persons Jigsaw", 26 *ELRev* (2001) 35, text at notes 77–81.

Along the lines of the fundamental choice that Advocate-General Tesauro had submitted to the Court in his Opinion in *Hünermund* between the liberalisation of intra-Community trade and the recognition of a right to trade, the doctrinal debate following the *Keck* judgment focuses on whether the law of free movement (of goods) should subject to its proportionality review only measures that *bar* market access or, more broadly, to all measures that simply *restrict* (more or less substantially) trade among Member States. According to the former view, advocated by Professor Weiler, while rules that bar market access are caught by Article 28 and must be justified, [m]arket regulation rules—whether selling arrangements or otherwise—that do not bar access, should not be caught unless discriminatory in law or fact.[344] There is thus perfect agreement between this view and the Court's assertion in *Keck* that, where the non-discriminatory conditions of the above-mentioned paragraph 16 are satisfied, national restrictions on selling arrangements are not "by nature such as to prevent their [foreign goods'] access to the market or to impede access any more than it impedes the access of domestic products".[345] Following this perspective, *Keck's* reference exclusively to "certain selling arrangements" is indeed inadequate, since there exist several other measures that, though not "selling arrangements", do not constitute "market access barriers", and thus should also not be caught by Article 28. In other words, the scope of application of the *Keck* doctrine is too strict.

According to the second view, advocated for example by Professor Weatherill, *Keck* should not be read as re-directing the law of the free movement toward "factual and legal equality of application to the exclusion of questions of market access and obstruction to the construction of cross-border commercial strategies."[346] This line of argument emphasises that even certain internal regulations causing serious hindrance to market access for imported products should not escape the prohibition of Article 28 simply because they fall within the definition of selling arrangements and are not discriminatory, in law and in fact. Thus, the Court is wrong in asserting in *Keck* that non-discriminatory selling arrangement are "by nature" incapable of seriously impeding or even preventing altogether market access. In other words, the scope of application of the *Keck* doctrine is too broad.[347]

---

[344] JHH Weiler, "Epilogue: Towards a Common Law of International Trade", in JHH Weiler (ed), *The EU, the WTO and the NAFTA: Towards a Common Law of International Trade?* (Oxford, OUP 2000) at 228. Cf in the field of movement of workers the Opinion of the Advocate-General in Case C–190/98, *Volker Graf v Filzmoser Maschinenbau GmbH* [2000] ECR I–493.
[345] Joined Cases C–267 and 268/91, *Keck & Mithouard* [1993] ECR 6097, para 17.
[346] S Weatherill, "After Keck: Some Thoughts on how to Clarify the Clarification", 33 *CMLRev* (1996) 885, at 904.
[347] Cf D Chalmers, "Repackaging the Internal Market—The Ramifications of the *Keck* Judgment", 19 *ELRev.* (1994) 385; L Gormley, "Reasoning Renounced? The Remarkable

Leaving aside the broader debate, let us now focus on the specific contours of the *Keck* judgment, in particular the meaning of "certain selling arrangements" and when a measure may be deemed to "affect in the same manner, in law and fact, the marketing of domestic and imported products."

(b) "Certain selling arrangements" (ie the objective element)   Although the Court of Justice in *Keck* clearly put forward a different normative approach depending on whether the national measure at issue is a rule relating to "product characteristics" or one relating to "selling arrangements", the Court did not provide in that decision for a definition of what precisely it meant by "certain selling arrangements". Subsequent *Keck* jurisprudence has however remedied this original lack of clarity, in particular with regard to the meaning of the concept of selling arrangements.[348] I fully agree with Oliver's suggestion that

> [i]t is the Court's very tenacity in continuing to apply that ruling—despite the torrent of adverse criticism—which has enabled it to clarify that judgment so effectively.[349]

From the Court's relative wealth of jurisprudence applying the *Keck* doctrine, it may be noted that the Court has applied the distinction between "product requirements" and "selling arrangement" in a very formalistic manner, employing as the discriminating criterion whether or not the particular measure at issue requires alteration of the product's physical identity or composition, independently of the measure's effects on market access for the regulated product. Accordingly, the concept of "selling arrangements" has been held to cover several types of

---

Judgment in *Keck & Mithouard"*, *European Business Law Review* (1994) 63; C Barnard, "Fitting the Remaining Pieces into the Goods and Persons Jigsaw", 26 *ELRev* (2001) 35. Also Opinion of Advocate-General Lenz in Case C–391/92, *Commission v Greece* (*Processed Milk*) [1995] ECR I–1621; and Opinion of Advocate-General Jacobs in Case C–412/93, *Société d'Importation Edouard Leclerc-Siplec v TFI Publicité SA and M6 Publicité SA* [1995] ECR I–179.

[348] P Oliver, "Some Further Reflections on the Scope of Art 28–30 (ex 30–36) EC", 36 *CMLRev* (1999) 783, at 793–94; G Tesauro, "The Community's Internal Market in light of the Recent Case-Law of the Court of Justice", *YEL* (1995) 1, at 7.
[349] P Oliver, "Some Further Reflections on the Scope of Art 28–30 (ex 30–36) EC", 36 *CMLRev* (1999) 783, at 794–95. Barnard notes the "enthusiasm" with which the Court applied its *Keck* ruling, C Barnard, "Fitting the Remaining Pieces into the Goods and Persons Jigsaw", 26 *ELRev* (2001) 35, at text note 59. Cf P Eeckhout, "After *Keck and Mithouard*: Free Movement of Goods in the EC, Market Access, and Non-Discrimination" T Cottier and P Mavroidis (eds), *Regulatory Barriers and the Principle of Non-Discrimination in World Trade Law* (Ann Arbor, the University of Michigan Press, 2000) at 202.

advertising regulations,[350] restrictions on when,[351] where or by whom[352] goods may be sold, and price controls.[353] Notwithstanding their actual lesser or greater impact on intra-Community trade or market access, all of these measures were found to constitute "selling arrangement" for purposes of *Keck* since they did not have any direct impact on the physical characteristics of the covered products. The legislation at issue did not require manufacturers to change the composition, packaging, labelling, etc. of their products.

For example in *De Agostini*,[354] the Court, reiterating its previous case-law on the subject, reached the conclusion that Swedish legislation prohibiting commercial television advertising directed specifically at children fell within the concept of "selling arrangements" since it prohibited a particular form of promotion of a particular method of marketing products, without imposing any alteration on the product's characteristics (at issue in that case was De Agostini's children's magazine "Everything about Dinosaurs"). Although it was noted that the legislation under review in that case affected *cross-border* advertising and was the only effective form of promotion enabling imported products to penetrate the Swedish market (there was no other advertising method for reaching children and their parents), the Court nonetheless found that the ban was a "selling arrangement". Following the a priori judgement or general assumption it had formulated in *Keck*—non-discriminatory selling arrangements are not by nature such as to prevent imported products from accessing the market or to impede such access any more than it impedes the access of domestic products—the Court has never inquired, at least for the

---

[350] Case C–292/92, *Hünermund v Landesapothekerkammer Baden-Württemberg* [1993] ECR I–6787 (no advertising of pharmaceutical products except inside pharmacists' shops); Case C–412/93, *Société d'Importation Edouard Leclerc-Siplec v TF1 Publicité SA and M6 Publicité SA* [1995] ECR I-179 (ban on television advertising by the distribution sector); Joined Cases C–34, 35 and 36/95, *Konsumentombudsmannen (KO) v De Agostini (Svenska) Förlag AB and Konsumentombusdsmannen (KO) v TV-Shop i Sverige AB (De Agostini)* [1997] ECR I–3843 (ban on commercial television advertisment directed at children); Case C–405/98, *Konsumentombudsmannen (KO) v Gourmet International Products (GIP) AB (Gourmet)* [2001] ECR I–1795 (restrictions on advertising of alcoholic beverages).
[351] Case C–401 and 402/92, *Criminal Proceedings Against Tankstation 't Heukske and J B E Boermans* [1994] ECR I–2199 (restrictions on opening hours of petrol stations); Case C–69/93, *Punto Casa v Sindaco del Comune di Capena* [1994] ECR I–2355 (restrictions on retail outlets Sunday opening hours); Joined Cases C–418–421, 460–462, and 464/93, 9–11, 14–15, 23–24, and 332/94, *Semeraro Casa Uno Srl v Sindaco del Comune di Erbusco* [1996] ECR I–2975 (idem).
[352] Case C–391/92, *Commission v Greece (Processed Milk)* [1995] ECR I–1621 (restriction to pharmacies alone of sales of milk for infants).
[353] Case C–63/94, *Belgapom v ITM Belgium* [1995] ECR I–2467. With regard to price controls, however, even pre-*Keck* jurisprudence has always employed a discrimination-based test. Cf P Oliver, *Free Movement of Goods in the European Community* (London, Sweet & Maxwell, 1996) at 95.
[354] Joined Cases C–34–36/95, *De Agostini* [1997] ECR I–3843. Cf J Stuyck's note on the case in 34 *CMLRev* (1997) 1445, at 1464–66.

purpose of determining the scope of application of the *Keck* doctrine,[355] into whether or not its assumptions have indeed been correct in any particular case. In the recent *Gourmet* case,[356] the Court applied *Keck* (ie it considered the measure under review a "selling arrangement") with regard to the Swedish legislation prohibiting, with only a few insignificant exceptions, the advertising of alcohol beverages, even if it implicitly recognised substantial adverse effects of the measure on intra-Community trade. The Court admitted in fact that the Swedish ban "not only prohibits a form of marketing a product but in reality prohibits producers and importers from directing any advertising messages at consumers".[357]

On the other hand, all national measures imposing on the manufacturer requirements relating, for example, to the composition or designation of the product will be excluded from the reach of the notion of "selling arrangements" and thus subject to the previous *Dassonville–Cassis de Dijon* doctrine, even if these apparently seem to affect selling in some manner.[358] For example, in *Familiapress*,[359] the Court found that Austrian legislation prohibiting publishers from including prize competitions (such as crossword puzzles) in their papers was not concerned with a selling arrangement within the meaning of the *Keck* judgment since the measure under review in that case affected the actual content of the product at issue. The Court argued that,

> even though the relevant national legislation is directed against a method of sales promotion, in this case it bears on the actual content of the products, in so far as the competitions in question form an integral part of the magazine in which they appear.[360]

Equally in *Clinique Laboratoires & Estée Lauder Cosmetics*,[361] the Court reviewed a German prohibition on the use of the name *Clinique* for

---

[355] See below discussion on the discrimination test, where the Court does seem to take into account, at least to a certain extent, the issue of market access.

[356] Case C–405/98, *Gourmet* [2001] ECR I–1795.

[357] *Ibid.*, para 20. Cf Case C–254/98, *Schutzverband Gegen Unlauteren Wettbewerb v TK-Heimdienst Sass GmbH* [2000] ECR I–151, para 24, where Austrian legislation requiring that bakers, butchers and grocers could "make sales on rounds in a given administrative district, only if they also trade from a permanent establishment in that administrative district or an adjacent municipality where they offer for sale the same goods as they do on rounds", was found to relate to "selling arrangements for certain goods in that it lays down the geographical areas in which each of the operators concerned may sell his goods by that method".

[358] D Chalmers, "Repackaging the Internal Market—The Ramifications of the *Keck* Judgment", 19 *ELRev* (1994) 385, text at notes 44–45.

[359] Case C–368/95, *Vereinigte Familiapress Zeitungsverlags- und Vertriebs GmbH v Heinrich Bauer Verlag* [1997] ECR I–3689.

[360] *Ibid.*, para 11.

[361] Case C–315/92, *Verband Sozialer Wettbewerb eV v Clinique Laboratoires SNC et Estée Lauder Cosmetics GmbH* [1994] ECR I–0317.

cosmetics on the basis of its *Dassonville–Cassis de Dijon* jurisprudence in light of the fact that the German measure at hand regulated a physical characteristic of the product at issue and thus implicitly imposed an alteration of the identity or composition of that same product.[362]

Following the Court's formalistic application of the notion of "selling arrangements", it appears that the *Keck* doctrine applies also with regard to those rules, which, though formally selling arrangements (ie measures regulating the manner in which products should be sold without altering the product's physical composition), totally or substantially prevent intra-Community trade. For example, the French one-year ban on the sale or hire of film video, which in *Cinétheque*[363] had been subject to the *Cassis de Dijon* proportionality review, would now in the light of *Keck* escape the reach of Article 28 unless the measure were found to discriminate in law or fact against imported products.[364] Similarly, the hypothetical case, put forward by White in his seminal Article preceding and anticipating the Court's turn in *Keck*,[365] of a ban on the sale of cigarettes on all days of the year other than Christmas day would also fall within the concept of selling arrangements as strictly interpreted by the Court.[366]

(c) The Discrimination Test: from Processed Milk *to* Gourmet   As previously noted, according to *Keck* national provisions restricting or prohibiting certain selling arrangements will not be caught by the prohibition of Article 28 unless they are found to discriminate in law or fact between domestic and imported products. Next to the formalisation of the "selling arrangements" category, reference to the concept of de facto discrimination constitutes the other element of novelty which, in *Keck*, the Court of Justice introduced in the law of the free movement of goods, at least within

---

[362] See, recently, Case C–390/99, *Canal Satélite Digital SL v Administracion General del Estado* [2002] ECR I–607, para 30, where the Court stated that "the need in certain cases to adapt the products in question to the rules in force in the Member State in which they are marketed prevents the abovementioned requirements [on operators of conditional-access television services to register in a national registry and obtain administrative certification of compliace with technical regulation] from being treated as selling arrangements within the meaning of paragraph 16 of [the *Keck & Mithouard* decision]". Cf Case C–470/93, *Verein gegen Unwesen in Handel und Gewerbe Köln e.V v Mars GmbH* [1995] ECR I–1923, paras. 11–14, where the Court applied its *Dassonville-Cassis de Dijon* jurisprudence to German legislation prohibiting the importation and marketing of a product lawfully marketed in another Member State, whose packaged units were increased in quantity during a short publicity campaign and *the wrapping marked "+ 10%"*.

[363] Joined Cases 60 and 61/84, *Cinéthèque SA v Fédération Nationale des Cinémas Francais* [1985] ECR 2605.

[364] Cf P Craig and G de Búrca, *EU Law* (Oxford, OUP, 1998) at 619, citing the Opinion of Advocate-General van Gerven in Joined Cases C–401 and 402/92, *Criminal Proceedings Against Tankstation 't Heustke and J B E Boermans* [1994] ECR I–2199, at 2220.

[365] E White, "In Search of the Limits to Art 30 of the EEC Treaty", 26 *CMLRev* (1989) 235, at 258.

[366] White, however, considered that this type of measure should be treated as a measure having equivalent effect for purposes of Art 28. Cf P Oliver, "Some Further Reflections on the Scope of Art 28–30 (ex 30–36) EC", 36 *CMLRev* (1999) 783, at 795.

the ambit of Article 28. It should be recalled that the Court's pre-*Keck* jurisprudence had simply employed the distinction between "distinctly" and "indistinctly" applicable measures or, in other words, between measures which *formally* discriminated on the basis of the product's origin and measures that did not. One of the praised advantages of the *Dassonville–Cassis de Dijon* formula was precisely that it avoided the issue of determining whether or not a measure that does not discriminate on its face is nevertheless discriminatory in its effects. By explicitly subjecting selling arrangements to the condition that they "affect in the same manner, in law and *fact*, the marketing of domestic products and of those from other Member States", *Keck* has formally introduced the concept of material or de facto discrimination into Article 28 of the Treaty.[367]

As both the case-law on old Article 95 (now 90) EC and that on Article III GATT indicate, establishing *factual* equality of national rules may be a complex undertaking.[368] This is especially evident if one considers that the non-discrimination conditions required by the *Keck* doctrine clearly refer to the measure's *effects* on the marketing of domestic and imported products, as the term *"affect"* employed in paragraph 16 of *Keck* clearly emphasises.

Oliver has recently suggested that the considerable uncertainty surrounding the concept of discrimination applicable to selling arrangements "may sadly prove to be the Achilles' heel of *Keck*."[369] In this section, I will try to shed some light on how the Court of Justice has so far dealt with claims of de facto discrimination for purposes of the *Keck* doctrine, by examining in chronological order five cases where the Court was called on to determine whether or not a selling arrangement affected in the same manner, *in fact*, the marketing of domestic and imported products. Besides a recent, more favourable attitude towards de facto discrimination arguments, from these few cases appears to emerge, once again, a very unstructured discrimination test which the Court centres on the inherently protectionist nature of the national measure under review.

In *Commission v Greece* (the so called *Processed Milk* case),[370] the Court was confronted with the claim that the non-discrimination condition imposed by *Keck* was not met by the selling arrangement under review. The Commission argued that Greek legislation restricting the sale of processed milk for infants exclusively to pharmacies fell foul of

---

[367] Under the *Keck* formula, the Court also required that the national provisions restricting selling arrangements "apply to all affected traders operating within the national territory". The actual meaning of this condition is not altogether clear and subsequent *Keck* jurisprudence does not provide any indication of its real value. At best it would seem to be covered by the broader condition of non-discrimination.

[368] S Weatherill and P Beaumont, *EC Law* (London, Penguin Books, 1995) at 538.

[369] Cf P Oliver, "Some Further Reflections on the Scope of Art 28–30 (ex 30–36) EC", 36 *CMLRev* (1999) 783, at 795.

[370] Case C–391/92, *Commission v Greece* (*Processed Milk*) [1995] ECR I–1621.

the prohibition of Article 28 since the Greek measure was a selling arrangement within the meaning of *Keck* and it materially discriminated against imported products. The Commission's argument was apparently based on the fact that Greece did not itself produce processed milk for infants. The Court rejected the Commission's claim, noting that,

> the applicability of Article 30 [now 28] of the Treaty to a national measure for the general regulation of commerce, which concerns all the products concerned without distinction according to their origin, cannot depend on such a purely fortuitous factual circumstance, which may, moreover, change with the passage of time. If it did, this would have the illogical consequence that the same legislation would fall under Article 30 [now 28] in certain Member States but fall outside the scope of that provision in other Member States.[371]

However, if the fact that the regulated product was not manufactured in the regulating State was not sufficient for a finding of material discrimination, the Court added that the situation would be different only if it was apparent that the legislation at issue protected domestic products which were similar to processed milk for infants from other Member States or which were in competition with milk of that type.[372] Since the Commission had not shown that to be the case,[373] the Court concluded that the Greek measure was not discriminatory and thus fell outside the scope of Article 28.

Making use of the well-known concepts of "protection", "similar products" and "competitive products" from the Court's jurisprudence relating to internal taxation, the *Processed Milk* ruling shows that the Court is not willing to base a finding of material discrimination on the purely fortuitous factual circumstance that the measure under review negatively affects only imported products. In order to justify a finding of material discrimination, the Court considers it necessary for the plaintiff to establish the measure's protective nature with regard to similar or competitive domestic products. Accordingly, the Court's ruling in the instant case should not be read as excluding statistical economic data for the purposes of determining the existence of material discrimination;[374] rather, it demonstrates the Court's emphasis on the rationale of the non-discrimination requirement, which is to strike down national measures that have the effect of protecting domestic products.

---

[371] *Ibid.*, para 17.
[372] *Ibid.*
[373] This confirms that the burden of proving discrimination is on the plaintiff and not on the defending Member State. Cf C Barnard, "Fitting the Remaining Pieces into the Goods and Persons Jigsaw", 26 *ELRev* (2001) 35, text at n 77.
[374] Cf P Oliver, "Some Further Reflections on the Scope of Art 28–30 (ex 30–36) EC", 36 *CMLRev* (1999) 783, at 796.

In *Semeraro Casa Uno Srl. v Sindaco del Comune di Erbusco* (and related cases),[375] the applicants, as well as the referring national court, argued that Italian legislation requiring all shops to close on Sundays violated the prohibition of Article 28 as interpreted by *Keck* on the ground that it had a differential impact on the marketing of domestic and imported goods. In summary, since out-of-town shopping centres sold more imported goods than did small shops and relied in particular on weekend shoppers, the effects of the prohibition on Sunday opening on the marketing of national and imported products were not *in fact* the same.[376]

The Court rejected the de facto discrimination argument essentially on the grounds of insufficiency of evidence. The Court stated categorically that,

> there is no evidence […] that, viewed as a whole, [the rules at issue] could lead to unequal treatment between national products and imported products as regard to access to the market.[377]

In particular, the fact that the national legislation had the effect of limiting the marketing of a product generally, and consequently its importation, could not justify, on that basis alone, a finding that access to the market for imported products was limited to a greater extent than for similar national products.[378]

In *De Agostini*,[379] for the first time, the Court seemed more receptive to a de facto discrimination claim. As previously noted, the case concerned a Swedish ban on television advertising directed at children under 12 (as well as a ban on misleading commercials for skincare products). Having determined that the measure at issue was a selling arrangement, the Court examined whether that same measure complied with the non-discrimination requirement of *Keck*. Although it left the final decision to the national court, the Court of Justice noted that,

> it cannot be excluded that an outright ban, applying in one Member State, of a type of promotion for a product which is lawfully sold there might have a greater impact on products from other Member States.[380]

The Court, however, did not give any instruction on how the national court should carry out this factual determination, except possibly that, as

---

[375] Joined Cases C–418–421, 460–462, and 464/93, 9–11, 14–15, 23–24, and 332/94, *Semeraro Casa Uno Srl v Sindaco del Comune di Erbusco* [1996] ECR I–2975.
[376] *Ibid.*, paras 17–19.
[377] *Ibid.*, para 24.
[378] *Ibid.*
[379] Joined Cases C–34–36/95, *De Agostini* [1997] ECR I–3843. Cf J Stuyck's note on the case in 34 *CMLRev* (1997) 1445, at 1464–66.
[380] Joined Cases C–34-36/95, *De Agostini*, [1997] ECR I–3843, para 42.

suggested by Oliver, the use of statistics may be a necessary element in showing the measure's "greater impact" on imported products.[381]

More insightful are two recent cases, where the Court has finally concluded that the facially origin-neutral selling arrangements under review did *not* in practice affect in the same manner the marketing of domestic products and that of products from other Member States.

As previously noted, *Heimdienst*[382] concerned Austrian legislation requiring bakers, butchers and grocers to maintain a permanent establishment in a particular administrative district if they wanted to make sales on rounds in that district or in an adjacent municipality.[383] Having determined that the Austrian measure was a selling arrangement, the Court also found that the legislation on rounds sales did not meet the non-discrimination requirements provided for in *Keck*. The Court explained its decision by noting, first of all, that the legislation under review imposed an obligation on bakers, butchers and grocers who *already* had a permanent establishment in another Member State and who wished to sell their goods on rounds in a particular administrative district in Austria to set up or purchase another permanent establishment in that administrative district or in an adjacent municipality, *whilst local economic operators already met the requirement as to a permanent establishment*.[384] In other words, borrowing from previous *Cassis de Dijon* jurisprudence on dual-burden rules, the Court considered that the Austrian legislation imposing additional market access costs on goods from other Member States compared to the ones borne by national products showed inherent discriminatory or protectionist features.

In this regard, it should be emphasised that the Court's finding appears to be based on nothing more than a general assumption of discrimination, very much in line with the arguments of those, like Marenco for example, who had interpreted the *Dassonville–Cassis de Dijon* jurisprudence as a mere application of the non-discrimination principle. Are *Cassis de Dijon*-type arguments surreptitiously making their way back into the *Keck* doctrine?

---

[381] Cf P Oliver, "Some Further Reflections on the Scope of Art 28–30 (ex 30–36) EC", 36 *CMLRev* (1999) 783, at 796.

[382] Case C–254/98, *Schutzverband gegen unlauteren Wettbewerb v TK-Heimdienst Sass GmbH* [2000] ECR I–151.

[383] The measure did not affect those traders established in Member States adjacent to Austria since, as is noted in the judgment "it is always open to traders in Member States adjacent to Austria to make deliveries direct to Austrian consumers on the other side of the border if they carry on business in a municipality adjacent to the Austrian Verwaltungsbezirk where they intend to make sales on rounds. Traders from other Member States are therefore at liberty to export the goods referred to in Art 53a of the GewO to Austria even if they do not have permanent establishment in Austria." Case C–254/98, *Heimdienst* [2000] ECR I–151, para 18.

[384] *Ibid.*, para 26.

A further argument advanced by the Court in *Heimdienst* does not help much in "structuring" the discrimination test under *Keck*. The Court noted the fact that the Austrian legislation affected both the sale of products from other parts of the national territory and the sale of products imported from other Member States, but did not modify its conclusion since,

> [f]or a national measure to be categorised as discriminatory or protective for the purposes of the rules on the free movement of goods, it is not necessary for it to have the effect of favouring national products as a whole or of placing only imported products at a disadvantage and not national products.[385]

This line of argument, originally put forward in the context of determining the existence of arbitrary discrimination for purposes of Article 30 (old 36) with regard to a measure adopted by, and applicable in, the Catalan region,[386] seems to deny the need, for purposes of determining the measure's discriminatory or protectionist nature, to compare *all domestic products* affected by the measure with *all imported products* similarly affected by that same measure. More correctly, this type of argument should be limited, as in the case at hand, to measures enacted by local administrative units.

Finally in the recent *Gourmet* case,[387] the Court found that Swedish legislation prohibiting producers and importers of alcoholic beverages from directing any advertising messages at consumers should be regarded as affecting the marketing of products from other Member States *more heavily* than the marketing of domestic products, once again because of the inherently protectionist features of the Swedish ban.[388] The Court noted that,

> in the case of products like alcoholic beverages, the consumption of which is linked to traditional social practices and to local habits and customs, a

---

[385] *Ibid.*, paras 27–28, citing an earlier decision in Joined Cases C–1 and 176/90, *Aragonesa de Publicidad and Publivía* [1991] ECR I–4151, para 24. The Court also rejected the contention of the Schutzverband that the measure's restrictive effects were too random and indirect to be regarded as impeding trade between Member States, observing that "goods from other Member States could never be offered for sale on rounds in an administrative district, such as an Austrian Verwaltungsbezirk, which is not situated in a border area." Case C–254/98, *Heimdienst* [2000] ECR I–151, para 30.

[386] Joined Cases C–1/90 and C–176/90, *Aragonesa de Publicidad and Publivía* [1991] ECR I–4151.

[387] Case C–405/98, *Gourmet* [2001] ECR I–1795. For a stimulating comment on the decision see A Biondi, "Advertising Alcohol and the Free Movement Principle: The *Gourmet* Decision", 26 *ELRev* (2001) 616.

[388] Case C–405/98, *Gourmet* [2001] ECR I–1795, para 25. While there was no dispute regarding the fact that an advertising ban on alcoholic beverages adversely *affected* the marketing of those products, the parties diverged on whether or not such effect was greater on imported products vis-à-vis domestic products.

prohibition of all advertising directed at consumers in the form of advertisements in the press, on the radio and on television, the direct mailing of unsolicited material or the placing of posters on the public highway is liable to impede access to the market by products from other Member States more than it impedes access by domestic products, with which consumers are instantly more familiar.[389]

The Court's finding that the measure under review was liable to affect in a different manner the market access capabilities of domestic and imported alcoholic beverages, appears to be based once again on a very general, unsubstantiated assumption. It is clear that the Court is not really interested in supporting its conclusion with more precise evidence, such as statistical data. The Court simply adds that its conclusion cannot be altered by the information provided by the Swedish Government concerning the relative increase in Sweden in the consumption of wine and whisky, which are mainly imported, in comparison with other products such as vodka, which is mainly of Swedish origin. The Court argued as follows:

> First, it cannot be precluded that, in the absence of the legislation at issue in the main proceedings, the change indicated would have been greater; [and] second, that information takes into account only some alcoholic beverages and ignores, in particular, beer consumption.[390]

Moreover, in order to show the inherently protectionist nature of the Swedish legislation as a whole, the Court noted the following two facts: (a) the Swedish legislation did not prohibit "editorial advertising" (ie the promotion in articles forming part of the editorial content of the publication) and (b) for various, principally cultural, reasons, domestic producers have easier access to that means of advertising vis-à-vis their competitors established in other Member States. For the Court, these circumstances are "liable to increase the imbalance inherent in the absolute prohibition on direct advertising".[391]

Although its reasoning in *Gourmet* is clearly based on the similar or competitive relationship between imported and domestic alcoholic beverages, the Court seems to have taken the existence of this relationship for granted, thus avoiding the complex and time-consuming determination of whether the products at issue were indeed similar or at least competitive.

In conclusion, although the Court seems to require a high threshold of discrimination (the inherently protectionist nature of a measure), in

---

[389] *Ibid.*, para 21.
[390] *Ibid.*, para 22.
[391] *Ibid.*, para 24.

practice the Court is willing to conclude that a measure is indeed discriminatory in effect on the basis of very general assumptions unsubstantiated by any statistical data with regard to the relevant markets and the relevant imported and domestic products. If the Court were to continue the approach followed in *Heimdienst* and *Gourmet*, a case like *Oosthoek*, where, in pre-*Keck* times, the Court held that legislation prohibiting the offer of free gifts to buyers of encyclopaedias (ie a selling arrangement) were caught by Article 28 since it might have forced a producer to adopt sales promotion or advertising schemes which differed as between States, might still today, in post-*Keck* times, fall within the scope of application of Article 28 on those same grounds.[392] Although the Court's reluctance to get its hands dirty with empirical evidence may be comprehensible on grounds of both pure judicial self-restraint and legal certainty,[393] *Keck*'s express reference to the concept of de facto discrimination would be for all practical purposes subverted if the Court were to continue this trend of simply making use of very general assumptions with regard to the adverse effects of internal marketing regulations on the competitive relationship between domestic and imported products.[394]

Furthermore, there have recently been attempts to explain the Court's case-law on the application of the non-discrimination requirements imposed by the *Keck* doctrine by reference to the concept of market access. As suggested most recently by Barnard, the *Keck* jurisprudence, as well as more generally the case-law on the free movement of both goods and persons, would seem to show that the Court of Justice is perhaps moving towards employing a global test of "prevention of direct and substantial hindrance of access to the market" as the benchmark for establishing a violation of any of the EC free movement principles.[395] Despite the strength of the arguments advanced *de jure condendo* by Barnard in favour

---

[392] This is the argument advanced in P Craig and G de Búrca, *EU Law* (Oxford, OUP, 1998) at 620. *Cf* also C Barnard, "Fitting the Remaining Pieces into the Goods and Persons Jigsaw", 26 *ELRev* (2001) 35, text at notes 87–93.

[393] With regard to the latter concern, Oliver has noted that "the dangers of introducing a case by case economic assessment and thus the use of statistics into Art 28 to 30—a virtually statistics-free zone until very recently." Especially, reliance on statistical data could "lead to perverse results, as the legality of a measure might vary from month to month." P Oliver, "Some Further Reflections on the Scope of Art 28–30 (ex 30–36) EC", 36 *CMLRev* (1999) 783, at 796.

[394] *Cf* P Eeckhout, "After *Keck and Mithouard*: Free Movement of Goods in the EC, Market Access, and Non-Discrimination" T Cottier and P Mavroidis (eds), *Regulatory Barriers and the Principle of Non-Discrimination in World Trade Law* (Ann Arbor, the University of Michigan Press, 2000) at 203, noting that "the broader the approach to non-discrimination under *Keck*, the less difference there will be between the approach to selling arrangements and classic *Cassis de Dijon* cases."

[395] C Barnard, "Fitting the Remaining Pieces into the Goods and Persons Jigsaw", 26 *ELRev* (2001) 35, at 53 *et seq*. *Cf* P Eeckhout, "After *Keck and Mithouard*: Free Movement of Goods in the EC, Market Access, and Non-Discrimination" T Cottier and P Mavroidis (eds), *Regulatory Barriers and the Principle of Non-Discrimination in World Trade Law* (Ann Arbor, the University

of adopting such a global test, I would argue that, at least with regard to its *Keck* jurisprudence, the Court does not seem to be moved at least predominantly by "market access" concerns. This impression is confirmed by examining the approach followed by the Court in the two most recent decisions on the matter: *Heimdienst* and *Gourmet*.

In those two cases, the national measures under review, respectively the Austrian restriction on rounds sales by bakers, butchers and grocers and the Swedish advertising ban of alcoholic beverages, appeared to have similar effects on the market access capabilities of the products involved. While neither of these measures *prevented* access to the respective national markets, they certainly *hindered* or *impeded* such access to a certain extent. Now, if one had to classify the measures under review in *Heimdienst* and *Gourmet* according to the intensity of their hindrance on market access, it would appear that the Swedish ban affected the market access of alcoholic beverages more than the Austrian restrictions on rounds sales by bakers, butchers and grocers. While in *Gourmet* even the Swedish Government accepted that the prohibition on advertising in Sweden affected sales of all alcoholic beverages, noting that the specific purpose of the Swedish legislation was indeed to reduce the consumption of alcohol,[396] in *Heimdienst* there is no indication that the products of non-established bakers, butchers and grocers could not be sold in a different manner without incurring any relevant loss of sales.[397] While the latter measure concerned a selling arrangement merely hindering or impeding access to a section of the Austrian market (sales on rounds by bakers, butchers and grocers in an Austrian Verwaltungsbezirk were permitted only if those traders had a permanent establishment in that district), the former case dealt with a selling arrangement coming close to substantially preventing non-domestic products access to the Swedish market.

Nevertheless, despite the different levels of market hindrance, the Court eventually found only the Austrian restriction in violation of Article 28 EC. The Court's more rigorous attitude in assessing the respective public policy justifications toward the Austrian restriction on rounds sales (not justified) vis-à-vis the Swedish advertising ban of alcoholic beverages (possibly justified) seems to suggest that the Court's emphasis was truly neither on the measure's discriminatory nor market access effects, rather on its

---

of Michigan Press, 2000) at 198 *et seq.*; D O'Keeffe and A Bavasso, "Four Freedoms, One Market and National Competence: In Search of a Dividing Line" in D O'Keeffe and A Bavasso (eds), *Judicial Review in European Union Law* (The Hague, Kluwer Law International, 2000) at 548 *et seq.*

[396] Case C–405/98, *Gourmet* [2001] ECR I–1795, para 14.
[397] As noted earlier, the Schutzverband restriction did not affect traders established in Member States *adjacent* to the Austrian administrative district in question, ie the small local traders who could not devise other more costly means of marketing their products.

proportionality or more generally on its overall reasonableness. It is thus time to turn to the issue of the "justification options".

B. Justification Options

1. De facto Discriminatory Selling Arrangements and the "Mandatory Requirements" Doctrine under EC Law

On the basis of the Court's fundamental statement in *Keck* that certain selling arrangements are not such as to hinder, directly or indirectly, actually or potentially, trade between Member States within the meaning of the *Dassonville* judgment, provided that they affect in the same manner, in law and fact, the marketing of domestic and imported products, it follows that discriminatory selling arrangements may still be justified on the basis of the dual approach envisaged by the *Dassonville–Cassis de Dijon* jurisprudence. Accordingly, while de jure discriminatory selling arrangements may rely exclusively on the exhaustive list of public policy exceptions of Article 30 (like any other "distinctly applicable measure"), de facto discriminatory selling arrangements may be justified also on the basis of the open-ended list of "mandatory requirements" (like any other "indistinctly applicable measure").

This dual approach was confirmed by the Court of Justice for the first time, though only implicitly, in *De Agostini*.[398] The Court noted that where it is shown that a provision restricting certain selling arrangements does not affect in the same way, in fact and in law, the marketing of national products and of products from other Member States,

> it is for the national court to determine whether the [advertising] ban is necessary to satisfy overriding requirements of general public importance or one of the aims listed in Article 36 [now 30] of the EC Treaty if it is proportionate to that purpose and if those aims or requirements could not have been attained or fulfilled by measures less restrictive of intra-Community trade.[399]

The justification avenue was actually applied by the Court in *Heimdienst*,[400] once it was established that the restriction on rounds sales

---

[398] Joined Cases C–34–36/95, *De Agostini* [1997] ECR I–3843. Cf J Stuyck's note on the case in 34 *CMLRev* (1997) 1445, at 1466, where it is noted that "a justification under *Cassis* is only possible if the national measure, albeit affecting imported and domestic products differently, are nevertheless "equally applicable", ie that they do not contain any formal discrimination between domestic products and products from other Member States."
[399] Joined Cases C–34–36/95, *De Agostini* [1997] ECR I–3843.
[400] Case C–254/98, *Schutzverband Gegen Unlauteren Wettbewerb v TK-Heimdienst Sass GmbH* [2000] ECR I–151.

did not meet the non-discrimination requirements provided for in *Keck*. The Court noted that in the view of the referring court the purpose of the national legislation was to protect the supplying of goods at short distance, to the advantage of local businesses, an objective which would otherwise be jeopardised in a country as topologically varied as Austria.[401] Thus, the Court considered whether that legislation was indeed justified on that basis.[402] In that connection, although it pointed out that aims of a purely economic nature could not justify a barrier to the fundamental principle of the free movement of goods, the Court stated that in certain circumstances it may be possible to justify an impediment to intra-Community trade on the basis that it is "necessary to avoid deterioration in the conditions under which goods are supplied at short distance in relatively isolated areas of a Member State". The Court, however, concluded that this was not the case at hand since,

> legislation such as that in point in the main proceedings, which applies to the whole of the national territory, is in any event disproportionate to that objective.[403]

Moreover, even with regard to the other ground of justification advanced by the Austrian Government (the protection of public health), the Court stated that this objective could be attained by measures that have effects less restrictive of intra-Community trade than a provision such as the establishment requirement. It gave the example of rules on refrigerating equipment in the vehicles used for the rounds.[404]

The protection of public health was also a reason advanced by the Swedish Government in *Gourmet*[405] to justify its prohibition on advertising alcoholic beverages, which the Court had found to affect the marketing of imported products more heavily than the marketing of domestic ones. Having accepted that rules restricting the advertising of alcoholic beverages in order to combat alcohol abuse might indeed reflect public health concerns, the Court noted that,

> [for these] concerns to be capable of justifying an obstacle to trade such as that inherent in the advertising ban at issue in the main proceedings, the measure concerned must also be proportionate to the objective to be achieved and must not constitute either a means of arbitrary discrimination or a disguised restriction on trade between Member States.[406]

---

[401] *Ibid.*, para 32.
[402] *Ibid.*
[403] *Ibid.*, para 34.
[404] *Ibid.*, paras 35–36.
[405] Case C–405/98, *Gourmet* [2001] ECR I–1795.
[406] *Ibid.*, paras 27–28.

On this issue both the Swedish Consumer Ombudsman and the intervening Governments claimed that the advertising prohibition at issue conformed with the proportionality requirements of Article 30, emphasising in particular that the prohibition was not absolute and did not prevent members of the public from obtaining information, if they wished (for example, in restaurants, on the Internet, in an "editorial context" or by asking the producer or importer to send advertising material). Moreover, recalling the Court of Justice's acknowledgement that Member States are at liberty, within the limits set by the Treaty, to decide on the degree of protection which they wish to afford to public health and on the way in which that protection is to be achieved, the Swedish Government maintained that the legislation at issue in the main proceedings constituted an *essential* component of its alcohol policy.[407]

On the other hand, noting that the Swedish policy on alcoholism was already catered for by (a) the existence of the monopoly on retail sales, (b) the prohibition on sales to persons under the age of 20 years and (c) the prohibition on information campaigns, Gourmet International Products (GIP) claimed that the outright prohibition on advertising laid down by the Swedish measure under review was indeed disproportionate. The protection sought could have been obtained by prohibitions of a more limited nature, concerning, for example, certain public places or the press aimed at children and adolescents.[408]

Confronted with a too-close-to-call decision, the Court took the easy way out by entrusting the national court with the final determination on the matter.[409] The Court noted that,

> the decision as to whether the prohibition on advertising at issue in the main proceedings is proportionate, and in particular as to whether the objective sought might be achieved by less extensive prohibitions or restrictions or by prohibitions or restrictions having less effect on intra-Community trade, calls for an analysis of the circumstances of law and of fact which characterise the situation in the Member State concerned, which the national court is in a better position than the Court of Justice to carry out.[410]

---

[407] *Ibid.*, para 29.

[408] *Ibid.*, para 30. The Commission submitted that the decision as to whether or not the prohibition on advertising at issue in the main proceedings was proportionate was a matter for the national court. However, it also stated that the prohibition "does not appear to be particularly effective, owing in particular to the existence of 'editorial' publicity and the abundance of indirect advertising on the Internet, and that requirements as to the form of advertising, such as the obligation to exercise moderation already found in the Alkoholreklamlagen, may suffice to protect the interest in question." *Ibid.*, para 31.

[409] For a critical view of the Court's decision to refer the proportionality back to the national court in *Gourmet* see A Biondi, "Advertising Alcohol and the Free Movement Principle: The *Gourmet* Decision", 26 *ELRev* (2001) 616 at 621.

[410] Case C–405/98, *Gourmet* [2001] ECR I–1795, para 33.

However, before divesting itself of the matter, the Court did point out one very interesting impression about the merits of the justification arguments advanced by the Swedish authorities. Citing its previous jurisprudence on the function of Article 30, second sentence,[411] the Court noted that there appeared to be

> no evidence [...] to suggest that the public health grounds on which the Swedish authorities rely have been diverted from their purpose and used in such a way as to *discriminate* against goods originating in other Member States or to *protect* certain national products *indirectly*.

With this statement, the Court emphasised, without resolving two important points: first, the longstanding unclear relationship between the proportionality principle and the requirements of Article 30, second sentence,[412] and secondly, the apparently overlapping role of, on the one hand, the requirements of the latter and, on the other, discrimination as the new violation threshold introduced by *Keck* for selling arrangements.[413] While from the Court's reasoning it appears that the concepts of "arbitrary discrimination" and "disguised restriction" for the purpose of Article 30, second sentence, should not be equated to the concept of de facto discrimination for purpose of determining whether or not certain selling arrangements are caught by the prohibition of Article 28, the Court's statements in *Gourmet* do not help in clarifying how and to what extent these concepts do indeed differ. In this regard, the extensive *Dassonville–Cassis de Dijon* jurisprudence may not be employed as an interpreting tool since, as has already been noted, that jurisprudence is not based, at least formally, on the notion of discrimination, and in particular on the notion of material discrimination.

---

[411] Case 34/79, *Regina v Henn and Darby* [1979] ECR 3795, para 21. In that case, the Court stated as follows: "20. According to the second sentence of Art 36 the restrictions on imports referred to in the first sentence may not 'constitute a means of arbitrary discrimination or a disguised restriction on trade between Member States'. 21 In order to answer the questions which have been referred to the court it is appropriate to have regard to the function of this provision, which is designed to prevent restrictions on trade based on the grounds mentioned in the first sentence of Art 36 from being diverted from their proper purpose and used in such a way as either to create discrimination in respect of goods originating in other Member States or indirectly to protect certain national products." See above in ch 2, the discussion on the 'justification options' for de jure discriminatory non-fiscal measures in EC law.

[412] "Such prohibitions or restrictions shall not, however, constitute a means of arbitrary discrimination or disguised restriction on trade between Member States". Art 30, second sentence. For a further discussion on Art 30, second sentence, see below ch 4 on 'proportionality' within the *Dassonville–Cassis de Dijon* 'rule of reason' approach.

[413] Even more puzzling would appear to be the Court's apparent, though not proven, reversal of the burden of proving 'arbitrary discrimination' for purposes of Art 30, second sentence, according to which it would be for the party claiming a violation of EC law to show evidence of discriminatory or protectionist intent.

Nevertheless, by comparing the Court's respective statements with regard to the relevance of discrimination under both Article 28 (as a condition for a finding of violation) and Article 30 (as a condition for a finding of justification), it may be possible to note a difference in emphasis. Where in the ambit of Article 28 the Court focuses principally on those features that point to the inherently discriminatory or protectionist *effects* of the measure at issue, under Article 30 it would appear that the Court's emphasis is on the evidence showing the discriminatory or protectionist *intent* of the Member State. By stressing the fact that there is no evidence suggesting that the public health grounds relied on by the Swedish authorities *have been diverted* from their purpose and *used in such a way* as to discriminate against imported goods or to protect certain national products, the Court seems to ground its assertion in the absence of discriminatory or protectionist "intent". Although it is clear that the Court is employing the requirements of Article 30, second sentence, as a mechanism for preventing the abuse or misuse of the general public policy exception, it is not altogether clear on what elements the Court based its statements. Could it be that the emphasis on the Member's discriminatory or protectionist "intent" represents a sign of the Court's willingness to look at those types of process-based deficiencies that have been employed by the Appellate Body in its application of the chapeau of Article XX GATT? Focusing on the Member State's "intent" is nothing other than reviewing the "purposive conduct" of the Member State in adopting the particular measure at issue, and thus may indeed imply a review of the *regulatory process* that has brought that same measure to life.

In this respect, the Appellate Body's reference to the principle of good faith when interpreting the chapeau of Article XX should be emphasised, since one application of this general principle prohibits the abusive exercise of a State's rights and enjoins that whenever the assertion of a right "impinges on the field covered by a treaty obligation, it must be exercised bona fide, that is to say, reasonably".[414] In other words, it would seem that within a justification inquiry, and in particular with regard to arguments based on Article 30, second sentence, emphasis should be more on the Member's "bad faith" *conduct* rather than simply on the "discriminatory" *effect* of the measure under review. As will be examined in the next chapter, these types of arguments have indeed been, though only rarely, employed within the context of an expanded

---

[414] Appellate Body Report on *United States—Import Prohibition of Certain Shrimp and Shrimp Products (US–Shrimp)*, WT/DS58/AB/R, circulated 12 Oct 1998, adopted 6 Nov 1998, para 158 citing B Cheng, *General Principles of Law as applied by International Courts and Tribunals* (Stevens & Sons, Ltd., 1953), ch 4, in particular, at 125 elaborates that "A reasonable and *bona fide* exercise of a right in such a case is one which is appropriate and necessary for the purpose of the right (ie in furtherance of the interests which the right is intended to protect). It should at the same time be *fair and equitable as between the parties* and not one which is calculated to procure for one of them an unfair advantage in the light of the obligation assumed. [...]" [emphasis added by the Appellate Body]. *Ibid.*, at fn 156.

proportionality review under the *Cassis de Dijon* "mandatory requirements" jurisprudence.[415]

These two recent cases show that the criteria employed by the Court of Justice in order to examine whether de facto discriminatory selling arrangements are justified on public policy grounds may be of two different kinds. On the one hand, one may find typical *proportionality*-type criteria that usually focus on whether the regulatory measure is the "least-trade restrictive" instrument to achieve a given public policy goal (*Heimdienst*). On the other, the Court is willing to impose *process*-type standards, which focus on the regulatory Member's "bad faith" conduct in adopting the discriminatory internal measure (*Gourmet*). Although the jurisprudence dealing with the issue of justification of de facto discriminatory selling arrangements is still developing, it is interesting to note the similar dual approach followed in WTO jurisprudence dealing with Article XX GATT in the previous section on de jure discriminatory non-fiscal regulation.

2.   Article XX GATT

It has already been noted that of the few cases in which a facially origin-neutral regulation has been claimed de facto to afford less favourable treatment to imported products, only once has the complaining party managed to successfully demonstrate to the Panel the existence of such hidden discrimination. It is thus easy to understand why in both GATT panel practice and WTO jurisprudence there has not really been any great need to invoke and apply the general exception provisions of Article XX GATT to justify measures in violation of the prohibition of de facto discrimination. However, there exists at least one instance where this provision has been applied in order to justify an origin-neutral measure with apparently de facto discriminatory effects vis-à-vis imported products; this is the case dealing with the French prohibition on public health grounds of asbestos and asbestos-containing products (the *Asbestos* dispute). This section will thus briefly examine the interpretation of the "necessity" requirement within the ambit of justifying a national regulation adopted in pursuance of public health objectives pursuant to Article XX(b).

(a) Justifying de facto discriminatory measures under Article XX(b): the Panel and Appellate Body Reports on Asbestos   In the *Asbestos* dispute, the Panel examined the applicability of Article XX GATT since it had previously found that the French regulations prohibiting the importation and sale of

---

[415] See below in ch 4, the discussion on "Art 30, second sentence, EC: substantive and procedural review?".

asbestos and asbestos-products were in violation of the National Treatment obligation of Article III:4. Following previous WTO jurisprudence, the Panel correctly divided its analysis under Article XX in two parts: first, "provisional justification" under subparagraph (b), and secondly, "further appraisal" under the chapeau of Article XX.

With regard to the first part, the Panel correctly noted that a party invoking Article XX(b) must prove (a) that the policy in respect of the measures for which Article XX is invoked falls within the range of policies designed to protect human life or health; and (b) the inconsistent measures for which the exception is invoked are necessary to fulfil the policy objective.[416] These two requirements clearly correspond respectively to the "suitability" and "necessity" prongs of the proportionality principle.

As regards the suitability requirement, the Panel noted that, inasmuch as they include the notion of "protection", the words "policies designed to protect human life or health" imply the existence of a *health risk*. Accordingly, in the case at hand, the Panel had to determine whether chrysotile asbestos, in its various forms relevant to the dispute, posed a risk to human life or health. The Panel noted that it did not have to examine the necessity of the policy goal, or, in other words, the choice made by France to protect its population against certain risks, or the level of protection of public health that France wishes to achieve. Its task was simply to determine if the French policy of prohibiting the use of chrysotile asbestos fell within the range of policies designed to protect human life or health.[417]

On the basis of the evidence before it, the Panel found that the EC had made a prima facie case for the existence of a health risk in connection with the use of chrysotile, in particular as regard to lung cancer and mesothelioma in the occupational sectors downstream of production and processing and for the public in general in relation to chrysotile cement products. Accordingly, the Panel concluded that the policy of prohibiting chrysotile asbestos implemented by the French Decree under review fell within the range of policies designed to protect human life or health within the meaning of Article XX(b) GATT.[418]

With regard to the question of whether the measure was "necessary" to protect human life or health, the Panel recalled the test set out in the GATT Panel Report on *Thai Cigarettes*, according to which a measure could be considered to be "necessary" in terms of Article XX(b) only if there are no alternative measures consistent with the General Agreement, or less inconsistent with it, which the Member Government

---

[416] Panel Report on *EC–Asbestos*, above n 236, para 8.169, citing Panel Report on *United States—Standards for Reformulated and Conventional Gasoline* (*Reformulated Gasoline*), WT/DS2/R, circulated 29 Jan 1996, adopted 20 May 1996, para 6.20.
[417] Panel Report on *EC–Asbestos*, above n 236, para 8.171.
[418] *Ibid.*, para 8.194.

could reasonably be expected to employ to achieve its health policy objectives.[419] Accordingly, in order to apply this "necessity" test, the Panel had to (a) establish *the scope* of the health policy objectives pursued by France, and (b) consider the existence of measures consistent, or less inconsistent, with the GATT 1994 which are *reasonably available* to the regulating Member.

Noting that France's objective was to halt the spread of the health risks connected with chrysotile, the Panel focused its inquiry on whether there indeed existed consistent or less inconsistent measures other than the ban, which were reasonably available in order to achieve the relevant public health objective. Despite Canada's arguments to the contrary, the Panel found that "controlled" or "safe use", consisting of precautionary measures to restrict the release of fibres and protect the airways and methods of decontaminating equipment and work clothing, was neither *sufficiently effective* in light of France's health policy objectives nor *reasonably available* in light of the economic and administrative realities facing the Member concerned. With regard to the former conclusion, the Panel also rejected Canada's reference to international standards (which appear to allow for "controlled use") since the levels of protection obtained by following such standards were lower than those established by France.[420] With regard to the latter conclusion, the Panel stressed the difficulty in imposing sophisticated occupational safety practices on the building sector and on Do-it-Yourself (DIY) enthusiasts or undeclared workers operating outside any proper framework or system of control.[421]

The Panel also concluded that the French measure at issue satisfied the conditions of the introductory clause of Article XX since the measure was not applied in a discriminatory manner (a finding of discrimination under Article III:4 is not relevant in terms of the introductory clause of Article XX) and it did not constitute a disguised restriction on international trade (employing the notion of "protective application" developed with regard to Article III:2, second sentence, the Panel concluded that from its design, architecture and revealing structure the French Decree did not have protectionist objectives).[422]

---

[419] *Ibid.*, para 8.199, citing the Panel Report on *Thai Cigarettes*, DS10/R, adopted on 7 Nov 1990, BISD 37S/200, para 75.

[420] Panel Report on *EC–Asbestos*, above n 236, paras 8.209–8.211.

[421] *Ibid.*, paras 8.212–8.214.

[422] *Ibid.*, paras 8.231–8.239. Note the Panel's following statement: "Admittedly, there is always the possibility that measures such as those contained in the Decree might have the effect of favouring the domestic substitute product manufacturers. This is a natural consequence of prohibiting a given product and in itself cannot justify the conclusion that the measure has a protectionist aim, as long as it remains within certain limits. In fact, the information made available to the Panel does not suggest that the import ban has benefited the French substitute fibre industry, to the detriment of third country producers, to such an extent as to lead to the conclusion that the Decree has been so applied as to constitute a disguised restriction on

The Appellate Body confirmed *in toto* the Panel findings on Article XX, although it limited itself to an analysis of the "provisional justification" under Article XX(b).

It is interesting to note that the Appellate Body could have avoided a review of the Panel's findings with regard to Article XX, since it had reversed the Panel's findings on Article III. In other words, there was no longer any need to justify a violation. There are however two possible explanations for the Appellate Body's examination of the Article XX(b) issue. First, the Appellate Body did not really find that chrysotile asbestos fibres and products containing them are not like substitute fibres and products containing them. The Appellate Body more simply established that the *evidence* supporting the Panel's finding of likeness was not sufficient. Accordingly, it might have been necessary in any case to examine the justification issue of the French measure under review. As a second possible explanation, it should be remembered that the Appellate Body had also reversed the Panel's finding with regard the applicability of the TBT Agreement, albeit without completing the analysis in that regard in light of the uncharted waters it would have found itself in. This finding might possibly have warranted a future revival of the dispute. However, having confirmed that the French measure is in any case justified under the general exception provision of Article XX(b), the Appellate Body implicitly discouraged Canada from pursuing a second *Asbestos* case under the TBT Agreement. As will be clarified in the chapter on the "reasonableness rule", it would appear in fact that the arguments dealt with under Article XX(b) would most likely pre-empt a TBT claim.

With regard to the Panel's finding on the "suitability" of the French measure to protect public health, the Appellate Body deferred to the Panel's discretion as the trier of facts in assessing the value of the evidence and the weight to be ascribed to that evidence. In the Appellate Body's view, the Panel's appreciation of the evidence was within the bounds of its discretion.

With regard to the Panel's finding on the "necessity" of the French measure, the Appellate Body emphasised the following points. First, contrary to Canada's claim, the Appellate Body found that there is no requirement under Article XX(b) to quantify the risk concerned. Drawing on its previous jurisprudence interpreting the Agreement on the Application of Sanitary and Phytosanitary Measures (SPS Agreement), the Appellate Body stated that "a risk may be evaluated either in quantitative or qualitative terms".[423]

---

international trade". *Ibid.* para 8.239. Cf G Verhoosel, *National Treatment and WTO Dispute Settlement: Adjudicating the Boundaries of Regulatory Autonomy* (Oxford, Hart Publishing, 2002) at 39.

[423] Appellate Body Report on *EC–Asbestos*, above n 275, para 167, citing Appellate Body Report on *EC–Hormones*, WT/DS48/AB/R, circulated 16 Jan 1998, adopted 13 Feb 1998, para 186.

Secondly, noting that WTO Members have the right to determine the level of protection of health that they consider appropriate in a given situation, the Appellate Body correctly emphasised the fundamental nature and scope of the test under Article XX(b): under such a test, a panel must simply determine whether the measure is reasonably related (ie suitable) to the goal of protecting health and whether there exist consistent or less inconsistent measures which are capable of achieving *the* level of protection set by the Member State. The Appellate Body's reference to its decision in *Korea–Beef* to the effect that in determining whether another alternative method is reasonably available, it is appropriate to consider (1) the extent to which the alternative measure "contributes to the realisation of the end pursued" as well as (2) the importance of the interests or values pursued, should be interpreted taking into account the restrictive nature of the proportionality test in Article XX. With regard to the first element, it should be emphasised that, in assessing the "necessity" of a national measure, the fundamental issue is indeed whether there exists an alternative measure which is (a) less restrictive of international trade and (b) capable of achieving the chosen level of protection. Accordingly, it will be necessary to appreciate the extent to which the alternative measure contributes to the realisation of the end pursued. With regard to the second element, it is understandable that, if the interest pursued is important, the inquiry will be somewhat less rigid and thus it would be easier to accept as "necessary" measures designed to achieve such interests.[424] In sum, as previously noted commenting the Appellate Body decision in *Korea–Beef*, reference to a "weighing and balancing process" should not be understood as permitting an inquiry over the "proportionality" *stricto sensu* of the public policy objective pursued by WTO Members.[425]

The Appellate Body also added that the fact that PCG fibres, which were allowed under certain conditions by French law, might pose a risk to health did not change the outcome of its conclusion since "the scientific evidence before the Panel indicated that the risk posed by the PCG fibres is, in any case, *less* than the risk posed by chrysotile asbestos fibres". In other words, the Appellate Body was not convinced that there was an *inconsistency* in the levels of protection with regard to apparently "similar" products.[426]

---

[424] D Osiro, "GATT/WTO Necessity Analysis: Evolutionary Interpretation and its Impact on the Autonomy of Domestic Regulation", 29 *Legal Issues of Economic Integration* (2002) 123 at 130.
[425] Cf J Trachtman, "Decisions of the Appellate Body of the WTO: *EC–Asbestos*", available at <www.ejil.com>.
[426] Appellate Body Report on *EC–Asbestos*, above n 275, para 168. It should be remembered that the basis on which the Appellate Body found that the two products were *not* similar under Art III:4 was the different level of risk which characterised asbestos and substitute products..

3.3   CONCLUSIONS

Following the ECJ decision in *Keck & Mithouard*,[427] it may be said that the National Treatment obligation is employed in both EC and WTO law in order to prohibit de facto discriminatory measures of both fiscal and non-fiscal nature restricting trade in goods. While Article III:2 GATT and Article 90 EC have since the beginning been interpreted in a similar manner to prohibit formally origin-neutral fiscal charges with discriminatory effects vis-à-vis imported products, until the decision in *Keck* Article 28 EC did not expressly include a prohibition of de facto discriminatory measures of a non-fiscal nature (Article III:4 GATT, on the contrary, did include such prohibition). As explained above, when confronted with the momentous question of whether Article 28 EC was indeed a provision which sought to liberalise trade between Member States, or more broadly to liberalise the pursuit of economic activities within a Member State even where there was no link with either "trade" or "market integration", the Court of Justice in *Keck* chose the former and subjected "certain selling arrangements" to the less intrusive test of non-discrimination. Despite their different scope of application, Article III:4 GATT and Article 28 EC thus embody inter alia a prohibition on de facto discrimination.

As noted in the introduction to this section, in the case of de facto discrimination the national measure does not in its terms differentiate between products on the basis of origin or nationality. This is why it is necessary to go behind the formal text of the origin-neutral measure under review and determine whether or not *in practice* that measure has the same protectionist effect as a measure formally discriminating on the basis of origin or nationality.

In order to accomplish this task, next to a comparison of the actual treatment afforded to *identical* imported and domestic products, it may also be appropriate to examine how *similar* imported and domestic products are treated. The relevance of taking into account the treatment afforded to "similar" products stems from the *competitive* relationship between "similar" products. By providing special treatment (ie in the form of a lower tax burden) to red apples, for example, the competitive opportunities of green apples might be negatively affected since consumers will tend to prefer the cheaper product. It is self-evident that the relationship between red and green apples exists only in as far as the two products are indeed "competitive", or, in other words, "substitutable" with regard to their end uses. Thus, for the purpose of determining whether a fiscal or non-fiscal measure discriminates *in fact* between imported and domestic products, it makes sense to compare the treatment afforded to "competitive" or "substitutable" products.

---

[427] Joined Cases C–267 and 268/91, *Keck & Mithouard* [1993] ECR 6097.

Recent WTO jurisprudence clearly confirms this interpretation. In the *Asbestos* dispute, the Appellate Body emphasised that the term "like products" in Article III:4 GATT is concerned with competitive relationships between and among products, and that it is thus important under Article III:4 to take account of evidence which indicates whether, and to what extent, the products involved are—or could be—in a competitive relationship in the marketplace.[428] The so-called *Border Tax Adjustment* criteria (ie the criteria enunciated in the Report of the Working Party on Border Tax Adjustment: (i) physical properties, (ii) end-uses, (iii) consumer's perception and preference, and (iv) tariff classification) are simply tools to assist in the task of sorting and examining the evidence capable of establishing the competitive relationship between the products at issue, and they should not dissolve the duty or the need to examine, in each case, *all* of the pertinent evidence.[429] Accordingly, while the Appellate Body did not want to constrain excessively the evidence relevant in determining whether two products are like for purposes of Article III:4, it did clarify that the likeness determination under Article III:4 was directed at establishing the competitive relationship of the products at issue.

From the Appellate Body decision in the *Asbestos* dispute, two interrelated points should be once more emphasised. First of all, the Appellate Body seems to suggest that for a finding of likeness not only do *all* of the relevant criteria have to be taken into account, but these criteria need to point overall to "likeness".[430] In other words, in line with the relevant burden of proof, the Appellate Body appears to make more difficult the case for "likeness" than that for "unlikeness". For example, taking the case of two products sharing several or even all physical characteristics (ie being "like" with regard to the physical properties criterion), if for some reason consumers perceive those same two products as two very different products (ie they are "unlike" with regard to consumers' tastes and habits), the Appellate Body's report in *Asbestos* seems to stand for the conclusion that the two products would probably fail the "likeness" requirement of Article III:4. I have suggested, moreover, that this reading may indirectly open the door, albeit in exceptional circumstances, for a finding that two physically identical products may nevertheless be found to be unlike for purposes of Article III:4 in light of consumers' perceptions with regard to strictly non-product related features (such as the characteristics of the producer or of the production methods). According to this view, this would be the only way for process-based distinctions *à la Shrimp/Turtle* or *Tuna/Dolphin* to be relevant for purposes of determining "likeness".

---

[428] Appellate Body Report on *EC–Asbestos*, above n 275, para 102.
[429] *Ibid.*, para 102.
[430] The Appellate Body emphasises that, if *any* of the relevant criteria suggests that the products are not like, the burden of proving likeness thus becomes quite heavy.

Secondly, while the recognition of the relevance of consumer preference for the purpose of the likeness determination does indeed in a way "[bring] into the picture the kinds of regulatory interests, which had under the GATT been taken into account through the *aims-and-effects* doctrine,"[431] the Appellate Body Report on *Asbestos* should not be taken as resurrecting such a doctrine, at least for the purpose of determining product likeness. Consumers may distinguish between physically similar products on the basis of a variety of factors, which may or may not be related to pure product characteristics, thus differentiating between whether shrimps are caught with turtle-friendly or unfriendly nets, whether car engines produce environment-unfriendly gases or not, or whether roof tiles are carcinogenic or not. The macroscopic difference between the *Asbestos* report and the *aims-and-effects* doctrine is that, while the latter focused on the often nationally-bias perspective of the regulator (ie whether the measure was aimed and had the effect of protecting domestic products), the former clearly adopts the more origin-neutral, market-based perspective of the consumer (ie whether the two products are competitive or substitutable in the eyes of consumers). Accordingly, following its earlier jurisprudence with regard to origin-neutral fiscal charges and Article III:2, the Appellate Body Report on *Asbestos* has, though only implicitly, rejected the *aims-and-effects* test as a tool to be employed for purposes of determining the likeness issue.

Always with regard to the issue of the types of products to be compared for the purpose of determining material discrimination, it should also be emphasised that the distinction between "similar" or "like" products and "competitive" or "substitutable" products—as the relevant relationship between the products—does not really change the type of analysis performed by both EC and WTO adjudicating bodies. As the interpretation of the non-discrimination obligations in Article 90 EC and Article III:2 GATT demonstrates, whether two products are similar or competitive is simply a matter of degree, with the former perhaps focusing more on physical properties and the latter on end uses and consumer's preference.

It should also be noted that, while Article III:2 and 4 GATT and Article 90 EC expressly refer to the relationship between the products as one of the normative elements of the non-discrimination rule, the *Keck* reading of Article 28 does not say anything about the type of relationship that must be established for a finding of de facto discrimination. This should not however mean that the non-discrimination requirement in *Keck* differs in this respect from those in Article III:2 and 4 GATT and Article 90 EC. Although it is undisputed that the focus of a discrimination analysis

---

[431] R Howse and E Tuerk, "The WTO Impact in Internal Regulations—A Case Study of the *Canada—EC Asbestos* Dispute" in G de Búrca and J Scott (eds), *The EU and the WTO: Legal and Constitutional Aspects* (Oxford, Hart Publishing, 2001) at 301.

under *Keck* has so far been on whether the selling arrangement at issue is inherently protectionist with regard to domestic products, it appears that all of the decisions so far rendered by the Court of Justice on selling arrangements are at least implicitly based on a finding of likeness between the products involved. However, it may be suggested that the lack of an express reference to the relationship between the products in the *Keck* non-discrimination doctrine stands as an indication that the principal normative element of the prohibition of de facto discrimination centres around the notion of the discriminatory or protectionist *effect* of the fiscal or non-fiscal measure, rather than on the concept of products' likeness.

This is possibly the greatest difference between the application of the non-discrimination principle in EC and WTO law respectively. While a finding of de facto discrimination under both Article 28 and Article 90 EC is based principally on whether the national measure protects domestic products as a whole, in WTO law and in particular under Article III GATT the same finding has so far focused mainly on whether the products involved are like or competitive. As noted in the introduction to this chapter, an origin-neutral measure will be deemed to discriminate de facto on the basis of the product's origin depending on (a) the relationship of the products at issue (whether identical, similar or competitive) *and* (b) the effect of the measure itself on domestic and imported products (whether discriminatory or protectionist). Thus both elements are necessary components for a finding of de facto discrimination. Nevertheless, the emphasis should be on whether the effects of the measure are "protectionist", rather than on the issue of the likeness of the products.[432] In this respect, a comparison between the non-discrimination rules in EC and WTO law produces valuable insights.

Among the four non-discrimination rules that have been examined in this chapter (Article III:2 and 4 GATT and Articles 90 and 28 EC), perhaps the rule that has reached the highest level of maturity is that contained in Article 90 EC, which requires that internal taxation does not afford protection to domestic products. In the relevant section, I have argued that, notwithstanding Article 90's apparently clear language[433] and the often

---

[432] For an example of a National Treatment provision in WTO law which does not make express reference to 'likeness' see Art 3 TRIPS. Cf Appellate Body Report on *United States—Section 211 Omnibus Appropriations Act of 1998 (Havana Club)*, WT/DS176/AB/R, circulated 2 Jan 2002, adopted 1 Feb 2002.

[433] Depending on the nature of the relationship between the imported and domestic products at issue, the wording of Art 90 provides for two different legal standards to be met by national fiscal measures in order to conform with the non-discrimination provisions of that Art. If the imported and domestic products are "similar products", the first para of Art 90 prohibits any tax applied to the imported products that is *"in excess of"* those applied to the similar domestic products. On the other hand, if the imported and domestic products are "competitive products", the second para of Art 90 prohibits a fiscal measure imposed by a Member if it is of such a nature *"as to afford protection to"* the domestic products. Thus in light

contrary view of legal commentators,[434] an examination of the case-law shows that the essential factor in determining a breach of either of the obligations enunciated in Article 90 is whether the internal taxation in question has the effect of protecting *domestic* products.[435] In other words, in order to establish a prima facie case of violation of both the *first* and *second* paragraph of Article 90, the complainant needs to demonstrate the discriminatory or protective nature of the measure under review (ie that the internal fiscal measure, though formally origin-neutral, has the *effect* of disfavouring in particular products from other Member States (discriminatory nature) or favouring in particular national production (protective nature)). In this context, the discrimination/protection dichotomy should simply be taken as emphasising a mere difference in perspective, although the two "perspectives" are very much related to one another. Accordingly, the only difference between the obligations in the first and second paragraphs of Article 90 rests on the level or magnitude of the measure's protectionist effect; while in the first instance the Court does not allow for even the smallest protectionist effect, in the second instance there exists a *de minimis* level under which the measure is not deemed to afford protection to domestic products.

It was emphasised moreover that reliance on the discriminatory or protectionist effect of the measure under review is merely the application of the uncontroversial purpose of Article 90, which is not to equalise internal taxation depending on the similarity of the products (all liqueur wines, ethyl alcohol or cars should be taxed equally), but to eliminate all forms of discrimination or protection, whether formal or material, *based on the origin of the product*.

---

of the two different terms employed in Art 90, the Court has stated that while the criterion indicated in the first para "consists in the comparison of tax burdens, [...] the second paragraph is based upon a more general criterion, in other words the protective nature of the system of internal taxation." Case 168/78, *Commission v France* (*Tax Arrangements Applicable to Spirits*) [1980] ECR 347, para 7.

[434] Cf L Daniele, *Il diritto materiale della Comunità Europea* (Milano, Giuffré, 2000) at 42–43; P Craig and G de Búrca, *EU Law* (Oxford, OUP, 1998) at 566; PJ Kuyper, "Booze and Fast Cars: Tax Discrimination under GATT and EC", *Legal Issues of European Integration* (1996) at 139–40; G Bermann, R Goebel, W Davey, E Fox, *Cases and Materials on European Community Law* (St. Paul, West Publishing, 1993) at 325; D Wyatt and A Dashwood, *The Substantive Law of the EEC* (London, Sweet and Maxwell, 1980) at 90. For a more "illuminated" view see A Easson, "Fiscal Discrimination: New Perspectives on Art 95 of the EEC Treaty", 18 *CMLRev* (1981) 521 at 540. Also for a more cautious approach see G Tesauro, *Diritto Comunitario* (Padova, Cedam, 1995) at 264; S Weatherill and P Beaumont, *EC Law* (London, Penguin Books, 1995) at 408–09.

[435] What Easson terms the "national dimension", A Easson, "Fiscal Discrimination: New Perspectives on Art 95 of the EEC Treaty", 18 *CMLRev* (1981) 521 at 540. Cf M Danusso and R Denton, "Does the European Court of Justice Look for a Protectionist Motive Under Art 95?", *LIEI* (1990) 67.

Moving to WTO rules with regard to the prohibition of de facto discrimination on grounds of nationality in the field of taxation, it has been suggested that the current approach developed by WTO panels and the Appellate Body with regard to Article III:2 GATT needs to be taken two steps further. Thus, the **first proposition** would be that the "protective application" of a fiscal measure as required by the principles set forth in Article III:1 is, and should be, deemed to exist only in so far as the measure predominantly favours domestic products as a whole. In practical terms, the higher tax must be imposed in the majority of cases on imported products. Clearly, in this regard, evidence that a specific national measure *disfavours predominantly imported* products may be submitted in order to prove the so called "protective application" requirement (ie the higher tax is imposed in the majority of cases on imported products). The **second proposition** would be that the difference in the role of the "principles" set forth in Article III:1 resides simply in the different structure of the burden of proof for the purpose of establishing a violation of the first and second sentences of Article III:2. In other words, the burden of proving or denying the existence of protectionist *effects* related to origin—the so-called "protective application" of the measure—is on the *complaining* Member when the products at issue are "directly competitive or substitutable" and rests on the *defendant* in the case the products are "like", respectively.

It is however interesting to note that, while both EC and, at least partially, WTO jurisprudence applying the prohibition of de facto discrimination in the realm of internal taxation focuses on the protectionist *effect* of the measure under review (in line with the concept of de facto discrimination), the Appellate Body's emphasis on the objective features of the measure under review, its design, architecture and structure, shows a greater willingness to radicate a finding of de facto discrimination (on the basis of the product's nationality) on the *objective features* of the measure itself. As noted above, this approach appears to be aimed at limiting as much as possible the risks connected with a purely effect-based analysis. In other words, WTO jurisprudence shows that, while the principal aim of the "protective application" calculation appears to be the determination of the protectionist *effect* of the measure under challenge, this calculation must principally be focused on the protectionist (and discriminatory) *features* of that same measure.

It follows that the "appropriate proportion" between *favoured* domestic products and *disfavoured* imported products will have to be determined on a case-by-case basis giving full consideration to all the relevant facts and all the relevant circumstances, focusing in particular on the design, architecture and structure of the measure in question. Accordingly, the "magnitude" of the dissimilar taxation between imported and domestic competitive products should play a relevant role, albeit complementary to a finding of protectionist effect. The greater the difference in the tax burden, the less the difference in the proportion between favoured domestic products and disfavoured imported products will need to be in order to establish that the fiscal measure has a protective application.

When one moves away from the field of internal taxation and into that of non-fiscal regulation, recent EC and WTO jurisprudence applying the prohibition of de facto discrimination as provided for in Article 28 EC and Article III:4 GATT respectively clearly indicates the centrality of the protectionist effect of the measure. This is evident in EC law from the analysis of the few post-*Keck* decisions dealing with apparently origin-neutral selling arrangements and in WTO law from the Appellate Body's *obiter dicta* in the recent *Asbestos* dispute.

In light of their relative novelty, it is difficult to forecast the type of non-discrimination standard that will eventually emerge from the two rules dealing with apparently origin-neutral non-fiscal regulations.

In the above analysis of the *Asbestos* dispute, it was noted that while the Appellate Body's rejection of the so called "diagonal approach" to the "less favourable treatment" requirement of Article III:4[436] cannot be denied, that decision does not illustrate all the relevant contours of the correct approach. I put forward at least two quite different ways in which the Appellate Body's new reading of the "less favourable treatment" requirement may be actually applied. According to one perspective, a measure may be found in violation of the National Treatment obligation of Article III:4 if it is established that at the time of the dispute the measure negatively affects imports more than domestic products considered as a whole. In other words, while it will still be necessary to show an *overall imbalance* of the measure's impact between the group of like domestic products (the majority of which fall within the more favoured sub-group of like products) and the group of like imported products (the majority of which falls within the more disfavoured sub-group of like products), it will be sufficient to prove, under a *pure discriminatory effect test*, that such imbalance has occurred in the past, is currently present or may happen in the future, without determining the causes of such imbalance.

Under the other approach, I suggested that a violation of Article III:4 may be found only if it is established that the measure under review

---

[436] L Ehring, "De facto Discrimination in WTO Law: National Treatment and Most-Favoured-Nation Treatment—or Equal Treatment?", *Jean Monnet Working Paper* (NYU School of Law, 2002) at 3, "Under the diagonal approach, one compares the treatment accorded to the disfavoured foreign goods with that enjoyed by the favoured domestic goods, e.g. domestic low-alcohol beer receives more favourable treatment than imported strong beer. This means that it is always possible to find a violation of Art III:4, as long as the disfavoured type is (potentially) imported and the favoured type exists domestically. Even when imported products overwhelmingly receive the better treatment and most domestic goods fall in the less advantageous category, there is still a violation."

inherently discriminates against imported products as a whole. According to this approach, which borrows partially from the rationale of the *aims-and-effects* doctrine, the existence of an overall imbalance between domestic and imported like products would not be enough for a finding of violation of the National Treatment obligation unless it were supported also by a finding that, under an *inherent discriminatory nature test*, the structural characteristics of the measure itself constitute the principal and direct cause for that imbalance.[437]

It is suggested that the correct approach to be followed in determining whether a given measure affords no less favourable treatment sits half-way between the two above-mentioned perspectives. While a finding that the origin-neutral measure under review is inherently discriminatory in nature should clearly be enough for a violation of the National Treatment principle, a mere showing of an overall imbalance between imported and domestic like products at any given time should not. As a preliminary matter, the interpreter should focus principally on the *object and purpose* of Article III:4, as specifically enunciated in Article III:1. As previously noted, the first paragraph of Article III states in relevant part that "internal regulations [...] should not be applied to imported or domestic *products* so as to afford *protection* to domestic production". Accordingly, the ultimate aim of determining whether an origin-neutral internal measure affords less favourable treatment to imported products, should be to pinpoint measures that afford *protection* to domestic products. It follows that an origin-neutral measure differentiating between two like products will be deemed to violate Article III:4 if it is found to favour *predominantly* domestic products considered as a whole. Moreover, in order to determine whether the measure favours predominantly domestic products, a Panel should, in line with current WTO jurisprudence, focus on all the relevant evidence pertaining to the case at hand under a case-by-case approach.[438] In this regard, previous GATT panel practice employing the *aims-and-effects* doctrine may represent a useful, albeit only indicative, reference in examining some of these elements. While I would not like to see the resuscitation of the *aims-and-effects* doctrine as it was originally employed (ie for purposes of determining likeness), it is here submitted that several of its tenets may indeed become useful in the context of determining the measure's discriminatory or protectionist nature.

---

[437] This appears to be the view proposed by the supported of the *aims-and-effects* doctrine, who tend to limit as much as possible any intrusion into national legitimate regulatory prerogatives. Cf R Howse and E Tuerk, "The WTO Impact in Internal Regulations—A Case Study of the *Canada–EC Asbestos* Dispute" in G de Búrca and J Scott (eds), *The EU and the WTO: Legal and Constitutional Aspects* (Oxford, Hart Publishing, 2001) at 297, fn 55.

[438] For a list of possible factors to be included in the analysis see above the section discussing the *Asbestos* dispute.

It is interesting to contrast this proposed approach to the prohibition of de facto discrimination in WTO law with the manner in which the Court of Justice has applied the non-discrimination test in its *Keck* jurisprudence. In the examination of the relevant EC case-law, it was noted that, although the Court of Justice appears to require a high threshold of discrimination focusing on the inherently protectionist nature of the incriminated measure, in practice the Court is willing to conclude that the measure is indeed discriminatory in effect on the basis of very general assumptions unsubstantiated by any statistical data relating to the relevant markets and the relevant imported and domestic products. If the Court were to continue the approach recently followed in *Heimdienst* and *Gourmet*, a case like *Oosthoek*, where, in pre-*Keck* times, the Court held that legislation prohibiting the offer of free gifts to buyers of encyclopaedias (ie a selling arrangement) were caught by Article 28 since it might have forced a producer to adopt sales-promotion or advertising schemes which differed as between States, might still today, in post-*Keck* times, fall within the scope of application of, and thus provisionally prohibited by, Article 28 on the basis of those same grounds. Although the Court's reluctance to get its hands dirty with empirical evidence may be comprehensible on grounds of both pure judicial self-restraint and legal certainty, *Keck*'s express reference to the concept of de facto discrimination would for all practical purposes be subverted if the Court were to continue this trend of simply making use of very general assumptions with regard to the adverse effects of internal marketing regulations on the competitive relationship between domestic and imported products. For all practical purposes, this interpretation would represent a hidden re-introduction of the pre-*Keck* reasonableness rule enunciated in *Dassonville–Cassis de Dijon*. As correctly noted by Professor Eeckhout "the broader the approach to non-discrimination under *Keck*, the less difference there will be between the approach to selling arrangements and classic *Cassis de Dijon* cases."[439]

* * *

As in the case of de jure discriminatory measures, once an origin-neutral measure has been found, albeit only covertly, to afford protection to domestic products, the regulating State may still avoid a final finding of violation by arguing that this de facto discriminatory treatment is justified on public policy grounds. In other words, the relationship between the non-discrimination obligation and the public policy justification is one

[439] P Eeckhout, "After *Keck and Mithouard*: Free Movement of Goods in the EC, Market Access, and Non-Discrimination" T Cottier and P Mavroidis (eds), *Regulatory Barriers and the Principle of Non-Discrimination in World Trade Law* (Ann Arbor, the University of Michigan Press, 2000) at 203.

of "rule" to "exception". In practical terms, however, in both EC and WTO law the dividing line between establishing a prima facie case of discrimination (the "rule") and providing for a public policy justification (the "exception") is not altogether clear in particular in the case of de facto discrimination. Both the jurisprudence and academic writings on the issue do not appear conclusive on whether the legitimate public policy purposes underlying an internal measure should be taken into account in determining the existence of discrimination contrary to Article III:2 and 4 GATT or Articles 28 and 90 EC, or whether those same public policy purposes should function exclusively as justification grounds once the measure has been found to violate the above mentioned non-discrimination provisions.

It is suggested that two different sets of reasons explain this uncertainty: one is *physiological* to the prohibition of de facto discrimination and the other is *contingent* on the specific National Treatment provisions adopted in EC and WTO law.

Let us start with the former set. The dividing line between establishing a prima facie case of de facto discrimination and providing for a public policy justification is not altogether clear because both determinations necessitate taking into consideration and evaluating practically the same features of the national measure under review. This explanation has to do with the concept of de facto discrimination and demonstrates that, with regard to a finding of both discrimination and public policy justification, there is an important difference between the case of de jure and de facto discrimination. If a de jure discriminatory tax or regulation by definition *intentionally* employs the origin of a product as the differentiating criterion, a de facto discriminatory tax or regulation, as demonstrated in the preceding section, merely employs an origin-neutral criterion that nonetheless happens to have an discriminatory *effect* on grounds of nationality or origin. In other words, while in the case of de jure discriminatory measures, discrimination is in the law and is thus easy to detect (and punish), within the realm of de facto discriminatory measures, discrimination is not in the law and thus must be determined on the basis of an analysis of the features and effects of the measure. Accordingly, if in the former case once discrimination has been established, the taxing or regulating Member needs to provide a reason for employing exactly the prohibited criterion (ie the nationality or origin of the product), in the latter case, the public policy justification focuses on providing a motive for treating two different products alike or differentiating the treatment of two like products on the basis of a facially origin-neutral criterion (such as the nature of ethyl alcohol—synthetic v natural—or the power rate of cars—above or below 16CV). In the case of origin-neutral taxation or non-fiscal regulation, assessing whether the measure has a de facto protectionist effect benefiting domestic products vis-à-vis imported ones may involve some of the same issues that are at the basis of determining whether the same measure may be justified on public policy grounds.

Empirical confirmation of the difficulty of drawing a clear dividing line between a determination of material discrimination and one of a public policy justification may be seen in the jurisprudential application of the prohibition of de facto discrimination in EC and WTO law with regard to both fiscal and non-fiscal measures. For example, it should be enough to recollect, first, the judge-made public policy exception to the non-discrimination rule of Article 90 EC that the Court of Justice read into the discrimination determination, and secondly, the failed attempt by certain GATT panels to introduce an *aims-and-effects* test for purposes of determining whether Members' measures violated the National Treatment obligation of Article III GATT.

This "physiological" ambiguity is worsened by what may be called the "contingent" ambiguity. This second reason for blurring the boundaries between the rule and the exception is that neither EC nor WTO law imposing the prohibition of de facto discrimination provides for an express and non-exhaustive public policy justification option. As mentioned several times in this chapter, where the GATT only provides for a *limited* set of public policy exceptions to the National Treatment obligations of Article III, in the EC Treaty derogations to the non-discrimination rules are either *absent* (ie with regard to Article 90) or *exhaustive* in nature (cf Article 30).

Thus, in EC law, both the non-discrimination rule in Article 90 relating to internal taxation as well as that enunciated by the ECJ in *Keck* with regard to selling arrangements have been judicially integrated with a *non-exhaustive* list of public policy justifications. As demonstrated in the analysis of the case-law, this list finds a limitation only with regard to purely fiscal policy objectives and aims of a purely economic nature that in the Court of Justice's view are not enough to justify respectively a tax system or a selling arrangement that, though origin-neutral on its face, is found to discriminate in practice on the basis of the origin or nationality of the product (*Humblot, Bananas*, and *Heimdienst*).

With regard to WTO law, on the other hand, commentators have voiced the potentially serious weakness of the rule-and-exception analysis (non-discrimination/public policy justification) noting that Article XX lists only ten policy goals capable of justifying national measures deviating from GATT obligations, thus leaving outside the coverage of the exception a host of other important or legitimate policy goals.[440] The prospect of these

---

[440] F Roessler, "Diverging Domestic Policies and Multilateral Trade Integration" in J Bhagwati and R E Hudec (eds), *Fair Trade and Harmonization: Prerequisites for Free Trade? Vol 2: Legal Analysis*, (Cambridge, MA, MIT Press, 1996) at 30; A Mattoo and A Subramanian, "Regulatory Autonomy and Multilateral Disciplines: The Dilemma and a Possible Resolution", 1 *JIEL* (1998) 303 at 313–14; R Howse and D Regan, "The Product/Process Distinction: An Illusory Basis for Disciplining 'Unilateralism' in Trade Policy", 11 *European Journal of International Law* (2000) 249 at 253.

objectives being broadened through political negotiation appearing not very likely, there have thus been several attempts within both GATT panel practice and academic writings to permeate the content of the non-discrimination "rule" with the features of the public policy "exception" in a way similar to what the Court of Justice *had to* do with regard to the non-discrimination rule of Article 90 EC. Among these attempts, I have examined in particular the *aims-and-effects* doctrine as well as the proposition to integrate the non-discrimination determination of Article III with an "economic efficiency" criterion or the "necessity" test.

Despite the above mentioned "physiological" and "contingent" uncertainties, I believe that even in WTO law the National Treatment principle should be interpreted as including the non-discrimination *rule* and the public policy *exception*. These two determinations can and should be distinct. While a finding of de facto discrimination should be based on an inquiry of the discriminatory or protectionist features of a measure, a finding of justification on public policy grounds should be based on an assessment of whether the apparently origin-neutral measure constitutes a reasonable and proportionate instrument to achieve a legitimate public policy objective. Accordingly, although both determinations make use of an examination of the objective features of the measure at issue, their function clearly differs. If the objective of a de facto discrimination assessment is to determine whether the effect of the regulatory treatment of products is *in fact* discriminatory or protectionist, the objective of an analysis of a public policy justification is to establish whether that same regulatory treatment of products is a "reasonable" attempt to achieve a legitimate public policy aim. At least within the realm of non-fiscal measures, in order to perform the "reasonableness" assessment both the Court of Justice and WTO adjudicating bodies have had recourse to the proportionality principle, and in particular its "suitability" and "least-trade restrictive" prongs.

However, a necessary precondition for keeping the "rule" and the "exception" separate is that the list of public policy justifications be somehow expanded. If in EC law judicial interpretation has succeeded in providing for and expanding the list of public policy justifications, WTO adjudicating bodies might find it much more difficult, even if not impossible, to follow the lead of the ECJ. As was suggested in the section on the justification options for de jure discriminatory non-fiscal measures, this situation may possibly be improved by an extensive interpretation of the exception provided in Article XX(d). Recent jurisprudence seems to indicate that a broader interpretation of the "objective connection" requirement (ie the connection between the inconsistent measure and the "laws and regulations" not inconsistent with the provisions of GATT, whose compliance the inconsistent measure has to secure) would arguably allow for Article XX(d) to function as the basis for including other legitimate policy objectives within the otherwise exhaustive list of Article XX.[441] Any risk of Members abusing this exception would be prevented by the rigorous requirements that the inconsistent measure be "necessary" to secure compliance (Article XX(d) "functional connection" requirement) and that it comply with the provisions of the introductory clauses of Article XX.

This more enlightened approach seems to have been endorsed by the Panel and the Appellate Body in their reports on *Korea—Measures Affecting Imports of Fresh, Chilled and Frozen Beef.*[442] While the Panel adopted a looser reading of the term "to secure compliance" under Article XX(d), the Appellate Body interpreted the term "necessary" for purposes of that same provision in quite a strict manner.

On a more practical level, however, there is no doubt that a provisional finding of discrimination does indeed influence the finding of justification. In the section examining the prohibition of de jure discrimination, it was found that in both EC and WTO law an origin-based fiscal or non-fiscal measure is very rarely justified on public policy grounds. With regard to the prohibition of de facto discrimination, the situation is, however, not so uniform. In EC law, in the taxation field, where the tax system differentiates between products on the basis of legitimate public policy purposes, the Court is willing to take account of these purposes (albeit within its discrimination assessment) only if the differentiating criterion is not *inherently discriminatory* against imported products (*Italian Ethyl Alcohol*, *Marsala*). In other words, an origin-neutral tax taken for a legitimate policy purpose (other than of a pure fiscal nature) with indirect discriminatory effects will most likely be deemed not to violate the prohibition of de facto discrimination if those discriminatory effects are not based on an inherently discriminatory criterion. With regard to selling arrangements, though the case-law is still developing, there appears to be, on the other hand, a certain reluctance on the part of the Court of Justice to justify a national measure on public policy grounds once it has found, on the basis of very general assumptions unsubstantiated by any statistical data relating to the relevant markets and the relevant imported and domestic products, that that same measure is indeed discriminatory in effect (*Heimdienst*, *Gourmet*).

When one moves to WTO law, the data is even more contradictory. As evidenced in the analysis of recent WTO jurisprudence with regard to the non-discrimination obligation in the field of internal taxation, Article XX has never really even been raised (let alone applied) in order to justify an

---

[441] G Verhoosel, *National Treatment and WTO Dispute Settlement* (Oxford, Hart Publishing, 2002) at 34, citing Appellate Body Report on *Reformulated Gasoline*, WT/DS2/AB/R, circulated 29 April 1996, adopted 20 May 1996, para 21.

[442] Appellate Body Report on *Korea—Measures Affecting Imports of Fresh, Chilled and Frozen Beef* (*Korea–Beef*), WT/DS161/AB/R and WT/DS169/AB/R, circulated 11 Dec 2000, adopted 10 Jan 2001.

origin-neutral tax that was found to violate the National Treatment obligation of Article III:2. While it is true that the non-existent role played by a fiscal measure's policy purposes in an Articles III:2/XX analysis may be due to the type of public policy justifications included in Article XX (which do not easily adapt to Member's fiscal policy objectives), there is however a sense that WTO adjudicating bodies are not afraid to strike down origin-neutral tax systems simply on the basis of their protectionist effects. This attitude appears to contrast with that shown in both GATT panel practice and WTO jurisprudence with regard to the prohibition of de facto discrimination in the realm of non-fiscal internal regulations. In the very few cases where a Member's origin-neutral measure has indeed been found to violate the National Treatment obligation of Article III:4, reference to the measure's public policy purposes has almost always reversed the provisional finding of de facto discrimination.

4

Judicial Integration—Third Layer: The Reasonableness Rule

U NDER THE HEADING "judicial integration—third layer" I will analyse the requirement that trade-restrictive national measures be "reasonable" or "proportionate" in the context of both EC and WTO law. This involves, in particular, comparing the legal approach stemming from the *Dassonville–Cassis de Dijon* jurisprudence of the European Court of Justice dealing with "indistinctly applicable measures" with that embodied in the two WTO sectoral agreements on Technical Barriers to Trade (TBT) and Sanitary and Phytosanitary Measures (SPS).

As will be examined in the following sections, neither approach provides for the abolition or reduction of a specific set of measures or the imposition of the non-discrimination principle. Rather each requires that Members exercise their regulatory prerogatives according to very general, albeit more intrusive, normative standards. Given their very general nature, these standards will inevitably have to be interpreted and applied by judiciary bodies on a case-by-case basis. Thus, they still fall within the category of instruments of "judicial integration" (as do the obligations stemming from the National Treatment principle). However, in light of their higher level of intrusiveness in the regulatory prerogatives of Members, these standards sit on the *deeper* end of the integration continuum and should thus be referred to as "third layer" instruments of judicial integration.

One preliminary note may be necessary at this point in order to facilitate the understanding of this chapter. As will be demonstrated in the ensuing analysis, the normative standards that are imposed under the "reasonableness rule" in both EC and WTO law are mainly represented by the several tenets of the "proportionality principle". As noted throughout the previous chapters, the principle of proportionality is also employed outside the "reasonableness rule", most notably as a tool to limit the availability of the public policy exceptions provided for in Article 30 EC and Article XX GATT to justify, for example, a violation of the ban on quantitative restrictions or of the National Treatment obligation.

There is, however, a distinct doctrinal difference between "proportionality" employed, on the one hand, within the ambit of a "public policy exception" and, on the other, within the "reasonableness rule". While in the former instance, the proportionality of a measure is assessed in order to justify an otherwise prohibited measure (because it constitutes a border measure or it discriminates against imported products), in the latter instance, the proportionality of a measure operates as the principal normative standard, ie the "primary norm". Notwithstanding the fact that both forms of proportionality review involve technically the same type of analysis (is the measure reasonably related to its objective?), this difference may influence not only several features of the actual review (ie burden of proof, list of public policy aims) but mostly the manner in which the proportionality review is actually carried out as well as its outcomes. In short, the *context* of a proportionality review constitutes a key element that must be taken into account. Consequently, while it is possible and useful to keep in mind the different applications of the principle of proportionality, it is equally very much important to examine these applications separately.

In order to emphasise the distinction between "proportionality" as the "exception" and "proportionality" as the "rule", I have preferred (a) to examine them in separate chapters and (b) to refer to the two legal approaches stemming, on the one hand, from the *Dassonville–Cassis de Dijon* jurisprudence of the ECJ and, on the other, from the TBT and SPS Agreements, as two examples of the "reasonableness rule".

4.1   ARTICLE 28 EC AND THE DASSONVILLE–CASSIS DE DIJON JURISPRUDENCE: "RULE OF REASON", "MANDATORY REQUIREMENTS" AND THE "PROPORTIONALITY PRINCIPLE"

The jurisprudential evolution of Article 28 EC is certainly remarkable. As evidenced in previous chapters, the European Court of Justice has employed the prohibition of "quantitative restrictions and measures having equivalent effect" in Article 28 in order to ban, first of all, non-pecuniary *border* measures (step 1), then all *distinctly applicable* measures (step 2), then any *unreasonable* measure affecting intra-Community trade (step 3), and most recently, "selling arrangements" formally or materially discriminating vis-à-vis imported products (step 4).

Steps 1, 2 and 4 have already been addressed in the chapter dealing with, respectively, the elimination or reduction of quantitative restrictions and equivalent measures, the prohibition of de jure discrimination and the prohibition of de facto discrimination. It is now the occasion to analyse step 3, which has constituted a fundamental element in the process of European integration. At the centre of this third step are two judgments rendered by the Court of Justice during the 1970s: *Dassonville*[1] and *Cassis de Dijon*.[2]

A. Dassonville and Cassis De Dijon: The Revolutionary Approach

In *Dassonville* the Court was faced with a Belgian rule requiring that spirits imported and sold as Scotch whisky had to be accompanied by an official document from the government of the country of origin (ie the UK) certifying that they were indeed what they claimed. While this rule could be defended as a measure protecting Belgian consumers, it clearly constituted an obstacle for importers wishing to purchase Scotch whisky in France and sell it back on the Belgian market.[3] In striking down the measure at issue, the Court gave a potentially very broad reading of the scope of application of Article 28 stating that,

> all trading rules capable of hindering, directly or indirectly, actually or potentially, intra-Community trade are to be considered as measures having an effect equivalent to quantitative restrictions.[4]

At the same time, the Court, albeit in a very obscure manner, seemed to limit the "strikingly, almost insanely, broad"[5] definition of "measures having equivalent effect" by noting that

> in the absence of a Community system guaranteeing for consumers the authenticity of a product's designation of origin, if a Member state takes measures to prevent unfair practices in this connection, it is however subject to the condition that these measures should be reasonable and that the means required should not act as a hindrance to trade between Member States.[6]

In this paragraph the Court is apparently saying that *reasonable* restraints may not be caught by the prohibition of Article 28, thus putting forward a

---

[1] Case 8/74, *Procureur de Roi v Dassonville* [1974] ECR 837.
[2] Case 120/78, *Rewe-Zentrale AG v Bundesmonopolverwaltung für Branntwein* (*Cassis de Dijon*) [1979] ECR 649.
[3] Technically, Belgian importers could buy the whisky directly from its country of origin and obtain the required certificate, but this would have meant paying a higher price. Differences in the price of whisky arose because the manufacturers sold at different prices to different countries, according to what the market could bear, and thus in France, where manufacturers were trying to break into the market, Scotch whisky was sold quite cheaply. G Davies, *European Union Internal Market Law* (London, Cavendish Publishing Ltd, 2002) at 21. Cf P Craig and G de Búrca, *EU Law* (Oxford, OUP, 1998) at 584 *et seq*; G Tesauro, *Diritto Comunitario* (Padova, CEDAM, 1995) at 270 *et seq*.
[4] Case 8/74, *Procureur de Roi v Dassonville* [1974] ECR 837, para 5.
[5] G Davies, *European Union Internal Market Law* (London, Cavendish Publishing Ltd., 2002) at 22.
[6] Case 8/74, *Procureur de Roi v Dassonville* [1974] ECR 837, para 6.

sort of "rule of reason" approach similar to the parallel concept employed in American antitrust law.

The full potential of the *Dassonville* "interpretation" of Article 28 was spelled out in *Cassis de Dijon*, where the Court was called on to review the validity of a German requirement imposing a minimum alcoholic strength (around 30 per cent) on all fruit liqueur. This requirement had the effect of impeding the importation into Germany of the traditional French blackcurrant liqueur "*Cassis de Dijon*", which contained less than the required minimum alcohol level. The core of the Court's decision may be found in the following two paragraphs.

First of all, paragraph 8 reads as follows:

> [although] in the absence of common rules relating to the production and marketing of alcohol it is for the Member States to regulate all matters relating to the production and marketing of alcohol and alcoholic beverages on their own territory... [o]bstacles to movement within the Community resulting from disparities between the national laws relating to the marketing of the products in question must be accepted in so far as those provisions may be recognised as being necessary in order to satisfy mandatory requirements relating in particular to the effectiveness of fiscal supervision, the protection of public health, the fairness of commercial transactions and the defence of the consumer.[7]

With *Cassis de Dijon* thus the Court abandoned any reference to the distinction between border and internal measures and endorsed the dichotomy originally devised by the Commission in Directive 70/50[8] between *distinctly* and *indistinctly* applicable measures. Accordingly, while the former are *directly* included in the concept of "measures having equivalent effect" and are thus provisionally prohibited as such by Article 28, the latter fall within the prohibition of that same Article *only if* they are found not to be necessary in order satisfy any legitimate public policy objective (ie if they

---

[7] Case 120/78, *Cassis de Dijon* [1979] ECR 649, para 8.
[8] Since its 1963 action programme the Commission had emphasised that Member States' rules governing the marketing of products, which dealt inter alia with shape, size, weight, composition, presentation (so-called "product standards"), which applied, at least formally, equally to domestic and imported products, could have a restrictive effect on the free movement of goods resulting from the *inherent disparities* between these rules. In Directive 70/50, the Commission introduced a *different* normative approach with regard indistinctly applicable measures: while "distinctly applicable" measures were prohibited once they were found *formally* to discriminate against imported products, "indistinctly applicable" measures fell within the scope of application of old Art 30 and thus had to be abolished *only if* their restrictive effects on the free movement of goods "exceeded the effects intrinsic to trade rules". As expressly specified by Art 3, this was the case in particular where (a) the restrictive effects on the free movement of goods are out of proportion to their purpose and (b) the same objective can be attained by other means which are less of a hindrance to trade. See Commission Directive 70/50 of 22 Dec 1969, OJ L 13 (1970) 29. Cf the discussion above in ch 2.

fail the "reasonableness" or "proportionality" test). This is, in other words, the realisation of the *Dassonville* rule of reason idea.[9]

Secondly, in paragraph 14, having determined that the German requirement did not serve a purpose which is in the general interest such as to take precedence over the requirements of the free movement of goods (ie it was indeed *not* necessary in order to satisfy consumer protection and public health), the Court concluded with the following statement:

> there was no valid reason why, provided that they have been lawfully produced and marketed in one of the Member States, alcoholic beverages should not be introduced into any other Member States; the sale of such products may not be subject to a legal prohibition on the marketing of beverages with an alcohol content lower than the limit set by the national rules.[10]

This statement is usually believed to encapsulate the *principle of mutual recognition* according to which any product imported from another Member State must in principle be admitted to the territory of the importing Member State if it has been lawfully produced (that is, conforms to the rules and processes of manufacture that are customarily and traditionally accepted in the exporting country) and is marketed in the territory of the latter.[11] In practical terms, *Cassis de Dijon* establishes a rebuttable presumption that, once goods have been lawfully marketed in one Member State, they should be admitted into any other Member State without restriction, unless the Member State of import can successfully demonstrate that the laws of the exporting Member State are *not* functionally equivalent to its own laws.[12] In other words, contrary to the Commission approach in Directive 70/50 setting the burden on the *exporter* to prove the "unreasonableness" of the equally applicable regulation of the *importing* State,[13] with *Cassis de Dijon* the burden is shifted on to the *importing* State that has to demonstrate the "reasonableness" of its equally applicable laws. In this manner, the Court considerably

[9] G Davies, *European Union Internal Market Law* (London, Cavendish Publishing Ltd., 2002) at 28. Cf P Craig and G de Búrca, *EU Law* (Oxford, OUP, 1998) at 607; G Tesauro, *Diritto Comunitario* (Padova, CEDAM, 1995) at 281.

[10] Case 120/78, *Cassis de Dijon* [1979] ECR 649, para 14.

[11] This is the interpretation given in Communication from the Commission concerning the consequences of the Judgment given by the Court of Justice on 20 Feb 1979 in Case 120/78 ("*Cassis de Dijon*") [OJ 1980, No C256/2].

[12] P Craig and G de Búrca, *EU Law* (Oxford, OUP, 1998) at 607.

[13] As correctly noted by Oliver, while de jure discriminatory measures were automatically considered to be measures of equivalent effect under Art 2 of Directive 70/50, Art 3 of that directive provided for a presumption that "indistinctly applicable measures" were compatible with old Art 30, which could have been rebutted by showing that the restrictive effects of the measure exceeded the effects that are intrinsic to trade rules. Cf P Oliver, *Free Movement of Goods in the European Community* (London, Sweet & Maxwell, 1996) at 89.

reduced market barriers stemming from regulatory disparities of the Member States (what I have previously referred to as the "regulatory overlap" phenomenon)[14] and at the same time furthered the creation of a unified market.[15]

The *Dassonville–Cassis de Dijon* doctrine may thus be summarised as follows: although all trading rules capable of hindering, directly or indirectly, actually or potentially, intra-Community trade are to be considered as measure having an effect equivalent to quantitative restrictions for the purposes of the prohibition in Article 28, except if justified under Article 30 (the *Dassonville* limb), in the absence of Community harmonisation, *indistinctly applicable measures* must be accepted in so far as they are *necessary* in order to satisfy *mandatory requirements* relating inter alia to the effective of fiscal supervision, the protection of public health, the fairness of commercial transaction and the defence of the consumer (the *Cassis de Dijon* limb).[16]

B.   The Dassonville–Cassis De Dijon "Rule of Reason" Doctrine: Uncovering the Court's "Formalist Sophistry"[17]

From a pure theoretical perspective, the Court has tried to explain its different approach with regard to "distinctly" and "indistinctly" applicable measures (ie origin-based and origin-neutral measures) in the following manner. Distinctly applicable measures, whether (inherently discriminatory) border or de jure discriminatory internal measures, are automatically

---

[14] I have referred to the "regulatory overlap" phenomenon to indicate the existence of several regulatory centres with limited territorial authority (the Member States) that, by imposing different product requirements within their jurisdictions, impeded or severely restricted the free circulation of goods within the greater market (the Common Market).

[15] E White, "In search of the Limits to Art 30 of the EEC Treaty", 26 *CMLRev.* (1989) 235 at 245 *et seq*, where it is noted that "the different legal and economic environment of the Member State of origin finds its expression in the different *characteristics* of an imported product compared with the national product. Consequently, as the judgment of the Court in *Cassis de Dijon* clearly shows, Member States are not entitled to require that imported products to have the same *characteristics* as are required of, or are traditional in, domestic products unless this is strictly necessary for the protection of some legitimate interest." For a recent case see Case C–14/02, *Atral SA v Belgium* [2003] ECR 0000 (Judgment of 8 May 2003), para 69.

[16] The connection between Directive 70/50 and the *Cassis de Dijon* jurisprudence is widely recognised in the legal literature. Cf P Craig and G de Búrca, *EU Law* (Oxford, OUP, 1998) at 605; S Weatherill and P Beaumont, *EC Law* (London, Penguin Books, 1995) at 494. Note however that the Court made the link between *Dassonville* and *Cassis de Dijon* for the first time in the post-*Cassis* decision in Case 788/79, *Gilli & Andres* [1980] ECR 2071. Cf D Chalmers, "Repackaging the Internal Market—the Ramifications of the *Keck* Judgment", 19 *ELRev* (1994) 385 at 386.

[17] JHH Weiler, "Epilogue: Towards a Common Law of International Trade" in JHH Weiler (ed), *The EU, the WTO and the NAFTA: Towards a Common Law of International Trade?* (Oxford, OUP, 2000) at 220.

caught by the prohibition of Article 28 as "measures having equivalent effect" to quantitative restrictions once they satisfy the *Dassonville* formula (capable of hindering, directly or indirectly, actually or potentially, intra-Community trade). These measures, however, may *subsequently* be justified on the basis of one of the public policy exceptions expressly provided for in Article 30 EC. At this later stage, usually referred to as the "justification" stage, a Member State may try to save its measure, which has been found to violate Article 28, by arguing that it has been taken in order to pursue one of the public policy goals included in Article 30 and that the measure is *reasonably* related to such a goal.

On the contrary, the "mandatory requirements" or "rule of reason" doctrine, hinted in *Dassonville* and fully elaborated in *Cassis de Dijon* focuses once again on the reasonableness of the relationship between the measure under review and its public policy objective. This doctrine is employed by the Court in order to determine whether an "indistinctly applicable measure" is *first of all* a measure having an "equivalent effect" within the meaning of Article 28. Accordingly, if an indistinctly applicable measure is *necessary* to satisfy mandatory requirements (ie any legitimate public policy), that measure falls outside the scope of application of Article 28 altogether. In other words, if justified on public policy grounds, an indistinctly applicable measure is not deemed to constitute a "measure having equivalent effect" to quantitative restrictions at all.

Several authors have criticised the approach followed by the ECJ in distinguishing between the general exception provision of Article 30 and "mandatory requirements", at least from a perspective of theoretical clarity.[18] According to these authors, the analysis should in fact be two-limbed. Is the national measure prohibited by the Treaty because it constitutes a restriction on trade? If yes, is it justified by any of the public policy exceptions? Yes or no. End of story. As clearly put by Professor Weiler, if one ignores the "formalist sophistry" advocated by the Court of Justice, which pretends that the doctrine of "mandatory requirements" simply qualifies what is or is not a violation of Article 28 as distinct from Article 30, which "redeems" or justifies a prima-facie violation,[19] the only meaningful doctrinal difference between distinctly and indistinctly applicable measures is that while the former may be justified exclusively by reference to the exhaustive list of public policy objectives included in Article 30,

---

[18] Cf JHH Weiler, "Epilogue: Towards a Common Law of International Trade" in JHH Weiler (ed), *The EU, the WTO and the NAFTA: Towards a Common Law of International Trade?* (Oxford, OUP, 2000) at 220, who refers to the Court of Justice doctrinal distinction as mere "formalist sophistry" and P Oliver, *Free Movement of Goods in the European Community*, above n 13, at 110 *et seq*.

[19] JHH Weiler, "Epilogue: Towards a Common Law of International Trade" in JHH Weiler (ed), *The EU, the WTO and the NAFTA: Towards a Common Law of International Trade?* (Oxford, OUP, 2000) at 220.

the latter enjoys the more generous open-ended list of public policy justifications provided for by the "mandatory requirements" doctrine.[20]

The overall complexity of the Court's *Dassonville–Cassis de Dijon* doctrine (as well as its subsequent ramifications—*Keck* for example) finds its roots in one simple fact: in the minds of the drafters of the Treaty of Rome, the original chapter on "Elimination of Quantitative Restrictions Between Member States" including old Articles 30–37 (now 28–31) was not meant to go beyond a prohibition of (inherently discriminatory) border measures. Indeed, this is the only starting point if one wants to really understand the multiple normative functions that the Court has attributed to the provisions of that chapter.

As argued in chapter 1, the prohibition of "quantitative restrictions and all measures having equivalent effect" in Article 28 was originally aimed at *border* measures. Given their highly damaging effect on the liberalisation of intra-Community trade as well as their inherently discriminatory nature, border measures had to be *eliminated* and could remain in place only in the exceptional circumstances expressly provided for in Article 30. The structure of the provisions in the chapter on "Elimination of Quantitative Restrictions Between Member States" was relatively clear. Article 28 constituted the "rule" and required the elimination of *a particular set of regulations, objectively identifiable*. More specifically, as previously explained, while *border measures* were the "objective element" of Article 28, their *elimination* and *prohibition* constituted the "normative content" of that Article. Then there was Article 30 recognising the possibility to allow those measures if justified on a limited set of "non-economic" public policy objectives. This represented the "exception".

Extending Articles 28/30's dual approach—rule and exception—to *formally* discriminatory or origin-based *internal* measures came without much ado both because the Treaty of Rome already contained a general prohibition on "any discrimination on grounds of nationality" (Article 12, ex 6, EC), and because, in practical terms, *formally* discriminatory internal measures had exactly the same negative effects on intra-Community trade as border measures (ie they constituted clear and unreasonable "obstacles" to the creation of the European internal market). However, as demonstrated above in the chapters on the principle of non-discrimination based on the nationality of the product (ie the National Treatment principle),

---

[20] *Ibid*; N Bernard, "Discrimination and the Free Movement in EC Law", 45 *ICLQ* (1996) at 93; D Martin, "'Discrimination', 'entraves' et 'raisons impérieuses' dans le Traité CE: trois concept en quête d'identité", *CDE* (1998) 261 at 275 *et seq*. As examined in the chapter on de jure discriminatory measures, there may be cases where this doctrinal difference does entail relevant practical consequences, in particular where the national measure deemed to constitute a prima facie violation of Art 28 is taken in order to pursue a public policy objective (such as consumer or environmental protection) that is not included in the exhaustive list of Art 30. See above ch 2.

from a purely theoretical perspective, the features of the "rule" *did* change: the "objective element" of the rule was now potentially also any *internal* regulation; and its "normative content" was the obligation not to discriminate on the basis of the origin of a product. Representing the very negation of the concept of trade among States, *formally* discriminatory (or, in the Court's language, "distinctly applicable") measures did not in principle require any broader justification. Thus, the "exception" did not (have to) change.

When it came to addressing origin-neutral (or "indistinctly applicable") internal measures, things became more complex. There were at least two approaches that could have been taken with regard to "indistinctly applicable measures"; one would have been to interpret the prohibition of Article 28 as a general ban on discriminatory measures, both de jure and de facto; the other would have been to go beyond the non-discrimination principle and introduce a different normative standard. First the Commission with its 70/50 directive and later the Court in *Dassonville* and *Cassis de Dijon* took the second option and focused the inquiry on the validity of origin-neutral (or indistinctly applicable) measures on the basis of their "reasonableness" or "proportionality".[21] In very general terms, a measure which, at least on its face, applied equally to both domestic and imported products (facially origin-neutral measure) is deemed to conform with basic principles of Community free movement law if that same measure is *reasonably related* to a legitimate public policy objective.[22]

The non-discrimination route, even if taken to its fullest potential (ie extending to de facto discriminatory measures), would have permitted maintaining the "rule and exception" approach as employed by the EC Treaty in the chapter on the elimination of quantitative restrictions: Article 28 would have prohibited any form of discrimination, whether direct or indirect, and Article 30 would have provided the Member States with the possibility of justifying discriminatory measures on public policy grounds (this is currently the approach characterising the GATT).

Adopting the second option, based on the "reasonableness" or "proportionality" of the national measure restricting intra-Community

---

[21] According to the Commission, indistinctly applicable measures fell foul of Art 28 only if their restrictive effect on the free movement of goods "exceeds the effects intrinsic to trade rules", in particular, where (a) "the restrictive effects on the free movement of goods are out of proportion to their purpose" and (b) "the same objective can be attained by other means which are less of a hindrance to trade". Art 3, Commission Directive 70/50 of 22 Dec 1969, OJ L 13 (1970) 29.

[22] This was to become the so-called requirement of proportionality which "entails that there be a reasonable relationship between a particular objective and the administrative or legislative means used to achieve that objective." G de Búrca, "The Principle of Proportionality and its Application in EC law", 13 *YEL* (1994) 105 at 105.

trade, clearly meant abandoning the dual approach for a single-limb approach: is the indistinctly applicable measure reasonably related to its objective? This is where the Court had to use the above-mentioned "formalist sophistry" in order to find some kind of textual basis for its novel (and revolutionary) approach. Indeed, the Court "moved" the inquiry as to the reasonableness or proportionality of the national regulation under review to the stage of determining whether that same regulation constituted a "measure having equivalent effect" within the meaning of Article 28. Thus, the Court differentiated in technical terms between justification under the "mandatory requirements" doctrine and justification under Article 30.[23]

The Court's "formalist sophistry" reveals the inherently different features of the two above-mentioned options. Determining whether a facially origin-neutral measure is *discriminatory in its effects* is, though very difficult, technically feasible, independently of an examination of the substantive merits of the measure itself. In its basic and broadest meaning, material discrimination will be found where a Member State's measure, even if formally origin-neutral, has the *effect* of favouring domestic production vis-à-vis imported competitive products. Thus, under the non-discrimination approach one can still distinguish between the "rule" and the "exception".

On the contrary, establishing whether that same measure is *reasonable* or *proportionate* necessarily involves an examination of the relationship between the measure and its purported policy objective. Thus, under the "rule of reason" approach there is not much sense in distinguishing between rule and exception.

Furthermore, the similarity between the structure of the analysis under Article 30 (the justification option) and that carried out under the "mandatory requirements" or "rule of reason" doctrine (whether indistinctly applicable measures constitute "measures having equivalent effect"), even with regard to the burden of proof (it is always the regulating Member State that has to "defend" its laws), is only apparent. Even masked behind the Court's formalist sophistry, the normative approaches with regard to, on the one hand, distinctly applicable measures (ie border and de jure discriminatory internal measures), and, on the other, indistinctly applicable ones (all facially origin-neutral regulations) are quite different.

First, under the two-step approach, a measure falls within the prohibition of Article 28 because (a) it is a "distinctly applicable rule" and (b) it is

---

[23] There seems to be general agreement that despite all there is indeed a difference between the objective justifications introduced by *Dassonville* and *Cassis de Dijon* with regard to indistinctly applicable measures and the public policy exceptions of Art 30 (ex 36). Cf G Davies, *European Union Internal Market Law* (London/Sydney, Cavendish, 2002) at 28.

deemed to be capable of hindering, directly or indirectly, actually or potentially, intra-Community trade. Once a measure is deemed to be prohibited then a distinctly applicable rule may be justified on public policy grounds or, in other words, by looking at its "substantive merits" or public policy objectives. Under the one-step approach, a measure is caught by that same prohibition if (a) it is an "indistinctly applicable rule", (b) it is deemed to be capable of hindering, directly or indirectly, actually or potentially, intra-Community trade and (c) it is found not to be reasonably or proportionately related with its purported policy objective. Leaving aside for a moment the second condition (the so-called *Dassonville* formula), the relevance of the measure's public policy objectives or its "substantive merits" varies depending on whether the measure under review is distinctly or indistinctly applicable. In the former case, a review of the measure's substantive merits comes always after a finding that the measure is prohibited by Article 28. In the latter, a prohibition finding is based principally on such a review.

Moreover, possibly as a direct consequence of the a priori value-judgement inherent in the prohibition of *distinctly* applicable measures, justification on public policy grounds for this type of measure has always been interpreted in a strict manner. It follows from this that the list of legitimate public policy grounds that Member States may employ to "defend" their laws is, under the two-step approach, exhaustive in character. On the other hand, under the one-step, reasonableness approach, in order to demonstrate the validity of their regulations, Member States may refer to an open-ended list of public policy objectives, emphasising once more that the focus of this type of approach is directly on the measure's substantive merits.

With regard to the so-called *Dassonville* formula, the issue of whether the measure under review "hinders, directly or indirectly, actually or potentially, intra-Community trade" functions as the *threshold question* that is necessary to delimit the scope of application of Article 28, in particular as it has been applied to indistinctly applicable measures. Although possible in theory, it is very unlikely that a "distinctly" applicable measure may be excluded from the prohibition of Article 28 on the basis that it lacks a potentially trade-restrictive effect.[24] With regard to "indistinctly" applicable measures, on the other hand, the *Dassonville* formula has indeed been employed in order to exclude having to review the reasonableness of facially origin-neutral regulations without any *indirect* or *potential* restrictive effect on trade between the Member States (the so-called "rule of remoteness"). As correctly noted by Oliver, this rule of

---

[24] C Costello, "Market Access All Areas—The Treatment of Non-Discriminatory Barriers to the Free Movement of Workers", 27 *Legal Issues of Economic Integration* (2000) 267 at 271–2.

remoteness should not be regarded as a *de minimis* test in disguise since a measure may constitute an actual and direct restriction even on a very small proportion of imports. On the other hand, a measure is deemed to be too remote and thus outside the terms of the *Dassonville* formula only when the *possibility* of it (even marginally) affecting imports is "too uncertain and indirect".[25]

In summary, while the "normative content" of the "rule" dealing with *distinctly applicable measures* is a ban on a specific type of inherently discriminatory measures (ie border measures shall be prohibited) and a non-discrimination requirement (ie product origin shall not be the differentiating criterion), the "normative content" of the "rule" dealing with *indistinctly applicable measures* is "reasonableness" or "proportionality" (ie internal measures shall be reasonably or proportionately related to their public policy objectives).[26] With regard to this latter rule, the *Dassonville* formula (ie the "threshold question") simply represents a flexible instrument to determine the rule's scope of application (ie the rule's "objective element").

At least from a strictly legal perspective, the judgment in *Keck* should be read in these same terms. Along the lines of the formalist sophistry employed in the *Dassonville–Cassis de Dijon* jurisprudence, the Court stated in that case that "selling arrangements" would not be deemed to hinder intra-Community trade within the terms of the *Dassonville* formula

---

[25] P Oliver, "Some Further Reflections on the Scope of Art 28–30 (ex 30–36) EC", 36 *CMLRev* (1999) 783 at 788–91, citing as instances where the Court found that the measure was too remote for purposes of the *Dassonville* formula Case 379/92, *Peralta* [1994] ECR 3453, and Case C–67/97, *Bluhme* [1998] ECR I–8033. For instances where the Court refused to apply a *de minimis* rule see Joined Cases 177 & 178/82, *Van de Haar* [1984] ECR 1797, and Case C–184/96, *Commission v France* (*Foie Gras*) [1998] ECR 6197. For a pre-*Keck* strict interpretation of the *Dassonville* formula see J Steiner, "Drawing the Line: Uses and Abuses of Art 30 EEC", *CMLRev.* (1992) 749 at 772–73, noting that "[t]he correct approach to the test is not to ask whether imports or trade in imported goods have been affected, or the volume of imports reduced, as a result of the measure, but whether the measure constitutes, actually or potentially, a *hindrance* to inter-state trade. Applied in this way, any 'qualifications' to the *Dassonville* principle remain firmly embedded within the rule" [emphasis original]. Note, however, that the author leaves out the further reference to "directly and *indirectly*", which clearly gives a broader meaning to "a hindrance to intra-community trade".

[26] Despite a certain appearance to the contrary in the Court's case-law, the *Dassonville–Cassis de Dijon* doctrine should not be interpreted as setting a "rule and exception" type of approach, whereby the "rule" is a general prohibition on all measures restricting intra-Community trade and the "exception" is the possibility to justify or redeem such measures on public policy grounds. Since any national regulatory measure is capable of restricting trade, this "rule" would not make any "normative" sense. Cf T Tridimas, *The General Principle of EC Law* (Oxford, OUP, 1999), "The notions of non-discrimination and proportionality have been used by the Court as conceptual tools for drawing the demarcation line between lawful and unlawful impediments to free movement […] if it is accepted that free movement goes beyond equal treatment and requires freedom of access to the market, then any obstacle to free access becomes an unlawful impediment unless objectively justified. Under [this] model, proportionality is elevated to the principal criterion for determining the dividing line between lawful and unlawful barriers to trade." *Ibid*, at 127.

(and thus they would not constitute a "measure having equivalent effect" prohibited by Article 28) so long as those provisions affect in the same manner, in law and in fact, the marketing of domestic and imported products. In reality, what the Court did in *Keck* was to exclude national regulations on the manner in which goods may be sold or used ("selling arrangements") from the scope of application of the "reasonableness rule" and to subject them to the less intrusive non-discrimination principle.[27] As argued in the previous chapter, it was a further reinterpretation of Article 28 in at least two ways: (a) it limited the scope of application of the *Dassonville–Cassis de Dijon* "rule of reason" approach and (b) it employed Article 28 as a fully-fledged "non-discrimination" obligation with regard to a specific category of regulations. Furthermore, by maintaining the underlying connection with the *Dassonville–Cassis de Dijon* doctrine, selling arrangements found to discriminate only *in fact* between domestic and imported products may be justified by the same open-ended list of public policy objectives available under the "rule of reason" approach.

In conclusion, the Court's jurisprudence shows four different "rules" stemming from Article 28. The first, and truly original, rule is a ban on import restrictions. The second rule, and the only plausible extension of the original scope of Article 28, is a prohibition of de jure discrimination on the basis of the product's nationality or origin covering any internal regulation. Violations of these two "rules" may be justified exclusively on the basis of the public policy exceptions exhaustively included in Article 30 (*Dassonville–Cassis de Dijon I* doctrine—*distinctly applicable measures*). The third rule is a general requirement that any regulation hindering, directly and indirectly, actually and potentially, intra-Community trade, must be reasonably or proportionately related to a legitimate public policy objective (*Dassonville–Cassis de Dijon II* doctrine—*indistinctly applicable measures*). The fourth rule, which constitutes an exception to the third rule, is a prohibition of de facto discrimination on the basis of the product's nationality that applies only to "selling arrangements". Violations of this latter rule may be justified on any public policy grounds (*Dassonville–Cassis de Dijon-Keck* doctrine—*selling arrangements*).

---

[27] As noted in the previous ch, the Court case law on the application of the *Dassonville–Cassis de Dijon* doctrine with regard to selling arrangements was not altogether consistent: while in some cases the application of Art 28 was excluded regardless of whether the rules were justified or not, in other, quite similar, cases, this type of measures were brought within the ambit of Art 28 and were subjected to the *Dassonville–Cassis de Dijon* proportionality review. G Tesauro, "The Community's Internal Market in light of the Recent Case-Law of the Court of Justice" in *YEL* (1995) 1 at 4; S Weatherill, "Current Developments in European Community Law: I. Free Movement of Goods" 50 *ICLQ* (2001) 158 at 160 *et seq*. Cf Opinion of AG Jacobs in Case C–412/93, *Société d'Importation Edouard Leclerc-Siplec v TF1 Publicité SA and M6 Publicité SA*. [1995] ECR I–0179, paras 27–33.

C.   Asymmetry Between "Normative Objectives" and "Legal Features"

A final and fundamental footnote should be emphasised. While there is no doubt that the several normative applications of Article 28 were taken in order to address specific issues facing the Community's integration process, I believe that often the broader reasons underlying each application are not automatically reflected in the "rules" themselves. In other words, there is to a certain extent an asymmetry between the original reasons for adopting a specific "rule" and the actual legal features and interpretation of that same "rule".

For example, the *Dassonville–Cassis de Dijon II* doctrine subjecting indistinctly applicable measures affecting intra-Community trade to the "rule of reason" may be *explained*, as noted earlier, by reference to the "regulatory overlap" phenomenon, and thus to either a very broad concept of "discrimination"[28] or the strict notion of "market access".[29] However, it seems that neither of these two concepts is sufficient to *describe* all the facets of the legal approach actually followed by the Court of Justice with regard to indistinctly applicable measures. This is quite clearly evidenced in the "text" and "interpretation" of the legal test delimiting the scope of application of the "rule of reason" (what I have called the "threshold question").

With regard to the "text", under the *Dassonville–Cassis de Dijon II* doctrine, a facially origin-neutral regulation is subject to a review of proportionality simply if it is deemed to be "capable of *hindering*, directly or indirectly, actually or potentially, intra-Community trade". Thus, the so-called *Dassonville* formula is *textually* quite broad, inasmuch as it goes beyond the concept of discrimination and encompasses mere *hindrances* to the circulation of Community goods.[30]

With regard to the "interpretation" of the legal test, the *Dassonville–Cassis de Dijon* jurisprudence shows that hindrances to intra-Community trade

---

[28] As suggested by Marenco in his seminal 1984 article, the true reason for the Court's finding in *Cassis de Dijon* was that "regulating alcohol beverages quality only on the basis of traditions developed within the national market automatically disadvantages imports". G Marenco, "Pour une interprétation traditionelle de la notion de mesure d'effet équivalent à une restriction quantitative", 20 *CDE* (1984) 291 at 306 [my translation].

[29] The Court's emphasis in its *Cassis de Dijon* judgment on the magnitude of the adverse effects on the free circulation of goods within the common market may be taken to suggest that the reason for invalidating the German minimum alcohol requirements was that they had the effect of *excluding* or *preventing* (rather than simply impeding) Community products from entering Member States' markets. The Court noted that "[i]n practice, the principle effect of requirements of this nature is to promote alcoholic beverages having a high alcohol content by *excluding* from the national market products of other Member States which do not answer that description." Case 120/78, *Cassis de Dijon* [1979] ECR 649, para 14 [emphasis added].

[30] For a pre-*Keck* strict interpretation of the *Dassonville* formula see J Steiner, "Drawing the Line: Uses and Abuses of Art 30 EEC", *CMLRev.* (1992) 749 at 772–73.

may be represented by measures which, though indistinctly applicable (ie facially origin-neutral), (a) specifically discriminate *in fact* between imported and domestic competitive products (*French Alcohol Advertising*), (b) generally disadvantage or prevent the importation of products from other Member States (*Cassis de Dijon*), and (c) simply negatively affect the circulation of goods within the Community (*Torfaen*).[31]

The *Dassonville* formula, in other words, has not represented a meaningful limitation to the (scope of) application of the "rule of reason" approach. The battle for the validity of a national measure was, at least until *Keck*, almost invariably won and lost on the issue of whether that measure was reasonably or proportionately related to a legitimate public policy objective.[32] In short, while a very broad concept of discrimination might have even been the principal motive inspiring the *Dassonville–Cassis de Dijon* approach with regard to indistinctly applicable measures, it was certainly *not* the normative rule subsequently applied by the Court, which on the contrary focused on an analysis of the "reasonableness" and "proportionality" of the national measure under review.[33]

I believe that *Keck* may be analysed, once again, in a similar manner. While the Court's clarification of its *Dassonville–Cassis de Dijon* approach could be said to be aimed at re-focusing Article 28 on what the Court had originally in mind when *Cassis de Dijon* was rendered (ie to defuse the "regulatory overlap" phenomenon), *Keck* did not modify the specific normative features of the "rule of reason" approach. As previously noted, with *Keck* the Court simply excluded from the scope of application of the *Dassonville–Cassis de Dijon* "rule of reason" approach national provisions

---

[31] Cf L Gormely, "'Actually or Potentially, Directly or Indirectly'? Obstacles to the Free Movement of Goods", 9 *YEL* (1989) 197. It should be emphasised that the reach recognised *on the field* to the "rule of reason" approach could probably not have been foreseen (even by the Court itself) at the time the *Dassonville* judgment was rendered. The extension of its scope of application is the product of a relatively quick process where the primary actors were not simply the Court of Justice and the Commission, but to a certain extent also private entities appreciating and consequently exploiting to the fullest the potentialities for liberalisation inherent in the basic free movement principles. In *Keck* the Court noted that it was necessary to re-examine and clarify its case-law on Art 28 "in view of the increasing tendency of traders to invoke Art 28 of the Treaty as a means of challenging any rules whose effect is to limit their commercial freedom even where such rules are not aimed at products from other Member States". Joined Cases C–267 and 268/91, *Keck & Mithouard* [1993] ECR I–6097, para 14.

[32] S Weatherill, "Recent Case Law Concerning the Free Movement of Goods: Mapping the Frontiers of Market Deregulation", 36 *CMLRev* (1999) 51 at 52–3.

[33] Incidentally, one of the most praised qualities of the new normative approach advance in the Court's *Dassonville–Cassis de Dijon* jurisprudence is precisely the abandonment of any reference to the concept of de facto discrimination on the basis of the product's origin. By adopting the distinction between "distinctly" and "indistinctly" applicable measures (ie between origin-based and origin-neutral measures), the Court was able to get rid of the problematic determination of whether a facially origin-neutral regulation constituted discrimination in fact. Cf P Eeckhout, *The European Internal Market and International Trade: A Legal Analysis* (Oxford, Clarendon Press, 1994) at 268.

restricting or prohibiting certain selling arrangements[34] and subjected these same provisions to a fully-fledged "non-discrimination" obligation. Accordingly, outside "selling arrangements" the Court will continue to apply the "traditional" *Dassonville–Cassis de Dijon* doctrine: distinctly applicable measures are prohibited if they cannot be justified on the basis of Article 30; indistinctly applicable measures capable of hindering, even indirectly or potentially, intra-Community trade (*threshold question*) are subject to a reasonableness or proportionality review (*normative standard*).

The fact that after *Keck* the Court appears to apply, even outside the ambit of selling arrangements, the so-called "threshold question" or *Dassonville* formula more cautiously, limiting the "reasonableness" review to measures with a "sufficient" impact on cross-border trade,[35] does not modify the conclusion that the normative structure of the *Dassonville–Cassis de Dijon* "rule of reason" approach has remained the same.

Once again, while it is important to note and emphasise the plausible goals underlying the Court's interpretation of the basic free movement norms, it is also very much crucial not to lose sight of the actual, more technical features of these norms.

D. Proportionality as the "Normative Standard": A Few Preliminary Remarks

The remainder of this section will focus on the "normative standard" of the *Dassonville–Cassis de Dijon II* doctrine, that is, the general *criteria* imposed by the Court on indistinctly applicable Member State measures capable of hindering, directly or indirectly, actually or potentially, intra-Community trade. In EC law parlance, these criteria as a whole are usually referred to as embodying the *principle of proportionality*, which generally requires that a Member State's measure be appropriate and necessary to achieve its objectives[36] or, put somewhat differently, that there

---

[34] P Eeckhout, "After *Keck and Mithouard*: Free Movement of Goods in the EC, Market Access, and Non-Discrimination" in T Cottier and P Mavroidis (eds), *Regulatory Barriers and the Principle of Non-Discrimination in World Trade Law* (Ann Arbor, University of Michigan Press, 2000).

[35] Several authors have emphasised the Court's post-*Keck* focus on market access even outside selling arrangements. Cf S Weatherill, "Recent Case Law Concerning the Free Movement of Goods: Mapping the Frontiers of Market Deregulation", 36 *CMLRev* (1999) 51 at 52–53; P Eeckhout, "After *Keck and Mithouard*: Free Movement of Goods in the EC, Market Access, and Non-Discrimination" in T Cottier and P Mavroidis (eds), *Regulatory Barriers and the Principle of Non-Discrimination in World Trade Law* (Ann Arbor, University of Michigan Press, 2000) at 198 *et seq*; C Barnard, "Fitting the Remaining Pieces into the Goods and Persons Jigsaw", 26 *ELRev.* (2001) 35 at 49 *et seq*.

[36] T Tridimas, "Proportionality in Community Law: Searching for the Appropriate Standard of Scrutiny" in E Ellis (ed), *The Principle of Proportionality in the Laws of Europe* (Oxford, Hart Publishing, 1999) at 65.

be a reasonable relationship between a particular objective and the administrative or legislative means used to achieve that objective.[37]

In order to set the stage for an analysis of the application by the Court of Justice of the principle of proportionality, three preliminary remarks should be noted.

First, in the European Communities, proportionality is used mainly in two contexts: to review the validity of (a) Member States' actions and (b) Community measures.[38] Although the principle of proportionality in its general meaning always requires that a measure be appropriate and necessary to achieving its objective, its fundamental function differs according to whether the measure under review is a Community or a Member State measure. Emphasising that the underlying interests which proportionality seeks to protect in each of the above cases are different, Tridimas notes:

> Where proportionality is invoked as a ground of review of Community pol-
> icy measures, the Court is called upon to balance a private against a public
> interest. The underlying interest, which the principle seeks to protect, is the
> rights of the individual but, given the discretion of the legislature, review of
> policy measures is based on the so-called "manifestly inappropriate test".
> [...] By contrast, where proportionality is invoked in order to challenge the
> compatibility with Community law of national measures affecting one of
> the fundamental freedoms, the Court is called upon to balance a
> Community against a national interest. The principle is applied as a market
> integration mechanism and the intensity of review is much stronger.[39]

In its former function, proportionality is perceived as a principle of "administrative validity". It has to do more with the rule of law[40] and

---

[37] G de Búrca, "The Principle of Proportionality and its Application in EC law", 13 *YEL* (1994) 105 at 105.

[38] With regard the issue of how the principle of proportionality managed to enter into the EC legal order, it is usually argued that the principle of proportionality may be derived from (a) several provisions of the Treaty (like Art 30 (ex 36) and 33 (ex 40), for example), (b) a reference to the parallel principle included in the national legal systems of the Member States, or (c) the principle of the Rule of Law. Cf J Schwarze, *European Administrative Law* (Sweet & Maxwell, 1997) at 710 *et seq*. It is undisputed, however, that the principle of proportionality, employed initially to safeguard fundamental rights vis-à-vis Community acts (principle of administrative validity), has subsequently been used by the ECJ in reviewing Member State measures violating the fundamental principles of free movement (market integration mechanism). Cf N Emiliou, *The Principle of Proportionality in European Law: A Comparative Study* (London, 1996) at 24; T Tridimas, "Proportionality in Community Law: Searching for the Appropriate Standard of Scrutiny" in E Ellis (ed), *The Principle of Proportionality in the Laws of Europe* (Oxford, Hart Publishing, 1999) at 65. Although only the "administrative validity function" of the proportionality principle has been recently codified in the EC Treaty (Art 5), its "market integration function" constitutes a general principle of EC law, as well.

[39] T Tridimas, "Proportionality in Community Law: Searching for the Appropriate Standard of Scrutiny" in E Ellis (ed), *The Principle of Proportionality in the Laws of Europe* (Oxford, Hart Publishing, 1999) at 65.

[40] *Ibid.*

the proper exercise of regulatory powers than with the attainment of liberalisation and integration.[41] This is the function of the principle of proportionality that has been codified in Article 5 of the EC Treaty, which now reads: "Any action by the Community shall not go beyond what is necessary to achieve the objectives of this Treaty."

In its latter function, proportionality is employed as an instrument of "trade liberalisation", since it imposes certain general conditions on the ability of Member States to adopt trade-restrictive regulations in the name of legitimate public policies such as the protection of public morality, public security, public health, the environment, the consumer. As will be explained in greater detail later, these conditions are, for example, that the trade-restrictive measure be "appropriate", "necessary", and/or "proportionate" to its public policy objective(s).

The difference between the two functions of proportionality is evident. Proportionality as an instrument of "administrative validity" is applied mainly to protect the fundamental rights of the citizens, and consequently limits the discretionary authority of Community institutions in the attainment of an integrated market (*protection of fundamental rights + limit on Communities regulatory prerogatives*). Proportionality as a mechanism of "market integration", on the other hand, is employed to limit the regulatory prerogatives of the Member States, and accordingly provides a guarantee for the four basic freedoms of movement (*protection of the freedoms of movement + limit on Member States' regulatory prerogatives*).[42]

This difference largely explains why the Court of Justice is much more tolerant in reviewing the proportionality of Community measures than when proportionality is employed as a market integration mechanism in reviewing Member States' measures.[43] Even aside from the criticism expressed towards such a double standard, this differentiation in the application of the proportionality principle demonstrates, on the one hand, the great flexibility and adaptability of the principle itself, and on the other, the need to keep the two functions of proportionality clearly

---

[41] This is true in particular when the proportionality principle is employed as a standard of review of a Community act, which an individual or undertaking claims is in violation of his or her fundamental rights (for example, the right of property). This characterisation may not be totally accurate in cases where the claimant or "offended" party is a Member State. In such circumstance, although the State may be acting on behalf of its citizens to protect their fundamental rights, it may be true as well that the action represents a disguised means of defending a national regulatory prerogative vis-à-vis the Communities.

[42] There would still be a difference if one were to consider the four freedoms of movement as fundamental rights of the Communities' citizens.

[43] Cf G Bermann, "Proportionality and Subsidiarity" in C Barnard and J Scott (eds), *The Law of the Single Market: Unpacking the Premises* (Oxford, Hart Publishing, 2002) at 75–6; F Jacobs, "Recent Developments in the Principle of Proportionality in European Community Law in E Ellis (ed), *The Principle of Proportionality in the Laws of Europe* (Oxford, Hart Publishing, 1999) at 21; Egger, "The Principle of Proportionality in Community Anti-Dumping Law" 18 *ELRev* (1993) 367.

separate. The present analysis will thus only deal with proportionality in its "trade liberalisation" or "market integration" function.[44]

Secondly, the concept of proportionality is sufficiently flexible to be capable of encompassing several regulatory criteria that may be employed in order to assess the reasonableness of a particular measure. Although the ECJ has never clearly endorsed this, even when invited to do so by its Advocates-General (in particular Van Gerven),[45] it has been said that the application of the principle of proportionality entails in effect a three-part test, much based on the equivalent and more developed principle employed in German law.[46] Accordingly, a measure will be deemed to comply with the proportionality principle if the measure (a) is *suitable* or *effective* to achieve a legitimate aim (suitability test), (b) is *necessary* to achieve that aim, namely, there are no other less restrictive means capable of producing that same result (the least restrictive alternative or necessity test), and (c) even if there are no less restrictive means, does not have an *excessive* or *disproportionate* effect on the applicant's interests (test of proportionality *stricto sensu*).[47]

As correctly noted by Jans, these three elements constitute an ascending series in terms of the intensity with which the Court of Justice can review national measures.[48] The "suitability" test involves an inquiry as to whether the regulatory instrument adopted by a Member is *technically capable* of achieving the public policy objective that is pursued. This assessment is mainly aimed at establishing a minimum level of "reasonableness" in the relation between the regulatory instrument and its public policy objective,

---

[44] For a recent analysis of the "administrative validity" function see G Bermann, "Proportionality and Subsidiarity" in C Barnard and J Scott (eds), *The Law of the Single Market: Unpacking the Premises* (Oxford, Hart Publishing, 2002) at 75 *et seq.*

[45] In the area of goods, see Opinion of Advocate-General Van Gerven in Case C–169/89, *Criminal Proceedings Against Gourmetterie Van den Burg* (*Dead Red Grouse*) [1990] ECR I–2143, para 8: "In the Court's case-law, the requirements of necessity and proportionality are frequently considered at the same time, in an analysis which closely revolves around the facts relied upon in support and the legal circumstances themselves. The assessment of the first requirement involves ascertaining whether there is a relationship of necessity between the measure adopted and the attainment of the objective pursued. This has two implications: in the first place, the existence of a causal connection between the measure adopted and the aim pursued, that is to say the measure is relevant or pertinent, and secondly there is no alternative to it which is less restrictive of the free movement of goods. The second requirement is concerned with the existence of a relationship of proportionality between the obstacle introduced, on the one hand, and, on the other, the objective pursued thereby and its actual attainment." In the area of services see Opinion of Advocate-General Van Gerven in Case C–159/90, *SPUC v Grogan* [1991] ECR I–4685.

[46] N Emiliou, *The Principle of Proportionality in European Law: A Comparative Study* (London, Kluwer, 1996) at 23 *et seq.*

[47] G de Búrca, "The Principle of Proportionality and its Application in EC law", 13 *YEL* (1994) 105 at 113. See also T Tridimas, "Proportionality in Community Law: Searching for the Appropriate Standard of Scrutiny" in E Ellis (ed), *The Principle of Proportionality in the Laws of Europe* (Oxford, Hart Publishing, 1999) at 68.

[48] J Jans, "Proportionality Revisited", 27 *Legal Issues of Economic Integration* (2000) 239 at 241.

without having to consider whether the Member State's measure is the "best" alternative in light of the specific objective pursued or the negative effects on other interests (such as the free movement of goods).

The "necessity" test, on the other hand, involves an inquiry as to whether among the several regulatory instruments capable of achieving the public policy objective pursued by the Member State the chosen measure is indeed the *least-trade restrictive*, or in other words, whether the chosen regulatory instrument is no more trade-restrictive than necessary to fulfil a legitimate public policy objective (this is why the "necessity" test is usually also known as the "least-trade restrictive" requirement). In this calculation, level of the trade-restrictiveness of the chosen measure will need to be taken into account and compared with that of all other alternative regulatory instruments. The difficult task in the necessity test, as will be shown in the following analysis, is not only to determine whether there exist other regulatory measures that affect trade to a lesser extent compared to the measure chosen by the Member State, but principally to establish whether these alternatives are indeed capable of achieving the specific public policy objective as *effectively* and *to the same extent* as the chosen measure.

Finally, the test of "proportionality *stricto sensu*" involves a determination of whether the measure's negative effects on intra-Community trade are *out of proportion* to the measure's benefits to a legitimate public policy objective. In other words, what is at stake under the test of proportionality *stricto sensu* is whether the chosen level of public policy protection (and the measure necessary to reach it) is out of proportion with respect to the principle of free circulation of goods. For example, an absolute ban on a certain substance for environmental protection purposes might be deemed to fail the test of proportionality *stricto sensu* if the environmental gains from such a ban are too minimal compared to the severe negative impact on trade stemming from the ban itself. With regard to national regulatory prerogatives, this is undoubtedly the more intrusive and thus problematic form of review, since it focuses on assessing the relative *values* of, on the one hand, non-economic, public policy objectives (such as public health, consumer protection or environmental protection), and, on the other, the aim of liberalising intra-Community trade.

The German-style reconstruction of the proportionality test, even if employed in that legal system mainly as an instrument of administrative validity,[49] constitutes a very useful starting point since it provides a fair idea of the issues that the Court may take into consideration in determining the "reasonableness" of Member States' measures. This is especially true in light of the often pragmatic, and at times confusing, approach taken by the ECJ in applying the *Dassonville–Cassis de Dijon* "rule of reason"

---

[49] N Emiliou, *The Principle of Proportionality in European Law: A Comparative Study* (London, Kluwer, 1996) at 25.

doctrine, where the activity of the Court can only be described as a form of balancing of interests with several disparate factors influencing the final outcome.[50]

Running the risk of being repetitive, the third and last point that I would like to emphasise is that the principle of proportionality, as a "trade liberalisation" or "market integration" instrument, is also employed outside the *Dassonville–Cassis de Dijon* "rule of reason" doctrine. For example, "border measures" (as well as all other "distinctly applicable measures") found to violate the prohibition of Article 28 may indeed be justified on the basis of one of the public policy exceptions listed in Article 30 if those measures comply with the proportionality principle. Likewise, a "selling arrangement" deemed to constitute de facto discrimination against imported products may also be justified on public policy grounds if it complies with the principle of proportionality. As previously noted, there is, however, a distinct difference between proportionality employed within the ambit of "distinctly applicable measures" or "selling arrangements", on the one hand, and product-related "indistinctly applicable measures", on the other. While in the two former instances the proportionality of the measure is assessed in order to justify an otherwise prohibited measure (because it constitutes a border measure or it discriminates against imported products), in the latter instance, the proportionality of the measure operates as the principal normative standard, or "primary norm". In other words, the "normative content" of the rules dealing with "distinctly applicable measures" and "selling arrangements" is either a ban on a type of inherently discriminatory measures (border measures) or a prohibition of discriminatory treatment vis-à-vis imported products. Within this context, proportionality operates as the exception for purposes of limiting the Member State's option to justify such measures on public policy grounds. On the other hand, with regard to the rule dealing with "indistinctly applicable measures" (ie the *Dassonville–Cassis de Dijon* "rule of reason" approach) proportionality *is* the "normative content" of the rule. An indistinctly applicable measure is deemed to be in breach of Article 28 (as extensively interpreted by the Court in its *Dassonville–Cassis de Dijon* jurisprudence), not simply because it is capable of hindering intra-Community trade, but principally because it does not comply with the principle of proportionality (in very simple terms, because it is *unreasonable*). Although technically the proportionality review of *distinctly* applicable measures under Article 30 involves the same type of analysis as in the proportionality assessment of *indistinctly* applicable measures under the *Dassonville–Cassis de Dijon*

---

[50] See G de Búrca, "The Principle of Proportionality and its Application in EC law", 13 *YEL* (1994) 105 at 147, and T Tridimas, *The General Principle of EC Law* (Oxford, OUP, 1999) at 124–25.

"rule of reason" doctrine (is the measure reasonably related to its objective?), the above mentioned doctrinal difference does have a certain influence in the manner in which the proportionality test is actually carried out.

E. What does Proportionality Actually Entail?

It is now time to turn to an examination of what the proportionality principle actually entails, or in other words, what are the *normative criteria* imposed by the Court on indistinctly applicable measures, applied by Member States, that are capable of hindering, directly or indirectly, actually or potentially, intra-Community trade. The following analysis of a very few of the many cases in which the Court has reviewed the reasonableness of Member States' origin-neutral regulations on the basis of its *Dassonville–Cassis de Dijon* "rule of reason" approach is not aimed at providing a comprehensive view of the application of the proportionality test in EC law. Its goal is the more limited one of offering a clearer theoretical reconstruction of the proportionality requirement with all its sub-concepts (suitability, necessity and proportionality *stricto sensu*). This in turn will hopefully allow for a useful comparison with the equivalent instruments employed in WTO law.

1. *Cassis De Dijon "Rule of Reason": "Suitability", "Necessity" and the Presumption of "Unreasonableness"*

Let us start with the very first and fundamental application of the proportionality principle by the Court of Justice. In *Cassis de Dijon*, as already noted, the Court of Justice stated that trade restrictive regulations,

> must be accepted in so far as those provisions may be recognised as being *necessary* in order to satisfy mandatory requirements relating in particular to the effectiveness of fiscal supervision, the protection of public health, the fairness of commercial transactions and the defence of the consumer.[51]

In that case, the German Government tried to defend its minimum alcohol content requirement by arguing that it had been established for the protection of public health and the protection of the consumer. The Court, however, was not convinced that such a requirement was indeed "necessary" in order to achieve either of these public policy objectives. With regard to the arguments advanced by the German Government relating to the protection of public health—eg avoiding the proliferation

---

[51] Case 120/78, [1979] ECR 649, para 8 [emphasis added].

of alcoholic beverages with low alcohol content,[52] the ECJ found that the consumer could obtain on the market an extremely wide range of weakly or moderately alcoholic products and furthermore a large proportion of alcoholic beverages with a high alcohol content freely sold on the German market is generally consumed in a diluted form.[53]

With regard to the argument based on the protection of the consumer against unfair practices, the Court stated that,

> [such protection could not be] taken so far as to regard the mandatory fixing of minimum alcohol contents as being an essential guarantee of the fairness of commercial transactions, since it is a simple matter to ensure that suitable information is conveyed to the purchaser by requiring the display of an indication of origin and of the alcohol content on the packaging of products.[54]

The Court attributed to the "necessary" requirement two distinct meanings that very much resemble the first two limbs of the proportionality principle. The ECJ rejected both public policy justifications advanced by Germany because the German measure was not an *effective* and *useful* means of achieving public health protection and because there were other means of pursuing consumer protection that were *less restrictive* compared to an outright ban. In other words, the German regulation did not comply with the "suitability test" and the "least restrictive" or "necessity test" respectively.[55]

It should be added that paragraph 14 of the Court's judgment, usually referred to as encapsulating the "principle of mutual recognition", simply clarified that the *burden of proof* lay with the importing State invoking the reasonableness of its trade-restrictive measure under review. Consequently, it may be said that once goods have been lawfully marketed in one Member State, the *presumption* is that they should be admitted into any other State without restriction, unless the State of import can successfully demonstrate that there exists a valid reason for subjecting those same goods to restrictive regulation.[56]

This is quite an important point to emphasise especially because it constitutes one of the principal differences between the *Dassonville–Cassis de Dijon* "rule of reason" approach and the "reasonableness rule" employed in the SPS and TBT Agreements. As will be examined in section 2, in both the SPS and TBT Agreements it is up to the *exporting*

---

[52] "… the purpose of the fixing of minimum alcohol contents by national legislation is to avoid the proliferation of alcoholic beverages on the national market, in particular alcoholic beverages with a low alcohol content, since, in its view, such products may more easily induce a tolerance towards alcohol than more highly alcoholic beverages." *Ibid.*, para 10.
[53] *Ibid.*, para 11.
[54] *Ibid.*, para 13.
[55] Identical issues and result in Case 788/79, *Criminal Proceedings Against Herbert Gilli and Paul Andres* [1980] ECR 2071.
[56] P Oliver, *Free Movement of Goods in the European Community*, above n 13, at 110 *et seq*.

Member to demonstrate objectively that the sanitary and phyto-sanitary measures as well as technical regulations of the *importing* Member do not conform with the reasonableness or proportionality requirements (mainly "suitability" and "necessity"). By contrast, under the *Dassonville–Cassis de Dijon* "rule of reason" approach, it is the *importing* Member that, at least in theory, is charged with the *onus* of proving the reasonableness of its "indistinctly applicable measures" that are deemed to hinder intra-Community trade.

The decision on the burden of proof was clearly a conscious choice of the European Court of Justice. As correctly noted by Oliver, Article 3 of Directive 70/50 incorporating the approach proposed by the Commission for dealing with the issue of "indistinctly applicable measures" set out a presumption that "indistinctly applicable measures" were indeed compatible with Article 28 EC. Such a presumption could have been rebutted by showing that the restrictive effects of the measure exceeded the effects intrinsic to trade rules. In other words, the Commission's approach in Directive 70/50 provided for a rebuttable presumption of "reasonableness".[57] Although the Court could have followed that same, more "conservative" approach, it decided to go the extra mile and established a rebuttable presumption of "unreasonableness" of any indistinctly applicable measure capable of hindering intra-Community trade.

Moreover, from the principle of mutual recognition established in *Cassis de Dijon*, it appears that the success of rebutting the presumption of "unreasonableness" depends on the importing Member State being able to prove that the exporting Member State's regulation is not "functionally parallel", to use Dashwood's expression, in achieving the importing Member State's desired objective. If the regulation of the exporting State is indeed functionally parallel to that of the importing State, then imposing the latter regulation would represent a violation of the proportionality principle, and in particular the necessity limb of such principle, a regulatory *duplication* being an *unnecessary* measure.[58]

2.   *French Woodworking Machines and "Functional Parallelism"*[59]

A case perfectly illustrating the application of "functional parallelism" is the *French Woodworking Machine* case,[60] where the Court had to determine

---

[57] *Ibid.*, at 89. See above in ch 2, s 2, the discussion on the Commission's official broad reading of Art 28 EC and Directive 70/50.

[58] P Craig and G de Búrca, *EU Law* (Oxford, OUP 1998) at 632.

[59] JHH Weiler, "The Constitution of the Common Marketplace: Text and Context in the Evolution of the Free Movement of Goods" in P Craig and G de Búrca (eds), *The Evolution of EU Law* (Oxford, OUP, 1999) at 365, accrediting the term to Alan Dashwood.

[60] Case 188/84, *Commission v France* [1986] ECR 419.

whether French safety requirements for woodworking machines were justified on public health grounds even if they were stricter than those prevailing in other Member States, as for example Germany. The Court carefully examined the policy objectives underlying the relevant French and German legislation. Although both rules had been adopted to further the protection of public health, the *levels of intended protection* of the two systems was clearly different. While the French rule was based on the idea that machine users must be protected from their own mistakes and that the machine must be designed as to limit the user's intervention to the absolute minimum, the German legislation was premised on the principle that the worker should receive thorough and continuing training so as to be capable of responding correctly if a machine did not function properly.

The Court recognised that while a Member State is free to require a product that has already received approval in another Member State to undergo a fresh process of examination and approval, it is not however entitled to prevent the marketing of a product originating in another Member State which provides *a level of protection* of the health and life of humans *equivalent* to that which the national rules are intended to ensure or establish. To require such imported products to comply strictly and exactly with the provisions or technical requirements laid down for products manufactured in the Member State of importation *when those imported products afford users the same level of protection* would be contrary to the principle of proportionality.[61] Nevertheless, in light of the higher level of protection which the French legislation was aiming at, and the Commission's failure to prove that imported woodworking machines (complying with German safety standards, for example) did in fact protect users equally well, the Court concluded that the French legislation was indeed justified on public health grounds and, accordingly, dismissed the Commission's claim.[62]

---

[61] *Ibid.*, para 16.

[62] The Court was also asked to review whether the French authorisation procedures violated EC law. "The Commission claims that the periods between the dates of the publication of the decrees and orders laying down the new rules and the dates on which certificates or approval became compulsory were too short. In many cases the French authorities were unable to process in sufficient time the documents submitted to them in support of applications for certificates or approval. Thus, for instance, it proved impossible to deliver by 1 March 1982 any of the certificates requested for surfacing machines although 125 applications had been submitted." *Ibid.*, para 24. The Court noted that "frequent and substantial delays on the part of the supervisory authorities in processing applications for certificates or approval may make importation more difficult and more costly and, accordingly, such delays may constitute measures having an effect equivalent to quantitative restrictions within the meaning of Art 30 of the Treaty." *Ibid.*, para 26. However, it dismissed the Commission's second complaint by stressing the lack of any discrimination between domestic and foreign goods: "[I]t appears from the documents before the Court that the delays affected the applications submitted by French manufacturers as well as those submitted by manufacturers from other Member States. There is no evidence to suggest that the French authorities gave priority to applications from French manufacturers." *Ibid.*, para 27.

It seems that as part of the inquiry into proportionality, the Court needs to determine whether the stricter national regulatory requirements of the importing State are really *necessary* in light of the parallel requirements imposed by the exporting State. In order to assess the necessity of the stricter legislation, the Court must first of all establish whether the public policy objectives underlying the two regulations are really equivalent or not. In this calculation, the Court must take into account not just their general purpose (for example, the protection of public health), but also the specific level and nature of protection of public health aimed at by each national legislation. If the general objectives and levels of protection at issue are indeed equivalent, then for the importing Member State to require a second authorisation in addition to that imposed by the exporting Member State would constitute a clearly *unnecessary duplication* of requirements in breach of the principle of proportionality.[63] Where the objectives or levels of protection of the respective legislation are *not* equivalent and the requirements of the exporting Member State do not in practice guarantee an equivalent level of protection, then, as in the instant case, the imposition by the importing State of a second set of safety requirements complies with the principle of proportionality, and in particular with its necessity limb.

No clear mention is made in the judgment under review of either the "suitability" or the "proportionality *stricto sensu*" of the French safety requirements. With regard to the former, the suitability of the French safety legislation was, in a way, implied in the parties' arguments. Moreover, not even the Commission raised the issue. In this respect, it should be noted that the three normative criteria constituting the proportionality principle are like the famous Russian dolls, where the smaller doll fits in the bigger doll. If a measure is deemed to be "necessary" or the "least restrictive" alternative to achieve a certain objective, it is also implicit in such a finding that that same measure is also "suitable". Similarly, a finding that a measure complies with the "proportionality *stricto sensu*" test should be understood as also complying with both the "suitability" and "necessity" criteria. Clearly, the opposite is not true.

---

[63] For two examples of dual-burden rules see Case C–293/93, *Ludomira Neeltje v Barbara Houtwipper* [1994] ECR I–429, where a national requirement concerning the hallmarking of precious metal had to take into account the "equivalent" requirement imposed by another State, even if it differed in its details; and Case 27/80, *Fietje* [1980] ECR 3839, where a labelling requirement which required the purchaser to be provided with sufficient information on the nature of the product, in order to prevent confusion with similar products, could be justified on the grounds of consumer protection only if the original label contained the same information required by the State of import.

It should be noted that even in the case where the general objectives and levels of protection are indeed equivalent, there may be other legitimate reasons for the apparent duplication. For example, if the authorisation authorities in the exporting country are not reliable or competent, then the importing country may require the product to undergo a second authorisation without this constituting an unnecessary duplication.

It is more difficult to explain rationally why the Court did not take into consideration whether the restrictive effects on intra-Community trade of the French requirements could be deemed to be *disproportionate* to the public safety benefits gained from such requirements (the proportionality *stricto sensu* test). By not even considering the issue, it appears that the Court was not really willing to strike down a national measure aimed at the protection of public health and safety only on the basis of its disproportionately restrictive effects on intra-Community trade.[64] It would thus appear that the Court shows a certain self-restraint in balancing the public policy benefits of national regulation vis-à-vis their adverse effects on intra-Community trade. As recently noted by Jans, "though the Court will not rule out a genuine balancing of interests in the context of a proportionality test, as a general rule it will not carry out such a test."[65]

3. Danish Bottles and "Proportionality Stricto Sensu"

One of the very few cases where the test of proportionality *stricto sensu* was *explicitly* applied by the ECJ in reviewing the validity of a Member State's indistinctly applicable measure is *Commission v Denmark*, more commonly known as the *Danish Bottles* case.[66] Under scrutiny, in that instance, was a Danish system requiring that all containers for beer and soft drinks be returnable. As spelled out by the Court, the main features of the challenged system were the following: (a) manufacturers could market beer and soft drinks only in re-usable containers; (b) the containers had to be approved by the National Agency for the Protection of the Environment;[67] and (c) an exception was envisaged that allowed a

---

[64] See the Court's following statements: "It should be noted in the first place that there are no Community rules governing the safety of woodworking machines and that the national laws on the matter have not been harmonised. *Consequently the Member States are entitled to introduce rules for the protection of the health and life of users of those machines.* Such rules fall within the scope of Art 30 *et seq.* [now 28–30] of the Treaty if, as in this case, they impede directly and actually the importation of machines which are lawfully in free circulation in another Member State. The Court has consistently held that under Art 36 [now 30] such national rules are compatible with the Treaty only to the extent to which they are necessary for the effective protection of the health and life of humans. *Although it is for the Member States to decide what degree of that protection they intend to ensure,* that protection must not constitute a means of arbitrary discrimination or a disguised restriction on trade between Member States." *Ibid.,* paras 13–15 [emphasis added].
[65] J Jans, "Proportionality Revisited", 27 *Legal Issues of Economic Integration* (2000) 239 at 248.
[66] Case 302/86, [1988] ECR 4607.
[67] The Agency could refuse approval of new kinds of container, especially if it considered that a container was not technically suitable for a system for returning containers or that the return system envisaged did not ensure that a sufficient proportion of containers were actually re-used or if a container of equal capacity, which were both available and suitable for the same use, had already been approved. *Ibid.,* para 2.

producer to market up to 3,000 hectolitres a year in non-approved containers, provided that such a deposit-and-return system was established.

Since it clearly restricted intra-Community trade, the Danish system fell within the net of Article 28 and was consequently subject to a proportionality review. The Danish Government argued in this respect that its system was justified on the basis of environmental protection, which the Court had already recognised as "one of the Community's essential objectives"[68] and thus one of the "mandatory requirements" for purposes of the *Dassonville–Cassis de Dijon* doctrine. Although it accepted that the protection of environment was a mandatory requirement which may limit the application of Article 28, the Court was not altogether convinced about the general proportionality of certain features of the Danish system under review.

While the Court found that the obligation to establish a deposit-and-return system for empty containers was indeed "an indispensable element of a system intended to ensure the re-use of containers" and as such it appeared "necessary to achieve the aims pursued by the contested rules",[69] the Court struck down the requirement to use approved containers (over and above the 3,000 hectolitre limit) because the restrictive effects on trade were *disproportionate* to the objective pursued.[70] In this latter regard, the Court stated as follows:

20. It is undoubtedly true that the existing system for returning approved containers *ensures a maximum rate of re-use* and therefore a very considerable degree of protection of the environment since empty containers can be returned to any retailer of beverages. Non-approved containers, on the other hand, can be returned only to the retailer who sold the beverages, since it is impossible to set up such a comprehensive system for those containers as well.

21. Nevertheless, the system for returning non-approved containers *is capable of protecting the environment* and, as far as imports are concerned, *affects only limited quantities of beverages* compared with the quantity of beverages consumed in Denmark owing to the restrictive effect which the requirement that containers should be returnable has on imports. In those circumstances, a restriction of the quantity of

---

[68] Case 240/83, *Procureur de la République v Association de Défense des Brûleurs d'Huiles Usagées* [1985] ECR 531.

[69] Case 302/86, *Danish Bottles* [1988] ECR 4607, para 13.

[70] It should be noted that the Danish government stated that for practical reasons its deposit-and-return system would not work if the number of approved containers were to exceed 30 or so, since the retailers taking part in the system would not be prepared to accept too many types of bottles owing to the higher handling costs and the need for more storage space. For that reason the Agency had followed the practice of ensuring that fresh approvals were normally accompanied by the withdrawal of existing approvals. *Ibid.*, para 15.

products which may be marketed by importers is *disproportionate to the objective pursued.* [emphasis added][71]

Although the Court might have employed clearer language,[72] it is evident that in these two paragraphs the Court was not really concerned with the "suitability" or "necessity" of the Danish measure, but rather with its "proportionality *stricto sensu*". The underlying issue was whether the (high) level of environmental protection guaranteed by the Danish measure was indeed proportionate to the severe negative effects that that same measure had on intra-Community trade. As noted by Scott,

> having regard to the limited quantity of imported beverages sold, or likely to be sold, in Denmark, the additional degree of environmental protection ensured by this measure was, in practice, marginal. Balancing the intensity of the restriction against the intensity of the benefit, the Court found that the measure was "disproportionate to the objective pursued".[73]

In more practical terms, reviewing the proportionality *stricto sensu* of the Danish system involved an inquiry into whether the specific level of environmental protection pursued by the national system was indeed excessive or disproportionate in light of the adverse effects that such a system had on intra-Community trade.[74] In the words of the Advocate-General Slynn,

> the level of protection required for one of the [mandatory requirements] must not, as I see it, be *excessive* or *unreasonable* and the measures taken to achieve the requirement must be necessary and proportional.[75]

---

[71] *Ibid.*, paras 20–21.
[72] The disproportion is between the trade restrictive effects and the public policy gains of a given measure; or, in other words, between the chosen level of public policy protection and the principle of free movement of goods.
[73] J Scott, *EC Environmental Law* (London, Longman 1998) at 69–70. Cf D French, "The Changing Nature of 'Environmental Protection': Recent Developments Regarding Trade and the Environment in the European Union and the World Trade Organisation", 47 *Netherlands International Law Review* (2000) 1.
[74] J Jans, "Proportionality Revisited", 27 *Legal Issues of Economic Integration* (2000) 239 at 250.
[75] Opinion of Advocate-General Sir Gordon Slynn in Case 302/86, *Danish Bottles* [1988] ECR 4607, delivered on 24 May 1988: "I also accept that it may be difficult by other methods to achieve the same high standard. Yet it does not seem to me that Denmark must succeed in this application unless the Commission can show that the same standard can be achieved by other specified means. There has to be a balancing of interests between the free movement of goods and environmental protection, even if in achieving the balance the high standard of the protection sought has to be reduced. The level of protection sought must be a reasonable level: I am not satisfied that the various methods outlined in the Council directive and referred to at the hearing—selective collection by governmental authorities or private industry, a voluntary deposit system, penalties for litter, education of the public as to waste

If there is no doubt that the Danish obligation to use approved containers was found not to be "reasonable" in the meaning of the *Dassonville–Cassis de Dijon* jurisprudence because it was "disproportionate" in the narrow sense, it is not altogether clear why the other obligation under review in that case (to establish a deposit-and-return system) was only subjected to the less intensive "necessity test".[76] The Court clearly noted in the above cited paragraphs that the deposit-and-return system had a grave restrictive effect on imports ("only limited quantities of [imported] beverages [...] owing to the restrictive effect which the requirement that containers should be returnable has on imports"). Nevertheless, the Court did not assess whether this effect was excessive or disproportionate in light of the measure's benefit for the environment. Should this conduct be taken as an implicit finding that this latter obligation was indeed proportionate even in the stricter sense?

Moreover, the Court's reasoning in *Danish Bottles* is blurred by the use of inconsistent terminology, and in particular by a failure clearly to distinguish between the concepts of proportionality *lato sensu* and proportionality *stricto sensu*. This may be noted, for example, in the Court's examination of the obligation to establish a deposit-and-return system, where the Court employed the term "proportionate" without clearly distinguishing whether it was using it in the strict or broad sense. The Court stated that,

> it must be observed that this [deposit-and-return] requirement is an *indispensable* element of a system intended to ensure the re-use of containers and therefore appears *necessary* to achieve the aims pursued by the contested rules. That being so, the restrictions which it imposes on the free movement of goods cannot be regarded as *disproportionate.*[77]

In light of the reference to terms such as "indispensable" and "necessary", it may be argued that in this context the Court's use of the concept of

---

disposal—are incapable of achieving a reasonable standard which impinges less on the provisions of Art 30. Accordingly, in my view, the Commission is entitled to the declaration it seeks and to its costs of these proceedings."

The AG is not criticising the "suitability" or "necessity" of the measure, but the level of protection which the Danish measure is aimed at. That level of protection is unreasonable, ie disproportionate, or in other words, the burden on the freedom of movement are excessive in comparison with the benefits of the measure. Cf Scott, *EC Environmental Law* (London, Longman, 1998) at 69–70, and M Montini, "The Nature and Function of the Necessity and Proportionality Principles in the Trade and Environment Context", 6 *RECIEL* (1997) 121 at 126–27.

[76] Cf D Geradin, "Trade and Environmental Protection: Community Harmonization and National Environmental Standards" 13 *YEL* (1993) 151, where the author also notes that the Court's analysis with regard to the proportionality of the Danish legislation "lacks clarity". *Ibid.*, at 157.

[77] Case 302/86, *Danish Bottles* [1988] ECR 4607, para 13 [emphasis added].

"proportionality" should be interpreted as referring to proportionality in the broad sense.

In any case, one can easily perceive the difference between the approach followed in the *Danish Bottles* case and that in the previous *French Woodworking Machines* case, where the Court did not examine at all whether the level of safety protection underlying the French legislation on woodworking machines was in any way out of proportion or unreasonable in light of the adverse effect on intra-Community trade. In the *Danish Bottles* case, on the contrary, the Court was (at least to a certain extent) ready to review the Danish Government's public policy choice itself in finding the level of environmental protection excessive and disproportionate, and consequently in striking down the national measure as incompatible with Community law.

Although it is not easy to determine the reason for the different approach followed in the two above mentioned cases, one plausible explanation (if an explanation needs to be found) may relate to the different nature of the public policy objectives underlying the safety regulation in the *French Woodworking Machines* case and the environmental policy in the *Danish Bottles* case. Possibly, the Court recognises a wider margin of discretion to Member States with regard to public safety regulation than for environmental protection laws, connected with the division of labour between the Community and the Member States themselves.[78]

4.   *"Necessity" or "Proportionality Stricto Sensu"? The Issue of the "Level of Protection"*

A confirmation of such a different approach based on the public policy ground justifying the measure can be seen in the Court's case law with regard to consumer protection legislation.[79] It is very difficult to find a

---

[78] J Jans, "Proportionality Revisited", 27 *Legal Issues of Economic Integration* (2000) 239, citing both goods and services cases where the Court showed unusual "self-restraint in the application of the proportionality principle": Case C–124/97, *Läärä* [1999] ECR I–6067 (regulating the passion for gambling, avoiding gambling-related crime); Case C–83/94 *Leifer* [1995] ECR I-3231 (foreign policy defense); Case C–394/97, *Heinonen* [1999] ECR I–3599 (public order connected with the consumption of alcohol). The explanation advanced by the author is that "the grounds put forward in justification of the measure […] do not as such constitute policy areas in which the Community could take regulatory action." *Ibid.*, at 250.

[79] For cases where the Court held that the national measure was not justified on consumer protection grounds, see Case 178/84, *Commission v Germany* (*German Purity Beer*) [1987] ECR 1227, where a German law required that "Bier" be made from barley, hops, yeast and water on the ground of consumer protection, while in other States beer could be made from other substances; Case 94/82, *De Kikvorsch Groothandel-Import-Export BV* [1983] ECR 947, where a Dutch law required that beer have a certain level of acidity usually exceeded by German beer; Case C–315/92, *Verband Sozialer Wettbewerb e V v Clinique Laboratoires SNC* [1994] ECR I–317, where a German law requiring that cosmetic products could not be sold with the name "Clinique" on the ground that it was to protect consumers from being misled into believing that the product had medicinal properties was not justified because there was no risk of consumer confusion. Cfr. Case C–293/93, *Ludomira Neeltje v Barbara Houtwipper* [1994]

case where the Court has relied upon consumer protection as a justification for an indistinctly applicable measure falling within the *Dassonville* formula.[80] Usually the Court appears to fail national measures taken for consumer protection because they violate the "least restrictive" test of the proportionality principle, suggesting for example that a labelling requirement can equally reach the same objective.[81]

Upon closer examination, however, many of these findings appear to be based at least in part on an implicit belief that these regulations excessively or disproportionately restrict intra-Community trade. In many of the consumer protection cases, the Court has implicitly or expressly disregarded the different levels of consumer protection which a Member State had decided to pursue in a manner that differs from the approach followed, for example, in the case of the French safety legislation, where the Court did distinguish between differing degrees of safety protection.[82] In *Cassis de Dijon*, for example, the Court found that the objective of the German Government to ensure that consumers be not misled into buying a liqueur, believing it to have a higher alcoholic content, could be achieved by a measure less restrictive than an outright ban, namely by requiring the product to carry a label displaying its alcoholic content. It has been noted that,

> what, in effect, the Court decides in *Cassis* is that the German policy of zero-tolerance to any consumer confusion does not override the societal interest in free movement of goods.[83]

In other words, by disregarding the differing levels of protection underlying the two national requirements, the Court made it almost certain that the

ECR I–429; and Case 27/80, *Fietje* [1980] ECR 3839. For a recent in-depth analysis of consumer protection cases see S Weatherill, "Recent Case Law concerning the Free Movement of Goods: Mapping the Frontiers of Market Deregulation", 36 *CMLRev* (1999) 51.

[80] One of the few cases where a national consumer protection measure was indeed found "reasonable" is Case 286/81, *Oosthoek's Uitgeversmaatschappij BV* [1982] ECR 4575. Reviewing a Dutch law strictly controlling the offer for sales promotion purposes of 'free gifts' to buyers of encyclopaedias, the Court found the measure justified on the grounds of consumer protection and fair trading, since free gifts might mislead the consumer about the real price of goods. S Weatherill and P Beaumont, *EC Law* (London, Penguin Books 1995) at 512.

[81] Beginning with *Cassis de Dijon* there are several examples of this type of case: Case 193/80, *Commission v Italy (Italian Vinegar)* [1981] ECR 3019; Case 261/81, *Rau v de Smedt (Margarine)* [1982] ECR 3961; Case 178/84, *Commission v Germany (German Purity Beer)* [1987] ECR 1227. Cf T Tridimas, *The General Principles of EC Law* (Oxford, OUP, 1999) at 137–38.

[82] See J Jans, "Proportionality Revisited", 27 *Legal Issues of Economic Integration* (2000) 239 at 252, who argues that in cases concerning consumer protection and misleading advertising "it is clearly the Court which ultimately establishes the level of protection in the Community. Higher levels of consumer protection in the Member States will be deemed to be contrary to the proportionality principle."

[83] JHH Weiler, "The Constitution of the Common Marketplace: Text and Context in the Evolution of the Free Movement of Goods", in P Craig and G de Búrca (eds), *The Evolution of EU Law* (Oxford, OUP, 1999) at 368.

stricter German rules were "unnecessary" or "not least-restrictive" because the (lower) consumer protection could indeed be achieved with a less restrictive measure, a labelling requirement for example.

Following this reasoning, it appears evident that in *Cassis de Dijon* (as in several other instances) the Court reviewed the German ban through the lens of the principle of proportionality *stricto sensu*, ie by balancing the trade-restrictive effects of the measure with its public policy benefits. By not taking into consideration the *level* or *degree* of consumer protection that the German measure was—or might have been—aimed at, the Court *indirectly* hinted that a high level of protection (zero consumer confusion) was disproportionate vis-à-vis the adverse effects of such high level of protection on intra-Community trade. In other words, the Court seems to influence the application and the final outcome of the proportionality inquiry depending on its willingness to take into account the specific (level of) public policy protection pursued by the Member State through the particular measure under review. Seen in this light, then, what may appear to be a review of the "necessity" or "least-restrictiveness" of a measure in reality becomes an assessment "in disguise" of its proportionality *stricto sensu*.[84]

Without negating the above mentioned self-restraint shown by the Court in subjecting equally applicable measures to the full potential of the proportionality review, there appear to be cases even outside the ambit of consumer legislation, where the Court carries out a balancing exercise *à la* proportionality *stricto sensu* without really appearing to do so.

Take for example the *Sandoz* case,[85] where the Court was faced with the question of whether a Dutch law prohibiting the addition of vitamins to food without government authorisation was proportionate to the protection of public health.[86] Noting scientific uncertainties with regard to the health risks of excessive consumption of vitamins over a prolonged period, and the difficulty in foreseeing or monitoring the quantities of vitamins consumed, the Court recognised the wide discretion to be left to the Member States, in particular with regard to the *degree of protection* of the health and life of humans they intend to assure. However, while national rules prohibiting, without prior authorisation, the marketing of foodstuffs to which vitamins have been added *are justifiable in principle* on the grounds of the protection of human health, proportionality still requires that the power of the Member States to prohibit imports from other

---

[84] J Jans, "Proportionality Revisited", 27 *Legal Issues of Economic Integration* (2000) 239 at 249, noting that "the question 'who decides the level of protection' is one that goes to the heart of the proportionality principle."

[85] Case 174/82, *Sandoz BV* [1983] ECR 2445.

[86] Sandoz was denied authorisation to import "muesli" bars and beverages, health foods containing Vitamins A and D, from Germany and Belgium, where they were lawfully marketed.

Member States be restricted to what is *necessary* to attain the legitimate aim of protecting health.[87] The Court noted that, in light of the above-mentioned scientific uncertainties and lack of relevant data, it was difficult to assess whether the marketing of the contested products was "compatible" with the need to protect health and thus concluded with the following general finding: in order to observe the principle of proportionality, Member States must authorise marketing when the addition of vitamins to foodstuffs meets a real need, especially a technical or nutritional one.[88]

Besides the inherent vagueness of the reference to "a real need, especially a technical or nutritional one", the standard under which the Court reviewed the Dutch measure is not altogether clear. On the one hand, the Court seems to suggest a sort of balancing exercise between the need to protect public health and the need to add vitamins to foodstuffs, which is structurally similar to the balancing that goes on under the test of proportionality *stricto sensu*: if the need to add vitamins is "real", in particular "technical or nutritional", then the importing Member State should authorise the marketing of the relevant products, notwithstanding possible harmful effects on human health and life. On the other hand, however, the Court does not take into account as part of such a balancing the restrictive effects on intra-Community trade, which is usually the case under the test of proportionality *stricto sensu*.[89] In a way, the *Sandoz* decision seems to suggest that the Court's aim was not simply to protect intra-Community trade as such, but rather to safeguard the more general freedom of trade in the broader sense.

Whatever type of balancing exercise the Court carried out in *Sandoz*, it appears that the type of review suggested in that case is capable of cutting quite deep into the regulatory prerogatives of the Member States. By finding that the public health risks considered in the Dutch measure do not "qualify" for the type of protection envisioned in that measure, the Court is in practice arrogating to itself (or allocating to national courts) the prerogative to determine the legitimate level of health protection under Community law. There appears to be a certain contradiction between this type of review and the Court's statements regarding the "wide margin of discretion left to the Member States". Moreover, where scientific data is either missing or uncertain, the Court seems to prefer "trade" (and thus "deregulation") to "health protection" (and thus Member States' regulation).[90]

---

[87] *Ibid.*, paras 17–18.
[88] *Ibid.*, paras 19–20.
[89] J Jans, "Proportionality Revisited", 27 *Legal Issues of Economic Integration* (2000) 239 at 252.
[90] In any event, it appears, from the judgment itself, that the Court was once again unwilling to decide the sensitive issue at hand and left the national court with the task of operating the balancing exercise and determining whether in this case the addition of vitamins met a "real need".

There seems to be a tendency in the Court's application of the proportionality principle to hide a finding of unreasonableness, which is based on the excessive or disproportionate effects of a measure on intra-Community trade. The Court appears to be conscious of the sensitivity of striking down a Member State's regulation on the basis of the test of pro-portionality *stricto sensu*. This is indirectly confirmed by cases where the Court more openly carried out a full proportionality review (including the proportionality *stricto sensu* limb) and found that the national meas-ure under review was indeed "reasonable".

Take, for example, the *Aragonesa* case,[91] where the Court was faced in *pre-Keck* times with a law enacted by the Parliament of a Spanish autonomous community (Catalonia) prohibiting, within the territory under its jurisdiction, the advertising of beverages having an alcoholic strength of more than 23 degrees in (a) the mass media, (b) streets and highways, with the exception of signs indicating centres of production and sale, (c) cinemas, and (d) public transport. Having determined that the Spanish law was capable of hindering imports from other Member States within the meaning of the *Dassonville* formula,[92] the Court exam-ined whether it was of such a nature as to protect public health and whether it was proportionate to the objective to be attained. With regard to the first point, the Court stated that it was sufficient to observe that advertising acts as an encouragement to consumption and the existence of rules restricting the advertising of alcoholic beverages in order to combat alcoholism "reflects" public health concerns.[93] The Court thus implicitly found, albeit in a very loose manner, that the advertising restriction was *suitable* to protect public health.

On the latter point, the Court emphasised that in the absence of any common or harmonised rules governing in a general manner the adver-tising of alcoholic beverages, it was for the Member States to decide (a) on the *degree of protection* which they wish to afford to public health and (b) on the *way* on which that protection is to be achieved. The Court, how-ever, subjected these prerogatives to the limits set by the Treaty and, in particular, to the principle of proportionality.[94] The Court noted that the national measure at issue restricted freedom of trade *only to a limited extent*, since it concerned only beverages having an alcoholic strength of more than 23 degrees,[95] and prohibited *only* advertising of such bever-ages in *specified* places some of which, such as public highways and

---

[91] Joined Cases C–1 and 176/90, *Aragonesa de Publicidad v Departamento de Sanidad* [1991] ECR I–4151.
[92] *Ibid.*, para 11.
[93] *Ibid.*, para 15.
[94] *Ibid.*, para 16.
[95] *Ibid.*, para 17. "In principle, the latter criterion does not appear to be manifestly unreason-able as part of a campaign against alcoholism."

cinemas, were particularly frequented by motorists and young persons (two categories of the population in regard to which the campaign against alcoholism was of quite special importance). On this basis, it concluded that the Spanish measure could not in any event "be criticised for being disproportionate to its stated objective."[96]

In *Aragonesa*, the Court's application of the proportionality review was clearly more straightforward than in *Sandoz*. Given the lack of harmonisation in the particular area at issue, the Court stressed the Member States' prerogative of deciding both the degree of public health protection and the manner in which such protection should be pursued, subject only to the requirements of proportionality. However, the Court was apparently satisfied with conditioning the exercise of such a prerogative on one fundamental requirement: that the restriction not be disproportionate to the stated objective, or more clearly, that the restrictive effects of a measure on trade not be out of proportion to its benefits to public health (ie the classic test of proportionality in the strict sense). The scope of the Spanish prohibition was so limited that the Court refused to consider the measure in breach of the proportionality *stricto sensu* standard.[97]

Thus, looking at the approach taken by the Court in these two cases, while the proportionality assessment in *Aragonesa* is characterised by a certain explicitness in employing arguments pertaining to the measure's proportionality *stricto sensu*, in *Sandoz* a similar balancing exercise is somehow carried out in disguise. It is not enough to distinguish the two cases by pointing to what the Court did a couple of years later in *Keck*, subjecting selling arrangements (such as those at issue in *Aragonesa*) to the milder discrimination-based approach. As previously noted, the difference in the two mentioned cases focuses on the manner in which the assessment of proportionality in the strict sense is carried out and appears to do with the Court's reluctance to strike down national measures on the basis of such a delicate balancing. Moreover, although both measures had been taken to protect public health, the different, more confused, approach in *Sandoz* may perhaps also be explained by the scientific uncertainty with which the Court was faced in that case. In *Aragonesa*, on the other hand, there was no issue concerning the basic scientific soundness of the relationship between restricting the advertisement of alcoholic beverages and the protection of public health. This difference might even explain the fact that only in *Sandoz* was the actual proportionality assessment eventually entrusted to the national court.

---

[96] *Ibid.*, para 18.
[97] The Court then went on to determine whether the advertising ban constituted arbitrary discrimination or a disguised restriction pursuant to the second sentence of Art 30. It excluded the existence of such discrimination or restriction exclusively because the measure was neither formally nor materially discriminatory. *Ibid.*, para 25.

Now, taking for granted that in both above mentioned cases the Court did subject a national measure adopted in the pursuit of sensitive public policy objectives to a fully-fledged proportionality review (including an inquiry into the proportionality of the level of protection chosen by the Member State), what could be the real reason for the different results reached by the Court with regard to the Spanish and Dutch legislation? Once again, if an explanation needs to be given, I would suggest comparing the relative restrictive nature of the two public health rules at issue in *Aragonesa* and *Sandoz*. While in the former case the advertising restriction could be said to have had only minimal adverse effects on intra-Community trade, in the latter case, the absolute ban on import of products containing certain additives constituted a clearly higher obstacle to free movement.[98]

In sum, notwithstanding the nature of the public interest pursued by the Member State, the Court will permit this latter type of measures only in exceptional circumstances.[99] As clearly stated by de Búrca,

> what determines the degree of scrutiny to which the Court will subject a State measure is not solely the kind of national interest invoked, but also the nature of the individual's Community right or interest and the degree to which it has been affected by that measure. The more severe the impact on the Community interest or aim, the lower the degree of deference to the national measure which the Court will display, even if the nature of the State's justification for that measure is one which would generally lead the Court to represent the State's assessment of necessity.[100]

The Court's tendency to limit the intensity of its proportionality review and thus "save" national measures with only minimally adverse effects on intra-Community trade may be noted in other pre-*Keck* cases dealing with "selling arrangements".

For example, in the *Cinéthèque* case,[101] at issue was whether a French law banning the sale or hire of videos of films during the first year in which the film was released complied with the *Dassonville–Cassis de Dijon* "rule of reason" doctrine. Although the Court held that the French law

[98] Cf the Court's decision in *Keck*, distinguishing between selling arrangements and product standards, above in ch 3.

[99] See Case C–131/93, *Commission v Germany* [1994] ECR I–3303. A German ban on imports of live European freshwater crayfish from Member States or from non-Member countries in free circulation in other Member States, in order to prevent the risks of crayfish plague and faunal distortion, failed the principle of proportionality because the German Government could have *adopted less restrictive measures*, such as submitting consignments of imported crayfish to health checks and only carrying out checks by sample if such consignments were accompanied by a health certificate, or confining itself to regulating the marketing of crayfish in its territory.

[100] G de Búrca, "The Principle of Proportionality and its Application in EC Law", 13 *YEL* (1994) 105 at 126.

[101] See Joined Cases 60 and 61/84, *Cinéthèque SA v Fédérationn Nationale des Cinémas Francais* [1985] ECR 2605.

restricted trade in the meaning of the *Dassonville* formula, it saved the law by arguing that the (temporary) ban was justified by the need to protect or enhance artistic works, a "mandatory requirement" pursuant to the *Cassis de Dijon* jurisprudence.

Interestingly enough, the ECJ did not bother to review the measure in terms of the three limbs of the proportionality test or the requirements of the second sentence of Article 30. It merely stated that,

> it must be conceded that a national system which, in order to encourage the creation of cinematographic works irrespective of their origin, gives priority, for a limited initial period, to the distribution of such works through the cinema, is so justified.[102]

This sentence reveals the grounds for the Court's finding of reasonableness. First of all, as noted above, the restrictive effects on the free circulation of goods is temporarily "limited" to a specific period. Moreover, the fact that the French system did not discriminate, in law or in fact,[103] between imported and domestic products also made it easier for the Court to consider the measure justified on public policy grounds.[104]

A further example of the Court's treatment of equally applicable measures falling within the category of "selling arrangements" is the so-called *Sunday Trading* saga. In *Torfaen*,[105] for example, B & Q was prosecuted for violation of the UK Sunday trading laws that prohibited retail shops from selling on Sundays, subject to exceptions for certain types of products. B & Q claimed that these laws constituted a violation of Article 28, since the effect of the laws was to reduce total turnover by about 10 per cent, with a corresponding diminution of imports from other Member States. Although imported goods were in no worse a position than domestic goods, since the reduction in sales would affect all goods indistinctly, the ECJ stated that such rules were caught by Article 28 as interpreted by the Court in its *Dassonville–Cassis de Dijon* jurisprudence. The Court emphasised that the Sunday trading laws reflected certain political and economic policy choices with regard to the working and non-working hours, and noted that, in the present state of Community law, although such rules were a matter for the Member States, "it is necessary to ascertain whether the effects of such national rules exceed what is

---

[102] *Ibid.*, para 23.
[103] The Court determined that the French system did not encourage the creation of domestic cinematographic works more than it did foreign ones, clearly excluding not just formal but also material discrimination.
[104] See T Tridimas, *The General Principles of EC Law*, at 140, "*Cinéthèque* and, more recently, *Alpine Investments* show that the wider the Court understands the scope of fundamental freedoms the less vigorously it is prepared to apply proportionality. Viewed in that light, a soft proportionality test is the *quid pro quo* for extending the scope of free movement."
[105] Case 145/88, *Torfaen BC v B & Q plc* [1989] ECR 3851.

necessary to achieve the aim in view."[106] Citing Article 3 of Commission Directive 70/50/EEC of 22 December 1969, the Court clarified that the prohibition laid down in Article 28 covered national measures governing the marketing of products where the restrictive effect of such measures on the free movement of goods "exceeds the effects intrinsic to trade rules". The Court once again avoided answering the question, adding that the determination of whether the effects of specific national rules do in fact remain within that limit is a question of fact to be determined by the national court.[107]

As a parenthesis, the reference to Article 3 of Commission Directive 70/50 is interesting in that Article 3 contains one, if not the first, clear elaboration of the proportionality principle with regard to its market integration function. As examined in the second chapter, just a few years prior to *Dassonville* with the aim of clarifying the meaning of the phrase "measures having equivalent effect" of Article 28, the Commission had established a different regime depending on whether the national measure was (formally) "discriminatory" or (facially) "equally applicable". Article 3 of Directive 70/50 prohibited this latter type of measures (governing the marketing of products which deal in particular with shape, size, weight, composition, presentation, identification or putting up) only "where the restrictive effect of such measures on the free movement of goods *exceeds the effects intrinsic to trade rules.*" Paragraph 2 of Article 3, then, specified that this condition would be found, in particular, where "the restrictive effects on the free movement of goods are *out of proportion* to their purpose; [or] the same objective can be attained by other means which are *less of a hindrance* to trade."[108] Although the concepts of "effects intrinsic to trade rules", "proportionality *stricto sensu*" and "less-restrictive means" were employed in Directive 70/50 to define the normative content of Article 28 with regard to product standards (measures dealing in particular with shape, size, weight, etc.), it is unsurprising that those exact concepts have been employed by the ECJ in reviewing the validity of any type of national measures including "selling arrangements" (at least up to *Keck*).

In any event, since the judgment in *Torfaen* failed to give adequate guidance to national courts, the ECJ was forced to take up again the controversy and solve the issue of whether Sunday trading laws complied

---

[106] *Ibid.*, para 14.

[107] *Ibid.*, para 16.

[108] Even though the Commission could not give a broad interpretation to the phrase "measures having equivalent effect" of Art 28 as including equally applicable measures, it nevertheless recognised in the preamble that "such measures may have a restrictive effect on the free movement of goods over and above that which is intrinsic to such rules," and accordingly urged the Member States to take all necessary steps to abolish them. Commission Directive 70/50, above n 21, Art 4.

with the proportionality principle. That is what the Court of Justice did in a few subsequent judgments, where those laws were finally found to be proportionate and lawful.[109] It is interesting, however, to note that the proportionality review performed by the Court in these later judgments never took up more than a few lines, and thus cannot even be referred to as a proper reviewing exercise. For example, in *Conforama*,[110] the Court noted first of all that it was for the Member States to regulate the employment of staff on Sundays in the furniture retailing sector and then added, with notable brevity, with regard to the proportionality of the measure that "the restrictive effects on trade which may stem from such rules do not seem disproportionate to the aim pursued."[111] Looking *ex-post facto* at the Court's willingness to perform a proportionality review of selling arrangements in these judgments, one might be tempted to say that the change in the Court's jurisprudence that took place only a year later in *Keck* did not come as a big surprise.

In conclusion, two brief observations deserve to be made with regard to the Court's pre-*Keck* jurisprudence dealing with selling arrangements. First, the review of proportionality is carried out with differing degrees of scrutiny, making proportionality a very flexible legal tool. Secondly, there appears to be a clear relation between the willingness to perform a thorough proportionality review of national measures and the potentially damaging effect of such measures on the building of the internal market.

5. Article 30, Second Sentence, EC: Substantive and Procedural Review?

There is a further issue that needs to be addressed in connection with the application of the proportionality test, particularly in the area of the free movement of goods: the function of the second sentence of Article 30 within the *Dassonville–Cassis de Dijon* "rule of reason" doctrine.

After providing that Articles 28 and 29 shall not preclude prohibitions or restrictions "justified on" certain public policy grounds, Article 30 affirms, in its second sentence, that "such prohibitions or restrictions shall not, however, constitute a means of arbitrary discrimination or a disguised restriction on trade between Member States." As noted throughout this study,[112] the Court has never been very clear on the real meaning of the requirements of Article 30, second sentence, and in particular in its

---

[109] Joined Cases C–306/88, 304/90, and 169/91, *Stoke-on-Trent CC v B&Q plc* [1992] ECR I–6457, 6493, 6635. See also Case C–312/89, *Union Département des Syndicats CGT de l'Aisne v SIDEF Conforama* [1991] ECR I–997; Case C–332/89, *Ministère Public v Marchandise* [1991] ECR I–1027.

[110] Case C–312/89, *Union Département des Syndicats CGT de l'Aisne v SIDEF Conforama* [1991] ECR I–997.

[111] *Ibid.*, para 12.

[112] See above the sections discussing the "justification options" with regard to non-pecuniary measures in chs 1–3.

relation to Article 30, first sentence, giving preference in practice to a very "unstructured" approach to the issue of public policy justification under Article 30. Notwithstanding the lack of "authoritative" clarity, the dominant view among scholars is that the second sentence of Article 30 has been interpreted by the Court of Justice as (one of) the legal bases of the proportionality test.[113] This reading has also been confirmed by the Court's statement that the purpose of the second sentence of Article 30 is to prevent restrictions on trade based on the grounds mentioned in the first sentence of Article 30 from being diverted from their proper purpose.[114] Although Article 30 does not contain any explicit reference to either a "necessity" or a "proportionality" requirement,[115] the principle of proportionality is indeed perceived as exercising a very similar function. By limiting the scope of application of the public policy exceptions of Article 30, the Court prevents possible abuses of such a provision and thus maintains a proper balance between multilateral liberalisation objectives and national regulatory prerogatives.

Since the Court has not always clearly distinguished between the original two-stage approach of Articles 28 and 30 (prohibition and justification) and the one-limb doctrine enunciated in *Dassonville* and *Cassis de Dijon* (rule of reason), the public policy grounds expressly listed in Article 30, as well as the requirements contained in the second sentence of Article 30,

---

[113] S Weatherill and P Beaumont, *EU Law* ((London, Penguin Books, 1995); MA Jarvis, *The Application of EC Law by National Courts—The Free Movement of Goods* (Oxford, OUP, 1998). The Court has at times expressly confirmed this. In Case 174/82, *Sandoz* [1983] ECR 2445, the ECJ stated that "the principle of proportionality which underlies the last sentence of Art 36 of the Treaty requires that the power of the Member States to prohibit imports of the products in question from other Member States should be restricted to what is necessary to attain the legitimate aim of protecting public health. Accordingly, national rules providing for such a prohibition are justified only if authorisations to market are granted when they are compatible with the need to protect health." *Ibid.*, para 18. See also case 178/84, *Commission v Germany* (*German Purity Beer*) [1987] ECR 1227, citing *Sandoz, Motte,* and Case 308/84, *Ministère Public v Mueller*, [1986] ECR 1511.

[114] Case 34/79, *Henn & Darby* [1979] ECR 3795.

[115] Art 30, first sentence, simply permits import restrictions "*justified on*" public policy grounds. It does not specify whether restrictions taken in the pursuit of a public policy objectives must be necessary or proportionate to these objectives. As noted earlier, the Court has at times interpreted the first sentence of Art 30 as indeed requiring that the measure be reasonably connected with its objective: in Case 251/78, *Firma Denkavit Futtermittel GmbH v Minister für Ernähung, Landwirtschaft und Forsten des Landes Nordrhein-Westfalen* [1979] ECR 3369, the Court explained in this term the concept of "a justified restriction" within the meaning of Art 30 of the Treaty: "Having regard to the foregoing considerations it is necessary, with reference to the question put by the national court, to ascertain next whether the restrictions of the kind laid down by the Viehseuchenverordnung 1957 keep within the restrictions placed by Art 36 [now 30] of the Treaty on the exceptions to the free movement of goods permitted by that provision. In fact it is clear from the wording thereof that the prohibitions or restrictions which it permits must be justified, that is to say *necessary for* attainment of its objective and may not constitute a means of arbitrary discrimination." *Ibid.*, para 21 [emphasis added].

have at times been applied also in reviewing the reasonableness and proportionality of *indistinctly* applicable measures.[116] Although it is, unsurprisingly, not quite clear in the case-law of the ECJ whether or not these requirements are distinct from the three limbs of the proportionality principle, there are cases where the Court seemed to have distinguished the two, at least from the point of view of the arguments employed.[117]

In the above mentioned *Aragonesa* case, the Court did not restrict its assessment of the Spanish advertising restriction to an assessment of proportionality but went on to determine whether such restriction constituted an "arbitrary discrimination or a disguised restriction" pursuant to Article 30, second sentence.[118] The Court excluded the existence of such discrimination or restriction solely on the basis that the measure was neither formally nor materially discriminatory. The relevant paragraph reads as follows,

> [...] On the one hand, it is clear from the documents before the Court that such legislation does not distinguish between products according to their origin. The restrictions which it imposes do not apply to beverages having an alcoholic strength of less than 23 degrees and therefore do not restrict imports of such beverages from other Member States. In regard to beverages having an alcoholic strength of more than 23 degrees, those restrictions affect both products, in not inconsiderable quantities, originating in the part of the national territory to which they apply and products imported from other Member States. On the other hand, the fact that that part of the national territory produces more beverages having an alcoholic strength of less than 23 degrees than beverages with a higher alcohol content is not in itself sufficient to cause such legislation to be regarded as liable to give rise to arbitrary discrimination or a disguised restriction on intra-Community trade.[119]

---

[116] As shown by some of the cases already examined, the Court has usually referred to Art 30 when reviewing the proportionality of both distinctly and indistinctly applicable measures taken for the protection of health and life of humans, animals and plants. Cf Case 40/82, *Commission v United Kingdom* (*UK Chickens*) [1982] ECR 2793; Case 174/82, *Sandoz* [1983] ECR 2445.

[117] See above in ch 3 the discussion on the different kinds of criteria employed by the Court of Justice in order to examine whether de facto discriminatory selling arrangements are justified on public policy grounds.

[118] "According to the applicants in the main proceedings, what should be compared, therefore, is not the situation of imported products with that of products from Spain as a whole but the situation of imported products with that of Catalan products. Since the majority of Catalan-produced alcoholic beverages have an alcohol content of less than 23 degrees, the measure at issue should be regarded as discriminatory and protective in nature, inasmuch as it seeks to discourage the consumption of beverages with a high alcohol content and thus places at a disadvantage beverages originating outside Catalonia, and inasmuch, on the other hand, as it does not restrict the advertising of beverages with a lower alcohol content, thus protecting locally-produced beverages." *Ibid.*, para 22.

[119] *Ibid.*, para 25.

It is interesting to note how the Court complements its reasonableness review with an assessment of whether the facially origin-neutral (indistinctly applicable) measure at issue may be deemed to constitute de facto discrimination between domestic and imported products. This should clearly demonstrate that the *Dassonville–Cassis de Dijon* "rule of reason" approach does not apply simply to *discriminatory* trade-restrictive measures but goes beyond the traditional prohibition of discrimination on the basis of nationality (before *Keck*, at times, even with regard to selling arrangements). As shown by the interpretation by WTO jurisprudence of a similar provision contained in the chapeau of Article XX GATT, it would be contradictory to employ the same standard both to limit the applicability of the "rule of reason" approach and as part of the "reasonableness" review itself.[120]

Very different arguments were used in *Commission v United Kingdom* (the so-called *UK Chickens* case),[121] where the Court had to review a ban on imports into the United Kingdom of poultry products, eggs and egg products from those Member States (including France) which did not have a policy of slaughtering flocks infected with Newcastle disease. The UK Government sought to justify this system on the grounds of the protection of animal health. The Court restated the purpose of the second sentence of Article 30,[122] and focused in particular on the prohibition of "disguised restriction".[123] It noted in particular that the *manner* in which the United Kingdom had introduced the new legislation on the importation of poultry products suggested that the real aim of the import ban was to block, for commercial and economic reasons, imports of poultry products from other

---

[120] Identical reasoning, though with opposite results, may be found in the similar *French Alcoholic Advertising* case, where the Court found the French advertising restriction in violation of Art 30, second sentence, because the national legislation constituted de facto discrimination vis-à-vis imported products: "It is therefore apparent that although the disputed legislation is in principle justified by concern relating to the protection of public health, none the less it constitutes arbitrary discrimination in trade between Member States to the extent to which it authorizes advertising in respect of certain national products whilst advertising in respect of products having comparable characteristics but originating in other member states is restricted or entirely prohibited. Legislation restricting advertising in respect of alcoholic drinks complies with the requirements of Art 36 [now 30] only if it applies in identical manner to all the drinks concerned whatever their origin." Case 152/78, *Commission v France (French Alcohol Advertising)* [1982] ECR 2299, para 17.

[121] Case 40/82, [1982] ECR 2793.

[122] "As the Court has already observed in its judgment of 14 Dec 1979 in Case 34/79, *Henn and Darby* (1979) ECR 3795, the second sentence of Art 36 [now 30] is designed to prevent restrictions on trade mentioned in the first sentence of that article from being diverted from their proper purpose and used in such a way as either to create discrimination in respect of goods originating in other Member States or indirectly to protect certain national products." *Ibid.*, para 36.

[123] "In reviewing the facts of the case, the court finds it appropriate to examine first the submissions of the Commission and the French Republic to the effect that the 1981 measures, in their effects on imports from other Member States except Ireland and Denmark, amount to a disguised restriction on intra-Community trade within the meaning of the second sentence of Art 36." *Ibid.*, para 35.

Member States, in particular from France.[124] The Court referred to (a) the pressure the UK Government had been subjected to from British poultry producers to block imports; (b) the fact that the UK Government did not find it necessary to discuss the effects of the new measures on imports with community institutions, the standing veterinary committee or the Member States concerned; (c) the fact that it did not even inform the Commission and the Member States concerned in good time; (d) the lack of any elaborate scientific studies or discussions, which had, by contrast, been carried out prior to the adoption of the previous legislation in 1964;[125] and (e) the way in which the United Kingdom dealt with French demands that French poultry products should be readmitted to Great Britain after France had fulfilled the three conditions required by the UK Government, by adding an additional fourth condition.[126]

All these facts, taken together, were sufficient for the Court to establish that the UK measure constituted a "disguised restriction on imports" of poultry products from other Member States. This expanded the scope of review of the national measure to include questions of procedural due process.[127] Although the aim of the Court of Justice seemed to be to determine the real goal of the UK measure,[128] the interesting issues in the reasoning of the Court are the factors taken into account in reviewing the validity of the national measure relating more to *how* the measure had been adopted than with its substantive content. The failure to discuss the matter with the Commission and the Member States concerned, or even

---

[124] *Ibid.*, para 37.

[125] "It should be noted, in this context, that when the United Kingdom abandoned, in 1964, the policy of non-vaccination and compulsory slaughter conducted till then in Great Britain, in order to adopt a policy of control of Newcastle disease by vaccination, this change of policy was thoroughly prepared by an elaborate report of a committee of experts, by various studies and by prolonged discussions among veterinary experts. The evidence available in the present case does not suggest that any comparable effort was made before the government decided, in 1981, to reintroduce the policy, which it had applied before 1964. The deduction must be made that the 1981 measures did not form part of a seriously considered health policy." *Ibid.*, para 38.

[126] "By refusing French imports on the ground that France had not closed its frontiers to poultry imports from non-Member countries where vaccine was still in use, the United Kingdom added in fact a fourth condition to the three which it had previously stated in its letter to the Commission of 27 August 1981, and which it still states in its defence in the present case as the only applicable conditions." *Ibid.*, para 39.

[127] J Scott, "On Kith and Kine (and Crustaceans): Trade and Environment in the EU and WTO", *Jean Monnet Working Paper* (Harvard Law School, 1999) at 30 *et seq*; M Maduro Poiares, *We, the Court: The ECJ and the European Economic Constitution* (Oxford, Hart Publishing, 1998) at 169 *et seq*.

[128] Oliver is critical of the view that a measure is not justified under Art 30 if it is enacted for protectionist reasons, since this approach would clearly lead to questionable results. "It would mean that, even where a measure was in itself undoubtedly justified under Art 30 it could nevertheless be held to fall outside the protection of that Art on the grounds that the Member State concerned had acted out of the wrong motives." P Oliver, *Free Movement of Goods in the European Community*, above n 13, at 185.

to inform them in good time, as well as the failure to carry out any elaborate scientific study upon which to base the legislation at issue were taken by the Court of Justice as indications of bad faith on the part of the UK Government and at the same time as evidence that the 1981 measure "did not form part of a seriously considered health policy."[129] There is thus a clear connection between respect of certain minimum criteria in the regulatory process followed by Member States and the ability of these same Member States to demonstrate the "good faith" and "legitimacy" of their trade-restrictive regulations.[130]

One should note the similarity of the arguments advanced by the Court in the *UK Chickens* case with those recently employed by the same Court in *Gourmet* on the issue of whether a de facto discriminatory selling arrangements was justified on public policy grounds. Although the Court's language is all but clear, I would argue that, like in the *UK Chickens* case, *Gourmet* appears to show the Court's willingness to impose *process*-type standards, which focus on the regulatory Member's "bad faith" conduct in adopting the discriminatory internal measure.[131]

However, the Court limited the reach of its "procedural" approach in the *UK Chickens* case by adding that, even under the incriminating circumstances of the case at hand, a national measure would not constitute a disguised restriction on imports if the Member State could show that the measure was the least restrictive measure available.[132] Accordingly, contrary to an apparent reading of Article 30,[133] even a "disguised restriction" could be justified if it met the "necessity test". Since there were in fact less stringent measures for obtaining the same standards of animal health, which the UK Government had in mind when it enacted the new legislation, the Court found the United Kingdom in breach of its obligations under the Treaty.

---

[129] Case 40/82, *UK Chickens* [1982] ECR 2793, para 39.

[130] See also Case 178/84, *German Purity Beer* [1987] ECR 1227. German law prohibited the use of additives in beer, on ground of public health, while additives were used to make beer in other States. Although the Court recognised the right of each Member States to decide what *degree of protection* of the health and life of humans they intend to ensure, in so far as there are uncertainties at the present state of scientific research and in the absence of Community legislation, the law was not justified because it was contrary to the principle of proportionality, in that case, (a) because the substance was not prohibited by the findings of international scientific research, (b) there was no reasonable procedure whereby traders could obtain authorisation for a specific additive, and (c) the additives were permitted by German law in beverages other than beer. Both the first and third factors clearly related to the manner in which the national law was enacted (a) and applied (c), employing several of the same factors used in GATT Art XX jurisprudence.

[131] See above the discussion in ch 3 on "De facto discriminatory selling arrangements and 'mandatory requirements' under EC law".

[132] Case 40/82, *UK Chickens* [1982] ECR 2793, para 40.

[133] "There is some difficulty in reconciling this reasoning with the language of Art 30 which suggests that, if a measure is caught by the second sentence, it cannot be justified." P Oliver, *Free Movement of Goods in the European Community*, above n 13, at 185.

It is evident how the approach followed by the Court in *UK Chickens*, though laudable in terms of the willingness of the Court to review procedural issues as well as substantive ones, does not clarify the structure of the test to be employed in reviewing a national measure adopted on public policy grounds, in particular with regard to the relationship between the requirements of Article 30, second sentence (prohibition on arbitrary discrimination and disguised restriction) and the three limbs of the proportionality principle.[134]

Furthermore, the Court's examination of the UK measure's *necessity* is tainted with the same ambiguity in applying the principle of proportionality. The Court, apparently without even realising, moved from arguing whether the measure was "necessary" to whether it was "proportionate *stricto sensu*". Although it recognised several times the right of the United Kingdom to pursue the *highest levels of freedom from animal disease*,[135] the Court then failed the UK measure because it constituted a disproportionate restriction on intra-Community trade in light of the nature of the risk the measure was aimed at preventing. Adopting an approach similar to the one in the *Danish Bottles* case, the Court stated that,

> the possibility of infection by imported poultry products would be so much due to sheer hazard that it cannot justify a complete prohibition of imports from Member States which admit the use of vaccine.[136]

In short, the level of protection pursued by the UK measure (zero tolerance with regard to poultry diseases) was out of proportion to the actual risk to animal health, especially in light of the substantial adverse effects that an import ban had on intra-Community trade: while the benefits to animal health were minimal, the adverse effect on trade were substantial. As noted earlier, such finding constitutes a typical analysis under the proportionality *stricto sensu* limb.

6.   A Few Concluding Remarks

Following this jurisprudential analysis of the application of the proportionality principle as the true "normative standard" of the *Dassonville–Cassis de Dijon* "rule of reason" doctrine, a few remarks should be noted.

---

[134] For another case where the Court seems to distinguish between proportionality and the second sentence of Art 30 see Joined Cases C–1 and 176/90, *Aragonesa de Publicidad v Departamento de Sanidad* [1991] ECR I–4151, para 17–19. The AG seems to be of the same opinion: "The question raised has little if any practical import, since the conditions governing the applicability of the *Cassis de Dijon* doctrine and of Art 36 are the same (absence of harmonisation, examination of the criteria of necessity and proportionality, prohibition of arbitrary discrimination or disguised restriction on trade)." Opinion of Advocate-General Van Gerven, para 14.

[135] *Ibid.*, paras 13, 40, and 41.

[136] *Ibid.*, para 44.

Despite the sometimes structural vagueness of the approach followed by the European Court of Justice in reviewing "indistinctly applicable measures" on the basis of the proportionality principle, in particular with regard to (a) the relationship between the limbs of the proportionality principle and the requirements in the second sentence of Article 30 and (b) the division of labour between the Court of Justice and national courts in the actual carrying out of the proportionality review, the factors taken into account by the Court in reviewing the proportionality *tout court* of a national measure may be both of a substantive and procedural character. Although they usually relate to the substantive soundness of the measure (ie "suitability", "necessity", or "proportionality *stricto sensu*"), they may also refer to the measure's compliance with procedural principles, in particular where the substantive soundness of the measure under review is "difficult" to assess (for example, where the measure involves morality or health choices), and the Court cannot but look at other criteria of review (for example, the *UK Chickens* and *German Purity Beer* cases).

The Court shows some degree of deference to Member States' regulatory prerogatives where the nature of the public policy objective pursued by the national measure under review is of a delicate nature, in particular by emphasising the Member States' discretion in determining the appropriate level of protection (compare *Woodworking Machines* with *Danish Bottles*). The Court appears to apply a stricter proportionality review when the national measure at issue has highly restrictive effects on intra-Community trade (for example, in the case of a total ban on imports). Notwithstanding the nature of the public interest pursued by the Member State (public health or security), the Court will permit this type of restriction only in exceptional circumstances (the *UK Chicken* and *German Crayfish* cases).

There is a clear tendency in the Court to fail measures which are substantially discriminatory (*Cassis de Dijon*, *Danish Bottles*, *UK Chickens*, *German Crayfish*), while on the other hand, the Court seems to be more willing to find a truly origin-neutral measure (ie de facto equally applicable measures) justified on public policy grounds (*Aragonesa*), sometimes without even carrying out a proportionality review (*Cinéthèque*), or simply by tossing the hot potato back to the national courts (*Sandoz* and *Torfaen*).

The Court's unwillingness to adopt a clear-cut distinction between the test of necessity and the test of proportionality *stricto sensu* may suggest (a) that the dividing line between the two principles is not (and cannot be) fixed, and (b) the sensitivity of striking down a national regulation on the basis of the disproportion between the measure's restrictive effects on intra-Community trade and the measure's public policy benefits. The above analysis has emphasised a tendency in the Court's application of proportionality to hide findings of unreasonableness based on the measure's "excessive" or "disproportionate" effects on intra-Community trade (proportionality in the strict sense) behind findings on the existence of other less-trade restrictive instruments (necessity). This may be indirectly confirmed by those cases where the Court more openly carried out a full proportionality review (including proportionality *stricto sensu* limb) and found that the national measure under review was indeed "reasonable". In any event, it is fundamental to emphasise that any time the Court disregards the particular level of protection pursued by the Member State in assessing the proportionality of a national measure, the Court, although it may appear to be reviewing only its "necessity", is indirectly assessing also the proportionality *stricto sensu* of the public policy objective underlying the measure at issue. Thus, there seems to be many more cases than would appear at first sight in which the Court has (albeit only indirectly) employed the highly intrusive and powerful principle of proportionality in the strict sense to review (and strike down) national measures.

4.2   REASONABLENESS IN WTO LAW: THE SPS AND TBT AGREEMENTS

The Agreement on the Application of Sanitary and Phytosanitary Measures (SPS Agreement) and the Agreement on Technical Barriers to Trade (TBT Agreement) undoubtedly represent two of the most innovative features of the Uruguay Round. Building on the previous plurilateral Agreement on Technical Barriers to Trade, or the so-called "Standards Code", which had been adopted in 1979 at the Tokyo Round, these two agreements deal with the growing problem of trade distortions arising from disparate national regulations, in particular in the area of health and safety standards, by adopting an approach which goes beyond the basic features of GATT 1947 (ie the reduction/elimination of border measures and the prohibition on discrimination based on nationality).[137]

In order to ensure that sanitary and phytosanitary measures and all other technical regulations are truly justified on public policy grounds and do not constitute disguised restrictions on international trade, the SPS and TBT Agreements have adopted an approach very much resembling that enunciated by the ECJ in its *Dassonville–Cassis de Dijon* "rule of reason" jurisprudence: setting aside the centrality of the non-discrimination principle, these Agreements provide for a set of rules, principles and

---

[137] During the Uruguay Round, following the elimination of agriculture-specific non-tariff measures as well as the reduction of tariffs, some countries feared that the lowering of border measures would be circumvented by disguised protectionist measures in the form of sanitary or phytosanitary regulations. This concern has been said to have provided a major driving force which led negotiators to create a separate Agreement dealing with sanitary and phytosanitary measures, the SPS Agreement, in parallel with the major agricultural trade negotiations. M Trebilcock and R Howse, *The Regulation of International Trade* (London-New York, Routledge 1999) at 145.

benchmarks which principally include several of the ramifications of the "reasonableness" or "proportionality" principle that have emerged in EC law under the "rule of reason" doctrine (as well as in GATT panel practice under Article XX GATT). In very general terms, for example, both Agreements provide for an obligation to show a *causal connection* between the measure adopted and the aim pursued (Articles 2.2 and 5.1–5.3 SPS and Articles 2.2 and 2.8 TBT); an obligation to choose the *means least restrictive* to trade capable of achieving the level of protection set by WTO Members (Articles 2.2, 4 and 5.5–5.6 SPS and Articles 2.2, 2.3 and 2.7 TBT); and perhaps even an obligation that the disadvantages on trade caused by technical regulations be *not disproportionate* to the public policy aims pursued by Members (Article 5.4 SPS and Article 2.2 TBT).

Next to the so-called "proportionality" requirements, the SPS and TBT Agreements also include other types of general obligations like, for example, "transparency" requirements (Article 7 SPS and Articles 2.5 and 2.9–2.11 TBT), "harmonisation" requirements (Article 3 SPS and Article 2.4–2.6 TBT), and "conformity procedures" requirements (Article 8 SPS and Articles 5–8 TBT). Despite their relevance, these further requirements will not be examined in this section since they are to a certain extent different from the traditional "proportionality" requirements.[138]

The following section will focus on those substantive provisions of both the SPS and TBT Agreements that have more or less explicitly incorporated into WTO law the "reasonableness" approach, as the new-generation instrument for balancing trade liberalisation objectives with the regulatory prerogatives of WTO Members.[139] In other words, this section will examine the "proportionality" requirements imposed by these two sector-specific Agreements on the exercise of regulatory authority by WTO Members.

As already emphasised in the introduction to this chapter, although there are clear and useful connections to be drawn between the interpretation and application of "proportionality" as a tool for limiting the availability of the public policy exception in Article XX GATT and "proportionality" as the primary normative requirement imposed on Members through the SPS and TBT Agreements, the reason for keeping the analysis of these principles separate, at least from a structural point of view, is the fundamental theoretical difference between the use of "proportionality" in these two areas.

---

[138] The "harmonisation" requirements, for example, appear to represent what we would call an instrument of "positive integration" *stricto sensu*, where the substantive rules or standards are not established directly by the relevant organisation (the WTO in this case) but indirectly through reference to the work of other international bodies. See above the brief discussion on these types of integration instruments in the "Introduction".

[139] Cf the preamble to the SPS Agreement where Members express their *desire* to establish a "multilateral framework of rules and disciplines to guide the development, adoption and enforcement of sanitary and phytosanitary measures in order to minimize their negative effects on trade".

Before examining the normative features of the proportionality requirements in the SPS and TBT Agreements, it is necessary to say a few words about the general scope of application of the SPS and TBT Agreements (ie the "objective element"), including in particular the relationship between the "proportionality requirements" of these two sectoral Agreements and the GATT.

A.   "Objective Element"

As stated in Article 1.1, the SPS Agreement applies to all (1) sanitary and phytosanitary measures (2) which may, directly or indirectly, affect international trade.

The first criterion delimits the type of measures that are regulated by the SPS Agreement. In order for a specific measure to be viewed as a "sanitary and phytosanitary measure" ("SPS measure"), reference must be made to the relevant definition provided for in Annex 1, paragraph 1, of the SPS Agreement: an SPS measure is (i) any measure applied to protect human, animal or plant life or health (ii) within the territory of the Member (iii) from risks arising from *either* the entry, establishment or spread of pests, disease, disease-carrying organisms or disease-causing organisms (so-called "pest- or disease-related" risks) *or* additives, contaminants, toxins or disease-causing organisms in foods, beverages or feedstuffs (so-called "food-borne" risks). Let us address these three issues in turn.

So far, in all the WTO disputes involving the SPS Agreement, the defending Member has always admitted that health protection was the purpose of the measure challenged. Accordingly, there has never been any discussion on whether the required relationship between the specific measure and the relevant aim (to protect life or health) must be ascertained on the basis of an objective or subjective criterion. This raises the question whether a panel should rely solely on the pre- or post-dispute "subjective" statements of the Member enacting the measure at issue or, alternatively, whether it should examine whether there is at least a minimum level of "objective" relationship between the measure and the aim pursued. It would seem more appropriate that, in the case of a defendant claiming that its measure was not aimed at protecting health within the meaning of the definition in Annex 1, the panel should base its decision on the applicability of the SPS Agreement on the more "objective" criterion of the rational relationship between the measure and its aim. Otherwise, a Member could easily avoid the stringent disciplines provided for by the SPS Agreement by simply "writing" in its sanitary regulation a different objective.[140]

---

[140] For a different view see J Pauwelyn, "The WTO Agreement on Sanitary and Phytosanitary (SPS) Measures as Applied in the First Three SPS Disputes: *EC–Hormones, Australia–Salmon* and *Japan–Varietals*, 3 *JIEL* (1999) 641 at 643–44.

With regard to the issue of "territoriality", the definition of an SPS measure in Annex 1 only specifies the place where the protected interest is located. In other words, although its purpose must be to protect human, animal or plant life or health *within* the territory of the importing country, the measure imposed may be defined in terms of elements occurring *outside* the territory of the importing country, thus potentially including also process requirements or certification.[141]

With regard to the issue of the types of risks, the distinction between "pest- or disease-related" risks and "food-borne" risks is only relevant for the type of "risk assessment" required by Article 5.1. Accordingly, this difference will be examined only within that context.

Once a measure has been deemed to constitute an SPS measure, the second additional criterion for the SPS Agreement to apply is that the measure needs to "directly or indirectly affect international trade". This is a criterion based on the extent of the measure's impact on international trade. Although there have been only few disputes up until now (in none of which this criterion has raised any controversy), it would seem that this condition does not represent any serious limitation on the applicability of the SPS Agreement. It would be sufficient to look at WTO jurisprudence interpreting the term "affect" with regard to the scope of application of Article III GATT to understand the breadth of this concept. By adding that the effect may even be simply "indirect", Article 1.1 clearly indicates a very broad application of the SPS disciplines. In this regard, it would appear that the criterion dealing with the extent of the measure's effect on international trade is possibly even broader than the *Dassonville* formula employed in EC jurisprudence to limit the scope of application of the "rule of reason" doctrine.

Contrary to the SPS Agreement, the TBT Agreement does not contain an express provision laying out the boundaries of its disciplines. Article 1 of this agreement simply provides that (a) all products, including industrial and agricultural products, shall be subject to the provisions of this Agreement, (b) purchasing specifications prepared by governmental bodies for production or consumption requirements of governmental bodies are not subject to the provisions of this Agreement, and (c) the provisions of this Agreement do not apply to sanitary and phytosanitary measures as defined in Annex A of the SPS Agreement.[142] The scope of the TBT Agreement may however be determined in more positive terms by looking at its preamble and its substantive provisions together with the definitions included in the Annexes. Accordingly, the TBT applies to (1) "technical regulations and standards" as well as to "procedures for assessment of

---

[141] Cf L Bartels, "Art XX of GATT and the Problem of Extraterritorial Jurisdiction: The Case of Trade Measures for the Protection of Human Rights", 36 *JWT* (2002) 353
[142] TBT Agreement, Art 1, paras 3–5.

conformity with such regulations and standards" (2) which are capable of creating "obstacles to international trade".

Once again, the first criterion limits the type of measures that are regulated by the TBT Agreement. Annex 1, paragraph 1, defines "technical regulation" as a

> document which lays down product characteristics or their related processes and production methods, including the applicable administrative provisions, with which compliance is mandatory. It may also include or deal exclusively with terminology, symbols, packaging, marking or labelling requirements as they apply to a product, process or production method.

Annex 1, paragraph 2 defines "standard" as a

> document approved by a recognised body, that provides, for common and repeated use, rules, guidelines or characteristics for products or related processes and production methods, with which compliance is not mandatory. It may also include or deal exclusively with terminology, symbols, packaging, marking or labelling requirements as they apply to a product, process or production method.

Annex 1, paragraph 3 defines "conformity assessment procedures" as "any procedure used, directly or indirectly, to determine that relevant requirements in technical regulations or standards are fulfilled."

The definition of "technical regulation" for purposes of determining the scope of the TBT Agreement was at issue in two recent disputes. In *Asbestos* the Panel drew a distinction between that part of the French legislation at issue that banned asbestos and asbestos products and that part that provided for certain limited exceptions, and found that the TBT Agreement did *not* apply to the former because a measure banning a product cannot be equated with a measure that specifies the product's characteristics. On appeal, the Appellate Body reversed the Panel's two-stage interpretative approach, noting that the part of the measure establishing a ban and the part providing limited exceptions had to be considered as a unified whole.[143]

With regard to the term "technical regulation" the Appellate Body noted in general terms that,

> the heart of the definition of a "technical regulation" is that a "document" must "lay down"—that is, set forth, stipulate or provide—"product *characteristics*" [where] the word "characteristics" has a number of synonyms

---

[143] Appellate Body Report on *European Communities—Measures Affecting Asbestos and Asbestos Containing Products* (*EC–Asbestos*), WT/DS155/AB/R, circulated 12 March 2001, adopted 5 April 2001, paras 63–65.

[that] include, in our view, any objectively definable "features", "qualities", "attributes", or other "distinguishing mark" of a product.[144]

In the Appellate Body's view, the examples given in Annex 1.1 ("terminology, symbols, packaging, marking or labelling") indicate that "product characteristics" include not only features and qualities intrinsic to the product itself, but also related "characteristics", such as the means of identification, the presentation and the appearance of a product.[145] Next, the Appellate Body emphasised that the definition of a "technical regulation" in Annex 1.1 of the TBT Agreement also states that *"compliance"* with the "product characteristics" laid down in the "document" must be *"mandatory"*. In other words, a "technical regulation" must regulate the "characteristics" of products in a binding or compulsory fashion.[146] The Appellate Body added that product characteristics might be prescribed or imposed with respect to products in either a positive or a negative form. In other words, technical regulations may provide, positively, that products must possess certain "characteristics", or they may require, negatively, that products must not possess certain "characteristics".[147] Accordingly, having interpreted the definition of "technical regulation" in the abstract, the Appellate Body examined whether the French measure was indeed a "technical regulation". In this regard, the Appellate Body reversed the panel's finding noting that the French legislation did not simply ban asbestos in its natural state, but it also prohibited asbestos in products and thus the measure challenged did describe a characteristic of products, even if only in negative form (ie products must not contain asbestos).[148]

More recently, in *Sardines* the Appellate Body returned to the issue of the definition of a "technical regulation" for purposes of determining the scope of application of the TBT Agreement.[149] This dispute concerned Council Regulation (EEC) 2136/89 regulating the name under which certain species of fish may be marketed in the European Community. The EC Regulation set forth common marketing standards for preserved sardines. Article 2 of the EC Regulation provided that only products meeting certain requirements could be marketed as preserved sardines. Among these requirements, the Regulation prescribed that such products had to be prepared exclusively from fish of the species "Sardina pilchardus Walbaum",

---

[144] *Ibid.*, para 67.
[145] *Ibid.*
[146] *Ibid.*, para 68.
[147] *Ibid.*, para 69.
[148] Cf R Howse and E Tuerk, "The WTO Impact on Internal Regulations—A Case Study of the Canada-EC Asbestos Dispute", in G de Búrca and J Scott (eds), *The EU and the WTO: Legal and Constitutional Aspects* (Oxford, Hart, 2001) at 306–7.
[149] Appellate Body Report on *European Communities—Trade Description of Sardines* (*EC–Sardines*), WT/DS231/AB/R, circulated 26 Sept 2002, adopted 23 Oct 2002.

which is found mainly around the coasts of the Eastern North Atlantic Ocean, in the Mediterranean Sea, and in the Black Sea.

Following the interpretation given in the *Asbestos* dispute, the Appellate Body emphasised the three criteria that a document must meet to fall within the definition of "technical regulation" in the TBT Agreement: *first*, the document must apply to an identifiable product or group of products; *secondly*, the document must lay down one or more characteristics of the product; *thirdly*, compliance with the product characteristics must be mandatory. The panel found that the EC Regulation at issue was a technical regulation as it laid down product characteristics for preserved sardines and made compliance with the provisions contained therein mandatory.[150] On appeal, the EC argued inter alia that, although the definition of "technical regulation" covers labelling requirement, it does not extend to "naming" rule. Thus, the Regulation under review did not meet the second criterion since it did not lay down product characteristics; rather it set out a "naming" rule. The Appellate Body rejected this interpretation and agreed fully with the Panel's holding that,

> the requirement to use exclusively *Sardina pilchardus* is a product characteristic as it objectively defines features and qualities of preserved sardines for the purposes of their "market[ing] as preserved sardines and under the trade description referred to in Article 7" of the EC Regulation.[151]

Contrary to the SPS Agreement, the TBT Agreement does not expressly limit its scope of application on the basis of the measure's negative impact on trade. However, this further criterion may easily be extrapolated from both the text and the objective of the Agreement. From its name,[152] its preamble[153] as well as several of its substantive provisions,[154] the TBT

---

[150] Panel Report on *European Communities—Trade Description of Sardines* (*EC–Sardines*), WT/DS231/R, circulated 29 May 2002, adopted 23 Oct 2002, para 7.35.

[151] Appellate Body Report on *EC–Sardines*, above n 149, para 190 citing Panel Report on *EC–Sardines*, above n 150, para 7.27. Cf J Trachtman, Decisions of the Appellate Body of the WTO, *EC–Sardines*, available at <www.ejil.com>, and A Appleton and V Heiskanen, "The *Sardines* Decision: Fish Without Chips?", paper presented at the London meeting of the World Trade Law Association in Nov 2002 (in file with author).

[152] Agreement on Technical *Barriers to Trade*.

[153] The fifth recital of the preamble includes the Members' *desire* "to ensure that technical regulations and standards including packaging, marking and labelling requirements, and procedures for assessment of conformity with technical regulations and standards do not create unnecessary *obstacles to international trade*". [second emphasis added]

[154] Art 2.2 reads in part as follows: "Members shall censure that technical regulations are not prepared, adopted or applied with a view to or with the effect of creating unnecessary *obstacles to international trade*. For this purpose, technical regulations shall not be more *trade-restrictive* than necessary to fulfil a legitimate objective, taking account of the risks non-fulfilment would create" [emphasis added]. Moreover, Art 2.5 states in part that "A Member

Agreement clearly applies to national technical regulations which are deemed to be "barriers" or "obstacles" to international trade. While there may be slight differences with regard to the extent of the negative impact on international trade required in the several provisions of the TBT, in any case there must be at least a certain minimum adverse effect on trade in order for the TBT discipline to come into play. Only future jurisprudence may tell whether the scope of application of the TBT will be as broad as that of the SPS Agreement.

B.   The Proportionality Requirements Under TBT and SPS as Independent from the GATT

Contrary to the proportionality requirements derived from the interpretation and application of the general public policy exception of Article XX GATT (where proportionality is only relevant when invoking exceptions capable of justifying an established GATT violation), in the SPS and TBT Agreements "the need for technical regulations and sanitary or phytosanitary measures to be proportionate in the sense of these agreements becomes a new independent obligation."[155] In other words, much like the *Dassonville–Cassis de Dijon* "rule of reason" doctrine, under both the SPS and TBT Agreements, all disciplines apply even if no prior discrimination has been found.[156]

The novelty of their normative structure has been more or less implicitly recognised by WTO jurisprudence, which has emphasised both the independent character and the different normative nature of the obligations included in the two sectoral Agreements. In *EC–Hormones*, despite the arguments of the EC to the contrary,[157] the Panel found that the SPS Agreement applies to all SPS measures affecting international trade *independently* of the

preparing, adopting or applying a technical regulation which *may have a significant effect on trade of other Members* shall [...] explain the justification for that technical regulation in terms of the provisions of para 2 to 4" [emphasis added].

[155] A Desmedt, "Proportionality in WTO Law", in 4 *JIEL* (2001) 441 at 461. Cf R Quick and A Blüthner, "Has the Appellate Body Erred? An Appraisal and Criticism of the Ruling in the WTO *Hormones Case*", 3 *JIEL* (1999) 603 at 627.

[156] J Pauwelyn, "The WTO Agreement on Sanitary and Phytosanitary (SPS) Measures as Applied in the First Three SPS Disputes: *EC–Hormones, Australia–Salmon and Japan–Varietals*, 3 *JIEL* (1999) 641 at 644; R Howse and E Tuerk, "The WTO Impact on Internal Regulations— A Case Study of the Canada–EC Asbestos Dispute", in G de Búrca and J Scott (eds), *The EU and the WTO: Legal and Constitutional Aspects* (Oxford, Hart, 2001) at 309.

[157] The EC had relied on the final paragraph of the preamble of the SPS which, in a not altogether unproblematic manner, states that the Agreement aims "to elaborate rules for the application of the provisions of GATT 1994 which relate to the use of sanitary and phytosanitary measures, in particular the provision of Art XX(b)". On the basis of this part of the preamble, the EC argued that the SPS was *not* a "self-standing" agreement but only interpreted and gave precision to the "application" of GATT 1994.

GATT and imposes obligations that go beyond and are additional to GATT.[158] In *EC–Asbestos*, the Appellate Body noted that,

> although the TBT Agreement is intended to "further the objective of GATT 1994", it does so through a *specialised legal regime* that applies solely to a limited class of measures. For these measures, the TBT Agreement imposes obligations on Members that seem to be *different* from, and *additional* to, the obligation imposed on Members under the GATT 1994.[159]

This did not mean, however, that the specific disciplines in the SPS and TBT may not operate *concurrently* with the more general GATT obligations: in other words, provided that it falls within their ambit of application, a measure may be subject at the same time to both the GATT and either the SPS or TBT Agreement.[160] This interpretation would be consistent with the way in which panels and the Appellate Body have understood the relationship between GATT and other WTO treaties. Without being able in the present study to address in more general terms the problematic issue of the relationships between the several disciplines (or Agreements) in WTO law, it is nevertheless necessary to emphasise what might be the consequence of a "concurrent" application of the GATT and either one of the TBT or SPS Agreement.[161]

There are two different scenarios depending on whether or not the national measure at issue has been adopted in order to pursue a public policy objective which is included in the exhaustive list of Article XX GATT.

In the first scenario (the measure under review is based on one of the public policies of Article XX), if a measure complies with either the

---

[158] Panel Reports on *European Communities—Measures Affecting Livestock and Meat (EC–Hormones)*, WT/DS48/R, circulated 18 Aug 1997, adopted 13 Feb 1998, para 8.36 (US panel) and para 8.39 (Canada panel). The Panel considered the substantive obligations of the SPS Agreement to go beyond and be additional to GATT principally on the basis of a textual interpretation of Art 1.1 SPS setting out the scope of application of the SPS Agreement. Cf R Quick and A Blüthner, "Has the Appellate Body Erred? An Appraisal and Criticism of the Ruling in the WTO *Hormones Case*", 3 *JIEL* (1999) 603 at 627. See further below.

[159] Appellate Body Report on *EC–Hormones*, WT/DS48/AB/R, circulated 16 Jan 1998, adopted 13 Feb 1998, para 80, [emphasis added].

[160] Cf R Howse and E Tuerk, "The WTO Impact on Internal Regulations—A Case Study of the Canada–EC Asbestos Dispute", in G de Búrca and J Scott (eds), *The EU and the WTO: Legal and Constitutional Aspects* (Oxford, Hart, 2001) at 308, where the authors argue that the Appellate Body in *Asbestos* appears to have endorsed a "concurrent" application of the GATT and TBT, by remarking that the TBT Agreement imposes obligations on members that seem to be different from, and additional to, the obligations imposed on members under the GATT.

[161] See E Montaguti and M Lugard, "The GATT 1994 and Other Annex 1A Agreements: Four Different Relationships?", 3 *JIEL* (2000) 473, and G Marceau and J Trachtman, "The Technical Barriers to Trade Agreement, the Sanitary and Phytosanitary Measures Agreement, and the General Agreement on Tariffs and Trade: A Map of the World Trade Organization Law of Domestic Regulation of Goods", 36 *JWT* (2002) 811.

SPS or the TBT Agreement, it is almost automatic that it would also be found to comply with any GATT obligation. This conclusion stems from the fact that, as will be examined below, several of the requirements provided for in the SPS and TBT Agreements are elaborations of the proportionality requirements provided for in Article XX as limitations of Members' right to justify a GATT violation on public policy grounds. In other words, if a measure complies with the more detailed and stringent proportionality requirements of the SPS and TBT, it should also comply with the looser proportionality requirements of Article XX and thus with GATT as a whole. In this scenario, the "concurrent" application of the GATT and either of the two sectoral Agreements should not result in any real conflict.

Since the SPS Agreement is applicable *only* to measures taken to protect human, animal or plant life or health (a public policy expressly included in Article XX GATT), an SPS measure complying with the SPS Agreement should always be deemed to comply with GATT obligations. Following this reasoning, it is suggested that the GATT-compatibility presumption established in Article 2.4 SPS, though rebuttable in theory, should be equated for all practical purposes to an unrebuttable presumption.

The same applies for a measure subject to the TBT Agreement which is based on any of the public policy objectives included in Article XX GATT. Even if the TBT Agreement does not provide for a GATT-compatibility presumption, for the same reasons as with regard to the SPS Agreement, a measure found to comply with the TBT should also be deemed to comply with the general exception provision of Article XX GATT and thus with GATT as a whole.

The situation changes once we move to the second scenario, ie a measure subject to the TBT Agreement which has been adopted in order to pursue a public policy objective which is *not* included in the exhaustive list of Article XX GATT. Contrary to the SPS Agreement, the TBT Agreement does not limit the legitimate public policies at which a technical measure may be aimed. In this second scenario, the concurrent application of the GATT and the TBT Agreement may cause certain unwanted results. Let us take the case of a technical regulation adopted for consumer protection (for example a labelling requirement), which de facto discriminates against imported products. According to the "concurrent application" theory, the regulation would thus be subject to both the TBT disciplines and Article III:4 GATT. Let us imagine, moreover, that the consumer regulations at issue were found to comply with the proportionality requirements of the SPS Agreement since that regulation was inter alia the least-trade restrictive instrument capable of achieving the appropriate level of consumer protection. However, analysed under the GATT, that same measure would violate Article III:4 as constituting de facto discrimination, and could *not* be justified on public policy grounds pursuant to Article XX. Indeed, even if the measure adopted by the Member is the least-trade restrictive alternative to achieve the level of consumer protection pursued by the Member, there would still be a GATT violation because consumer protection is *not* included in the exhaustive list of public policy justifications of Article XX.[162]

True, this situation would exist even if the TBT Agreement had not been enacted. As evidenced in the section on the prohibition of material discrimination, because of the exhaustive character of Article XX GATT, a facially origin-neutral measure with de facto discriminatory effects vis-à-vis imported products may be held to violate WTO law even if it is *reasonably* based on legitimate public policy purposes. Consequently, it would seem appropriate to employ (or to interpret) the TBT Agreement in order to remedy this problem and avoid such unwanted results. This would be possible only if the TBT Agreement were considered as a *lex specialis* at least with regard to the general obligations and rights in Article III and XX GATT. I believe that this would be the correct interpretation of the relationship between the TBT and GATT. Accordingly, a measure falling within the definition of a technical regulation or standard for purposes of the TBT Agreement would be reviewed under this agreement to the exclusion of Article III and XX GATT.[163]

Within the TBT Agreement, some of these same issues arise, in an even more problematic manner, in the relationship between the non-discrimination obligation of Article 2.1 (including both MFN and NT) and the general necessity requirement of Article 2.2. If the two principles were interpreted as two concurrent obligations, the relevance of the whole novel approach introduced by the TBT Agreement would be put in great jeopardy. Since the TBT does not provide for a provision such as that in Article XX GATT where public policy objectives are taken into account in order to justify de jure or de facto discriminatory measures, a TBT violation could be established simply by showing that a specific measure discriminates in law or fact vis-à-vis imported products. Although this reading, which would render the whole TBT Agreement nugatory, cannot be accepted, it is difficult to put forward a reasonable solution that would deal with Article 2.1 TBT (other than that of ignoring such provision).[164]

---

[162] This is true unless a broad interpretation of Art XX(d) GATT, as suggested in ch 2, is taken.

[163] For a somewhat different interpretation of the relationship between the TBT and Arts III/XX GATT regime, see R Howse and E Tuerk, "The WTO Impact on Internal Regulations—A Case Study of the Canada–EC Asbestos Dispute", in G de Búrca and J Scott (eds), *The EU and the WTO: Legal and Constitutional Aspects* (Oxford, Hart, 2001) at 310 *et seq*.

[164] For possible solutions to this problem see G Marceau and J Trachtman, "The Technical Barriers to Trade Agreement, the Sanitary and Phytosanitary Measures Agreement, and the General Agreement on Tariffs and Trade: A Map of the World Trade Organization Law of Domestic Regulation of Goods", in 36 *JWT* (2002) 811, at 874–75.

C.   "Normative Content"

In the preceding section on the scope of application of the SPS and TBT, we already had a chance to appreciate the lack of clarity in the relationship between the two sectoral Agreements (in particular the relationship between the TBT Agreement and the more general disciplines of the GATT). Unfortunately, the picture does not improve when one moves from the "objective element" to the "normative content" of the several substantial obligations, and in particular of the proportionality features, provided for in both the SPS and TBT Agreements. For example, as will be emphasised below, a certain preliminary confusion arises from the existence in both Agreements (in particular in the SPS Agreement) of both general and specific provisions, the relationship of which is often not clearly spelled out.

With the aim of clarifying the normative standards imposed on WTO Members by these two Agreements, this section will examine the SPS and TBT through the lens of the several elements of the proportionality principle.

1.   *The "Suitability" Requirement or the Need to Establish a "Rational Relationship" between the Measure and the Legitimate Public Policy Objective*

The requirement that the regulatory measure be "suitable" to achieve a legitimate public policy objective pursued by the Members is more or less explicit in both the SPS and TBT Agreements. One should remember that the "suitability" requirement mandates that the regulatory instrument adopted by a Member be *technically capable* of contributing to the public policy objective which that same Member intends to pursue. This requirement is usually aimed at establishing a minimum level of "reasonableness" in the relation between the regulatory instrument and its public policy objective and it does not require that the national measure be the "best" (ie indispensable) alternative in light of (a) the specific objective pursued (the "least-trade restrictive" test) or (b) the negative effects on other interests such as, in our case, the liberalisation of international trade (the "proportionality *stricto sensu*" test).

As emphasised above in the section addressing the *Dassonville–Cassis de Dijon* "rule of reason" approach in EC law, the "suitability" requirement is usually *implied* in the broader requirement that a measure be "necessary" to achieve a specified public policy objective. Desmedt notes correctly in this regard that the word "necessary" includes inter alia the obligation to show a causal link between the measure and the aim.[165]

---

[165] A Desmedt, "Proportionality in WTO Law", 5 *JIEL* (2001) 441 at 454.

Accordingly, since both the SPS and the TBT expressly provide that Members shall ensure that SPS measures and technical regulations are respectively "applied only to the extent *necessary* to protect human, animal or plant life or health"[166] and "not prepared, adopted or applied with a view to or with the effect of creating *unnecessary* obstacles to international trade",[167] it follows that the suitability standard is also part of the general proportionality requirements of the two Agreements at issue.

In more practical terms, however, the suitability requirement is employed for different purposes as well as in a different manner depending on whether one is addressing the SPS or the TBT Agreement. With regard to the latter, the suitability test appears to function for the purpose and in a manner which is almost identical to the corresponding concept in EC law. The first *substantive* obligation imposed by the TBT on WTO Members is the requirement that any technical regulation or standard must be *capable of contributing* to a *legitimate* public policy goal. Contrary to the SPS Agreement (where the legitimacy of the public policy purpose of an SPS measure—the protection of human, animal, or plant life or health—is *not* put into question), under the TBT a Member may take any technical measure necessary to achieve *any* legitimate objectives. Article 2.2 TBT simply provides for a non-exhaustive list of legitimate objectives including national security requirements, the prevention of deceptive practices, the protection of human health or safety, animal or plant life or health, or the environment.

Much like the "rule of reason" doctrine of *Dassonville–Cassis de Dijon*, under the TBT Agreement the legitimacy of the objective of a technical measure can be called into question and is thus the first substantial requirement to be met by a technical regulation or standard. However, besides the principal inquiry into whether a stated objective is indeed legitimate,[168] it will also be necessary to determine whether there is a "rational relationship" between the adopted measure and the legitimate public policy objective, or, in short, whether the measure is *suitable to* or *capable of* contributing to its stated goal. Without an inquiry into such a relationship, there would be no sense in requiring that the measure's objective be *legitimate*. Moreover, the suitability requirement in the TBT is not articulated in much detail and it is thus left to the "judiciary" to attribute to it the appropriate meaning. It would seem in this regard wise to employ the concept of suitability as simply requiring a minimum level of

---

[166] Art 2.2 SPS.

[167] Art 2.2, first sentence, TBT.

[168] G Marceau and J Trachtman, "The Technical Barriers to Trade Agreement, the Sanitary and Phytosanitary Measures Agreement, and the General Agreement on Tariffs and Trade: A Map of the World Trade Organization Law of Domestic Regulation of Goods", in 36 *JWT* (2002) 811 at 836 inquiring into the issue of determining the legitimacy of the public policy objective.

"reasonableness" in the relation between the regulatory instrument and the legitimate public policy objective pursued by the Member. The jurisprudence on Article XX GATT interpreting the connector "relating to" should provide valuable "know-how" for future application of the TBT.

Within the SPS Agreement, on the other hand, the "suitability" test plays a somewhat different function and its normative content is articulated in a much more detailed manner. First of all, as examined in the previous section, the suitability concept is employed in order to determine whether a national measure is indeed subject to the disciplines provided for in the SPS Agreement. In order to determine whether or not the SPS Agreement applies, it is not sufficient for the defending Member to argue that the challenged measure is or is not applied to protect human, animal or plant life or health. At least where the issue is complicated, the treaty interpreter will need to verify the existence of a minimum "rational link" between the measure and its stated goals.

Moreover, under the SPS Agreement, the "suitability" principle has been formulated in a more detailed manner. One may consider the general obligations in Article 2.2 (an SPS measure must be "based on scientific principles" and it cannot be "maintained without sufficient scientific evidence"),[169] as well as the more specific requirement in Article 5.1 (an SPS measure must be "based on a risk assessment"),[170] to be simply more or less detailed elaborations of the need to demonstrate a "rational relationship" between the measure and the objective pursued. Let us now examine these more specific applications of the "suitability" requirement.

WTO jurisprudence has thus far determined that the obligation in Article 5.1 constitutes a specific application of the more general principles set out in Article 2.2,[171] as well as that the two Articles should always be read together.[172] It is thus not surprising that in the three disputes so far brought under the SPS Agreement panels have focused more on the

---

[169] Art 2.2 SPS reads as follows: "Members shall ensure that any sanitary or phytosanitary measure is applied only to the extent necessary to protect human, animal or plant life or health, is based on scientific principles and is not maintained without sufficient scientific evidence, except as provided for in para 7 of Art 5."

[170] Art 5.1 SPS reads as follows: "Members shall ensure that their sanitary or phytosanitary measures are based on an assessment, as appropriate to the circumstances, of the risks to human, animal or plant life or health, taking into account risk assessment techniques developed by the relevant international organizations."

[171] Panel Reports on *EC–Hormones*, above n 158, paras 8.93 (US panel) and 8.96 (Canada panel).

[172] Appellate Body Report on *EC–Hormones*, above n 159, para 180, "Arts 2.2 and 5.1 should constantly be read together. Art 2.2 informs Art 5.1: the elements that define the basic obligation set out in Art 2.2 impart meaning to Art 5.1", confirmed in Appellate Body Report on *Japan—Measures Affecting Agricultural Products* (*Japan–Varietals*), WT/DS76/AB/R, circulated 22 Feb 1999, adopted 19 March 1999, paras 75–6.

specific requirements of Article 5.1 than on the more general obligations of Article 2.2.[173] Although the requirements of Article 5.1 should be interpreted by taking into account the more general principles in Article 2.2,[174] it seems more appropriate to start the assessment of the measure's "suitability" from the more specific discipline of Article 5.1 and then move on to the more general discipline of Article 2.2 in the event that the measure under review is found to comply with the former.[175] WTO panels have mainly focused on Article 5.1 also because the measures under review have all been found to violate the specific requirements of Article 5.1 and thus there has not been any need to make use of the more general obligations of Article 2.2. In *Australia–Salmon*, the Appellate Body noted that an SPS measure that is *not* based on a risk assessment within the meaning of Article 5.1 can be presumed to be *neither* based on scientific principles *nor* maintained with sufficient scientific evidence as provided for by Article 2.2.[176]

As interpreted by the Appellate Body in the *EC–Hormones* dispute,

> the requirement that an SPS measure be "based on" a risk assessment is a substantive requirement that there be a rational relationship between the measure and the risk assessment.[177]

Accordingly, in order to determine whether an SPS measure complies with Article 5.1, panels and the Appellate Body have focused *first* on whether there is indeed a "risk assessment" and *second* on whether the measure at issue is indeed "rationally related to" that risk assessment. Let us next examine these two elements in turn.

As defined in Annex A, paragraph 4, "risk assessment" is (a) the evaluation of the likelihood of entry, establishment or spread of a pest or

---

[173] This has certainly be the case in the first two SPS cases, *EC–Hormones* and *Australia–Salmon*. In the third and last case, *Japan–Varietals*, the panel, however, began its analysis with the third requirement in Art 2.2 ("is not maintained without sufficient scientific evidence"). See further below.

[174] This is the reading to be attributed to the following statement by the Appellate Body with regard to the relationship between Art 2.2 and 5.1 SPS: "We are, of course, surprised by the fact that the Panel did not begin its analysis of this whole case by focusing on Art 2 that is captioned 'Basic Rights and Obligations', an approach that appears logically attractive." Appellate Body Report on *EC–Hormones*, above n 159, para 250.

[175] *Contra* R Quick and A Blüthner, "Has the Appellate Body Erred? An Appraisal and Criticism of the Ruling in the WTO *Hormones Case*", 3 *JIEL* (1999) 603 at 629, arguing that panels are "well advised to follow the 'direct' route of applying Art 2 SPS instead of the 'complex and direct' route of Art 5 SPS."

[176] Appellate Body Report on *Australia—Measures Affecting the Importation of Salmon* (*Australia–Salmon*), WT/DS18/AB/R, circulated 20 Oct 1998, adopted 6 Nov 1998, paras 137–38.

[177] Appellate Body Report on *EC–Hormones*, above n 159, para 193. In other words, "a panel has to determine whether an SPS measure is sufficiently supported or reasonably warranted by the risk assessment". *Ibid.*, para 186.

disease within the territory of an importing Member according to the sanitary or phytosanitary measures which might be applied ("disease or pest" risk assessment definition) or (b) the evaluation of the potential for adverse effects on human or animal health arising from the presence of additives, contaminants, toxins or disease-causing organisms in food, beverages or feedstuffs ("food-borne" risk assessment definition).

With regard to the meaning of "risk assessment", WTO jurisprudence has clarified the following general issues: (1) a Member imposing an SPS measure does not necessarily have to conduct the required risk assessment itself but it can use assessments carried out by other Members or international organisations; (2) there is no requirement to make a "quantitative" evaluation, since risk assessment can either be quantitative or qualitative; (3) risk assessment needs to be specific enough, or, in other words, it must address the particular substance or kind of risk at issue; and (4) *some* evaluation of the likelihood or probability of the relevant risk is not sufficient as a risk assessment within the meaning of Article 5.1.[178]

More specifically, in applying the two definitions of risk assessment mentioned above, WTO jurisprudence has listed the following requirements depending on whether the risk assessment is required for "food-borne" risks or for disease or pest risks. In the former case, risk assessment within the meaning of Article 5.1 must (i) *identify* adverse effects and (ii) *evaluate* the *potential* of occurrence of these effects.[179] In the case of disease or pest risk, risk assessment within the meaning of Article 5.1 must (i) *identify* the diseases whose entry, establishment or spread a Member wants to prevent within its territory, as well as the potential biological and economic consequences associated with the entry, establishment or spread of these diseases; (ii) *evaluate the likelihood* of entry, establishment or spread of these diseases, as well as the associated potential biological and economic consequences; and (iii) evaluate the likelihood of entry, establishment or spread of these diseases *according to the SPS measures which might be applied*.[180]

There are two distinctions between the meaning of "risk assessment" required for "food-borne" risks or for disease or pest risks. First and foremost, the degree of risk differs depending on whether the assessment is

---

[178] Cf J Pauwelyn, "The WTO Agreement on Sanitary and Phytosanitary (SPS) Measures as Applied in the First Three SPS Disputes: *EC–Hormones, Australia–Salmon and Japan–Varietals*, 3 *JIEL* (1999) 641 at 646; and J Scott, "On Kith and Kine (and Crustaceans): Trade and Environment in the EU and WTO" in JHH Weiler (ed), *The EU, the WTO and the NAFTA: Towards a Common Law of International Trade?* (Oxford, OUP, 2000).

[179] Panel Reports on *EC–Hormones*, above n 158, para 8.98 (US panel) and para 8.101 (Canada panel).

[180] Appellate Body Report on *Australia–Salmon,* above n 176, para 121 and Appellate Body Report on *Japan–Varietals*, above n 172, para 112.

on "disease or pest" risks or on "food-borne" risks. In the words of the Appellate Body in *Australia–Salmon*,

> while the second requires only the evaluation of the *potential* for adverse effects on human or animal health, the first type of risk assessment demands an evaluation of the *likelihood* of entry, establishment or spread of a disease, and of the associated potential biological and economic consequences.[181]

This substantive difference in the type of risk assessment prescribed by the SPS Agreement depending on the nature of the risk appears to indicate a higher threshold of tolerance for trade-restrictive measures adopted to prevent food-borne risks on human or animal health grounds. Even if it is not altogether clear whether this distinction was intended by the drafters of the SPS Agreement and whether it is either politically or scientifically justified, the Appellate Body could not but define "risk assessment" within the meaning of Article 5.1 on the basis of the above mentioned textual difference.

The second and minor difference is that the evaluation of the likelihood of disease or pest risk must be performed *expressly* with regard to "the SPS measures which might be applied" (ie the measures which reduce the relevant risks). In other words, in the case of an assessment of disease or pest risk, Members must clearly evaluate or assess the *relative effectiveness* of any applicable measures in reducing the overall risk of disease.[182]

With regard to the definition of "risk assessment" for purposes of Article 5.1, it should also be noted that Articles 5.2 and 5.3 indicate some of the factors that Members must take into account in their risk assessments. These are for example, "available scientific evidence", "relevant processes and production methods", "relevant inspection, sampling and testing methods", etc. (Article 5.2), as well as "the potential damage in terms of loss of production or sales in the event of the entry, establishment or spread of a pest or disease", and "the costs of control or eradication in the territory of the importing Member" (Article 5.3). In *EC–Hormones*, the Appellate Body interpreted the list of factors in Article 5.2 first as a non-exhaustive list[183] and second as including also non-scientific factors

---

[181] Appellate Body Report on *Australia–Salmon*, above n 176, para 123, fn 69 [emphasis original].

[182] Panel Report on *Australia–Salmon*, WT/DS18/R, circulated 12 June 1998, adopted 6 Nov 1998, para 8.90, confirmed in Appellate Body Report on *Australia–Salmon*, above n 176, para 132.

[183] Appellate Body Report on *EC–Hormones*, above n 159, para 187, "there is nothing to indicate that the listing of factors that may be taken into account in a risk assessment of Art 5.2 was intended to be a closed list". For a criticism of this interpretation see R Quick and A Blüthner, "Has the Appellate Body Erred? An Appraisal and Criticism of the Ruling in the WTO *Hormones Case*", 3 *JIEL* (1999) 603 at 617, stating that "In extending the range of factors to be taken into account in a risk-analysis procedure, the AB exceeds its own goals by stating

(contrary to what had been suggested by the Panel). In this latter respect, the Appellate Body's criticism of the panel's strict scientific approach should be emphasised. The relevant paragraph reads as follows:

> [...] to the extent that the Panel purports to exclude from the scope of a risk assessment in the sense of Article 5.1, all matters not susceptible of quantitative analysis by the empirical or experimental laboratory methods commonly associated with the physical sciences, we believe that the Panel is in error. Some of the kinds of factors listed in Article 5.2 such as "relevant processes and production methods" and "relevant inspection, sampling and testing methods" are not necessarily or wholly susceptible of investigation according to laboratory methods of, for example, biochemistry or pharmacology. [...] It is essential to bear in mind that the risk that is to be evaluated in a risk assessment under Article 5.1 is not only risk ascertainable in a science laboratory operating under strictly controlled conditions, but also risk in human societies as they actually exist, in other words, the actual potential for adverse effects on human health in the real world where people live and work and die.[184]

Commentators have reacted in very different manner to these general statements on the nature of the risk assessment required by the SPS Agreement. While some have heavily criticised the Appellate Body for having interpreted the notion of "risk assessment" in an unnecessarily broad manner in conflict with the intentions of the drafters of the SPS, which required scientific justification,[185] others have praised the "institutional sensitivity" to national regulatory authorities that the Appellate Body has shown in *Hormones* with regard to the notion of risk assessment.[186]

In my view, the above quoted statements simply show the Appellate Body's willingness to favour a very pragmatic and flexible approach to the issue of risk assessment. Although "scientific principles" as well as "scientific evidence" should be at the basis of Member's sanitary and phytosanitary measures, the Appellate Body emphasises that "science" is not an infallible tool and that Members should be free to evaluate health and life risks also on the basis of other non-scientific factors. If this more contextual approach to risk assessment does not mean that risk should be evaluated exclusively or even predominantly on the basis of these other non-scientific factors, then neither can the risk relevant for purposes of

'that there is no indication that Art 5.2 SPS must be understood as a closed list'. Such statement has no textual basis either."

[184] Appellate Body Report on *EC–Hormones*, above n 159, para 187.
[185] R Quick and A Blüthner, "Has the Appellate Body Erred? An Appraisal and Criticism of the Ruling in the WTO *Hormones Case*", 3 *JIEL* (1999) 603 at 618–19.
[186] R Howse, "Adjudicative Legitimacy and Treaty Interpretation in International Trade Law: The Early Years of WTO Jurisprudence" in JHH Weiler (ed), *The EU, the WTO and the NAFTA: Towards a Common Law of International Trade?* (Oxford, OUP, 2000) at 64 *et seq*.

the SPS disciplines be evaluated exclusively within the parameters of "laboratory science". This is the meaning of the Appellate Body's statement that the risk to be evaluated in a risk assessment "is not only risk ascertainable in a science laboratory operating under strictly controlled conditions, but also risk in human societies as they actually exist". This shows the Appellate Body's preference for a balanced approach based on scientific principles and evidence filtered through other non-scientific realities, which should and do influence the way risks are perceived and regulated.[187]

In this regard, it is interesting to note that Article 5.3 specifies that, in assessing the risk to animal or plant life or health (and thus excluding human life or health),[188] Members may take into account also relevant *economic* factors such as "the potential damage in terms of loss of production or sales in the event of entry, establishment or spread of a pest or disease" or "the cost of control or eradication in the territory of the importing Member". The reference to other non-scientific factors should confirm the appropriateness of the contextual approach followed by the Appellate Body in interpreting Article 5.2. Risk assessment cannot be performed in a "science laboratory" without taking into consideration also "relevant economic factors".

Two issues should be emphasised. First, the SPS Agreement requires the taking into account of economic factors *only* with regard to risks to animal and plant life or health and not to human life or health. Is it not appropriate (or morally wrong) to assess the potential damage in terms of economic cost of a risk to human life or health? Moreover, the SPS Agreement expressly requires the taking into account, next to scientific evidence, of *only* economic factors. But should not broader environmental or moral concerns have a place in risk assessment? In these two respects there appears to be room for improvement.

Once it has been determined that a "risk assessment" actually exists, it is necessary to establish whether the SPS measure adopted by the Member is indeed "based on" or "rationally related to" that risk assessment.[189] According to the Appellate Body, Article 5.1 requires that the results of

---

[187] For a more critical and in depth analysis of the Appellate Body Report on *EC–Hormones* see J Scott, "On Kith and Kine (and Crustaceans): Trade and Environment in the EU and WTO" in JHH Weiler (ed), *The EU, the WTO and the NAFTA: Towards a Common Law of International Trade?* (Oxford, OUP, 2000). For a positive assessment of the role of science in WTO law cf W Maruyama, "A New Pillar of the WTO: Sound Science", *International Lawyer* (Fall, 1998), 651.

[188] As well as "determining the measure to be applied for achieving the appropriate level of sanitary or phytosanitary protection from such risk".

[189] In the three SPS disputes to date, SPS measures have been usually found to breach Art 5.1 because there was not a proper risk assessment. In *EC–Hormones*, the Appellate Body found that the EC measure was in violation of Art 5.1 because of the absence of an assessment of the risk with regard to the existence and level of risk arising in the present case from abusive use of hormones and the difficulties of control of the administration of hormones for growth

the risk assessment must "sufficiently warrant—that is to say, reasonably support—the SPS measure at stake."[190] The degree of rational relationship between the measure and the risk assessment is possibly better understood in another momentous statement by the Appellate Body in its *EC–Hormones* report:

> We do not believe that a risk assessment has to come to a monolithic conclusion that coincides with the scientific conclusion or view implicit in the SPS measure. The risk assessment could set out both the prevailing view representing the "mainstream" of scientific opinion, as well as the opinions of scientists taking a divergent view. Article 5.1 does not require that the risk assessment must necessarily embody only the view of a majority of the relevant scientific community. In some cases, the very existence of divergent views presented by qualified scientists who have investigated the particular issue at hand may indicate a state of scientific uncertainty. Sometimes the divergence may indicate a roughly equal balance of scientific opinion, which may itself be a form of scientific uncertainty. In most cases, responsible and representative governments tend to base their legislative and administrative measures on "mainstream" scientific opinion. In other cases, equally responsible and representative governments may act in good faith on the basis of what, at a given time, may be a divergent opinion coming from qualified and respected sources. By itself, this does not necessarily signal the absence of a reasonable relationship between the SPS measure and the risk assessment, especially where the risk involved is life-threatening in character and is perceived to constitute a clear and imminent threat to public health and safety. Determination of the presence or absence of that relationship can only be done on a case-to-case basis, after account is taken of all considerations rationally bearing upon the issue of potential adverse health effects.[191]

Accordingly, the Appellate Body held that a measure is rationally related to a risk assessment even if that measure adopts the minority opinion stemming from such assessment. This divergent opinion is, however, viable only in as much as it comes from "qualified" and "respected" sources. The Appellate Body's use of the concept of "minority" or "divergent opinion" should be viewed as a clever attempt to illustrate the *level*

---

promotion purposes. Appellate Body Report on *EC–Hormones*, above n 159, paras 207–9. In *Australia–Salmon*, the Appellate Body held that a risk assessment within the meaning of Art 5.1 as defined in the Annex did not exist (failure of the 2nd and 3rd requirement). Appellate Body Report on *Australia–Salmon*, above n 176, para 135. In *Japan–Varietals*, the Appellate Body failed the Japanese measure on the basis of Art 5.1 because there was no risk assessment whatsoever with regard to certain products. Appellate Body Report on *Japan–Varietals*, above n 172, para 113.

[190] Appellate Body Report on *EC–Hormones*, above n 159, para 193, confirmed in Appellate Body Report on *Japan–Varietals*, above n 172, para 76.
[191] Appellate Body Report on *EC–Hormones*, above n 159, para 194.

of "reasonable" or "rational relationship" which is needed for an SPS measures to comply with the requirement of Article 5.1. In real life, the results of a risk assessment may indeed be quite disparate and hard to evaluate in terms of majority and minority opinion. There may be more than two opinions, all of which may be equally supported by the scientific community. Even in the event that a majority opinion does exist, there may be several minority opinions which could either come from "qualified" and "respected" sources or be based on quite extremist theories. By stating that "rationality" or "reason" is not found exclusively in "mainstream" opinion, the Appellate Body is clearly emphasising that, in order for an SPS measure to be considered to be "based on" risk assessment, it is sufficient for that measure to show a certain minimum level of reasonable connection with the assessment of risk. In short, an SPS measure does not have to be the best possible option available, but rather one that has *some* rational basis in the results of the risk assessment.

This reading seems to be confirmed by the flexible approach adopted by the Appellate Body in interpreting one of the more general requirements in Article 2.2 (ie SPS measures shall not be maintained without sufficient scientific evidence). The only dispute where the requirement of "sufficient scientific evidence" has been addressed is *Japan–Varietals*. In that case, the Appellate Body noted that "sufficiency" requires the existence of a sufficient or adequate relationship between two elements, *in casu*, between the SPS measure and the scientific evidence.[192] In other words, the obligation that an SPS measure not be maintained without sufficient scientific evidence requires that there be a "rational or objective relationship between the SPS measure and the scientific evidence". In the Appellate Body's view, this determination is to be carried out on a case-by-case basis and will depend upon the particular circumstances of the case, including the characteristics of the measure at issue and the quality and quantity of the scientific evidence.[193]

It should thus be clear now that both the obligations in Article 2.2 and in Article 5.1 should be viewed as representing more or less detailed elaborations of the "suitability" requirement or, in other words, of the need to demonstrate a "rational relationship" between the measure and the objective pursued. Like the suitability requirement, the two SPS obligations focus on the capability of the measure to address the SPS issue of concern. In order to determine this capability it is necessary, first of all, to determine the issue of concern. If in very general terms the issue of concern is "the protection of human, animal or plant life or health", in more specific terms it is either "the risk of entry, establishment or spread of a pest or

---

[192] Appellate Body Report on *Japan–Varietals*, above n 172, para 73.
[193] *Ibid.*, para 84.

disease within the territory of a Member" or "the risk of adverse effects on human or animal health arising from the presence of additives, contaminants, toxins etc. in food, beverages or feedstuff". Determining for example whether a particular measure is rationally related to the protection of plant health or to the assessment of the risk of entry of a pest with adverse effects on plant health involves qualitatively the same type of inquiry. The only and relevant difference between these determinations is that in the latter case the parameters for review are elaborated in much more detail. Regulatory measures may not simply relate, for example, generally to the protection of plant health; rather, they have to relate expressly to the results of a specific assessment of the risks to plant health.

Let us take the case of *Japan–Varietals*, where the SPS measure under review was the "varietal testing requirement" that Japan imposed, as part of its plant protection regime, as a condition for lifting the import prohibition on certain products (like apricot, cherry, plum, pear, quince, peach, apple and walnuts, imported as fresh fruit) in relation to which Japan claimed that codling moth, a plant pest, may occur. The Japanese measure worked in the following manner: in order to obtain an exemption from the import prohibition, the exporting country had to propose an alternative measure which would achieve a level of protection equivalent to that met by the import prohibition. The exporting country bore the burden of proving that the proposed alternative would guarantee the appropriate level of protection. In practice, the alternative measure proposed was disinfestation. With respect to hosts of codling moth, disinfestation consists of fumigation with methyl bromide ("MB") or a combination of MB fumigation and cold storage (as required in the treatment approved by Japan for apples). However, since exemptions were granted on a variety-by-variety basis, the exporting country had to test and demonstrate the efficacy of the MB treatment for *each variety* of products it wished to export to Japan.[194] The United States alleged inter alia that this varietal testing requirement was in violation of Article 2.2 SPS, since there was *no scientific evidence* of a variation in the efficacy of disinfestation depending on the type of variety treated. The United States submitted that the quarantine treatment approved for one variety of a product had always proven to be effective for all other tested varieties of the same product (whether apples, cherries, walnuts, nectarines, etc.).

Japan defended its measure by pointing to the existence of a sufficient amount of literature and scientific data, indicating the possible presence of a statistically significant difference in the efficacy of known disinfestation measures across varieties of the same product (mainly or even exclusively

[194] For example, while Red Delicious and Golden Delicious apples had been tested and already approved by Japan, Gala, Granny Smith, Jonagold, Fuji, and Braebum apples were at the time of the dispute still pending approval.

related to different levels of sorption[195] of the fruit), and that such a difference could require application of a different treatment.

Although the experts advising the panel did not exclude that there *may* be differences between varieties of the products in dispute which *may*, in turn, be relevant for quarantine purposes (ie which *may* affect the efficacy of an MB treatment approved for one variety of a product if applied to another variety of the same product), they advised that the question whether varietal differences, if any, were significant for quarantine purposes *could not be determined on the basis of the evidence before the Panel*.[196] Accordingly, the Panel concluded that it had not been sufficiently demonstrated that there was a rational or objective relationship between the varietal testing requirement and the scientific evidence submitted to the Panel.[197]

The *Japan–Varietals* dispute shows that the inquiry on whether the SPS measure under review is rationally related to scientific evidence as required by Article 2.2 SPS equates to an assessment of the suitability of the measure, ie whether the measure at issue is reasonably related to the public policy goal pursued by the Member (in the specific case, the protection of plant life or health). In other words, since the requirement of separate testing for each variety of the same product lacked scientific justification and thus could not be deemed to contribute in any specific manner to the protection of plant health, the Japanese SPS measure under review was found not to be "suitable" or "capable" of achieving its purported public policy objective. The same concept applies to Article 5.1 SPS, which requires that there be a rational relationship between the SPS measure and the

---

[195] "Sorption" is defined as "the sum of adsorption, absorption and chemisorption". Adsorption is a physical surface effect and results from the attraction of molecules to the surface of products and other materials in the fumigation chamber. Absorption is also a physical process whereby the chemical enters into the product and other materials in the fumigation chamber. Chemisorption is an irreversible reaction in which residues are left in the fumigated products and materials. When the pest takes in the fumigant while in a product, or takes in the fumigant while on the surface of the fruit, it may die. Panel Report on *Japan–Varietals*, WT/DS76/R, circulated 27 Oct 1998, adopted 19 March 1999, para 2.16.
[196] *Ibid.*, para 8.33. The original fn (n 260) to this statement reads as follows:

"See Transcript, paras 10.274–10.279. As noted in the previous fn, *Dr. Heather* stated unambiguously: '*I don't believe that the occurrence of the differences has been proven and that they may be relevant for quarantine purposes*'. See also the introductory statement by *Dr. Ducom*: '*the questions of the Panel are relevant but often there is no clear response to give because we miss data on the exact subject on variety by variety testing*' (Transcript, para 10.39, italic added). See also *Mr. Taylor*: '*one of the things that has come out from this meeting which I have found extremely interesting is that we do need more information before we can say categorically that variety in fruit is a major factor affecting the efficacy of treatment*' (Transcript, para 10.266, italics added)."

[197] *Ibid.*, para 8.42. The Panel noted that "[w]hen we asked the experts advising the Panel whether, in their expert opinion, there is an objective or rational relationship between, on the one hand, the varietal testing requirement imposed by Japan for MB treatment and, on the other hand, any of the evidence submitted by the parties, they stated unanimously that—even though in theory there may be relevant varietal differences—to date there is not sufficient evidence in support of the varietal testing requirement."

risk assessment. If the SPS measure under review does not rationally relate to the risk assessment prescribed by the SPS Agreement, it means that the Member's measure is not capable of contributing in any relevant manner to the pursuit of the regulatory objective.

Notwithstanding the basic structural identity between the "suitability" requirement and the two obligations set out in Articles 2.2 and 5.1, the more detailed character of these two latter obligations makes them more specific as well as rigid. While a general "suitability" requirement may leave some flexibility in assessing the reasonableness of the relationship between the measure and its aim, the obligation to maintain SPS measures on sufficient scientific evidence (2.2) and to base them on risk assessment (5.1) does not allow for such a broad flexibility and thus may be viewed as representing stricter normative standards.

If the contextual approach employed by the Appellate Body in defining "risk assessment" within the meaning of Article 5.1 SPS were confirmed, the increased specificity and thus rigidity of the "suitability" requirements in the SPS Agreement should be welcomed as a development favouring legal certainty. One should never forget that the SPS Agreement in general and its proportionality disciplines in particular are principally aimed at providing national regulators with "appropriate" as well as "clear" normative standards capable of finding the right balance between multilateral trade liberalisation and national regulatory prerogatives.

2. The "Necessity" Requirement or the Need to Establish that the Measure is the "Least-Trade Restrictive" Alternative to Achieve the Legitimate Public Policy Objective

If the requirements that a measure is "applied to the extent *necessary* to protect human, animal or plant life or health" (Article 2.2 SPS) or is "not

---

As it is usually the case, the experts' answers do not appear as clear-cut as reported by the panel. Cf Transcript, paras 10.167–10.174: Dr. Ducom: "… the arguments are not statistically good. Scientifically, they may be good, but in practice they may be too narrow. But the answer is really difficult." Mr Taylor: "I have to agree with Dr. Ducom. The answer is very difficult otherwise perhaps we would not be here. Again I think in theory there may be some differences which perhaps exist, but in practice it is difficult to show these and it seems very difficult in fact to say that at this time the differences that might make the difference between treatments efficacious and non-efficacious have not yet been reached and therefore I think at this moment in time that the evidence is not sufficiently strong although in theory it does have some possible validity. But at this stage, as Dr. Ducom has said, and in practical terms, it's very difficult to say yes there is something which is sufficiently demonstrated to show that there is a real problem which has to be addressed in terms of maybe variety-by-variety testing, and which could lead to differences in the treatment techniques that are used." Dr Heather: "More to agree with both of my colleagues. I'd say yes there is a relationship but it is an incomplete one but this is a real world and to totally complete the relationship of these and decide on how important it is, I think would probably be beyond the resources even of the United States and Japan in the time available, and I'm not sure that it would really add anything of great value to the argument." *Ibid.*, para 8.35, fn 265.

prepared, adopted or applied with a view to or with the effect of creating *unnecessary* obstacles to international trade" (Article 2.2 TBT) may be interpreted as including the "suitability" requirement, their principal function is to impose on Members a duty to adopt the *least-trade restrictive* measure. This second function of the "necessity" requirement *lato sensu* involves an inquiry into whether, among the several regulatory instruments capable of achieving the public policy objective pursued by the Member, the chosen regulatory instrument is no more trade-restrictive than necessary to fulfil a legitimate public policy objective. This is why the "necessity" requirement *stricto sensu* is usually also known as the "least-trade restrictive" requirement.

Let us start with the "necessity" requirement in the SPS Agreement. Article 5.6 of the SPS Agreement requires in relevant part that

> when establishing or maintaining sanitary or phytosanitary measures to achieve the appropriate level of sanitary or phytosanitary protection, Members shall ensure that such measures are not more trade-restrictive than required to achieve their appropriate level of sanitary or phytosanitary protection, taking into account technical and economic feasibility.

In the *Salmon* dispute, where Article 5.6 was applied for the first time,[198] the Panel interpreted the meaning of "not more trade restrictive than required" mainly on the basis of a footnote to that provision.[199] From this footnote, the Panel inferred a three-limbed test: the SPS measure in place is inconsistent with the SPS Agreement if there is an alternative SPS measure which: (a) is reasonably available taking into account technical and economic feasibility; (b) achieves the Member's appropriate level of sanitary or phytosanitary protection; and (c) is significantly less restrictive to trade than the sanitary measure contested.[200] These three elements are cumulative in nature and the complaining Member bears the burden of proving that those three elements are met. This approach was confirmed by the Appellate Body in its *Australia –Salmon* report, as well as in the later dispute on *Japan–Varietals*.[201]

---

[198]Although it was invoked in the earlier *EC–Hormones* dispute, both the Panel and Appellate Body had refrained from making findings on the necessity requirements of Arts 2.2 and 5.6 SPS, since the EC measure had already been found to violate Arts 3 and 5 of the SPS. Cf Panel Reports on *EC–Hormones*, above n 158, para 8.271 (US panel) and para 8.274 (Canada panel); and Appellate Body Report on *EC–Hormones*, above n 159, para 252.

[199]"For purposes of paragraph 6 of Art 5, a measure is not more trade-restrictive than required unless there is another measure, reasonably available taking into account technical and economic feasibility, that achieves the appropriate level of sanitary or phytosanitary protection and is significantly less restrictive to trade."

[200]Panel Report on *Australia–Salmon*, above n 182, para 8.167, confirmed in Appellate Body Report on *Australia–Salmon*, above n 176, para 194.

[201]Appellate Body Report on *Japan–Varietals*, above n 172, para 95.

The first and third elements of the three-limb test of Article 5.6 appear to render the least-trade restrictive obligation less rigid. In particular, echoing the first interpretation of the "necessity" requirement in Article XX GATT by the *Section 337* Panel, the first element requires that the alternatives to be considered be *reasonably* available taking into account technical and economic feasibility. Accordingly, in the selection of the least-trade restrictive measure, Members are able to choose among the several alternatives, taking into consideration what is reasonably available in technical and economic terms. In this regard, Article 5.3 SPS suggests a few relevant economic factors to be considered when assessing the risks on animal or plant life or health (not human life or health) and determining the measure to be applied.[202]

Moreover, the third element mandates that the least trade-restrictive alternative must be *significantly* less restrictive to trade. Even this requirement would seem to give more leeway to Members in adopting SPS measures in compliance with the "necessity" principle. From the few cases so far decided on the basis of the SPS Agreement, it is hard to evaluate how much more leeway this further requirement does actually afford. In the two disputes in which the three-limb test of Article 5.6 was applied, the first and third elements did not raise any particular problem, mainly because the defending Members (Australia and Japan) did not come forward with any argument or evidence to rebut the complainants' arguments.

On the other hand, the focus of both of the SPS disputes concerning salmon and several agricultural products with regard to the "necessity" requirement was mainly on the second element of the three-limb test of Article 5.6.[203] In order to establish whether or not a measure achieves the appropriate level of protection chosen by a Member, it is necessary to determine what the level of protection of the Member in question actually is. As correctly noted by Pauwelyn, "a decision on this matter often goes to the heart of a Member's capacity to select the health regulation it considers to be appropriate to sufficiently protect its population, animal or plants."[204]

In the *Salmon* dispute, the Appellate Body rejected the Panel's finding that the level of protection implied or reflected in a sanitary measure or

---

[202] Reference may be had to the arguments advanced by Thailand in defending its restrictions on the importation of cigarettes in Panel Report on *Thailand—Restrictions on Importation of and Internal Taxes on Cigarettes* (*Thai Cigarettes*), DS10/R, adopted on 7 Nov 1990, BISD 37S/200. See above ch 1.

[203] Cf J Pauwelyn, "The WTO Agreement on Sanitary and Phytosanitary (SPS) Measures as Applied in the First Three SPS Disputes: *EC–Hormones, Australia–Salmon* and *Japan–Varietals*, 3 *JIEL* (1999) 641 at 652; A Desmedt, "Proportionality in WTO Law", 5 *JIEL* (2001) 441 at 456.

[204] J Pauwelyn, "The WTO Agreement on Sanitary and Phytosanitary (SPS) Measures as Applied in the First Three SPS Disputes: *EC–Hormones, Australia–Salmon* and *Japan–Varietals*, 3 *JIEL* (1999) 641 at 652.

regime imposed by a WTO Member can be presumed to be at least as high as the level of protection considered to be appropriate by that Member. In other words, in the Appellate Body's view, the level of protection that the measure actually affords (in light of the measure's features) may not always coincide with the level of protection aimed at by the regulating Member. In the *Salmon* dispute, the Appellate Body noted that the level of protection *reflected* in the SPS measure at issue (ie the import prohibition) is undisputedly a "zero-risk level" of protection, although Australia had explicitly determined that its *appropriate* level of protection is "... a high or 'very conservative' level of sanitary protection aimed at reducing risk to 'very low levels', 'while not based on a zero-risk approach'."[205] According to the Appellate Body, the "appropriate level of protection" (a notion defined in paragraph 5 of Annex A as the "level of protection deemed appropriate by the Member establishing a sanitary or phytosanitary measure") is a *prerogative* of the Member concerned and should clearly be distinguished from the "SPS measure" itself.[206]

The Appellate Body's interpretation of the obligation in Article 5.6 SPS conforms to the traditional function of the "necessity" requirement. While "necessity" is employed to impose on Members the duty to choose the regulatory instrument with the least restrictive effects on trade, it should not be used to pass judgement on the appropriateness of the level of protection that each Member wishes to achieve. In other words, under the "necessity" requirement there is no balancing of different competing interests.[207]

At the same time, however, each Member's prerogative to choose its own level of protection should not render such requirement "nugatory". The Appellate Body stated that the SPS Agreement contains an implicit obligation on the treaty interpreter to determine the appropriate level of protection of the regulating Member (it would otherwise be impossible to examine whether alternative SPS measures would achieve the appropriate level of protection). Accordingly, an importing Member is not free to determine its level of protection with such vagueness or equivocation that the application of the relevant provisions of the SPS Agreement becomes impossible. While in this case Australia had determined its appropriate level of protection and had done so with sufficient precision to make the application of Article 5.6 possible, in the Appellate Body's view, there may be cases where a Member does not determine its appropriate level of protection with sufficient precision. In these circumstances, the appropriate level of protection will need to be established by panels on the basis of the

---

[205] Appellate Body Report on *Australia–Salmon*, above n 176, paras 196–7, citing Panel Report on *Australia–Salmon*, above n 182, para 8.107.
[206] Appellate Body Report on *Australia–Salmon*, above n 176, paras 199–200.
[207] Cf A Desmedt, "Proportionality in WTO Law", 5 *JIEL* (2001) 441 at 457.

level of protection reflected in the SPS measure actually applied. Otherwise, a Member's failure to comply with the implicit obligation to determine its appropriate level of protection—with sufficient precision—would allow it to escape from its obligations under this Agreement and, in particular, its obligations under Articles 5.5 and 5.6.[208]

On the basis of these further statements, it is clear that the prerogative of WTO Members in choosing their level of SPS protection should not be overestimated, since "it does not represent a *carte blanche* for legitimising SPS measures."[209] In any event, future disputes will certainly demonstrate the difficulty for Panels of determining the "appropriate level of protection", which constitutes an indispensable step in assessing the "necessity" of an SPS measure.[210]

The Appellate Body eventually reversed the Panel's finding of violation in *Australia–Salmon* on the basis of insufficient factual evidence. The Appellate Body stated that, although there may well be a violation of Article 5.6, and possibly Article 2.2,

> we are unable to come to a conclusion on these issues due to the insufficiency of the factual findings of the Panel and of facts that are undisputed between the parties.[211]

The *Japan–Varietals* dispute followed a very similar path. Although both the Panel and the Appellate Body confirmed the general interpretation of the obligation in Article 5.6, the Panel's finding of violation was eventually reversed by the Appellate Body on the basis that it was reached in a manner inconsistent with the rules on the burden of proof. In particular, the Appellate Body agreed first of all with the Panel that "testing by product" did not constitute an alternative measure (to testing by product's variety) capable of achieving the appropriate level of protection set by Japan.[212] At the same time, the Appellate Body noted that "determination of sorption levels", which the Panel had found to represent an alternative measure meeting all of the elements of Article 5.6, had been *suggested* by the experts advising the Panel and *not* by the United States.

---

[208] Appellate Body Report on *Australia–Salmon*, above n 176, paras 205–7.

[209] Cf A Desmedt, "Proportionality in WTO Law", 5 *JIEL* (2001) 441 at 458.

[210] See above the discussion in chapter 2 over the Appellate Body Report on *Korea—Measures Affecting Imports of Fresh, Chilled and Frozen Beef* (*Korea–Beef*), WT/DS161/AB/R and WT/DS169/AB/R, circulated 11 Dec 2000, adopted 10 Jan 2001, para 178, where the same issue was dealt with by the Appellate Body in a somewhat unclear manner.

[211] Appellate Body Report on *Australia–Salmon*, above n 176, para 213.

[212] The panel concluded that " […] after having carefully examined all the evidence before us in light of the opinions we received from the experts advising the Panel, we are not convinced that there is sufficient evidence before us to find that testing by product would achieve Japan's appropriate level of protection for any of the products at issue." Panel Report on *Japan–Varietals*, above n 195, para 8.84, cited in Appellate Body Report on *Japan–Varietals*, above n 172, para 96.

The Appellate Body emphasised that the United States did not establish a prima facie case of inconsistency with Article 5.6 based on claims relating to the "determination of sorption levels", since it did not even *argue* that the "determination of sorption levels" was an alternative measure meeting the three elements of Article 5.6.[213]

These findings are interesting in two respects. First of all, they explain why in both above-mentioned disputes, while the Appellate Body found that the SPS measures under review failed the "suitability" requirement of Article 5.1, it also concluded that those same measures complied with the "necessity" requirement of Article 5.6. It is often the case that a measure which violates the "suitability" requirement is also in violation of the "necessity" or "least-trade restrictive" requirement. However, the Article 5.6 findings on the measure's "necessity" were predicated on procedural grounds and, as the Appellate Body expressly emphasised in *Australia–Salmon*, should not be deemed to exclude that the SPS measures at issue did not also violate the "necessity" requirement.

Secondly, both findings of the Appellate Body in *Australia–Salmon* and *Japan–Varietals* clearly show that the burden of proof is on the complaining Member (ie the Member claiming that the export of its products into the market of another Member (importing Member) is restricted by the importing Member's "unreasonable" regulation). Establishing the existence of other less-trade restrictive measures capable of achieving the *same* level of protection as set by the regulating Member may constitute a quite burdensome task. In this regard, it may be noted that the allocation of the burden of proof constitutes one of the principal differences between the "reasonableness" approach enunciated in EC law under the *Dassonville–Cassis de Dijon* doctrine and the "reasonableness" disciplines found in the SPS Agreement. As noted earlier, according to the decision in *Cassis de Dijon*, the burden of proving the reasonableness of "indistinctly applicable" measures hindering intra-Community trade is on the *importing/regulating* Member. The relevance of the so-called principle of "mutual recognition" enunciated in *Cassis de Dijon* is represented by the establishment of a rebuttable presumption of the "unreasonableness" of any regulation hindering intra-Community trade.[214]

Moving to the TBT Agreement, it should first of all be noted that, perhaps even more than the SPS Agreement, one of the cornerstone obligations of the TBT Agreement is the requirement that "technical regulations shall not be more trade-restrictive than necessary to fulfil a legitimate objective, taking account of the risks non-fulfilment would create."

It has been suggested that in light of the similar wording in the SPS Agreement, a similar three-limbed test should be used to review a

---

[213] Appellate Body Report on *Japan–Varietals*, above n 172, paras 125–31.

[214] See above section on the *Dassonville–Cassis de Dijon* "rule of reason" approach.

measure's consistency with this requirement. Thus, in order to show a violation of Article 2.2, second sentence, one would have to prove that there is another measure which (1) is reasonably available, (2) fulfils the Member's legitimate objective[215] and (3) is significantly less trade restrictive than the chosen measure.[216] I share this suggestion for at least two sets of reasons. First, this approach would have the advantage of interpreting the "necessity" or "least-trade restrictive" obligations in the SPS and TBT Agreements in a uniform manner, increasing their general understanding as well as their normative value. Secondly, the interpretation advanced in the footnote to Article 5.6 SPS conforms almost exactly to the "necessity" principle as it has been developed under Article XX GATT. The only relevant difference is the addition of the requirement that the alternative measure needs to be *significantly* less trade-restrictive. If this addition is interpreted as a *de minimis* requirement, according to which national regulators enjoy a certain minimum leeway in selecting the appropriate technical regulation, there should not be any major problems in extending the detailed definition of "necessity" contained in the SPS Agreement to the corresponding obligation of Article 2.2 of the TBT Agreement.

Before concluding this section on the "necessity" requirement, it is worth commenting briefly on the "equivalence" provisions of both the SPS and TBT Agreements. Article 4 SPS provides in part that,

> Members shall accept the sanitary or phytosanitary measures of other Members as equivalent, even if these measures differ from their own or from those used by other Members trading in the same product, if the exporting Member objectively demonstrates to the importing Member that its measures achieve the importing Member's appropriate level of sanitary or phytosanitary protection.

Similarly, Article 2.7 TBT provides that,

> Members shall give positive consideration to accepting as equivalent technical regulations of other members, even if these regulations differ from their own, provided they are satisfied that these regulations adequately fulfil the objectives of their own regulations.

Leaving aside the fundamental question of the normative strength of these two provisions (Members *shall* accept versus Members *shall give*

---

[215] As previously noted, contrary to the SPS Agreement, the TBT does not limit the type of legitimate public policy objectives which may be relevant in order to determine the "necessity" of a technical regulation. Art 2.2, third sentence, contains a non-exhaustive list of such legitimate objectives.

[216] Cf A Desmedt, "Proportionality in WTO Law", 5 *JIEL* (2001) 441 at 459.

positive consideration to accepting), there is a clear relationship between an equivalence requirement and the "necessity" principle. As noted by Weiler, this type of obligation (which may be defined as "equivalence", "mutual recognition" or "functional parallelism") is,

> a very conservative and fully justified application of the principle of proportionality. For a Member State to insist on a specific technical standard even if a different standard is functionally parallel in achieving the desired result, is to have adopted a measure which is not the least restrictive possible.[217]

Although I agree with Weiler's important doctrinal point, it is essential to emphasise the qualitatively different nature of the equivalence requirements vis-à-vis the more traditional least-trade restrictive obligation. While in the latter the regulating Member is required to choose the measure, among the several regulatory options, with the least restrictive effects on trade, in the former the Member needs to examine the regulatory situation in the country where the foreign good is produced and determine whether the exporting Member's regulation is capable of achieving in equally effective manner the objectives or the level of protection set by the importing Member.[218]

The difference from the EC law concept of "mutual recognition" may once again be found in the allocation of the burden of proving equivalence. While in EC law it is the *importing* Member that needs to establish the "necessity" of its regulations (ie the non-equivalence of the exporting Member's rules), in both the SPS and TBT Agreements it is up to the *exporting* Member to demonstrate objectively that its regulations are capable of achieving in equally effective manner the objectives or the level of protection pursued by the importing Member.

Although in all the disputes so far decided on the basis of the TBT or SPS Agreements the "equivalence" obligations have not played any part whatsoever, these provisions may in the future represent an important instrument for eliminating "unnecessary obstacles to international trade".

3. A "Proportionality Stricto Sensu" Requirement in WTO Law?

The question whether WTO law and in particular the SPS or TBT Agreements contain the requirement of proportionality *stricto sensu* has lately been at centre stage in both academic and diplomatic circles. As noted earlier with regard to the proportionality principle in EC law, the

---

[217] JHH Weiler, "Epilogue: Towards a Common Law of International Trade" in JHH Weiler (ed), *The EU, the WTO and the NAFTA: Towards a Common Law of International Trade?* (Oxford, OUP, 2000) at 221.

[218] Cf P Eeckhout, *The European Internal Market and International Trade: A Legal Analysis* (Oxford, Clarendon 1994) at 78 *et seq.*

requirement of "proportionality *stricto sensu*" involves an assessment of whether the negative effects of a measure on intra-Community trade are *out of proportion* with its benefits in terms of a legitimate public policy objective. In other words, what is at stake with the test of proportionality *stricto sensu* is whether the chosen level of public policy protection (and the measure necessary to reach it) is out of proportion to the principle of trade liberalisation.

With regard to the regulatory prerogatives of Members, this is undoubtedly a more intrusive and thus problematic form of review, since it focuses on assessing the relative *values* of, on the one hand, non-economic, public policy objectives (such as public health, consumer protection or environmental protection), and, on the other, the aim of liberalising international trade. While the two requirements previously examined deal with the question whether the regulatory *measure* is "suitable" and "necessary" to achieve a determined public policy objective, the review of "proportionality *stricto sensu*" focuses on the "reasonableness" of the regulatory *objective* itself. Allowing for a true balancing of differing competing interests, this latter requirement is thus capable of influencing the level of protection that Members are allowed to pursue. A particular objective or level of protection is deemed to violate the requirement of proportionality *stricto sensu* if it is found to have disproportionately negative effects on international trade.

While neither sectoral Agreement explicitly includes the requirement of proportionality *stricto sensu*, there are a few provisions, at least in the SPS, which might appear to influence the prerogatives of Members in choosing their appropriate level of protection.

The first provision in this regard is contained in Article 5.5 of the SPS Agreement, which provides, in part, as follows:

> With the objective of achieving consistency in the application of the concept of appropriate level of sanitary or phytosanitary protection against risks to human life or health, or to animal and plant life or health, each Member shall avoid arbitrary or unjustifiable distinctions in the levels it considers to be appropriate in different situations, if such distinctions result in discrimination or a disguised restriction on international trade.

As noted by the Appellate Body in both *EC–Hormones* and *Australia–Salmon* disputes,[219] an important part of the context of Article 5.5 is Article 2.3 of the SPS Agreement, which provides that,

> Members shall ensure that their sanitary and phytosanitary measures do not arbitrarily or unjustifiably discriminate between Members where identical or similar conditions prevail, including between their own territory

[219] Appellate Body Report on *EC–Hormones*, above n 159, para 212, and Appellate Body Report on *Australia–Salmon*, above n 176, para 240.

and that of other Members. Sanitary and phytosanitary measures shall not be applied in a manner which would constitute a disguised restriction on international trade.

In the Appellate Body's view, when read together with Article 2.3, Article 5.5 may be seen as "marking out and elaborating a particular route leading to the same destination set out in Article 2.3."[220] Like the relationship between Articles 5.1–5.3 and 5.6, on the one hand, and Article 2.2 SPS, on the other, Article 5.5 SPS should be viewed as a specific application of the more general principle contained in Article 2.3 SPS.

According to WTO jurisprudence, the three elements necessary for there to be a violation of Article 5.5 SPS are the following: (a) that the Member concerned adopts *different* appropriate levels of sanitary protection in several "different situations"; (b) that those levels of protection exhibit differences which are *arbitrary* or *unjustifiable*; and (c) that the measure embodying those differences results in *discrimination* or a *disguised restriction on international trade*.[221]

Although an arbitrary or unjustifiable inconsistency in the levels of sanitary or phytosanitary protection is not enough for an Article 5.5 violation, the right of WTO Members to determine their appropriate level of protection is nevertheless conditioned by this provision. If the third requirement (ie the measure embodying those differences in levels of protection results in "discrimination" or "disguised restriction on international trade") is interpreted in a broad manner (especially with regard to the existence of a "disguised restriction" on trade),[222] then Article 5.5 may indeed exercise a relevant limitation on the Members' ability to set their own appropriate level of sanitary or phytosanitary protection. It is for this reason that Article 5.5 SPS, although structurally focused on the prohibition of "arbitrary or unjustifiable discrimination" and "disguised restriction on international trade", shares certain normative functions similar to the requirement of proportionality *stricto sensu*.

In the SPS Agreement, there is however a provision that appears to deal much more specifically with the balancing exercise that characterises the proportionality *stricto sensu* requirement. Article 5.4 SPS provides that,

Members should, when determining the appropriate level of sanitary or phytosanitary protection, take into account the objective of minimising negative trade effects.

---

[220] Appellate Body Report on *EC–Hormones*, above n 159, para 212.

[221] *Ibid*., para 214 and Appellate Body Report on *Australia–Salmon*, above n 176, para 140.

[222] Appellate Body Report on *Australia–Salmon*, above n 176, paras 159–78. Cf J Pauwelyn, "The WTO Agreement on Sanitary and Phytosanitary (SPS) Measures as Applied in the First Three SPS Disputes: *EC–Hormones, Australia–Salmon* and *Japan–Varietals*, 3 *JIEL* (1999) 641 at 655, noting a more flexible approach in *Australia–Salmon* compared to the previous *EC–Hormones* dispute.

While Article 5.4 does not expressly require that the negative trade effects of SPS measures be *proportionate* to the protection of human, animal and plant life or health, it may certainly be interpreted as providing a sort of balancing obligation whereby, in setting out their appropriate level of sanitary or phytosanitary protection, WTO Members need to avoid regulatory measures with *excessive* trade restrictive effects. The normative strength of Article 5.4 SPS, however, appears to be limited by the use of the term "should", indicating that the provision is simply hortatory.

A confirmation of the hortatory nature of Article 5.4 SPS provision may be inferred from the fact that it has almost never been applied in the three disputes so far decided on the basis of the SPS Agreement. The only reference to Article 5.4 in dispute settlement reports to date is in the panel report on *Australia–Salmon*. Following the argument by Australia,[223] the Panel hinted that the determination of the level of protection is subject to certain conditions specified in the SPS Agreement, including inter alia Article 5.4.[224] However, in its review of the panel report in the *Salmon* dispute, the Appellate Body did not refer to this provision. On the contrary, the Appellate Body appeared in that case to deny the possibility of limiting the right of WTO Members to set their own appropriate level of protection. In the Appellate Body's view, the determination of the appropriate level of protection (ie "the level of protection deemed appropriate by the Member establishing a sanitary measure") is "a *prerogative* of the Member concerned and not of a panel or of the Appellate Body."[225] Although this statement was made specifically with regard to the panel's application of the least-trade restrictive requirement of Article 5.6 SPS, it might be interpreted as a *dictum* covering the entire SPS Agreement.

If we move from the SPS to the TBT Agreement, there appear to be even fewer, if any, provisions that might impose the type of balancing obligation that characterises the test of proportionality *stricto sensu*. Some have interpreted the language in Article 2.2 TBT, second sentence ("technical regulations shall not be more trade-restrictive than necessary to fulfil a legitimate objective, *taking account of the risks non-fulfilment would create*") as imposing an additional requirement on the defending Member.[226] Not only does the measure have to be the least trade-restrictive available, it also must be *proportional*, which is to say that the marginally greater risk of a less trade restrictive measure would need to be balanced against

---

[223] Panel Report on *Australia–Salmon*, above n 182, para 4.170.
[224] *Ibid.*, paras 8.172–173.
[225] Appellate Body Report on *Australia–Salmon*, above n 176, para 199.
[226] R Hudec, "GATT Constraints on National Regulation: Requiem for an 'Aim and Effects' Test", 32 *The International Lawyer* (1998) 623. More cautiously, A Desmedt, "Proportionality in WTO Law", 5 *JIEL* (2001) 441 at 459.

the degree to which the measure is less trade restrictive. As noted by Desmedt,

> [u]nder the TBT Agreement, when taking into account the risks of non-fulfilment of a legitimate objective, a panel could arguably find that the obstacle to international trade outweighs those risks [...] a technical measure could be considered disproportionate even though an alternative less trade-restrictive measure is not really available.[227]

I would tend to disagree with this reading for two sets of reasons. First, as examined in the previous section, Article 2.2, second sentence, of the TBT Agreement incorporates the necessity requirement (ie that technical regulation not be more trade restrictive than necessary to achieve a legitimate objective). The reference to the "risks of non-fulfilment" should be read in this perspective: rather than an *additional* inquiry into the proportionality of the measure in the stricter sense, this reference is a specification of one of the several elements to be assessed in order to determine its *necessity*. When a panel is deciding whether the adopted measure is the least-trade restrictive among the several regulatory alternatives "capable" of achieving a legitimate public policy objective, it also needs to take into account risks of non-fulfilment, ie the risks of not fulfilling that specific legitimate objective. It would appear that this specification makes the "necessity" requirement of Article 2.2 TBT possibly less rigid, since the one element which is expressly included in that Article for purposes of the "necessity" assessment is, rather than the negative effects on trade (cf Article 5.4 SPS), the risks of not fulfilling the specific public policy objective.

The second argument excluding a proportionality *stricto sensu* requirement in Article 2.2 comes from the express recognition in the preamble to the TBT Agreement that,

> no country should be prevented from taking measures necessary to ensure the quality of its exports, or for the protection of human, animal or plant life or health, of the environment, or for the prevention of deceptive practices, *at the levels it considers appropriate.* [emphasis added]

Contrary to the SPS Agreement, where such an express recognition of Members' regulatory prerogatives is not to be found, the TBT Agreement clearly excludes any interference in the ability of WTO Members to determine their own appropriate level of (human health, environment and consumer) protection.[228]

---

[227] A Desmedt, "Proportionality in WTO Law", 5 *JIEL* (2001) 441 at 459–60.
[228] Cf R Howse and E Tuerk, "The WTO Impact on Internal Regulations—A Case Study of the Canada–EC Asbestos Dispute", in G de Búrca and J Scott (eds), *The EU and the WTO: Legal and Constitutional Aspects* (Oxford, Hart, 2001) at 317, fn 91. The fact that the draft TBT

My conclusion is that, although there are certain elements at least in the SPS Agreement that appear to limit, even if only in an indirect manner, WTO Members' prerogative to decide their appropriate level of protection, a full proportionality *stricto sensu* obligation does not seem to be part of the reasonableness rule in the SPS and TBT Agreements.

4.3 CONCLUSIONS

There are a number of features in common between the "reasonableness" approaches in EC and WTO law, stemming respectively from the *Dassonville–Cassis de Dijon* jurisprudence of the Court of Justice dealing with "indistinctly applicable measures" and from the Agreements on Technical Barriers to Trade (TBT Agreement) and on the Application of Sanitary and Phytosanitary Measures (SPS Agreement). Extending beyond the non-discrimination principle, both rules mandate that trade-restrictive national measures be "reasonable" or "proportionate" taking into consideration the measure's public policy objectives as well as the restriction on intra-State trade.

However, it is perhaps more interesting in this conclusion to point out the principal differences between these two approaches.

At least on a purely formal level, the "reasonableness" rule of the TBT and SPS differs from the parallel *Dassonville–Cassis de Dijon* "rule of reason" doctrine with respect to the allocation of the burden of proof. Similar to the Commission approach in Directive 70/50,[229] both the TBT and the SPS Agreements place the burden on the *exporting* Member to prove the "unreasonableness" of the *importing* State internal measure (*Australia–Salmon* and *Japan–Varietals*). On the other hand, with *Cassis de Dijon* the burden is shifted on to the *importing* State that has to demonstrate the "reasonableness" of its equally applicable laws, once the measure has been deemed to be capable of hindering, directly or indirectly, actually or potentially, intra-Community trade. As shown in WTO

Agreement used in discussions during the Uruguay Round, contained a footnote to Art 2.2 stating that this provision intended to "ensure proportionality between regulations and the risk non-fulfilment of legitimate objectives would create" does not affect this interpretation of Art 2.2, second sentence, if only because the later elimination of that footnote might be an indication of rejection by the Members of such an interpretation. Cf A Desmedt, "Proportionality in WTO Law", 5 *JIEL* (2001) 441 at 459; and "The Uruguay Round's Technical Barriers to Trade Agreement" (WWF International Research Report, Jan 1993).

[229] As already emphasised, Oliver correctly noted that while de jure discriminatory measures were automatically considered to be measures of equivalent effect under Art 2 of Directive 70/50, Art 3 of that directive provided for a presumption that "indistinctly applicable measures" were compatible with Art 28 (ex 30) EC, which could have been rebutted by showing that the measure's restrictive effects exceeded the effects intrinsic to trade rules. Cf P Oliver, *Free Movement of Goods in the European Community*, above n 13, at 89.

jurisprudence, establishing for example the existence of other less-trade restrictive measures capable of achieving the same level of protection chosen by the regulating Member may indeed constitute a quite burdensome task. Accordingly, by shifting the relevant *onus* on the regulating State, the European Court of Justice has considerably reduced the impact of market barriers stemming from the Member States' regulatory disparities (the so-called issue of "regulatory overlap")[230] and at the same time furthered the creation of a unified market.

A further difference exists in the extent to which the proportionality principle is employed as a normative standard limiting a Member's regulatory prerogatives. It has been noted that in theoretical terms the application of the principle of proportionality entails a three-part test based on the equivalent and more developed German notion of *Verhältnismässigkeit* that includes a review of the measure's "suitability", "necessity" and "proportionality *stricto sensu*". Accordingly, a measure will be deemed to comply with the proportionality principle if the measure (a) is *suitable* or *effective* to achieve a legitimate aim, (b) is *necessary* to achieve that aim, namely, there are no other less restrictive means capable of producing that same result, and (c) even if there are no less restrictive means, does not have an *excessive* or *disproportionate* effect on the applicant's interests.[231] As correctly noted by Jans, these three elements constitute an ascending series in terms of the intensity with which national measures are subject to judicial review.[232]

However, while the "reasonableness rule" in WTO law centres exclusively on the "suitability" and "necessity" limbs of the proportionality test, the *Dassonville–Cassis de Dijon* "rule of reason" doctrine extends also to a review of proportionality *stricto sensu*. In other words, while WTO law imposes on WTO Members normative standards that focus respectively on whether national measures are technically capable of achieving the chosen public policy objective (suitability) and whether the chosen regulatory instrument is no more trade-restrictive than necessary to fulfil that public policy objective (necessity), EC law includes also a determination of whether the measure's negative effects on intra-Community trade are *out of proportion* to its benefits with respect to the legitimate public policy objective (proportionality *stricto sensu*).

---

[230] I have referred to the "regulatory overlap" phenomenon to indicate the existence of several regulatory authorities with limited territorial competencies (the Member States), which, by imposing different product requirements within their jurisdictions, impeded or severely restricted the free circulation of goods within the greater market (the Common Market).

[231] G de Búrca, "The Principle of Proportionality and its Application in EC law", 13 *YEL* (1994) 105 at 113, see T Tridimas, "Proportionality in Community Law: Searching for the Appropriate Standard of Scrutiny" in E Ellis (ed), *The Principle of Proportionality in the Laws of Europe* (Oxford, OUP, 1999) at 68.

[232] J Jans, "Proportionality Revisited", 27 *Legal Issues of Economic Integration* (2000) 239 at 241.

In relation to Member States' regulatory prerogatives, this last criterion is undoubtedly the most "intrusive" and, thus problematic, form of review, since it involves an assessment of the relative *values* of, on the one hand, non-economic public policy objectives (such as public health, consumer protection or environmental protection), and, on the other, the aim of liberalising intra-Community trade.

The real difference between EC and WTO law with regard to the extent to which the proportionality principle is applied may be appreciated only by looking at the "loose" manner in which the Court of Justice has applied the "necessity" test. It was noted that in order to determine whether among the several regulatory instruments capable of achieving the public policy objective pursued by the Member State, the chosen measure is indeed the *least-trade restrictive*, the level of trade-restrictiveness of the chosen measure will need to be taken into account and compared with that of all other alternative regulatory instruments. The difficult task in the "necessity" calculation, as evidenced in the present analysis of both EC and WTO law, is not only to determine whether there exist other regulatory measures that affect trade to a lesser extent compared to the measure chosen by the Member State; it is principally to establish whether these alternatives are indeed capable of achieving the specific public policy objective as *effectively* and *to the same extent* as the chosen measure. While WTO jurisprudence on the application of the necessity test (under both Article XX GATT as well as under the reasonableness approach of the TBT and SPS) has so far correctly understood and applied this standard, thus recognising the right of Members to set their *appropriate* level of protection, ECJ case-law, on the other hand, shows a certain tendency to hide a review of the appropriate level of protection (ie a review of the "proportionality *stricto sensu*") behind what appears to be an assessment of "necessity". It was noted that even in the famous *Cassis de Dijon* decision, by not taking into consideration the *level* or *degree* of consumer protection that the German measure was—or might have been—aimed at, the Court of Justice *indirectly* hinted that a high level of protection (zero consumer confusion) was in any case disproportionate vis-à-vis the adverse effects that such high level of protection had on intra-Community trade (no importation of Cassis into Germany).[233] Seen in this light, then, what may appear to be a review of the measure's "necessity" or "least-restrictiveness", in reality becomes an assessment "in disguise" of its proportionality *stricto sensu*.

The unwillingness of the Court of Justice to adopt a clear-cut distinction between the test of necessity and the test of proportionality *stricto sensu* may suggest not just that the dividing line between the two standards is

---

[233] JHH Weiler, "The Constitution of the Common Marketplace: Text and Context in the Evolution of the Free Movement of Goods", in P Craig and G de Búrca (eds), *The Evolution of EU Law* (Oxford, OUP, 1999) at 368.

not as fixed as it might otherwise appear, but principally the high degree of sensitivity of striking down a national regulation on the basis of the disproportion between the trade-restrictive effects and the public policy benefits of the measure. Substituting its own value judgment for that of the Members (often reached by a democratically elected legislative body) clearly constitutes an extraordinary intrusion into national regulatory sovereignty. This is often the (difficult) task of a constitutional court. It might occasionally be the task of the ECJ, but it certainly should not be the task of the Appellate Body. Accordingly, WTO law *does* not, and I also believe *should* not, include, even in its more modern "reasonableness" disciplines embodied in the TBT and SPS Agreements, the principle of "proportionality *stricto sensu*".

A third and final distinction appears to rest on the higher degree of specificity of the TBT and SPS proportionality requirements vis-à-vis the requirements of the *Dassonville–Cassis de Dijon* "rule of reason". This is evidenced not only in the way in which these requirements are formulated in the two WTO sectoral Agreements, but also in the manner in which they are applied by WTO adjudicating bodies.

In the analysis of the proportionality requirements of the SPS Agreement, I have emphasised, for example, that notwithstanding the basic structural identity between the "suitability" requirement and the two obligations set out in Articles 2.2 and 5.1 SPS, these two latter obligations have a more detailed character, which makes them both more specific as well as more rigid. While a general "suitability" requirement may leave some flexibility in assessing the reasonableness of the relationship between the measure and its aim, the obligation to maintain SPS measures on "sufficient scientific evidence" (2.2) and to base them on "risk assessment" (5.1) does not allow for such a broad flexibility and thus may be viewed as imposing stricter normative standards on Members. This more detailed and thus stricter normative character of the SPS "suitability" requirements appears to be counterbalanced by the flexible and pragmatic approach that has been taken with regard to the definition of "risk assessment". Although "scientific principles" as well as "scientific evidence" should be at the basis of each Member's sanitary and phytosanitary measures, the Appellate Body has correctly emphasised that "science" is not an infallible tool and that Member States should be free to evaluate health and life risks also on the basis of other non-scientific factors. If this more contextual approach to risk assessment does not mean that risk should be evaluated exclusively or even predominantly on the basis of these other non-scientific factors, equally the risk that is relevant for the purposes of the SPS disciplines cannot be evaluated exclusively within the parameters of "laboratory science". This shows the Appellate Body's preference for a balanced approach based on scientific principles and evidence as filtered through other non-scientific realities, which should and do influence the way risks are perceived and regulated.

Accordingly, if the contextual approach employed by the Appellate Body in defining "risk assessment" within the meaning of Article 5.1 SPS is confirmed in future jurisprudence, the increased specificity and thus rigidity of the "suitability" requirements in the SPS Agreement should be welcomed as an element favouring legal certainty. One should never forget that the "reasonableness" or "proportionality" principle with all its related normative tenets is principally aimed at providing national regulators with "appropriate" as well as "clear" normative standards. In this regard the "reasonableness" rule in WTO law (in particular in the SPS and TBT Agreements) as applied so far by WTO adjudicating bodies appears to be more capable than its EC counterpart in providing national regulators with *clearer* normative standards. While this is due partly to the different origins of the two "reasonableness" disciplines ("legislative" in WTO law and "jurisprudential" in EC law), I believe that the principal reason for such a difference in the level of specificity stems from the awareness of WTO adjudicating bodies (and in particular the Appellate Body) that in WTO law the margins for covert interpretative manoeuvres are much more limited than those within which the ECJ has operated in the last three decades.

5

Conclusion

I T IS APPROPRIATE to end this comparative study with some
conclusions on the process of "trade liberalisation" in the European
Union and the World Trade Organisation.

In his remarks on an *ensemble* of papers contributed to the first book of
the first volume stemming from the research project on the role of law in
the process of European integration as seen against the American federal
experience,[1] Donald Kommers noted that "federalism is an evolutionary
process that defies universal definition".[2] From the analysis of a few basic
legal instruments involving (a) the obligation to reduce or eliminate border measures, (b) the prohibitions of de jure and (c) de facto discrimination based on nationality, and (d) the rule of reasonableness which has
been employed by the EU and the WTO in order to liberalise trade in
goods among their respective Members, the same evolutionary process
may also be seen in the development of trade liberalisation or, if you will,
economic integration. This may be noted by looking at the above-
mentioned instruments from both a static (or structural) perspective as
well as from a more dynamic (or interpretative) one.

From a static perspective, given their different "normative content"
and "objective element", the cocktail of *rules* that is adopted in order to
bring down barriers to international trade is directly dependent on the
level of liberalisation (ie integration) that the participating Member States
collectively pursue. In chapter 1, it was noted, for example, that while the
GATT dealt with the issue of internal regulation "simply" by imposing on
its Members a National Treatment obligation, the Treaty of Rome
included more advanced instruments aimed at the ambitious goal of harmonising all Member States' internal regulations affecting the establishment or functioning of the common market (Articles 94–95 EC).
Moreover, as examined in chapter 4, only recently has the WTO gone
beyond the non-discrimination principle and included in its spectrum of

---

[1] M Cappelletti, M Seccombe, J Weiler (eds), *Integration Through Law—Europe and the
American Federal Experience*, Vols 1–6 (Berlin/New York, Walter de Gruyter, 1986).
[2] D Kommers, "Federalism and European Integration: A Commentary" in M Cappelletti,
M Seccombe, J Weiler (eds), *Integration Through Law—Europe and the American Federal
Experience, Vol 1: Methods, Tools and Institutions, Book 1: A Political, Legal and Economic
Overview* (Berlin/New York, Walter de Gruyter, 1986) at 615.

trade-liberalising tools more detailed disciplines imposing on its Members several normative standards (such as reasonableness or proportionality) in the field of sanitary and technical regulation.

The evolutionary nature of integration may also be perceived by taking a more dynamic view, focusing on the "interpretation" or "application" of the several trade-liberalising instruments. The history of the interpretation of Article 28 EC is perhaps the paradigm of such an evolution. As was demonstrated in all four chapters, the Court of Justice has employed the apparently innocuous prohibition of "quantitative restrictions and measures having equivalent effect" in Article 28 EC as a means of imposing, first of all, a ban on non-pecuniary *border* measures (step 1), a prohibition of de jure (or formally) discriminatory *internal* measures (step 2), a requirement that any indistinctly applicable measure affecting intra-Community trade be *reasonable* or *proportionate* (step 3), with the exception of "selling arrangements" which, most recently, have been required not to discriminate in law or in fact vis-à-vis imported products (step 4).

In observing the remarkable evolution of the interpretation of Article 28 EC, a few other central points may be emphasised. First, it is certainly premature at this stage to claim an equivalence in the content of the legal instruments employed in EC and WTO law to liberalise trade, in other words, the existence of a single, unified theory of free trade.[3] I feel that constructing such a theory would not do justice to the complexities and uncertainties surrounding not simply the various legal provisions but also the socio-political-economic contexts in which the EC and the WTO function.

Secondly, and as a confirmation of the first point, the evolutionary *process* of integration does not follow exclusively mono-directional, linear patterns, but is rather characterised by "trial-and-error" developments as well as "diagonal" patterns. For example, the decision of the Court of Justice in *Keck* could be seen as a sign of the Court's desire both to retrace its steps (ie to limit the scope of application of its long-standing, pro-market *Dassonville–Cassis de Dijon* "rule of reason" doctrine) and to promote the use of other integration strategies (ie harmonisation, or subsidiarity).

---

[3] Cf P Eeckhout, "After *Keck and Mithouard*: Free Movement of Goods in the EC, Market Access, and Non-Discrimination", in T Cottier and P Mavroidis (eds), *Regulatory Barriers and the Principle of Non-Discrimination in World Trade Law* (Ann Arbor, Michigan University Press, 2000) at 204, "The question can be raised, however, whether at present the difference is not rather one of quantum than of quality. It is clear that in the EC there is a much more developed body of case-law, complemented by a high level of harmonisation of legislation. The quantity of intervention is therefore much higher than in the WTO. But, as was noted, the basic concepts are similar, and when one looks at the approach to the interpretation of those concepts in WTO law, one discovers great potential for the development of far-reaching case-law." For a somewhat different view, JHH Weiler, "Epilogue: Toward a Common Law of International Trade", in JHH Weiler (ed), *The EU, the WTO and the NAFTA: Towards a Common Law of International Trade?* (Oxford, OUP, 2000).

Thirdly, there is no doubt today that the evolution of Article 28 EC was a *jurisprudential* affair. It was the European Court of Justice that, after a first foundational period from 1963 to the mid-1970s during which the Community legal structure was "constitutionalised",[4] single-handedly carried the Community and its Member States forward in their pursuit of the single market. What was a prohibition on, at most, "distinctly applicable measures" (ie the original function of Article 30 EEC) became after *Dassonville* and *Cassis de Dijon* the "mighty" requirement that all "indistinctly applicable measures" hindering intra-Community trade be *reasonable* or *proportionate*, where the burden of proving reasonableness was placed on importing Members (thus, the so called principle of "mutual recognition"). In contrast, at the multilateral level, the inclusion of the reasonableness rule as a tool for increasing the liberalisation of international trade in goods (ie the disciplines of the TBT and SPS Agreements) has occurred at the end of a long negotiating process among "sovereign" States based on consensus, and not certainly at the hand of the seven-member Appellate Body of the WTO. Thus, Article XI GATT was kept, contrary to its European counterpart (Article 28 EC), as the instrument requiring the elimination of a specific type of national regulations (non-pecuniary border measures) and, I believe wisely, nothing more.[5]

The quasi-"legislative" role of the Court of Justice may be detected also in other areas of the law of the free movement of goods. For example, following a very strict interpretation of the public policy exception of Article 30 EC, the Court of Justice requires not simply that the national measure at issue be somehow connected with (ie "justified on grounds of") one of the relevant public policies listed in that provisions, but, more rigorously, than that same measure comply with the so called "proportionality principle" (which entails in effect the three sub-tests of "suitability", "least restrictive alternative" or "necessity", and "proportionality *stricto sensu*"). As noted throughout the present analysis,[6] the Court has never been very clear on either the legal basis of the proportionality principle or its relationship with the requirements of Article 30, second sentence (prohibiting "arbitrary discrimination" and "disguised restriction"). Thus, following the Court's preference for its "unstructured" approach to the issue of public policy justification under Article 30, it has been emphasised that (a) the various tests constituting the proportionality principle have become the central requirements in an Article 30 analysis and (b) the conditions

---

[4] JHH Weiler, "The Transformation of Europe", 100 *Yale LJ* (1991) 2403 at 2413 *et seq.*

[5] Cf JHH Weiler, "Epilogue: Toward a Common Law of International Trade", in JHH Weiler (ed), *The EU, the WTO and the NAFTA: Towards a Common Law of International Trade?* (Oxford, OUP, 2000) who argues on the contrary that, although the GATT never took Art XI seriously, recent WTO jurisprudence would seem to suggest a different future development.

[6] See above sections discussing the "justification options" with regard to non-pecuniary measures in chs 1, 2 and 3.

provided for in the second sentence of Article 30 have been practically absorbed by the proportionality test and only very rarely constitute a further ground of appraisal.[7]

Another example of judicial intervention, this time to correct an apparent gap in the original EC Treaty, is the Court of Justice's recognition of a *"de facto* derogation clause" to the National Treatment obligation imposed on Member States in the taxation field. Accordingly, Member States may plead *any* social policy to justify either an origin-based or origin-neutral fiscal measure which has been found to violate the non-discrimination principle of Article 90 EC.[8] It is clear, however, that the Court will take account of public policy purposes formally *within* its "discrimination" assessment. In other words, if the Court is persuaded of the legitimacy of the policy purposes underlying the differential tax burdens on similar or competitive products, it will simply reject any claim of "discrimination", instead of "justifying" it.[9]

It should not be too difficult to contrast this uninhibited approach[10] with the more conservative and textually-faithful approach shown by WTO jurisprudence (and in particular the Appellate Body). For example, with regard to the interpretation of the justification provision of Article XX GATT, WTO jurisprudence has demonstrated a willingness to follow more strictly the text of the "general exception" provision even if this has meant having to deal with, and reconcile, the two distinct features of Article XX: on the one hand, the several and different "connectors" qualifying the public policy interests found in Article XX, subletters (a) to (j) (ie "necessary", "related to", "essential", etc.) and, on the other hand, the general requirements of the Chapeau of Article XX (ie prohibition on "arbitrary and unjustifiable discrimination" and "disguised restrictions on international trade").[11]

Moreover, with regard to the possibility of expanding the coverage of the public policy justification of Article XX, which lists only ten policy goals, recent WTO jurisprudence has fought back several attempts to follow the steps of the European Court of Justice (in its interpretation of Article 90 EC) and permeate the content of the non-discrimination "rule" with the features of the public policy "exception". In chapter 3, the first

---

[7] See in particular the discussion in chs 1 and 2.

[8] JHH Weiler, "The Constitution of the Common Marketplace: Text and Context in the Evolution of the Free Movement of Goods" in P Craig and G de Búrca (eds), *Evolution of EU Law* (Oxford, OUP, 1999) at 365.

[9] See above chs 2 and 3 on the National Treatment principle, in particular the section on the prohibition of de facto discriminatory fiscal charges in EC law.

[10] One should remember that pursuant to old Art 164 (now 220) EC the task of the Court of Justice is to "ensure that in the interpretation and application of the Treaty the law is observed".

[11] See above ch 2, the discussion on the "justification options" for formally discriminatory non-fiscal regulation.

and most known among these attempts was examined: the so called *aims-and-effects* doctrine. This approach was professed in a few Panel Reports (not all of them adopted by GATT Members), at the beginning of the 1990s when panels began to be confronted with claims that apparently origin-neutral measures were in violation of the National Treatment obligations (ie claims of de facto discrimination).[12] The *aims-and-effects* doctrine attempted to redefine the "like product" concept of GATT Article III on the basis of the *purpose* of Article III, which is to ensure that internal taxation and regulation "should not be applied to imported or domestic products so as to afford protection to domestic production." Accordingly, in determining whether two products that are subject to different treatment are "like products" for purposes of Article III:2 (and 4), it would be necessary to consider whether such *product differentiation* is being made "so as to afford protection to domestic production" *or* it is pursuing legitimate policy purposes unrelated to the protection of domestic products.[13] As noted in that discussion, although the *aims-and-effects* doctrine was eventually rejected with force by WTO jurisprudence, inter alia, on the basis of the doctrine's inconsistency with the wording of Article III:2, first sentence, and the risk of making the general exception provision of Article XX GATT redundant,[14] several of its tenets may well become useful in the context of determining the discriminatory or protectionist nature of a measure.[15]

The pros and cons of the respective approaches of the European Court of Justice and WTO adjudicating bodies may be analysed, first of all, from the perspective of the interpretation of each trade-liberalising "rule". While the liberal and "unstructured" approach pursued by the Court of Justice holds greater flexibility and thus improves the ability to reach the right result in the specific case, it does not much help the cause of the "certainty of the law" and thus the ability of the "rule" to provide a *normative standard* for national regulators (as well as courts) to follow. On the other hand, the more rigorous and "textually-faithful" approach followed by WTO jurisprudence favours the certainty and thus the positive normative function of the "rules", this may at the same time lose the flexibility necessary to find the "appropriate" or "correct" solution for each specific case.

However, notwithstanding these differences in these initial approaches to the issue of interpretation, there does seem to be an inherent propensity

---

[12] Panel Report on *United States—Measures Affecting Alcoholic and Malt Beverages* (*Malt Beverages*), DS23/R, adopted on 19 June 1992, BISD 39S/206; *United States—Taxes on Automobiles*, unadopted, GATT Doc. DS31/R, reprinted in 33 ILM 1397.

[13] See Panel Report on *Malt Beverages*, above n 12, para 5.25.

[14] See both the Panel and the Appellate Body Reports in *Japan–Alcoholic II* and above the discussion in ch 3 in the section on "fiscal charges restricting trade in goods".

[15] See above ch 3, the discussion on the interpretation of the "less favourable treatment" requirement.

for these two types of interpretation to reach, in the long run, a similar balance between the competing interests (flexibility + appropriate case-specific end-result *v* rigidity + certainty of the law). Let us take the example of the prohibition of de facto discrimination as it is applied to fiscal charges. In EC law, in light of the absence of an express exception provision capable of justifying on public policy grounds a national pecuniary measure that is found to violate the National Treatment provision of Article 90 EC, the European Court has employed its "power" to read within the non-discrimination principle a "*de facto* derogation clause". The ambivalence of the ensuing case law has perplexed many EC experts. However, following an examination of this apparently confusing application of Article 90 (chapter 3), it would appear that, at least in overall terms, the Court of Justice operates according to very basic and simple criteria. First of all, public policy arguments play a role only where the internal pecuniary measure under review is deemed to have some *discriminatory effects* against imported products (ie internal taxation, albeit formally origin-neutral, has the effect of disfavouring *in particular* products from other Member States—discriminatory nature—or favouring *in particular* national production—protective nature). Secondly, pure fiscal policy objectives are not enough to justify a tax system that, while origin-neutral on its face, is found to discriminate in practice on the basis of the product's origin or nationality. Thirdly, where the tax system differentiates between products on the basis of more specific public policy purposes, the Court will be willing to take account of these purposes, albeit within its discrimination assessment, only if the differentiating criterion is not *inherently* discriminatory against imported products.

This contrasts dramatically with the rigorous interpretation within WTO jurisprudence of the almost identical provision in Article III:2. For example, the requirement of the first sentence of Article III:2 (imported products shall not be subject to internal taxes in excess of those applied to like domestic products) has been interpreted by WTO adjudicating bodies in a very literal manner, with the consequence of transforming the *National* Treatment obligation into the much broader *Equal* Treatment obligation ("like products" must be taxed identically).[16] However, notwithstanding this initial rigorous (and, I believe, incorrect) interpretation, there are already signs in the jurisprudence predicting a future modification in the interpretation of the GATT National Treatment obligation. To a certain extent, this modification would go in the direction of the above-mentioned interpretation adopted by the Court of Justice. Although in the context of Article III:4 (ie non-fiscal internal regulation), the recent

---

[16] L Ehring, "*De Facto* Discrimination in WTO Law: National Treatment and Most-Favoured-Nation Treatment—or Equal Treatment?", *Jean Monnet Working Paper* (NYU School of Law, 2002); CD Ehlermann, "Some Personal Experiences as Member of the Appellate Body of the WTO", *EUI Policy Paper* (No 9, 2002) at 35.

Appellate Body *dicta* on the meaning of "less favourable treatment" in *Asbestos* (the famous paragraph 100 of the AB Report) appear to stress the centrality of the measure's protectionist effects vis-à-vis domestic products (a measure violates Article III only if it predominantly favours domestic products as a whole).

A similar evolution may be seen with regard to the application of "proportionality" used both as an instrument to limit the availability of the public policy exception of Article 30 EC and Article XX GATT, and as an independent normative standard (ie within the *Dassonville–Cassis de Dijon* "rule of reason" approach and the reasonableness disciplines of the SPS and TBT Agreements).[17]

In other words, despite the clear difference in the approaches of the European Court of Justice and the WTO adjudicating bodies to the interpretation of these basic rules, in the long run these approaches have led to similar and correct results. In more general terms, it may be noted that a fundamental feature of any type of "judicial integration" rules (such as the National Treatment principle or the reasonableness principle) is that their real normative value is intimately related to the long process of interpretation carried out by the "judiciary".

Differences, however, remain. For example, the Court of Justice "readings" of Article 28 EC are clearly inconceivable within the WTO context. Even a broadening of the list of public policy justifications in Article XX GATT through the dispute settlement mechanism appears at the moment highly unlikely.[18] The inability of the political arm of the WTO to function as a "filter" to prevent sensitive cases from ending up before WTO adjudicators or to provide for the necessary amendments to the substantive rules imposes on the judicial arm of the WTO a need to "proceed with extraordinary circumspection and care" in exercising its functions.[19]

Thus the lack of any viable mechanism to adapt the rules drafted more than 50 years ago to current needs will certainly put enormous strains on the dispute settlement mechanism and, as a consequence, on the WTO system as a whole. For example, as the focus of disputes moves from *origin-based* national measures to *origin-neutral* ones, the interpretation of Article XX GATT "is likely to raise some of the most difficult questions that the WTO will face."[20] As the present analysis has shown, the issue of justification on grounds of public policy is not controversial as long as we are dealing with measures *directly* and *expressly* discriminating on the

---

[17] See above respectively, chs 2–3 and ch 4.

[18] See above discussion of Art XX(d) in ch 2, section on the "justification options" for non-fiscal regulation, for a possible way to broaden the coverage of Art XX GATT.

[19] CD Ehlermann, "Some Personal Experiences as Member of the Appellate Body of the WTO", *EUI Policy Paper* (No 9, 2002) at 42–3.

[20] D McRae, "GATT Art XX and the WTO Appellate Body" in M Bronckers and R Quick (eds), *New Directions in International Economic Law* (London, Kluwer Law International, 2000) at 233.

basis of the origin or nationality of products. By contrast, when we start tackling origin-neutral regulations affecting the transnational circulation of products simply because of the existence of multiple regulators (ie de facto discriminatory measures), the question of public policy justifications of such measures becomes a very "problematic" and "sensitive" exercise.

This is problematic because the dividing line between establishing a prima facie case of discrimination (the "rule") and making out a public policy justification (the "exception") is not altogether clear in the case of origin-neutral measures with discriminatory effects vis-à-vis imported products. Both EC and WTO jurisprudence applying the National Treatment obligations demonstrate the problematic nature of establishing what constitutes (de facto) discrimination. It is sensitive because in dealing with origin-neutral measures with discriminatory effects vis-à-vis imported products, it is quite difficult for the judiciary to strike the "appropriate" balance between the trade-liberalising "rule" and the national public policy "exception", in particular considering the inherent bias in the "rule" versus "exception" approach towards liberalisation vis-à-vis the pursuit of public policy objectives. Moreover, GATT/WTO case-law has so far focused excessively on the "likeness" component of the National Treatment norm, which, though necessary in order to establish discrimination, it is not sufficient for a finding of discrimination on grounds of nationality or protectionism.

This is where looking at the EC experience affords valuable insights for the future of the WTO. First of all, despite the above-mentioned uncertainties, it has been suggested here that even in WTO law the non-discrimination *rule* should be distinguished from the public policy *exception*. While a finding of de facto discrimination should be based on an inquiry as to the discriminatory or protectionist features of a measure, a finding of justification on public policy grounds should be based on an assessment of whether the measure (apparently origin-neutral) is a reasonable and proportionate instrument to achieve a legitimate public policy objective. Accordingly, although both determinations make use of an examination of the objective features of the challenged measure, their function clearly differs. If the objective of a de facto discrimination assessment is to determine whether the effect of the regulatory treatment of products is *in fact* protectionist, the objective of a public policy justification analysis is to establish whether that same regulatory treatment is indeed a "reasonable" attempt to achieve a legitimate public policy aim.

However, there may still be problems even if WTO jurisprudence eventually endorses the correct reading of the National Treatment principle (as suggested in the present analysis). It has been noted that, in light of the exhaustive nature of the public policy list in Article XX GATT, there may still be cases where it will be impossible for the judiciary to even attempt to strike a balance between trade liberalisation and national regulatory prerogatives. Although this is indeed a difficult problem, one may advance two relevant points. First, it is indeed possible to broaden the coverage of Article XX GATT through a more flexible interpretation of Article XX(d) GATT, as suggested in chapter 2. Secondly, the absence of certain important public policy objectives in Article XX has been cured at least to a certain extent by the introduction of the TBT Agreement, which permits Members to adopt technical regulations for the pursuit of *any* legitimate public policy objective, as long as the requirements provided for in the Agreement itself are met. This means that Members may adopt a technical regulation for the protection of consumers (a policy objective not found in Article XX GATT) as long as such regulation conforms with the TBT Agreement disciplines (even if the regulation might be deemed to have discriminatory effects vis-à-vis imported products).[21] This would be possible only if, as I argued in chapter 4, the TBT Agreement were considered as *lex specialis* at least with regard to the general obligations and rights in Article III and XX of the GATT (ie a measure falling within the definition of a technical regulation or standard for purposes of the TBT Agreement would be reviewed under the latter to the exclusion of Articles III and XX GATT).

As a further insight from the EC experience, one may argue for the abandonment of the dual approach underlying the National Treatment principle (ie the non-discrimination "rule" vis-à-vis the public policy "exception") and for the adoption of other types of normative standards that are better capable of achieving the appropriate balance between trade-liberalisation efforts and the pursuit of legitimate public policy goals. In this respect, the disciplines recently provided for in the TBT and SPS Agreements including more elaborated and detailed forms of two of the elements of the proportionality principle ("suitability" and "necessity"), are clearly steps in the right direction. As noted in chapter 4, despite the usual difficulty in the actual implementation of these general standards, the increased specificity and consequent rigidity of the proportionality requirements in these recent Agreements should be welcomed as an element favouring overall legal certainty.

Once again, one should not forget that the general principles employed for the liberalisation and regulation of the transnational movement of products are principally aimed at providing national regulators with "appropriate" as well as "clear" normative standards. In this regard, the "reasonableness" rules in WTO law (in particular in the SPS and TBT Agreements) as applied so far by WTO adjudicating bodies appear to be more capable than their EC counterparts of providing national regulators with *clear* normative standards. While this is due partially to the different

---

[21] See above ch 4, the discussion on the relationship between the TBT Agreement and the GATT.

origin of the two "reasonableness" disciplines ("legislative" in WTO law and "jurisprudential" in EC law), I believe that the principal reason for such a difference in the level of specificity stems from the awareness of WTO adjudicating bodies (and in particular the Appellate Body) that, in WTO law, the margins for covert interpretative manoeuvres are much more limited (if not precluded) when compared to those within which the ECJ has operated over the last three decades. Moreover, by limiting such disciplines to "suitability" and "necessity" and thus excluding the more sensitive review of "proportionality *stricto sensu*", it may be suggested that even the WTO adjudicating bodies would be able to handle the task of giving actual content to such general principles.[22]

In addition, the experience with the application of the proportionality principle in the context of Articles 28 and 30 EC and that of Article XX GATT shows that there are possible gains to be made by employing both "substantive" and "procedural" elements in assessing the reasonableness or proportionality of origin-neutral internal measures. As recently argued by several scholars, reliance on an examination of the legislative *process* behind the measure under review might be a more accurate means of assessing the legitimacy of national regulatory measures.[23]

There is, however, no doubt that whatever development there might be in WTO law, the use of instruments of "judicial integration" will have the inevitable effect of entrusting a relevant, though, difficult, role to the dispute settlement system and in particular the Appellate Body.

---

[22] G Verhoosel, *National Treatment and WTO Dispute Settlement* (Oxford, Hart Publishing, 2002) at 106 *et seq*.

[23] M Maduro Poiares, *We, the Court: The ECJ and the European Economic Constitution* (Oxford, Hart Publishing, 1998); J Scott, "On Kith and Kine (and Crustaceans): Trade and Environment in the EU and WTO", *Jean Monnet Working Paper* (Harvard Law School, 1999); C Joerges, "'Good Governance' in the European Internal Market—Two Competing Legal Conceptualisations of European Integration and their Synthesis" in A von Bogdandy, P Mavroidis and Y Mény (eds), *European Integration and International Co-ordination—Studies in Transnational Economic Law in Honour of Claus-Dieter Ehlermann* (The Hague/London/New York, Kluwer Law International, 2002).

Bibliography

ADINOLFI G, *L'organizzazione mondiale del commercio: profili istituzionali e normativi* (Padova, CEDAM, 2001).

AHN D, "Environmental Disputes in the GATT/WTO: Before and After *US–Shrimp* Case", 20 *Mich J Int'l L* (Summer, 1999) 819.

APPLETON A AND HEISKANEN V, "The *Sardines* Decision: Fish Without Chips?", paper presented at the London meeting of the World Trade Law Association in Nov 2002 (in file with author).

APPLETON A, "GATT Article XX's Chapeau: A Disguised 'Necessary' Test?: The WTO Appellate Body's Ruling in *United States—Standards for Reformulated and Conventional Gasoline*", 6 *RECIEL* (1997) 131.

——"*Shrimp/Turtle*: Untangling the Nets", 2 *JIEL* (1999) 477.

BALASSA B (ed), *Studies in Trade Liberalization: Problems and Prospects for the Industrial Countries* (Baltimore, Johns Hopkins Press, 1967).

BALDWIN R, *Nontariff Distortions of International Trade* (Washington DC, The Brookings Institution, 1970).

BARENTS R, "Charges of Equivalent Effect to Customs Duties", 15 *CMLRev* (1978) 415.

BARNARD C AND J SCOTT (eds), *The Law of the Single European Market: Unpacking the Premises* (Oxford, Hart Publishing, 2002).

BARNARD C, "Fitting the Remaining Pieces into the Goods and Persons Jigsaw", 26 *ELRev* (2001) 35.

BARTELS L, "Article XX of GATT and the Problem of Extraterritorial Jurisdiction: The Case of Trade Measures for the Protection of Human Rights", 36 *JWT* (2002) 353.

BEVIGLIA ZAMPETTI A AND SAUVÉ P (eds), *New Dimension of Market Access in a Globalising World Economy* (Paris, Organisation for Economic Co-operation and Development, 1996).

BÉRAUD RC, "Les mesures d'effet équivalent au sens des Articles 30 et suivants du Traité de Rome", *Revue Trimestrelle de Droit Européen* (1968) 265.

BERMANN G, GOEBEL R, DAVEY W, FOX E, *Cases and Materials on European Community Law* (St. Paul, West Publishing, 1993).

BERNARD N, "Discrimination and the Free Movement in EC Law", 45 *ICLQ* (1996) 82.

BIONDI A, "Advertising Alcohol and the Free Movement Principle: The *Gourmet* Decision", 26 *ELRev* (2001) 616.

BHAGWATI J AND HUDEC R E (eds), *Fair Trade and Harmonization: Prerequisites for Free Trade? Vol 2: Legal Analysis*, (Cambridge, MA, MIT Press, 1996).

CAPPELLETTI M, SECCOMBE M, WEILER J (eds), *Integration Through Law—Europe and the American Federal Experience, Vol 1: Methods, Tools and Institutions, Book 1: A Political, Legal and Economic Overview* (Berlin/New York, Walter de Gruyter, 1986).

CAPPELLETTI M, SECCOMBE M, WEILER J (eds), *Integration Through Law—Europe and the American Federal Experience, Vol 1: Methods, Tools and Institutions, Book 2: Political Organs, Integration Techniques and Judicial Process* (Berlin/New York, Walter de Gruyter, 1986).

CARTABIA M AND WEILER JHH, *L'Italia in Europa—Profili istituzionali e costituzionali* (Bologna, Il Mulino, 2000).

CASS D, "The 'Constitutionalization' of International Trade Law: Judicial Norm-Generation as the Engine of Constitutional Development in International Trade", 12 *EJIL* (2001) 39.

CHALMERS D, "Repackaging the Internal Market—the Ramifications of the Keck Judgement", 19 *ELRev* (1994) 385.

CHARNOVITZ S, "Exploring Environmental Exceptions in GATT Article XX", 25 *JWT* (1991) 37.

——"The WTO Panel Decision on US Clean Air Act Regulations", *International Environment Reporter* (6 March 1996).

COMBA A, *Il Neo Liberismo Internazionale* (Milano, Giuffré Editore, 1995).

CONDON B, "Reconciling Trade and Environment: A Legal Analysis of European and North American Approaches", 8 *Cardozo Journal of International and Comparative Law* (2000) 1.

COREA C, "Implementing National Public Health Policies in the Framework of WTO Agreements" 34 *JWT* (2000) 89.

COSTELLO C, "Market Access All Areas—The Treatment of Non-Discriminatory Barriers to the Free Movement of Workers", 27 *Legal Issues of Economic Integration* (2000) 267

COTTIER T AND MAVROIDIS P (eds), *Regulatory Barriers and the Principle of Non-Discrimination in World Trade Law* (Ann Arbor, University of Michigan Press, 2000).

COTTIER T, "A Theory of Direct Effect in Global Law", in A von Bogdandy, P Mavroidis and Y Mény (eds), *European Integration and International Co-ordination—Studies in Transnational Economic Law in Honour of Claus-Dieter Ehlermann* (The Hague/London/New York, Kluwer Law International, 2002).

CRAIG P AND DE BÚRCA G (eds), *Evolution of EU Law* (Oxford, OUP, 1999).

——*EU Law* (Oxford, OUP, 1998).

DANIELE L, *Il diritto materiale della Comunità Europea* (Milano, Giuffré, 2000).

DANUSSO M AND DENTON R, "Does the European Court of Justice Look for a Protectionist Motive Under Article 95?", *LIEI* (1990), 67.

DAVEY W AND PAUWELYN J, "MFN Unconditionality: A Legal Analysis of the Concept in View of its Evolution in the GATT/WTO Jurisprudence with Particular Reference to the Issue of 'Like Product'", in Cottier T and Mavroidis P (eds), *Regulatory Barriers and the Principle of Non-Discrimination in World Trade Law* (Ann Arbor, The University of Michigan Press, 1999).

DAVEY W, "Has the WTO Dispute Settlement System Exceeded its Authority? A Consideration of Deference Shown by the System to Member Government Decisions and its Use of Issue-Avoidance Techniques", 4 *JIEL* (2001) 79.

DAVIES G, *European Union Internal Market Law* (London/Sydney, Cavendish, 2001).

De Búrca G, "The Principle of Proportionality and its Application in EC law", 13 *YEL* (1994) 105.

——and Scott J (eds), *The EU and the WTO: Legal and Constitutional Aspects* (Oxford, Hart Publishing, 2001).

De Vergottini G, *Diritto Costituzionale Comparato* (Padova, CEDAM, 1999).

Demaret P, "The Non-Discrimination Principles and the Removal of Fiscal Barriers to Intra-Community Trade", in Cottier T and Mavroidis P (eds), *Regulatory Barriers and the Principle of Non-Discrimination in World Trade Law* (Ann Arbor, The University of Michigan Press, 2000).

Desmedt A, "Proportionality in WTO Law", 4 *JIEL* (2001) 441.

Dougan M, "Minimum Harmonisation and the Internal Market", 37 *CMLRev* (2000) 853.

Dunkley G, *The Free Trade Adventure, the WTO, the Uruguay Round and Globalism—A Critique* (London/New York, Zed Books, 2000).

Eeckhout P, *The European Internal Market and International Trade: A Legal Analysis* (Oxford, Clarendon Press, 1994).

——"The European Court of Justice and the Legislature", 18 *Yearbook of European Law* (1998) 1.

——"After *Keck and Mithouard*: Free Movement of Goods in the EC, Market Access, and Non-Discrimination" Cottier T and Mavroidis P (eds), *Regulatory Barriers and the Principle of Non-Discrimination in World Trade Law* (Ann Arbor, the University of Michigan Press, 2000).

——"Constitutional Concepts for Free Trade in Services" in de Burca G and Scott J (eds), *The EU and the WTO: Legal and Constitutional Aspects* (Oxford, Hart, 2001).

——"Judicial Enforcement of WTO Law in the European Union—Some Further Reflections", 5 *JIEL* (2002) 91.

Ehlermann CD, *Das Verbot der Wassnahmen gleicher Wirkung in der Rechtsprechung des Gerichthofes: Festschrift für Ipsen* (1985).

——"The Internal Market Following the Single European Act", 24 *CMLRev* (1987) 361.

——and Campogrande G, "Rules on Services in the EEC: A Model for Negotiating World-Wide Rules?" in Petersmann EU and Hilf M (eds) *The New GATT Round of Multilateral Trade Negotiations–Legal and Economic Problems* (Deventer-Boston, Kluwer Law and Taxation Publishers, 1991).

——"Some Personal Experiences as Member of the Appellate Body of the WTO", *European University Institute, Policy Paper* (No 9, 2002).

Ehlermann CD and Ehring L, "WTO Dispute Settlement and Competition Law: Views from the Perspective of the Appellate Body's Experience", *European University Institute, Policy Papers* (No 12, 2002).

El-Agran A (ed), *International Economic Integration* (London, Macmillan, 1982).

Ellis E (ed), *The Principle of Proportionality in the Laws of Europe* (Oxford, OUP, 1999).

Emiliou N, *The Principle of Proportionality in European Law: A Comparative Study* (London, Kluwer, 1996).

——and D O'Keefe (eds), *The European Union and World Trade Law: After the GATT Uruguay Round* (London, John Wiley & Sons, 1996).

——(eds), *Legal Aspects of Integration in the European Union* (London, Kluwer Law International, 1997).

EHRING L, "*De Facto* Discrimination in WTO Law: National Treatment and Most-Favoured-Nation Treatment—or Equal Treatment?", *Jean Monnet Working Paper* (NYU School of Law, 2002).

EASSON A, "Fiscal Discrimination: New Perspectives on Art 95 of the EEC Treaty", 18 *CMLRev* (1981) 521.

EGGER, "The Principle of Proportionality in Community Anti-Dumping Law" 18 *ELRev* (1993) 367.

ESTY D AND GERADIN D, "Market Access, Competitiveness, and Harmonisation: Environmental Protection in Regional Trade Agreements", 21 *Harvard Environmental Law Review* (1997) 265.

FARBER D AND HUDEC R, "GATT Legal Restraints on Domestic Environmental Regulations" in Bhagwati J and Hudec R (eds), *Fair Trade and Harmonization: Prerequisites for Free Trade*, Vol 2 (Cambridge, MA MIT Press, 1996).

FAUCHALD OK, *Environmental Taxes and Trade Discrimination* (London, Kluwer Law International, 1998).

FRENCH D, "The Changing Nature of 'Environmental Protection': Recent Developments Regarding Trade and the Environment in the European Union and the World Trade Organisation", XLVII *Netherlands International Law Review* (2000) 1.

GAINES S, "The WTO's Reading of the GATT Article XX Chapeau: A Disguised Restriction on Environmental Measures", 22 *U Pa J Int'l Econ L* (Winter, 2001) 739.

GATT, *Analytical Index: Guide to GATT Law and Practice*, 6th edn (1994).

GEORGE S, *Remettre l'OMC à sa Place* (Mille et nuits, département de la Librairie Arthème Fayard, 2001).

GERADIN D, "Trade and Environmental Protection: Community Harmonisation and National Environmental Standards", 13 *YEL* (1993) 151.

——*Trade and the Environment: A Comparative Study of EC and US Law*, (Cambridge, CUP, 1997).

GORMLEY L "Actually or Potentially, Directly or Indirectly? Obstacles to the Free Movement of Goods", 9 *YEL* (1989) 197.

——"Reasoning Renounced? The Remarkable Judgment in *Keck and Mithouard*", *European Business Law Review* (1994) 63.

HANDOL J, *Free Movement of Persons in the EU* (Chichester, John Wiley and Sons, 1995).

HATZOPOULOS V, "Exigences essentielles, impératives ou impérieuse: *une* théorie, *des* théories ou pas de théorie du tout?", 34 *RTD eur.* (1998) 191.

——"Recent Developments of the Case Law of the ECJ in the Field of Services", 37 *CMLRev* (2000) 43.

HAZARD J, *The Soviet System of Government* (Chicago/London, University of Chicago Press, 1968).

HILF M, JACOBS F AND PETERSMANN EU (eds), *The European Community and GATT* (Deventer-Boston, Kluwer, 1986).

HILF M, "Power, Rules and Principles—Which Orientation for WTO/GATT Law?", 4 *JIEL* (2001) 111.

HILSON C, "Discrimination in Community free movement law", 24 *ELRev* (1999) 445.

HOEKMAN B, "Market Access Through Multilateral Agreement: From Goods to Services", 15 *The World Economy* (Nov 1992) 721.

——AND C PRIMO BRAGA, "Protection and Trade in Services: A Survey", *World Bank paper* (March 1997).

——AND D KONAN, "Deep Integration, Nondiscrimination, and Euro-Mediterranean Free Trade", paper presented at the Conference on "Regionalism in Europe: Geometries and Strategies After 2000", Bonn, Nov 6–8, 1998.

——AND KOSTECKI M, *The Political Economy of the World Trading System—The WTO and Beyond* (Oxford, OUP, 2001).

HORVAT B, *The Theory of International Trade—An Alternative Approach* (London, MacMillan, 1999).

HOWSE R, "Adjudicative Legitimacy and Treaty Interpretation in International Trade Law: The Early Years of WTO Jurisprudence" in JHH Weiler (ed), *The EU, the WTO and the NAFTA: Towards a Common Law of International Trade?* (Oxford, OUP, 2000).

——AND REAGAN D, "The Product/Process Distinction: An Illusory Basis for Disciplining 'Unilateralism' in Trade Policy", 11 *European Journal of International Law* (2000) 249.

——"Managing the Interface between International Trade Law and the Regulatory State: What Lessons Should (and Should Not) Be Drawn from the Jurisprudence of the United States Dormant Commerce Clause", in Cottier T and Mavroidis P (eds), *Regulatory Barriers and the Principle of Non-Discrimination in World Trade Law* (Ann Arbor, University of Michigan Press, 2000).

——AND TUERK E, "The WTO Impact on Internal Regulations—A Case Study of the Canada–EC Asbestos Dispute" in de Burca G and Scott J (eds), *The EU and the WTO: Legal and Constitutional Aspects* (Oxford, Hart, 2001).

HUDEC R, "The Product-Process Doctrine in GATT/WTO Jurisprudence", in Bronckers M and Quick R (eds), *New Directions in International Economic Law* (London, Kluwer Law International, 2000).

——"GATT/WTO Constraints on Domestic Regulation: Requiem for an 'Aims and Effects' Test", 32 *The International Lawyer* (1998) 623.

IAPADRE L (ed), *Costruire regole nella globalizzazione—Conferenza nazionale sul "Millenium Round"* (Bologna, Il Mulino, 2000).

JACKSON J, *World Trade and the Law of GATT* (New York, The Bobs-Merrill Co., 1969).

——*The Jurisprudence of GATT and the WTO* (Cambridge, CUP, 2000).

——"Comments on *Shrimp/Turtle* and the Product/Process Distinction", 11 *European Journal of International Law* (2, 2000) 303.

——DAVEY W AND SYKES A, *Legal Problems of International Economic Relations: Cases and Materials* (St. Paul Minnesota, West Publishing Co., 1995).

JACOBS F, "Recent Developments in the Principle of Proportionality in European Community Law in E Ellis (ed), *The Principle of Proportionality in the Laws of Europe* (Oxford, OUP, 1999).

JANS J, "Analysis", 11 *Journal of Environmental Law* (1999).

——"Proportionality Revisited", 27 *Legal Issues of Economic Integration* (2000) 239.

JANSEN B AND LUGARD M, "Some Considerations on Trade Barriers Erected for Non-Economic Reasons and WTO Obligations", 2 *JIEL* (1999) 530.

JARVIS MA, *The Application of EC Law by National Courts—The Free Movement of Goods* (Oxford, OUP, 1998).

JOVANOVIC M, *International Economic Integration* (London/New York, Routledge, 1998).

KAHLER M, *International Institutions and the Political Economy of Integration* (Washington DC, The Brookings Institution, 1995).

KURTZ J, "A General Investment Agreement in the WTO? Lessons from Chapter 11 of NAFTA and the OECD Multilateral Agreement on Investment", *Jean Monnet Working Paper* (NYU School of Law, 2002).

KUYPER PJ, "Booze and Fast Cars: Tax Discrimination Under GATT and the EC", 23 *Legal Issues of European Integration* (1996) 129.

LESTER S AND LEITNER K, *Dispute Settlement Commentary, European Communities–Asbestos (Appellate Body Report)* at 13 (2001), available at <http://www.worldtradelaw.net/dscsamples/index.htm>, visited 19 Feb 2002.

MADURO POIARES M, *We, the Court: The ECJ and the European Economic Constitution* (Oxford, Hart Publishing, 1998).

MALANCZUK P, *Akehurst's Modern Introduction to International Law* (London and New York, Routledge, 1997).

MARCEAU G AND TRACHTMAN J, "The Technical Barriers to Trade Agreement, the Sanitary and Phytosanitary Measures Agreement, and the General Agreement on Tariffs and Trade: A Map of the World Trade Organization Law of Domestic Regulation of Goods", 36 *JWT* (2002) 811.

MARENCO G, "Pour une interprétation traditionelle de la notion de mesure d'effet équivalent à une restriction quantitative", 20 *CDE* (1984) 291.

MARTIN D, "'Discrimination', 'entraves' et 'raisons impérieuses' dans le traité CE: trois concept en quête d'identité", 34 *CDE* (1998) 261.

MAAS C, "Should the WTO Expand GATT Article XX: An Analysis of *United States—Standards for Reformulated and Conventional Gasoline*", 5 *Minn J Global Trade* (1996) 415.

MARUYAMA W, "A New Pillar of the WTO: Sound Science", 32 *The International Lawyer* (Fall, 1998), 651.

MASCLET J, "Les Articles 30, 36 et 100 du traité CEE à la lumière de l'arrêt «cassis de Dijon»", *RDE* (1980) 23.

MATTERA A, "L'arrêt «cassis de Dijon»: une nouvelle approche pour la réalisation et le bon fonctionnemment du marché intérieur", *Revue du marché commun* (1980) 505.

MATTOO A AND MAVROIDIS P, "Trade, Environment and the WTO: The Dispute Settlement Practice Relating to Article XX of GATT", in EU Petersmann (ed) *International Trade Law and the GATT/WTO Dispute Settlement System* (London, Kluwer Law International, 1997).

MATTOO A, "National Treatment in the GATS: Corner-Stone or Pandora's Box?", 31 *JWT* (1997) 113.

——AND SUBRAMANIAN A, "Regulatory Autonomy and Multilateral Disciplines: The Dilemma and a Possible Resolution", 1 *JIEL* (1998) 303.

MAVROIDIS P, "Trade and Environment after the Shrimps-Turtles Litigation", 34 *JWT* (2000) 73.

MCGEE A AND WEATHERILL S, "The Evolution of the Single Market—Harmonisation or Liberalisation", 53 *The Modern Law Review* (Sept 1990) 578.

MCGINNIS J AND MOVSESIAN M, "The World Trade Constitution" 114 *Harvard Law Review* (2000) 511.

MEIJ A AND WINTER J, "Measures Having an Effect Equivalent to Quantitative Restrictions", 13 *CMLRev* (1976) 79.

Memorandum della Commissione sul Programma della Comunità nella seconda tappa (Bruxelles, 1962).

MENGOZZI P, "I servizi nell'Organizzazione Mondiale del Commercio" in SIDI (Società Italiana di Diritto Internazionale), *Diritto ed organizzazione del commercio internazionale dopo la creazione della Organizzazione Mondiale del Commercio*, Il Convegno, Milano 5–7 giugno 1997 (Editoriale Scientifica, 1998).

——(ed), *International Trade Law on the 50th Anniversary of the Multilateral Trade System* (Milano, Giuffré, 1999).

MCRAE D, "GATT Article XX and the WTO Appellate Body" in Bronckers M and Quick R (eds), *New Directions in International Economic Law* (London, Kluwer Law International, 2000).

MIGLIORINI L, *Le Restrizioni all'esportazione nel diritto internazionale* (Padova, CEDAM, 1993).

MONTAGUTI E AND LUGARD M, "The GATT 1994 and Other Annex 1A Agreements: Four Different Relationships?", 3 *JIEL* (2000) 473.

MONTINI M, "The Nature and Function of the Necessity and Proportionality Principles in the Trade and Environment Context", 6 *RECIEL* (1997) 121.

MORTELMANS K, "Article 30 of the EEC Treaty and Legislation Relating to Market Circumstances: Time to Consider a New Definition?", 28 *CMLRev* (1991) 115.

MOVSESIAN M, "Sovereignty, Compliance, and the World Trade Organisation: Lessons from the History of Supreme Court Review", 20 *Michigan Journal of International Law* (1999) 775.

MUSSELLI I, "Alla ricerca di un difficile equilibrio tra commercio e diritti sociali: la nozione di 'similarità' dei prodotti ex Art III del GATT", *Riv Dir Comm Int* (2001) 873.

NEUMAYER E, "Greening the WTO Agreements—Can the Treaty Establishing the European Community be of Guidance", 35 *JWT* (2001) 145.

NICOLAIDES P, "Economic Aspects of Services: Implications for a GATT Agreement", 23 *JWT* (1989) 123.

NOTARO N, *Judicial Approaches to Trade and Environment: The EC and the WTO, alias The Comparative Disadvantage of Dolphins and Turtles* (London, Cameron May International Law Publishers, 2003).

O'KEEFFE D AND BAVASSO A, "Four Freedoms, One Market and National Competence: In Search of a Dividing Line" in O'Keeffe D and Bavasso A (eds), *Judicial Review in European Union Law* (The Hague, Kluwer Law International, 2000).

OLIVER P, *Free Movement of Goods in the European Community* (London, Sweet and Maxwell, 1996)

——"Some Further Reflections on the Scope of Articles 28–30 (Ex 30–36) EC", 36 *CMLRev* (1999) 783.

OPPERMANN T AND CASCANTE J , "Dispute Settlement in the EC: Lessons for the GATT/WTO Dispute Settlement System?", in Petersmann EU (ed) *International Trade Law and the GATT/WTO Dispute Settlement System* (London, Kluwer Law International, 1997).

OSIRO D, "GATT/WTO Necessity Analysis: Evolutionary Interpretation and its Impact on the Autonomy of Domestic Regulation", 29 *Legal Issues of Economic Integration* (2002) 123.

PALMER A, WTO *European Communities—Measures Affecting Asbestos And Asbestos-Containing Products*, Report Of The Appellate Body, 10 *RECIEL* (2001) 340.

PAUWELYN J, "The WTO Agreement on Sanitary and Phytosanitary (SPS) Measures as Applied in the First Three SPS Disputes: *EC–Hormones, Australia–Salmon and Japan–Varietals*, 2 *JIEL* (1999) 641.

——"The Nature of WTO Obligations", *Jean Monnet Working Paper* (NYU School of Law, 2002).

PEABODY G, "The Lobster Size Conflict: Use of United States-Canada Free Trade Agreement Dispute Resolution Procedures", 1 *Territorial Sea Journal* (1991) 273.

PELKMANS J, "Removing Regulatory Access Barriers: The Case of 'Deep' Integration", *OECD Paper* (Feb 1996).

PETERSMANN EU, *International and European Trade and Environmental Law after the Uruguay Round* (London—The Hague–Boston, Kluwer Law International, 1995).

——*The GATT/WTO Dispute Settlement System—International Law, International Organisations and Dispute Settlement* (London/The Hague/Boston, Kluwer Law International, 1997).

——"From 'Negative' to 'Positive' Integration in the WTO: Time for 'Mainstreaming Human Rights' into WTO Law?", 37 *CMLRev* (2000) at 1363.

PICOD F , "La nouvelle approche de la Cour de justice en matière d'entraves aux échanges", 34 *RTD eur* (1998) 169.

PICONE P AND SACERDOTI G, *Diritto internazionale dell'economia : raccolta sistematica dei principali atti normativi internazionali ed interni con testi introduttivi e note* (Milano, Angeli, 1989).

PICONE P AND LIGUSTRO A, *Diritto dell'Organizzazione Mondiale del Commercio* (Padova, CEDAM, 2002).

PINDER J, "Positive Integration and Negative Integration: Some Problems of Economic Union in the EEC", 24 *World Today* (1968) 90.

QUADRI R, MONACO R, Trabucchi A (eds), *Commentario al Trattato Istitutivo della Comunità Economica Europea* Vol 1 (Milano, Giuffré Editore, 1965).

QURESHI A, *International Economic Law* (London, Sweet and Maxwell, 1999).

QUICK R AND BLÜTHNER A, "Has the Appellate Body Erred? An Appraisal and Criticism of the Ruling in the WTO *Hormones Case*", 2 *JIEL* (1999) 603.

RADICATI DI BROZOLO L, "Un primo confronto tra la liberalizzazione delle telecomunicazioni nel sistema del WTO e della Comunità Europea" in SIDI (Società Italiana di Diritto Internazionale), *Diritto ed organizzazione del commercio internazionale dopo la creazione della Organizzazione Mondiale del Commercio*, Il Convegno, Milano 5–7 giugno 1997 (Editoriale Scientifica, 1998).

REGAN D, "Regulatory Purpose and 'Like Products' in Article III:4 of the GATT (With Additional Remarks on Article III:2)", 36 *JWT* (3, 2002) 443.

ROBSON P, *The Economics of International Integration* (1998).

ROESSLER F, "Diverging Domestic Policies and Multilateral Trade Integration" in Bhagwati J and Hudec R E (eds), *Fair Trade and Harmonization: Prerequisites for Free Trade? Vol 2: Legal Analysis*, (Cambridge, MA, MIT Press, 1996).

——"Increasing Market Access under Regulatory Heterogeneity: The Strategies of the World Trade Organisation", in OECD, *Regulatory Reform and International Market Openness* (1996).

SAUVÉ P AND STERN R (eds), *GATS 2000—New Directions in Services Trade Liberalisation* (Washington DC, Brookings Institution Press, 2000).

SCHARPF F, "Balancing Positive and Negative Integration: the Regulatory Options for Europe", *Policy Papers Robert Schuman Centre* (No 4, 1997).

SCHOENBAUM T, "International Trade and Protection of the Environment: The Continuing Search for Reconciliation", 91 *Am J Int'l L* (April, 1997) 268.

SCOTT J, "GATT and Community Law: Rethinking the 'Regulatory Gap'" in Shaw J and More G (eds), *New Legal Dynamics of European Union* (New York, Clarendon Press, 1995).

——*EC Environmental Law* (London, Longman, 1998).

——"On KITH AND KINE (and Crustaceans): Trade and Environment in the EU and WTO", *Jean Monnet Working Paper* (Harvard Law School, 1999).

——"Mandatory or Imperative Requirements in the EU and the WTO" in Barnard C and Scott J (eds), *The Law of the Single European Market: Unpacking the Premises* (Oxford, Hart Publishing, 2002).

SCHWARZE J, *European Administrative Law* (London, Sweet and Maxwell, 1997).

SHAW S AND SCHWARTZ R, "Trade and Environment in the WTO: State of Play", 36 *JWT* (2002) 129.

SNAPE R, "Principles in Trade in Services" in Messerlin P and Sauvant K (eds), *The Uruguay Round Services in the World Economy* (Washington, DC, World Bank, 1990).

SNELL J, "True Proportionality and Free Movement of Goods and Services", *European Business Law Review* (Jan/Feb 2000) 50.

——*Goods and Services in EC Law—A Study of the Relationship Between the Freedoms* (Oxford, OUP, 2002).

SNYDER F, *International Trade and Customs Law of the European Union* (London, Butterworths, 1998).

——(ed), *The Europeanisation of Law* (Oxford, Hart Publishing, 2000).

——(ed), *Regional and Global Regulation of International Trade* (Oxford, Hart Publishing, 2002).

SIDI (Società Italiana di Diritto Internazionale), *Diritto ed organizzazione del commercio internazionale dopo la creazione della Organizzazione Mondiale del Commercio*, Il Convegno, Milano 5–7 giugno 1997, (Editoriale Scientifica, 1998).

STAKER C, "Free Movement of Goods in the EEC and Australia: A Comparative Study", 10 *YEL* (1990) 209.

STEINBERG R, "Trade-Environment Negotiations in the EU, NAFTA, and WTO: Regional Trajectories of Rule Development", 91 *American Journal of International Law* (1997) 231.

STEINER J, "Drawing the Line: Uses and Abuses of Article 30 EEC", 29 *CMLRev* (1992) 749.

STONE SWEET A AND SANDHOLZ W, "Integration, Supranational Governance and the Institutionalization of the European Polity" in Stone Sweet A and Sandholz W (eds), *European Integration and Supranational Governance* (Oxford, OUP, 1998).

STUYCK J, "Note on Joined Cases C–34, 35 and 36/95, *Konsumentombudsmannen (KO) v De Agostini (Svenska) Förlag AB* and *Konsumentombudsmannen (KO) v TV-Shop i Sverige AB*, [1997] ECR I–3843", 34 *CMLRev* (1997) 1445.

TESAURO G, *Diritto Comunitario* (Padova, Cedam, 1995).
——"The Community's Internal Market in light of the Recent Case-Law of the Court of Justice", *YEL* (1995) 1.
TINBERGEN J, *International Economic Integration* (Amsterdam, 1954).
TORGERSEN OA, "The Limitations of the Free Movement of Goods and the Freedom to Provide Services—In Search of a Common Approach", *European Business Law Review* (Sept/Oct 1999) 371.
TRACHTMAN J, "Trade in Financial Services under GATS, NAFTA and the EC: A Regulatory Jurisdiction Analysis", 34 *Columbia Journal of Transnational Law* (1995) 37.
——"The Theory of the Firm and the Theory of the International Economic Organization: Toward Comparative Institutional Analysis", *Northwestern Journal of International Law and Business* (Winter-Spring 1996–1997) 471.
——Decisions of the Appellate Body of the WTO, *EC–Asbestos*, available at <www.ejil.com>.
——Decisions of the Appellate Body of the WTO, *EC–Sardines*, available at <www.ejil.com>.
TREBILCOCK M AND HOWSE R, *The Regulation of International Trade* (London/New York, Routledge 1999).
TRIDIMAS T, *The General Principle of EC Law* (Oxford, OUP, 1999).
——"Proportionality in Community Law: Searching for the Appropriate Standard of Scrutiny" in E Ellis (ed), *The Principle of Proportionality in the Laws of Europe* (Oxford, OUP, 1999).
The Uruguay Round's Technical Barriers to Trade Agreement, WWF International Research Report (Jan 1993).
USHER J, *General Principles of EC Law* (London, Longman, 1998).
VAN CALSTER G, "Export Restrictions—A Watershed for Article 30", 25 *ELRev* (2000) 335.
VAN GERVEN W, "The Recent Case Law of the Court of Justice Concerning Articles 30 and 36 of the EEC Treaty", 14 *CMLRev* (1977) 5.
VENTURINI G, *L'organizzazione mondiale del commercio* (Milano, Giuffrè, 2000).
VERHOOSEL G, *National Treatment and WTO Dispute Settlement* (Oxford, Hart Publishing, 2002).
VERLOREN VAN THEMAT P, "La libre circulation des marchandises apres l'arrêt 'Cassis de Dijon'", 18 *CDE* (1982) 123.
VERMULST E, WAER P AND BOURGEOIS J (eds), *Rules of Origin in International Trade: a Comparative Study* (Ann Arbor, University of Michigan Press, 1994).
VIPIANA PM, *Introduzione allo studio del principio di ragionevolezza nel diritto pubblico* (Padova, CEDAM, 1993).
VOGEL D, "The WTO, International Trade and Environmental Protection: European and American Perspective", *EUI Working Paper* (N 34, 2002).
VON BOGDANDY A, MAVROIDIS P AND MÉNY Y (eds), *European Integration and International Co-ordination—Studies in Transnational Economic Law in Honour of Claus-Dieter Ehlermann* (The Hague/London/New York, Kluwer Law International, 2002).
ZEDALIS R, "Product *v* Non-Product Based Distinctions in GATT Article III Trade and Environment Jurisprudence: Recent Developments", *European Environmental Law Review* (April, 1997).

WALKER S, *Environmental Protection v Trade Liberalisation: Finding the Balance—An Examination of the Legality of Environmental Regulation under International Trade Law Regimes* (Bruxelles, Faculté Saint-Louis, 1993).

WEATHERILL S AND BEAUMONT P, *EC Law* (London, Penguin Books, 1995).

WEATHERILL S, "After Keck: Some Thoughts on how to Clarify the Clarification", 33 *CMLRev* (1996) 885.

——"Recent Case Law Concerning the Free Movement of Goods: Mapping the Frontiers of Market Deregulation", 36 *CMLRev* (1999) 51.

——"Current Developments in European Community Law: I Free Movement of Goods" 50 *ICLQ* (2001) 158.

WEILER JHH, "The Transformation of Europe", 100 *Yale L J* (1991) 2403.

——"The Constitution of the Common Marketplace: Text and Context in the Evolution of the Free Movement of Goods", in Craig P and de Burca G (eds), *The Evolution of EU Law* (Oxford, OUP, 1999).

——(ed), *The EU, the WTO and the NAFTA: Towards a Common Law of International Trade?* (Oxford, OUP, 2000).

——"The Rule of Lawyers and the Ethos of Diplomats: Reflections on the Internal and External Legitimacy of WTO Dispute Settlement", *Jean Monnet Working Paper* (Harvard-NYU School of Law, 2000).

WHITE E, "In Search of the Limits to Articles 30 of the EEC Treaty" 26 *CMLRev* (1989) 235.

WIENER J, *Globalization and the Harmonization of Law* (London-New York, Pinter, 1999).

WIERS J, "Regional and Global Approaches to Trade and Environment: the EC and the WTO", 25 *Legal Issues of European Integration* (1998) 93.

——*Trade and Environment in the EC and the WTO: a Legal Analysis* (Groningen, Europa Law Publishing, 2002).

WYATT D AND DASHWOOD A, *The Substantive Law of the EEC* (London, Sweet and Maxwell, 1980).

ZEDALIS R, "Labeling of Genetically Modified Foods—The Limits of GATT Rules", 35 *JWT* (2001) 301.

——"Product *v* Non-Product Based Distinctions in GATT Article III Trade and Environment Jurisprudence: Recent Developments", *European Environmental Law Review* (April 1997) 108.

ZWEIGERT K AND KÖTZ H, *Introduction to Comparative Law* (Oxford, OUP 1998).

Index